D1222339

Illustrated 2003 Building Code Handbook

Illustrated
2003 Building Code
Handbook

Terry L. Patterson, NCARB
University of Oklahoma

McGraw-Hill

*New York   Chicago   San Francisco
Lisbon   London   Madrid   Mexico City
Milan   New Delhi   San Juan   Seoul
Singapore   Sydney   Toronto*

Released from
Samford University Library

Samford University Library

The McGraw-Hill Companies

Library of Congress Cataloging-in-Publication Data

Patterson, Terry L.
   Illustrated 2003 building code handbook/Terry L. Patterson.
     p.cm.
   Includes index.,
   ISBN 0-07-142365-6
   1. Buildings–Standards. 2. Standards. engineering. I. Title.

TH420.P38 2003
690'.2'18—dc   2003059391

Copyright © 2004 by The McGraw-Hill Companies, Inc. All rights reserved. Printed in the United States of America. Except as permitted under the United States Copyright Act of 1976, no part of this publication may be reproduced or distributed in any form or by any means, or stored in a data base or retrieval system, without the prior written permission of the publisher.

1 2 3 4 5 6 7 8 9 0   DOC/DOC   0 9 8 7 6 5 4 3

ISBN 0-07-142365-6

The sponsoring editor for this book was Cary Sullivan, the editing supervisor was Caroline Levine, and the production supervisor was Pamela Pelton. It was set in Bookman, Graphite MM, Lucida Math, and Times by Jennie M. Patterson. The art director for the cover was Margaret Webster-Shapiro.

Printed and bound by R. R. Donnelley.

This book is printed on acid-free paper

McGraw-Hill books are available at special quantity discounts to use as premiums and sales promotions, or for use in corporate training programs. For more information, please write to the Director of Special Sales, Professional Publishing, McGraw-Hill, Two Penn Plaza, New York, NY 10121-2298.

Information contained in this work has been obtained by The McGraw-Hill Companies, Inc. ("McGraw-Hill") from sources believed to be reliable. However, neither McGraw-Hill nor its authors guarantee the accuracy or completeness of any information published herein and neither McGraw-Hill nor its authors shall be responsible for any errors, omissions, or damages arising out of use of this information. This work is published with the understanding that McGraw-Hill and its authors are supplying information but are not attempting to render engineering or other professional services. If such services are required, the assistance of an appropriate professional should be sought.

TH
420
.P38
2004

To my wife, Jennie M. Patterson

Contents

Preface

Every effort has been made to provide accurate clarifications of the code sections selected. To this end, I attended public hearings and have examined hundreds of proposals for changes that were subsequently approved or disapproved since the first drafts of the code. Proposal reasoning and comments of the technical committees were studied for additional insight to intentions. Dozens of professionals have been queried regarding the model codes on which the new code is based. I attended BOCA seminars to get a better grasp of that code, which has a dominant presence in the new code. Every section of the handbook was traced back to its origin in a model code or change proposal to verify accuracy and intent. Commentaries for all three model codes and the 2000 edition of the *International Building Code* were studied. Some section sources located in other standards such as accessibility regulations, fire codes, and BCMC (Board for the Coordination of the Model Codes) reports were examined. Every cited reference that is included was examined for content and accuracy. Through this research it has become apparent that in spite of the best intentions of the code sponsors, there will be differences of opinion regarding interpretation. The individual who proposed the original version of a section is not the person providing the official interpretation at the job site. Original intent is easily obscured in the several stages of review, modification, and approval that occur between the first proposal to the final interpretation at the local level. Consequently, the meaning imparted by the actual phrasing in the code dominates original intent. This problem will be greater than ever before in the new code given the varying traditions of building officials in enforcing their own model codes.

Many actual building projects are used in the handbook to illustrate how real buildings comply with code requirements. This has been done for two reasons. It is intended to bring a sense of reality to students studying the code who otherwise would find it remote from their life experience. It also provides an opportunity to explore code intent as related to complex building circumstances. This is not possible using only imaginary examples having simple rectangular shapes that neatly fit into conditions described in the code.

Terry L. Patterson
Norman Oklahoma

Acknowledgments

A large work such as this handbook cannot be the result of a single person's efforts. Many people provided important assistance. First, I thank my wife, Jennie M. Patterson, for her significant and lengthy effort on this project. Jennie produced virtually all of the graphics for the examples from architectural firms, all the tables and supporting calculations, the index, and the table of contents. She edited the whole work and developed the raw manuscript into a camera-ready format. She kept the computers running with the necessary maintenance and software management. This handbook would not be possible without Jennie's competent and timely contributions.

I am indebted to David Pendley, C.B.O., E.I.T. for his indispensable help to me in understanding the *BOCA National Building Code*, the *Uniform Building Code*, and the *International Building Code*. David is the Building Official for the City of North Richland Hills, Texas. He presently provides code interpretations, technical assistance, and building code administration to architects, engineers, builders, inspectors, and plan examiners, using the ICC *International Building Code* within the North Richland Hills jurisdiction. He graduated from the University of Nebraska School of Engineering and Technology in Lincoln, Nebraska, with a B.S. degree in Construction Management. David's experience includes that of serving as Chief Plans Examiner for the City of Fort Worth, Texas, and serving as the Building Official for Beatrice, Nebraska, and Norman, Oklahoma. David is a CABO/ICC Certified Building Official, an ICBO Certified Code Official, an ICBO Building Plans Examiner, an ICBO/ICC Building Inspector, an ICBO Plumbing Inspector, an ICBO/ICC Mechanical Inspector, a SBCCI Commercial Energy Plans Examiner, and is licensed as an Engineering Intern in Texas and Oklahoma. David's extensive and competent assistance with the model codes in no way implies responsibility on his part for my interpretations of the 2003 *International Building Code* in this handbook. Any errors or misunderstandings are entirely my responsibility as the sole author of the handbook.

Many thanks go to my graduate assistants for their important help. Srdan Kalajdzic was especially helpful in identifying examples from architectural working drawings that illustrate code requirements. He also produced a large number of the generic details for the handbook. Srdan performed his tasks with his usual high level of dependability and competence. Many thanks to Rene Spineto, who produced a large number of generic details and some graphics for the architectural project examples. Thanks to Arvind Vishnu Ram for his high-quality graphic production of numerous generic details. Thanks to Dana A. Templeton for her administrative help and some graphic work on the architectural project examples. Thanks to Kevin Zhou for his help with the production of generic details. Many thanks to Brett W. Johnson for his assistance in verifying numbers and titles of sections and standards referenced in the second edition as well as his Internet work in updating contact information for organizations providing referenced standards to the code. I am also grateful for the continued support of the University of Oklahoma College of Architecture for my publishing efforts.

Lin Li, who recently graduated with a master's degree in architecture, provided the excellent project design and artwork used on the cover of this handbook. Thanks go to Lin for her creative contribution.

Many thanks are due the following architectural firms who generously permitted me to select examples from their work to illustrate methods of compliance with the code.

Alt Breeding Schwarz
Architects, LLC
209 Main Street
Annapolis, MD 21401

Ankrom Moisan
Associated Architects
6720 S.W. Macadam
Portland, OR 97219

C. Allen Mullins, Architect
P.O. Box 21
Bear Creek, PA 18602

Cromwell Architects Engineers
101 South Spring St.
Little Rock, AR 72201

David Woodhouse Architects
811 West Evergreen Avenue
Chicago, IL 60622

Gossen Livingston
Associates, Inc.
420 South Emporia
Wichita, KS 67202

HKS, Inc.
1919 McKinney Avenue
Dallas, TX 75201

HKT Architects, Inc.
35 Medford Street
Somerville, MA 02143

The Hollis and Miller
Group, Inc.
220 NW Executive Way
Lee's Summit, MO 64063

Overland Partners, Inc. P.C.
5101 Broadway St.
San Antonio, TX 78209

PBK Architects, Inc.
11 Greenway Plaza
Houston, TX 77046

Perkins Eastman Architects,
115 Fifth Avenue
New York, NY 10003

Phillips Metsch Sweeney Moore
Architects
Marc A. Phillips, Proj. Architect
Santa Barbara, CA 93103

Spencer Godfrey Architects
1106 S. Mays
Round Rock, Texas 78664

Stephen Wen + Associates,
Architects, Inc.
77 North Mentor Avenue
Pasadena, CA 91106

Vogt Architectural Services
9000 Old Cedar Avenue
Bloomingtron, MN 55420

Watkins Hamilton Ross
Architects, Inc.
20 Greenway Plaza, Suite 450
Houston, Texas 77046

Wilson Darnell Mann, P.A.
105 N. Washington
Wichita, KS 67202

I thank the following people for their helpful responses to my questions for the first edition of the handbook regarding various sections of model codes in their jurisdictions.

Gene Abbot
Building Official
City of Lakeville
20195 Holyoke Avenue
Lakeville, MN 55044

Thomas Anderson
ICBO Director
Chief Building Inspector
City of Hopkins
1010 S First Street
Hopkins, MN 55343

Dick Bower
Building Official
City of Soldotna
177 N. Birch Street
Soldotna, AK 99669

Christopher Caruso
Building Official
Drawer W
Clinton, PA 15026

Kenneth Elsberry
Building Official
City of Dallas
120 Main Street
Dallas, GA 30132

John Graber
Civil Engineering Technician
USDA Forest Service
Suite 680
310 W. Wisconsin Avenue
Milwaukee, WI 53203

Robert Hegner
Building Official
City of Northfield
801 S. Washington St.
Northfield, MN 55057

Frank P. Hodge, Jr.
Building Official
Town of Hilton Head Island
1 Town Center Ct.
Hilton Head Island, SC 29928

Charles M. Huss, R.C.I.
Project Specialist
Maniilaq Health Center
P.O. Box 256
Kotzebue, AK 99752

Douglas Lalim
Building Official
City of Williston
1011 18th St., West
Williston, ND 58801

Clayton Larson
Chief Building Official
City of Coon Rapids
11155 Robinson Drive, NW
Coon Rapids, MN 55433

Duane Lasley
Building Official
City of Duluth
City Hall, Room 210
411 West First
Duluth, MN 55802

John J. Mayo
Building Official
Certified Building Inspector
Certified Environmental
Inspector
Lac Du Flambeau, WI 54538

Rick Murray
Building Official
City of Fulton
City Hall
Fulton, MO 65251

Aslam Rana
Building Inspector Services
Director
City of Dothan
126 N. Saint Andrews, Rm 315
Dothan, AL 36303

Donald Ranes
Building Official
County of Natrona
Suite 200
120 West First Street
Casper, WY 82601

Jerry Ratzlaff
Building Official
Ramsey County
524 Fourth Avenue, Suite 7
Devil's Lake, ND 58301

James Rich
Building Official
City of Hermantown
5255 Maple Grove Road
Hermantown, MN 55811

Bruce J. Spiewak, AIA
Consulting Architect
375 Morgan Lane, Unit 405
West Haven, CT 06516

J.P. Swanson
Building Official
City of Big Lake
802 Kjellbergs
Monticello, MN 55362

Murray Ward
Building Official
City of Grand Rapids
420 N. Pokgama
Grand Rapids, MN 55744

Many thanks go to Samuel Ray Moore, Architect of Oklahoma City and to John C. Womack, AIA, of the School of Architecture, Oklahoma State University for their help in launching the first edition of this project. And, special thanks to Cary Sullivan, Senior Editor at McGraw-Hill, for her advice and help in seeing the second edition of this handbook through to a successful conclusion and for her continued support of my work.

Introduction

Purpose.

This handbook clarifies the sections of the 2003 *International Building Code* that are the most useful to designers, detailers, estimators, and students. It is not directed to specifiers or engineers. It is not intended to be a substitute for the code, but an aid to understanding it.

The 2003 *International Building Code* is owned by the International Code Council, Inc., of Falls Church, Virginia. This handbook is neither sponsored nor approved by this agency, which has no relationship to this project.

Code language.

In their analysis of proposed change 1005.1-1 to the "First Draft" of the *International Building Code,* the Means of Egress Technical Subcommittee rejected the language of the proposal as being "commentary, not code text." This single statement succinctly summarizes the problem with codes for many people who must comply with them.

"Code text" is the language of building codes, a pseudo-legal kind of language intended to minimize variations in interpretation and withstand legal challenges. As in legal documents, the penalty for this special style is clarity to people who are not specialists in the language. The difficult language might be justified if interpretations among users and officials were consistent. This is not the case, as a visit to any internet code-discussion site will verify. Code questions posted on such sites often generate conflicting responses from code officials and other knowlegable parties.

Building codes have other readability problems. Sentences are often long and convoluted. Some items in the first part of a sentence affect some items in the second and third parts of the sentence but all items are not necessarily affected by all other items. Sorting out the relationships between words is complicated by the fact that some phrases affect previous or subsequent sentences and some do not. Too much substantive content is joined by too few words of clarification. Another problem in reading a code is letting expectations affect interpretation. The logic on which the code is based is not always accessible to the user and does not always reflect the experience of the professional. Statistics, tests, tradition, and other data and trends in life safety on which codes are based may not be available to the average user. In most cases, taking the literal meaning of code statements is more effective than is applying common sense. Since this approach is not 100 percent reliable, however, doubt makes the mental discipline required for understanding even more challenging.

Handbook language.

The language of this handbook accommodates the needs of design and production professionals and students. It is one of illustrations, tables, outlines, and lists. Common phrasing is substituted for legalistic wording. Lengthy and convoluted code sentences are broken down into line items. Quick and easy readability is the goal.

Format.

Drawings and diagrams illustrate numerous requirements. Actual building projects as well as generic examples are included. Tables are provided, many of which are based on mathematical equations that would otherwise require computation by the user. Large code tables are broken down into smaller tables and reformatted to reduce the number of variables that must be reconciled. Footnotes are integrated into the body of each table or the body of the text, which eliminates the fine print that is difficult to read and easily overlooked. Exceptions are integrated into the body of the basic requirements. This eliminates reversals of requirements where exceptions supercede the main text.

Several common-sense shortcuts were taken in the handbook to facilitate readability. First, the handbook refers to the *International Building Code* simply as the code. The code consistently modifies references to residential occupancies as follows: "R-3 as applicable in Section 101.2." This indicates that the *International Residential Code* governs 1- and 2- family dwellings and townhouses $\leq$ 3 stories. By use of this phrase, the code is indicating to which residential occupancies it applies. It is sufficient to understand that the code does not address residences governed by the *International Residential Code*. Consequently, the reference to 101.2 is omitted throughout the handbook. Where sprinklers are addressed, the code typically refers to section 903.3.1.1 or 903.3.1.2. These sections essentially require that sprinklers comply with NFPA 13 and 13R respectively. In many places listing these sections as references, the handbook simply refers to sprinklers with the phrase "as per NFPA 13" or "13R" in the body of the requirement. The code refers to sprinklers as being automatic. Since it is understood that all sprinklers are to be automatic, the handbook omits this term.

The code often refers to "buildings and structures" so as not to exclude constructions such as stadiums, which may not be considered buildings. The handbook usually refers only to "buildings," which must be understood to include all the structures that the code governs. The handbook utilizes mathematical and other symbols instead of words to the greatest extent possible so as to provide visual relief to the text. For example, the symbols $\geq$ and $\leq$ are substituted, where readibililty is enhanced, for the terms "minimum" and "maximum." The code reports frequently that certain cases must comply with the code. Such comments are omitted as it must be understood that every entry of the code requires compliance.

The shortcuts and plain language used by the handbook lack the legal precision of the code. The code attempts to provide regulations that cannot be circumvented. The handbook makes selected regulations more accessible to designers, detailers, and estimators. Consequently, common sense must be applied to the guidance provided.

The need to refer to other pages in order to grasp the concept of a code requirement is minimized. Numerical references to other code sections are eliminated from the main text. Descriptions of such referenced data, the data itself, or the subject of the referenced data is substituted. This provides a more easily read text without the disruption of numbers that add no apparent meaning to the paragraph. The cited section number along with its name are listed below the body of the requirement text in italics. Comments on the citation are added where necessary for clarification. The reader may turn to the cited section if desired. The following example illustrates the contrast in formats:

Code entry:

407.2 Corridors. "Corridors in occupancies in Group I-2 shall be continuous to the exits and separated from other areas in accordance with Section 407.3 except spaces conforming to Sections 407.2.1 through 407.2.4."

Handbook clarification:
407.2 Corridors

- The enclosure of occupancy I-2 corridors is governed as follows:
  - Each corridor must be continuous to an exit.
  - Corridors may be open to the spaces indicated below where design and construction meet minimum requirements for fire safety:
    Waiting areas.
    Nurses' stations.
    Mental health treatment areas.
    Gift shops.
  - Otherwise, corridors must be separated from other spaces for purposes of smoke protection.

    Note: The following are cited as sources of requirements for the spaces opening to a corridor:
    407.2.1, "Spaces of unlimited area," which addresses waiting rooms.
    407.2.2 "Nurses' stations."
    407.2.3 "Mental health treatment areas."
    407.2.4 "Gift shops."
    407.3, "Corridor walls," for walls required to separate corridors from other spaces.

Focus for design.

The handbook focuses on code sections affecting design decisions at the schematic stage and design development phases such as in Chapters 3, 4, 5, 10, 11, 12, 30, and 32. Designers are provided with a clarification of requirements affecting floor plan configuration and building massing. Required heights, widths, lengths, clearances, and distances are among the data clarified. These sections are of particular interest to students, as much studio work is schematic in nature.

Focus for detailing.

The handbook focuses on code sections affecting detailing decisions in the working drawing phase such as in Chapters 6, 7, 8, 9, 14, 15, 18, 19, 21, 22, 23, 24, 25, 26, and 31. Detailers are provided with a clarification of requirements affecting material choices and detail configuration. Clarification of these sections also helps the designer make spatially related decisions based on probable relative cost of the options as driven by fire protection requirements. These sections are of particular interest to students since they narrow the choices for material selection and detail composition.

Focus for cost estimating.

The handbook focus on code sections affecting detailing also helps estimators prepare construction bids. Where architectural working drawings require that the builder "meet current code requirements," this handbook can provide options for code compliance where certain detailing is vague or missing in the project drawings.

Sections de-emphasized.

Material that is solely specification oriented is generally omitted from the handbook. That is, requirements referring to only specifications, tests, procedures, administration, other codes and standards, and paragraphs not related to space planning or detailing are not addressed. Chapters 1, 17, 33, and parts of other chapters are this type. These subjects are typically the responsibility of professionals who are familiar with code language. Specification type data is included in the handbook only where it is mixed with design and detailing information.

Requirements that are engineering oriented are generally omitted. This refers mainly to Chapter 16. Engineers and architects with responsibilities in Chapter 16 typically have the experience to respond directly to code language. Certain loading requirements from Chapter 16 are included in the handbook, as they may be useful to students and production personnel who need to approximate member sizes for detailing purposes.

Within chapters addressed by the handbook, certain paragraphs are omitted that are administrative in nature and contain no technical content. For example, sections are distributed throughout the code that establish the applicability of subsequent subsections. For these to be useful, they must be referred to periodically as subsequent sections are studied. This requires turning pages, which interrupts concentration. In lieu of these scope-type paragraphs, the applicability of each section is reported in the handbook within the section itself, where such is not self-evident. Other sections are also omitted where they do not contribute to the needs of designers and detailers. Some of these are scattered and some are grouped. Theses various omissions result in occasional gaps in section numbering. When a numbered paragraph is selected for clarification, however, every item under the number is addressed.

In order to keep handbook chapter numbering continuous and consistent with the code, a few "place holder" pages are inserted to identify de-emphasized chapters that lack significant material of interest to designers, detailers, and estimators. Chapters 1, 2, 13, 17, 20, 27, 28, and 33 have such pages. For most of these, material of minor interest is included. For example, Chapter 17 deals with testing, a subject not featured in the handbook. Sections on performance labels for materials and assemblies were included on the Chapter 17 "place holder" page. Such label information is of general interest to the detailer and is of more value than would be an empty page. Code Chapters 13 and 28 merely refer to other codes with no further information, so the "place holder" pages for these chapters are correspondingly brief.

Code errors.

This handbook is based on the first printing of the 2003 *International Building Code,* which contains errors. Included are common typographical errors, obsolete section reference numbers, and occasional omitted phrases or superfluous phrases. Where these were discovered, verification of the correct meaning was determined for use in this handbook and where necessary intent was verified informally by Building Officials and Code Administrators (BOCA) staff. BOCA provides this service to its members without charge and is an excellent resource for understanding the code. BOCA, of course, is not responsible for the use in this handbook of any information provided. It is anticipated that errors in the code will be corrected by errata and/or in a future supplement issued by the International Code Council.

Any conceptual errors where found in the code are not corrected. A few of this type occur where an omission or conflict is apparent which does not result from a mechanical error but from an oversight in phrasing. It is not the purpose of this handbook to improve on the requirements of the code but only to clarify its wording. Such corrections should be effected by the code change process, which only the International Code Council can accomplish.

Illustrated 2003 Building Code Handbook

1

Administration

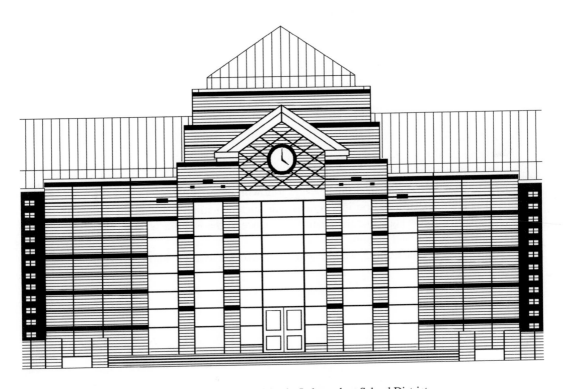

High School 6, Cypress-Fairbanks Independent School District.
Harris County, Texas. *(partial elevlation)*
PBK Architects, Inc. Houston, Texas.

106 Construction Documents

106.1.2 Means of egress

- Construction documents must show the following:
  - All parts of the means of egress as follows:
    Location.
    Construction.
    Size.
- For occupancies other than R-2 and R-3, the following is required:
  - Construction documents must show the number of occupants as follows:
    On every floor.
    In all rooms and spaces.

106.1.3 Exterior wall envelope

- Construction documents must describe the exterior wall envelope as follows:
  - Information must be adequate to verify code compliance, including the following:
    Wall intersections with dissimilar materials.
    Wall intersections with the roof.
    Wall intersections with eaves.
    Wall intersections with parapets.
    Means of drainage.
    Waster-resistive membrane.
    Details around openings.
    Flashing.
    Corners.
    End details.
    Control joints.
- Construction documents must include the following information:
  - Manufacturers' installation instructions and documentation verifying the following:
    That the following maintain weather resistance of the exterior wall envelope:
      Penetration and opening details.
  - Description of the exterior wall system as tested and the test method.

106 Construction Documents

106.2 Site plan

- Construction drawings submitted for approval must include a site plan showing the following:
  - Site plan must show to scale the following information:
    - Size and location of the following:
      - New and existing construction.
      - Distances to lot lines.
    - Established street grades.
    - Proposed finished grades:
      - Applicable flood-related aspects as follows:
        - Flood hazard areas.
        - Floodways.
        - Design flood elevations.
  - Site plan must be prepared in accordance with a boundary line survey.
- Where demolition will occur, the site plan must show the following:
  - Construction to be demolished and to remain.
- The building official may waive the site plan requirement as follows:
  - For alteration or repair or where otherwise warranted.

NOTES

2

Definitions

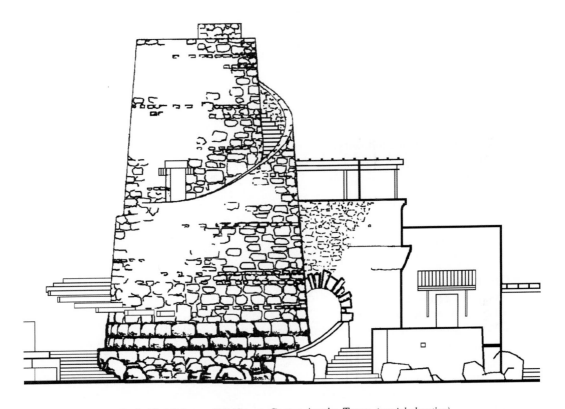

Lady Bird Johnson Wildflower Center. Austin, Texas. *(partial elevation)*
Overland Partners, Inc. San Antonio, Texas.

202 Definitions *(part 1 of 2)*

- **Court**
  - An uncovered space open to the sky.
  - Enclosed on ≥ 3 sides by one of the following:
    Exterior building walls.
    Other enclosing elements.

- **Dwelling**
  - A building containing one of the following:
    1 dwelling unit.
    2 dwelling units.
  - To be occupied for living purposes by one of the following means.

- **Grade floor opening**
  - One of the following:
    Window.
    Other opening.
  - Sill height is ≤ 44" from adjacent grade as follows:
    Above finished grade.
    Below finished grade.

- **Habitable space**
  - A space in a building for the following:
    Sleeping.
    Eating.
    Cooking.
  - Does not include the following:
    Bathrooms.
    Toilet rooms.
    Closets.
    Halls.
    Storage spaces.
    Utility spaces.
    Similar spaces.

- **Occupiable space**
  - A room or enclosed space.
  - Designed for human occupancy.
  - Where people congregate for the following:
    Amusement.
    Education.
    Similar purposes.
    Labor.
  - Has means of egress.
  - Has lighting.
  - Has ventilation.

202 Definitions *(part 2 of 2)*

- **Skylight, unit**
  - Factory-assembled glazed fenestration unit.
  - Contains one panel of glazing as follows:
    Transmits natural light.
  - Penetrates the roof assembly as follows:
    Provides a weather barrier.

- **Skylights and sloped glazing**
  - Any of the following:
    Glass.
    Transparent glazing material.
    Translucent glazing material.
  - Installed at a slope ≥ 15° from vertical.
  - The following glazing is included:
    In skylights.
    In solariums.
    In sun spaces.
    In roofs.
    In sloped walls.

- **Sleeping unit**
  - A space where people sleep.
  - Can include permanent living facilities.
  - Can include permanent eating facilities.
  - Can include only one of the following:
    Sanitation facilities.
    Kitchen facilities.
  - Not part of a dwelling unit.

- **Story**
  - The segment of a building between the following levels:
    Upper surface of a floor.
    Upper surface of the floor or roof directly above.
  - For floors other than the top floor, a story is measured in one of the following ways:
    From top to top of successive tiers of beams.
    From top to top of successive tiers of finished floor surfaces.
  - For the top floor, a story is measured as follows:
    From top of finished floor to top of ceiling joists where there is a ceiling.
    From top of finished floor to top of roof rafters where there is no ceiling.

- **Story above grade plane**
  - A story with its finished floor surface above the grade plane.
  - A basement with a finished floor surface at one of the following levels:
    > 6' above grade plane.
    > 6' above the finished ground level for > 50% of the building perimeter.
    > 12' above the finished ground level at any point.

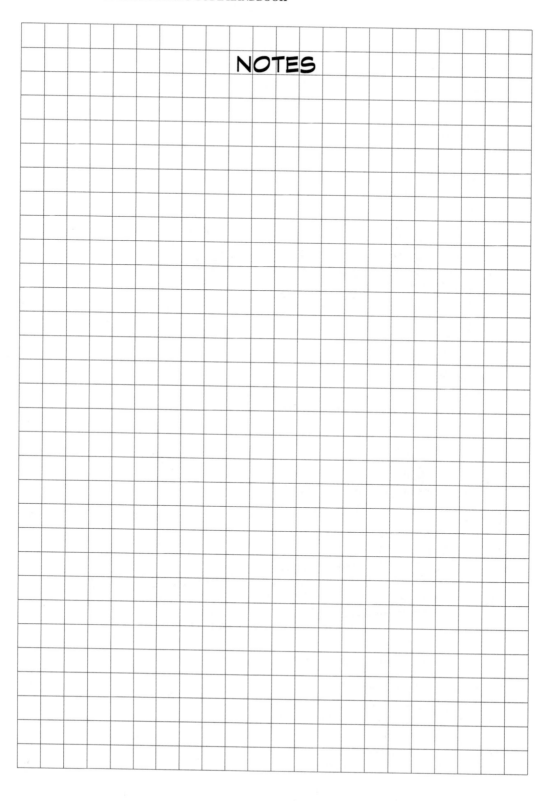

NOTES

3

Use and Occupancy
Classification

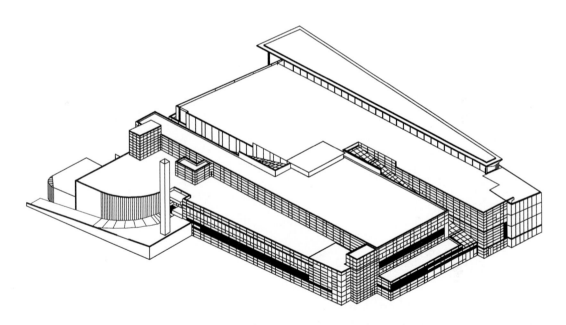

University of Connecticut New Downtown Campus at Stamford, Connecticut.
Perkins Eastman Architects, P.C. New York, New York.

302 Classification

302.1 General

- Buildings or parts of buildings are classified as one or more of the following occupancy categories:
  - A—Assembly:
    - A-1.
    - A-2.
    - A-3.
    - A-4.
    - A-5.
  - B—Business.
  - E—Educational.
  - F—Factory and Industrial:
    - F-1.
    - F-2.
  - H—High Hazard:
    - H-1.
    - H-2.
    - H-3.
    - H-4.
    - H-5.
  - I—Institutional:
    - I-1.
    - I-2.
    - I-3.
    - I-4.
  - M—Mercantile.
  - R—Residential:
    - R-1.
    - R-2.
    - R-3.
    - R-4.
  - S—Storage:
    - S-1.
    - S-2.
  - U—Utility and Miscellaneous.
- Buildings not listed in one of the occupancy categories by the code are to be assigned to the category with the most similar fire hazard.

302 Classification

302.1.1 Incidental use areas* *(part 1 of 2)*

- The following spaces are not governed by this section:
    - Areas within and serving a dwelling unit.
    - Areas incidental to a main occupancy with both the following characteristics:
        Designated as an occupancy different from the main occupancy.
        Located in a building designated as mixed occupancy building.

    Note: 302.3, "Mixed occupancies," is cited as governing this type of incidental space.

- The following spaces are governed by this section:
    - Areas incidental to the main occupancy as described in this section.
- Occupancy classification of incidental use areas is as follows:
    - Same as the main occupancy in which they are located.
- The following areas require one of the conditions listed below:
    - Areas:
        Furnace rooms:
            With any equipment > 400,000 Btu/h input.
        Rooms with boilers having both the following characteristics:
            > 15 psi.
            > 10 horsepower.
        The following spaces in occupancy E or I-2:
            Laboratories not classified as H.
            Vocational shops not classified as H.
        Laundry rooms > 100 sf.
        Storage rooms > 100 sf.
        Waste collection rooms > 100 sf.
        Linen collection rooms > 100 sf.
    - Conditions:
        Separation with fire-resistance rating ≥ 1 hr.
        Automatic fire-extinguishing system in the space.
- Refrigerant machinery rooms require one of the conditions listed below:
    - Separation with fire-resistance rating ≥ 1 hr.
    - Sprinklers in the space.
- The following areas require a separation with a fire-resistance rating ≥ 1 hr:
    - I-3 padded cells.
    - I-2 waste collection rooms.
    - I-2 linen collection rooms.
- Parking garages require one of the following options:
    - Separation with a fire-resistance rating ≥ 2 hr.
    - Both conditions as follows:
        Separation with a fire-resistance rating ≥ 1 hr.
        Automatic fire-extinguishing system in the space.

    Note: 406.2, "Parking garages," is cited as governing these facilities.

*Source: IBC Table 302.1.1.

302 Classification

302.1.1 Incidental use areas* *(part 2 of 2)*

- Incinerator rooms require both the following:
  - Separation with a fire-resistance rating ≥ 2 hr.
  - Sprinklers in the space.
- The following paint shops require one of the conditions listed below:
  - Paint shops:
    Where not classified as H.
    Where located in other than F.
  - Conditions:
    Separation with a fire-resistance rating ≥ 2 hr.
    Automatic fire-extinguishing system in the space.
- Battery systems with all the following characteristics have requirements as listed below:
  - Characteristics:
    Stationary lead-acid systems.
    Liquid capacity > 100 gallons.
    Used for any of the following:
      Facility standby power.
      Emergency power.
      Uninterrupted power supply.
  - Requirements in occupancies B, F, H, M, S, U:
    Fire barriers with a fire-resistance rating ≥ 1 hr.
    Floor-ceiling assemblies with a fire-resistance rating ≥ 1 hr.
  - Requirements in occupancies A, E, I, R:
    Fire barriers with a fire-resistance rating ≥ 2 hr.
    Floor-ceiling assemblies with a fire-resistance rating ≥ 2 hr.
- Hydrogen cutoff rooms have the following requirements:
  - In occupancies B, F, H, M, S, U:
    Fire barriers with a fire-resistance rating ≥ 1 hr.
    Floor-ceiling assemblies with a fire-resistance rating ≥ 1 hr.
  - In occupancies A, E, I, R:
    Fire barriers with a fire-resistance rating ≥ 2 hr.
    Floor-ceiling assemblies with a fire-resistance rating ≥ 2 hr.

Source: IBC Table 302.1.1

302 Classification

302.1.1.1 Separation

- This section addresses the fire-resistance-rated separations required for incidental use areas.
- Required separations are to be fire barriers.
- The following applies where a fire-extinguishing system is provided in lieu of a fire barrier:
  - The space must be separated from the rest of the building with construction that resists the passage of smoke as follows:

    Partitions must extend from the floor to the underside of the following where applicable:

    The fire-rated floor/ceiling assembly.

    The roof/ceiling assembly.

    The floor deck above.

    The roof deck above.

    Doors must close automatically when smoke is detected.

    Doors may not have openings which transfer air.

    Doors may not be undercut more than indicated below:

Table 302.1.1.1   Maximum Undercut of Doors

Door type	Material below door	Clearance below door
Swinging, builders hardware	Rigid floor tile	$^5/_8$"
All types	Raised noncombustible sill	$^3/_8$"
All types	Floor with no sill	$^3/_4$"
All types	Floor covering	$^1/_2$"

Source: NFPA 80, "Fire Doors and Windows," Table 1-11.4.

302.2 Accessory use areas

- The following fire barriers are not governed by this section:
  - As required for accessory areas of occupancy H.

    Note: 302.3.1, "Two or more uses," addresses fire barriers for occupancy H.

  - As required for incidental use areas.

    Note: 302.1.1, "Incidental use areas," addresses fire barriers for selected incidental use areas.

- In other cases, fire barriers are not required where all the following conditions are met:
  - Accessory use occupies ≤ 10% of any floor area.
  - Accessory use meets both the following requirements:

    Height limits based on occupancy and construction type.

    Area limits based on occupancy and construction type.

    Note: IBC Table 503 lists height and area limitations based on occupancy and construction type.

302 Classification

302.2.1 Assembly areas

- This section addresses assembly areas that are accessory to nonassembly occupancies.
- Such accessory areas are not considered separate occupancies as follows:
  - Where the assembly area has ≤ 750 sf.
  - Where the assembly area is accessory to occupancy E.
  - Where the following assembly areas have < 100 occupants:
    Religious educational rooms.
    Religious auditoriums.

302.3 Mixed occupancies

- This section does not govern the following:
  - Separation of certain parking garages from other occupancies.

    Note: 508, "Special Provisions," is cited as the source of requirements for the separation of parking garages excluded from this section.

  - Separation of the following occupancies from other occupancies:
    H-2.
    H-3.
    H-4.
    H-5.

    Note: 302.3.2, "Separated uses," is cited as the source of requirements for separation of these occupancies from others.

  - Areas of the following occupancies where required to be in detached buildings:
    H-1.
    H-2.
    H-3.

    Note: Table 415.3.2, "Required Detached Storage," is cited as the source of requirements for occupancies that must be in detached buildings.

  - Certain accessory uses limited in size.

    Note: 302.2, "Accessory use areas," is cited as the source of requirements for these spaces.

  - Certain incidental use areas.

    Note: 302.1.1, "Incidental use areas," is cited as the source of requirements for these spaces.

- Other buildings having > 1 use are governed by subsequent sections of this chapter.

  Note: The following sections are cited as sources of requirements for these buildings:
  302.3.1, "Nonseparated uses."
  302.3.2, "Separated uses."

302 Classification

302.3.1 Nonseparated uses

- Each area within a building is to have an occupancy classification based on use.
- Construction type required for the entire building is determined as follows:
  - Highest type required for any occupancy in the building based on both the following:
    Building height as if each occupancy were the sole occupancy of the building.
    Building area as if each occupancy were the sole occupancy of the building.
- Where applicable, the most restrictive high-rise rules for any occupancy in the building apply to the entire building.

    Note: Section 403, "High-Rise Buildings," is cited as the source of such requirements.

- The most restrictive fire protection system requirements for any occupancy in the building apply to the entire building.

    Note: Chapter 9, "Fire Protection Systems," is cited as the source of requirements.

- This section does not require fire-resistance-rated separations between different uses:
  - This section does not preclude other sections from requiring such separations.
- Otherwise, each use is governed by requirements applicable to its own classification.

302.3.2 Separated uses *(part 1 of 15)*

- This section applies where uses of mixed occupancy classifications are to be separated.
- Each area within a building is to have an occupancy classification based on use.
- Adjacent occupancies must be separated as follows:
  - By one or both the following constructions with the appropriate fire-resistance rating:
    Fire barrier walls.
    Horizontal assemblies.

    Note: IBC Table 302.3.2, "Required Separation of Occupancies," is cited as the source of fire-resistance ratings required for occupancy separations.

- Each fire area must comply with the following:
  - Requirements pertinent to its occupancy classification.
  - Height limitations based on the following:
    Occupancy classification.
    Construction type.
- The sum of the following ratios in each story must be ≤ 1:
  - Area of each occupancy ÷ its allowable area.
- Some fire-resistance ratings required for separations can be reduced as follows:
  - Ratings for the following occupancies cannot be reduced:
    H, I-2.
  - Buildings must be sprinklered.
  - Ratings can be reduced by 1 hr with the following restrictions:
    Rating cannot be reduced to < 1 hr.
    Rating cannot be reduced to < the rating required for the following:
      Floor construction based on construction type.

Case study: Fig. 302.3.2. In order to separate the occupancy A-3 area (cafeteria and gymnasium) from the other occupancies in this building, a fire barrier is required at the perimeter of the space. IBC Table 302.3.3 indicates that where A-3 is to be separated from E, such a barrier must have a 2-hr fire-resistance rating. The same rating is required for walls separating A-3 from B and S-2 occupancies which also occur in this plan. The gymnasium and cafeteria are separated from the adjacent B, S-2, and E occupancies by 2-hr walls. The A-3 space, therefore, is in its own fire area separate from the adjacent occupancies.

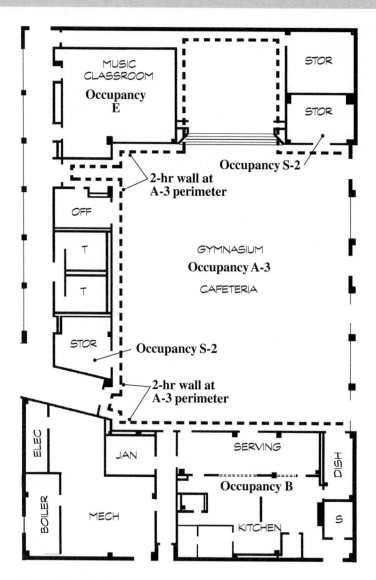

Fig. 302.3.2. Partial floor plan at cafeteria wing. New Jasper Pre-K–2nd Grade School. Jasper, Texas. PBK Architects, Inc. Houston, Texas.

302 Classification

302.3.2 Separated uses *(part 2 of 15)*

- This part of the section governs fire-resistance ratings for separations of occupancy A.
- The table below shows separations required between A and the occupancies listed as follows:
  - A restaurant kitchen is not required to be separated from seating served.
  - The table does not apply to separations of the following like occupancies:
    A-1 and A-1.
    A-2 and A-2.
    A-3 and A-3.
    A-4 and A-4.
    A-5 and A-5.

Table 302.3.2a   Occupancy A: Fire-Resistance Ratings for Occupancy Separations

Occupancies	Ratings in hrs
With sprinklers:	
A	1
B	1
E	1
F-1	2
F-2	1
H-2, H-5	4
H-3	3
H-4	2
I-1, I-3, I-4	1
I-2	2
M	1
R	1
S-1	2
S-2	1
U	1
Without sprinklers:	
A	2
B	2
E	2
F-1	3
F-2	2
M	2
R	2
S-1	3
S-2	2
U	1

With sprinklers:

A — 1 — A, B, E, F-2, I-1, I-3, I-4, M, R, S-2, U

A — 2 — F-1, H-4, I-2, S-1

A — 3 — H-3

A — 4 — H-2, H-5

Without sprinklers:

A — 1 — U

A — 2 — A, B, E, F-2, M, R, S-2

A — 3 — F-1, S-1

Source: IBC Table 302.3.2.

302 Classification

302.3.2 Separated uses *(part 3 of 15)*

- This part of the section governs fire-resistance ratings for separations of occupancy B.
- Storage areas in occupancy B with any of the following characteristics do not require separation:
  - Storage < 10% of floor area.
  - Storage < 1000 sf.
  - Storage with both the following:
    Area < 3000 sf.
    Area is sprinklered.
- The table below shows separations required between B and the occupancies listed:

Table 302.3.2b   Occupancy B: Fire-Resistance Ratings for Occupancy Separations

Occupancies	Ratings in hrs
With sprinklers:	
A	1
E	1
F-1	2
F-2	1
H-2	2
H-3, H-4, H-5	1
I-1, I-3, I-4	1
I-2	2
M	1
R	1
S-1	2
S-2	1
U	1
Without sprinklers:	
A	2
E	2
F-1	3
F-2	2
M	2
R	2
S-1	3
S-2	2
U	1

With sprinklers:

B | 1 — A, E, F-2, H-3, H-4, H-5, I-1, I-3, I-4, M, R, S-2, U

B | 2 — F-1, H-2, I-2, S-1

Without sprinklers:

B | 1 — U

B | 2 — A, E, F-2, M, R, S-2

B | 3 — F-1, S-1

Source: IBC Table 302.3.2.

302 Classification

302.3.2 Separated uses *(part 4 of 15)*

- This part of the section governs fire-resistance ratings for separations of occupancy E.
- Accessory assembly uses in occupancy E are not separate occupancies.
- The table below shows separations required between E and the occupancies listed:

Table 302.3.2c   Occupancy E: Fire-Resistance Ratings for Occupancy Separations

Occupancies	Ratings in hrs
With sprinklers:	
A	1
B	1
F-1	2
F-2	1
H-2	4
H-3, H-5	3
H-4	2
I-1, I-3, I-4	1
I-2	2
M	1
R	1
S-1	2
S-2	1
U	1
Without sprinklers:	
A	2
B	2
F-1	3
F-2	2
M	2
R	2
S-1	3
S-2	2
U	1

E 1 A, B, F-2, I-1, I-3, I-4, M, R, S-2, U

E 2 F-1, H-4, I-2, S-1

E 3 H-3 H-5

E 4 H-2

E 1 U

E 2 A, B, F-2, M, R, S-2

E 3 F-1 S-1

Source: IBC Table 302.3.2.

302 Classification

302.3.2 Separated uses *(part 5 of 15)*

- This part of the section governs fire-resistance ratings for separations of occupancy F-1.
- The table below shows separations required between F-1 and the occupancies listed:

Table 302.3.2d   Occupancy F-1: Fire-Resistance Ratings for Occupancy Separations

Occupancies	Ratings in hrs
With sprinklers:	
A	2
B	2
E	2
F-2	2
H-2	2
H-3, H-4, H-5	1
I-1, I-3, I-4	2
I-2	3
M	2
R	2
S	2
U	2

F-1 **1**   H-3 H-4 H-5

F-1 **2**   A, B, E, F-2, H-2, I-1, I-3, I-4, M, R, S, U

F-1 **3**   I-2

Occupancies	Ratings in hrs
Without sprinklers:	
A	3
B	3
E	3
F-2	3
I	3
M	3
R	3
S	3
U	3

F-1 **1**   A, B, E, F-2, I, M, R, S, U

Source: IBC Table 302.3.2.

302 Classification

302.3.2 Separated uses *(part 6 of 15)*

- This part of the section governs fire-resistance ratings for separations of occupancy F-2.
- The table below shows separations required between F-2 and the occupancies listed:

Table 302.3.2e   Occupancy F-2: Fire-Resistance Ratings for Occupancy Separations

Occupancies	Ratings in hrs
With sprinklers:	
A	1
B	1
E	1
F-1	2
H-2	2
H-3, H-4, H-5	1
I-1, I-3, I-4	1
I-2	2
M	1
R	1
S-1	2
S-2	1
U	1

F-2 — 1 — A, B, E, H-3, H-4, H-5, I-1, I-3, I-4, M, R, S-2, U

F-2 — 2 — F-1, H-2, I-2, S-1

Occupancies	Ratings in hrs
Without sprinklers:	
A	2
B	2
E	2
F-1	3
M	2
R	2
S-1	3
S-2	2
U	1

F-2 — 1 — U

F-2 — 2 — A, B, E, M, R, S-2

F-2 — 3 — F-1, S-1

Source: IBC Table 302.3.2.

302 Classification

302.3.2 Separated uses *(part 7 of 15)*

- This part of the section governs fire-resistance ratings for separations of occupancies H-2 and H-3.
- The table below shows separations required between H-2 and the occupancies listed:

Table 302.3.2f   **Occupancy H-2: Fire-Resistance Ratings for Occupancy Separations**

Occupancies	Ratings in hrs
With sprinklers:	
A	4
B	2
E	4
F	2
H-3	1
H-4, H-5	2
I	4
M	2
R	4
S	2
U	1

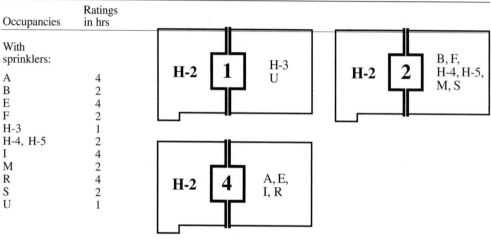

Source: IBC Table 302.3.2.

- The table below shows separations required between H-3 and the occupancies listed:

Table 302.3.2g   **Occupancy H-3: Fire-Resistance Ratings for Occupancy Separations**

Occupancies	Ratings in hrs
With sprinklers:	
A	3
B	1
E	3
F	1
H-2, H-4, H-5	1
I-1	4
I-2, I-3, I-4	3
M	1
R	3
S	1
U	1

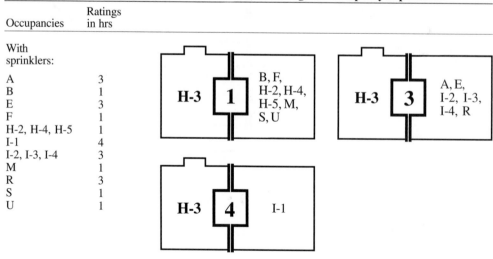

Source: IBC Table 302.3.2.

302 Classification

302.3.2 Separated uses *(part 8 of 15)*

- This part of the section governs fire-resistance ratings for separations of occupancies H-4 and H-5.
- The table below shows separations required between H-4 and the occupancies listed:

Table 302.3.2h   Occupancy H-4: Fire-Resistance Ratings for Occupancy Separations

Occupancies	Ratings in hrs
With sprinklers:	
A	2
B	1
E	2
F	1
H-2	2
H-3, H-5	1
I	4
M	1
R	4
S	1
U	1

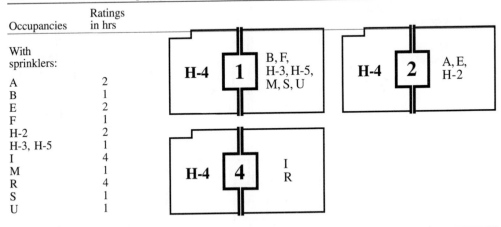

Source: IBC Table 302.3.2.

- The table below shows separations required between H-5 and the occupancies listed:

Table 302.3.2i   Occupancy H-5: Fire-Resistance Ratings for Occupancy Separations

Occupancies	Ratings in hrs
With sprinklers:	
A	4
B	1
E	3
F	1
H-2	2
H-3, H-4	1
I-1, I-2, I-3	4
I-4	3
M	1
R	4
S	1
U	3

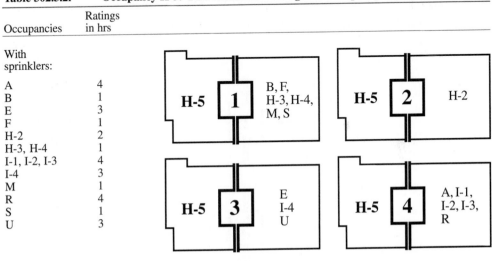

Source: IBC Table 302.3.2.

302 Classification

302.3.2 Separated uses *(part 9 of 15)*

- This part of the section governs fire-resistance ratings for separations of occupancies I-1 and I-2.
- The table below shows separations required between I-1 and the occupancies listed:

Table 302.3.2j   **Occupancy I-1: Fire-Resistance Ratings for Occupancy Separations**

Occupancies	Ratings in hrs
With sprinklers:	
A	1
B	1
E	1
F-1	2
F-2	1
H-2, H-3, H-4, H-5	4
I-2	2
I-3, I-4	1
M	1
R	1
S-1	3
S-2	2
U	1

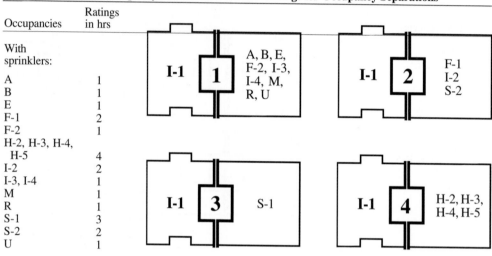

Source: IBC Table 302.3.2.

- The table below shows separations required between I-2 and the occupancies listed:

Table 302.3.2k   **Occupancy I-2: Fire-Resistance Ratings for Occupancy Separations**

Occupancies	Ratings in hrs
With sprinklers:	
A	2
B	2
E	2
F-1	3
F-2	2
H-3	3
H-2, H-4, H-5	4
I-1	2
M	2
R	2
S-1	3
S-2	2
U	1

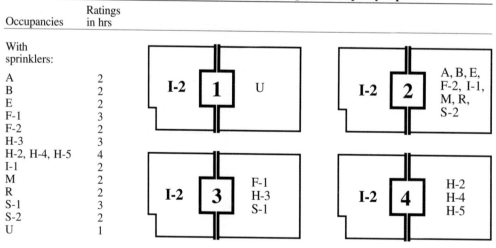

Source: IBC Table 302.3.2.

302 Classification

302.3.2 Separated uses *(part 10 of 15)*

- This part of the section governs fire-resistance ratings for separations of occupancies I-3 and I-4.
- The table below shows separations required between I-3 and the occupancies listed:

Table 302.3.2l **Occupancy I-3: Fire-Resistance Ratings for Occupancy Separations**

Occupancies	Ratings in hrs
With sprinklers:	
A	1
B	1
E	1
F-1	2
F-2	1
H-3	3
H-2, H-4, H-5	4
I-1, I-4	1
I-2	2
M	1
R	1
S-1	2
S-2	1
U	1

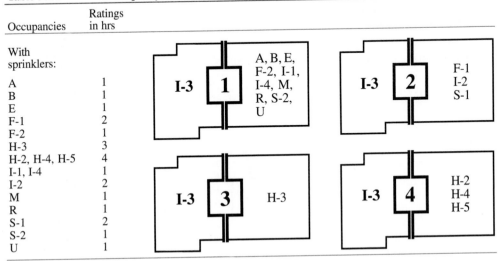

Source: IBC Table 302.3.2.

- The table below shows separations required between I-4 and the occupancies listed:

Table 302.3.2m **Occupancy I-4: Fire-Resistance Ratings for Occupancy Separations**

Occupancies	Ratings in hrs
With sprinklers:	
A	1
B	1
E	1
F-1	2
F-2	1
H-2, H-4	4
H-3, H-5	3
I-2	2
I-1, I-3	1
M	1
R	1
S-1	2
S-2	1
U	1

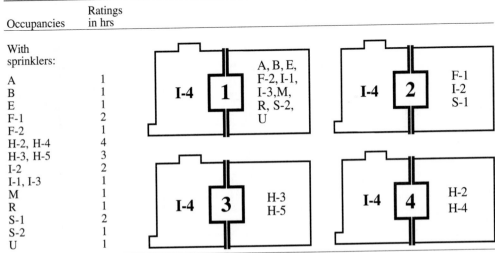

Source: IBC Table 302.3.2.

302 Classification

302.3.2 Separated uses *(part 11 of 15)*

- This part of the section governs fire-resistance ratings for separations of occupancy M.
- Storage areas in occupancy M with any of the following characteristics do not require separation:
  - Storage < 10% of floor area.
  - Storage < 1000 sf.
  - Storage with both the following:
    Area < 3000 sf.
    Area is sprinklered.
- The table below shows separations required between M and the occupancies listed:

Table 302.3.2n   Occupancy M: Fire-Resistance Ratings for Occupancy Separations

Occupancies	Ratings in hrs
With sprinklers:	
A	1
B	1
E	1
F-1	2
F-2	1
H-2	2
H-3, H-4, H-5	1
I-2	2
I-1, I-3, I-4	1
R	1
S-1	2
S-2	1
U	1
Without sprinklers:	
A	2
B	2
E	2
F-1	3
F-2	2
R	2
S-1	3
S-2	2
U	1

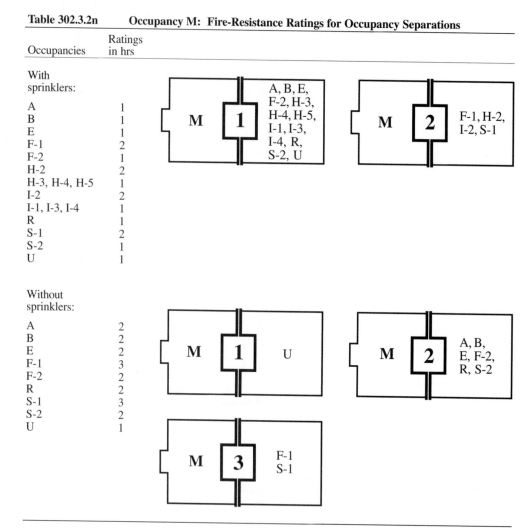

Source: IBC Table 302.3.2.

302 Classification

302.3.2 Separated uses *(part 12 of 15)*

- This part of the section governs fire-resistance ratings for separations of occupancy R.
- The table below shows separations required between R and the occupancies listed as follows:
  - The table does not apply to separations between the following like occupancies:

    R-1 and R-1.

    R-2 and R-2.

    R-3 or R-4 and R-3 or R-4.

Table 302.3.2o   Occupancy R: Fire-Resistance Ratings for Occupancy Separations

Occupancies	Ratings in hrs
With sprinklers:	
A	1
B	1
E	1
F-1	2
F-2	1
H-2, H-4, H-5	4
H-3	3
I-2	2
I-1, I-3, I-4	1
M	1
R	1
S-1	2
S-2	1
U	1

R 1 — A, B, E, F-2, I-1, I-3, I-4, M, R, S-2, U

R 2 — F-1, I-2, S-1

R 3 — H-3

R 4 — H-2, H-4, H-5

Occupancies	Ratings in hrs
Without sprinklers:	
A	2
B	2
E	2
F-1	3
F-2	2
M	2
R	2
S-1	3
S-2	2
U	1

R 1 — U

R 2 — A, B, E, F-2, M, R, S-2

R 3 — F-1, S-1

Source: IBC Table 302.3.2.

302 Classification

302.3.2 Separated uses *(part 13 of 15)*

- This part of the section governs fire-resistance ratings for separations of occupancy S-1.
- Occupancy separation is not required for incidental storage areas in occupancy B or M if any of the following conditions apply:
  - Storage is < 10% of floor area.
  - Storage area is < 1000 sf.
  - Storage with both the following:
    - Area < 3000 sf.
    - Area is sprinklered.
- The table below shows separations required between S-1 and the occupancies listed:

Table 302.3.2p   Occupancy S-1: Fire-Resistance Ratings for Occupancy Separations

Occupancies	Ratings in hrs
With sprinklers:	
A	2
B	2
E	2
F	2
H-2	2
H-3, H-4, H-5	1
I-1, I-2	3
I-3, I-4	2
M	2
R	2
S-2	2
U	2

S-1 [1] H-3 H-4 H-5

S-1 [2] A, B, E, F, H-2, I-3, I-4, M, R, S-2, U

S-1 [3] I-1 I-2

Without sprinklers:	
A	3
B	3
E	3
F	3
M	3
R	3
S-2	3
U	3

S-1 [3] A, B, E, F, M, R, S-2, U

Source: IBC Table 302.3.2.

302 Classification

302.3.2 Separated uses *(part 14 of 15)*

- This part of the section governs fire-resistance ratings for separations of occupancy S-2.
- Occupancy separation is not required for incidental storage areas in occupancy B or M if any of the following conditions apply:
  - Storage is < 10% of floor area.
  - Storage area is < 1000 sf.
  - Storage with both the following:

    Area < 3000 sf.

    Area is sprinklered.
- Separation for areas used for private or pleasure vehicles may be reduced by 1 hr.
- The table below shows separations required between S-2 and the occupancies listed:

Table 302.3.2q   Occupancy S-2: Fire-Resistance Ratings for Occupancy Separations

Occupancies	Ratings in hrs
With sprinklers:	
A	1
B	1
E	1
F-1	2
F-2	1
H-2	2
H-3, H-4, H-5	1
I-1, I-2	2
I-3, I-4	1
M	1
R	1
S-1	2
U	1

S-2 — 1 — A, B, E, F-2, H-3, H-4, H-5, I-3, I-4, M, R, U

S-2 — 2 — F-1, H-2, I-1, I-2, S-1

Occupancies	Ratings in hrs
Without sprinklers:	
A	2
B	2
E	2
F-1	3
F-2	2
M	2
R	2
S-1	3
U	1

S-2 — 1 — U

S-2 — 2 — A, B, E, F-2, M, R

S-2 — 3 — F-1, S-1

Source: IBC Table 302.3.2.

302 Classification

302.3.2 Separated uses *(part 15 of 15)*

- This part of the section governs fire-resistance ratings for separations of occupancy U.
- An occupancy U carport is not required to be separated from R-3 where both the following conditions apply:
  - The carport is 100% open on ≥ 2 sides.
  - There is no enclosed use above the carport.
- The table below shows separations required between U and the occupancies listed:

Table 302.3.2r   **Occupancy U: Fire-Resistance Ratings for Occupancy Separations**

Occupancies	Ratings in hrs
With sprinklers:	
A	1
B	1
E	1
F-1	2
F-2	1
H-2, H-3, H-4	1
H-5	3
I	1
M	1
R	1
S-1	2
S-2	1
Without sprinklers:	
A	1
B	1
E	1
F-1	3
F-2	1
M	1
R	1
S-1	3
S-2	1

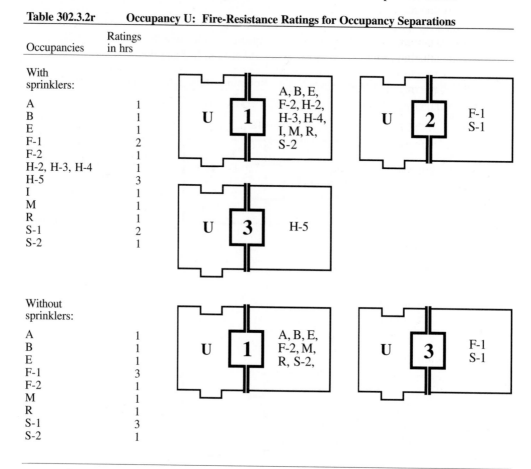

Source: IBC Table 302.3.2.

302.4 Spaces used for different purposes

- A space used for different purposes must comply with the following:
  - Requirements applicable to each purpose.

303 Assembly Group A

303.1 Assembly Group A *(part 1 of 3)*

- Buildings or parts of buildings where people gather for activities such as the following:
  Civic.
  Religious.
  Waiting for transportation.
  Social.
  Recreation.
  Consumption of food or drink.
- A gathering space is part of the occupancy served where both the following apply:
  - The gathering space has < 50 occupants.
  - The gathering space is accessory to the occupancy served.
- A gathering space is part of the occupancy served where both the following apply:
  - The gathering space has < 750 sf.
  - The gathering space is accessory to the occupancy served.

  Note: 302.2.1, "Assembly areas," is cited as the basis for this rule, but no additional information is provided in the reference section.

- A gathering space is designated as occupancy E where all the following apply:
  - The space is accessory to occupancy E.
  - The space occupies ≤ 10% of any floor area.
  - The space meets both the following requirements:
    Height limits based on occupancy and construction type.
    Area limits based on occupancy and construction type.

  Note: 302.2, "Accessory use areas," is cited as the criteria for accessory spaces in occupancy E, the applicable requirements of which are included in the summary above.
  IBC Table 503 lists height and area limitations based on occupancy and construction type.

- A gathering space is designated as occupancy A3 where all the following apply:
  - The space is one of the following:
    Religious education room.
    Religious auditorium.
  - The space is accessory to a church.
  - The space has < 100 occupants.
  - The space occupies ≤ 10% of any floor area.
  - The space meets both the following requirements:
    Height limits based on occupancy and construction type.
    Area limits based on occupancy and construction type.

  Note: 302.2, "Accessory use areas," is cited as the criteria for religious accessory spaces used for gathering, the applicable requirements of which are included in the summary above.

303 Assembly Group A

303.1 Assembly Group A *(part 2 of 3)*

- Assembly spaces are divided into the following designations:
  - A-1:
    - For the production and viewing of any of the following:
      - Performing arts.
      - Motion pictures.
    - Includes the following building types among others:
      - Theaters.
      - Movie theaters.
      - Television studios with audience seating.
      - Radio studios with audience seating.
      - Symphony and concert halls.
    - Typically with fixed seating.
  - A-2:
    - For the consumption of food and/or drink.
    - Includes the following building types among others:
      - Banquet halls.
      - Taverns and bars.
      - Nightclubs.
      - Restaurants.
  - A-3:
    - Spaces for the following functions:
      - Worship.
      - Recreation.
      - Amusement.
      - Gatherings not assigned to other assembly categories.
    - Includes the following building types among others:
      - Amusement arcades.
      - Funeral parlors.
      - Art galleries.
      - Gymnasiums, no spectator seating.
      - Indoor swimming pools, no spectator seating.
      - Bowling alleys.
      - Indoor tennis courts, no spectator seating.
      - Churches.
      - Lecture halls.
      - Community halls.
      - Libraries.
      - Courtrooms.
      - Museums.
      - Dance halls, no food or drink.
      - Passenger waiting areas.
      - Exhibition halls.
      - Pool and billiard parlors.

303 Assembly Group A

303.1 Assembly Group A *(part 3 of 3)*

- A-4:
  - Spaces for viewing indoor sporting activities as follows:
    - With spectator seating.
  - Includes the following building types among others:
    - Arenas.
    - Skating rinks.
    - Swimming pools.
    - Tennis courts.
- A-5:
  - Spaces for the following functions:
    - Participating in outdoor activities.
    - Viewing outdoor activities.
  - Includes the following building types among others:
    - Amusement park structures.
    - Bleachers.
    - Grandstands.
    - Stadiums.

303.1.1 Nonaccessory assembly use

- A gathering space with the following characteristics is designated as occupancy B:
  - Building or tenant space.
  - < 50 occupants.

304 Business Group B

304.1 Business Group B

- Includes buildings or parts of buildings used for the following:
  - Offices.
  - Professional transactions.
  - Service transactions.
  - Storage of records.
  - Storage of accounts.

- Includes the following building types among others:
  - Airport traffic control towers.
  - Electronic data processing.
  - Animal hospital.
  - Animal kennel.
  - Engineer's office.
  - Animal pound.
  - Architect's office.
  - Laboratories, testing and research.
  - Attorney's office.
  - Laundry pickup/drop off.
  - Bank.
  - Laundry, self-service.
  - Barber shop.
  - Motor vehicle showroom.
  - Beauty shop.
  - Physician's office.
  - Car wash.
  - Print shop.
  - Civic administration.
  - Clinic, outpatient.
  - Post Office.
  - Dentist.
  - Professional services.
  - Dry cleaning pickup/drop off.
  - Radio station.
  - Dry cleaning, self-service.
  - Telephone exchange.
  - Educational functions above 12th grade.
  - TV station.

Case study: Fig. 304.1. Because people gather in the conference room of the architect's office, it must be determined whether or not the space is to be designated as a business occupancy like the office in general or as an assembly occupancy. This is done by computing the number of occupants based on the use of the space, which is assembly in nature. According to IBC Table 1004.1.2, 15 sf per occupant are assigned for an assembly use having tables and chairs. This yields an occupant load of 19 for the room. Subsection 303.1 indicates that an accessory gathering space with < 50 occupants is considered to be same occupancy as that served. The conference room is designated, therefore, as occupancy B and must comply with means of egress requirements for a business.

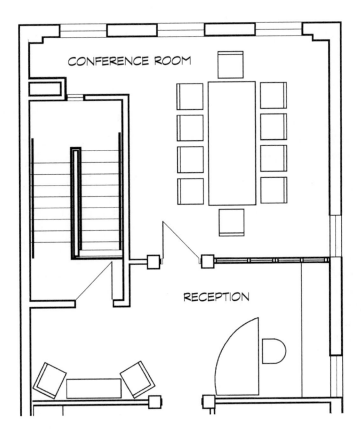

Fig. 304.1. Partial floor plan. Alterations to 209 Main Street, Annapolis, Maryland. Alt Breeding Schwarz Architects, LLC. Annapolis, Maryland.

305 Educational Group E

305.1 Educational Group E

- Includes buildings or parts of buildings used as follows:
  - ○ Buildings with both the following characteristics:
    Serving 12th grade and lower.
    Serving ≥ 6 people at one time.
- Does not include the following spaces which are designated as occupancy A-3:
  - ○ Where all the following apply:
    The space has one of the following uses:
    Religious education room.
    Religious auditorium.
    The space is accessory to a church.
    The space has < 100 occupants.
    The space occupies ≤ 10% of any floor area.
    The space meets height limits based on the following:
    Occupancy type.
    Construction type.
    The space meets area limits based on the following:
    Occupancy type.
    Construction type.

  Note: 302.2, "Accessory use areas," is cited as the criteria for religious accessory spaces used for gathering, the applicable requirements of which are included in the summary above.
  IBC Table 503 lists height and area limitations based on occupancy and construction type.

305.2 Day care

- Occupancy E includes buildings or parts of buildings serving the following purposes with all the characteristics listed below:
  - ○ Purposes:
    Educational.
    Supervisory.
    Personal care.
  - ○ Characteristics of services:
    Serving > 5 children.
    Serving children > 2½ years old.

306 Factory Group F

306.1 Factory Industrial Group F

- Includes buildings or parts of buildings used for any of the following functions, which are not classified as occupancy H or S:
  - Assembling.
  - Disassembling.
  - Fabricating.
  - Finishing.
  - Manufacturing.
  - Packaging.
  - Repair.
  - Processing operations.

306.2 Factory Industrial F-1 Moderate-Hazard Occupancy

- Includes factory and industrial functions not classified as F-2: Low Hazard including the following:

Aircraft	Recreational vehicles
Publishing	Athletic equipment
Bicycles	Rug making
Automobiles	Business machines
Bakeries	Boat fabrication
Electronics	Beverages > 12% alcohol
Brushes	TV studio, no audience
Rug cleaning	Photographic film
Brooms	Electric generation plants
Disinfectants	Construction and agricultural machinery
Dyeing	Food processing
Jute products	Musical instruments
Metals	Hemp products
Shoes	Cameras
Printing	Canvas and fabric similar to canvas
Dry cleaning	Leather products
Upholstering	Photographic equipment
Clothing	Optical products
Carpet making	Refuse incineration
Appliances	Cabinet making and door and sash millwork
Machinery	Engine manufacaturing and rebuilding
Trailers	Paper mills and paper products
Motor vehicles	Soap and detergent
Furniture	Carpet cleaning
Textiles	Motion picture studio, no audience
Laundries	Plastic products
Tobacco	Wood distillation

306 Factory Group F

306.3 Factory Industrial F-2 Low-Hazard Occupancy

- Includes factory and industrial functions as follows:
  - Use of noncombustible materials in the following:
    Manufacturing.
    Fabrication.
  - Does not cause a significant fire hazard in the following:
    Processing.
    Finishing.
    Packing.
  - Includes product types and processes similar to the following:
    Beverages $\leq$ 12% alcohol.
    Ceramic products.
    Gypsum.
    Metal products fabrication.
    Brick and masonry.
    Foundries.
    Metal product assembly.
    Glass products.
    Ice.

307 High-Hazard Group H

307.1 High-Hazard Group H

- Includes buildings or building areas containing materials with the 3 conditions listed:
  - With any of the following characteristics:
    Readily support combustion.
    Risk of explosion.
    Extremely rapid oxidation as follows:
      Potential for explosion if contained.
    Pose a health hazard.
  - Used in any of the following ways:
    Manufacturing.
    Processing.
    Generation of materials.
    Storage.
  - With quantities in excess of limits defining significant hazard.

    Note: The following tables are cited as listing limits of hazardous materials:
      IBC Table 307.7(1), "Maximum Allowable Quantity per Control Area of Hazardous Materials Posing a Physical Hazard."
      IBC Table 307.7(2), "Maximum Allowable Quantity per Control Area of Hazardous Material Posing a Health Hazard."

307.3 High-Hazard Group H-1 *(part 1 of 2)*

- Buildings containing materials with risk of explosion are classified as H-1 as follows:
  - Division 1.1:
    Risk of near simultaneous explosion of all material.
  - Division 1.2:
    No risk of near simultaneous explosion of all material.
    Risk of projectiles upon explosion.
  - Division 1.3:
    No risk of near simultaneous explosion of all material.
    Risk of limited explosion.
    Risk of limited projectiles upon explosion.
    Risk of fire.
    Does not include the following materials which are classified as H-2:
      Materials with either of the following conditions that prevents fire from producing a near simultaneous explosion of all material:
        Confinement of the substance.
        Configuration of the substance.

307 High-Hazard Group H

307.3 High-Hazard Group H-1 *(part 2 of 2)*

○ Division 1.4:

  Risk of limited explosion.

  No risk of significant projectiles upon explosion.

  Fire does not result in near simultaneous explosion of all material.

  Does not include the following materials which are classified as H-3:

    Materials not regulated as explosives by the following agency:

      Bureau of Alcohol, Tobacco, and Firearms.

    Materials used in proccesses that do not produce either of the following:

      Explosion of other products.

      Explosivelike combustion of other products.

○ Division 1.5:

  Potential for near simultaneous explosion of all material.

  Minimal risk for near simultaneous explosion of all material.

  Explosives have very low sensitivity.

○ Division 1.6:

  No risk of near simultaneous explosion of all material.

  Virtually no risk of accidental explosion.

  Explosives have extremely low sensitivity.

○ Organic peroxides, unclassified detonatable:

  Derivative of hydrogen peroxide.

  High risk of explosion.

○ Oxidizers, Class 4:

  Substances which yield oxygen in a fire.

  Risk of spontaneous combustion.

  Risk of explosion with any of the following:

    Contamination.

    Thermal shock.

    Physical shock.

○ Unstable (reactive) materials of the two classes listed below:

  Class 3 detonatable:

    Not an explosive.

    Risk of explosive reaction when subjected to the following:

      Strong initiating source.

      Thermal or physical shock at high temperatures and pressures.

  Class 4:

    Not an explosive.

    Risk of explosive when subjected to the following:

      Thermal or physical shock at normal temperatures and pressures.

○ Detonatable pyrophoric materials:

  Substances which can spontaneously combust at low temperatures.

307 High-Hazard Group H

307.4 High-Hazard Group H-2

- Buildings containing materials subject to the following risks:
  - Accelerated burning.
  - Extremely rapid oxidation:
    Potential for explosion if contained.
- Two types of substances and their storage methods classified as H-2:
  - Liquids:
    Flammable:
      Class I: Flash point < 100°F.
    Combustible:
      Class II: Flash point ≥ 100°F, < 140°F.
      Class III-A: Flash point ≥ 140°F, < 200°F.
  - Oxidizers, Class 3:
    Substances which yield oxygen in a fire.
    Causes high increase in burning rate of other materials.
    Undergoes vigorous decomposition when subjected to the following:
      Contamination.
      Heat.
  - Storage methods:
    In open systems.
    Closed systems > 15 psi.
- Selected examples of other H-2 substances:
  - Combustible dust.
  - Flammable cryogenic liquids:
    Liquids with boiling point < 150°F.
  - Flammable gases:
    Compressed gas that burns in air.
  - Organic peroxides, Class I:
    Derivative of hydrogen peroxide.
    Burns very rapidly.
  - Pyrophoric materials:
    Risk of spontaneous combustion at low temperatures.
  - Class 3, nondetonable unstable (reactive) materials:
    Not an explosive.
    Vigorous chemical reaction when subjected to the following:
      Strong initiating source.
      Thermal or physical shock at high temperatures and pressures.
  - Class 3 water-reactive materials:
    Reacts explosively to water without the following:
      Confinement.
      Heat.

307 High-Hazard Group H

307.5 High-Hazard Group H-3 *(part 1 of 2)*

- Buildings containing materials with any of the following characteristics:
  - ○ Readily support combustion.
  - ○ Risk of explosion.
  - ○ Risk of extremely rapid oxidation:
      Potential for explosion if contained.
- Categories of H-3 substances include but are not limited to the following:
  - ○ 2 types of liquids contained as indicated below:
      Liquids:
        Flammable:
          Class I: Flash point $< 100°F$.
        Combustible:
          Class II: Flash point $\geq 100°F$ and $< 140°F$.
          Class III-A: Flash point $\geq 140°F$ and $< 200°F$.
      Contained as follows:
        In closed systems.
        @ < 15 psi.
  - ○ Combustible fibers.
  - ○ Oxidizing cryogenic fluids:
      Liquids with boiling point $< 150°F$.
  - ○ Consumer fireworks:
      Division 1.4G substances as follows:
        No risk of near simultaneous explosion of all materials due to the following:
          Detonation of individual products.
          Fire.
        No significant projectile risk.
        Can include products not considered explosives by the following:
          Bureau of Alchohol, Tobacco, and Firearms.
  - ○ Flammable solids:
      Do not include the following:
        Blasting products.
        Explosives.
      Solids that have the following characteristics:
        Readily ignite.
        Burn rapidly, vigorously, and persistently.

307 High-Hazard Group H

307.5 High-Hazard Group H-3 *(part 2 of 2)*

- 2 classes of organic peroxides:
  Derivatives of hydrogen peroxide.
  Class II:
    Burns rapidly.
    Severe risk of vigorous chemical reaction due to the following:
      Heat.
      Friction.
      Shock.
  Class III:
    Burns rapidly.
    Moderate risk of vigorous chemical reaction due to the following:
      Heat.
      Friction.
      Shock.
- 2 classes of oxidizers:
  Substances which yield oxygen in a fire.
  Class 2:
    Can cause moderate increase in burning rate of other materials.
    Can cause spontaneous combustion of other materials.
  Class 3:
    Where contained in closed systems < 15 psi.
    Causes high increase in burning rate of other materials.
    Undergoes vigorous decomposition when subjected to the following:
      Contamination.
      Heat.
- Oxidizing gases:
  Sometimes yield oxygen.
  Enhance burning of other materials.
- Tire storage with all the following characteristcs:
  ≥ 10,000 tires.
  Passenger vehicle tires:
    Average size.
    Tire weight = about 25 lbs.
- Class 2 unstable (reactive) materials:
  Not an explosive.
  Subject to any of the following:
    Rapid chemical reaction in the following conditions:
      Normal temperatures and pressures.
    Vigorous chemical reaction in the following conditions:
      High temperatures and pressures.
- Class 2 water-reactive materials:
  Contact with water can yield the following:
    A potentially explosive substance.

307 High-Hazard Group H

307.6 High-Hazard Group H-4

- Buildings containing health hazards among the following:
  - Corrosive substances:
    - Chemicals that cause any of the following upon contact with living tissue:
      - Visible destruction.
      - Irreversible alterations.
  - Toxic substances:
    - Lethal chemicals.
  - Highly toxic substances:
    - Chemicals that are lethal in smaller dose than are toxic substances.

  Note: Health hazards include the following substances among others: Paint remover, ammonia, oven cleaner, bleach, pesticides, radioactive materials, lime, cement, battery acid, iodine, fertilizer, calcium chloride, salts, weed killer, drain cleaner.

307.7 Group H-5 structures

- Includes buildings with either of the following processes using substances listed below:
  - Processes:
    - Semiconductor fabrication.
    - Semiconductor research and development.
  - Substances:
    - Hazardous production materials (HPM) as follows:
      - Where HPM are present in quantities greater than certain code limits.
      - Examples include any of the following among others:
        - Flammable substances:
          - Substances that ignite easily and burn readily.
        - Combustible liquids:
          - Liquids that burn but do not ignite as easily as flammable liquids.
        - Corrosive liquids:
          - Liquids that damage living tissue on contact.
          - Damage to nonliving materials is not required for a liquid to be corrosive.
        - Oxidizing substances:
          - Substances that enhance burning by the release of oxygen.
        - Organic peroxides:
          - Substances that have a risk of fire or explosion.
        - Toxic materials:
          - Substances that are poisionous to humans.

  Note: The following tables are cited as sources of limits above which HPM result in an H-5 classification:
    IBC Table 307.7(1), "Maximum Allowable Quantity per Control Area of Hazardous Materials Posing a Physical Hazard."
    IBC Table 307.7(2), "Maximum Allowable Quantity per Control Area of Hazardous Material Posing a Health Hazard."
    415.9, "Group H-5," is cited as the source of requirements for H-5 structures.

307 High-Hazard Group H

307.9 Exceptions *(part 1 of 3)*

- This section addresses buildings and parts of buildings containing hazardous materials that do not warrant an occupancy H classification.
- Regardless of quantity, materials listed in this section must comply with the following:
  - They require the occupancy classification with which they are the most compatible.
  - They must comply with applicable code requirements.

  Note: The following are cited as sources of applicable code requirements:
  > *Section 414, "Hazardous Materials."*
  > *Pertinent sections of the IBC.*
  > *International Fire Code.*

- Buildings with quantities of hazardous materials < the limits defining a significant hazard.

  Note: The following tables are cited as defining limits of hazardous materials:
  > *IBC Table 307.7(1), "Maximum Allowable Quantity per Control Area of Hazardous Materials Posing a Physical Hazard."*
  > *IBC Table 307.7(2), "Maximum Allowable Quantity per Control Area of Hazardous Material Posing a Health Hazard."*
  > *The International Fire Code is also cited as governing these materials.*

- Buildings with control areas housing quantities of hazardous materials that are < the limits defining a significant hazard.

  Note: 414.2, "Control areas," is cited as providing requirements for such areas.

- Buildings housing the application of flammable finishes.

  Note: The following flammable or combustible substances are included among others: paint, varnish, lacquer, stain, fiberglass resins or other liquids applied by spray or dip tank; powders applied by spray, electrostatic processes, or fluidized beds; dual-component coatings or liquids applied by brush or roller in amounts > 1 gallon.
  > *The following are cited as governing these processes:*
  > *Section 416, "Application of Flammable Finishes."*
  > *International Fire Code.*

- Storage and sale of flammable and combustible liquids as follows:
  - In occupancy M.

  Note: International Fire Code is cited as governing these liquids.

307 High-Hazard Group H

307.9 Exceptions *(part 2 of 3)*

- Buildings housing liquids or gases with all the following characteristics:
  - Flammable or combustible.
  - In closed systems.
  - For operating the following:
    Machinery.
    Equipment.
- Cleaning establishments in either of the following cases:
  - Using combustible liquid solvents meeting all the following conditions:
    Flash point $\geq$ 140F°.
    Contained in closed systems.
    In equipment listed by an approved testing agency.
    In areas separated from the rest of the building as follows:
      By construction with a fire-resistance rating $\geq$ 1 hr.
  - Using liquid solvents meeting all the following conditions:
    Flash point $\geq$ 200F°.
- Liquor stores with no bulk storage.
- Liquor distributors with no bulk storage.
- Buildings housing refrigeration systems.
- Storage or use of agricultural materials as follows:
  - Used on the property where stored.
- Buildings housing stationary batteries meeting all the following conditions:
  - Where used for any of the following:
    Facility emergency power.
    Uninterruptible power supply.
    Telecommunication facilities.
  - Where batteries comply with all the following:
    Batteries must have safety venting caps.
    Ventilation is provided.

  Note: International Mechanical Code is cited as governing ventilation requirements for the batteries.

- Buildings housing corrosives in the following categories:
  - Personal or household products as follows:
    Contained in original packaging.
    Used in retail display.
  - Common building materials.

307 High-Hazard Group H

307.9 Exceptions *(part 3 of 3)*

- Buildings used for aerosol storage as follows:
  - Buildings are to be classified as S-1.
  - Buildings must comply with the *International Fire Code.*
- Buildings housing the display and storage of the following hazardous materials where the conditions listed below apply:
  - Materials:
    Nonflammable solid materials.
    Nonflammable liquids.
    Noncombustible liquids.
  - Conditions:
    Quantities are < than the limits defining significant hazard.
    Where one of the following occupancies applies:
    M, S.

  Note: 414.2.4, "Hazardous material in Group M display and storage areas and in Group S storage areas," is cited as governing these materials.
  The following tables define the limits of hazardous materials:
  IBC Table 307.7(1), "Maximum Allowable Quantity per Control Area of Hazardous Materials Posing a Physical Hazard."
  IBC Table 307.7(2), "Maximum Allowable Quantity per Control Area of Hazardous Material Posing a Health Hazard."

- Buildings storing materials as follows:
  - Industrial explosives in the following occupancies:
    B, F, M, S.
  - The following materials in the occupancies indicated below:
    Materials:
    Black powder.
    Smokeless propellant.
    Small arms primers.
    Occupancies:
    M, R-3.

  Note: The International Fire Code is cited as the governing quantity limits and other requirements for the explosive materials.

308 Institutional Group I

308.1 Institutional Group I

- Includes buildings or parts of buildings where occupants are physically limited as follows:
  - Occupants live in a supervised environment.
  - Occupants receive the following due to health or age:
    Medical treatment.
    Other care.
    Other treatment.
  - Occupants are housed for penal or correctional purposes as follows:
    Occupants are detained.
    Liberty of occupants is restricted.

308.2 Group I-1

- Includes buildings or parts of buildings wherein people live in a residential environment as follows:
  - >16 occupants are housed for reasons related to the following:
    Age.
    Mental disability.
    Other reasons.
  - Occupants can respond to an emergency without assistance.
  - Personal care services are provided as follows:
    Occupants are supervised.
    Services are provided 24 hrs/day.
  - The following facility types among others in this category:
    Residential board and care facilities.
    Assisted living facilities.
    Halfway houses.
    Group homes.
    Congregate care facilities.
    Social rehabilitation facilities.
    Alcohol and drug centers.
    Convalescent facilities.
- The following facilities that are otherwise similar to those above are not included:
  - Facilities with ≤ 5 people are governed by one of the following:
    Occupancy R-3 requirements.
    International Residential Code requirements.
  - Facilities with ≥ 6 people and ≤ 16 people are classified as occupancy R-4.

308 Institutional Group I

308.3 Group I-2

- Includes buildings or parts of buildings used for medical related purposes as follows:
  - Functions:

Medical	Surgical	Psychiatric
Nursing	Custodial care	

  - Characteristics:
    > 5 persons are housed.
    Clients are housed 24 hrs/day.
    Clients are not capable of self-preservation.
  - Facility types include the following:
    Hospitals.
    Intermediate care nursing homes.
    Skilled care nursing homes.
    Mental hospitals.
    Detoxification facilities.
- Facilities which are otherwise similar are not included as follows:
  - Facilities with ≤ 5 people are governed by one of the following:
    Occupancy R-3 requirements.
    International Residential Code.

308.3.1 Child care facility

- I-2 includes child care facilities as follows:
  - Care is provided 24 hrs/day.
  - > 5 children are served.
  - Children are ≤ 2½ years old.

308.4 Group I-3

- Includes buildings wherein occupants are restrained for security purposes as follows:
  - > 5 restrained occupants.
  - Occupants are not capable of self-preservation due to security measures.
  - Facility types among others include the following:

Prisons	Jails	Reformatories
Detention centers	Correctional centers	Prerelease centers

  - Occupancy I-3 is subdivided into 5 conditions as follows:
    Degree of restraint is increased with each higher condition number.

    Note: The following sections are cited as having requirements affecting occupancy I-3:
    408.1, "General," which identifies section 408, "Group I-3" as governing this occupancy.
    308.4.1–5, "Condition 1," "Condition 2," "Condition 3," "Condition 4," and "Condition 5."

308 Institutional Group I

308.4.1 Condition 1

- This section addresses the least restrained condition of occupancy I-3.
- Detainees may move freely without restraint to the exterior from the following areas:
  - Sleeping areas.
  - Other spaces occupied by detainees.
- Such buildings may be constructed as occupancy R.

308.4.2 Condition 2

- This section addresses the occupancy I-3 condition of restraint at the next higher level above that of condition 1.
- Detainees may move freely between smoke compartments.
- Locked exits prevent free egress to the exterior.

308.4.3 Condition 3

- This section addresses the occupancy I-3 condition of restraint at the next higher level above that of condition 2.
- Detainees may move freely within a smoke compartment such as the following:
  - A residential unit containing the following:
    Individual sleeping units.
    Group activity spaces.
- Egress between smoke compartments is controlled by remote-controlled locks.

308.4.4 Condition 4

- This section addresses the occupancy I-3 condition of restraint at the next higher level above that of condition 3.
- Detainee movement between spaces is restricted by remote-controlled locks as follows:
  - From the following within a smoke compartment:
    Sleeping units.
    Activity spaces.
    Other spaces occupied by detainees.
  - Between smoke compartments.

308.4.5 Condition 5

- This section addresses the most restrained condition of occupancy I-3.
- Movement between occupied spaces is restricted by manual-release locks as follows:
  - From the following within a smoke compartment:
    Sleeping units.
    Activity spaces.
    Other spaces occupied by detainees.
  - Between smoke compartments.

308 Institutional Group I

308.5 Group I-4, day care facilities

- Care during religious functions at places of worship are not governed by this section.
- Buildings wherein persons receive custodial care as follows:
  - Occupants served may be of any age.
  - Care is < 24 hrs/day.
  - Care is by individuals other than the following:
    Parents.
    Guardians.
    Relatives by blood.
    Relatives by marriage.
    Relatives by adoption.
  - Care is at a location other than the home of person receiving care.
- Similar facilities caring for ≤ 5 persons are governed by one of the following:
  - Occupancy R-3 requirements.
  - *International Residential Code.*

308.5.1 Adult care facility

- A facility providing supervision and personal care for adults as follows:
  - Care is provided < 24 hrs/day.
  - Care is provided for > 5 adults.
  - Adults are unrelated.
- Such facilities are classified as follows:
  - I-4 where occupants require help to respond to an emergency.
  - A-3 where occupants do not require help to respond to an emergency.

308.5.2 Child care facility

- Day care service is classified as occupancy I-4 where the following apply:
  - Care is provided < 24 hrs/day.
  - Care is provided for > 5 children.
  - Children cared for are ≤ 2½ years old.
- Day care service is classified as occupancy E where all the following apply:
  - Care is provided < 24 hrs/day.
  - Care is provided for > 5 children.
  - Care is provided for ≤ 100 children.
  - Children cared for are ≤ 2½ years old.
  - Childcare rooms are on level of exit discharge.
  - Each childcare room has an exit door directly to the outside.

309 Mercantile Group M

309.1 Mercantile Group M

- Includes buildings or parts of buildings used for the display and sale of merchandise as follows:
  - Involves stocks of the following incidental items accessed by the public:
    Goods.
    Wares.
    Merchandise.
  - Includes the following functions:
    Department stores.
    Drug stores.
    Markets.
    Motor vehicle service stations.
    Retail stores.
    Wholesale stores.
    Sales rooms.

309.2 Quantity of hazardous materials

- This section addresses hazardous materials stored or displayed in an occupancy M control area.
- The total amount of the following hazardous materials must be within permitted limits:
  - Nonflammable solids.
  - Nonflammable liquids.
  - Noncombustible liquids.

  Note: IBC Table 414.2.4, "Maximum Allowable Quantity per Indoor and Outdoor Control Area in Group M and S Occupancies: Nonflammable Solids and Nonflammable and Noncombustible Liquids," is cited as listing quantity limitations.

310 Residential Group R

310.1 Residential Group "R" *(part 1 of 2)*

- Includes buildings or parts of buildings with sleeping accommodations as follows:
  - Those not classified as occupancy I.
- Residential spaces are divided into the following designations:
  - R-1:

    Residents are primarily transient.

    Includes the follfowing building types:

    Hotels.

    Motels.

    Boarding houses.

  - R-2:

    Residents are primarily permanent.

    Buildings with 1 of the following:

    > 2 dwelling units.

    Sleeping accommodations.

    Includes the following building types:

Apartment houses	Dormitories	Fraternities
Sororities	Monasteries	Boarding houses
Convents	Hotels	Timeshare vacation properties
Motels		

  - R-3:

    Residents are primarily permanent.

    Buildings with < 3 dwelling units.

    Not classified as any of the following:

    R-1, R-2, I.

    Not governed by the *International Residential Code*.

    Includes day care facilities as follows:

    Care is provided for ≤ 5 persons.

    Care is for persons of any age.

    Care provided < 24 hrs/day.

  Note: Adult and child care facilities in a 1-family home may comply with the International Residential Code.

  - R-4:

    Residential care/assisted living facilities as follows:

    Number of residents served is > 5 and ≤ 16.

    Must comply with one of the following:

    R-3 construction requirements as follows:

    Unless superseded by other code requirements.

    International Residential Code where the facility qualifies.

  Note: 101.2, "Scope," is cited as defining the scope of jurisdiction of the International Residential Code.

311 Storage Group S

311.1 Storage Group S

- Includes buildings or parts of buildings used for storage that are not classified as occupancy H.

311.2 Moderate-hazard storage, Group S-1

- Includes storage not classified as S-2.
- Includes the following types of storage:

Books	Aerosols, Levels 2 and 3
Buttons	Burlap bags
Canvas belting	Furniture
Aircraft repair	Baskets
Paper bags	Leather belting
Boots	Bamboo
Shoes	Paper in rolls
Cardboard boxes	Glue
Cloth bags	Cordage
Wax candles	Paper in packs
Furs	Leather
Mucilage	Cardboard
Tobacco products	Grain
Linoleum	Horn
Woolen apparel	Noncelluloid combs
Paste	Lumber
Silk	Photo engraving
Resilient flooring	Sugar
Upholstery	Soap
Mattresses	Bulk tire storage
Rattan	

- Includes motor vehicle repair garages containing limited hazardous materials.

  Note: The following are cited as governing repair garages:
  IBC Table 307.7(1), "Maximum Allowable Quantity per Control Area of Hazardous Materials Posing a Physical Hazard."
  406.6, "Repair garages."

311 Storage Group S

311.3 Low-hazard storage, Group S-2

- Includes the storage of noncombustible materials as follows:
  - Packaging allowed for stored materials includes the following:
    On wood pallets.
    In paper cartons with single-thickness divisions.
    In paper wrappings.
    In paper cartons without divisions.

  - Characteristics of all stored products:
    A negligible amount of the following plastic trim materials is allowed:
    Knobs.
    Handles.
    Film wrapping.
  - Items allowed to be stored, among others, are as follows:

Empty glass bottles	Frozen foods
Washers and dryers	Glass
Cement in bags	Gypsum board
Crayons	Metals
Electrical motors	Soapstones
Mirrors	Meats
Dry cell batteries	Food products
Pottery	Stoves
Electrical coils	Empty cans
Talc	Chalk
Open parking garages	Metal cabinets
Porcelain	Ivory
Closed parking garages	Inert pigments

Beverages ≤ 12% alcohol in the following containers:
    Metal.
    Glass.
    Ceramic.

Dairy products in nonwaxed coated paper containers.
Foods in noncombustible containers.
Fresh vegetables in nonplastic containers.
Fresh fruits in nonplastic containers.
Metal desks with plastic tops and trim.
Noncombustible liquids in glass bottles.
Oil-filled distribution transformers.
Distribution transformers that are not oil-filled.

312 Utility and Miscellaneous Group U

312.1 General

- Occupancy U includes the following types of buildings and structures:
  - Accessory buildings.
  - Miscellaneous buildings not classified in another occupancy.
  - Building types and structures include the following:
    Agricultural buildings.
    Barns.
    Carports.
    Fences > 6' high.
    Stables.
    Tanks.
    Towers.
    Livestock shelters.
    Private garages.
    Greenhouses.
    Sheds.
  - Aircraft hangars are included as follows:
    Where accessory to a 1- or 2-family residence.

    Note: 412.3, "Residential aircraft hangars," is cited as governing these structures.

  - Grain silos are included as follows:
    Where accessory to a building in occupancy R.

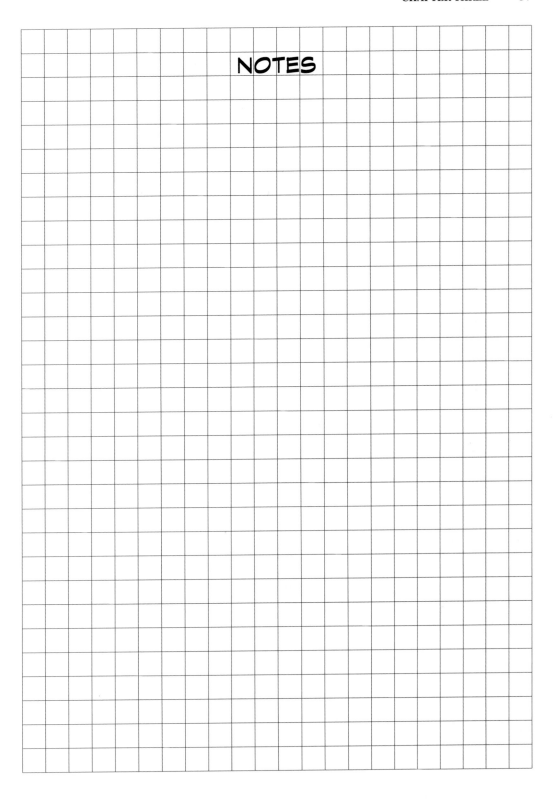

NOTES

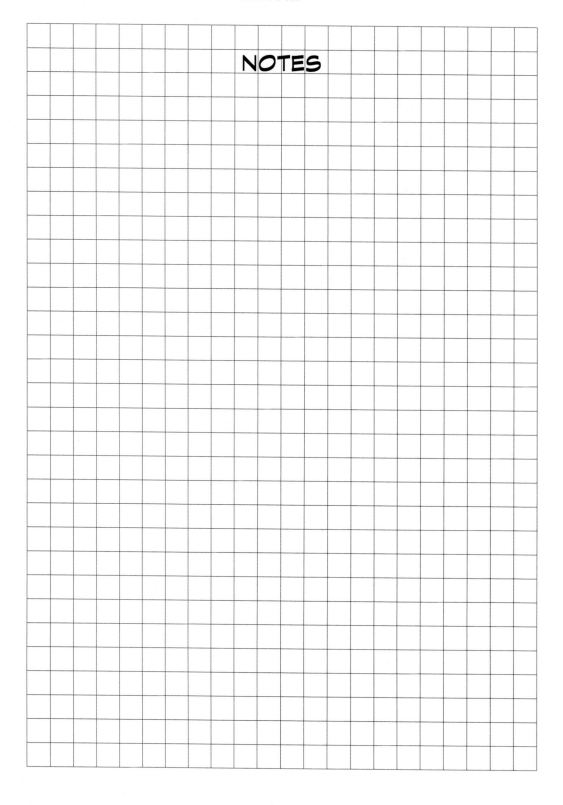

NOTES

4

Special Detailed Requirements Based on Use and Occupancy

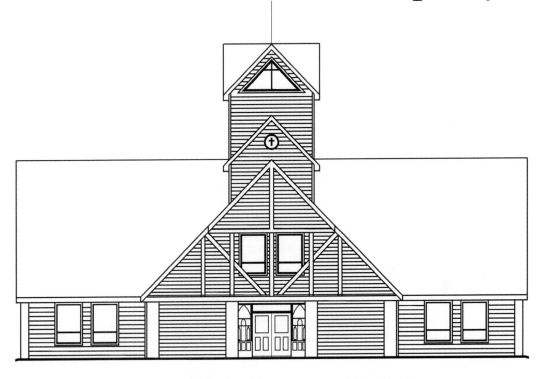

Glad Tidings Assembly of God Church. Naticoke, Pennsylvania.
Mullins and Weida, Architect and Associate. Bear Creek, Pennsylvania.

402 Covered Mall Buildings

402.1 Scope

- This section does not apply to foyers and lobbies in the following occupancies:
  B, R-1, R-2.
- Otherwise, this section applies to covered mall buildings where both of the following apply:
  - Building is ≤ 3 floor levels at every location.
  - Building is ≤ 3 stories above grade.
- Covered mall buildings are required to meet one of the following sets of requirements:
  - Applicable sections of the code in total excluding this section.
  - This section plus applicable sections of the code other than those addressed by this section.

402.2 Definitions

- **Anchor building**
  - Located on the exterior perimeter of the mall building.
  - Is in an occupancy other than H.
  - Has direct access to a covered mall building.
  - Has required means of egress separate from the mall.

- **Covered mall building**
  - A single building housing tenants similar to the following types:
    Retail stores.
    Eating and drinking establishments.
    Entertainment and amusement facilities.
    Passenger transportation terminals.
    Offices.
    Similar functions.
  - ≥ 2 tenants have a main entrance into ≥ 1 mall areas.
  - Anchor buildings are not part of the covered mall building.

- **Food court**
  - A public seating area in the mall area.
  - Serves adjacent tenants that provide food preparation.

- **Gross leasable area**
  - Total floor area for tenant occupancy including tenant storage.
  - Area of tenant occupancy is measured to the following:
    To the outside of an individual tenant's walls.
    To the centerline of shared tenant walls.

- **Mall**
  - Covered common pedestrian area in a covered mall building.
  - Provides access for ≥ 2 tenants.
  - Has ≤ 3 levels open to each other.

402 Covered Mall Buildings

402.4 Means of egress

- Means of egress is required for the spaces listed below:
  - Each tenant space.
  - The covered mall building.
- Means of egress must comply with both of the following:
  - This section.
  - The code.
- Means of egress requirements of this section govern in the following case:
  - Where they conflict with requirements of other code sections.

402.4.1 Determination of occupant load

- Occupant load allowed in a tenant space is governed by the code.
- Means of egress requirements for a tenant space is based on the permitted occupant load of the space.

402.4.1.1 Occupant formula

- This section addresses occupant load for means of egress in a covered mall building.
- The square feet required per occupant is calculated by the equation below as follows:
  - Gross leasable area does not include anchor buildings:

  Sf required per person = (0.00007 × gross leasable area in sf) + 25

  Note: Occupant load = gross leasable area ÷ sf required per person.

402.4.1.2 OLF range

- This section addresses the range permitted for square feet per occupant as calculated for various sizes of covered mall buildings.
  - The sf required per person in covered mall buildings must be ≤ 50.
  - 30 sf per occupant may be used where the sf required per person is calculated to be < 30.

402.4.1.3 Anchor buildings

- The occupant load of a covered mall building does not include the following:
  - The occupant load of anchor buildings opening into the mall.

402.4.1.4 Food courts

- The occupant load of a food court is determined by requirements elsewhere in the code.
  Note: Section 1003, "General Means of Egress," is cited as the source of requirements.

- The occupant load of the food court is added to the occupant load of the covered mall building as derived from gross leasable area.

402 Covered Mall Buildings

402.4.2 Number of means of egress

- This section addresses tenant spaces in covered mall buildings.
- ≥ 2 means of egress are required in either of the following cases:
  - Travel distance for other than employees from any point in a tenant space to the mall > 75'.
  - Tenant space has an occupant load > 50.

402.4.3 Arrangements of means of egress

- This section addresses assembly spaces in covered mall buildings.
- Assembly spaces with occupant loads ≥ 500 are governed as follows:
  - Entrance to assembly space must be immediately adjacent to a main entrance of the mall.
  - ≥ ½ the required means of egress for the assembly space must open directly to outside the mall building.

402.4.3.1 Anchor building means of egress

- The required means of egress for an anchor building is governed as follows:
  - It must be separate from the means of egress for the mall.
- Means of egress requirements for the mall do not include the following:
  - The occupant load of anchor buildings that open into the mall.
- Mall means of egress may not pass through anchor buildings.
- A mall terminating at an anchor building is a dead end in the following circumstance:
  - Where at the termination there is no means of egress independent from the anchor building.

402.4.4 Distance to exits

- This section addresses travel distance in a covered mall building.
- Travel distance must be ≤ 200' in the following cases:
  - From any point in a tenant space to the mall.
  - From any point in a tenant space to an exit.
  - From any point in a mall to an exit.

402.4.5 Access to exits

- Dead ends are permitted in malls in the following case:
  - Where dead-end length is ≤ 2 × its width at the narrowest point.
- Otherwise, where > 1 exit is required in a mall, the following applies:
  - At all mall locations, travel in different directions to separate exits must be possible.
- The width of the following routes from a mall must be ≥ 66":
  - Exit passageway.
  - Exit access corridor.

402 Covered Mall Buildings

402.4.5.1 Exit passageway enclosures

- This section addresses exit passageway enclosures that provide a secondary means of egress from a tenant space.
- Doors from a tenant space to such enclosures are governed as follows:
  - The doors must be 1-hr fire doors.
  - One of the following types of closing systems is required:
    The doors must be self-closing.
    The doors must be automatically closed by smoke detection.

402.4.6 Service areas fronting on exit passageways

- The following service areas may open directly into exit passageways where separated as indicated below:
  - Service areas:
    Mechanical rooms.
    Electrical rooms.
    Building service areas.
    Service elevators.
  - Service areas must be separated from the exit passageway by both the following:
    Walls with 1-hr fire-resistance rating.
    Opening protectives rated at 1 hr.

402.5 Mall width

- Malls are considered corridors for purposes of required egress.
- Requirements for mall widths and clearances specified in this section supercede those listed elsewhere in the code.

  Note: 1005.1, "Minimum required egress width," is cited as the section having requirements that are superceded by requirements in this section.

402.5.1 Minimum width

- Mall width must accommodate the occupant load served.
- Mall width must be ≥ 20'.
- A clear exit width ≥ 10' wide by ≥ 8' high is required in a mall between any projection of a tenant space and any of the following:
  - Kiosk.
  - Vending machine.
  - Bench.
  - Display opening.
  - Food court.
  - Other obstruction to means of egress travel.

402 Covered Mall Buildings

402.6 Types of construction

- The area of covered mall buildings including anchor buildings is governed as follows:
  - Area is not limited where the buildings have all of the following characteristics:
    The buildings are one of the following construction types:
    I, II, III, IV.
    The following buildings are surrounded on all sides by permanent open space $\geq 60'$:
    Covered mall building.
    Attached anchor buildings.
    Parking garage.
    The anchor buildings are ≤ 3 stories high.

    Note: The following are cited as governing height and area of anchor buildings > 3 stories:
    Section 503, "General height and area limitations."
    Section 504, "Height modifications."
    Section 506, "Area modifications."
    The following are cited as governing the construction type of parking garages:
    406.3, "Open parking garages."
    406.4, "Enclosed parking garages."

402.7 Fire-resistance-rated separation

- A separation with a fire-resistance rating is not required between the following spaces:
  - Between a tenant space and the mall.
  - Between a food court and the mall.
  - Between a food court and adjacent tenant spaces.

402.7.1 Attached garage *(part 1 of 2)*

- Where a parking garage is located >10' away from the following buildings, the requirements listed below apply:
  - Buildings:
    Covered mall building.
    Anchor building.
  - Requirements:
    The walls separating the two structures must meet fire-resistance requirements.
    The following elements connecting to the garage must meet code requirements:
    Pedestrian walkways.
    Tunnels.

    Note: The following are cited as the source of applicable requirements:
    IBC Table 602, "Fire-Resistance Rating Requirements for Exterior Walls Based on Fire Separation Distance."
    3104, "Pedestrian Walkways and Tunnels."

402 Covered Mall Buildings

402.7.1 Attached garage *(part 2 of 2)*

- A covered mall building and attached parking garage are separate buildings as follows:
  - ○ Where the following garage types are separated from the mall building as indicated:
    Garage types:
    Garages for vehicles carrying ≤ 9 passengers each.
    Open garages.
    Separation:
    Fire barrier with a fire-resistance rating ≥ 2 hrs.

402.7.2 Tenant separations

- No separation wall is required between a tenant space and the mall.
- Fire partitions are required between tenant spaces.

  Note: Section 708, "Fire Partitions," is cited as the source of applicable requirements.

402.7.3 Anchor building separation

- Anchor buildings with all the following characteristics are governed as indicated below:
  - ○ Characteristics:
    ≤ 3 stories above grade.
    Is classified as an occupancy that is permitted for tenants in the building.
  - ○ Requirements:
    They must be separated from the covered mall building as follows:
    By fire barriers with the following fire-resistive rating:
    2 hrs.

  Note: Section 706, "Fire Barriers," is cited as governing these barriers.

- Other anchor buildings are governed as follows:
  They must be separated from the covered mall building as follows:
  By fire walls.

  Note: Section 706, "Fire Barriers," is cited as governing these fire walls.

402.7.3.1 Openings between anchor building and mall

- This section does not apply to the following openings:
  - ○ Between occupancy R-1 sleeping units and the mall.
- Openings between anchor buildings and the mall are governed as follows:
  - ○ Openings are not required to be protected where anchor buildings have the following construction types:
    Type 1.
    Type 2.

402 Covered Mall Buildings

402.8 Automatic sprinkler system

- Sprinklers are not required in open parking garages.

  Note: 406.2, "Parking garages," is cited as describing qualifying garages.

- Otherwise, covered mall buildings and connected buildings must be sprinklered as follows:
  - As per NFPA 13.
  - Prior to occupation by any tenant, the sprinkler system must be complete and operable throughout the covered mall building.
  - Empty tenant spaces must be protected with operable sprinklers as follows:
    Where approved alternative systems are not provided.
  - Mall sprinklers must be independent from the following:
    Sprinklers for tenant spaces.
    Sprinklers for anchor buildings.
  - Sprinklers of the same system serving more than one tenant are governed as follows:
    They must be controlled independently.

402.8.1 Standpipe system

- A standpipe system is required in covered mall buildings.

  Note: 905.3.3, "Covered mall buildings," is cited as applicable to this requirement.

402.9 Smoke control

- Smoke control is required in a covered mall building where it is required for atriums.

  Note: Section 404, "Atriums," is cited as the source of requirements for smoke control.

402.10 Kiosks *(part 1 of 2)*

- This section governs kiosks and like constructions in a mall as follows:
  - Temporary.
  - Permanent.
- Kiosks must be constructed of one of the following:
  - Noncombustible materials.
  - Fire-retardant-treated wood.

    Note: 2303.2, "Fire-retardant-treated wood," is cited as governing this material.

  - Foam plastics as follows:
    With a heat release rate ≤ the following:
    100 kW.
    105 Btu/h.

    Note: UL 1975, "Fire Tests of Foam Plastics Used for Decorative Purposes," is cited as the required test for heat release using exhibit booth protocol.

402 Covered Mall Buildings

402.10 Kiosks *(part 2 of 2)*

- o Aluminum composite material (ACM) with both the following characteristics:
  Flame spread index $\leq$ 25.
  Smoke-developed index $\leq$ 450.

  Note: ASTM E 84, "Tests Methods for Surface Burning Characteristics of Building Materials," is cited as governing the tests for ACM. Tests are required for the material in the maximum thickness used in the kiosk.

- Kiosks must have both of the following approved systems:
  - o Fire detection.
  - o Fire suppression.
- $\geq$ 20' separation is required between the following and other structures in a mall:
  - o Kiosks.
  - o Groups of kiosks.
- The following must be $\leq$ 300 sf in area:
  - o Kiosks.
  - o Groups of kiosks.

402.11 Security grilles and doors

- Security grilles or doors of the following types in a required means of egress have requirements as indicated below:
  - o Types:
    Horizontal sliding.
    Vertical.
  - o Requirements:
    They must remain fully open during occupancy by the public.
    They may not be closed while the served space has the following conditions:
      Where > 10 persons occupy a space with 1 exit.
      Where > 50 persons occupy a space with >1 exit.
    They must be operable when the served space is occupied as follows:
      From inside the space.
      Without special knowledge or effort.
- Where $\geq$ 2 exits are required, the following applies:
  - o Security grilles or doors are limited to $\leq$ ½ the exits.

402.12 Standby power

- Standby power is required in mall buildings > 50,000 sf as follows:
  - o Systems must be able to operate emergency voice/alarm systems.

402 Covered Mall Buildings

402.13 Emergency voice/alarm communication system

- Emergency voice/alarm systems are required in covered mall buildings > 50,000 sf of total floor area.
- Mall emergency voice/alarm systems must be accessible to the fire department as follows:
  - Where such systems are required.
  - Where such systems are not required but are provided.

  Note: 907.2.12.2, "Emergency voice/alarm communication system," is cited as governing the locations and characteristics of such systems.

402.14 Plastic signs

- Plastic signs are restricted in size and detail in covered mall buildings as follows:
  - Within every store as follows:
      On every level.
  - From side wall to side wall of each tenant space facing the mall.
  - By requirements of this section series.

  Note: The following are cited as the source of sign requirements in this section series:
      402.14.1, "Area."
      402.14.2, "Height and width."
      402.14.3, "Location."
      402.14.4, "Plastics other than foam plastics."
      402.14.5, "Foam plastics."

402.14.1 Area

- Plastic signs are limited to ≤ 20% of the tenant façade facing the mall.

402.14.2 Height and width

- The size of plastic signs is limited as follows:
  - Vertical dimension must be ≤ 36" for horizontal signs.
  - Vertical dimension must be ≤ 96" for vertical signs.
  - Horizontal dimension must be ≤ 36" for vertical signs.

402.14.3 Location

- Plastic signs must be ≥ 18" from adjacent tenants:
  - Measured to the center of the common wall between tenants.

402 Covered Mall Buildings

402.14.4 Plastics other than foam plastics

- This section does not apply to the following:
  - Foam plastics used in signs.
- Other plastics are to be light-transmitting plastics complying with one of the following:
  - Specifications listed elsewhere in the code.

    Note: The following sections are cited as alternatives for governing the plastics:
    2606.4, "Specifications."
    803.2.1, "Acceptance criteria," is an alternative when tests are in accordance
    with NFPA 286, "Standard Method of Fire Test for Evaluating Contribution of
    Wall and Ceiling Interior Finish to Room Fire Growth."

  - Specifications as follows:
    Self-ignition temperature $\geq 650°F$.
    Flame-spread index ≤ 75.
    Smoke-developed index ≤ 450.

    Note: The following are cited as describing tests for verifying the properties above:
    ASTM D 1929, "Standard Test Method for Determining Ignition Temperature
    of Plastics."
    ASTM E 84, "Standard Test Methods for Surface Burning Characteristics of
    Building Materials."

402.14.4.1 Encasement

- The backs and edges of plastic signs in the mall must be enclosed with metal.

402.14.5 Foam plastics

- Foam plastics used in signs are governed as follows:
  - The sign must have a heat release rate ≤ 150 kW.

    Note: UL 1975, "Fire Test of Foamed Plastic Used for Decorative Purposes," is cited
    as describing the test verifying heat release rate.

  - The foam plastics must have the properties specified in subsequent sections.

    Note: The following sections specify the required properties:
    402.14.5.1, "Density."
    402.14.5.2, "Thickness."

- Foam plastic signs meeting plastic-sign requirements need not have the following:
  - Flame-spread index ≤ 75.
  - Smoke-developed index ≤ 450.

    Note: 402.14, "Plastic signs," is cited as governing in lieu of the specified flame
    spread and smoke-developed indexes.
    2603.3, "Surface-burning characteristics," is cited as the source of flame
    spread and smoke-developed indexes which do not apply in this case.

402 Covered Mall Buildings

402.14.5.1 Density

- The density of foam plastic must be $\geq$ 20 lbs/cu ft.

402.14.5.2 Thickness

- The thickness of foam plastic signs must be $\leq \frac{1}{2}''$.

402.15 Fire department access to equipment

- Areas housing the following controls are to be identified for use by the fire department:
  - Controls for air-conditioning systems.
  - Controls for automatic fire-extinguishing systems.
  - Controls for other detection, suppression, or control elements.

403 High-Rise Buildings

403.1 Applicability

- Buildings not governed by this section include the following:
  - Airport traffic control towers.
  - Open parking garages.
  - Occupancy A-5 buildings.
  - Occupancy F-2 buildings that require large heights to accommodate equipment such as the following:
    - Craneways.
    - Rolling mills.
    - Structural metal fabrication.
    - Production and distribution of power.
  - Buildings with the following occupancies:
    - H-1, H-2, H-3.

  Note: The following are cited as governing the buildings above:
  Section 412, "Aircraft-Related Occupancies."
  406.3, "Open parking garages."
  303.1, "Assembly Group A."
  503.1.2, "Special industrial occupancies," for buildings with large equipment.
  Section 415, "Groups H-1, H-2, H-3, H-4 and H-5."

- Otherwise, buildings governed by this section are as follows:
  - Buildings with occupied floors > 75' above lowest level of fire department vehicle access.

403.2 Automatic sprinkler system *(part 1 of 2)*

- Sprinklers are not required in buildings used only to house telecommunications equipment as follows, with the conditions listed below:
  - Equipment:
    - Telecommunications equipment.
    - Associated electrical power distribution equipment.
    - Batteries.
    - Standby engines.
  - Conditions:
    - Automatic fire detection system is required in equipment spaces.
    - Fire barriers must isolate equipment spaces as follows:
      - Walls must have a fire-resistance rating ≥ 1 hr.
      - Floor/ceiling assemblies must have a fire-resistance rating ≥ 2 hrs.

  Note: 907.2, "Where required," is cited as governing the fire detection system.

- Sprinklers are not required in open parking garages.

  Note: 406.3, "Open parking garages," is cited as governing these facilities.

- Other high-rise buildings are required to be sprinklered as per NFPA 13.

403 High-Rise Buildings

403.2 Automatic sprinkler system *(part 2 of 2)*

- Secondary water systems for sprinklers are required as follows:
  - For high-rise buildings in Seismic Design Categories C, D, E, or F as follows:
    To equal the hydraulically calculated demand.
    To have a duration ≥ 30 minutes.

  Note: 903.3.5.2, "Secondary water supply," is cited as the source of requirements.

403.3 Reduction in fire-resistance rating

- Reduction in requirements for fire-resistance ratings is permitted as follows:
  - Where sprinkler control valves are equipped as follows for specified conditions:
    Valves have supervisory initiating devices for each floor.
    Valves have water-flow initiating devices for each floor.

  Note: The following are cited as indicating the rating reductions permitted. They also define additional conditions required for such reductions:
  403.3.1, "Type of construction."
  403.3.2, "Shaft enclosures."

403.3.1 Type of construction

- Where sprinkler control valves are equipped as follows, required fire-resistance ratings may be reduced as indicated below:
  - Control valves:
    Valves have supervisory initiating devices for each floor.
    Valves have water-flow initiating devices for each floor.
  - Reductions in fire-resistance ratings permitted:
    Type IA may be reduced to Type IB.
    Type IB may be reduced to Type IIA in the following occupancies:
    A, B, E, F-2, H, I, R, S-2, U.

  Note: The following are cited as applicable to the reductions described above:
  IBC Table 601, "Fire-Resistance Rating Requirements for Building Elements," lists construction types and fire-resistance ratings that may be reduced.
  403.3, "Reduction in fire-resistance rating," is cited as the source of conditions required for rating reductions.

  - Height and area limitations of the original construction type apply to the following:
    The reduced construction type.

403.3.2 Shaft enclosures *(part 1 of 2)*

- This section does not apply to the following enclosures:
  - Exit enclosures.
  - Elevator hoistway enclosures.

403 High-Rise Buildings

403.3.2 Shaft enclosures *(part 2 of 2)*

- The fire-resistance rating required for other fire barriers enclosing vertical shafts may be reduced as follows:
  - Rating reduced to $\geq$ 1 hr in the following case:

    Where sprinklers are provided in the shaft at the following locations:

    At the top.

    At every other floor.

  Note: 403.3, "Reduction in fire-resistance rating," lists the conditions permitting the reduction described in this section.

403.4 Emergency escape and rescue

- Such openings are not required in high-rise buildings.

  Note: Section 1025, "Emergency Escape and Rescue," is cited as the source for opening requirements waived by this section.

403.5 Automatic fire detection

- Smoke detection is required in high-rise buildings.

  Note: 907.2.12.1, "Automatic fire detection," is cited as the source of requirements for smoke detection in this type of building.

403.6 Emergency voice/alarm communication systems

- An emergency voice/alarm communication system is required in high-rise buildings.

  Note: 907.2.12.2, "Emergency voice/alarm communication system," is cited as the source of requirements for such systems.

403.7 Fire department communications system

- A 2-way communication system is required in high-rise buildings for fire department use as follows:
  - The system must connect the fire command center to the following locations:

    Elevators.

    Every lobby.

    Emergency and standby power rooms.

    Fire pump rooms.

    Areas of refuge.

    Within enclosed exit stairways:

    At each floor level.

  Note: 907.2.12.3, "Fire department communication system," is cited as the source of requirements for such systems. A partial summary of requirements is provided above.

403 High-Rise Buildings

403.8 Fire command

- A fire command center is required in high-rise buildings as follows:
  - Location to be approved by the fire department.

    Note: Section 911, "Fire Command Center," is cited as the source of requirements for such a facility.

403.10 Standby power

- Standby power is required for the following:
  - Fire command centers.
  - Electric fire pumps.
  - Ventilation for smokeproof enclosures.
  - Fire detection systems for smokeproof enclosures.
  - Elevators.

    Note: Section 2702, "Emergency and standby power systems," is cited as governing the standby power required.
    403.10.2, "Standby power loads," is cited as the source of loads requiring standby power.

403.10.1 Special requirements for standby power systems

- Where a generator inside a building provides standby power, the following applies:
  - The generator system must be located in its own room:
    The room must be enclosed with 2-hr fire barrier assemblies.
- The fire command center must provide the following:
  - System supervision.
  - Manual-start capability.
  - Transfer features.

403.10.2 Standby power loads

- Standby power loads include the following:
  - Fire command centers.

    Note: 403.8, "Fire command," is cited as the source of requirements for a fire command center. It establishes the need for such and refers to Section 911, "Fire Command Center," for its requirements.

  - Electric fire pumps.
  - Ventilation for smokeproof enclosures.
  - Fire detection systems for smokeproof enclosures.
  - Elevators.

    Note: Section 3003, "Emergency Operations," is cited as the source of requirements for elevator standby power.

403 High-Rise Buildings

403.11 Emergency power systems

- Emergency power is required for the following:
  - Exit signs.
  - Lighting for means of egress.
  - Lighting in elevator cars.
  - Emergency voice communication systems.
  - Alarm systems.
  - Fire detection systems.
  - Fire alarm systems.

  > *Note: Section 2702, "Emergency and standby power systems," is cited as governing the standby power required.*
  > *403.11.1, "Emergency power loads," is cited as the source of loads requiring emergency power.*

403.11.1 Emergency power loads

- Emergency power is required for the following:
  - Exit signs.
  - Lighting for means of egress.

  > *Note: Chapter 10, "Means of egress," is cited as the source of requirements for exit signs and egress lighting.*

  - Lighting in elevator cars.
  - Emergency voice communication systems.
  - Alarm systems.
  - Fire detection systems.
  - Fire alarm systems.

403.12 Stairway door operation

- This section addresses stairway doors that are not exit discharge doors.
- Such doors may be locked so as to prevent opening from the stairway side in the following case:
  - Where the doors can be unlocked as follows:
    - Simultaneously.
    - Without being unlatched.
    - By a signal from the fire command station.

403.12.1 Stairway communications system

- This section addresses stairways where doors are locked from the stairway side.
- A 2-way communication system is required in the stairway as follows:
  - To be connected to an approved and continuously attended station.
  - To be located at every 5th floor or at more frequent intervals.

403 High-Rise Buildings

403.13 Smokeproof exit enclosures

- The following required stairways must meet requirements for smokeproof enclosures:
  - Stairways serving floors > 75' above lowest access level for fire department vehicles.

   Note: The following sections are cited as having applicable requirements:
   909.20, "Smokeproof enclosures."
   1019.1.8, "Smokeproof enclosures."

404 Atriums

404.1 General

- In the following occupancies, enclosure of vertical openings is not required as noted:
  - Occupancies A, B, E, F, I, M, R, S, U.
  - Where vertical openings comply with this section series.

404.1.1 Definition

- **Atrium**
  - The following are not considered to be stories for this definition:
        Balconies in assembly occupancies.
        Mezzanines.

    Note: Section 505, "Mezzanines," is cited as the source of mezzanine requirements.

  - Openings through floors for the following are not included:
        Enclosed stairways.
        Elevators.
        Hoistways.
        Escalators.
        Plumbing.
        Electrical services.
        Air conditioning.
        Other equipment.
  - Openings through floors defined as a mall are not included.
  - Openings through floor(s) with both the following characteristics are included:
        Openings connecting ≥ 2 floor levels.
        Openings are closed at the top.

404.2 Use

- Atrium floors may serve any use where both of the following apply:
  - Use is approved.
  - Individual space is sprinklered as per NFPA 13.
- Otherwise, atrium floors may serve only the following:
  - Low-fire-hazard uses.
- The following components of an atrium must be approved:
  - Materials.
  - Decorations.

    Note: International Fire Code is cited as the source of requirements with which materials and decorations must comply.

404 Atriums

404.3 Automatic sprinkler protection

- The following areas are not required to be sprinklered with the condition listed below:
  - Areas:
    - Above an atrium.
    - On levels adjacent to an atrium.
  - Condition:
    - Where separated from the atrium as follows:
      - By fire barriers with a fire-resistance rating ≥ 2 hrs.
- Sprinklers at the ceiling of an atrium are not required as follows:
  - Where the ceiling is > 55' above the floor.
- Otherwise, a sprinkler system is required as follows:
  - Required throughout a building containing an atrium.
  - Must be approved.

404.4 Smoke control

- In general, smoke control is required in atriums.

  Note: Section 909, "Smoke Control Systems," is cited as governing such systems.

- In certain cases, smoke control is not required in atriums.

  Note: The following are cited as alternative sources of conditions which permit smoke control to be omitted from an atrium:
  707.2, "Shaft enclosure required,"exceptions 2, 7, 8, or 9.

404 Atriums

404.5 Enclosure of atriums

- Space adjacent to an atrium need not be separated from the atrium as follows:
    - Such space is limited to that on any 3 floors.
    - Such space must be included in the volume of the atrium as follows:
        For the smoke-control design.
- In other cases, atriums must be separated from adjacent spaces by any of the following:
    - Fire-barrier wall with a fire-resistance rating of 1 hr.
    - Glass block wall with a $^3/_4$-hr fire protection rating.

    Note: Section 2110, "Glass Unit Masonry," is cited as governing glass block.

    - A glass wall having all the following characteristics:
        Glass wall must function as a smoke partition.
        Sprinklers with all the following characteristics must be provided along the glass:
            Located in one of the following arrangements:
                On both the atrium side and the room side of the glass wall.
                On only the room side of the glass wall in the following case:
                    Where there is no walkway on the atrium side.
            Spaced $\leq$ 6' apart.
            Located $\geq$ 4" and $\leq$ 12" from the glass wall.
            Upon activation sprinklers must wet the entire surface of the glass.
        Glass must be set in a gasketed frame which can deflect as follows:
            Prior to sprinkler activation.
            Without breaking the glass.

404.6 Standby power

- Smoke control equipment must be connected to standby power.

    Note: 909.11, "Power systems," is cited as the source of requirements for smoke control system power supply.

404.7 Interior finish

- $\geq$ Class B finishes are required for walls in atriums as follows:
    - Sprinklers do not warrant a reduction of this class.

404.8 Travel distance in atriums

- Means of egress travel through an atrium is governed as follows:
    - On levels other than the lowest level:
        Travel distance within the atrium is limited to $\leq$ 200'.

405 Underground Buildings

405.1 General

- Spaces governed as underground buildings have both the following characteristics:
  - Floors > 30' below the lowest exit discharge.
  - Floors occupied by humans.
- The following are not underground buildings:
  - 1- and 2-family dwellings as follows:
    Sprinklered.

    Note: 903.3.1.3, "NFPA 13D sprinkler systems," is cited as governing the sprinkler system.

  - Parking garages as follows:
    With automatic fire-suppression systems.

    Note: 405.3, "Automatic sprinker system," is cited as governing the fire-suppression systems.

  - Transit systems as follows:
    With fixed guideways.
  - The following facilities:
    Grandstands.
    Bleachers.
    Stadiums.
    Arenas.
    Similar facilities.
  - A building story with all the following characteristics:
    Lowest story of a building.
    The only story that otherwise qualifies as an underground building.
    An area ≤ 1500 sf.
    < 10 occupants.

405.2 Construction requirements

- The construction type required for the underground part of the building is as follows:
  - Type I.

405.3 Automatic sprinkler system

- Underground portions of the building must be sprinklered as follows:
  - At the highest level of exit discharge.
  - At all levels below the highest level of exit discharge.

    Note: The following are cited as governing the sprinkler system:
    903.3.1.1, "NFPA 13 sprinkler systems."
    903.4, "Sprinkler system monitoring and alarms," for water-flow switches and control valves.

405 Underground Buildings

405.4.1 Number of compartments

- A building with a floor > 60' below the lowest exit discharge is governed as follows:
  - It must be divided into ≥ 2 compartments as follows:
    Compartments are to be about equal in size.
    Compartments must extend as follows:
    Through all underground levels.
    To the highest level of exit discharge serving the underground levels.
  - The lowest story is not required to be compartmentalized as follows:
    Where it has both the following characteristics:
    ≤ 1500 sf.
    < 10 occupants.

405.4.2 Smoke barrier penetration

- Compartments must be separated as per all the following:
  - The separation must be ≥ 1-hr fire barrier.
  - The separation must run from floor slab to floor deck above.
  - Openings in the separation are governed as follows:
    Doors must automatically close by a signal from a smoke detection system.
    Doors must have the following to minimize smoke passage:
    Gaskets.
    Drop sills.

  Note: 715.3, "Fire door and shutter assemblies," is cited as governing the doorways.

    Other openings are limited to the following:
    Fire-stopped openings as follows:
    For plumbing piping.
    For electrical conduit.

  Note: Section 712, "Penetrations," is cited as governing fire-stopped openings.

- Each compartment's air system must be independent of other compartments.

405.4.3 Elevators

- Where elevators are provided to compartments the following applies:
  - Direct access to an elevator is required for each compartment.
  - The following is required where an elevator serves > 1 compartment:
    An elevator lobby is required with all the following characteristics:
    A 1-hr fire barrier must separate the lobby from the compartments.
    Doors require gaskets.
    Doors required drop sills.
    Doors must close automatically upon a signal from a smoke detection system.

  Note: 907.10, "Fire safety functions," is cited as the source of requirements for the smoke detection system.

405 Underground Buildings

405.5.1 Smoke control systems

- A smoke control system is required for underground buildings as follows:
  - ○ The system must contain smoke within the area of the fire origin.
  - ○ The system must limit smoke in the means of egress to maintain its viability.

  Note: Section 909, "Smoke Control Systems," is cited as the source of requirements for the smoke control system.

405.5.2 Smoke exhaust system

- Compartments in underground buildings require smoke control systems as follows:
  - ○ Each compartment must have its own system.
  - ○ The system must be activated automatically.
  - ○ Manual control of the system must be possible.

  Note: 907.2.18, "Underground buildings with smoke exhaust system," is cited as the source of requirements for the smoke control system.

405.6 Fire alarm systems

- A fire alarm system is required as follows:
  - ○ Where the lowest level is > 60' below the lowest exit discharge.

  Note: 907.2.19, "Underground buildings," is cited as the source of requirements for the fire alarm system.

405.7 Public address

- A public address system is required as follows:
  - ○ Where a fire alarm system is not required.

  Note: 907.2.19.1, "Public address system," is cited as the source of requirements for the public address system.

405.8.1 Number of exits

- Each floor requires ≥ 2 exits.
- Where compartments exist, each requires the following:
  - ○ ≥ 1 exit.
  - ○ An exit access doorway to the adjacent compartment.

  Note: 405.4, "Compartmentation," is cited as the source of criteria for requiring compartments.

405 Underground Buildings

405.8.2 Smokeproof enclosure

- Stairways for floors > 30' below their exit discharge have the following requirement:
  - They must meet smokeproof enclosure requirements.

  Note: 1019.1.8, "Smokeproof enclosures," is cited as the source of requirements for smokeproof enclosures.

405.9 Standby power

- Standby power is required for the following systems:
  - Smoke control.
  - Ventilation for smokeproof enclosures.
  - Fire detection for smokeproof enclosures.
  - Fire pumps.
  - Elevators.

  Note: The following are cited as sources of requirements for standby power:
  Section 2702, "Emergency and Standby Power Systems."
  405.9.1, "Standby power loads," lists the systems needing standby power.

405.9.1 Standby power loads

- The following systems are standby power loads:
  - Smoke control.
  - Ventilation for smokeproof enclosures.
  - Fire detection for smokeproof enclosures.
  - Fire pumps.
  - Elevators.

  Note: Section 3003, "Emergency Operations," is cited as the source of requirements for elevator standby power.

405.9.2 Pick-up time

- Standby power must supply power to connected loads as follows:
  - ≤ 60 seconds after power failure.

405 Underground Buildings

405.10 Emergency power

- Emergency power is required for the following systems:
  - Emergency voice communication.
  - Emergency alarms.
  - Fire alarms.
  - Fire detection.
  - Lighting for elevator cars.
  - Lighting for means of egress.
  - Illumination of exit signs.

  Note: The following are cited as sources of requirements for emergency power:
  Section 2702, "Emergency and Standby Power Systems."
  405.10.1, "Emergency power loads," lists systems needing emergency power.

405.10.1 Emergency power loads

- The following are emergency power loads:
  - Emergency voice communication.
  - Emergency alarms.
  - Fire alarms.
  - Fire detection.
  - Lighting for elevator cars.
  - Lighting for means of egress.
  - Illumination of exit signs.

  Note: Chapter 10, "Means of Egress," is cited as the source of requirements for illumination of means of egress and exit signs.

405.11 Standpipe system

- Standpipe systems are required in the following:
  - Underground buildings.

  Note: Section 905, "Standpipe Systems," is cited as governing these systems.

406 Motor-Vehicle-Related Occupancies

406.1 Private garages and carports

406.1.1 Classification

- Occupancy U buildings or parts of buildings are limited as follows:
  - Area must be ≤ 1000 sf where area increases are not permitted.
  - Height must be ≤ 1 story.

    Note: 406.1.2, "Area increase," is cited as the source of increases permitted to the area limit.

406.1.2 Area increase

- An occupancy U storage of the following vehicles may be ≤ 3000 sf where the conditions listed below apply:
  - Vehicles:
    Private motor vehicles.
    Pleasure-type motor vehicles.
  - Conditions:
    No repair work is done.
    No fuel is dispensed.
    For a mixed-occupancy building, the following is required:
      The exterior wall for the occupancy U area is governed as follows:
        It must meet requirements for the major occupancy.
        Openings must be protected as per requirements of the major occupancy.
      The floor area permitted for the building is governed as follows:
        The area is that permitted by the major occupancy.
    For a building housing only occupancy U, the following is required:
      The exterior wall is governed as follows:
        It must meet requirements for R-1 or R-2.
        Openings must be protected as per requirements for R-1 or R-2.
- More than one occupancy U area ≤ 3000 sf is allowed in the same building as follows:
  - Where each 3000 sf of occupancy U is isolated from the occupancies listed below by fire walls with the fire-resistance ratings indicated:

    Table 406.1.2   Occupancy U: Fire-Resistance Rating for Separation

Occupancy	Construction type	Rating
A, B, E, F-2, H-4, I, R, S-2, U	II, V	≥ 2 hr
A, B, E, F-2, H-4, I, R, S-2, U	I, III, IV	≥ 3 hr
F-1, H-3, H-5, M, S-1	I, II, III, IV, V	≥ 3 hr
H-2	I, II, III, IV, V	≥ 4 hr

    Source: IBC Table 705.4.

    Note: Section 706, "Fire Barriers," is cited as the source of requirements for fire walls applicable to this occupancy U separation.

406 Motor-Vehicle-Related Occupancies

406.1.3 Garages and carports

- Carports must meet the following requirements:
  - Open on ≥ 2 sides.
  - Floor surface must be one of the following:
    Approved noncombustible material.
    Asphalt on grade.
  - Parking surface must be sloped toward one of the following:
    A drain.
    The main vehicle entry.
- Carports open on < 2 sides must comply with the follwing:
  - Garage requirements.

    Note: This section (406, "Motor-vehicle-related occupancies,") is cited as the source of requirements for garages.

406.1.4 Separation *(part 1 of 2)*

- A private garage must be separated from the following spaces by the materials indicated:
  - Space to be separated from garage:
    Dwelling.
    Attic of dwelling.
  - Materials to use for separation:
    ½" gypsum board.
    Gypsum board to be applied to garage side of wall.
- A private garage must be separated from habitable space overhead as follows:
  - By ⅝" Type X gypsum board or equivalent.
- Doors between a private garage and a dwelling must be one of the following types:
  - Any of the following materials ≥ 1⅜" thick:
    Solid wood.
    Solid-core steel.
    Honeycomb-core steel.
  - 20-minute fire-protection-rated door.

    Note: 715.3.3, "Door assemblies in corridors and smoke barriers," is cited as governing the fire-protection-rated door option.

- Openings in the following location are not permitted:
  - Between a private garage and a sleeping room.
- A carport with both the following characteristics is not required to be separated from occupancy R-3:
  - Completely open on ≥ 2 sides.
  - No enclosed area above the carport.

406 Motor-Vehicle-Related Occupancies

406.1.4 Separation *(part 2 of 2)*

- Ducts in the following locations must have the characteristics shown below:
  - Duct locations:
      In private garages.
      Penetrating a wall between a private garage and a dwelling unit.
      Penetrating a ceiling between a private garage and a dwelling unit.
  - Required characteristics:
      Sheet steel ≥ 0.019" thick.
      No openings into the garage.

406.2 Parking garages

406.2.1 Classification

- Parking garages are classified as one of the following:
  - Open parking garage.
  - Enclosed parking garage.

    Note: The following are cited as sources of requirements for parking garages:
        406.3, "Open parking garages."
        406.4, "Enclosed parking garages."
        Section 508, "Special Provisions," addresses, for the most part, parking garages
            in relationship to specific occupancies.

406.2.2 Clear height

- A clear height of ≥ 7' is required at each floor level of a parking garage in the following areas:
  - Vehicle traffic areas.
  - Pedestrian traffic areas.
- Areas serving required van-accessible parking must comply with accessibility requirements.

    Note: The following are cited as sources of requirements for van-accessible parking:
        1106.5, "Van spaces."
        ICC/ANSI A117.1, "Accessible and Usable Buildings and Facilities."

406.2.3 Guards

- This section addresses guards in parking garages.
- Guards are required at locations with all the following characteristics:
    At interior or exterior vertical openings:
        On the floors or roofs.
        Where vehicles parked or moved.
    Where the vertical distance to the adjacent surface directly below is > 2'-6".

    Note: Section 1012, "Guards," is cited as the source of applicable requirements.

Case study: Fig. 406.2.2. There are two levels of parking under the living units of this building. The upper parking level has headroom dictated by the significant floor to floor height of the first floor which houses retail shops. Here clear height in the parking garage is never less than 13'-1". The lower level of parking has a reduced floor to floor dimension with retail space spanning over the ramp. The lowest clear height on the ramp under the retail shop mezzanine is 7'-1⅝". 7' - 11" is provided under the lowest beam elsewhere. Headroom under the ramp drops to 7' at the end of 2 parking spaces beyond which vehicles may not pass due to the presence of wheel-stops. The parking garage complies with the code requirement to provide 7' clear height in vehicle and pedestrian traffic areas.

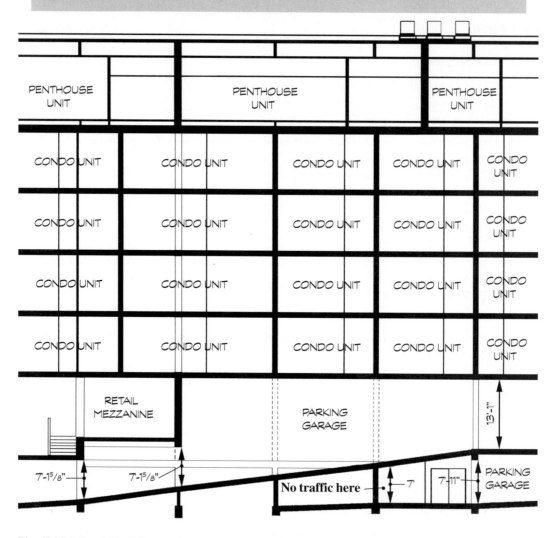

Fig. 406.2.2. Partial building section. McKenzie Lofts. Portland, Oregon. Ankrom Moisan Associated Architects. Portland, Oregon.

406 Motor-Vehicle-Related Occupancies

406.2.4 Vehicle barriers

- This section addresses barriers in parking garages.
- Parking areas must be provided with the following as applicable where pedestrian or vehicular access is not obstructed:
  - Interior walls.
  - Exterior walls.
  - Vehicle barriers.
- Vehicle barriers are to be provided at the following locations:
  - At the ends of drive lanes.
  - At the ends of parking spaces where the floor elevation changes > 12".
- Vehicle barriers are to be ≥ 2' high.

  Note: 1607.7, "Loads on handrails, guards, grab bars and vehicular barriers," is cited as the source of structural requirements for vehicle barriers.

406.2.5 Ramps

- Vehicle ramps in parking garages cannot serve as an exit.

406.2.6 Floor surfaces

- The floor surface of a parking garage must be one of the following:
  - Concrete.
  - Material similar to concrete as follows:
    Noncombustible.
    Nonabsorbent.
  - Asphalt on grade.
- The parking surface must be sloped toward one of the following:
  - A drain.
  - The main vehicle entry.

406.2.7 Mixed separation

- Parking garages are to be separated from other occupancies according to the fire-resistance separation requirement for each individual occupancy.

  Note: 302.1.1, "Incidental use areas," is cited as the source of requirements for separating parking garages from other occupancies.

406 Motor-Vehicle-Related Occupancies

406.2.8 Special hazards

- The connection of a parking garage to a room containing a fuel-fired appliance is governed as follows:
  - Where the source of appliance ignition is < 18" above the floor:
    A vestibule providing 2 doors between the spaces is required.
  - Where the source of appliance ignition is ≥ 18" above the floor:
    1 door is permitted in lieu of a vestibule.

406.2.9 Attached to rooms

- A parking garage may not open directly to a sleeping room.

406.3 Open parking garages

406.3.1 Scope

- Parking garages must comply with other requirements of the code as follows:
  - Where they are not superseded by this section.

406.3.2 Definitions *(part 1 of 2)*

- **Mechanical-access open parking garages**
  - Machines similar to the following move vehicles to and from street level:
    Parking machines.
    Lifts.
    Elevators.
    Mechanical devices.
  - The public is not permitted above street level.

- **Open parking garage**
  - Used for parking or storage of private vehicles as follows:
    Includes ≤ 1000 sf of accessory functions on grade-level tier as follows:
      Office.
      Waiting room.
      Toilet.
    Includes mechanical room serving the building.
    May be constructed under occupancies A, I, B, M, R.

  - *Note: 406.3.4, "Uses," is cited as governing the use of open parking garages. These requirements are summarized above.*

  - Vehicles are moved to and from street level by their own power.
  - Interior walls are to be open as follows:
    Open area to be > 20% of the wall area.
    Open area to be evenly distributed.

406 Motor-Vehicle-Related Occupancies

406.3.2 Definitions *(part 2 of 2)*

- ○ Openings in exterior walls for natural ventilation at each level are required as follows:
    To be on ≥ 2 sides of the building.
    To be uniformly distributed.
    Area of openings to be ≥ 20% of the total building perimeter wall area at each tier.
    Total length of openings at each level to be ≥ 40% of building perimeter as follows:
        Where they are not evenly distributed on opposite sides of the building.
    Total length of openings at each level does not have a minimum as follows:
        Where they are evenly distributed on opposite sides of the building.

    Note: 406.3.3.1, "Openings," is cited as governing the required openings of an open parking garage. These requirements are summarized above.

- **Ramp-access open parking garages**
    - ○ An open parking garage with one of the following configurations:
        Parking floors are sloped and serve as ramps between levels.
        Ramps provide access between floors for vehicles.
    - ○ Vehicles travel between floors and the street by their own power.

406.3.3 Construction

- Open parking garages must be one of the following types of construction:
    - ○ Type I.
    - ○ Type II.
    - ○ Type IV.

    Note: The following are cited as having applicable requirements:
        Chapter 16, "Structural Design."
        406.2.4, "Vehicle barriers."

406.3.3.1 Openings

- Openings in exterior walls for natural ventilation at each level are required as follows:
    - ○ To be on ≥ 2 sides of the building.
    - ○ To be uniformly distributed.
    - ○ Area of openings to be ≥ 20% of the total building perimeter wall area at each tier.
    - ○ Total length of openings at each level to be ≥ 40% of the building perimeter as follows:
        Where they are not evenly distributed on opposite sides of the building.
    - ○ Total length of openings at each level does not have a minimum in the following case:
        Where they are evenly distributed on opposite sides of the building.
- Interior walls are to be open as follows:
    - ○ Open area to be > 20% of the wall area.
    - ○ Open area to be evenly distributed.

406 Motor-Vehicle-Related Occupancies

406.3.4 Uses

- Limited mixed uses are permitted in an open parking garage building.

  Note: The following sections are cited as governing the mixed uses permitted:
    302.3, "Mixed occupancies."
    402.7.1, "Attached garage."
    406.3.13, "Prohibitions."
    508.3, "Group S-2 enclosed parking garage with Group S-2.open parking garage above."
    508.4, "Parking beneath Group R."
    508.7, "Open parking garage beneath Groups A, I, B, M and R."

406.3.5 Area and height

- The following is limited for open parking garages:
  - Height.
  - Area.

  Note: Chapter 5, "General Building Heights and Areas," is cited as governing these aspects of occupancy S-2.
    302.3, "Mixed Occupancies," is cited as having applicable requirements.

406.3.5.1 Single use *(part 1 of 2)*

- This section governs open parking garages.
- Only the following are permitted to be housed in garages governed by this section:
  - Private vehicles.
  - Any of the following functions restricted as indicated below:
    Functions:
      Office.
      Waiting room.
      Toilet rooms.
    Restrictions:
      At grade level only.
      Sum of all areas must be ≤ 1000 sf.
      Separation from the garage is not required.
- In garages with a spiral floor or sloped floor, area is limited as follows:
  - The area of the projected plan at any horizontal section is limited to that for a parking tier.
- In garages with a continuous spiral type floor, a tier is defined as follows:
  - Each 9'-6" height or portion thereof constitutes a parking tier.
- Parking tier clear heights are governed as follows:
  - Height must be ≥ 7' where mechanical parking-access devices are not used.
  - Height < 7' is permitted where approved and where mechanical parking-access devices are used.

406 Motor-Vehicle-Related Occupancies

406.3.5.1 Single use *(part21 of 2)*

- Areas of garages are governed as follows:
  - ○ Area in Type I construction is not limited.
  - ○ Area per tier in other permitted construction types is as follows:
    Limited to ≤ 50,000 sf.
- Heights of garages are governed as follows:
  - ○ Not limited in Type IA construction.
  - ○ In other types of construction height is limited as indicated in the following table:

Table 406.3.5.1   Height Limits of Open Parking Garages

Type of construction	Height of garages with ramp access	Height of garages with mechanical access	
		without sprinklers	with sprinklers
IB	12 tiers	12 tiers	18 tiers
IIA	10 tiers	10 tiers	15 tiers
IIB	8 tiers	8 tiers	12 tiers
IV	4 tiers	4 tiers	4 tiers

Source: IBC Table 406.3.5.

Note: The following are cited as governing garage height and area:
IBC Table 406.3.5, "Open Parking Garages Area and Height."
406.3.6, "Area and height increases."

406.3.6 Area and height increases *(part 1 of 3)*

- This section addresses open parking garages with openings in excess of the minimum.
- Area is unlimited in garages with the following characteristics:
  - ○ Type IB or Type II construction.
  - ○ Opening on each side must be ≥ 50% of the inside wall area as follows:
    Openings to be uniformly distributed on each side.
  - ○ Height ≤ 75'.
  - ○ Every point on the tier must be ≤ 200' from such openings measured horizontally.
- For garages with the following openings, height and area limitations are indicated below:
  - ○ Openings:
    ≥ ¾ of the building perimeter must have sides open.
    A side that is open must have ≥ 50% of its area open as measured inside the wall.
    An open side must have its openings uniformly distributed along its length.
  - ○ Area per tier:
    Area is unlimited for garages of Type I construction.
    Area per tier for other permitted construction types is limited as follows:
      Where ¾ of the building perimeter is open, area must be ≤ 62,500 sf.
      Where all the building perimeter is open, area must be ≤ 75,000 sf.

06 Motor-Vehicle-Related Occupancies

406.3.6 Area and height increases *(part 2 of 3)*
- ○ Height:

  Height is unlimited for garages of Type IA construction.

  Height limitations for other construction types are listed below:

Table 406.3.6a	Increased Height Limits of Open Parking Garages		
Type of construction	Height of garages with ramp access	Height of garages with mechanical access	
		without sprinklers	with sprinklers
IB	13 tiers	13 tiers	19 tiers
IIA	11 tiers	11 tiers	16 tiers
IIB	9 tiers	9 tiers	13 tiers
IV	5 tiers	5 tiers	5 tiers

- For the following conditions, tier areas may be increased above the maximum otherwise required and as indicated below:
  - ○ Conditions:

    Garage height must be ≤ 1 tier less than the maximum otherwise permitted.

    Openings must be located on ≥ 3 sides of the garage.

    Openings must a clear height ≥ 30".

    Openings must extend for ≥ 80% of the length of each side where they are located.

    Every point on the tier must be ≤ 200' from such an opening measured horizontally.

    Openings must face one of the following:

    Street ≥ 30' wide for the full opening length.

    Yard ≥ 30' wide for the full opening length as follows:

    Yard must have access to a street.

    Standpipes are required on each such tier.
  - ○ Tier areas are limited only by the total garage areas indicated in the following tables:

Table 406.3.6b	Limitations for Total Garage Area with Ramp Access	
Type of construction	Height of garage with ramp access	Total garage area
IIA	≤ 9 tiers	≤ 500,000 sf
IIB	≤ 7 tiers	≤ 400,000 sf
IV	≤ 3 tiers	≤ 200,000 sf

406 Motor-Vehicle-Related Occupancies

406.3.6 Area and height increases *(part 3 of 3)*

Type of construction	Height of garage with mechanical access	Total garage area
Table 406.3.6c	**Limitations for Total Garage Area with Mechanical Access**	
Without sprinklers:		
IIA	≤ 9 tiers	≤ 500,000 sf
IIB	≤ 7 tiers	≤ 400,000 sf
IV	≤ 3 tiers	≤ 200,000 sf
With sprinklers:		
IIA	≤ 14 tiers	≤ 750,000 sf
IIB	≤ 11 tiers	≤ 600,000 sf
IV	≤ 3 tiers	≤ 200,000 sf

406.3.7 Location on property

- This section addresses open parking garages.
- Exterior walls and openings must have fire resistance as required for other building types based on the following conditions:
  ○ Construction type.
  ○ Occupancy.
  ○ Fire separation distance.

    Note: The following are cited as the source of requirements for the components above:
    IBC Table 601, "Fire-Resistance Rating Requirements for Building Elements."
    IBC Table 602, "Fire-Resistance Rating Requirements for Exterior Walls Based on Fire Separation Distance."

- The distance required between a garage and its property lines is similar to that for any building type based on the following:
  ○ The fire resistance of exterior walls and openings.
  ○ Construction type.
  ○ Occupancy.
  ○ Fire separation distance.

    Note: The following are cited as sources for determining distance to property line:
    IBC Table 602, "Fire-Resistance Rating Requirements for Exterior Walls Based on Fire Separation Distance."
    Section 704, "Exterior Walls."

406 Motor-Vehicle-Related Occupancies

406.3.8 Means of egress

- This section addresses open parking garages.
- Exit stairways are governed as follows:
  - Where only parking attendants have access:
    $\geq$ 2 exit stairways are required.
    Exit stairways must be $\geq$ 3' wide.
  - Where persons other than parking attendants have access:
    Means of egress requirements applicable to the occupancy apply.

  Note: Chapter 10, "Means of Egress," is cited as governing open parking garages.

- Lifts are governed as follows:
  - May be provided for employee use only.
  - Must be enclosed by noncombustible materials.

406.3.9 Standpipes

- Standpipes are required in open parking garages as for any building type based on the following:
  - Building height.
  - Building area.
  - Occupant load.
  - Nature of building.

  Note: Chapter 9, "Fire Protection Systems," is cited as governing standpipes.

406.3.10 Sprinkler systems

- Where sprinklers are required in open parking garages, they must comply with requirements similar to those for most other occupancies.

  Note: Chapter 9, "Fire Protection Systems," is cited as governing sprinklers.

406.3.11 Enclosure of vertical openings

- This section addresses open parking garages.
- Where the public has access, the following applies:
  - Vertical openings must be enclosed as required for means of egress.
- Where only parking attendants have access:
  - $\geq$ 2 exit stairways are required.
  - Exit stairways must be $\geq$ 3' wide.
- Lifts must be enclosed by noncombustible materials.
- Other vertical openings are not required to be enclosed.

  Note: 406.3.8, "Means of egress," is cited as governing vertical openings and is partially summarized above.

406 Motor-Vehicle-Related Occupancies

406.3.12 Ventilation

- In open parking garages more ventilation than that provided by required openings is not required.

    Note: 406.3.3.1, "Openings," is cited as the source of requirements for openings.

406.3.13 Prohibitions

- The following uses are not permitted in open parkng garages:
  - Vehicle repairs.
  - Parking of the following vehicles:
    Buses.
    Trucks.
    Similar vehicles.
  - Partial or complete closing of required openings in exterior walls as follows:
    By tarpaulins.
    By any other means.
  - Dispensing fuel.

406.4 Enclosed parking garages

406.4.1 Heights and areas

- This section addresses enclosed parking garages.
- Garages and parts of garages that do not qualify as an open parking garage are governed as follows:
  - They must meet height and area limitations based on construction type.
- Parking is permitted on the roofs of enclosed parking garages.

    Note: IBC Table 503, "Allowable Height and Building Areas," is cited as the source of requirements with which enclosed parking garages must comply.

406.4.2 Ventilation

- Mechanical ventilation is required for enclosed parking garages.

    Note: International Mechanical Code is cited as the source governing such ventilation.

406.5 Motor fuel-dispensing facilities

406.5.1 Construction

- Motor fuel-dispensing facilities are governed by the following:
  - This section series.
  - Other standards.

    Note: International Fire Code is cited as governing motor fuel-dispensing facilities.

406 Motor-Vehicle-Related Occupancies

406.5.2 Canopies

- This section addresses canopies over fuel dispensing pumps.
- Canopies and canopy supports must be constructed of one or more of the following:
  - Noncombustible materials.
  - Fire-retardant-treated wood.
  - Heavy timber as follows:
    Sizes must comply with Type IV construction.
  - Construction having a 1-hr fire-resistance rating.

    Note: Chapter 23, "Wood," is cited as the source of requirements for fire-retardant-treated wood.

- Combustible materials at canopies must comply with one of the following:
  - They must be shielded from the pumps by one or more of the following:
    Noncombustible materials.
    Heavy timber as follows:
      Sizes must comply with Type IV construction.
  - Plastics are governed as follows:
    Must be covered by one of the following:
      Aluminum ≥ 0.010" thick.
      Corrosion-resistant steel with a base metal thickness ≥ 0.016".
    Must be tested in the same form as installed as follows:
      Must have a flame spread ≤ 25.
      Must have a smoke-developed index ≤ 450.
      Must have a self-ignition temperature ≥ 650°F.

    Note: The following are cited as the standards with which the plastics must comply:
      ASTM E 84, "Standard Test Method for Surface Burning Characteristics of Building Materials."
      ASTM D 1929, "Standard Test Method for Determining Ignition Temperature of Plastics."

  - Light-transmitting plastics are governed as follows:
    Panels must be located ≥ 10' from any building on the same property.
    Panels must face yards or streets ≥ 40' wide on other sides.
    Total area of all panels must be ≤ 1000 sf.
    Area of a single panel must be ≤ 100 sf.
- Canopy height is governed as follows:
  - Clear height in the drive area must be ≥ 13'-6".

407 Group I-2

407.1 General

- Occupancy I-2 is governed by the following:
  - This section.
  - Other sections of the code.

407.2 Corridors

- The enclosure of occupancy I-2 corridors is governed as follows:
  - Each corridor must be continuous to an exit.
  - Corridors may be open to the spaces indicated below where design and construction meet minimum requirements for fire safety:
    Waiting areas.
    Nurses' stations.
    Mental health treatment areas.
    Gift shops.
  - Otherwise, corridors must be separated from other spaces for purposes of smoke protection.

  Note: The following are cited as sources of requirements for space opening to a corridor:
  407.2.1, "Spaces of unlimited area," which addresses waiting rooms.
  407.2.2, "Nurses' stations."
  407.2.3, "Mental health treatment areas."
  407.2.4, "Gift shops."
  407.3, "Corridor walls," for walls required to separate corridors from other
  spaces.

407.2.1 Spaces of unlimited area *(part 1 of 2)*

- Waiting and similar areas may be open to a corridor only where all of the following apply:
  - The areas may not be used for the following:
    Patient sleeping rooms.
    Treatment rooms.
    Hazardous uses.
    Incidental uses having their own separation requirements.

  Note: 302.1.1, "Incidental use areas," is cited as a source of requirements for incidental
  use areas and identifies areas that may not open to a corridor.

  - The area must be constructed as corridors are required to be constructed.
  - The area must be protected by a fire detection system.
  - One of the following is required for a smoke compartment open to a corridor:
    The corridor must be protected by a fire detection system.
    The entire smoke compartment must be protected by quick-response sprinklers.

407 Group I-2

407.2.1 Spaces of unlimited area *(part 2 of 2)*

- Access to required exits may not be obstructed by the layout of the area.

  Note: The following are cited as sources of requirements for this section:
  Section 907, "Fire Alarm and Detection Systems," governs the fire detection systems required by this section.
  903.3.2, "Quick-response and residential sprinklers," refers to NFPA standards required for any quick-response sprinklers used.

407.2.2 Nurses' stations

- The following areas may be open to corridors where they have all the characteristics listed below:
  - Areas:
    Doctors' spaces.
    Nurses' spaces.
  - Required characteristics:
    Use of areas:
    Charting.
    Communications.
    Related clerical work.
    Construction of areas:
    Areas must be constructed according to requirements for the corridor.

407.2.3 Mental health treatment areas

- Where any of the following spaces are open to the corridor, they must comply with all the requirements listed below:
  - Spaces:
    Spaces housing patients who are not capable of self-preservation.
    Group meeting spaces.
    Multipurpose therapeutic spaces.

  Note: 302.1.1, "Incidental use areas," is cited as identifying spaces which are prohibited from being open to corridors and thus are not addressed by this section.

  - Requirements:
    Each smoke compartment is limited to 1 such space open to the corridor.
    Space must have continuous supervision by staff.
    Each space must be $\leq$ 1500 sf.
    Space layout does not obstruct access to required exits.
    Walls and ceilings are constructed as corridors are required to be constructed.
    Space must have a fire detection system.

  Note: Section 907.2, "Where required," is cited as the source of requirements for the fire detection system required by this section.

407 Group I-2

407.2.4 Gift shops

- Gift shops may be open to the corridor where all the following apply:
  - The gift shop must be < 500 sf.
  - The gift shop must be sprinklered.
  - The gift shop storage area must be sprinklered.

  Note: 302.1.1, "Incidental use areas," is cited as having applicable requirements.

407.3 Corridor walls

- Corridor walls must be smoke partitions.

407.3.1 Corridor doors

- This section governs corridor doors in occupancy I-2.
- The following doors must meet protection requirements consistent with the fire-resistance rating of their walls:
  - Doors in walls enclosing the following:
    - Incidental use spaces.
    - Vertical opening.
    - Exits.

  Note: 302.1.1, "Incidental use areas," is cited as the source listing incidental areas requiring protected doors.
  715.3, "Fire door and shutter assemblies," is cited as the source of protection requirements for doors in fire-resistance-rated walls.

- Doors in other corridor walls are governed as follows:
  - A fire-protection rating is not required.
  - Self-closing devices are not required.
  - Automatic closing devices are not required.
  - Doors must limit the transfer of smoke.
  - Positive latching is required.
  - Roller latches are prohibited.

407.3.2 Locking devices

- The following locking devices in occupancy I-2 are governed as indicated below:
  - Locking devices:
    - Those restricting access to the patient room from the corridor.
    - Those operable only by staff from the corridor side.
  - Requirements:
    - In mental health facilities:
      - Such locks may restrict the means of egress for patient rooms.
    - In other facilities:
      - Such locks may not restrict the means of egress for patient rooms.

407 Group I-2

407.4 Smoke barriers

- This section addresses the requirement for smoke barriers in occupancy I-2.
- The following stories must be divided as indicated below:
  - Stories:
    - Where patients sleep.
    - Where patients receive treatment.
    - Other stories where the occupant load is ≥ 50.
  - Requirements:
    - Story must be divided by smoke barriers.
    - Story must have ≥ smoke compartments:
      - Area of compartment must be ≤ 22,500 sf.
      - Travel in the compartment is limited as follows:
        - From any point to a smoke-barrier door must be ≤ 200'.

  Note: Section 709, "Smoke Barriers," is cited as the source of requirements for such components.

407.4.1 Refuge area

- This section addresses refuge area requirements in smoke compartments of occupancy I-2.
- The area required for refuge in a smoke compartment is computed as follows:
  - For floors where patients are confined to a bed or litter:
    - Refuge area required per patient is ≥ 30 sf:
      - Patient count includes only those from the adjoining compartment.
  - For floors where patients are not confined to a bed or litter:
    - Refuge area required per occupant is ≥ 6 sf:
      - Occupant count includes only those from the adjoining compartment.
- The refuge area required in smoke compartments is to be distributed in one or more of the following locations:
  - Corridors.
  - Patient rooms.
  - Treatment rooms.
  - Lounges.
  - Dining areas.
  - Other low-hazard areas.

  Note: The area required for refuge is in addition to the area required to meet means of egress minimums.

407.4.2 Independent egress

- This section addresses means of egress from smoke compartments in occupancy I-2.
- Each smoke compartment requires a means of egress as follows:
  - Egress may not return to the compartment of origin.

407 Group I-2

407.5 Automatic sprinkler system

- Smoke compartments with patient sleeping units must be sprinklered as follows:
  - As per NFPA 13.
  - Using one of the following systems:
    Quick-response sprinklers.
    Residential sprinklers.

  Note: 903.3.2, "Quick response and residential sprinklers," is cited as the source of requirements for these sprinkler types.

407.6 Automatic fire detection

- This section addresses the following locations in occupancy I-2:
  - Corridors in nursing homes as follows:
    Intermediate-care facilities.
    Skilled nursing facilities.
  - Corridors in detoxification facilities.
  - Spaces open to corridors.

  Note: 407.2, "Corridors," is cited as identifying spaces permitted to be open to corridors.

- Smoke detection is not required for locations addressed by this section where either of the following conditions exists:
  - Condition 1:
    Each patient sleeping unit must have smoke detectors as follows:
    Both the following must be provided at the attending nurses' station:
    Audible alarm.
    Visual alarm.
    Detectors must have a visual display on the corridor side of the sleeping unit.
    Detectors must meet minimum applicable standards.

  Note: UL 268, "Smoke Detectors for Fire Protective Signaling Systems," is cited as the standard applicable to smoke detectors.

  - Condition 2:
    Patient sleeping units must have doors equipped as follows:
    Doors must have the following automatic closing devices:
    Closing devices must have integral smoke detectors as follows:
    On the room side.
    Installed according to their listing.
    Detectors must perform the necessary alert.

- All other locations addressed by this section must have a fire detection system.

  Note: Section 907, "Fire Alarm and Detection Systems," is cited as governing the required fire detection system.

407 Group I-2

407.7 Secured yards

- Yard areas may be secured as follows where the conditions listed below exist:
  - Security:
    Surrounded by fencing.
    Gates provided with locks.
  - Required conditions:
    The following safe dispersal area must be provided:
    The area must be located as follows:
    Between the building and the fencing.
    $\geq 50'$ from the building.
    The following net area must be provided for each patient:
    30 sf for the following:
    Bed patients.
    Litter patients.
    6 sf for the following:
    Ambulatory patients.
    Occupants who are not patients.

408 Group I-3

408.1 General

- Occupancy I-3 must comply with the following:
  - This section.
  - Other applicable sections of the code.

  Note: 308.4, "Group I-3," is cited as a section applicable to this occupancy.

408.2 Mixed occupancies

- The following applies where an I-3 space occurs in an area with a different occupancy designation:
  - The larger area must meet requirements for its occupancy designation.
  - The following applies where means of egress must be locked for security purposes:
    The release of occupants must be possible at all times.
- Where means of egress from the following I-3 occupancies pass through other use designations, the requirements indicated below apply:
  - I-3 occupancies:
    Detention.
    Correctional.
  - Requirements:
    Egress through a horizontal exit into an occupancy that does not meet I-3 egress requirements is permitted as follows:
      The other occupancy must meet its own egress requirements.
      The other occupancy may not be a high-hazard use.
    In all other cases the means of egress must comply with I-3 requirements.

408.3 Means of egress

- Means of egress for I-3 occupancies are governed by the following:
  - This section governs those aspects addressed.
  - Other code requirements govern aspects not addressed in this section.

  Note: Chapter 10, "Means of Egress," is cited as governing egress issues not covered in this section.

408.3.1 Door width

- Resident sleeping-unit doors must have a clear width of $\geq$ 2'-4".

408.3.2 Sliding doors

- Horizontal sliding doors in an occupancy I-3 means of egress are governed as follows:
  - Doors must fully open under the following conditions:
    With an opening force $\leq$ 50 lbs in either of the following circumstances:
      Simultaneously with a force $\leq$ 50 lbs applied $\perp$ to the door.
      With no other force applied to the door.

408 Group I-3

408.3.3 Spiral stairs

- Spiral stairs may be used in occupancy I-3 for staff operational purposes.

    Note: 1003.3.3.9, "Spiral stairways," is cited as governing such stairs.

408.3.4 Exit discharge

- Exits may discharge from an I-3 occupancy into one of the following areas with the requirements indicated below:
  - Areas:
      Fenced courtyard.
      Walled courtyard.
  - Requirements:
      Enclosed yard must accommodate all occupants in a zone as follows:
      Zone to be located ≥ 50' from the building.
      Size of zone must provide ≥ 15 sf per person.

408.3.5 Sallyports

- Sallyports may be located in an occupancy I-3 means of egress as follows:
  - Where unobstructed travel through them is possible during emergencies.

408.3.6 Vertical exit enclosures

- A vertical exit enclosure of an I-3 occupancy may have glazing where all the following conditions apply:
  - Only one required vertical exit enclosure per building may have glazing.
  - Glazing is permitted only in the following:
      In doors at landings.
      In interior walls at landings serving enclosure access.
  - Stairway is limited to serving ≤ 4 floor levels.
  - Doors must be fire doors with the larger fire-protection rating of the following:
      ≥ that required for the fire-resistance rating of their wall.
      ≥ ¾ hour.
  - Total glazed area at each floor must be ≤ 5000 sq in.
  - Individual panels of glazing must be ≤ 1296 sq in.
  - Sprinklers must protect both sides of the glazing by wetting the entire surfaces.
  - Glazing must be in a gasketed frame as follows:
      Frame must be able to deflect prior to sprinkler activation without breaking the glass.
  - Obstructions such as the following are not allowed between the sprinklers and the glazing:
      Curtains and curtains rods.
      Drapes and drapery traverse rods.
      Similar obstructions.

    Note: 714.2, "Fire door and shutter assemblies," is cited as the source of fire-protection ratings for fire doors as based on the fire-resistance rating of their walls.

408 Group I-3

408.4.1 Remote release

- In occupancy I-3, remote control of locks is not required where all the following apply:
  - In restraint condition 4.
  - Locks that must be opened to move occupants to an area of refuge from a smoke compartment are governed as follows:
    They must number ≤ 10.
    The number of separate keys needed for all the locks is limited to ≤ 2.
    Movement of all occupants to the area of refuge must be possible in ≤ 3 minutes.
- Otherwise, locks on required doors in a means of egress of occupancy I-3 must have a remote release capability as follows:
  - Devices activating lock releases must be in a location remote from the resident living areas.
  - Locks preventing egress in the following conditions of restraint must meet the requirement indicated below:
    Conditions of restraint:
      Condition 3.
      Condition 4.
    Requirement:
      Locks must be releasable in ≤ 2 minutes as follows:
        By the minimum staff available.
        At any time.

408.4.2 Power-operated doors and locks *(part 1 of 2)*

- Emergency power for the following door mechanisms is not required in occupancy I-3 for the conditions indicated below:
  - Mechanisms:
    Power-operated sliding doors.
    Power-operated locks for swinging doors.
  - Conditions:
    In occupancy I-3 restraint condition 4:
      ≤ 10 locks must be opened to move occupants to an area of refuge.
      ≤ 2 separate keys are needed for all the locks.
      Movement of all occupants to the area of refuge must be possible in ≤ 3 minutes.

  Note: The exception to 408.4.1, "Remote release," is cited as applicable and is summarized above.

408 Group I-3

408.4.2 Power-operated doors and locks *(part 2 of 2)*

- Otherwise, the following door mechanisms must comply with requirements indicated below:
  - Mechanisms:
    Power-operated sliding doors.
    Power-operated locks for swinging doors.
  - Requirements:
    Manual release mechanism at the door must be provided.
    One of the following must be provided:
      Remote mechanical release for the door mechanisms.
      Emergency power to door mechanisms.

408.4.3 Redundant operation

- In occupancy I-3, the following mechanisms must have the redundant systems listed below:
  - Locks:
    Remote release, mechanically operated sliding doors.
    Remote release, mechanically operated locks.
  - Redundant systems:
    Mechanically operated release mechanism at each door.
    Redundant remote release mechanism.

408.4.4 Relock capability

- Doors in occupancy I-3 that are unlocked remotely in an emergency are governed as follows:
  - Doors may not relock automatically upon closing without the following action:
    Specific action is required at the control location to permit relocking.

408.5 Vertical openings

- This section addresses occupancy I-3 resident's housing areas.
- Floor levels of such areas may be open to the same space without vertical enclosure where all the following apply:
  - Staff can observe the normally occupied areas on all levels open to the same open space.
  - The means of egress can accommodate the egress of all occupants from the interconnected spaces at the same time.
  - The vertical distance between the highest and lowest floor surfaces of the interconnected levels is $\leq 23'$.
  - $\geq \frac{1}{2}$ the means of egress capacity of each story are through exits that do not open to another story open to the interconnected spaces.
- All other openings through floors must be enclosed.

  Note: Section 707, "Shaft and Vertical Exit Enclosures," is cited as the source of requirements for enclosing openings through floors.

408 Group I-3

408.6 Smoke barrier

- This section addresses the division of occupancy I-3 stories into smoke compartments.
- Spaces with the following characteristics are not required to be protected by smoke barriers:
  - Spaces must exit directly to one of the following locations:
    A public way.
    A building separated from resident housing by one of the following:
      Construction with a fire-resistance rating ≥ 2 hours.
      50' of open space.
    A secure yard or court with a holding space as follows:
      Holding space provides ≥ 6 sf per occupant including the following:
        Staff.
        Residents.
        Visitors.
      Holding space is located ≥ 50' from resident housing.
  - The locking methods for doors in the exit system must meet the following:
    Restraint-condition requirements for the space.
- Otherwise, each of the following stories must be subdivided as indicated below:
  - Stories:
    Where residents sleep.
    With an occupant load ≥ 50 persons.
  - Division requirements:
    Each story must be divided into ≥ 2 smoke compartments by smoke barriers.

  Note: Section 709, "Smoke Barriers," is cited as the source of requirements for these components.

408.6.1 Smoke compartments

- Smoke compartments in occupancy I-3 must have the following characteristics:
  - Number of residents in each compartment must be ≤ 200.
  - Travel distance between the following must be ≤ 150':
    Any room door required for exit access.
    The nearest door in a smoke barrier.
  - Travel distance between the following must be ≤ 200':
    Any point in the smoke compartment.
    The nearest door in a smoke barrier.

408 Group I-3

408.6.2 Refuge area

- This section addresses refuge areas in occupancy I-3 smoke compartments.
- A refuge area is required in each smoke compartment as follows:
  - ≥ 6 sf is required for each occupant seeking refuge.
  - The occupant count for computing refuge area is based on the following:
      The occupant load of the adjacent smoke compartment.
  - The occupant count for computing refuge area does not include the following:
      Original occupants in the smoke compartment housing the refuge area.
  - The refuge area must be immediately available for occupation in a fire emergency.

    Note: The required refuge area is in addition to the area required for the original occupants of the smoke compartment.

408.6.3 Independent egress

- This section addresses smoke compartments formed by smoke barriers in occupancy I-3.
- A means of egress is required from each smoke compartment as follows:
  - Means of egress may not require occupants to return to the smoke compartment from which they departed.

408.7.1 Occupancy conditions 3 and 4

- This section addresses the separation required in occupancy I-3 restraint conditions 3 and 4.
- Where travel distance on the following routes is > 50', the requirement indicated applies:
  - Route:
      Beginning in a sleeping area.
      Passing through the common space.
      To an access corridor.
  - Requirement:
      Common spaces and adjacent sleeping areas must be separated as follows:
        By a smoke-tight partition.

408.7.2 Occupancy condition 5

- This section addresses separations required in occupancy I-3 restraint condition 5.
- Each sleeping area must be separated from the following adjacent spaces by smoke-tight partitions:
  - Other sleeping areas.
  - Corridors.
  - Common spaces.
- A smoke-tight partition must separate the following areas from each other:
  - Exit access corridor.
  - Common space.

408 Group I-3

408.7.3 Openings in room face

- This section addresses sleeping rooms in occupancy I-3 restraint conditions 2, 3, 4, and 5.
- Openings in the solid face of sleeping rooms must meet the following requirements:
    Area of openings includes the following:
      Grilles.
      Food passages.
      Door undercuts.
      All other openings.
    - Area of all openings combined is limited to ≤ 120 sq in.
    - Openings must be located ≤ 3' above the floor.
    - In restraint condition 5, openings must be closeable from the room side.

408.7.4 Smoke-tight doors

- Doors in smoke-tight partitions are governed as follows:
    - Doors must be substantial.
    - Doors must resist the passage of smoke.
    - The following are not required on cell doors:
      Latches.
      Door closers.

    Note: Section 408.7, "Subdivision of resident housing areas," is cited as identifying partitions that must be smoke-tight. The section identifies such partitions by referring to the following:
    408.7.1, "Occupancy conditions 3 and 4."
    408.7.2, "Occupancy condition 5."

408.8 Windowless buildings

- A windowless building or part of a building is defined as having one or more of the following characteristics:
    - The building has windows that do not open.
    - The building has windows that are not readily breakable.
    - The building does not have windows.
- Each windowless building requires an engineered smoke control system as follows:
    - Windowless smoke compartments must be provided with one of the following types of ventilation:
      Mechanical.
      Natural.

    Note: Section 909, "Smoke Control Systems," is cited as the source of requirements for ventilating smoke control compartments.

410 Stages and Platforms

410.2 Definitions *(part 1 of 2)*

- **Fly gallery**
  - A floor level above a stage:
    - For the movement of scenery.
    - For controlling other stage effects.

- **Gridiron**
  - Structural framing over a stage supporting equipment:
    - For hanging and flying scenery.
    - For supporting other stage effects.

- **Pinrail**
  - A rail on or above a stage:
    - For holding belaying pin to which lines are fastened.

- **Platform**
  - A raised area within a building.
  - Used for any of the following purposes:
    - Worship.
    - Music.
    - Plays.
    - Entertainment.
    - Head table for special guests.
    - Lecturers or speakers.
    - Boxing ring.
    - Wrestling ring.
    - Theater-in-the-round stage.
    - Similar activities.
  - None of the following devices are present:
    - Overhead hanging curtains.
    - Drops.
    - Scenery.
    - Stage effects other than lighting and sound.

- **Platform, temporary**
  - A platform installed for ≤ 30 days.

- **Proscenium wall**
  - A wall between the stage and one of the following:
    - Auditorium.
    - Assembly seating area.

410 Stages and Platforms

410.2 Definitions *(part 2 of 2)*

- **Stage**
  - A space in a building used for either of the following:
    Entertainment.
    Presentations.
  - Includes the following elements:
    Performance area.
    Spaces adjacent to performance area as follows:
      Not separated by fire-resistance-rated construction.
      Backstage.
      Support areas.
    Overhead hanging curtains.
    Drops.
    Scenery.
    Stage effects other than the following:
      Lighting.
      Sound.
  - Stage height is measured from the lowest point on the stage floor to the following:
    The highest point on the underside of one of the following:
      Roof deck above the stage.
      Floor deck above the stage.

410 Stages and Platforms

410.3.1 Stage construction

- Stage floors may be constructed as follows where all the conditions indicated below apply:
  - Construction:
    Wood deck.
    Nominal thickness ≥ 2".
  - Conditions:
    Stage is separated from other areas.
    Stage floor construction is one of the following types:
      Type II B.
      Type IV.

    Note: 410.3.5, "Proscenium curtain," is cited as governing the separation of the stage from other areas in this case.

- A stage floor is not required to have a fire-resistance rating where all the following conditions apply:
  - Building is one of the following construction types:
    Type II A.
    Type III A.
    Type V A.
  - The space below the stage is provided with the following:
    An automatic fire-extinguishing system.

    Note: The following are cited as governing the options for the fire-extinguishing system required above:
      Section 903, "Automatic Sprinkler Systems."
      Section 904, "Alternative Automatic Fire-Extinguishing Systems."

- Stage finished floors may be constructed out of one of the following materials where the condition below applies:
  - Materials:
    Wood.
    Approved noncombustible materials.
  - Condition:
    Openings in stage floors must have trap doors with the following characteristics:
      Tight fitting.
      Solid wood.
      With approved safety locks.
- In all other cases, stages must be constructed as follows:
  - Using materials required for the building construction type.

410 Stages and Platforms

410.3.1.1 Stage height and area

- Stage area is measured including the following:
  - Performance area.
  - Spaces adjacent to performance area as follows:
      Not separated by fire-resistance-rated construction.
      Backstage.
      Support areas.
- Stage height is measured from the lowest point on the stage floor to the following:
  - The highest point on the underside of one of the following:
      Roof deck above the stage.
      Floor deck above the stage.

410.3.2 Galleries, gridirons, catwalks and pinrails

- Floors of the following may be constructed out of any approved material:
  - Fly galleries.
  - Catwalks.
- Materials for beams supporting only the following elements are governed as indicated below:
  - Elements:
      Theater equipment:
        Portable.
        Fixed.
      Gridirons.
      Galleries.
      Catwalks.
  - Beam materials:
      Must be approved.
      Must meet requirements of the construction type for the building.
      Are not required to have a fire-resistance rating.
- For application of code requirements, the following elements do not constitute any of the components listed below:
  - Elements:
      Fly galleries.
      Gridirons.
      Catwalks.
  - Components:
      Floors.
      Stories.
      Mezzanines.
      Levels.

410 Stages and Platforms

410.3.3 Exterior stage doors

- Where protection is required for the following openings, the requirement below applies:
  - Openings:
    Exterior exit doors from the stage.
  - Requirement:
    Such doors must be fire doors.

    Note: Section 715, "Opening Protectives," is cited as governing fire doors as required above.

- The following exterior openings from a stage are governed as indicated below:
  - Openings:
    Exterior exit doors.
    Exterior doors for loading and unloading.
  - Requirements:
    Vestibules required as follows:
      Where doors may be open while the theater is occupied.
      To prevent air drafts into the auditorium.

410.3.4 Proscenium wall

- The following applies where stage height is > 50'.
  - All areas of the stage must be separated from the seating area as follows:
    By a proscenium wall:
      Wall must have a fire-resistance rating ≥ 2 hr.
    Wall must be continuous between the foundation and roof.

410.3.5 Proscenium curtain

- This section applies to stages with a height > 50'.
- One of the following curtains is required for the proscenium opening:
  - A water curtain as per NFPA 13.
  - A curtain of approved material to function as follows:
    Curtain must intercept the following:
      Hot gases.
      Flames.
      Smoke.
    A glow in the curtain from a stage fire is limited as follows:
      Glow must not show on the auditorium side for ≤ 20 minutes.
    Curtain must close from completely open as follows:
      Must close in ≤ 30 seconds.
      The last 8' of closing must take ≥ 5 seconds.

410 Stages and Platforms

410.3.6 Scenery

- Materials for stage sets and scenery are governed as follows:
  - Combustible materials must be flame resistant.
  - Foam plastics are regulated by other provisions.

    Note: The following are cited as governing the above listed materials as indicated:
    Section 805, "Decorations and Trim," for combustible materials.
    Section 2603, "Foam Plastic Insulation," for foam plastics.
    International Fire Code for combustible materials and foam plastics.

410.4 Platform construction

- This section governs permanent platforms.
- Fire-retardant-treated wood may be used for platforms where all the following conditions are present:
  - The building of one of the following types of construction:
    - Type I.
    - Type II.
    - Type IV.
    - The platform is ≤ 30" above the main floor.
    - The platform is ≤ $\frac{1}{3}$ the room area.
    - The platform is ≤ 3000 sf.
- In other cases, materials must meet requirements for the building construction type.
- Platform floors must have a fire-resistance rating ≥ 1 hr in the following case:
  - Where the space under the floor is used for the following:
    - Storage.
    - Purpose other than the following:
      - Equipment.
      - Wiring.
      - Plumbing.
  - The underside of the platform floor need not be protected in the following case:
    - Where the space under the floor is used only for the following:
      - Equipment.
      - Wiring.
      - Plumbing.

410.4.1 Temporary platforms

- This section addresses platforms installed for ≤ 30 days.
- Any material allowed by the code may be used for temporary platforms.
- The space under a temporary platform and above the building floor is not permitted to be used for any purposes except the following service to platform equipment:
  - Plumbing.
  - Electrical wiring.

410 Stages and Platforms

410.5.1 Separation from stage

- Stages must be separated from the following spaces as indicated below:
  - Spaces:
    Dressing rooms.
    Scene docks.
    Property rooms and storerooms.
    Workshops.
    Compartments appurtenant to the stage.
    Other parts of the building.
  - Where the stage height is > 50':
    The following separations are required with the characteristics indicated below:
    Separations:
    Fire barrier walls.
    Horizontal assemblies.
    Characteristics required:
    Fire-resistance rating ≥ 2 hrs.
    Approved opening protectives.
  - Where the stage height is ≤ 50':
    The following separations are required with the characteristics indicated below:
    Separations:
    Fire barrier walls.
    Horizontal assemblies.
    Characteristics required:
    Fire-resistance rating ≥ 1 hr.
    Approved opening protectives.

410.5.2 Separation from each other

- The following spaces must be separated from each other as indicated below:
  - Spaces:
    Dressing rooms.
    Scene docks.
    Property rooms and storerooms.
    Workshops.
    Compartments appurtenant to the stage.
  - Separation:
    The following separations are required with the characteristics listed below:
    Separations:
    Fire barrier walls.
    Horizontal assemblies.
    Characteristics required:
    Fire-resistance rating ≥ 1 hr.
    Approved opening protectives.

410 Stages and Platforms

410.5.3 Opening protectives

- This section governs doorways to dressing and appurtenant rooms.
- Doorways other than the following may not connect dressing rooms and appurtenant spaces to the stage:
  - Doors to trunk rooms.
  - Doors other than those necessary at stage level.
- Doorways must be protected with fire door assemblies.

  Note: Section 715, "Opening Protectives," is cited as governing fire door assemblies as required above.

410.5.4 Stage exits

- ≥ 1 approved means of egress is required from the following locations:
  - Each side of the stage.
  - Each side of the space under the stage.
- ≥ 1 means of escape is required from the following locations:
  - Each fly gallery.
  - The gridiron.
- The gridiron may have one of the following access devices to a scuttle in the stage roof:
  - Steel ladder.
  - Alternating tread stairway.
  - Spiral stairway.

410.6 Automatic sprinkler system *(part 1 of 2)*

- Sprinklers are not required under stages areas with all of the following characteristics:
  - The space has a clear height < 4'.
  - The space is used only for storage of tables and chairs.
  - Concealed space is separated from other spaces by Type X gypsum board ≥ ⅝" thick.
- Sprinklers are not required for stages with all of the following characteristics:
  - Stages with ≤ 1000 sf.
  - Stages ≤ 50' in height as follows:
    Where the following are not retractable vertically:
    Curtains.
    Scenery.
    Other combustible hangings.
  - Combustible hangings are limited to the following:
    One main curtain.
    Borders.
    Legs.
    One backdrop.

410 Stages and Platforms

410.6 Automatic sprinkler system (*part 2 of 2*)

- Otherwise, stages require an automatic fire-extinguishing system in the following locations:
  - Under the roof above the gridiron.
  - Under the gridiron.
  - In tie and fly galleries.
  - Behind the proscenium wall of the stage.
  - In spaces accessory to the stage as follows:
    Dressing rooms.
    Lounges.
    Workshops.
    Storerooms.

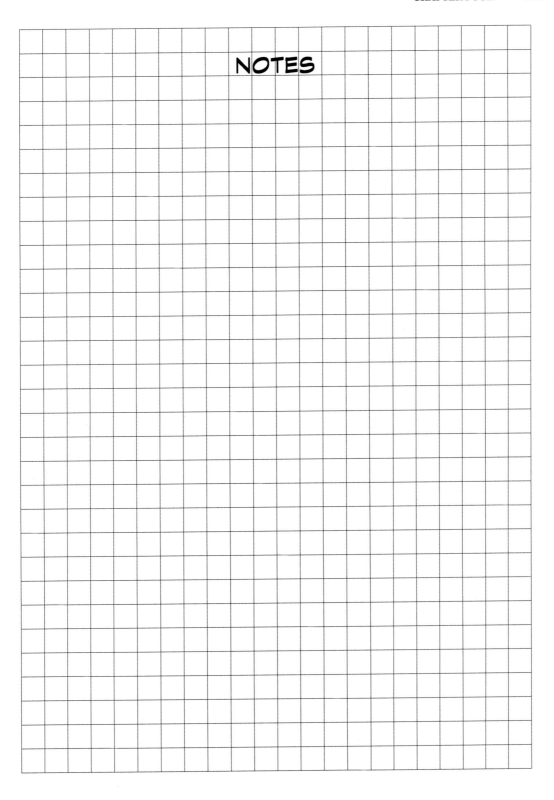

NOTES

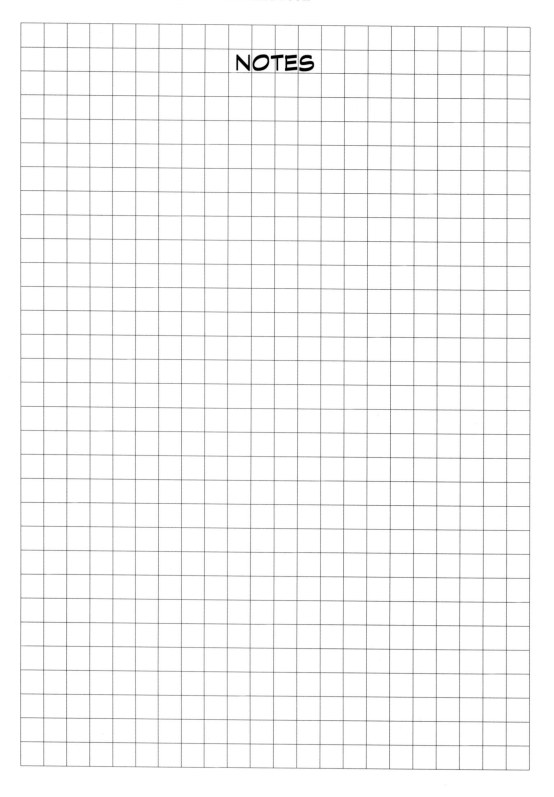

NOTES

5

General Building Heights and Areas

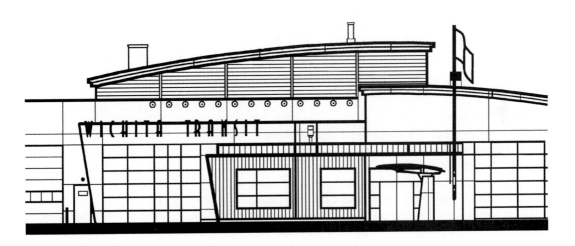

Wichita Transit Storage, Administration, and Maintenance Facility.
Wichita, Kansas. *(partial elevation)*
Wilson Darnell Mann, P.A., Architects. Wichita, Kansas.

502 Definitions

502.1 Definitions *(part 1 of 2)*

- **Area, building**
  - Area within the inside surfaces of the following perimeters as applicable:
    Exterior walls.
    Exterior walls and fire walls.
  - Areas of the following elements are not included:
    Vent shafts.
    Courts.
  - Usable area outside the exterior walls is included where is under the following:
    Roof above.
    Floor above.

- **Basement**
  - A story that is below the grade plane as follows:
    Partly.
    Completely.
  - A basement is considered a story above the grade plane as follows:
    Where the finished floor above the basement is > any of the following:
    6' above the grade plane.
    6' above the finished grade as follows:
    For > half the total building perimeter.
    12' above the finished ground surface at any point.

  Note: Section 202, "Definitions," is cited as clarifying the meaning of a "story above grade plane." The essence of that definition is included above.

- **Grade plane**
  - Average level of finished grade at the building.
  - Points of elevation are taken at the building in the following cases:
    Where grade is level to a building façade.
    Where grade slopes down to a building façade.
  - Where grade slopes away from a building façade, the following apply:
    Where the property line is ≤ 6' from the building:
    Grade plane is based on the following:
    Average level of lowest points between building and property line.
    Where the property line is > 6' from the building:
    Grade plane is based on the following:
    Average level of lowest points ≤ 6' from the building.

  Note: When more than 4 corner points are used to determine the grade plane, points should be evenly distributed along any façade.

502 Definitions

502.1 Definitions *(part 2 of 2)*

- **Height, building**
  - Vertical distance between the following levels:
    Grade plane.
    Roof as follows:
      The top of a flat roof.
      A level halfway between the highest and lowest points of a sloped roof.

- **Height, story**
  - Floors below the top floor:
    Vertical distance between the following:
      Top of a finished floor.
      Top of the finished floor next above it.
  - Top floor:
    Vertical distance between the following:
      Top of the finished floor and one of the following as applicable:
        The top of the ceiling joists.
        The top of the roof rafters as follows:
          Where there is no ceiling.

- **Industrial equipment platform**
  - A platform and associated components as follows:
    Elevated walkways.
    Stairs.
    Ladders.
  - Platform is unoccupied.
  - Located in occupancy F.
  - Used exclusively for one or both of the following:
    Mechanical systems.
    Industrial process equipment.
  - Not part of a mezzanine.

    Note: 505.5, "Industrial equipment platforms," is referenced.

- **Mezzanine**
  - A level or levels between the following:
    Floor and ceiling of a story.
  - Has a total floor area $\leq$ $^1/_3$ that of the space where it is located.

    Note: Section 505, "Mezzanines," is referenced.

- **Story**
  - The space between the following:
    The top surface of a floor and one of the following:
      The top surface of the next floor above.
      The top surface of the roof as follows:
        Where there is no floor above.

503 General Height and Area Limitations

503.1 General *(part 1 of 4)*

- Building height and area are limited by this section as per construction type and occupancy.
- Each part of a building enclosed is considered to be a separate building as follows:
    - Within the exterior walls.
    - Within the exterior walls and fire walls where applicable.
- Height and area limitations are subject to modification elsewhere in the code.
- Maximum area per floor and building height by occupancy are shown in the tables provided in this section on the following pages, 127–130.

    Note: The following are referenced as having applicable requirements:
    406.3, "Open parking garages," for occupancy S-2 facilities of this type.
    406.1, "Private garages and carports," for occupancy U facilities of this type.

> **Case study: Fig. 503.1A.** The occupancy B building is Type IIB construction and is not sprinklered. A maximum height of 55' and 4 stories is permitted for this category of building. The building is 2 stories and 38'-4" high, measured to the average height of the highest roof; thus, it is in compliance with the code regarding height.

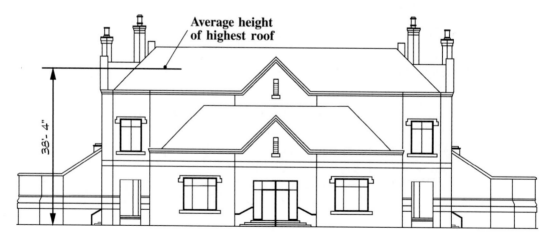

Fig. 503.1A. East elevation. Country Club Park Building One. Wichita, Kansas. Gossen Livingston Associates, Inc., Architecture. Wichita, Kansas.

503 General Height and Area Limitations

503.1 General *(part 2 of 4)*

Table 503.1a   Maximum Building Height and Area per Floor

Occ.	Height	IA	IB	IIA	IIB	IIIA	IIIB	IV	VA	VB
\multicolumn{11}{l}{Occupancy A: maximum height in stories and feet}
A	Feet	UL	160	65	55	65	55	65	50	40
A-1	Stories	UL	5	3	2	3	2	3	2	1
A-2	"	UL	11	3	2	3	2	3	2	1
A-3	"	UL	11	3	2	3	2	3	2	1
A-4	"	UL	11	3	2	3	2	3	2	1
A-5	"	UL	UL	UL	UL	UL	UL	UL	UL	UL
\multicolumn{11}{l}{Occupancy A: maximum area per floor in square feet}
A-1	SF	UL	UL	15,500	8,500	14,000	8,500	15,000	11,500	5,500
A-2	"	UL	UL	15,500	9,500	14,000	9,500	15,000	11,500	6,000
A-3	"	UL	UL	15,500	9,500	14,000	9,500	15,000	11,500	6,000
A-4	"	UL	UL	15,500	9,500	14,000	9,500	15,000	11,500	6,000
A-5	"	UL	UL	UL	UL	UL	UL	UL	UL	UL
\multicolumn{11}{l}{Occupancy B: maximum area in square feet}
B	Feet	UL	160	65	55	65	55	65	50	40
B	Stories	UL	11	5	4	5	4	5	3	2
\multicolumn{11}{l}{Occupancy B: maximum area per floor in square feet}
B	SF	UL	UL	37,500	23,000	28,500	19,000	36,000	18,000	9,000
\multicolumn{11}{l}{Occupancy E: maximum height in stories and feet}
E	Feet	UL	160	65	55	65	55	65	50	40
E	Stories	UL	5	3	2	3	2	3	1	1
\multicolumn{11}{l}{Occupancy E: maximum area per floor in square feet}
E	SF	UL	UL	26,500	14,500	23,500	14,500	25,500	18,500	9,500

Source: IBC Table 503.
UL = unlimited, Occ. = occupancy, SF = square feet.

503 General Height and Area Limitations

503.1 General *(part 3 of 4)*

Table 503.1b   Maximum Building Height and Area per Floor

					Type of construction					
Occ.	Height	IA	IB	IIA	IIB	IIIA	IIIB	IV	VA	VB
Occupancy F: maximum height in stories and feet										
F	Feet	UL	160	65	55	65	55	65	50	40
F-1	Stories	UL	11	4	2	3	2	4	2	1
F-2	Stories	UL	11	5	3	4	3	5	3	2
Occupancy F: maximum area per floor in square feet										
F-1	SF	UL	UL	25,000	15,500	19,000	12,000	35,500	14,000	8,500
F-2	SF	UL	UL	37,500	23,000	28,500	18,000	50,500	21,500	13,000
Occupancy H: maximum height in stories and feet										
H	Feet	UL	160	65	55	65	55	65	50	40
H-1	Stories	1	1	1	1	1	1	1	1	NP
H-2	"	UL	3	2	1	2	1	2	1	1
H-3	"	UL	6	4	2	4	2	4	2	1
H-4	"	UL	7	5	3	5	3	5	3	2
H-5	"	3	3	3	3	3	3	3	3	2
Occupancy H: maximum area per floor in square feet										
H-1	SF	21,000	16,500	11,000	7,000	9,500	7,000	10,500	7,500	NP
H-2	"	21,000	16,500	11,000	7,000	9,500	7,000	10,500	7,500	3,000
H-3	"	UL	60,000	26,500	14,000	17,500	13,000	25,500	10,000	5,000
H-4	"	UL	UL	37,500	17,500	28,500	17,500	36,000	18,000	6,500
H-5	"	UL	UL	37,500	23,000	28,500	19,000	36,000	18,000	9,000
Occupancy I: maximum height in stories and feet										
I	Feet	UL	160	65	55	65	55	65	50	40
I-1	Stories	UL	9	4	3	4	3	4	3	2
I-2	"	UL	4	2	1	1	NP	1	1	NP
I-3	"	UL	4	2	1	2	1	2	2	1
I-4	"	UL	5	3	2	3	2	3	1	1
Occupancy I: maximum area per floor in square feet										
I-1	SF	UL	55,000	19,000	10,000	16,500	10,000	18,000	10,500	4,500
I-2	"	UL	UL	15,500	11,000	12,000	NP	12,000	9,500	NP
I-3	"	UL	UL	15,000	10,000	10,500	7,500	12,000	7,500	5,000
I-4	"	UL	60,500	26,500	13,000	23,500	13,000	25,500	18,500	9,000

Source: IBC Table 503.
UL = unlimited, Occ. = occupancy, SF = square feet, NP = not permitted.

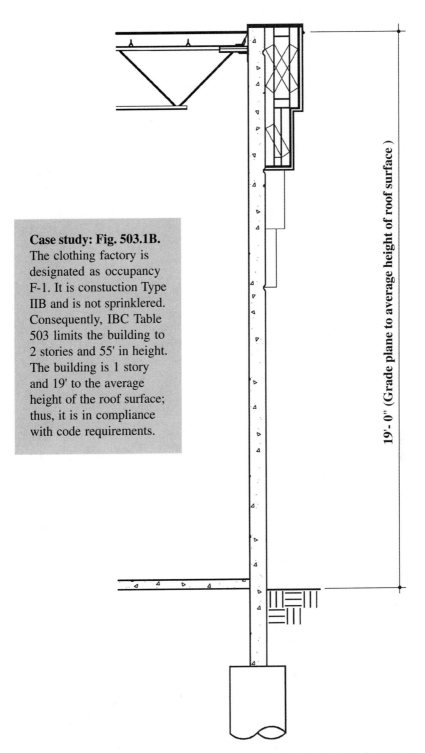

Case study: Fig. 503.1B. The clothing factory is designated as occupancy F-1. It is constuction Type IIB and is not sprinklered. Consequently, IBC Table 503 limits the building to 2 stories and 55' in height. The building is 1 story and 19' to the average height of the roof surface; thus, it is in compliance with code requirements.

19'- 0" (Grade plane to average height of roof surface)

Fig. 503.1B. Wall section. Garments to Go. Bastrop, Texas. Spencer Godfrey Architects. Round Rock, Texas.

503 General Height and Area Limitations

503.1 General *(part 4 of 4)*

Table 503.1c   **Maximum Building Height and Area per Floor**

Occ.	Height		Type of construction								
		IA	IB	IIA	IIB	IIIA	IIIB	IV	VA	VB
Occupancy M: maximum height in stories and feet										
M	Feet	UL	160	65	55	65	55	65	50	40
M	Stories	UL	11	4	4	4	4	4	3	1
Occupancy M: maximum area per floor in square feet										
M	SF	UL	UL	21,500	12,500	18,500	12,500	20,500	14,000	9,000
Occupancy R: maximum height in stories and feet										
R	Feet	UL	160	65	55	65	55	65	50	40
R-1	Stories	UL	11	4	4	4	4	4	3	2
R-2	"	UL	11	4	4	4	4	4	3	2
R-3	"	UL	11	4	4	4	4	4	3	3
R-4	"	UL	11	4	4	4	4	4	3	2
Occupancy R: maximum area per floor in square feet										
R-1	SF	UL	UL	24,000	16,000	24,000	16,000	20,500	12,000	7,000
R-2	"	UL	UL	24,000	16,000	24,000	16,000	20,500	12,000	7,000
R-3	"	UL	UL	UL	UL	UL	UL	UL	UL	UL
R-4	"	UL	UL	24,000	16,000	24,000	16,000	20,500	12,000	7,000
Occupancy S: maximum height in stories and feet										
S	Feet	UL	160	65	55	65	55	65	50	40
S-1	Stories	UL	11	4	3	3	3	4	3	1
S-2	Stories	UL	11	5	4	4	4	5	4	2
Occupancy S: maximum area per floor in square feet										
S-1	SF	UL	48,000	26,000	17,500	26,000	17,500	25,500	14,000	9,000
S-2	SF	UL	79,000	39,000	26,000	39,000	26,000	38,500	21,000	13,500
Occupancy U: maximum height in stories and feet										
U	Feet	UL	160	65	55	65	55	65	50	40
U	Stories	UL	5	4	2	3	2	4	2	1
Occupancy U: maximum area per floor in square feet										
U	SF	UL	35,500	19,000	8,500	14,000	8,500	18,000	9,000	5,500

Source: IBC Table 503.
UL = unlimited, Occ. = occupancy, SF = square feet.

503 General Height and Area Limitations

503.1.1 Basements

- Basement areas are not included in the total area permitted as follows:
  - Where the basement area < that allowed for a 1-story building.

503.1.2 Special industrial occupancies

- The following buildings and structures are not required to meet height and area limitations based on occupancy and construction type:
  - Those containing low-hazard industrial processes as follows:
    Processes requiring large areas and heights to accommodate the following:
      Building with craneways.
      Rolling mills.
      Structural metal fabrication shops and foundries.
      Production and distribution of power as follows:
        Electric.
        Gas.
        Steam.

  Note: IBC Table 503, "Allowable Height and Building Areas," is cited as listing the limitations from which these buildings are exempt.

503.1.3 Buildings on same lot

- Multiple buildings on the same lot may be considered to be either of the following:
  - Separate buildings.
  - A single building where all of the following apply:
    Height of each building meets the following:
      Height limits based on occupancy and construction type as modified.
    Sum of areas of the buildings meets the following:
      Area limits based on occupancy and construction type as modified.
    The individual structures meet applicable code requirements.
    The group of structures meet applicable code requirements as a single building.

  Note: The following are cited as providing limits for the buildings described above:
  IBC Table 503, "Allowable Height and Building Areas," provides the base limits.
  Section 504, "Height Modifications," alters the limits based on conditions.
  Section 506, "Area Modifications," alters the limits based on conditions.

503 General Height and Area Limitations

503.1.4 Type I construction

- Buildings of Type I construction, which are allowed unlimited height or area based on occupancy and construction type, are governed as follows:
  - These buildings are not subject to the conditions that are required for unlimited or increased height or area in other cases or construction types.

    Note: 504.3, "Roof structures," is cited as having limitations for unlimited-height buildings which do not apply here.
    503.1.2, "Special industrial occupancies," is cited as having limitations for unlimited-height buildings which do not apply here.
    Section 507, "Unlimited Area Buildings," is cited as a source of conditions for unlimited-area buildings which do not apply here.

503.2 Party walls

- A party wall must be constructed as a fire wall as follows:
  - Where located on a property line.
  - When located between adjacent buildings.
  - When used for joint service by the two buildings.
- Fire walls serving as party walls define separate buildings on each side.

    Note: Section 705, "Fire Walls," is cited as governing such construction.

504 Height Modifications

504.1 General

- Height of the following buildings is unlimited where all the conditions indicated apply:
  - Buildings:
    Aircraft hangars.
    Aircraft paint hangars.
    Buildings in which aircraft are manufactured.
  - Conditions:
    Automatic fire-extinguishing system is required.
    Building is surrounded by public ways or yards as follows:

    Width of yard is ≥ 1½ × hangar height.

    Note: Chapter 9, "Fire Protection Systems," is cited as governing the fire-extinguishing system required above.

- Height limits of other buildings based on the following may be increased only as permitted in this section series:
  - Occupancy.
  - Construction type.

504.2 Automatic sprinkler system increase *(part 1 of 4)*

- This section lists maximum heights of buildings sprinklered as per NFPA 13 as follows:
  - Maximum heights listed for the following do not constitute limit increases over those required for building without sprinklers:
    Occupancy I-2 in the following construction types:
    IIB, III, IV, V.
    Occupancies H-1, H-2, H-3, H-5.
    Buildings having unlimited height without sprinklers.

    Note: IBC Table 503, "Allowable Height and Building Areas," is cited as the source of height limits for buildings without sprinklers.

- These heights are allowed in addition to permitted area increases as follows:
  - Where sprinklered as per NFPA 13.

    Note: The following are cited as providing area increases:
    506.2, "Frontage increase."
    506.3, "Automatic sprinkler system increase."

- This section does not apply to the following cases:
  - Where sprinklers are used to achieve a 1-hr fire-resistance rating reduction.

    Note: Table 601, "Fire-resistance Rating Requirements for Building Elements," footnote d is cited as permitting a reduction in ratings due to the presence of sprinklers.

- Adjusted maximum height in feet and stories is listed in tables on the following pages, 134–137.

504 Height Modifications

504.2 Automatic sprinkler system increase *(part 2 of 4)*

- This table lists maximum heights of buildings sprinklered as per NFPA 13.

Table 504.2a **Maximum Height of Sprinklered Buildings**

| Occ. | Height | Type of construction | | | | | | | | |
		IA	IB	IIA	IIB	IIIA	IIIB	IV	VA	VB
Occupancy A:										
A	Feet	UL	180	85	75	85	75	85	70	60
A-1	Stories	UL	6	4	3	4	3	4	3	2
A-2	"	UL	12	4	3	4	3	4	3	2
A-3	"	UL	12	4	3	4	3	4	3	2
A-4	"	UL	12	4	3	4	3	4	3	2
A-5	"	UL	UL	UL	UL	UL	UL	UL	UL	UL
Occupancy B:										
B	Feet	UL	180	85	75	85	75	85	70	60
B	Stories	UL	11	6	5	6	5	6	4	3
Occupancy E:										
E	Feet	UL	180	85	75	85	75	85	70	60
E	Stories	UL	6	4	3	4	3	4	2	2
Occupancy F:										
F	Feet	UL	180	85	75	85	75	85	70	60
F-1	Stories	UL	12	5	3	4	3	5	3	2
F-2	Stories	UL	12	6	4	5	4	6	4	3
Occupancy H:										
H	Feet	UL	160	65	55	65	55	65	50	40
H-1	Stories	1	1	1	1	1	1	1	1	NP
H-2	"	UL	3	2	1	2	1	2	1	1
H-3	"	UL	6	4	2	4	2	4	2	1
H-5	"	3	3	3	3	3	3	3	3	2
Occupancy H-4:										
H-4	Feet	UL	180	85	75	85	75	85	70	60
H-4	Stories	UL	8	6	4	6	4	6	4	3

UL = unlimited, Occ. = occupancy.

Case study: Fig. 504.2A. The occupancy B building is sprinklered and is Type VB construction. This qualifies the builidng for an increase in height from limits of 40' and 2 stories for buildings that are unsprinklered to limits of 60' and 3 stories. The building is 2 stories and 30'-8" high, measured to the average height of the roof behind the parapet (just below the top of the spandrel glass). Thus, the building complies with the code requirements for height.

Fig. 504.2A. Partial elevation. AmberGlen Business Center. Hillsboro, Oregon. Ankrom Moisan Associated Architects. Portland, Oregon.

504 Height Modifications

504.2 Automatic sprinkler system increase *(part 3 of 4)*

- This table lists maximum heights of buildings sprinklered as per NFPA 13.

Table 504.2c   Maximum Height of Sprinklered Buildings

Occ.	Height	IA	IB	IIA	IIB	IIIA	IIIB	IV	VA	VB
Occupancy I:										
I	Feet	UL	180	85	75	85	75	85	70	60
I-1	Stories	UL	10	5	4	5	4	5	4	3
I-3	"	UL	5	3	2	3	2	3	3	2
I-4	"	UL	6	4	3	4	3	4	2	2
Occupancy I-2:										
I-2	Feet	UL	180	85	55	65	55	65	50	40
I-2	Stories	UL	5	3	1	1	NP	1	1	NP
Occupancy M:										
M	Feet	UL	180	85	75	85	75	85	70	60
M	Stories	UL	12	5	5	5	5	5	4	2
Occupancy S:										
S	Feet	UL	180	85	75	85	75	85	70	60
S-1	Stories	UL	12	5	4	4	4	5	4	2
S-2	Stories	UL	12	6	5	5	5	6	5	3
Occupancy U:										
U	Feet	UL	180	85	75	85	75	85	70	60
U	Stories	UL	6	5	3	4	3	5	3	2

UL = unlimited, NP = not permitted, Occ. = occupancy.

504 Height Modifications

504.2 Automatic sprinkler system increase *(part 4 of 4)*

- This table lists maximum heights of buildings sprinklered as per NFPA 13R.

Table 504.2d   Maximum Height of Sprinklered Buildings

Occ.	Height	IA	IB	IIA	IIB	IIIA	IIIB	IV	VA	VB
					Type of construction					
Occupancy R:										
R	Feet	UL	160	65	65	65	60	65	60	60
R-1	Stories	UL	11	4	4	4	4	4	4	3
R-2	"	UL	11	4	4	4	4	4	4	3
R-3	"	UL	11	4	4	4	4	4	4	4
R-4	"	UL	11	4	4	4	4	4	4	3

UL = unlimited, Occ. = occupancy.

Case study: Fig. 504.2B. The structure houses an occupancy B area separated from an occupancy S-1 warehouse by a fire wall. Construction is Type IIIA. The warehouse is limited to 4 stories and 85' in height based on the fact that it is sprinklered. The height of the 1-story warehouse from the grade plane to the average height of the roof is 42'. The warehouse is within height limitations for a sprinklered S-1 building of this type of construction.

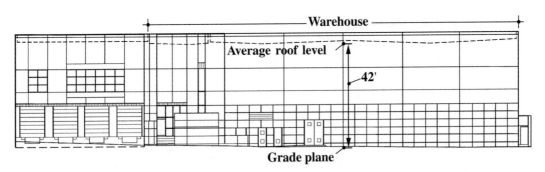

Fig. 504.2B. Elevation. New Warehouse Addition. Los Angeles, California. Stephen Wen + Associates, Architects, Inc. Pasadena, California.

504 Height Modifications

504.3 Roof structures

- The following elements are governed as indicated below:
  - Elements:
    - Towers.
    - Spires.
    - Steeples.
    - Other roof structures.
  - Requirements:
    - Elements must be constructed with materials according to construction type.
    - Elements may not be used for the following:
      - Habitation.
      - Storage.
    - Elements are unlimited in height as follows:
      - Where constructed of noncombustible materials.
    - Elements must be ≤ 20' above allowable building height as follows:
      - Where constructed of combustible materials.

Note: 1509.1, "Type of construction," is cited as providing alternatives to materials requirements.

   Chapter 15, "Roof Assemblies and Rooftop Structures," is cited as the source for additional requirements.

505 Mezzanines

505.1 General

- Mezzanines are considered to be a part of the floor below.
- The areas of mezzanines are included in the computation of fire areas.
- The clear height above a mezzanine floor must be ≥ 7'.
- The clear height below a mezzanine floor construction must be ≥ 7'.
- The areas of mezzanines are not included in the area limit per floor as based on occupancy and construction type.
- Mezzanines are not considered to be a story when computing the number of stories in the height of a building as limited by occupancy and construction type.

  Note: The following are cited as sources of requirements applicable as indicated:
  503.1, "General," which includes IBC Table 503, "Allowable Height and Building Areas."
  Section 702, "Definitions," defines fire area as referred to above.

505.2 Area limitation

- Mezzanine areas in industrial space that are exempt from the height and area limitations are governed as follows:
  - In Type 1 and 2 construction:
    The total area of all mezzanines in a space must be ≤ ²/₃ the area of the space.
- Mezzanine areas in all other occupancies are governed as follows:
  - The total area of all mezzanines in a space must be ≤ ¹/₃ the area of the space.
- The following are not included in determining the size of a space containing a mezzanine:
  - Enclosed areas within the space.
  - The area of the mezzanine.

  Note: 503.1.2, "Special industrial occupancies," is cited as defining the spaces exempt from height and area limitations.

505 Mezzanines

505.3 Egress

- ≥ 2 means of egress are required from a mezzanine as follows:
  - Where its occupant load exceeds that listed below.
  - Where its common path of travel would otherwise exceed that listed below:

Table 505.3   Length Limits for Common Path of Egress Travel

Occupancy	Occupant load	Common path with sprinklers	Common path without sprinklers
A, E, M, U	> 50	75'	75'
B, F	> 50	100'	75'
B tenant space, S, U	> 30	100'	100'
H-1, H-2, H-3	> 3	25'	not permitted
H-4, H-5	> 10	75'	not permitted
I-1, I-4, R	> 10	75'	75'
I-3	> 10	100'	100'

> *Note: 1013.3, "Common path of egress travel," is cited as the source of limits for egress travel, a partial summary of which is provided in the table above.*
> *1014.1, "Exit or exit access doorways required," is cited as identifying spaces requiring only 1 means of egress. The occupant load thresholds from that section are included in the table above.*

- Length of egress travel on a mezzanine stairway is included in travel distance as follows:
  - As measured on a line connecting the tread nosings.
- Accessible mezzanines must have accessible means of egress as follows:
  - ≥ 1 is required.
  - 2 accessible means of egress are required from each accessible space as follows:
    Where > 1 means of egress is required from the space.

> *Note: 1003.2.13, "Accessible means of egress," is cited as the source of requirements for accessible means of egress, some of which are summarized above.*

505.4 Openness (*part 1 of 2*)

- Mezzanines are not required to be open to the space in which they are located in any of the following cases:
  - Where the total occupant load of all the enclosed mezzanine areas totals ≤ 10.
  - Where both of the following apply:
    The mezzanine has ≥ 2 means of egress.
    ≥ 1 means of egress has direct access to an exit from the mezzanine.
  - Where enclosed portions are ≤ 10% of the total of the mezzanine areas.
- Mezzanines with both of the following conditions may be glazed on all sides:
  - Located in an industrial facility.
  - Used for control of equipment.

505 Mezzanines

505.4 Openness (*part 2 of 2*)

- Mezzanines are not required to be open to the surrounding space where all of the following conditions apply:
  - In occupancy F.
  - The building qualifies for having unlimited area.
  - The building is sprinklered as per NFPA 13.
  - The building is adjacent to public ways or yards ≥ 60' wide on all sides.
  - A fire alarm system is provided throughout the building.
  - Notification devices are located throughout the mezzanine.
  - Sprinkler flow must initiate the fire alarm system.

    Note: The following are cited as the sources of requirements applicable to this section.
    507.2, "Sprinklered, one-story," provides requirements for buildings qualifying to be unlimited in area, a partial summary of which is provided above.
    507.3, "Two-story," provides requirements for buildings qualifying to be unlimited in area, a partial summary of which is provided above.
    NFPA 72, " National Fire Alarm Code," governs the fire alarm systems.

- All other mezzanines must be open to the surrounding space as follows:
  - The following are permitted:
    Walls ≤ 42" above the mezzanine floor.
    Columns.
    Posts.

505.5 Industrial equipment platforms

- Platforms are not considered to be a part of the floor below.
- The areas of platforms are not included in the area limit per floor based on occupancy and construction type.
- Platforms are not considered to be a story when computing the number of stories in the height of a building as limited by occupancy and construction type.

    Note: 503.1, "General," which includes IBC Table 503, "Allowable Height and Building Areas," is cited as the source of heights and areas based on occupancy and construction type as indicated above.

- The areas of platforms are not included in the computation of fire areas.
- Platforms may not be a part of a mezzanine.
- Platforms and the following components may not serve as a means of egress from a building:
  - Components providing access to platforms:
    Walkways.
    Stairs.
    Ladders.

505 Mezzanines

505.5.1 Area limitations

- This section addresses industrial equipment platforms.
- The combined-areas platforms in a space is limited as follows:
  Area must be ≤ ²/₃ the area of the space.
- The combined areas of platforms and mezzanines in the same space is limited as follows:
  Area must be ≤ ²/₃ the area of the space.

  Note: 505.2, "Area limitation," is cited as the source of the limit on mezzanine area, which also applies when mezzanines are in the same space as a platform.

505.5.2 Fire suppression

- Sprinklers are required above and below industrial equipment platforms as follows:
  ○ Where the building is required to be sprinklered.
  ○ Where the space is not exempt from sprinkler requirements.

  Note: 903.3, "Installation requirements," is cited as referencing standards which exempt spaces from a requirement for sprinklers.

505.5.3 Guards

- Guards are required along the open sides of platforms as follows:
  ○ Where an open side is > 30" above the floor below.

  Note: 1012.1, "Where required," is cited as the source of requirements for guards which are partially summarized above.

506 Area Modifications

506.1 General

- Area per floor limits based on occupancy and construction type may be increased as follows:

> **Limit of area per floor**
> **+ Additional square footage allowed due to frontage**
> **+ Additional square footage allowed due to the presence of sprinklers**
> _____
> **Increased limit of area per floor**

- Additional square footage allowed is determined by the % increase allowed as follows:

Additional square footage allowed = (% increase added ÷ 100) ✕ Limit of area per floor

Note: The following are cited as sources of applicable requirements:
IBC Table 503, "Allowable Height and Building Areas."
506.2, "Frontage increase," describes area increases permitted by frontage.
506.3, "Automatic sprinkler system increase," lists increases based on sprinklers.

506.1.1 Basements

- The area of a single basement need not be included in the total building area as follows:
  - Where the basement area is ≤ that permitted for a 1-story building.

506.2 Frontage increase *(part 1 of 4)*

- This section addresses increases to limits to area per floor based on occupancy and construction type as permitted by minimum frontage requirements.
- The area limit may be increased where the following frontage conditions exist:
  - > 25% of the building perimeter must adjoin one of the following:
    A public way ≥ 20' wide.
    An open space ≥ 20' wide.
- The % increase in area permitted by frontage is listed in the following tables:
  - Tables are based on the following equation:

% increase in area = (% of open perimeter - 25%) ✕ (width of open space ÷ 30)

"Open perimeter" = perimeter adjoining a public way or open space.
"Width of open space ÷ 30" is limited to ≤ 2 where both the following apply:
    The building has < 60' of the open space required for unlimited area.
    The building qualifies for unlimited area in all other respects.
"Width of open space ÷ 30" is limited to ≤ 1 for other buildings.

Note: 506.2.1, "Width limits," is cited as governing width. The section establishes a
maximum to the % increase in area as determined using the above equation
by limiting the value of "width of open space ÷ 30" as indicated above.
Section 507, "Unlimited area buildings," sets forth requirements for buildings
to qualify for unlimited area.

506 Area Modifications

506.2 Frontage increase *(part 2 of 4)*

- The table below indicates the permitted % increase to the limit of area per floor as follows:
  - ○ Based on % of open perimeter from 26% to 49%.
  - ○ For frontage widths 20' to 30'.

Table 506.2a   **% Increase in Area per Floor due to Frontage**

% open	Width of frontage										
	20'	21'	22'	23'	24'	25'	26'	27'	28'	29'	30'
26	0.67	0.70	0.73	0.77	0.80	0.83	0.87	0.90	0.93	0.97	1.00
27	1.33	1.40	1.47	1.53	1.60	1.67	1.73	1.80	1.87	1.93	2.00
28	2.00	2.10	2.20	2.30	2.40	2.50	2.60	2.70	2.80	2.90	3.00
29	2.67	2.80	2.93	3.07	3.20	3.33	3.47	3.60	3.73	3.87	4.00
30	3.33	3.50	3.67	3.83	4.00	4.17	4.33	4.50	4.67	4.83	5.00
31	4.00	4.20	4.40	4.60	4.80	5.00	5.20	5.40	5.60	5.80	6.00
32	4.67	4.90	5.13	5.37	5.60	5.83	6.07	6.30	6.53	6.77	7.00
33	5.33	5.60	5.87	6.13	6.40	6.67	6.93	7.20	7.47	7.73	8.00
34	6.00	6.30	6.60	6.90	7.20	7.50	7.80	8.10	8.40	8.70	9.00
35	6.67	7.00	7.33	7.67	8.00	8.33	8.67	9.00	9.33	9.67	10.00
36	7.33	7.70	8.07	8.43	8.80	9.17	9.53	9.90	10.27	10.63	11.00
37	8.00	8.40	8.80	9.20	9.60	10.00	10.40	10.80	11.20	11.60	12.00
38	8.67	9.10	9.53	9.97	10.40	10.83	11.27	11.70	12.13	12.57	13.00
39	9.33	9.80	10.27	10.73	11.20	11.67	12.13	12.60	13.07	13.53	14.00
40	10.00	10.50	11.00	11.50	12.00	12.50	13.00	13.50	14.00	14.50	15.00
41	10.67	11.20	11.73	12.27	12.80	13.33	13.87	14.40	14.93	15.47	16.00
42	11.33	11.90	12.47	13.03	13.60	14.17	14.73	15.30	15.87	16.43	17.00
43	12.00	12.60	13.20	13.80	14.40	15.00	15.60	16.20	16.80	17.40	18.00
44	12.67	13.30	13.93	14.57	15.20	15.83	16.47	17.10	17.73	18.37	19.00
45	13.33	14.00	14.67	15.33	16.00	16.67	17.33	18.00	18.67	19.33	20.00
46	14.00	14.70	15.40	16.10	16.80	17.50	18.20	18.90	19.60	20.30	21.00
47	14.67	15.40	16.13	16.87	17.60	18.33	19.07	19.80	20.53	21.27	22.00
48	15.33	16.10	16.87	17.63	18.40	19.17	19.93	20.70	21.47	22.23	23.00
49	16.00	16.80	17.60	18.40	19.20	20.00	20.80	21.60	22.40	23.20	24.00

506 Area Modifications

506.2 Frontage increase *(part 3 of 4)*

- The table below indicates the permitted % increase to the limit of area per floor as follows:
  - Based on % of open perimeter from 50% to 79%.
  - For frontage widths 20' to 30'.

Table 506.2b   **% Increase in Area per Floor due to Frontage**

% open	Width of frontage										
	20'	21'	22'	23'	24'	25'	26'	27'	28'	29'	30'
50	16.67	17.50	18.33	19.17	20.00	20.83	21.67	22.50	23.33	24.17	25.00
51	17.33	18.20	19.07	19.93	20.80	21.67	22.53	23.40	24.27	25.13	26.00
52	18.00	18.90	19.80	20.70	21.60	22.50	23.40	24.30	25.20	26.10	27.00
53	18.67	19.60	20.53	21.47	22.40	23.33	24.27	25.20	26.13	27.07	28.00
54	19.33	20.30	21.27	22.23	23.20	24.17	25.13	26.10	27.07	28.03	29.00
55	20.00	21.00	22.00	23.00	24.00	25.00	26.00	27.00	28.00	29.00	30.00
56	20.67	21.70	22.73	23.77	24.80	25.83	26.87	27.90	28.93	29.97	31.00
57	21.33	22.40	23.47	24.53	25.60	26.67	27.73	28.80	29.87	30.93	32.00
58	22.00	23.10	24.20	25.30	26.40	27.50	28.60	29.70	30.80	31.90	33.00
59	22.67	23.80	24.93	26.07	27.20	28.33	29.47	30.60	31.73	32.87	34.00
60	23.33	24.50	25.67	26.83	28.00	29.17	30.33	31.50	32.67	33.83	35.00
61	24.00	25.20	26.40	27.60	28.80	30.00	31.20	32.40	33.60	34.80	36.00
62	24.67	25.90	27.13	28.37	29.60	30.83	32.07	33.30	34.53	35.77	37.00
63	25.33	26.60	27.87	29.13	30.40	31.67	32.93	34.20	35.47	36.73	38.00
64	26.00	27.30	28.60	29.90	31.20	32.50	33.80	35.10	36.40	37.70	39.00
65	26.67	28.00	29.33	30.67	32.00	33.33	34.67	36.00	37.33	38.67	40.00
66	27.33	28.70	30.07	31.43	32.80	34.17	35.53	36.90	38.27	39.63	41.00
67	28.00	29.40	30.80	32.20	33.60	35.00	36.40	37.80	39.20	40.60	42.00
68	28.67	30.10	31.53	32.97	34.40	35.83	37.27	38.70	40.13	41.57	43.00
69	29.33	30.80	32.27	33.73	35.20	36.67	38.13	39.60	41.07	42.53	44.00
70	30.00	31.50	33.00	34.50	36.00	37.50	39.00	40.50	42.00	43.50	45.00
71	30.67	32.20	33.73	35.27	36.80	38.33	39.87	41.40	42.93	44.47	46.00
72	31.33	32.90	34.47	36.03	37.60	39.17	40.73	42.30	43.87	45.43	47.00
73	32.00	33.60	35.20	36.80	38.40	40.00	41.60	43.20	44.80	46.40	48.00
74	32.67	34.30	35.93	37.57	39.20	40.83	42.47	44.10	45.73	47.37	49.00
75	33.33	35.00	36.67	38.33	40.00	41.67	43.33	45.00	46.67	48.33	50.00
76	34.00	35.70	37.40	39.10	40.80	42.50	44.20	45.90	47.60	49.30	51.00
77	34.67	36.40	38.13	39.87	41.60	43.33	45.07	46.80	48.53	50.27	52.00
78	35.33	37.10	38.87	40.63	42.40	44.17	45.93	47.70	49.47	51.23	53.00
79	36.00	37.80	39.60	41.40	43.20	45.00	46.80	48.60	50.40	52.20	54.00

506 Area Modifications

506.2 Frontage increase *(part 4 of 4)*

- The table below indicates the permitted % increase to the limit of area per floor as follows:
  - Based on % of open perimeter from 80% to 100%.
  - For frontage widths 20' to 30'.

Table 506.2c   % Increase in Area per Floor due to Frontage

% open	Width of frontage										
	20'	21'	22'	23'	24'	25'	26'	27'	28'	29'	30'
80	36.67	38.50	40.33	42.17	44.00	45.83	47.67	49.50	51.33	53.17	55.00
81	37.33	39.20	41.07	42.93	44.80	46.67	48.53	50.40	52.27	54.13	56.00
82	38.00	39.90	41.80	43.70	45.60	47.50	49.40	51.30	53.20	55.10	57.00
83	38.67	40.60	42.53	44.47	46.40	48.33	50.27	52.20	54.13	56.07	58.00
84	39.33	41.30	43.27	45.23	47.20	49.17	51.13	53.10	55.07	57.03	59.00
85	40.00	42.00	44.00	46.00	48.00	50.00	52.00	54.00	56.00	58.00	60.00
86	40.67	42.70	44.73	46.77	48.80	50.83	52.87	54.90	56.93	58.97	61.00
87	41.33	43.40	45.47	47.53	49.60	51.67	53.73	55.80	57.87	59.93	62.00
88	42.00	44.10	46.20	48.30	50.40	52.50	54.60	56.70	58.80	60.90	63.00
89	42.67	44.80	46.93	49.07	51.20	53.33	55.47	57.60	59.73	61.87	64.00
90	43.33	45.50	47.67	49.83	52.00	54.17	56.33	58.50	60.67	62.83	65.00
91	44.00	46.20	48.40	50.60	52.80	55.00	57.20	59.40	61.60	63.80	66.00
92	44.67	46.90	49.13	51.37	53.60	55.83	58.07	60.30	62.53	64.77	67.00
93	45.33	47.60	49.87	52.13	54.40	56.67	58.93	61.20	63.47	65.73	68.00
94	46.00	48.30	50.60	52.90	55.20	57.50	59.80	62.10	64.40	66.70	69.00
95	46.67	49.00	51.33	53.67	56.00	58.33	60.67	63.00	65.33	67.67	70.00
96	47.33	49.70	52.07	54.43	56.80	59.17	61.53	63.90	66.27	68.63	71.00
97	48.00	50.40	52.80	55.20	57.60	60.00	62.40	64.80	67.20	69.60	72.00
98	48.67	51.10	53.53	55.97	58.40	60.83	63.27	65.70	68.13	70.57	73.00
99	49.33	51.80	54.27	56.73	59.20	61.67	64.13	66.60	69.07	71.53	74.00
100	50.00	52.50	55.00	57.50	60.00	62.50	65.00	67.50	70.00	72.50	75.00

Case study: Fig. 506.2. The sports and fine arts center is divided into three buildings, A, B, and C by fire walls. Building A contains A-1, A-3, and B occupancies. Building B is occupancy A-3. Building C contains A-3 and B occupancies. The occupancies within buildings A and C are not separated by 2-hr walls as per IBC Table 302.3.3 so the buildings have "nonseparated uses" governed by 302.3.2. In this case, the most restrictive area limitation of the occupancies in each building dictates the area permitted.

Building A is construction Type IIB and is sprinklered. IBC Table 503 permits 8500 sf per floor for occupancy A-1 (the most restrictive case in this building). 506.1 allows this limit to be increased due to open area around the building and to the presence of sprinklers. Building A has an open frontage ≥ 30' deep at 90% of its perimeter. 506.2 permits an area increase of 65% or 5525 sf based on the frontage. 506.3 permits an area increase equal to twice the original limit, or 17,000 sf. The new limit of area per floor is, therefore, *8500 sf + 5525 sf + 17,000 sf = 31,025 sf.* Building A has 31,010 sf on the 1st floor and less on the 2nd floor; thus, it complies with the limit of 31,025 sf per floor.

Building B is construction Type IIB and is sprinklered. IBC Table 503 permits 9500 sf for occupancy A-3. 506.1 allows this limit to be increased due to open area around the builidng and to the presence of sprinklers. Building B has an open frontage ≥ 30' deep at 58% of its perimeter. 506.2 permits an area increase of 33% or 3135 sf based on the frontage. 506.3 permits an area increase equal to twice the original limit, or 19,000 sf. The new limit of area per floor is, therefore, *9500 sf + 3135 sf + 19,000 sf = 31,635 sf.* Building B has 7176 sf on the 1st floor and less on the 2nd floor; thus, it complies with the limit of 31,635 sf per floor.

Building C is construction Type IIA and is not sprinklered. IBC Table 503 permits 15,500 sf per floor for occupancy A-3 (the more restrictive case in this building). Building C has an open frontage ≥ 30' deep at 85% of its perimeter. 506.2 permits an area increase of 60% or 9300 sf based on the frontage. The new limit of area per floor is, therefore, *15,500 sf + 9300 sf = 24,800 sf.* Building C has 23,365 sf on the 1st floor and less on the 2nd floor; thus, it complies with the limit of 24,800 sf per floor.

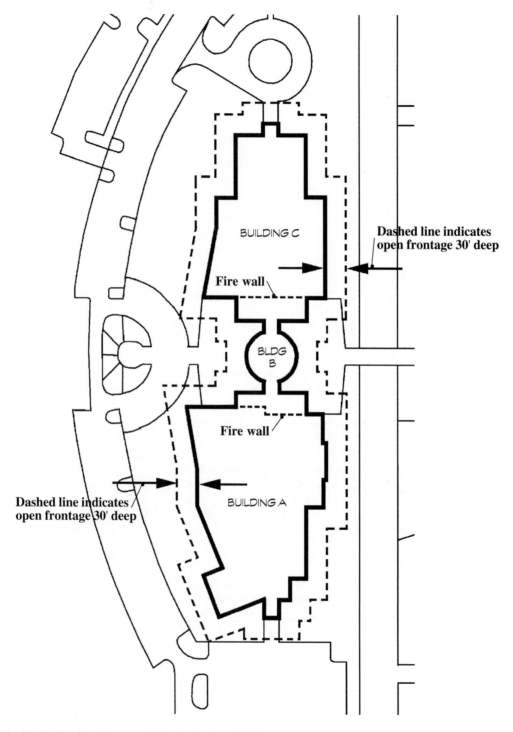

Fig. 506.2. Site plan. Newman University Sports and Fine Arts Center. Wichita, Kansas. Gossen Livingston Associates, Inc., Architecture. Wichita, Kansas.

506 Area Modifications

506.2.1 Width limits

- *W* as used in the equation for increased area limits based on frontage is as follows:
  - *W* is the width of public way or open space at the perimeter of a building.
  - *W* must be ≥ 20'.
  - *W* ÷ 30 is limited to a value ≤ 2.0 where both the following apply:
    The building has < 60' of the open space required to qualify for unlimited area.
    The building qualifies for unlimited area in all other respects.
  - *W* ÷ 30 is limited to a value ≤ 1.0 for other buildings.
  - A weighted average is used for W in the following case:
    Where the open space varies between 20' and 30' in width.

    Note: Section 507, "Unlimited area buildings," is cited as the source of requirements for buildings to qualify for unlimited area.

506.2.2 Open space limits

- This section addresses the frontage used as a basis for increasing the limits of area per floor.
- Open space qualifying as frontage is governed as follows:
  - It must be one of the following:
    Located on the same lot.
    Dedicated for public use.
  - It must be accessed by one of the following:
    From a street.
    By an approved fire lane.

506.3 Automatic sprinkler system increase *(part 1 of 3)*

- This section does not apply to the following cases:
  - Where sprinklers are used to achieve a 1-hr fire-resistance rating reduction.

    Note: Table 601, "Fire-resistance Rating Requirements for Building Elements," footnote d is cited as permitting a reduction in ratings due to the presence of sprinklers.

- Area increases permitted in this section are in addition to the following:
  - Height and story count increases permitted due to the presence of sprinklers.

    Note: 504.2, "Automatic sprinkler system increase," is cited as permitting height and story count increases due to the presnece of sprinklers.

- No increase in area is allowed due to sprinklers in H-1, H-2, or H-3 occupancies.
- In buildings of other occupancies, area per floor limits are increased as follows:
  - Where the building is sprinklered as per NFPA 13.
  - Increases are listed in the tables on the following pages.

    Note: IBC Table 503, "Allowable Height and Building Areas," is cited as the source of areas that may be increased by the presence of sprinklers.

506 Area Modifications

506.3 Automatic sprinkler system increase *(part 2 of 3)*

- This table lists area increases for multistory buildings sprinklered as per NFPA 13.

Table 506.3a   Added Area per Floor in SF for Sprinklered Multistory Buildings

Occ.	IA	IB	IIA	IIB	IIIA	IIIB	IV	VA	VB
A-1	UL	UL	31,000	17,000	28,000	17,000	30,000	23,000	11,000
A-2	UL	UL	31,000	19,000	28,000	19,000	30,000	23,000	12,000
A-3	UL	UL	31,000	19,000	28,000	19,000	30,000	23,000	12,000
A-4	UL	UL	31,000	19,000	18,000	19,000	30,000	23,000	12,000
A-5	UL	UL	UL	UL	UL	UL	30,000	UL	UL
B	UL	UL	75,000	46,000	57,000	38,000	72,000	36,000	18,000
E	UL	UL	53,000	29,000	47,000	29,000	51,000	37,000	19,000
F-1	UL	UL	50,000	31,000	38,000	24,000	71,000	28,000	17,000
F-2	UL	UL	75,000	46,000	57,000	36,000	101,000	43,000	26,000
H-4	UL	UL	75,000	35,000	57,000	35,000	72,000	36,000	13,000
H-5	UL	UL	75,000	46,000	57,000	38,000	72,000	36,000	18,000
I-1	UL	110,000	38,000	20,000	33,000	20,000	36,000	21,000	9,000
I-2	UL	UL	31,000	22,000	24,000	NP	24,000	19,000	NP
I-3	UL	UL	30,000	20,000	21,000	15,000	24,000	15,000	10,000
I-4	UL	121,000	53,000	26,000	47,000	26,000	51,000	37,000	18,000
M	UL	UL	43,000	25,000	37,000	25,000	41,000	28,000	18,000
R-1	UL	UL	48,000	32,000	48,000	32,000	41,000	24,000	14,000
R-2	UL	UL	48,000	32,000	48,000	32,000	41,000	24,000	14,000
R-3	UL	UL	UL	UL	UL	UL	UL	UL	UL
R-4	UL	UL	48,000	32,000	48,000	32,000	41,000	24,000	14,000
S-1	UL	96,000	52,000	35,000	52,000	35,000	51,000	28,000	18,000
S-2	UL	158,000	78,000	52,000	78,000	52,000	77,000	42,000	27,000
U	UL	71,000	38,000	17,000	28,000	17,000	36,000	18,000	11,000

SF = square feet, NP = not permitted, UL = unlimited, Occ. = occupancy.

506 Area Modifications

506.3 Automatic sprinkler system increase *(part 3 of 3)*

- This table lists area increases for one-story buildings sprinklered as per NFPA 13.

Table 506.3b   Added Area per Floor in SF for Sprinklered 1-Story Buildings

Occ.	IA	IB	IIA	IIB	IIIA	IIIB	IV	VA	VB
A-1	UL	UL	46,500	25,500	42,000	25,500	45,000	34,500	16,500
A-2	UL	UL	46,500	28,500	42,000	28,500	45,000	34,500	18,000
A-3	UL	UL	46,500	28,500	42,000	28,500	45,000	34,500	18,000
A-4	UL	UL	46,500	28,500	42,000	28,500	45,000	34,500	18,000
A-5	UL	UL	UL	UL	UL	UL	45,000	UL	UL
B	UL	UL	112,500	69,000	85,500	57,000	108,000	54,000	27,000
E	UL	UL	79,500	43,500	70,500	43,500	76,500	55,500	28,500
F-1	UL	UL	75,000	46,500	57,000	36,000	106,500	42,000	25,500
F-2	UL	UL	112,500	69,000	57,000	54,000	151,500	64,500	39,000
H-4	UL	UL	112,500	52,500	85,500	52,500	108,000	54,000	19,500
H-5	UL	UL	112,500	69,000	85,500	57,000	108,000	54,000	27,000
I-1	UL	165,000	57,000	30,000	49,500	30,000	54,000	31,500	13,500
I-2	UL	UL	46,500	33,000	36,000	NP	36,000	28,500	NP
I-3	UL	UL	45,000	30,000	31,500	22,500	36,00	22,500	15,000
I-4	UL	181,500	79,500	39,000	70,500	39,000	76,500	55,500	27,000
M	UL	UL	64,500	37,500	55,500	37,500	61,500	42,000	27,000
R-1	UL	UL	72,000	48,000	72,000	48,000	61,500	36,000	21,000
R-2	UL	UL	72,000	48,000	72,000	48,000	61,500	36,000	21,000
R-3	UL	UL	UL	UL	UL	UL	UL	UL	UL
R-4	UL	UL	72,000	48,000	72,000	48,000	61,500	36,000	21,000
S-1	UL	144,000	78,000	52,500	78,000	52,5000	76,500	42,000	27,000
S-2	UL	237,000	117,000	78,000	117,000	78,000	115,500	63,000	49,500
U	UL	106,500	57,000	25,500	42,000	25,500	54,000	27,000	16,500

NP = not permitted, SF = square feet, UL = unlimited, Occ. = occupancy.

506 Area Modifications

506.4 Area determination

- This section does not apply to buildings of unlimited area.

  Note: Section 507, "Unlimited Area Buildings," is cited as the source of requirements for the unlimited area buildings excluded from this section.

- Buildings sprinklered as per NFPA 13R are governed as follows:
  - The total area allowed for the building is calculated as follows:

  Total building area = Allowable area/floor × number of stories

  Note: 506.1, "General," is cited as specifying the method used to determine the allowable area/floor of a building.
  903.3.1.2, "NFPA 13R sprinkler systems," is cited as governing the sprinklers.

- The total area allowed for other buildings > 1 story is calculated as follows:

  Area per floor permitted by occupancy and construction type
  + Additional area permitted due to the presence of frontage
  + Additional area permitted by the presence of sprinklers

  Adjusted area permitted per floor

  Total building area allowed is as follows:

  Area for 2-story buildings = Adjusted area permitted per floor × 2
  Area for ≥ 3-story buildings = Adjusted area permitted per floor × 3

  Note: 506.1, "General," is cited as specifying the method for determining the allowable area per floor which is summarized above. The limit of area on each floor determined by the section may not be exceeded.
  IBC Table 503, "Allowable Height and Building Areas," provides the area per floor permitted by occupancy and construction type.
  506.2, "Frontage increase," provides the method for determining the increase in area permitted based on frontage.
  506.3, "Automatic sprinkler system increase," provides the method for determining the increase in area permitted based on sprinklers.

507 Unlimited Area Buildings

507.1 Unsprinklered, one-story

- Buildings in the following occupancies are not limited in area where they meet both of the criteria indicated below:
  - Occupancies:
    F-2, S-2.
  - Requirements:
    The building must be 1 story.
    Any of the following open areas must contact the entire perimeter of the building:
    Public ways and yards ≥ 60' wide.

507.2 Sprinklered, one-story

- Rack storage facilities meeting all the following criteria are not limited in area:
  - Buildings of any height are included.
  - Building must be Type I or Type II construction.
  - Public does not have access to the building.
  - Any of the following open areas must contact the entire perimeter of the building:
    Public ways and yards ≥ 60' wide.
  - The building must conform to other rack storage requirements.

  Note: NFPA 231C, "Rack Storage of Materials," is cited as a source of requirements.

- Occupancy A-4 areas housing indoor participant sports such as the following are governed as indicated below:
  - Sports areas:
    Tennis.
    Skating.
    Swimming.
    Equestrian activities.
  - Requirements:
    Sprinklers are not required in sports areas.
    Sports areas must have exit doors opening directly to the outdoors.
    The building must have manual fire alarm activation switches.

  Note: Section 907, "Fire Alarm and Detection Systems," is cited as applicable.

- In other cases, buildings in the following occupancies may have unlimited area if they meet all the conditions listed below:
  - Occupancies:
    A-4 with construction type I, II, III, IV.
    B, F, M, S.
  - Conditions:
    Building must be 1 story.
    Building must be sprinklered as per NFPA 13.
    Any of the following open areas must contact the entire building perimeter:
    Public ways and yards ≥ 60' wide.

507 Unlimited Area Building

507.3 Two-story

- 2-story buildings in the following occupancies are not limited in areas where both of the conditions below apply:
  - Occupancies:
    B, F, M, S.
  - Conditions:
    Building must be sprinklered as per NFPA 13.
    One or both of the following open areas must contact the entire perimeter of the building:
      Public ways and yards ≥ 60' wide.

507.4 Reduced open space

- This section addresses the reduction of width for the open space required at the perimeter of unlimited area buildings.
- Such open space may be reduced from ≥ 60' to ≥ 40' as follows:
  - Reduced width may occur on ≤ 75% of the building perimeter.
  - A fire-resistance rating of ≥ 3 hrs is required as follows:
    For exterior walls facing the reduced width.
    For protectives at openings in exterior walls facing the reduced width.
- Reduced width is permitted for the facilities listed below where they comply with the following requirements:
  - Requirements:
    Facilities must meet the requirements of this section.
    Facilities must meet the requirements for having unlimited area.
  - Facilities:
    1-story buildings as follows:
      Occupancy F-2 or S-2:
        Unsprinklered.
      Occupancies A-4, B, F, M, S:
        Sprinklered.
    2-story buildings as follows:
      Occupancies B, F, M, S:
        Sprinklered.

  Note: The following are cited as sources of requirements defining buildings of unlimited area that otherwise require a perimeter of open space 60' wide. A partial summary of such requirements is provided above.
  507.1, "Nonsprinklered, one-story."
  507.2, "Sprinklered, one story."
  507.3, "Two story."

Case study: Fig. 507.3. The 2-story office building is not limlited in area based on the facts that it is occupancy B, it is sprinklered, and it has the necessary open space around it. The dashed line shown is 60' from the structure, thus, indicating that the yards and public ways surrounding the building are all larger than the 60' minimum required.

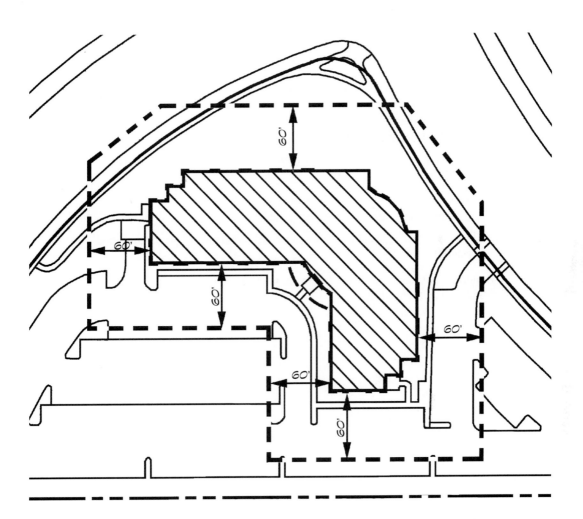

Fig. 507.3. Site plan. AmberGlen Business Center. Hillsboro, Oregon. Ankrom Moisan Associated Architects. Portland, Oregon.

507 Unlimited Area Buildings

507.5 Group A-3 buildings

- The following buildings are not limited in area where all the requirements listed are met:
  - Buildings:
    Church.
    Community hall.
    Dance hall.
    Exhibition hall.
    Gymnasium.
    Lecture hall.
    Indoor swimming pool.
    Tennis court.
  - Requirements:
    Building must be 1 story.
    Building must be in occupancy A-3.
    Building must have Type I or II construction.
    Building may not have a stage:
      Platforms are permitted.
    Building must be sprinklered.

    Note: 903.3.1.1, "NFPA 13 sprinkler systems," is cited as the source of requirements for the specified sprinklers.

    Assembly floor must be ≤ 21" above street or grade level.
    All exits must have ramps to street or grade level.

    Note: 1010.1, "Scope," is cited as the source of requirements for the specified ramps.

    Building must have one of the following on each side:
    Public way ≥ 60' wide.
    Yard ≥ 60' wide.

507 Unlimited Area Buildings

507.6 High-hazard use groups

- This section addresses H-2, H-3, or H-4 fire areas where located in unlimited area buildings of occupancy F or S.

    Note: IBC Table 302.3.2, "Required Separation of Occupancies," is cited as governing the fire-resistance ratings of fire barriers.

- Where an H-2, H-3 or H-4 fire area is located at the perimeter of the building, the following applies:
  - The area of the occupancy H fire area is limited to the smaller of the following:
    - ≤ 10% of the F or S building area.
    - ≤ the following area limit to be increased as indicated below:
      - Area limit as based on the following:
        - The occupancy of the fire area.
        - The construction type of the F or S building.
      - Area limit may be increased due to open frontage as follows:
        - The "% of open perimeter" used in the computation is based on the following:
          - Length of fire area walls facing required frontage ÷ perimeter of fire area.

    Note: IBC Table 503, "Allowable Height and Building Areas," is cited as the source of area limit based on the fire area occupancy and the construction type of the F or S building.
    506.2, "Frontage increase," is cited as the source of method for increasing the area limit from Table 503.

- Where an H-2, H-3 or H-4 fire area is located away from the perimeter of a building, the following applies:
  - The area of the occupancy H fire area is limited as follows:
    - Area must be ≤ 25% of the area limit based on the following:
      - The occupancy of the fire area.
      - The construction type of the F or S building.

    Note: IBC Table 503, "Allowable Height and Building Areas," is cited as the source of area limit based on the fire area occupancy and the construction type of the F or S building.

507.7 Aircraft paint hangar

- Aircraft hangers are not limited in area where all the following requirements are met:
  - Building must be 1 story.
  - Building must be occupancy H-2.
  - Building must have one of the following on each side:
    - Public way ≥ 1.5 × building height.
    - Yard ≥ 1.5 × building height.
  - Building must comply with other code requiremets for aircraft paint hangars.

    Note: 412.4, "Aircraft paint hangars," is cited as a source of requirements.

507 Unlimited Area Buildings

507.8 Group E buildings

- Occupancy E buildings may have unlimited area where all the following apply:
  - Building is 1 story.
  - Building is one of the following types of construction:
    Type II.
    Type IIIA.
    Type IV.
  - Each classroom has ≥ 2 means of egress.
  - Each classroom has ≥ 1 means of egress with a direct exit to the exterior.

    Note: Section 1017, "Exits," is cited as governing this exit.

  - Building must have one of the following on each side:
    Public way ≥ 60' wide.
    Yard ≥ 60' wide.
  - Building must be sprinklered.

    Note: 903.3.1.1, "NFPA 13 sprinkler systems," is cited as the source of requirements for the specified sprinklers.

507.9 Motion picture theaters

- Motion picture theaters meeting all the foll owing requirements are not limited in area:
  - Building must be Type I or II.
  - Building must be 1 story.
  - Building must have one of the following on each side:
    Public way ≥ 60' wide.
    Yard ≥ 60' wide.
  - Building must be sprinklered.

    Note: 903.3.1.1, "NFPA 13 sprinkler systems," is cited as the source of requirements for the specified sprinklers.

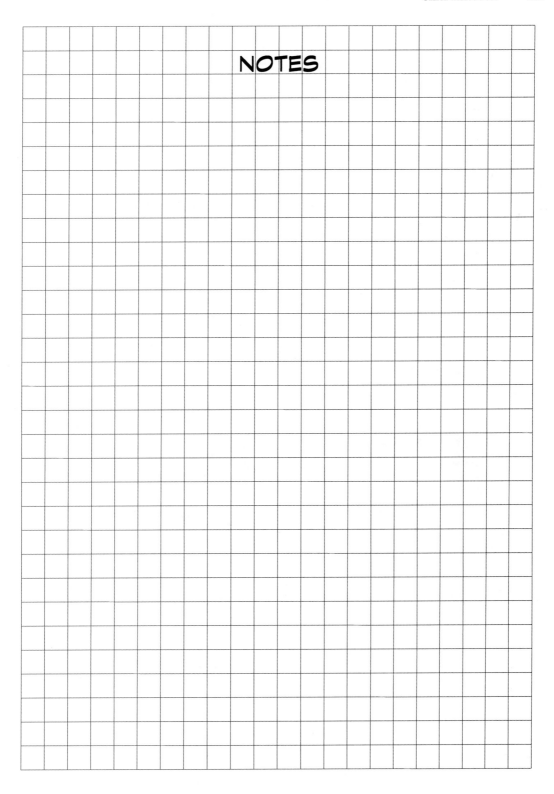

NOTES

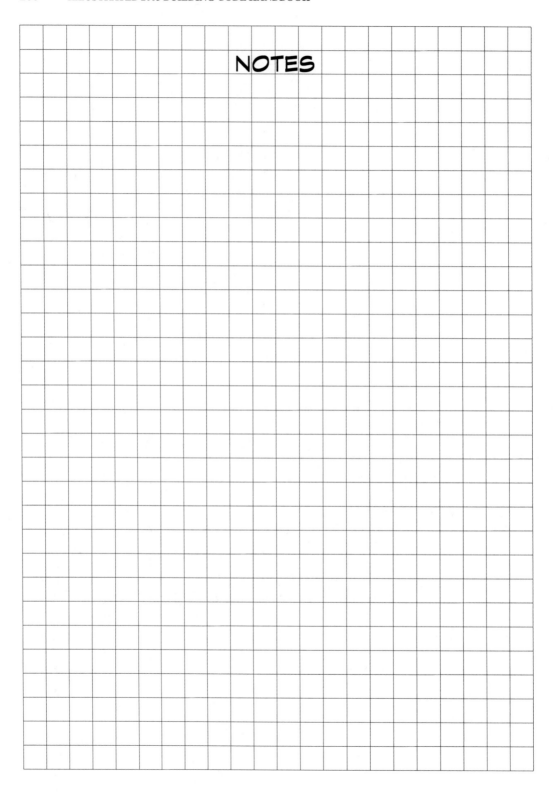

NOTES

6

Types of Construction

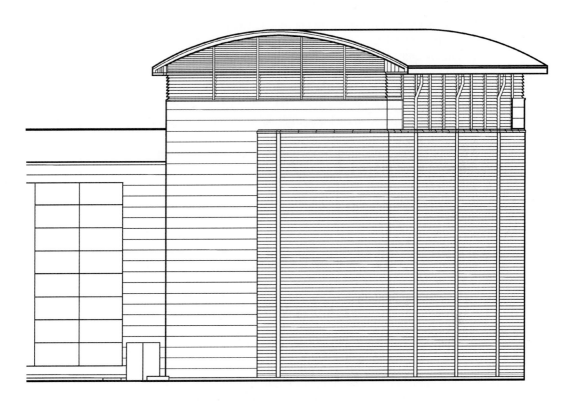

Montachusett Regional Vocational-Technical High School.
Fitchburg, Massachusetts. *(partial elevation)*
HKT Architects, Inc. Somerville, Massachusetts.

602 Construction Classification

602.1 General *(part 1 of 10)*

- The following buildings and structures are governed by this section:
  - New construction.
  - Alterations.
  - Additions to height.
  - Additions to area.
- The following apply to buildings and structures governed by this section:
  - They must be classified in 1 of the 5 construction types described in this section.
  - Where all elements of the roof construction are ≥ 20' above the floor directly below, the guidelines listed below apply to the following occupancies and construction types:

    Occupancies:

    A, B, E, F-2, I, R, S-2, and U.

    Construction types:

    I, II, III A, IV, VA.

    Guidelines:

    The following roof members do not require fire protection:

    Structural members.

    Framing and decking.

    The following roof members may be fire-retardant-treated wood:

    Structural members.

    Framing and decking.
  - Heavy timber is permitted in roof construction where the fire-resistance rating required is ≤ 1 hr.
  - Fire-retardant-treated wood may be used in the following components where all the conditions indicated below apply:

    Components:

    Roof girders.

    Roof trusses.

    Roof construction.

    Conditions:

    The building must be one of the following:

    ≤ 2 stories.

    Construction Type II.

    Construction Type I with both of the following characteristics:

    ≤ 2 stories.

    Roof is ≥ 20' above the top floor.

  Note: The following are cited as applying to this section:

  IBC Table 601, "Fire-Resistance Rating Requirements for Building Elements," the contents of which are summarized above and on the following pages.

  IBC Table 602, "Fire-Resistance Rating Requirements for Exterior Walls Based on Fire Separation Distance," the contents of which are summarized above and on the following pages.

602 Construction Classification

602.1 General *(part 2 of 10)*

> *Note: The following sections supplement requirements for the 5 construction types:*
>   *602.2, "Types I and II."*
>   *602.3, "Type III."*
>   *602.4, "Type IV."*
>   *602.5, "Type V."*

● Type IA buildings and structures must have the fire-resistance ratings listed below:

Table 602.1a   Fire-Resistance Ratings for Type IA Buildings and Structures

Construction Type IA components	Fire-resistance rating
Structural frame supporting a floor:	
Columns	≥ 3 hr
Members connected to columns:	
Girders, trusses, beams, spandrels	≥ 3 hr
Bracing members for gravity loads	≥ 3 hr
Structural frame supporting only a roof:	
Columns	≥ 2 hr
Members connected to columns:	
Girders, trusses, beams, spandrels	≥ 2 hr
Bracing members for gravity loads	≥ 2 hr
Exterior load-bearing walls other than party walls	≥ 3 hr
Interior load-bearing walls:	
Supporting a floor	≥ 3 hr
Supporting only a roof	≥ 2 hr
Exterior nonload-bearing walls other than party walls:	
All occupancies:	
Fire separation ≥ 30'	≥ 0 hr
Occupancy R-3 and U where serving R-3:	
Fire separation distance < 3'	≥ 1 hr
Fire separation distance ≥ 3'	≥ 0 hr
Occupancies A, B, E, F-2, I, R-1, R-2, R-4, S-2, U:	
Fire separation distance < 30'	≥ 1 hr
Occupancies F-1, M, S-1:	
Fire separation distance < 10'	≥ 2 hr
Fire separation distance ≥ 10' < 30'	≥ 1 hr
Occupancy H:	
Fire separation distance < 10'	≥ 3 hr
Fire separation distance ≥ 10' < 30'	≥ 2 hr
Interior nonload-bearing walls and partitions	≥ 0 hr
Floor construction:	
Beams and joists not connected to columns	≥ 2 hr
Other construction	≥ 2 hr
Roof construction:	
Beams and joists not connected to columns	≥ 1½ hr
Other construction	≥ 1½ hr

Source: IBC Tables 601 and 602.

> *Note: 503.2, "Party walls," defines the wall and requires that it be a fire wall.*
>   *Section 705, "Fire Walls," provides fire-resistance ratings and other requirements.*

602 Construction Classification

602.1 General *(part 3 of 10)*

- Type IB buildings and structures must have the fire-resistance ratings listed below:

Table 602.1b   Fire-Resistance Ratings for Type IB Buildings and Structures

Construction Type IB components	Fire-resistance rating
Structural frame supporting a floor:	
Columns	≥ 2 hr
Members connected to columns:	
Girders, trusses, beams, spandrels	≥ 2 hr
Bracing members for gravity loads	≥ 2 hr
Structural frame supporting only a roof:	
Columns	≥ 1 hr
Members connected to columns:	
Girders, trusses, beams, spandrels	≥ 1 hr
Bracing members for gravity loads	≥ 1 hr
Exterior load-bearing walls other than party walls:	
Occupancy H:	
Fire separation distance < 5'	≥ 3 hr
Fire separation distance ≥ 5'	≥ 2 hr
All other occupancies	≥ 2 hr
Interior load-bearing walls:	
Supporting a floor	≥ 2 hr
Supporting only a roof	≥ 1 hr
Exterior nonload-bearing walls other than party walls:	
All occupancies:	
Fire separation ≥ 30'	≥ 0 hr
Occupancy R-3 and U where serving R-3:	
Fire separation distance < 3'	≥ 1 hr
Fire separation distance ≥ 3'	≥ 0 hr
Occupancies A, B, E, F-2, I, R-1, R-2, R-4, S-2, U:	
Fire separation distance < 30'	≥ 1 hr
Occupancies F-1, M, S-1:	
Fire separation distance < 5'	≥ 2 hr
Fire separation distance ≥ 5' < 30'	≥ 1 hr
Occupancy H:	
Fire separation distance < 5'	≥ 3 hr
Fire separation distance ≥ 5' < 30'	≥ 2 hr
Interior nonload-bearing walls and partitions	≥ 0 hr
Floor construction:	
Beams and joists not connected to columns	≥ 2 hr
Other construction	≥ 2 hr
Roof construction:	
Beams and joists not connected to columns	≥ 1 hr
Other construction	≥ 1 hr

Source: IBC Tables 601 and 602.

Note: 503.2, "Party walls," defines the wall and requires that it be a fire wall.
Section 705, "Fire Walls," provides fire-resistance ratings and other requirements.

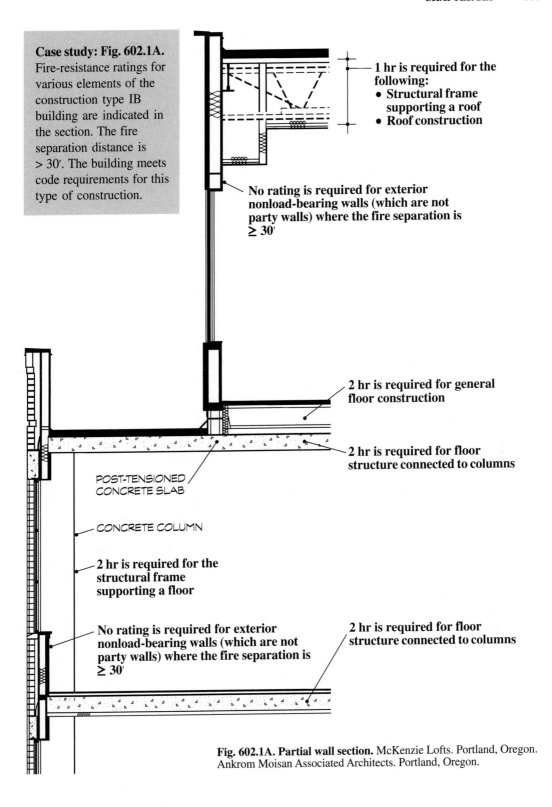

Case study: Fig. 602.1A.
Fire-resistance ratings for various elements of the construction type IB building are indicated in the section. The fire separation distance is > 30'. The building meets code requirements for this type of construction.

1 hr is required for the following:
- **Structural frame supporting a roof**
- **Roof construction**

No rating is required for exterior nonload-bearing walls (which are not party walls) where the fire separation is ≥ 30'

2 hr is required for general floor construction

2 hr is required for floor structure connected to columns

POST-TENSIONED CONCRETE SLAB

CONCRETE COLUMN

2 hr is required for the structural frame supporting a floor

No rating is required for exterior nonload-bearing walls (which are not party walls) where the fire separation is ≥ 30'

2 hr is required for floor structure connected to columns

Fig. 602.1A. Partial wall section. McKenzie Lofts. Portland, Oregon. Ankrom Moisan Associated Architects. Portland, Oregon.

602 Construction Classification

602.1 General *(part 4 of 10)*

- Type IIA buildings and structures must have the fire-resistance ratings listed below:
  - Reduction based on sprinklers is for sprinklers as follows:
    Sprinklers not otherwise required or used to increase area or height.

Table 602.1c   Fire-Resistance Ratings for Type IIA Buildings and Structures

Construction Type IIA components	With sprinklers	Other conditions
Structural frame supporting a floor or roof:		
Columns	≥ 0 hr	≥ 1 hr
Members connected to columns:		
Girders, trusses, beams, spandrels	≥ 0 hr	≥ 1 hr
Bracing members for gravity loads	≥ 0 hr	≥ 1 hr
Exterior load-bearing walls other than party walls:		
Occupancies A, B, E, F-2, I, R, S-2, U	≥ 1 hr	≥ 1 hr
Occupancies F-1, M, S-1:		
Fire separation distance < 5'	≥ 2 hr	≥ 2 hr
Fire separation distance ≥ 5' < 30'	≥ 1 hr	≥ 1 hr
Occupancy H:		
Fire separation distance < 5'	≥ 3 hr	≥ 3 hr
Fire separation distance ≥ 5' < 10'	≥ 2 hr	≥ 2 hr
Fire separation distance ≥ 10' < 30'	≥ 1 hr	≥ 1 hr
Interior load-bearing walls	≥ 0 hr	≥ 1 hr
Exterior nonload-bearing walls other than party walls:		
All occupancies:		
Fire separation distance ≥ 30'	≥ 0 hr	≥ 0 hr
Occupancy R-3 and U where serving R-3:		
Fire separation distance < 3'	≥ 1 hr	≥ 1 hr
Fire separation distance ≥ 3'	≥ 0 hr	≥ 0 hr
Occupancies A, B, E, F-2, I, R-1, R-2, R-4, S-2, U:		
Fire separation distance < 30'	≥ 1 hr	≥ 1 hr
Occupancies F-1, M, S-1:		
Fire separation distance < 5'	≥ 2 hr	≥ 2 hr
Fire separation distance ≥ 5' < 30'	≥ 1 hr	≥ 1 hr
Occupancy H:		
Fire separation distance < 5'	≥ 3 hr	≥ 3 hr
Fire separation distance ≥ 5' < 10'	≥ 2 hr	≥ 2 hr
Fire separation distance ≥ 10' < 30'	≥ 1 hr	≥ 1 hr
Interior nonload-bearing walls and partitions	≥ 0 hr	≥ 0 hr
Floor construction:		
Beams and joists not connected to columns	≥ 0 hr	≥ 1 hr
Other construction	≥ 0 hr	≥ 1 hr
Roof construction:		
Beams and joists not connected to columns	≥ 0 hr	≥ 1 hr
Other construction	≥ 0 hr	≥ 1 hr

Source: IBC Tables 601 and 602.

Note: 503.2, "Party walls," defines the wall and requires that it be a fire wall.
Section 705, "Fire Walls," provides fire-resistance ratings and other requirements.

602 Construction Classification

602.1 General *(part 5 of 10)*

- Type IIB buildings and structures must have the fire-resistance ratings listed below:

Table 602.1d   Fire-Resistance Rating for Type IIB Buildings and Structures

Construction Type IIB components	Fire-resistance rating
Structural frame supporting a floor or roof:	
Columns	≥ 0 hr
Members connected to columns:	
Girders, trusses, beams, spandrels	≥ 0 hr
Bracing members for gravity loads	≥ 0 hr
Exterior walls other than party walls:	
Load-bearing walls and nonload-bearing walls:	
Occupancy R-3 and U where serving R-3:	
Fire separation distance < 3'	≥ 1 hr
Fire separation distance ≥ 3'	≥ 0 hr
Occupancies A, B, E, F-2, I, R-1, R-2, R-4, S-2, U:	
Fire separation distance < 10'	≥ 1 hr
Fire separation distance ≥ 10'	≥ 0 hr
Occupancies F-1, M, S-1:	
Fire separation distance < 5'	≥ 2 hr
Fire separation distance ≥ 5' <10'	≥ 1 hr
Fire separation distance ≥ 10'	≥ 0 hr
Occupancy H:	
Fire separation distance < 5'	≥ 3 hr
Fire separation distance ≥ 5' < 10'	≥ 2 hr
Fire separation distance ≥ 10' < 30'	≥ 1 hr
Fire separation distance ≥ 30'	≥ 0 hr
Interior load-bearing walls	≥ 0 hr
Interior nonload-bearing walls and partitions	≥ 0 hr
Floor construction:	
Beams and joists not connected to columns	≥ 0 hr
Other construction	≥ 0 hr
Roof construction:	
Beams and joists not connected to columns	≥ 0 hr
Other construction	≥ 0 hr

Source: IBC Tables 601 and 602.

> *Note: 503.2, "Party walls," defines the wall and requires that it be a fire wall.*
> *Section 705, "Fire Walls," provides fire-resistance ratings and other requirements.*

602 Construction Classification

602.1 General *(part 6 of 10)*

- Type IIIA buildings and structures must have the fire-resistance ratings listed below:
  - Reduction based on sprinklers is for sprinklers as follows:
    Sprinklers not otherwise required or used to increase area or height.

Table 602.1e   Fire-Resistance Ratings for Type IIIA Buildings and Structures

Construction Type IIIA components	With sprinklers	Other conditions
Structural frame supporting a floor or roof:		
Columns	≥ 0 hr	≥ 1 hr
Members connected to columns:		
Girders, trusses, beams, spandrels	≥ 0 hr	≥ 1 hr
Bracing members for gravity loads	≥ 0 hr	≥ 1 hr
Exterior load-bearing walls other than party walls:		
Occupancy H:		
Fire separation distance < 5'	≥ 3 hr	≥ 3 hr
Fire separation distance ≥ 5'	≥ 2 hr	≥ 2 hr
All other occupancies	≥ 2 hr	≥ 2 hr
Interior load-bearing walls	≥ 0 hr	≥ 1 hr
Exterior nonload-bearing walls other than party walls:		
All occupancies:		
Fire separation distance ≥ 30'	≥ 0 hr	≥ 0 hr
Occupancy R-3 and U where serving R-3:		
Fire separation distance < 3'	≥ 1 hr	≥ 1 hr
Fire separation distance ≥ 3'	≥ 0 hr	≥ 0 hr
Occupancies A, B, E, F-2, I, R-1, R-2, R-4, S-2, U:		
Fire separation distance < 30'	≥ 1 hr	≥ 1 hr
Occupancies F-1, M, S-1:		
Fire separation distance < 5'	≥ 2 hr	≥ 2 hr
Fire separation distance ≥ 5' < 30'	≥ 1 hr	≥ 1 hr
Occupancy H:		
Fire separation distance < 5'	≥ 3 hr	≥ 3 hr
Fire separation distance ≥ 5' < 10'	≥ 2 hr	≥ 2 hr
Fire separation distance ≥ 10' < 30'	≥ 1 hr	≥ 1 hr
Interior nonload-bearing walls and partitions	≥ 0 hr	≥ 0 hr
Floor construction:		
Beams and joists not connected to columns	≥ 0 hr	≥ 1 hr
Other construction	≥ 0 hr	≥ 1 hr
Roof construction:		
Beams and joists not connected to columns	≥ 0 hr	≥ 1 hr
Other construction	≥ 0 hr	≥ 1 hr

Source: IBC Tables 601 and 602.

Note: 503.2, "Party walls," defines the wall and requires that it be a fire wall.
  Section 705, "Fire Walls," provides fire-resistance ratings and other requirements.

Case study: Fig. 602.1B. The sprinklered construction Type IIIA occupancy S-1 warehouse meets the fire-resistance-rating requirements of IBC Table 601 as indicated in the illustration.

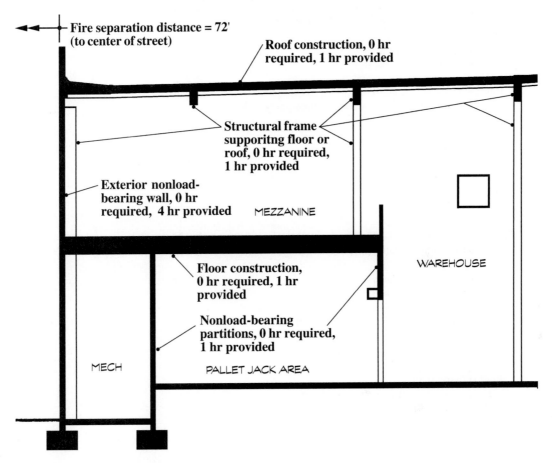

Fire separation distance = 72'
(to center of street)

Roof construction, 0 hr required, 1 hr provided

Structural frame supporitng floor or roof, 0 hr required, 1 hr provided

Exterior nonload-bearing wall, 0 hr required, 4 hr provided

MEZZANINE

Floor construction, 0 hr required, 1 hr provided

WAREHOUSE

Nonload-bearing partitions, 0 hr required, 1 hr provided

MECH

PALLET JACK AREA

Fig. 602.1B. Partial section. New Warehouse Addition. Los Angeles, California. Stephen Wen + Associates, Architects, Inc. Pasadena, California.

602 Construction Classification

602.1 General *(part 7 of 10)*

- Type IIIB buildings and structures must have the fire-resistance ratings listed below:

Table 602.1f   Fire-Resistance Rating for Type IIIB Buildings and Structures

Construction Type IIIB components	Fire-resistance rating
Structural frame supporting a floor or roof:	
Columns	≥ 0 hr
Members connected to columns:	
Girders, trusses, beams, spandrels	≥ 0 hr
Bracing members for gravity loads	≥ 0 hr
Exterior load-bearing walls other than party walls:	
Occupancy H:	
Fire separation distance < 5'	≥ 3 hr
Fire separation distance ≥ 5'	≥ 2 hr
All other occupancies	≥ 2 hr
Interior load-bearing walls	≥ 0 hr
Exterior nonload-bearing walls other than party walls:	
All occupancies:	
Fire separation distance ≥ 30'	≥ 0 hr
Occupancy R-3 and U where serving R-3:	
Fire separation distance < 3'	≥ 1 hr
Fire separation distance ≥ 3'	≥ 0 hr
Occupancies A, B, E, F-2, I, R-1, R-2, R-4, S-2, U:	
Fire separation distance < 30'	≥ 1 hr
Occupancies F-1, M, S-1:	
Fire separation distance < 5'	≥ 2 hr
Fire separation distance ≥ 5' < 30'	≥ 1 hr
Occupancy H:	
Fire separation distance < 5'	≥ 3 hr
Fire separation distance ≥ 5' < 10'	≥ 2 hr
Fire separation distance ≥ 10' < 30'	≥ 1 hr
Interior nonload-bearing walls and partitions	≥ 0 hr
Floor construction:	
Beams and joists not connected to columns	≥ 0 hr
Other construction	≥ 0 hr
Roof construction:	
Beams and joists not connected to columns	≥ 0 hr
Other construction	≥ 0 hr

Source: IBC Tables 601 and 602.

> *Note: 503.2, "Party walls," defines the wall and requires that it be a fire wall.*
> *Section 705, "Fire Walls," provides fire-resistance ratings and other requirements.*

602 Construction Classification

602.1 General *(part 8 of 10)*

- Type IV buildings and structures must have the fire-resistance ratings or meet Heavy Timber requirements as listed below:

Table 602.1g   Fire-Resistance Rating or Heavy Timber Requirements for Type IV Buildings and Structures

Construction Type IV components	Fire-resistance rating or heavy timber requirements
Structural frame supporting a floor or roof:	
Columns	Heavy timber
Members connected to columns:	
Girders, trusses, beams, spandrels	Heavy timber
Bracing for gravity loads	Heavy timber
Exterior load-bearing walls other than party walls:	
Occupancy H:	
Fire separation distance < 5'	≥ 3 hr
Fire separation distance ≥ 5'	≥ 2 hr
All other occupancies	≥ 2 hr
Interior load-bearing walls	≥ 1 hr or Heavy timber
Exterior nonload-bearing walls other than party walls:	
All occupancies:	
Fire separation distance ≥ 30'	≥ 0 hr
Occupancy R-3 and U where serving R-3:	
Fire separation distance < 3'	≥ 1 hr
Fire separation distance ≥ 3'	≥ 0 hr
Occupancies A, B, E, F-2, I, R-1, R-2, R-4, S-2, U:	
Fire separation distance < 30'	≥ 1 hr
Occupancies F-1, M, S-1:	
Fire separation distance < 5'	≥ 2 hr
Fire separation distance ≥ 5' < 30'	≥ 1 hr
Occupancy H:	
Fire separation distance < 5'	≥ 3 hr
Fire separation distance ≥ 5' < 10'	≥ 2 hr
Fire separation distance ≥ 10' < 30'	≥ 1 hr
Interior nonload-bearing walls and partitions	≥ 1 hr or code alternatives
Floor construction:	
Beams and joists not connected to columns	Heavy timber
Other construction	Heavy timber
Roof construction:	
Beams and joists not connected to columns	Heavy timber
Other construction	Heavy timber

Source: IBC Tables 601 and 602.

Note: 503.2, "Party walls," defines the wall and requires that it be a fire wall.
Section 705, "Fire Walls," provides fire-resistance ratings and other requirements.
602.4.6, "Partitions," is cited as a source of requirements for nonload-bearing walls and partitions. Alternatives to 1-hr construction are ≥ 1" thick matched boards and laminated construction ≥ 4" thick.

602 Construction Classification

602.1 General *(part 9 of 10)*

- Type VA buildings and structures must have the fire-resistance ratings listed below:
  - Reduction based on sprinklers is for sprinklers as follows:
    Sprinklers not otherwise required or used to increase area or height.

Table 602.1h   Fire-Resistance Ratings for Type VA Buildings and Structures

Construction Type VA components	With sprinklers	Other conditions
Structural frame supporting a floor or roof:		
Columns	≥ 0 hr	≥ 1 hr
Members connected to columns:		
Girders, trusses, beams, spandrels	≥ 0 hr	≥ 1 hr
Bracing members for gravity loads	≥ 0 hr	≥ 1 hr
Exterior load-bearing walls other than party walls:		
Occupancies A, B, E, F-2, I, R, S-2, U	≥ 1 hr	≥ 1 hr
Occupancies F-1, M, S-1:		
Fire separation distance < 5'	≥ 2 hr	≥ 2 hr
Fire separation distance ≥ 5'	≥ 1 hr	≥ 1 hr
Occupancy H:		
Fire separation distance < 5'	≥ 3 hr	≥ 3 hr
Fire separation distance ≥ 5' < 10'	≥ 2 hr	≥ 2 hr
Fire separation distance ≥ 10'	≥ 1 hr	≥ 1 hr
Interior load-bearing walls	≥ 0 hr	≥ 1 hr
Exterior nonload-bearing walls other than party walls:		
All occupancies:		
Fire separation distance ≥ 30'	≥ 0 hr	≥ 0 hr
Occupancy R-3 and U where serving R-3:		
Fire separation distance < 3'	≥ 1 hr	≥ 1 hr
Fire separation distance ≥ 3'	≥ 0 hr	≥ 0 hr
Occupancies A, B, E, F-2, I, R-1, R-2, R-4, S-2, U:		
Fire separation distance < 30'	≥ 1 hr	≥ 1 hr
Occupancies F-1, M, S-1:		
Fire separation distance < 5'	≥ 2 hr	≥ 2 hr
Fire separation distance ≥ 5' < 30'	≥ 1 hr	≥ 1 hr
Occupancy H:		
Fire separation distance < 5'	≥ 3 hr	≥ 3 hr
Fire separation distance ≥ 5' < 10'	≥ 2 hr	≥ 2 hr
Fire separation distance ≥ 10' < 30'	≥ 1 hr	≥ 1 hr
Interior nonload-bearing walls and partitions	≥ 0 hr	≥ 0 hr
Floor construction:		
Beams and joists not connected to columns	≥ 0 hr	≥ 1 hr
Other construction	≥ 0 hr	≥ 1 hr
Roof construction:		
Beams and joists not connected to columns	≥ 0 hr	≥ 1 hr
Other construction	≥ 0 hr	≥ 1 hr

Source: IBC Tables 601 and 602.

> *Note: 503.2, "Party walls," defines the wall and requires that it be a fire wall.*
> *Section 705, "Fire Walls," provides fire-resistance ratings and other requirements.*

602 Construction Classification

602.1 General *(part 10 of 10)*

- Type VB buildings and structures must have the fire-resistance ratings listed below:

Table 602.1i   Fire-Resistance Rating for Type VB Buildings and Structures

Construction Type VB components	Fire-resistance rating
Structural frame supporting a floor or roof:	
Columns	≥ 0 hr
Members connected to columns:	
Girders, trusses, beams, spandrels	≥ 0 hr
Bracing members for gravity loads	≥ 0 hr
Exterior walls other than party walls:	
Load-bearing walls and nonload-bearing walls:	
Occupancy R-3 and U where serving R-3:	
Fire separation distance < 3'	≥ 1 hr
Fire separation distance $\geq$ 3'	≥ 0 hr
Occupancies A, B, E, F-2, I, R-1, R-2, R-4, S-2, U:	
Fire separation distance < 10'	≥ 1 hr
Fire separation distance $\geq$ 10'	≥ 0 hr
Occupancies F-1, M, S-1:	
Fire separation distance < 5'	≥ 2 hr
Fire separation distance $\geq$ 5' < 10'	≥ 1 hr
Fire separation distance $\geq$ 10'	≥ 0 hr
Occupancy H:	
Fire separation distance < 5'	≥ 3 hr
Fire separation distance $\geq$ 5' < 10'	≥ 2 hr
Fire separation distance $\geq$ 10' < 30'	≥ 1 hr
Fire separation distance $\geq$ 30'	≥ 0 hr
Interior load-bearing walls	≥ 0 hr
Interior nonload-bearing walls and partitions	≥ 0 hr
Floor construction:	
Beams and joists not connected to columns	≥ 0 hr
Other construction	≥ 0 hr
Roof construction:	
Beams and joists not connected to columns	≥ 0 hr
Other construction	≥ 0 hr

Source: IBC Tables 601 and 602.

Note: 503.2, "Party walls," defines the wall and requires that it be a fire wall.
Section 705, "Fire Walls," provides fire-resistance ratings and other requirements.

602 Construction Classification

602.1.1 Minimum requirements

- The following applies to detailing that complies with a construction type higher than required:
  - Other components of the occupancy need not comply with the higher construction type.

602.2 Types I and II

- Construction Types I and II require noncombustible materials for the following:
  - Structural frame:
    Columns.
    Members connected to columns:
      Girders.
      Trusses.
      Spandrels.
    Bracing members for gravity loads.
  - Load-bearing walls:
    Exterior.
    Interior.
  - Nonload-bearing walls and partitions:
    Exterior.
    Interior.
  - Floor construction including the following:
    Beams not connected to columns.
    Joists not connected to columns.
    Other construction.
  - Roof construction including the following:
    Beams not connected to columns.
    Joists not connected to columns.
    Other construction.

602.3 Type III

- In construction Type III, building elements are of the following materials:
  - Noncombustible materials are required for exterior walls as follows:
    Where exterior wall assemblies have fire-resistance rated at ≤ 2 hrs:
      Fire-retardant-treated wood is allowed therein.
  - The following materials are allowed for interior building elements:
    Any material permitted by the code.

  Note: 2303.2, "Fire-retardant-treated wood," is cited as the source of requirements for this material.

602 Construction Classification

602.4 Type IV

- Construction Type IV consists of heavy timber (HT) construction as follows:
  - Noncombustible materials are required for exterior walls as follows:
    Where exterior wall assemblies have fire-resistance rated at ≤ 2 hrs:
    Fire-retardant-treated wood is allowed therein.
  - Interior building elements are required as follows:
    Solid or laminated wood.
    Contain no concealed spaces.
  - Details are governed by this section.

    Note: 2303.2, "Fire-retardant-treated wood," is cited as the source of requirements for this material.

602.4.1 Columns

- Construction Type IV wood columns are governed as follows:
  - Columns must be continuous or stacked with approved connections.
  - Columns must sawn as a single piece or be glue-laminated.
  - Column dimensions are required as follows:

Loads supported	Width	Depth
Floor loads	≥ 8"	≥ 8"
Roof and ceiling loads only	≥ 6"	≥ 8"

602.4.2 Floor framing

- Construction Type IV wood beams and girders are governed as follows:
  - Members must be sawn as a single piece or be glue-laminated.
  - Minimum nominal member dimensions are as follows:

Component	Width	Depth
Beams and girders	≥ 6"	≥ 10"
Arches springing from floor line and supporting floor loads	≥ 8"	≥ 8"
Members of trusses supporting floor loads	≥ 8"	≥ 8"

602 Construction Classification

602.4.3 Roof framing

- Construction Type IV roof framing members are governed as follows:
  - Parallel members spaced on either side of another member must have all of the following characteristics:
    - Assembled of ≥ 2 members.
    - Each member must have a nominal thickness ≥ 3".
    - Open space between spaced members requires the following:
      - Space must be closed by one of the following means:
        - Continuous blocking between spaced members as follows:
          - Nominal thickness ≥ 2".
        - Continuous wood cover plate as follows:
          - Nominal thickness ≥ 2".
          - Applied to underside of members.
  - Splice plates must have a nominal thickness ≥ 3".
  - Other roof framing members are governed as follows:
    - Required widths may be reduced with sprinklers as follows:
      - Sprinklers must be located under the roof deck.
    - Individual framing members must have the nominal dimensions listed below:

Table 602.4.3   Nominal Dimensions of Individual Roof Framing Members

Components supporting no floor loads	Width with sprinklers	Width with no sprinklers	Depth
Framed or glue-laminated arches:			
Where they spring from floor line or grade:			
In the upper half of height	≥ 6"	≥ 6"	≥ 6"
In the lower half of height	≥ 6"	≥ 6"	≥ 8"
Where they spring from the following:			
Top of walls or wall abutments	≥ 3"	≥ 4"	≥ 6"
Framed timber trusses	≥ 3"	≥ 4"	≥ 6"
Other roof framing	≥ 3"	≥ 4"	≥ 6"

602 Construction Classification

602.4.4 Floors

- This section addresses floors in Type IV construction.
- No concealed spaces in floors are permitted.
- The wood decking system must be one of the following:
  - Structural decking laid flat:
    Nominal thickness in the vertical dimension must be ≥ 3".
    Either sawn or glue-laminated is required.
    One of the following edge details for decking members is required:
      Splined.
      Tongue-and-groove.
    One of the following types of subflooring is required:
      Nominal 1" tongue-and-groove flooring laid ⊥ to or diagonally across decking.
      ½" particle board.
  - Structural decking laid on edge:
    Nominal dimensions required:
      Thickness in the vertical dimension must be ≥ 4".
    Horizontal dimension must be < the vertical dimension.
    Adjacent members must have continuous contact.
    Members must be securely spiked together.
    One of the following types of sub-flooring is required:
      Nominal 1" wood flooring.
      $^{15}/_{32}$" wood structural panel.
      ½" particle board.
- Butt-joints of lumber must be staggered as follows:
  - So joints are not aligned at locations other than on supports.
- A gap ≥ ½" is required between floors and walls as follows:
  - Gaps must be closed by one of the following means:
    Molding attached to the wall as follows:
      Molding must permit movement in the floor due to expansion and contraction.
    Masonry wall corbeling below the floor edge.

602 Construction Classification

602.4.5 Roofs

- This section addresses roofs in Type IV construction.
- Concealed spaces are not permitted in roof systems.
- Wood roof decks must be one of the following types:
  - Decking laid flat as follows:
    - Either sawn or glue-laminated is required.
    - One of the following edge details for plank decking is required:
      - Splined.
      - Tongue-and-groove.
    - Nominal thickness in the vertical dimension must be ≥ 2".
  - Decking laid on edge as follows:
    - Nominal thickness in the vertical dimension must be ≥ 3".
    - Horizontal dimension must be < the vertical dimension.
    - Adjacent members must have continuous contact.
    - Members must be securely spiked together.
  - Wood structural panels with both of the following characteristics:
    - Thickness ≥ 1$^1/_8$".
    - Exterior glue.
  - Other types of decking with both of the following characteristics:
    - ≥ the fire resistance as the other options above.
    - ≥ structural properties as the other options above.

602.4.6 Partitions

- Partitions in Type IV construction must be one of the following:
  - Solid wood with ≥ 2 layers of one of the following:
    - 1" thick matched boards.
    - 4" thick laminated construction.
  - Construction with a fire-resistance rating of 1 hr.

602.4.7 Exterior structural members

- Construction Type IV requires exterior wood columns and arches to have both of the following:
  - A fire separation distance ≥ 20'.
  - Sizes complying with heavy timber size requirements.

602.5 Type V

- Construction Type V permits any material otherwise allowed by the code for the following:
  - Structural elements.
  - Exterior and interior walls.

Case study: **Fig. 602.5.** The building is an example of Type V construction. In this category, materials are neither restricted nor specified so long as they are permitted by the code for building construction. This applies to both exterior and interior walls as well as structural components. Type V construction is not limited to the materials in this example. This represents only one particular combination.

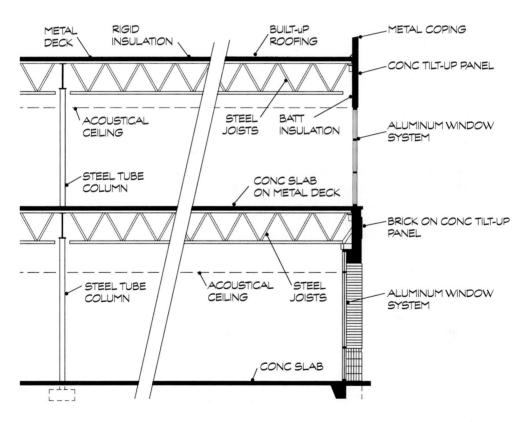

METAL DECK

RIGID INSULATION

BUILT-UP ROOFING

METAL COPING

CONC TILT-UP PANEL

ACOUSTICAL CEILING

STEEL JOISTS

BATT INSULATION

ALUMINUM WINDOW SYSTEM

STEEL TUBE COLUMN

CONC SLAB ON METAL DECK

BRICK ON CONC TILT-UP PANEL

STEEL TUBE COLUMN

ACOUSTICAL CEILING

STEEL JOISTS

ALUMINUM WINDOW SYSTEM

CONC SLAB

Fig. 602.5. Partial building section. AmberGlen Business Center. Hillsboro, Oregon. Ankrom Moisan Associated Architects. Portland, Oregon.

603 Combustible Material in Type I and II Construction

603.1 Allowable materials *(part 1 of 5)*

- This section lists combustible materials permitted in Type I and II construction.

   Note: The following are cited as requiring compliance:
   603.1.1, "Ducts."
   603.1.2, "Piping."
   603.1.3, "Electrical."

- Fire-retardant-treated wood in the following applications:
   - Nonload-bearing construction as follows:
      Partitions with a required fire-resistance rating ≤ 2 hrs.
      Exterior walls with no fire-resistance rating required.
   - In the following components where all the conditions indicated below apply:
      Components:
         Roof girders.
         Roof trusses.
         Roof construction.
      Conditions:
         The building must be one of the following:
            ≤ 2 stories.
            Construction Type II.
            Construction Type I with both of the following characteristics:
               ≤ 2 stories.
               Roof is ≥ 20' above the top floor.
- Insulation with the following conditions:
   - Layered between noncombustible materials as follows:
      No airspace.
      Flame spread index is ≤ 100.
   - Layered between the following components with the conditions indicated below:
      Components:
         Finished floor.
         Solid decking.
      Conditions:
         No air space.
         Flame spread index is ≤ 200.
   - Other insulation as follows:
      Other than foam.
      With a flame spread index ≤ 25.
      Either of the following types:
         Thermal insulation.
         Acoustical insulation.

603 Combustible Material in Type I and II Construction

603.1 Allowable materials *(part 2 of 5)*

- Plastics regulated by the code as follows:
  - Foam plastics.
  - Light-transmitting plastics.

    Note: Chapter 26, "Plastic," is cited as the source of requirements for the plastics.

- Interior finishes as follows:
  - Floor finishes.
  - Other finishes.
- Interior trim and millwork such as the following:
  - Doors and door frames.
  - Window sash and window frames.
- In the following applications located ≤ 15' above grade:
  - Show windows including the following related elements:
    Nailing or furring strips.
    Wood bulkheads below show windows.
    Frames.
    Aprons.
    Show cases.
- Finish flooring applied to one of the following is permitted:
  - Directly to a floor slab.
  - To wood sleepers in gymnasiums with no blocking of sleeper spaces required.
  - To wood sleepers in bowling facilities as follows:
    Spaces between sleepers are fire blocked in the following locations:
      At the juncture of alternate lanes.
      At the ends of each lane.
  - To wood sleepers, the following fire-resistance-rated floors with fire blocking as indicated:
    Floors:
      Masonry.
      Concrete.
    Blocking:
      Spaces between sleepers must be sealed in one of the following ways:
        Spaces filled with an approved material to obstruct the free flow of the following:
          Flames.
          Products of combustion.
        Spaces divided into areas ≤ 100 sf by fire blocking including the following:
          Spaces filled solid under permanent partitions.

    Note: 717.2.7, "Concealed sleeper spaces," is cited as applicable and is partially summarized above.

603 Combustible Materials in Type I and II Construction

603.1 Allowable materials *(part 3 of 5)*

- Roof coverings in one of the following classifications:
  - Class A.
  - Class B.
  - Class C.
- Partitions with the following characteristics may be constructed of the materials listed below:
  - Characteristics:
    Used to subdivide the following of a single tenant:
    Store.
    Offices.
    Similar spaces.
    Partitions may not create a corridor serving ≥ 30 occupants.
  - Materials:
    Any of the following are permitted for partitions ≤ 6' high:
    Fire-retardant-treated wood.
    1-hr fire-resistant-rated construction.
    Wood panels.
    Similar light construction.
- Platforms.

  Note: Section 410, "Stages and Platforms," is cited as the source of requirements for platforms permitted in combustible materials.

- Blocking such as for the following is permitted:
  - Handrails.
  - Millwork.
  - Cabinets.
  - Window frames.
  - Door frames.
- The following materials at exterior walls are permitted:
  - Combustible exterior wall coverings.
  - Appendages such as follows:
    Balconies.
    Bay windows.
    Oriel windows.
    Similar appendages.

  Note: Chapter 14, "Exterior Walls," is cited as the source of requirements for combustible materials permitted at exterior walls.

- Sealing materials between materials of exterior walls as follows:
  - Mastics.
  - Caulking.

603 Combustible Materials in Type I and II Construction

603.1 Allowable materials *(part 4 of 5)*

- Exterior plastic veneer.

  Note: 2605.2, "Exterior use," is cited as the source of requirements for plastic veneer on building exteriors.

- Nailing or furring strips.

  Note: 803.4, "Application," is cited as the source of requirements for furring.

- Heavy timber in the following locations:
  - In roof construction where a fire-resistance rating ≤ 1 hr is required.
  - Columns and arches outside a building as follows:
    Where a fire-separation distance ≥ 20' is provided.
  - In balconies and similar projections outside the building.

  Note: The following are cited as sources of requirements for the heavy timber:
    Footnote C of IBC Table 601, "Fire-Resistance Rating Requirements for Building Elements."
    602.4.7, "Exterior structural members."
    1406.3, "Balconies and similar projections."

- Combustible ingredients or components as follows:
  - Aggregates in gypsum concrete mixtures.
  - Aggregates in portland cement concrete mixtures.
  - Approved materials in assemblies meeting required fire-resistance ratings as follows:
    Admixtures.
    Component materials.

  Note: 703.2.2, "Combustible components," is cited as the source establishing the acceptability of combustible ingredients, a summary of which is provided above.

- Sprayed fire-resistive cementitious and mineral fiber materials.

  Note: 1704.11, "Sprayed fire-resistant materials," is cited as the source of requirements for such materials."

- Materials protecting penetrations in fire-resistance-rated assemblies.

  Note: Section 712, "Penetrations," is cited as the source of requirements for materials sealing penetrations against fire hazard.

- Materials in joints between components of assemblies with fire-resistance ratings.

  Note: Section 713, "Fire-Resistant Joint Systems," is cited as the source of requirements.

603 Combustible Materials in Type I and II Construction

603.1 Allowable materials *(part 5 of 5)*

- Materials as follows:
  - Class A finish materials.
  - Combustible piping.
  - Combustible materials relating to building services.

    Note: 717.5, "Combustibles in concealed spaces in Type I or II construction," is cited as listing materials permitted in concealed spaces, a partial summary of which is provided above.

- Certain materials exposed in plenums.

    Note: International Mechanical Code Section 602, "Plenums," is cited as the source of combustible materials permitted in plenums.

603.1.1 Ducts

- Nonmetallic ducts are permitted.

    Note: The International Mechanical Code is cited as governing nonmetallic ducts.

603.1.2 Piping

- Combustible piping is permitted.

    Note: The following are cited as governing combustible piping:
    The International Mechanical Code.
    The International Plumbing Code.

603.1.3 Electrical

- The following combustible electrical components are permitted:
  - Wiring insulation.
  - Tubing.
  - Raceways.
  - Related components.

    Note: The ICC Electrical Code is cited as governing these materials.

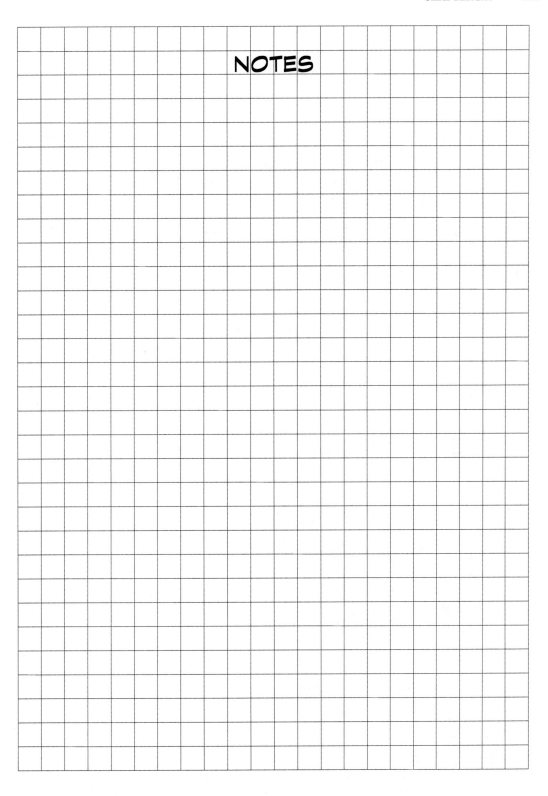

NOTES

NOTES

7

Fire-Resistance-Rated Construction

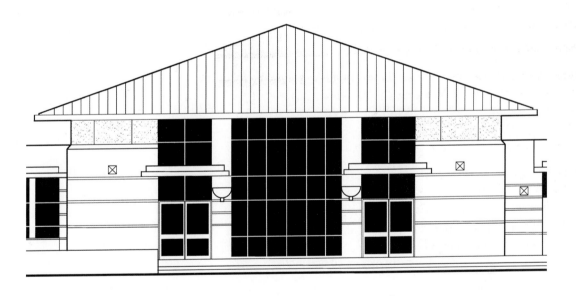

Lee's Summit Police and Court Facility. Lee's Summit, Missouri. *(partial elevation)*
The Hollis and Miller Group, Inc. Lee's Summit, Missouri.

702 Definitions

702.1 Definitions *(part 1 of 8)*

- **Annular space**
  - The gap around a component that is penetrating an assembly.

- **Combination fire/smoke damper**
  - A listed device.
  - Installed in any of the following locations:
    Air ducts.
    Air transfer openings.
  - Closes automatically upon detection of the following:
    Heat.
    Smoke.
  - Inhibits the flow of the following:
    Air.
    Smoke.
  - Capable of being adjusted from a remote command station where required.

- **Draft stop**
  - One of the following:
    A material.
    A device.
    A construction.
  - Installed to limit the movement of air within the following types of concealed spaces:
    Crawl spaces.
    Floor-ceiling assemblies.
    Roof-ceiling assemblies.
    Attics.
    Similar spaces.

- **Fire area**
  - The area surrounded by one or more of the following barriers:
    Fire walls.
    Fire barriers.
    Exterior walls.
    Horizontal fire-resistance-rated assemblies.

- **Fire barrier**
  - A fire-resistance-rated assembly in either of the following orientations:
    Vertical.
    Horizontal.
  - Designed to limit the spread of fire.
  - Any openings in the barrier protected.

702 Definitions

702.1 Definitions *(part 2 of 8)*

> **Case study: Fig. 702.1A.** TJI joists rest on 2"× 4" bearing plates which sit on a concrete slab. An air space results between the slab and each joist through which air can flow in the concealed space. Draft stop materials placed under periodic joists isolate small areas of continuous air space between which no air can move.

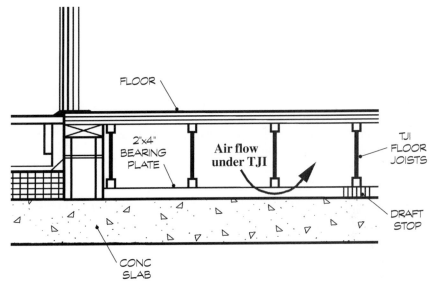

Fig. 702.1A. Detail at raised floor. McKenzie Lofts. Portland, Oregon. Ankrom Moisan Associated Architects. Portland, Oregon.

- **Fire damper**
    - A listed device.
    - Installed in any of the following locations:
        Air ducts.
        Air distribution systems.
        Smoke control systems.
    - Closes automatically upon detection of heat.
    - Limits air flow and passage of flame.
    - Categorized as one of two types:
        A static system closes in case of fire.
        A dynamic system continues to operate during a fire:
            Tested for closure during airflow.
            Rated for closure during airflow.

702 Definitions

702.1 Definitions *(part 3 of 8)*

- **Fire door**
  - The door in a fire door assembly.

- **Fire door assembly**
  - An assembly of the following:
    Fire door.
    Door frame.
    Hardware.
    Accessories.
  - Provides fire protection to an opening at a defined level.

- **Fire partition**
  - A vertical assembly.
  - Limits the spread of fire.
  - Any openings in the partition are protected.

- **Fire-protection rating**
  - Pertains to an assembly protecting an opening.
  - The length of time an assembly can contain a fire as follows:
    Measured in one of the following units:
      Hours.
      Minutes.

    Note: Section 715, "Opening Protectives," is cited as the source of tests used to determine fire-protection rating.

- **Fire resistance**
  - Ability to resist the transmission of the following:
    Excessive heat.
    Hot gases.
    Flames.

- **Fire-resistance rating**
  - The length of time an assembly or component can function in a fire as follows:
    Confine a fire.
    Perform assigned structural task.

    Note: Section 703, "Fire-Resistance Ratings and Fire Tests," is cited as the source of methods for determining fire-resistance ratings.

Case study: Fig. 702.1B. The selection of walls are among several types used at the hospital. The fire-resistance-rated walls shown are similar to those tested by Underwriters Laboratories, Inc.® and described in their publication, *Fire Resistance Directory*, or those listed in the Gypsum Association's *Fire Resistance Design Manual*, which are tested by several agencies. The numbers under the fire-resistance ratings shown in the wall sections indicate the index number under which descriptions of the walls are provided in the reference publications. Wall assemblies and horizontal assemblies are not considered to have a fire-resistance rating unless they have been tested by a recognized agency. Two walls without fire-resistance ratings are also shown.

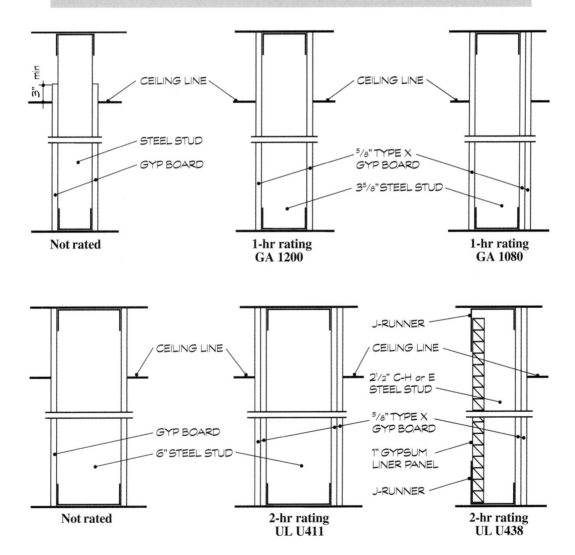

Fig. 702.1B. Selected wall sections. Methodist Community Health Center. Sugar Land, Texas. HKS, Inc., Architects, Engineers, Planners. Dallas, Texas.

702 Definitions

702.1 Definitions *(part 4 of 8)*

- **Fire-resistant joint system**
  - Assembly of elements is as follows:
    Retards the passage of fire through joints as follows:
      In fire-resistance-rated assemblies.
      Between fire-resistance-rated assemblies.
      For a specified length of time.
    System is fire-resistance-rated.

  Note: The following are cited as alternative standards governing these systems:
    ASTM E 1966, "Test Method for Fire-Resistant Joint System."
    UL 2079, "Tests for Fire Resistance of Building Joint Systems."

Case study:Fig. 702.1C. Measurement of fire separation distances in the example are ⊥ to the face of each exterior wall of the building extending to interior lot lines or to the center of the street.

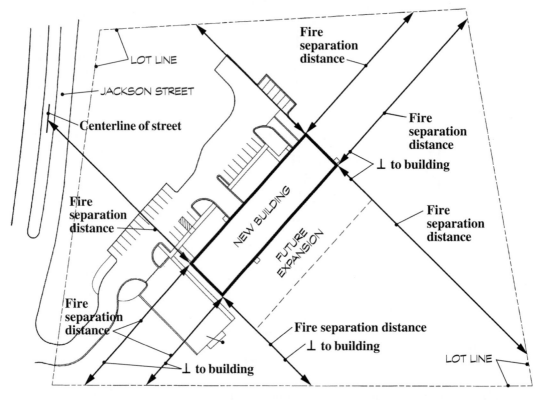

Fig. 702.1C. Site plan. Garments to Go. Bastrop, Texas. Spencer Godfrey Architects. Round Rock, Texas.

702 Definitions

702.1 Definitions *(part 5 of 8)*

- **Fire separation distance**
  - The distance measured from the building face to any of the following:
    Closest interior lot line.
    Centerline of a street.
    Centerline of an alley.
    Centerline of a public way.
    An imaginery line between two buildings in the following case:
      Buildings on the same lot.
  - The distance is measured ⊥ to the building wall.

- **Fire wall**
  - Has a fire-resistance rating.
  - Openings in wall are protected.
  - Wall retards the spread of fire.
  - Wall extends from foundation to or through roof.
  - Wall is detailed so as to remain standing as follows:
    In case of construction collapse on either side.

- **Fire window assembly**
  - A window that resists the passage of fire due to the following:
    Its construction.
    Its glazing.

- **Fireblocking**
  - Building materials installed in concealed spaces to prevent the spread of fire.

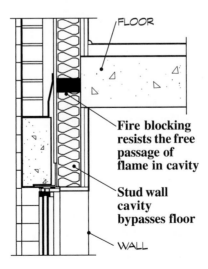

Fig. 702.1D. Detail at floor-wall intersection. McKenzie Lofts. Portland, Oregon. Ankrom Moisan Associated Architects. Portland, Oregon.

702 Definitions

702.1 Definitions *(part 6 of 8)*

- **Floor fire door assembly**
  - An assembly including the following:
    Fire door.
    Frame.
    Hardware.
    Accessories.
  - Installed horizontally.
  - Provides fire protection at a defined level as follows:
    To an opening through a floor with a fire-resistance rating.

  Note: 712.4.6, "Floor fire doors," is cited as governing these doors. Tests and other requirements are included, some of which are summarized above.

- **Joint**
  - A linear gap in fire-resistance-rated construction.
  - Allows independent movement in any plane resulting from any of the following:
    Thermal expansion and contraction.
    Seismic activity.
    Wind.
    Other loading.

- **Membrane penetration**
  - An opening through any of the following surface membranes:
    Wall.
    Floor.
    Ceiling.

- **Membrane-penetration fire-stop**
  - Any of the following:
    A material.
    A device.
    A construction.
  - Prohibits the passage of flame and heat as follows:
    Through membrane openings serving the following:
      Cables.
      Cable trays.
      Conduit.
      Tubing.
      Pipes.
      Similar items.
  - Is effective for a specified length of time.

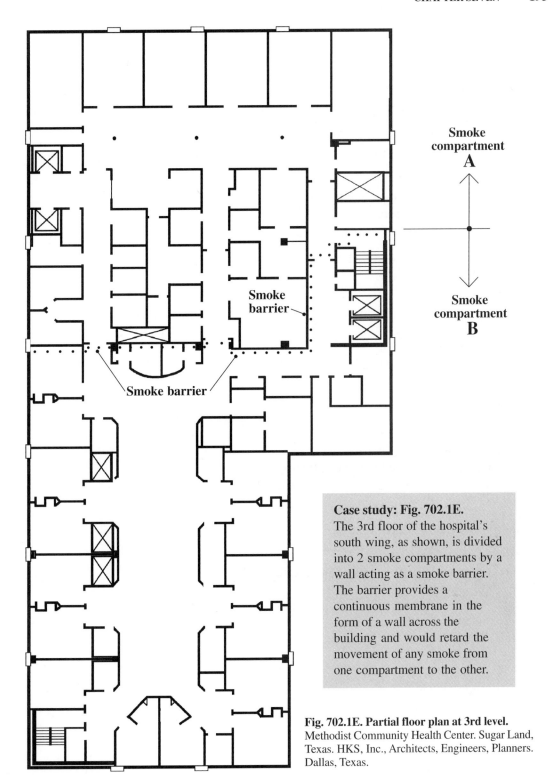

Smoke
compartment
A

Smoke
barrier

Smoke barrier

Smoke
compartment
B

Case study: Fig. 702.1E.
The 3rd floor of the hospital's
south wing, as shown, is divided
into 2 smoke compartments by a
wall acting as a smoke barrier.
The barrier provides a
continuous membrane in the
form of a wall across the
building and would retard the
movement of any smoke from
one compartment to the other.

Fig. 702.1E. Partial floor plan at 3rd level.
Methodist Community Health Center. Sugar Land,
Texas. HKS, Inc., Architects, Engineers, Planners.
Dallas, Texas.

702 Definitions

702.1 Definitions *(part 7 of 8)*

- **Penetration firestop**
  - A material or assembly protecting either of the following openings:
    An opening passing through an entire assembly.
    An opening through a membrane on one side of an assembly.

- **Self-closing**
  - A door equipped with a device as follows:
    Device closes the door after it is opened.
    Device must be approved.

- **Shaft**
  - An enclosed space.
  - Extends through ≥ 1 stories.
  - Connects vertical openings in any of the following:
    Floors.
    Floor and roof.

- **Shaft enclosure**
  - Any of the following elements surrounding a shaft:
    Walls.
    Other construction.

- **Smoke barrier**
  - A continuous membrane.
  - Oriented vertically or horizontally.
  - Examples include the following assemblies:
    Wall.
    Floor.
    Ceiling.
  - Limits the movement of smoke.

- **Smoke compartment**
  - A space surrounded by smoke barriers as follows:
    All sides.
    Above.
    Below.

702 Definitions

702.1 Definitions *(part 8 of 8)*

- **Smoke damper**
  - A listed device.
  - Installed in any of the following locations:
    - Air ducts.
    - Openings for the transfer of air.
  - Limits the passage of the following:
    - Air.
    - Smoke.
  - Operates automatically upon detection of smoke.
  - Can be adjusted from a remote location where required.

- **Splice**
  - Connection of fire-resistant joint systems as follows:
    - To form a continuous system by either of the following methods:
      - Factory process.
      - Field process.

- **T rating**
  - The length of time that a penetration firestop system is able to limit temperature rise as follows:
    - Temperature rise through the penetration is limited by the fire-stop.
    - The rise above initial temperature on the nonfire side is as follows:
      - Rise limited to 325°F.

  Note: ASTM E 814, "Standard Test Method of Fire Tests of Through-Penetration Fire Stops," is cited as governing the method for determining T ratings.

- **Through-penetration**
  - An opening completely through an assembly.

- **Through-penetration firestop system**
  - Either of the following that prevents the spread of fire through penetrations:
    - Materials.
    - Products.
  - The system is fire-resistance-rated.
  - The system is effective for a specified length of time.
  - The system the following ratings:
    - F rating.
    - T rating.

  Note: *ASTM E 814, "Standard Test Method of Fire Tests of Through-Penetration Fire Stops," is cited as governing the method for determining T ratings.*

704 Exterior Walls

704.2 Projections

- This section governs building projections extending beyond the floor area as follows:
  - Cornices and eave overhangs.
  - Exterior balconies and stairways.
  - Similar architectural projections.
- Combustible projections must comply with requirements for combustible materials.

    Note: Section 1406, "Combustible Materials on the Exterior Side of Exterior Walls," is cited as governing the projections listed above.
    1013.5, "Egress balconies," is cited as providing additional requirements.
    Section 1022, "Exterior Exit Ramps and Stairways," is cited as providing additional requirements.

- Projections may not extend closer to the lot line than either of the following points:
  - A point > 12" into the zone in which openings are not permitted.
  - A point ²/₃ the distance from the property line to a point requiring protection for openings.

    Note: 704.8, "Allowable area of openings," is cited as applicable to this subsection.

Case study: Fig. 704.2. A projection from the warehouse faces a street. The fire separation distance is 67'- 6". IBC Table 704.8 indicates that for distances > 30', openings are not regulated by the table; thus, the extent of this projection on the second floor is not limited. Because the building is Type III construction, the projection may be constructed of any approved material. It is constructed of noncombustible materials.

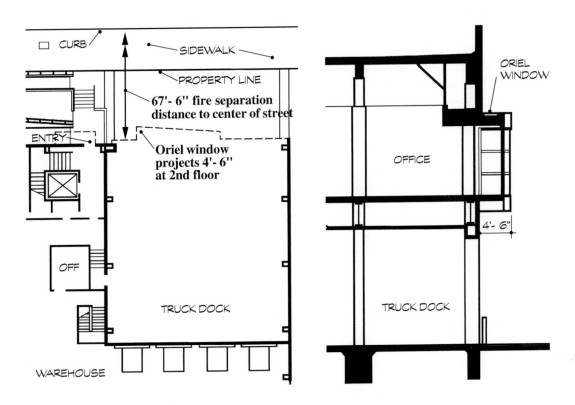

CURB

SIDEWALK

PROPERTY LINE

67'- 6" fire separation distance to center of street

ENTRY

Oriel window projects 4'- 6" at 2nd floor

OFF

TRUCK DOCK

WAREHOUSE

ORIEL WINDOW

OFFICE

4'- 6"

TRUCK DOCK

Fig. 704.2. Partial plan and section at truck dock. New Warehouse Addition. Los Angeles, California. Stephen Wen + Associates, Architects, Inc. Pasadena, California.

704 Exterior Walls

704.2.1 Type I and II construction

- This section addresses projections from walls of Type I and II construction.
- Combustible materials complying with the requirements listed below are permitted for the following types of projections:
  - Projections:
    Balconies.
    Porches
    Decks.
    Exterior stairways that are not required exits.
    Similar projections.
  - Requirements:
    Projections must be ≤ 50% of the building perimeter at each floor.
    Heavy timber is permitted.
    Combustible materials are permitted with the following fire-resistance ratings:
      ≥ 2 hours for projections from walls of Type I construction.
      ≥ 1 hour for projections from walls of Type II A construction.
      ≥ 0 hours for projections from walls of Type II B construction.
    Fire-retardant-treated wood is permitted on buildings ≤ 3 stories high.
    Untreated wood is permitted for the following elements where they are ≤ 42" in height:
      Pickets.
      Rails.
      Similar guardrail devices.

  Note: 1406.3, "Balconies and similar projections," is cited as governing projections of combustible materials, a partial summary of which is provided above.

- The following windows are governed as indicated below:
  - Windows:
    Bay windows.
    Oriel windows.
  - Requirements:
    For buildings ≤ 3 stories:
      Fire-retardant-treated wood is permitted.
    For other buildings:
      Window construction must match the building construction type.

  Note: 1406.4, "Bay windows and oriel windows," is cited as the source of requirements for such projections, a partial summary of which is provided above.

- Otherwise, noncombustible materials are required for projections.

704 Exterior Walls

704.2.2 Type III, IV or V construction

- Any approved material is permitted for projections as follows:
  - From walls of Types III, IV, and V construction.

704.2.3 Combustible projections

- This section applies to combustible projections in the following locations:
  - Where openings are not allowed.
  - Where openings are required to be protected.
- Combustible projections in occupancy R-3 may be Type V construction.
- In other cases, combustible projections must comply with one of the following:
  - Have ≥ 1-hour fire-resistance rating.
  - Be heavy timber construction.
  - Requirements listed below for the following types of projections:
    Projections:
    Balconies.
    Porches.
    Decks.
    Exterior stairways that are not required exits.
    Similar projections.
    Requirements:
    Projections must be ≤ 50% of the building perimeter at each floor.
    Combustible materials must have the following fire-resistance ratings:
    ≥ 2 hrs for projections from walls of Type I construction.
    ≥ 1 hr for projections from walls of the following construction types:
    II A, III A, IV, V A.
    ≥ 0 hr for sprinklered projections from walls of the following construction types:
    III A, IV, V A.
    ≥ 0 hr for projections from walls of the following construction types:
    II B, III B, V B.
    Fire-retardant-treated wood is permitted on buildings ≤ 3 stories high.
    Untreated wood is permitted for the following elements where they are ≤ 42" in height:
    Pickets.
    Rails.
    Similar guardrail devices.

Note: 1406.3, "Balconies and similar projections," is cited as the third option for combustible materials, a partial summary of which is provided above.

704 Exterior Walls

704.3 Buildings on the same lot and buildings containing courts

- Where opening protection is otherwise required in court walls:
  - Such protection is not required where all the following conditions apply:
    - ≤ 2 levels open onto the court.
    - The sum of the following areas is ≤ the allowable area for the building:
      - Building area.
      - Court area.
    - Building is not occupancy I.
- In other courts > 1 story, the following applies:
  - A line is assumed to be located between facing walls as follows:
    - To determine the wall protection required.
    - To determine the opening protection required.
    - To determine the requirements for roof covering.
- ≥ 2 buildings may be regulated as 1 building where they meet the following conditions:
  - They are located on the same lot.
  - The sum of their areas is ≤ the area limit for 1 building as follows:
    - Where the following differs among buildings, the smallest area limit governs:
      - Occupancy classification.
      - Construction type.
- In other cases where buildings are on the same lot, the following applies:
  - A line is assumed to be located between buildings > 1 story as follows:
    - So that requirements for the following can be determined:
      - Wall protection.
      - Opening protection.
      - Roof covering.
    - Where a new building is adjacent to an existing building:
      - The assumed line is located as follows:
        - Adjacent wall and openings of the existing building must comply with the following:
          - Fire resistance based on construction type.
          - Fire resistance based on fire separation distance.
          - Opening size limitations based on the following:
            - Protection.
            - Fire separation distance.

  Note: The following are cited as sources of requirements for the adjacent walls and openings of existing buildings indicated above:
  704.5, "Fire-resistance ratings."
  704.8, "Allowable area of openings."

704.4 Materials

- Exterior walls are required to be of materials as follows:
  - Materials within the designated construction type.

704 Exterior Walls

704.5 Fire-resistance ratings *(part 1 of 5)*

- Exterior walls are rated with regard to fire separation distance as follows:
  - Where fire separation distance >5':
    Walls are rated for fire exposure on the inside.
  - Where fire separation distance ≤ 5':
    Walls are rated for fire exposure on both sides.
- Type I construction exterior walls must have the fire-resistance ratings listed below:

Table 704.5a	Fire-Resistance Ratings for Type I Construction Exterior Walls
Exterior walls	Fire-resistance rating
Type IA load-bearing walls	≥ 3 hr
Type IA nonload-bearing walls:	
All occupancies:	
Fire separation distance ≥ 30'	≥ 0 hr
Occupancies R-3 and U where serving R-3:	
Fire separation distance < 3'	≥ 1 hr
Fire separation distance ≥ 3'	≥ 0 hr
Occupancies A, B, E, F-2, I, R-1, R-2, R-4, S-2, U:	
Fire separation distance < 30'	≥ 1 hr
Occupancies F-1, M, S-1:	
Fire separation distance < 10'	≥ 2 hr
Fire separation distance ≥ 10' < 30'	≥ 1 hr
Occupancy H:	
Fire separation distance < 10'	≥ 3 hr
Fire separation distance ≥ 10' < 30'	≥ 2 hr
Type IB load-bearing walls:	
Occupancy H:	
Fire separation distance < 5'	≥ 3 hr
Fire separation distance ≥ 5'	≥ 2 hr
All other occupancies	≥ 2 hr
Type IB nonload-bearing walls:	
All occupancies:	
Fire separation distance ≥ 30'	≥ 0 hr
Occupancies R-3 and U where serving R-3:	
Fire separation distance < 3'	≥ 1 hr
Fire separation distance ≥ 3'	≥ 0 hr
Occupancies A, B, E, F-2, I, R-1, R-2, R-4, S-2, U:	
Fire separation distance < 30'	≥ 1 hr
Occupancies F-1, M, S-1:	
Fire separation distance < 5	≥ 2 hr
Fire separation ratings ≥ 5 < 30'	≥ 1 hr
Occupancy H:	
Fire separation distance < 5'	≥ 3 hr
Fire separation distance ≥ 5' < 30'	≥ 2 hr

Source: IBC Tables 601 and 602.

704 Exterior Walls

704.5 Fire-resistance ratings *(part 2 of 5)*

- Type II construction exterior walls must have the fire-resistance ratings listed below:

Table 704.5b   Fire-Resistance Ratings for Type II Construction Exterior Walls

Exterior walls	Fire-resistance rating
Type IIA load-bearing walls:	
Occupancies A, B, E, F-2, I, R, S-2, U	≥ 1 hr
Occupancies F-1, M, S-1:	
Fire separation distance < 5'	≥ 2 hr
Fire separation distance ≥ 5'	≥ 1 hr
Occupancy H:	
Fire separation distance < 5'	≥ 3 hr
Fire separation distance ≥ 5' < 10'	≥ 2 hr
Fire separation distance ≥ 10'	≥ 1 hr
Type IIA nonload-bearing walls:	
All occupancies:	
Fire separation distance ≥ 30'	≥ 0 hr
Occupancies R-3 and U where serving R-3:	
Fire separation distance < 3'	≥ 1 hr
Fire separation distance ≥ 3'	≥ 0 hr
Occupancies A, B, E, F-2, I, R-1, R-2, R-4, S-2, U:	
Fire separation distance < 30'	≥ 1 hr
Fire separation distance ≥ 30'	≥ 0 hr
Occupancies F-1, M, S-1:	
Fire separation distance < 5'	≥ 2 hr
Fire separation distance ≥ 5' < 30'	≥ 1 hr
Occupancy H:	
Fire separation distance < 5'	≥ 3 hr
Fire separation distance ≥ 5' < 10'	≥ 2 hr
Fire separation distance ≥ 10' < 30'	≥ 1 hr
Type IIB load-bearing walls and nonload-bearing walls:	
Occupancies R-3 and U where serving R-3:	
Fire separation distance < 3'	≥ 1 hr
Fire separation distance ≥ 3'	≥ 0 hr
Occupancies A, B, E, F-2, I, R-1, R-2, R-4, S-2, U:	
Fire separation distance < 10'	≥ 1 hr
Fire separation distance ≥ 10'	≥ 0 hr
Occupancies F-1, M, S-1:	
Fire separation distance < 5'	≥ 2 hr
Fire separation distance ≥ 5' <10'	≥ 1 hr
Fire separation distance ≥ 10'	≥ 0 hr
Occupancy H:	
Fire separation distance < 5'	≥ 3 hr
Fire separation distance ≥ 5' < 10'	≥ 2 hr
Fire separation distance ≥ 10' < 30'	≥ 1 hr
Fire separation distance ≥ 30'	≥ 0 hr

Source: IBC Tables 601 and 602.

704 Exterior Walls

704.5 Fire-resistance ratings *(part 3 of 5)*

- Type III construction exterior walls must have the fire-resistance ratings listed below:

Table 704.5c   Fire-Resistance Ratings for Type III Construction Exterior Walls

Exterior walls	Fire-resistance rating
Type IIIA load-bearing walls:	
Occupancy H:	
Fire separation distance < 5'	≥ 3 hr
Fire separation distance ≥ 5'	≥ 2 hr
All other occupancies	≥ 2 hr
Type IIIA nonload-bearing walls:	
All occupancies:	
Fire separation distance ≥ 30'	≥ 0 hr
Occupancies R-3 and U where serving R-3:	
Fire separation distance < 3'	≥ 1 hr
Fire separation distance ≥ 3'	≥ 0 hr
Occupancies A, B, E, F-2, I, R-1, R-2, R-4, S-2, U:	
Fire separation distance < 30'	≥ 1 hr
Occupancies F-1, M, S-1:	
Fire separation distance < 5'	≥ 2 hr
Fire separation distance ≥ 5' < 30'	≥ 1 hr
Occupancy H:	
Fire separation distance < 5'	≥ 3 hr
Fire separation distance ≥ 5' < 10'	≥ 2 hr
Fire separation distance ≥ 10' < 30'	≥ 1 hr
Type IIIB load-bearing walls:	
Occupancy H:	
Fire separation distance < 5'	≥ 3 hr
Fire separation distance ≥ 5'	≥ 2 hr
All other occupancies	≥ 2 hr
Type IIIB nonload-bearing walls:	
All occupancies:	
Fire separation distance ≥ 30'	≥ 0 hr
Occupancies R-3 and U where serving R-3:	
Fire separation distance < 3'	≥ 1 hr
Fire separation distance ≥ 3'	≥ 0 hr
Occupancies A, B, E, F-2, I, R-1, R-2, R-4, S-2, U:	
Fire separation distance < 30'	≥ 1 hr
Occupancies F-1, M, S-1:	
Fire separation distance < 5'	≥ 2 hr
Fire separation distance ≥ 5' <30'	≥ 1 hr
Occupancy H:	
Fire separation distance < 5'	≥ 3 hr
Fire separation distance ≥ 5' < 10'	≥ 2 hr
Fire separation distance ≥ 10' < 30'	≥ 1 hr

Source: IBC Tables 601 and 602.

704 Exterior Walls

704.5 Fire-resistance ratings *(part 4 of 5)*

- Type IV construction exterior walls must have the fire-resistance ratings listed below:

Table 704.5d   Fire-Resistance Ratings for Type IV Construction Exterior Walls

Exterior walls	Fire-resistance rating
Type IV load-bearing walls:	
Occupancy H:	
Fire separation distance < 5'	≥ 3 hr
Fire separation distance ≥ 5'	≥ 2 hr
All other occupancies:	≥ 2 hr
Type IV nonload-bearing walls:	
All occupancies:	
Fire separation distance ≥ 30'	≥ 0 hr
Occupancies R-3 and U where serving R-3:	
Fire separation distance < 3'	≥ 1 hr
Fire separation distance ≥ 3'	≥ 0 hr
Occupancies A, B, E, F-2, I, R-1, R-2, R-4, S-2, U:	
Fire separation distance < 30'	≥ 1 hr
Occupancies F-1, M, S-1:	
Fire separation distance < 5'	≥ 2 hr
Fire separation distance ≥ 5' < 30'	≥ 1 hr
Occupancy H:	
Fire separation distance < 5'	≥ 3 hr
Fire separation distance ≥ 5' < 10'	≥ 2 hr
Fire separation distance ≥ 10' < 30'	≥ 1 hr

Source: IBC Tables 601 and 602.

704 Exterior Walls

704.5 Fire-resistance ratings *(part 5 of 5)*

- Type V construction exterior walls must have the fire-resistance ratings listed below:

Table 704.5e   Fire-Resistance Ratings for Type V Construction Exterior Walls

Exterior walls	Fire-resistance rating
Type VA load-bearing walls:	
Occupancies A, B, E, F-2, I, R, S-2, U	≥ 1 hr
Occupancies F-1, M, S-1:	
Fire separation distance < 5'	≥ 2 hr
Fire separation distance ≥ 5'	≥ 1 hr
Occupancy H:	
Fire separation distance < 5'	≥ 3 hr
Fire separation distance ≥ 5' < 10'	≥ 2 hr
Fire separation distance ≥ 10'	≥ 1 hr
Type VA nonload-bearing walls:	
All occupancies:	
Fire separation distance ≥ 30'	≥ 0 hr
Occupancies R-3 and U where serving R-3:	
Fire separation distance < 3'	≥ 1 hr
Fire separation distance ≥ 3'	≥ 0 hr
Occupancies A, B, E, F-2, I, R-1, R-2, R-4, S-2, U:	
Fire separation distance < 30'	≥ 1 hr
Occupancies F-1, M, S-1:	
Fire separation distance < 5'	≥ 2 hr
Fire separation distance ≥ 5' < 30'	≥ 1 hr
Occupancy H:	
Fire separation distance < 5'	≥ 3 hr
Fire separation distance ≥ 5' < 10'	≥ 2 hr
Fire separation distance ≥ 10' < 30'	≥ 1 hr
Type VB load-bearing walls and nonload-bearing walls:	
Occupancies R-3 and U where serving R-3:	
Fire separation distance < 3'	≥ 1 hr
Fire separation distance ≥ 3'	≥ 0 hr
Occupancies A, B, E, F-2, I, R-1, R-2, R-4, S-2, U:	
Fire separation distance < 10'	≥ 1 hr
Fire separation distance ≥ 10'	≥ 0 hr
Occupancies F-1, M, S-1:	
Fire separation distance < 5'	≥ 2 hr
Fire separation distance ≥ 5' < 10'	≥ 1 hr
Fire separation distance ≥ 10'	≥ 0 hr
Occupancy H:	
Fire separation distance < 5'	≥ 3 hr
Fire separation distance ≥ 5' < 10'	≥ 2 hr
Fire separation distance ≥ 10' < 30'	≥ 1 hr
Fire separation distance ≥ 30'	≥ 0 hr

Source: IBC Tables 601 and 602.

704 Exterior Walls

704.6 Structural stability

- Exterior walls must be detailed to remain standing during a fire as follows:
  - For a length of time equal to its fire-resistance rating.
- Exterior walls must extend above the roof or to a lower height as per the fire hazard.

  Note: 704.11, "Parapets," is cited as governing exterior wall height.

704.7 Unexposed surface temperature *(part 1 of 4)*

- This section addresses a surface of an exterior wall as follows:
  - Surface is subject to a rise in surface temperature due to fire on the other side of the wall.
  - Surface is not directly exposed to fire.
- In the following cases the rise of temperature on the unexposed surface is not limited to 250°F as otherwise required:
  - Where the fire separation distance is > 20'.
  - Where the fire separation distance is ≤ 20':
    The allowable area of protected openings is reduced by subtracting the following amount:

    Amount subtracted = Wall area not including openings × Equivalent Opening Factor

    Equivalent Opening Factors are based on the following equation:

    $$\textbf{Factor} \;=\; \frac{(\textbf{Average °F of surface not exposed to fire} + \textbf{460°F})^4}{(\textbf{Fire-resistance temperature coefficient} + \textbf{460°F})^4}$$

    Fire-resistance temperature coefficients are as follows:

Wall fire-resistance rating	Fire-resistance temperature coefficient
1 hr	1700°F
2 hr	1850°F
3 hr	1925°F
4 hr	2000°F

    Equivalent Opening Factors as derived from the equation above are provide as follows:
    In parts 2, 3, and 4 of this section.
    For every 10°F of unexposed surface temperature.
    From 410°F to 2000°F.

  Note: ASTM E 119, "Standard Test Methods for Fire Tests of Building Construction and Materials," is cited as the standard that requires a 250°F limit of temperature rise on an unexposed surface.
  704.8, "Allowable area of openings," is cited as a factor in identifying protected windows that are subject to the temperatuare rise limit of ASTM E 119. Key requirements therein are integrated into this section.

704 Exterior Walls

704.7 Unexposed surface temperature *(part 2 of 4)*

- Reduced allowable area of protected openings is calculated as follows:

    Allowable area – (Wall area not including openings × Equivalent Opening Factor)
- Equivalent Opening Factors are provided in the table below as follows:
    - From 410°F to 940°F.
    - Based on the following:

        Average temperature in °F of the unexposed wall surface.

        Fire-resistance rating of the wall.

Table 704.7a   Equivalent Opening Factors for Exterior Walls (410°F–940°F)

Surface Temp.,°F	Wall fire-resistance rating				Surface Temp.,°F	Wall fire-resistance rating			
	1 hr	2 hr	3 hr	4 hr		1 hr	2 hr	3 hr	4 hr
410	0.026	0.020	0.018	0.016	680	0.078	0.059	0.052	0.046
420	0.028	0.021	0.019	0.016	690	0.080	0.061	0.054	0.048
430	0.029	0.022	0.019	0.017	700	0.083	0.064	0.056	0.049
440	0.030	0.023	0.020	0.018	710	0.086	0.066	0.058	0.051
450	0.032	0.024	0.021	0.019	720	0.089	0.068	0.060	0.053
460	0.033	0.025	0.022	0.020	730	0.092	0.070	0.062	0.055
470	0.034	0.026	0.023	0.020	740	0.095	0.073	0.064	0.057
480	0.036	0.027	0.024	0.021	750	0.098	0.075	0.066	0.059
490	0.037	0.029	0.025	0.022	760	0.102	0.078	0.068	0.060
500	0.039	0.030	0.026	0.023	770	0.105	0.080	0.071	0.063
510	0.041	0.031	0.027	0.024	780	0.109	0.083	0.073	0.065
520	0.042	0.032	0.029	0.025	790	0.112	0.086	0.075	0.067
530	0.044	0.034	0.030	0.026	800	0.116	0.089	0.078	0.069
540	0.046	0.035	0.031	0.027	810	0.120	0.091	0.080	0.071
550	0.048	0.037	0.032	0.028	820	0.123	0.094	0.083	0.073
560	0.050	0.038	0.033	0.030	830	0.127	0.097	0.086	0.076
570	0.052	0.040	0.035	0.031	840	0.131	0.100	0.088	0.078
580	0.054	0.041	0.036	0.032	850	0.135	0.103	0.091	0.080
590	0.056	0.043	0.038	0.033	860	0.139	0.107	0.094	0.083
600	0.058	0.044	0.039	0.034	870	0.144	0.110	0.097	0.085
610	0.060	0.046	0.041	0.036	880	0.148	0.113	0.100	0.088
620	0.063	0.048	0.042	0.037	890	0.153	0.117	0.103	0.091
630	0.065	0.050	0.044	0.039	900	0.157	0.120	0.106	0.093
640	0.068	0.051	0.045	0.040	910	0.162	0.124	0.109	0.096
650	0.070	0.053	0.047	0.041	920	0.167	0.127	0.112	0.099
660	0.072	0.055	0.049	0.043	930	0.171	0.131	0.115	0.102
670	0.075	0.057	0.050	0.045	940	0.176	0.135	0.119	0.105

704 Exterior Walls

704.7 Unexposed surface temperature *(part 3 of 4)*

- Reduced allowable area of protected openings is calculated as follows:
  Allowable area – (Wall area not including openings × Equivalent Opening Factor)
- Equivalent Opening Factors are provided in the table below as follows:
  - From 950°F to 1480°F.
  - Based on the following:
    Average temperature in °F of the unexposed wall surface.
    Fire-resistance rating of the wall.

Table 704.7b   Equivalent Opening Factors for Exterior Walls (950°F–1480°F)

Surface Temp.,°F	Wall fire-resistance rating				Surface Temp.,°F	Wall fire-resistance rating			
	1 hr	2 hr	3 hr	4 hr		1 hr	2 hr	3 hr	4 hr
950	0.182	0.139	0.122	0.108	1220	0.366	0.280	0.246	0.218
960	0.187	0.143	0.126	0.111	1230	0.375	0.286	0.252	0.223
970	0.192	0.147	0.129	0.114	1240	0.384	0.293	0.258	0.228
980	0.198	0.151	0.133	0.117	1250	0.393	0.300	0.264	0.233
990	0.203	0.155	0.137	0.121	1260	0.402	0.307	0.270	0.239
1000	0.209	0.160	0.140	0.124	1270	0.411	0.315	0.277	0.245
1010	0.215	0.164	0.144	0.128	1280	0.421	0.322	0.283	0.250
1020	0.220	0.168	0.148	0.131	1290	0.431	0.329	0.290	0.256
1030	0.226	0.173	0.152	0.135	1300	0.441	0.337	0.297	0.262
1040	0.233	0.178	0.156	0.138	1310	0.451	0.345	0.303	0.268
1050	0.239	0.183	0.161	0.142	1320	0.461	0.352	0.310	0.274
1060	0.245	0.187	0.165	0.146	1330	0.472	0.361	0.317	0.280
1070	0.252	0.192	0.169	0.150	1340	0.482	0.369	0.324	0.287
1080	0.258	0.198	0.174	0.154	1350	0.493	0.377	0.332	0.293
1090	0.265	0.203	0.178	0.158	1360	0.504	0.385	0.339	0.300
1100	0.272	0.208	0.183	0.162	1370	0.515	0.394	0.347	0.306
1110	0.279	0.213	0.189	0.166	1380	0.527	0.403	0.354	0.313
1120	0.286	0.219	0.193	0.170	1390	0.538	0.411	0.362	0.320
1130	0.294	0.224	0.198	0.175	1400	0.550	0.420	0.370	0.327
1140	0.301	0.230	0.203	0.179	1410	0.562	0.429	0.378	0.334
1150	0.309	0.236	0.208	0.183	1420	0.574	0.439	0.386	0.341
1160	0.316	0.242	0.213	0.188	1430	0.586	0.448	0.394	0.348
1170	0.324	0.248	0.218	0.193	1440	0.599	0.458	0.403	0.356
1180	0.332	0.254	0.224	0.198	1450	0.611	0.467	0.411	0.363
1190	0.341	0.260	0.229	0.202	1460	0.624	0.477	0.420	0.371
1200	0.349	0.267	0.235	0.207	1470	0.637	0.487	0.429	0.379
1210	0.357	0.273	0.240	0.212	1480	0.651	0.497	0.438	0.387

704 Exterior Walls

704.7 Unexposed surface temperature *(part 4 of 4)*

- Reduced allowable area of protected openings is calculated as follows:

    Allowable area – (Wall area not including openings × Equivalent Opening Factor).

- Equivalent Opening Factors are provided in the table below as follows:
    - From 1490°F to 2000°F.
    - Based on the following:

        Average temperature in °F of the unexposed wall surface.

        Fire-resistance rating of the wall.

Table 704.7c   Equivalent Opening Factors for Exterior Walls (1490°F–2000°F)

Surface Temp.,°F	Wall fire-resistance rating				Surface Temp.,°F	Wall fire-resistance rating			
	1 hr	2 hr	3 hr	4 hr		1 hr	2 hr	3 hr	4 hr
1490	0.664	0.508	0.447	0.395	1750	NA	0.838	0.737	0.651
1500	0.678	0.518	0.456	0.403	1760	NA	0.853	0.751	0.663
1510	0.692	0.529	0.465	0.411	1770	NA	0.869	0.764	0.675
1520	0.706	0.540	0.475	0.420	1780	NA	0.884	0.778	0.687
1530	0.720	0.551	0.485	0.428	1790	NA	0.900	0.792	0.700
1540	0.735	0.562	0.495	0.437	1800	NA	0.916	0.806	0.712
1550	0.750	0.573	0.504	0.446	1810	NA	0.933	0.821	0.725
1560	0.765	0.585	0.515	0.455	1820	NA	0.949	0.835	0.738
1570	0.780	0.596	0.525	0.464	1830	NA	0.966	0.850	0.751
1580	0.796	0.608	0.535	0.473	1840	NA	0.983	0.865	0.764
1590	0.811	0.620	0.546	0.482	1850	NA	1.000	0.880	0.778
1600	0.827	0.632	0.557	0.492	1860	NA	NA	0.895	0.791
1610	0.843	0.645	0.567	0.501	1870	NA	NA	0.911	0.805
1620	0.860	0.657	0.578	0.511	1880	NA	NA	0.927	0.819
1630	0.877	0.670	0.590	0.521	1890	NA	NA	0.943	0.833
1640	0.893	0.683	0.601	0.531	1900	NA	NA	0.959	0.847
1650	0.911	0.696	0.613	0.541	1910	NA	NA	0.975	0.861
1660	0.928	0.709	0.624	0.552	1920	NA	NA	0.992	0.876
1670	0.946	0.723	0.636	0.562	1930	NA	NA	NA	0.891
1680	0.963	0.737	0.648	0.573	1940	NA	NA	NA	0.906
1690	0.982	0.750	0.660	0.583	1950	NA	NA	NA	0.921
1700	1.000	0.764	0.673	0.594	1960	NA	NA	NA	0.937
1710	NA	0.779	0.685	0.605	1970	NA	NA	NA	0.952
1720	NA	0.793	0.698	0.617	1980	NA	NA	NA	0.968
1730	NA	0.808	0.711	0.628	1990	NA	NA	NA	0.984
1740	NA	0.823	0.724	0.640	2000	NA	NA	NA	1.000

704 Exterior Walls

704.8 Allowable area of openings *(part 1 of 2)*

- This part of the section addresses the allowable area of unprotected openings in exterior walls of buildings without sprinklers.
- Unprotected openings are not limited in buildings as follows:
  - Where the following components are not required to have fire-resistance ratings:
      Exterior bearing walls.
      Exterior nonload-bearing walls.
      Exterior structural frame.
- For other cases, the % of an exterior wall in each story that may be occupied by unprotected openings varies with the fire separation distance as follows:

Table 704.8a   % of an Exterior Wall That May Be Occupied by Unprotected Openings

Occupancy	Fire separation distance	Unprotected openings limit of coverage
R-3, accessory to R-3	≤ 3'	Not permitted
R-3	> 3' ≤ 5'	≤ 25%
"	> 5'	Not limited
H-2, H-3	≤ 15'	Not permitted
"	> 15' ≤ 20'	25%
"	> 20' ≤ 25'	45%
"	> 25' ≤ 30'	70%
"	> 30'	Not limited
Open parking garages	≤ 5'	Not permitted
"	> 5' ≤ 10'	10%
"	> 10'	Not limited
Other occupancies	≤ 5'	Not permitted
"	> 5' ≤ 10'	10%
"	> 10' ≤ 15'	15%
"	> 15' ≤ 20'	25%
"	> 20' ≤ 25'	45%
"	> 25' ≤ 30'	70%
"	> 30'	Not limited

Source: IBC Table 704.8.

- Where a fire wall separates buildings of different heights, the following applies:
  - Where the fire wall does not extend above the lower roof:
      Openings in the lower roof are not permitted ≤ 10' from the fire wall.

  Note: 705.6.1, "Stepped buildings," is cited as the source of requirements for buildings of different heights.

704 Exterior Walls

704.8 Allowable area of openings *(part 2 of 2)*

- This part of the section addresses the allowable area of protected openings and combinations of protected and unprotected openings in exterior walls of buildings without sprinklers.
- Where a fire wall separates buildings of different heights, the following applies:
  - Where the fire wall extends above the lower roof:
    The wall plane within 15' of the lower roof is governed as follows:
    Openings must have a ¾-hr fire-protection rating.
  - Where the fire wall stops below the lower roof:
    Openings are not permitted in the lower roof ≤ 10' from the fire wall.
- For other cases, the % of an exterior wall in each story that may be occupied by protected openings varies with the fire separation distance as follows:

Table 704.8b **% of an Exterior Wall That May Be Occupied by Protected Openings**

Occupancy	Fire separation distance	Protected openings limit of coverage
R-3, accessory to R-3	≤ 3'	Not permitted
R-3	> 3' ≤ 5'	≤ 25%
"	> 5'	Not limited
Open parking garages	≤ 3' Not permitted	
"	> 3' ≤ 5'	15%
"	> 5' ≤ 10'	25%
"	> 10'	Not limited
Other occupancies	≤ 3'	Not permitted
"	> 3' ≤ 5'	15%
"	> 5' ≤ 10'	25%
"	> 10' ≤ 15'	45%
"	> 15' ≤ 20'	75%
"	> 20'	Not limited

Source: IBC Table 704.8.

- Protected and unprotected openings in the same wall of a story are governed as follows:
  - The sum of their areas, each in % of that allowed, may not be > 100%.
  - Where a surface of an exterior wall on the side away from a fire has a temperature rise > 250°F, the following applies:
    Where fire separation distance is ≤ 20':
    Allowable areas of protected and unprotected openings are reduced as shown below:

Allowable area − (Wall area not including openings × Equivalent Opening Factor)

Note: 704.7, "Unexposed surface temperature," provides Equivalent Opening Factors.
ASTM E 119, "Standard Test Methods for Fire Tests of Building Construction and Materials," is the standard limiting temperature rise on unexposed surfaces.

704 Exterior Walls

704.8.1 Automatic sprinkler system

- This section addresses allowable areas of unprotected openings in exterior walls of sprinklered buildings as per NFPA 13.
- The % of an exterior wall in each story that may be occupied by unprotected openings varies with the fire separation distance as follows:

Table 704.8.1   % of an Exterior Wall That May Be Occupied by Unprotected Openings: with Sprinklers

Occupancy	Fire separation distance	Unprotected openings, building sprinklered
R-3, accessory to R-3	≤ 3'	Not permitted
R-3	> 3' ≤ 5'	≤ 25%
"	> 5'	Not limited
H-1	≤ 5'	Not permitted
"	> 5' ≤ 10'	10%
"	> 10' ≤ 15'	15%
"	> 15' ≤ 20'	25%
"	> 20' ≤ 25'	45%
"	> 25' ≤ 30'	70%
	> 30'	Not limited
H-2, H-3	≤ 15'	Not permitted
"	> 15' ≤ 20'	25%
"	> 20' ≤ 25'	45%
"	> 25' ≤ 30'	70%
"	> 30'	Not limited
Open parking garages	≤ 3'	Not permitted
"	> 3' ≤ 5'	15%
"	> 5' ≤ 10'	25%
"	> 10'	Not limited
Other occupancies	≤ 3'	Not permitted
"	> 3' ≤ 5'	15%
"	> 5' ≤ 10'	25%
"	> 10' ≤ 15'	45%
"	> 15' ≤ 20'	75%
"	> 20'	Not limited

Source: IBC Table 704.8.

704 Exterior Walls

704.8.2 First story

- This section applies to buildings other than occupancy H.
- Unprotected opening area in exterior walls is not limited where all the following apply:
  - In the 1ˢᵗ story.
  - Where the wall faces either of the following open spaces:

    A street with a fire separation distance >15'.

    An unoccupied open space ≥ 30' wide with all the following characteristics:

      Has access from a street by a posted fire line.

      With one of the following conditions:

        Located on the same lot.

        Dedicated to public use.

  Note: International Fire Code is cited as the source governing posted fire lanes.

704.9 **Vertical separation of openings** *(part 1 of 2)*

- This section does not apply to the following:
  - Buildings ≤ 3 stories.
  - Sprinklered buildings as per NFPA 13 or NFPA 13R.
  - Open parking garages.

  Note: The following are cited as governing the specified sprinkler systems.
      903.3.1.1, "NFPA 13 sprinkler systems."
      903.3.1.2, "NFPA 13R sprinkler systems".

- Other buildings where both of the following conditions exist are governed as indicated below:
  - Conditions:

    The horizontal distance between an upper and lower opening is ≤ 5'.

    The opening in the lower story is not protected.

  Note: 715.4.8, "Exterior fire window assemblies," is cited as the source of requirements for windows qualifying as protected.

Case study: Fig. 704.8.2. The extent of the canopy on this building is subject to restriction based on the fire hazard associated with the proximity of adjacent buildings. Since openings are also vulnerable to such a fire hazard, the need for protected openings is used as a measure of the hazard. In this case, the canopy is on the first story (most accessible to the fire department), thus, qualifying the building to be without protected openings if the fire separation distance is > 15'. The fire separation distance is measured to the center of the street on a line ⊥ to the building wall. This shortest distance is 95' for this project. Consequently, the projection of the canopy is not limited. Since the canopy is constructed of noncombustible materials it is not subject to limitations for combustible materials. The canopy, therefore, complies with the code in all respects.

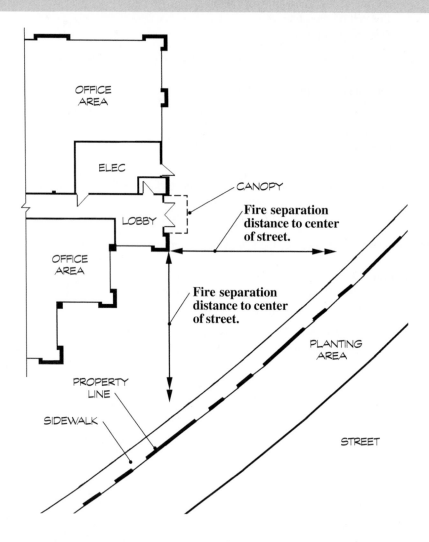

Fig. 704.8.2. Partial floor plan at canopy. AmberGlen Business Center. Hillsboro, Oregon. Ankrom Moisan Associated Architects. Portland, Oregon.

704 Exterior Walls

704.9 Vertical separation of openings *(part 2 of 2)*

○ Requirements:

Vertical separation of upper and lower windows is required by one of the following:

A vertical assembly as follows:

Provides ≥ 3' between openings.

Has a fire-resistance rating ≥ 1 hr.

Is one of the following components:

Spandrel girder.

Exterior wall.

Other similar assembly.

Flame barrier as follows:

Extends ≥ 30" horizontally beyond the exterior wall plane.

Has a fire-resistance rating ≥ 1 hr.

The rise of temperature on the barrier surface not exposed to a fire is not limited to 250°F by this section.

Note: ASTM E 119, "Standard Test Methods for Fire Tests of Building Construction and Materials," is cited as the standard limiting temperature rise on unexposed surfaces.

704.10 Vertical exposure

• This section addresses buildings on the same lot.

• The following applies to openings above the roof of an adjoining building:

○ Openings do not require approved protectives as follows:

Where the lower roof has all the following characteristics:

Construction has a fire-resistance rating ≥ 1 hr.

Rated construction extends ≥ 10' from the wall with the window.

Supporting structure for the rated construction complies with the following:

It has a fire-resistance rating ≥ 1 hr for its full length.

• In other cases, windows above a roof with all of the following conditions are governed as indicated below:

○ Conditions:

The window is in one of the following locations:

An adjacent building.

An adjoining building.

The window is < 15' vertically from the lower roof.

The lower roof and/or the higher wall is within a 15' fire separation distance.

○ Requirements:

The openings must be provided with approved protectives.

Note: The 15' fire separation distance is measured from each building to an imaginary line between them; thus, buildings closer than 30' to each other would cause one or both to be within the 15' fire separation distance by a literal interpretation.

704 Exterior Walls

704.11 Parapets

- Parapets are not required on exterior walls in any of the following cases:
  - Where walls need not have a fire-resistance rating based on fire separation distance.

    Note: IBC Table 602, "Fire-Resistance Rating Requirements for Exterior Walls Based on Fire Separation Distance," is cited as the source of applicable requirements.

  - Where no floor of the building has an area > 1000 sf.
  - Where walls terminate at either of the following roofs:
    Roofs having a fire-resistance rating ≥ 2 hrs.
    Roofs with construction of noncombustible materials including the following:
      Roof deck.
      Supporting construction.
  - Where fire separation distance permits unprotected openings in ≥ 25% of the wall.

    Note: 704.8, "Allowable area of openings," is cited as the source governing % of wall coverage permitted for openings based on fire separation distance.

- Parapets are not required on exterior walls in any of the following cases:
  - Where walls terminate at the bottom of the roof deck with all the following conditions:
    Wall has a fire-resistance rating ≥ 1 hr.
    Roof/ceiling framing and supports have a fire-resistance rating ≥ 1 hr as follows:
      Where roof framing is ‖ to the exterior wall:
        Rating extends ≥ 4' from interior face of exterior wall for the following:
          Occupancies R and U.
        Rating extends ≥ 10' from interior face of exterior wall for other occupancies.
      Where roof framing is not ‖ to the exterior wall:
        The entire span and its supports have a fire-resistance rating ≥ 1 hr.
    Roof openings are > 5' from the rated wall in the following occupancies:
      R, U.
    Roof openings are > 10' from the rated wall in other occupancies.
    The entire roof covering is ≥ Class B.
  - Where walls terminate at bottom of the roof deck with all the following conditions:
    In one of the following occupancies:
      R-2, R-3.
    In one of the following construction types:
      Types III, IV, V.
    Roof deck is constructed of one of the following for a distance of ≥ 4' from the wall:
      Approved noncombustible materials.
      Fire-retardant-treated wood.
    Roof covering is ≥ Class C.
    Roof is protected with Type X ⁵/₈" gypsum board as follows:
      Board is mounted immediately under the roof deck.
      Board is supported by ≥ nominal 2" ledgers attached to sides of roof framing.
      Board protection is installed a distance ≥ 4' from the wall.
- Other exterior walls must have parapets.

704 Exterior Walls

704.11.1 Parapet construction

- Parapets must have the same fire-resistance rating as required for the wall below.
- Parapets must have noncombustible surfaces subject to both of the following conditions:
  - On sides adjacent to a roof surface.
  - Covering the area within 18" from the top of the parapet including the following:
    Coping and counterflashing.
- Parapet height must be ≥ 30" above its intersection with the roof surface.
- Where the roof slopes toward the parapet at a slope > 2:12, the following applies:
  - Parapet height must be the greater of the following:
    A height ≥ 30" above the intersection of parapet and roof surface.
    A height ≥ the highest point of the roof as follows:
      Within a distance from the parapet equal to the following fire separation distance:
      The fire separation distance requiring protection of wall openings.

704.12 Opening protection *(part 1 of 2)*

- This section addresses openings required to be protected as follows:
  - Based on fire separation distance.
  - Based on relationships to openings above and below.
  - Based on relationships to lower roofs.

  Note: The following sections are cited as regulating openings governed by this section:
  704.8, "Allowable area of openings," limits size vs. fire separation distance.
  704.9, "Vertical separation of openings."
  705.10, "Vertical exposure," addresses openings exposed to lower roofs.

- Where both of the following conditions apply, openings are not required to have fire protective assemblies:
  - The building is sprinklered as per NFPA 13.
  - The exterior openings are protected by an approved water curtain as follows:
    Must be as per NFPA 13.
    Must utilize automatic sprinklers approved for use in water curtains.

704 Exterior Walls

704.12 Opening protection *(part 2 of 2)*

- In other cases, windows must be protected as follows:
    - Where walls must have a fire-resistance rating > 1 hr based on fire separation distance: Windows must have a fire-protection rating ≥ 1½ hrs.
    - Where walls must have a fire-resistance rating ≥ 1 hr based on fire separation distance: Windows must have a fire-protection rating ≥ ¾ hr.
    - Where windows are required to be protected due to exposure to one of the following, the requirement below applies:
        Exposure conditions:
            To windows above or below.
            To a roof below.
        Requirement:
            Windows must have a fire-protection rating of ≥ ¾ hr.
    - Where windows in walls not fire-resistance-rated are required to be protected due to exposure based on one of the following, the requirement below applies:
        Exposure conditions:
            Due to fire separation distance.
            To windows above or below.
            To a roof below.
        Requirement:
            Windows must have a fire-protection rating of ≥ ¾ hr.

    Note: 715.4.8, "Exterior fire window assemblies," is cited as governing windows addressed by this section. The section is partially summarized above.

- Other openings governed by this section must be protected with fire doors or shutters.

    Note: 715.3, "Fire door and shutter assemblies," is cited as governing these protectives.

704.12.1 Unprotected openings

- Where protected openings are not required:
    - The following may be constructed of any approved material:
        Windows.
        Doors.
    - The following must meet applicable code requirements:
        Glass and glazing.
        Plastic.

    Note: Section 704, "Exterior Walls," is cited as the source requiring protected openings. Chapter 24, "Glass and Glazing," is cited as the governing standard. Chapter 26, "Plastic," is cited as the governing standard.

704 Exterior Walls

704.13 Joints

- Where exterior walls may have unprotected openings, the following applies:
  - Joints in the walls need not comply with fire-resistant joint system requirements.
- Where exterior walls are required by this section to have a fire-resistance rating:
  - Joints at such walls must comply with fire-resistant joint system requirements.

  Note: Section 713, "Fire-Resistant Joint Systems," is cited as the source of requirements for joints in walls with a fire-resistance rating.

704.13.1 Voids

- This section addresses the void created by the intersection of an exterior curtain wall assembly and a floor/ceiling assembly.
- The void must be sealed as follows:
  - With an approved material.
  - Sealant material must be installed securely.
  - Sealant material must prevent the passage of the following:
    Flame.
    Hot gases.

  Note: 713.4, "Exterior curtain wall/floor intersection," is cited as governing the protection of such voids, a partial summary of which is provided above.

705 Fire Walls

705.1 General

- The following applies to each part of a building completely separated from adjacent parts by a fire wall:
  - Each part is considered to be a separate building.
- Where a fire wall occurs where a fire barrier wall is also required, the following applies:
  - The more restrictive requirements of each governs.
- Fire walls serving as party walls on lot lines may not have openings.

  Note: 503.2, "Party walls," is cited as a source of requirements for such walls, the content of which is summarized above.

705.2 Structural stability

- Fire walls must be constructed to remain standing during a fire as follows:
  - For a time period equal to its fire-resistance rating.
  - Regardless of any collapse of adjacent construction.

705.3 Materials

- In the following types of construction, fire walls must be built of an approved noncombustible material:
  - Types I, II, III, IV.

705.4 Fire-resistance rating

- Fire-resistance ratings required for fire walls are as follows:

Table 705.4   Fire-Resistance Ratings Required for Fire Walls

Construction type	Occupancy	Fire-resistance rating
II, V	A, B, E, H-4, I, R-1, R-2, U	≥ 2 hr
I, III, IV	A, B, E, H-4, I, R-1, R-2, U	≥ 3 hr
I, II, III, IV, V	F-1, H-3, H-5, M, S-1	≥ 3 hr
I, II, III, IV, V	H-1, H-2	≥ 4 hr
I, II, III, IV, V	F-2, R-3, R-4, S-2	≥ 2 hr

Source: IBC Table 705.4.

  Note: The following are cited as sources of requirements for H occupancies:
  415.4, "Special provisions for Group H-1 occupancies," addresses building size and configuration, roof and floor construction, and materials with multiple hazards.
  415.5, "Special provisions for Group H-2 and H-3 occupancies," addresses building size, configuration, construction, and special requirements pertaining to protection from water.

705 Fire Walls

705.5 Horizontal continuity

- Fire walls must be continuous between exterior walls.
- Fire walls must terminate at exterior walls in one of the following configurations:
  - Fire walls may extend past the exterior surface of the exterior as follows:
    For a distance ≥ 18".
  - Fire walls may terminate at the interior surface of the following where all the conditions indicated below apply to the exterior wall:
    Surfaces:
       Combustible exterior sheathing.
       Combustible exterior siding.
    Conditions:
       Wall has a fire-resistance rating ≥ 1 hr as follows:
         Extending ≥ 4' on both sides of the fire wall.
         Openings in this 4' length must have fire assemblies as follows:
           With a fire-protection rating ≥ ¾ hr.
  - Fire walls may terminate at the interior surface of the following where the condition indicated below applies:
    Surfaces:
       Noncombustible sheathing.
       Noncombustible siding.
       Noncombustible exterior material.
    Conditions:
       The noncombustible extends ≥ 4' on both sides of the fire wall.
  - Fire walls may terminate at the interior surface of the following where the condition indicated below applies:
    Surface:
       Noncombustible exterior sheathing.
    Condition:
       Where the building is sprinklered as follows:
         On each side of the fire wall.
         Sprinklers to be in compliance with one of the following:
         NFPA 13.
         NFPA 13R.

705 Fire Walls

705.5.1 Exterior walls

- This section addresses exterior walls on each side of a fire wall that meet each other at the end of the fire wall.
- The angle formed by the exterior walls meeting each other is measured as follows:
  - From outside face to outside face across the exterior of the building.
- Exterior walls that meet at an angle < 180° require protection as follows:
  - A fire-resistance rating ≥ 1 hr is required in the following location:
    Extending ≥ 4' on both sides of the fire wall:
      Openings in this 4' length must be protected as follows:
      With a fire-protection rating ≥ ¾ hr.
- Exterior walls that meet at an angle ≥ 180° are governed as follows:
  - They do not require the fire-resistance rating otherwise required by this section.

705 Fire Walls

705.5.2 Horizontal projecting elements

- This section addresses the relationship between fire walls and horizontal projecting elements as follows in the location indicated below:
  - Projections:
    Balconies.
    Roof overhangs.
    Canopies.
    Marquees.
    Architectural projections.
  - Location:
    Where they occur ≤ 4' from a fire wall.
- Fire walls need not extend to the outer edge of projecting elements in the following cases:
  - Where projections without concealed spaces comply with the following:
    Exterior wall behind and below the projection must be as follows:
    The wall must have a fire-resistance rating ≥ 1 hr:
    Rating must extend along both sides of the fire wall as follows:
    For a distance ≥ the depth of the projection.
    Openings in this rated zone must have the following:
    A fire-protection rating ≥ ¾ hr.
  - Where noncombustible projections with concealed spaces comply with the following:
    A wall with a fire resistance rating ≥ 1 hr must extend through the concealed space.
    The projecting element must be separated from the building as follows:
    Separating construction must have a fire-resistance rating ≥ 1 hr:
    Rating must extend along both sides of the fire wall as follows:
    For a distance ≥ the depth of the projection.
    The 1-hr-rated wall need not extend under the projected element in the following case:
    Where the exterior wall has a fire resistance rating ≥ 1 hr:
    Rating must extend along both sides of the fire wall as follows:
    For a distance ≥ the depth of the projection.
    Openings in this rated zone must have the following:
    A fire-protection rating ≥ ¾ hr.
  - Where combustible projections with concealed spaces comply with the following:
    Fire wall must extend through the concealed space to outer edge of projection.
    Exterior wall behind and below the projecting element must comply with the following:
    The wall must have a fire-resistance rating ≥ 1 hr:
    Rating must extend along both sides of the fire wall as follows:
    For a distance ≥ the depth of the projection.
    Openings in this rated zone must have the following:
    A fire-protection rating ≥ ¾ hr.
- In other cases fire walls must extend to the outer edge of projecting elements.

705 Fire Walls

705.6 Vertical continuity *(part 1 of 2)*

- This section does not address the upper termination fire walls in the following case:
  - Where fire walls separate certain buildings with different roof levels.

    Note: 705.6.1, "Stepped buildings," is cited as the source governing the tops of fire walls separating such buildings.

- The top of 2-hr fire-resistance-rated fire walls may terminate as follows if the listed conditions are met:
  - Terminations:
    At the underside of the roof sheathing.
    At the underside of the roof deck.
    At the underside of the roof slab.
  - Conditions:
    Elements of the lower roof assembly must have a fire-resistance rating ≥ 1 hr as follows:
      The roof assembly for a distance ≥ 4' from the wall.
      The entire length of components supporting the rated roof assembly.
    No openings are permitted in the roof as follows:
      ≤ 4' from the fire wall.
    The buildings on both sides of the fire wall require roofing as follows:
      ≥ Class B.
- Fire walls may terminate as follows if all the listed conditions are met:
  - Terminations:
    At the underside of noncombustible roof sheathing.
    At the underside of a noncombustible roof deck.
    At the underside of a roof slab.
  - Conditions:
    No openings are permitted in the roof as follows:
      ≤ 4' from the fire wall.
    The buildings on both sides of the fire wall require roofing as follows:
      ≥ Class B.

705 Fire Walls

705.6 Vertical continuity *(part 2 of 2)*

- Fire walls may terminate as follows if all the listed conditions are met:
    - Terminations:
        At the underside of combustible roof sheathing.
        At the underside of a combustible roof deck.
    - Conditions:
        Buildings must be one of the following types:
            Type III.
            Type IV.
            Type V.
        No openings are permitted in the roof as follows:
            ≤ 4' from the fire wall.
        The buildings on both sides of the fire wall require roofing as follows:
            ≥ Class B.
        One of the following applies to an area extending to ≥ 4' from both sides of the fire wall:
            The roof sheating or deck is constructed of the following:
                Fire-retardant-treated wood.
            ⁵/₈" Type X gypsum board is applied as follows:
                Underneath the roof sheathing or deck.
                Supported on ≥ 2" ledgers attached to roof framing.
- Where buildings having any of the following occupancies are located above enclosed parking garages, the condition indicated below applies:
    - Occupancies:
        A, B, M, R.
    - Condition:
        The bottom of the fire wall may terminate at the following location:
            At the horizontal separation between the garage and the building above.

    Note: 508.2, "Group S-2 enclosed parking garage with Groups A, B, M or R above," is cited as the source of requirements qualifying garages for this type of fire wall termination.

- The bottoms of fire walls in other buildings terminate at the foundations.
- In cases other than those addressed above in this section, the following applies:
    - Fire walls must extend to a level ≥ 30" above the roofs on each side of the fire wall.

705 Fire Walls

705.6.1 Stepped buildings

- This section addresses fire walls with both of the following characteristics:
  - The fire wall serves as an exterior wall.
  - The fire wall separates buildings with roofs at different levels.
- Such fire wall must terminate at its top in one of the following ways:
  - The fire wall must terminate at a level ≥ 30" above the lower roof as follows:
    The exterior wall above the lower roof is governed as follows:
    It must have a fire-resistance rating ≥ 1 hr from both sides:
    This rated zone must extend for a height ≥ 15' above the lower roof:
    Openings in this zone must have a fire-protection rating ≥ ¾ hr.
- Such a fire wall must terminate at the underside of one of the following elements of the lower roof with other conditions meeting all the requirements listed below:
  - Roof elements:
    Roof sheathing.
    Roof deck.
    Roof slab.
  - Conditions:
    The lower roof assembly must have a fire-resistance rating ≥ 1 hr as follows:
    The rating must extend for a distance ≥ 10' from the fire wall.
    The support system for the rated roof assembly is governed as follows:
    It must have a fire-resistance rating ≥ 1 hr for its full length.
    No openings are permitted in the lower roof ≤ 10' from the fire wall.

705.7 Combustible framing in fire walls

- The wall thickness between combustible members penetrating a fire wall from opposite sides is governed as follows:
  - Where the fire wall is concrete or masonry:
    A wall thickness ≥ 4" between embedded ends of members is required.
- Where the fire wall is hollow or has hollow units:
  - Hollow spaces must be filled solid as follows:
    For the full thickness of the wall.
    For a distance ≥ 4" in the following locations:
    Above members.
    Below members.
    Between members.
    Filler materials to be as follows:
    Noncombustible.
    Approved for fireblocking.

705 Fire Walls

705.8 Openings

- Openings are not allowed in fire walls serving as party walls.

  Note: 503.2, "Party walls," is cited as governing fire walls acting as party walls, the requirements of which are summarized above.

- Openings through other fire walls are governed as follows:
  - The sum of opening widths at a floor level must be ≤ 25% of the wall length.
  - Area of each opening must be ≤ 120 sf where either building is without sprinklers.
  - Area of each opening is not limited where the building is sprinklered as per NFPA 13.
  - Openings must be protected.

  Note: 715.3, "Fire door and shutter assemblies," governs the protection of openings in fire walls.

706 Fire Barriers

706.1 General

- This series of sections governs fire barriers used for the following:
  - To separate the following from other areas:
    Shafts.
    Exits.
    Exit passageways.
    Horizontal exits.
    Incidental use areas.
  - To separate different occupancies from each other.
  - To subdivide an occupancy into separate fire areas.
  - To isolate other areas as follows:
    Where a fire barrier is required by either of the following:
    This code.
    The *International Fire Code.*

706.2 Materials

- Materials of the following fire barriers must conform to the building construction type:
  - Walls.
  - Floor assemblies.

706.3.1 Shaft enclosures

- Fire barriers isolating shafts are governed as follows:
  - Basements are included in the number of stories connected by a shaft.
  - Mezzanines are not included in the number of stories connected by a shaft.
  - Where shafts connect < 4 stories:
    The greater of the following fire-resistance is required up to a maximum of 2 hrs:
    ≥ 1 hr.
    ≥ the fire-resistance rating of the floor penetrated.
  - Where shafts connect ≥ 4 stories:
    A fire-resistance rating ≥ 2 hrs is required.

  Note: 707.4, "Fire-resistance rating," is cited as the source of requirements for this fire barrier's isolating shafts. The section is summarized above and also cites Section 706, "Fire Barriers," as the source of further requirements.

706 Fire Barriers

706.3.2 Exit enclosures

- Fire barriers isolating exits are governed as follows for most cases:
  - Basements are included in the number of stories connected by a shaft.
  - Mezzanines are not included in the number of stories connected by a shaft.
  - Where exits connect < 4 stories:
    A fire-resistance rating of ≥ 1 hr is required.
  - Where exits connect ≥ 4 stories:
    A fire-resistance rating ≥ 2 hrs is required.

  Note: 1019.1, "Enclosures required," is cited as the source of requirements for exit enclosures. A partial summary is provided above which excludes the 9 exceptions listed in the section.

706.3.3 Exit passageway

- Exit passageways must be enclosed with fire barriers as follows:
  - Enclosure must have a fire-resistance rating ≥ the larger of the following:
    1 hr.
    The rating required for any connecting exit enclosure.

  Note: 1020.1, "Exit passageway," is cited as the source of applicable requirements. The section refers to additional sections, key requirements of which are summarized above and which require compliance with Section 706, "Fire Barriers."

706.3.4 Horizontal exit

- The separation between areas provided by an horizontal exit must have a fire-resistance rating ≥ 2 hr.

  Note: 1021.1, "Horizontal exits," is cited as the source of applicable requirements. The section requires compliance with additional sections including Section 706, "Fire Barriers." A key requirement thus referenced is summarized above.

706.3.5 Incidental use areas

- Fire barriers isolating incidental use areas are governed as follows:
  - They must have fire-resistance ratings based on the function of the incidental space.

  Note: IBC Table 302.1.1, "Incidental Use Areas," is cited as the source of fire-resistance ratings for the areas.

706 Fire Barriers

706.3.6 Separation of mixed occupancies

- Fire barriers required for separating mixed occupancies are governed as follows:
  - They must have a fire-resistance rating based on the separated occupancies.

    Note: 302.3, "Mixed occupancies," establishes where fire barriers are required to separate mixed occupancies.

    302.3.2, "Separated uses," is cited as the source of fire-resistance ratings based on the separated occupancies.

706.3.7 Single-occupancy fire areas

- A fire-resistance rating ≥ 4 hr is required for fire barriers dividing the following occupancies into separate fire areas:
  - H-1.
  - H-2.
- A fire-resistance rating ≥ 3 hr is required for fire barriers dividing the following occupancies into separate fire areas:
  - F-1.
  - H-3.
  - S-1.
- A fire-resistance rating ≥ 2 hr is required for fire barriers dividing the following occupancies into separate fire areas:
  - A, B, E, F-2, H-4.
  - H-5, I, M, R, S-2.
- A fire-resistance rating ≥ 1 hr is required for fire barriers dividing the following occupancy into separate fire areas:
  - U.

Source: IBC Table 706.3.7.

706 Fire Barriers

706.4 Continuity of fire barrier walls

- Shaft enclosures are not required to extend to the underside of a roof deck as follows:
  - Where the fire-resistance rating of the shaft's top closure is ≥ the larger of the following:
    The fire-resistance rating of the highest floor penetrated by the shaft.
    The fire-resistance rating of the shaft walls.

    Note: 707.12, "Enclosure at the top," is cited as governing the top of a shaft, a partial summary of which is provided above.

- In all other cases, fire barrier walls must extend continuously between the following levels:
  - Top of floor/ceiling assembly located below the fire barrier wall.
  - Underside of one of the following elements as applicable:
    Floor slab or deck above the fire barrier wall.
    Roof slab or deck above the fire barrier wall.
- Fire barrier walls must be securely attached at upper and lower terminations.
- Fire barrier walls must be continuous through concealed spaces such as follows:
  - Space above a suspended ceiling.
- Construction supporting fire barrier walls is governed as follows:
  - Applications with of the following characteristics are not required to have a fire-resistance rating ≥ than the barrier supported:
    Walls separating incidental use areas from other building areas.
    Walls with a fire-resistance rating = 1 hr.
    Walls located in the following types of construction:
      Type IIB.
      Type IIIB.
      Type VB.

    Note: IBC Table 302.1.1, "Incidental Use Areas," is cited as the source listing incidental use areas requiring 1-hr rated walls.

  - Applications that separate storage tank areas of H-2 occupancies from other uses must have a fire-resistance rating ≥ the larger of the following:
    ≥ 2 hr.
    ≥ fire-resistance rating required for building elements based on construction type.

    Note: 415.7.2.1, "Mixed occupancies," is cited as the source of requirements for tank storage.
    IBC Table 601, "Fire-Resistance Rating Requirements for Building Elements," is cited as the source for ratings based on construction type.

  - All other applications must have the following fire-resistance rating:
    ≥ the fire barrier supported.
- At each floor, fire stops are required as follows:
  - In any hollow vertical spaces within a fire barrier wall.

706 Fire Barriers

706.6 Exterior walls

- Exterior walls separating an exterior exit stairway from the interior are governed as follows:
  - For buildings < 4 stories:
    A fire-resistance rating ≥ 1 hr is required.
  - For buildings ≥ 4 stories:
    A fire-resistance rating ≥ 2 hr is required.

    Note: 1022.6, "Exterior ramps and stairway protection," is cited as governing exterior walls at these elements. A partial summary is provided above.

- Exterior walls on a required fire-resistance-rated enclosure are governed as follows:
  - Fire-resistance ratings required for enclosure separations do not apply.
  - The walls must comply with fire-resistance rating requirements for exterior walls.

    Note: Section 704, "Exterior Walls," is cited as governing exterior wall fire-resistance requirements.

706.7 Openings

- This section does not apply to fire doors serving an exit enclosure.
- Openings in a fire barrier must be protected.

    Note: Section 715, "Opening Protectives," is cited as governing such protectives.

- Openings in a fire barrier must meet one of the following conditions:
  - Openings must comply with both of the following:
    Buildings on both sides of the fire barrier must be sprinklered.
    The sum of opening widths is limited to 25% of the wall length.

    Note: 903.3.1.1, "NFPA sprinkler systems," is cited as governing the sprinklers.

  - Openings must have both of the following:
    An opening protective assembly tested by applicable standards.
    A fire-resistance rating ≥ the wall.

    Note: ASTM E 119, "Standard Test Methods for Fire Tests of Building Construction and Materials," is cited as the applicable test for opening protective assemblies.

  - Openings must meet both of the following size restrictions:
    Each opening is limited to an area ≤ 120 sf.
    The sum of openings widths is limited to ≤ 25% of the wall length.
- Openings in exit enclosures must meet additional requirements specific to their location.

    Note: 1020.4, "Openings and penetrations," is cited as the source of additional requirements for openings in exit enclosures.

706 Fire Barriers

706.8.1 Prohibited penetrations

- Required exit doors are permitted in an exit enclosure fire barrier.
- The following penetrations of an exit enclosure fire barrier must meet the requirements for preventing the passage of fire:
    - Equipment and ductwork necessary for independent pressurization of the enclosure.
    - Sprinkler piping.
    - Standpipes.
    - Electrical conduit serving the enclosure must terminate in a steel box ≤ 16 sq in.

    Note: 1020.5, "Penetrations," is cited as the source of applicable requirements.

- Other penetrations into an exit enclosure are not permitted.

707 Shaft Enclosures

707.1 General

- This section addresses vertical shafts as follows:
  - Where required to protect openings and penetrations through the following:
    - Floor/ceiling assemblies.
    - Roof/ceiling assemblies.

707.2 Shaft enclosure required *(part 1 of 3)*

- A shaft enclosure is not required for the following case:
  - For an opening through a floor/ceiling assembly with both of the following characteristics:
    - The opening is contained entirely within an individual dwelling unit.
    - The opening connects ≤ 4 stories.
- A shaft enclosure is not required for the following case:
  - For an opening through a floor/ceiling assembly meeting all of the following conditions:
    - The building is sprinklered as per NFPA 13.
    - The opening serves one of the following:
      - An escalator.
      - A stairway not required for means of egress.
    - The area of the opening is limited to one of the following:
      - ≤ 2 × the projected area of the escalator.
      - ≤ 2 × the projected area of the stairway.
    - The opening is protected by a draft curtain.
    - The opening is protected by closely spaced sprinklers as per NFPA 13.
    - The opening ≤ 4 stories in the following occupancies:
      - A, E, F, H, I, R, S, U.
- A shaft enclosure is not required for the following:
  - An opening through a floor/ceiling assembly meeting all of the following conditions:
    - The building is sprinklered as per NFPA 13.
    - The opening serves one of the following:
      - An escalator.
      - A stairway not required for means of egress.
    - Power-operated automatic shutters protect the opening at every floor as follows:
      - Shutters are approved.
      - Shutters are of noncombustible materials.
      - Shutters have a fire-resistance rating ≥ 1½ hr.
      - Shutters close immediately upon detection of smoke.
      - Shutters completely surround and seal the opening well.
      - Shutters move ≤ 30 fpm.
      - Shutters have a leading edge that controls movement as follows:
        - Shutters stop upon meeting an obstacle.
        - Shutters resume movement when the obstacle is removed.
      - Escalator stops when shutters begin to close.

Note: 907.10, "Fire safety functions," is cited as the source governing smoke detectors.

707 Shaft Enclosures

707.2 Shaft enclosure required *(part 2 of 3)*

- A shaft enclosure is not required for the following:
  - Penetrations as follows through a floor/ceiling assembly meeting the requirement indicated below:
    - Penetrations:
      - Pipe.
      - Tube.
      - Conduit.
      - Wire.
      - Cable.
      - Vents.
    - Requirement:
      - Penetrations must meet requirements for protection against the passage of fire.

  Note: 712.4, "Horizontal assemblies," is cited as the source of protection requirements for the penetrations listed above.

- A shaft enclosure is not required for the following:
  - Duct penetrations through a floor/ceiling assembly as follows:
    - Ducts are required to have dampers or meet protection requirements in lieu of dampers.

  Note: 712.4.4, "Ducts and air transfer openings," is cited as the source of applicable requirements.

  - Grease ducts are not governed by this section.

  Note: The International Mechanical Code is cited as governing grease ducts.

- A shaft enclosure is not required for the following:
  - An opening through a floor/ceiling assembly meeting the requirements for the following locations:
    - Covered malls.
    - Atriums.
- A shaft enclosure is not required for the following:
  - Masonry chimneys as follows:
    - Where approved.
    - Where the annular space is protected at each floor.

  Note: 717.2.5, "Ceiling and floor openings," is cited as the source of requirements for fireblocking at openings around chimneys.

707 Shaft Enclosures

707.2 Shaft enclosure required *(part 3 of 3)*

- A shaft enclosure is not required for the following:
  - An opening through a floor/ceiling assembly meeting the following requirements:
    Opening is located in an occupancy other than the following:
      I-2, 1-3.
    Opening connects ≤ 2 stories.
    Opening is not concealed in the building construction.
    Opening is not open to a corridor in the following locations:
      In occupancy I, R.
      On a nonsprinklered floor in any occupancy.
    Opening is separated from openings in other floors as follows:
      By construction meeting shaft enclosure requirements.
    Opening does not serve a required means of egress in other than special cases.

    Note: 1019.1, "Enclosures," is cited as the source listing special cases where stairways serving a means of egress need not be enclosed.

- A shaft enclosure is not required for the following:
  - Automobile ramps as follows:
    In open parking garages.
    In enclosed closed parking garages.

    Note: The following are cited as governing the construction of the garages listed above:
      406.3, "Open parking garages."
      406.4, "Enclosed parking garages."

- A shaft enclosure is not required for the following:
  - A floor opening connecting a floor and a mezzanine above.
- A shaft enclosure is not required for the following:
  - Joints with a fire-resistant joint protection system.

    Note: Section 713, "Fire-Resistant Joint Systems," is cited as governing the joints indicated above.

- A shaft enclosure is not required as follows:
  - Where other sections of the code permit its omission.
- In all other cases, the following applies:
  - Openings through floor/ceiling assemblies require the following:
    A shaft enclosure meeting the requirements of this section.

707.3 Materials

- Materials for shaft construction must be as follows:
  - Consistent with the type of construction for the building.

707 Shaft Enclosures

707.4 Fire-resistance rating

- Shaft enclosures are governed as follows:
    - Basements are included in the number of stories connected by a shaft.
    - Mezzanines are not included in the number of stories connected by a shaft.
    - Where they connect < 4 stories:
        The greater of the following fire-resistance ratings is required up to a maximum of 2 hrs:
        ≥ 1 hr.
        ≥ the fire-resistance rating of the floor penetrated.
    - Where they connect ≥ 4 stories:
        A fire-resistance rating ≥ 2 hrs is required.

    Note: Section 706, "Fire Barriers," is cited as the source of requirements for the construction of shafts.

707.5 Continuity

- Shaft enclosures must extend continuously between the following levels:
    - Top of floor/ceiling assembly below.
    - Underside of one of the following elements above:
        Floor slab or deck.
        Roof slab or deck.
- Shaft enclosures must be securely attached.
- Shaft enclosures must be continuous through concealed spaces such as follows:
    - Space above a suspended ceiling.
- Construction supporting shaft enclosures is governed as follows:
    - It must have a fire-resistance rating ≥ that of the shaft enclosure supported.
- Where shaft enclosure walls have hollow vertical spaces:
    - Fire stops are required at each floor level.

707.6 Exterior walls

- Exterior walls separating an exterior exit stairway from a building interior are governed as follows:
    - They must have the following fire-resistance rating at buildings < 4 stories:
        ≥ 1 hr.
    - They must have the following fire-resistance rating at buildings ≥ 4 stories:
        ≥ 2 hr.

    Note: 1022.6, "Exterior ramps and stairway protection," is cited as governing these walls, a partial summary of which is provided above.

- Exterior walls that are part of a shaft enclosure are governed as follows:
    - Fire-resistance-rated enclosure requirements do not apply to the walls.
    - The walls must comply with fire-resistance rating requirements for exterior walls.

    Note: Section 704, "Exterior Walls," is cited as governing these walls.

707 Shaft Enclosures

707.7 Openings

- Openings in shaft enclosures must be one of the following:
  - Self-closing.
  - Automatic closing by smoke detection.
- Openings in shaft enclosures must meet opening protective requirements.

  Note: Section 715, "Opening Protectives," is cited as the source of requirements for opening protectives.

707.7.1 Prohibited openings

- The only openings permitted in a shaft enclosure are those required for the function of the shaft.

707.8 Penetrations

- Penetrations in shaft enclosures must be protected as required for fire barriers.

  Note: Section 712, "Penetrations," is cited as governing these penetrations.

707.8.1 Prohibited penetrations

- The only penetrations permitted in a shaft enclosure are those required for the function of the shaft.
- The only ducts permitted to penetrate a shaft enclosure are those necessary for independent pressurization of the shaft.

  Note: 1020.5, "Penetrations," is cited as the source permitting pressurization ducts to penetrate a shaft enclosure.

707.10 Enclosure at the bottom *(part 1 of 3)*

- This section addresses shafts that terminate at a point above the bottom of the building.
- The room in which a shaft terminates is not required to have the following characteristics where the shaft meets all the requirements indicated below:
  - Characteristics:
    The room need not be separated from the building as follows:
      By fire-resistance rated construction.
    The bottom of the shaft need not have opening protectives.
  - Requirements:
    The shaft must contain no combustibles.
    There may be no openings in the shaft enclosure as follows:
      To the interior of the building.
    There may be no penetrations through the shaft enclosure as follows:
      To the interior of the building.

707 Shaft Enclosures

707.10 Enclosure at the bottom *(part 2 of 3)*

- The room in which a shaft terminates is not required to have the following characteristics where the shaft meets all the requirements indicated below:
  - Characteristics:
    The room need not be separated from the building as follows:
    By fire-resistance rated construction.
  - Requirements:
    There may be no openings into the shaft enclosure as follows:
    To the interior of the building other than at the bottom.
    There may be no penetrations of the shaft enclosure as follows:
    To the interior of the building other than at the bottom.
    One of the following conditions must be provided:
    The room must have an approved automatic fire-suppression system.
    Draftstopping materials as follows must be provided in the location indicated below:
    Materials:
    ½" gypsum board.
    ³/₈" wood structural panel.
    ³/₈" particleboard.
    Other approved materials.
    Location:
    Materials must seal around penetrating items at the bottom of the shaft.

  Note: 717.3.1, "Draft-stopping materials," is cited as the source of materials permitted for this function, a summary of which is provided above.

- A shaft enclosure containing either of the following functions must comply with the requirements indicated below:
  - Functions:
    Laundry chute.
    Refuse chute.
  - Requirements:
    The shaft may not be used for any other purpose.
    The shaft must terminate at the bottom in a room as follows:
    Room must be separated from the rest of the building as follows:
    By construction with a fire-resistance rating ≥ 1 hr.
    Openings into the room must be protected as follows:
    By protectives with a fire-protection rating ≥ ¾ hr.
    Openings into the room must be one of the following:
    Self-closing.
    Automatic-closing activated by smoke detection.
    Refuse chutes may not terminate in the following room:
    An incinerator room.

  Note: 707.13.4, "Termination room," is cited as the source of requirements for the termination room serving laundry and refuse chutes.

707 Shaft Enclosures

707.10 Enclosure at the bottom *(part 3 of 3)*

- Other shafts must comply with one of the following requirements:
  - The shaft must be enclosed at the lowest level as follows:
    - By construction with the greater of the following fire-resistance ratings:
      - That of the lowest floor through which the shaft penetrates.
      - That required for the shaft enclosure.
  - The shaft must terminate in a room as follows:
    - The room function must relate to the function of the shaft.
    - The room must be separated from the rest of the building as follows:
      - By construction with the following:
        - A fire-resistance rating ≥ that required for the shaft enclosure.
        - Opening protectives providing the following fire protection:
          - ≥ than the fire protection required for the shaft enclosure.
  - The shaft must be protected with a fire damper as follows:
    - Dampers must be approved.
    - Dampers must be installed as per their listing.
    - Dampers must be installed in the shaft enclosure at the lowest floor level penetrated.

707.12 Enclosure at the top

- Shaft enclosures terminating at a point lower than the roof deck are governed as follows:
  - They must be enclosed at the top with construction as follows:
    - Construction having the greater of the following:
      - Fire-resistance rating ≥ that of the highest floor penetrated.
      - Fire-resistance rating ≥ that required for the shaft enclosure.

707.13 Refuse and laundry chutes

- This section addresses the following:
  - Chutes other than those contained in a single dwelling unit as follows:
    - Laundry chutes.
    - Refuse chutes.
  - Access to chutes.
  - Termination rooms.
  - Incinerator rooms.

707 Shaft Enclosures

707.13.1 Refuse and laundry chute enclosures

- This section addresses shaft enclosures for the following:
  - Refuse chute.
  - Laundry chute.
- Such shaft enclosure may not be used for other purposes.
- Fire-resistance ratings required for such shaft enclosures are as follows:
  - Where they connect < 4 stories:
    The greater of the following fire-resistance ratings is required up to a maximum of 2 hrs:
    ≥ 1 hr.
    ≥ the fire-resistance rating of the floor penetrated.
  - Where they connect ≥ 4 stories:
    A fire-resistance rating ≥ 2 hrs is required.

  Note: 707.4, "Fire-resistance rating," is cited as the source of applicable requirements, a summary of which is provided above.

- Openings into such shafts as follows required fire protection:
  - Openings from access rooms.
  - Openings from termination rooms.
  - All other openings.

  Note: Section 715, "Opening Protectives," is cited as the source of requirements for protecting the openings indicated above, in addition to requirements of this section.

- Exit access corridors may not have openings into chutes.
- Protection for shaft openings must be one of the following:
  - Self-closing.
  - Automatic-closing by one of the following means:
    Activated by heat or smoke as follows:
    Between the shaft and termination room.

  Note: 907.10, "Fire safety functions," is cited as the source of requirements for fire detectors.

707.13.2 Materials

- Shaft enclosures for the following types of chutes require materials as indicated below:
  - Chutes:
    Laundry chute.
    Refuse chute.
  - Materials:
    Must be consistent with the building construction type.

707 Shaft Enclosures

707.13.3 Refuse and laundry chute access rooms

- Chute access openings must be in rooms enclosed as follows:
  - Room construction must have a fire-resistance rating ≥ 1 hr.
  - Openings to access rooms must have protectives as follows:
    With a fire-protection rating ≥ ¾ hr.
    Which close by one of the following means:
      Self-closing.
      Automatic-closing when activated by smoke.

707.13.4 Termination room

- This section governs the following rooms with functions as indicated below:
  - Rooms:
    Laundry.
    Refuse.
  - Functions:
    Receives discharge from chutes.
    Does not receive discharge from chutes.
- Rooms receiving chutes discharge are governed as follows:
  - Room must be separated from the rest of the building as follows:
    Room construction must have a fire-resistance rating ≥ 1 hr.
    Openings to the room must have protectives as follows:
      With a fire-protection rating ≥ ¾ hr.
    Opening protectives must close by one of the following means:
      Self-closing.
      Automatic-closing activated by smoke.
  - Incinerator rooms may not receive refuse by chute.
- Rooms that do not receive chute discharge are governed as follows:
  - Incinerators rooms require the following:
    Must be separated from the rest of the building as follows:
      By ≥ 2 hr fire-resistance-rated construction.
    Room must be sprinklered.
  - The following rooms where > 100 sf are governed as indicated below:
    Rooms:
      Laundry rooms.
      Waste collection.
      Linen collection.
    Requirement:
      Must be separated from the rest of the building as follows:
        By ≥ 1-hr fire-resistance-rated construction.

  Note: IBC Table 302.1.1, "Incidental Use Areas," is cited as the source for fire protection requirements for refuse and laundry rooms without chutes, a partial summary of which is provided above.

707 Shaft Enclosures

707.13.6 Automatic fire sprinkler system

- The following chutes must be sprinklered:
  - Rubbish chutes.
  - Linen chutes.
- Sprinklers for chutes must comply with the following:
  - Characteristics:
    - Must be approved.
    - Must be automatic.
    - Must have access for servicing.
  - Locations:
    - Required at the top of chutes.
    - Required at alternate floors in the following case:
      - Where chutes pass through ≥ 3 floors.

> *Note: 903.2.12.2, "Rubbish and linen chutes," is cited as the source of requirements for sprinklers in chutes, a summary of which is provided above.*

707.14 Elevator and dumbwaiter shafts

- Elevator hoistways and dumbwaiter enclosures are governed by this section.
- Shaft enclosures are governed as follows:
  - Where they connect < 4 stories:
    - The greater of the following fire-resistance ratings is required up to a maximum of 2 hrs:
      - ≥ 1 hr.
      - ≥ the fire-resistance rating of the floor penetrated.
  - Where they connect ≥ 4 stories:
    - A fire-resistance rating ≥ 2 hrs is required.

> *Note: The following are cited as sources of requirements pertaining to the above shafts:*
> *707.4, "Fire-resistance rating," a summary of which is provided above.*
> *Chapter 30, "Elevators and Conveying Systems."*

707.14.1 Elevator lobby *(part 1 of 2)*

- A fire-resistance-rated separation between an elevator lobby and the connecting corridor is not required where all the following conditions are met:
  - The building is an office building.
  - The lobby is on the street-level floor.
  - The entire street-level floor is sprinklered.

> *Note: 903.3.1.1, "NFPA 13 sprinkler systems," is cited as governing the required sprinkler system.*

707 Shaft Enclosures

707.14.1 Elevator lobby *(part 2 of 2)*

- This section does not apply where elevators are not required to have a shaft enclosure.

  Note: 707.2, "Shaft enclosure required," is cited as the source of conditions that do not require a shaft enclosure for an elevator.

- The following doors must comply with requirements listed below:
  - Doors in addition to hoistway doors and elevator car doors as follows:
    Located at the point of access to elevators.
    Located between the hoistway doors and the lobby or corridor.
  - Requirements for additional doors:
    Doors must be readily openable from car side as follows:
    Without a key or tool.
    Without special knowledge.
    Without special effort.

  Note: 3002.6, "Prohibited doors," is cited as defining additional door requirements which are summarized above.

    Doors must be tested for air leakage as follows:
    With no artificial seal applied to the bottom.

  Note: UL 1784, "Air Leakage Tests of Door Assemblies," is cited as describing the test that additional doors must pass.

- A fire-resistance-rated separation between an elevator lobby and the connecting corridor is not required where all the following conditions are present:
  - The building is among the following occupancies:
    A, B, E, F, H, I-1, I-2, I-4, M, R, S, U.
  - The building is ≤ 4 stories above the lowest level of fire department vehicle access.
  - The building is sprinklered throughout as follows:
    Including the elevator lobby.
    Including corridors leading to the elevator lobby.

  Note: The following are cited as alternative requirements for the sprinkler system:
  903.3.1.1, "NFPA 13 sprinkler systems."
  903.3.1.2, "NFPA 13R sprinkler systems."

- In all other cases, elevators opening into a fire-resistance-rated corridor require an elevator lobby as follows:
  - A lobby is required at each floor where elevators open into such a corridor.
  - The lobby must separate the elevators from the corridor with fire barriers as follows:
    With the required opening protection.
  - The lobby must have ≥ 1 means of egress.

  Note: The following are cited as sources of applicable requirements:
  1004.3.2.1, "Construction," governs fire-resistance ratings for corridors.
  Chapter 10, "Means of Egress," governs the means of egress for the lobby.

708 Fire Partitions

708.1 General

- This series of sections governs the following walls:
  - Walls between dwelling units in the same building.
  - Walls separating sleeping units in the following occupancies:
    R-1 hotels.
    R-2.
    I-1.
  - Walls in covered malls between tenant spaces.

    Note: 402.7.2, "Tenant separations," is cited as a source of requirements for these walls.

  - Corridor walls.

    Note: 1016.1, "Construction," is cited the source of requirements for corridor walls. The section excludes certain corridor walls in occupancies E and R, in open parking garages, in a limited range of B occupancies, and in many occupancies with a sprinkler system.

708.2 Materials

- Fire partitions must be constructed of materials as follows:
  - Consistent with building construction type.

708.3 Fire-resistance rating *(part 1 of 2)*

- Walls governed by this section series must have fire-resistance ratings as follows:
  - $\geq$ ½ hr is required where all the following apply:
    Corridor walls.
    Occupancy R.
    Corridor occupant load >10.
    The building is sprinklered.

  Note: The following is cited as governing sprinkler systems that meet the sprinkler requirement:
  903.3.1.1, "NFPA 13 sprinkler systems."

708 Fire Partitions

708.3 Fire-resistance rating *(part 2 of 2)*

- ○ ≥ ½ hr is required where all the following apply:
  - The wall is a separation for any of the following:
    - Dwelling unit.
    - Sleeping unit.
  - The construction type of the building is any of the following:
    - Type IIB.
    - Type IIIB.
    - Type VB.
  - The building is sprinklered.

    Note: 903.3.1.1, "NFPA 13 sprinkler systems," is cited as governing the required sprinkler system.

- ○ ≥ 1 hr is required for all other fire partitions.

    Note: Table 1016.1, "Corridor Fire-Resistance Rating," is cited as listing exceptions to the 1-hr requirement for corridor walls. The table and Section 1016.1, "Construction," identify corridor walls which need no fire-resistance rating as well as listing other requirements.

708.4 Continuity *(part 1 of 3)*

- This section addresses the upper and lower points of termination for a fire partition.
- A fire partition is not required to extend into a crawl space as follows:
  - ○ Where the floor above the crawl space has the following:
    - A fire-resistance rating ≥ 1 hr.
- Requirements listed below apply to the corridor ceiling adjacent to the following membrane:
  - ○ Membrane:
    - Membrane is located on the room side of the corridor wall.
    - Membrane is fire-resistance-rated.
    - Membrane extends to the underside of one of the following as applicable:
      - Fire-resistance-rated floor above.
      - Fire-resistance-rated roof above.
  - ○ Requirements:
    - Corridor ceiling may be protected by ceiling materials as follows:
      - As required for a fire-resistance rating ≥ 1 hr for one of the following:
        - A roof system.
        - A floor system.
- Corridor walls may terminate as follows:
  - ○ At the upper membrane of the corridor ceiling in the following case:
    - Where the corridor ceiling complies with the same requirements as for the walls.

708 Fire Partitions

708.4 Continuity *(part 2 of 3)*

- Fire partitions between mall tenant spaces are governed as follows:
  - They are not required to extend above the following height:
    The underside of a ceiling in the following case:
    Where the ceiling is not part of a fire-resistance-rated assembly.
  - A wall is not required in the following spaces:
    In the attic above tenant separation walls.
    In the ceiling spaces above tenant separation walls.

    Note: 402.7.2, "Tenant separations," is cited as the source requiring tenant spaces to be separated by fire partitions.

- Fireblocking or draftstopping is not required in the following locations:
  - At the line of a fire partition in either of the following cases:
    In occupancy R-2 buildings where all the following conditions apply:
    In buildings $\geq$ 4 stories.
    Where the attic has draftstops isolating areas $\leq$ the smaller of the following:
    Area above every two dwelling units.
    3000 sf.
    In sprinklered buildings as follows:
    Sprinklers are also installed in the following spaces:
    Combustible floor/ceiling spaces.
    Combustible roof/ceiling spaces.

    Note: The following are cited as governing sprinkler systems that meet the sprinkler requirement:
    903.3.1.1, "NFPA 13 sprinkler systems."
    903.3.1.2, "NFPA 13R sprinkler systems."

- Construction supporting a fire partition is governed as follows:
  - Supporting construction need not have a fire-resistance rating $\geq$ that of the partition supported in the following cases:
    Tenant separation walls.
    Sleeping unit separation walls.
    Exit access corridor walls in buildings of the following construction types:
    Types IIB, IIIB, VB.
  - Supporting construction must have a fire-resistance rating $\geq$ that of the partition supported in the following types of construction:
    Types I, IIA, IIIA, IV, VA.

708 Fire Partitions

708.4 Continuity *(part 3 of 3)*

- In all other cases, fire-partition continuity is required as follows:
  - Partitions must extend to the following termination levels:
       Top of floor assembly below.
       Underside of one of the following above:
         Floor slab or deck.
         Roof slab or deck.
         Fire-resistance-rated floor/ceiling assembly.
         Fire-resistance-rated roof/ceiling assembly.
  - Partitions must be securely attached to the termination points.
  - Combustible partitions that do not reach the deck above are governed as follows:
       One of the following is required in the gap between the partition and the deck:
         Space is to be fire-blocked with one of the following materials held securely in place:
           2" nominal lumber.
           2 layers of 1" nominal lumber with staggered joints.
           0.719" wood structural panel with joints backed by the same material.
           0.75" particle board with joints backed by the same material.
           Gypsum board.
           Cement fiber board.
           Batts of mineral wool or glass fiber.
           Blankets of mineral wool or glass fiber.
           Loose-fill insulation only as follows:
             Must be specifically tested in the form and manner of the actual application.
             Ability to remain in place must be demonstrated.
             Ability to retard the spread of fire and hot gases must be demonstrated.
           Other approved material.
         Space is to be draft-stopped with one of the following materials adequately supported:
           0.5" gypsum board.
           0.375" wood structural panel.
           0.375" particle board.
           Other approved material.

    Note: The following are cited as sources of fire-blocking and draft-stopping materials, a summary of which is provided above:
       717.2.1, "Fireblocking materials."
       717.3.1, "Draftstopping materials."

708.5 Exterior walls

- Exterior walls as part of a required fire-resistance-rated enclosure are governed as follows:
  - Such walls must comply with fire-resistance requirements for exterior walls.
  - Fire-resistance-rated enclosure requirements do not apply.

  Note: Section 704, "Exterior Walls," is cited as governing fire-resistance requirements.

709 Smoke Barriers

709.2 Materials

- Materials for smoke barriers must conform to the construction type for the building.

709.3 Fire-resistance rating

- Smoke barriers with both the following characteristics are not required to have a fire-resistance rating $\geq$ 1 hr:
  - Located in occupancy I-3.
  - Constructed of $\geq$ 0.10" thick steel.
- Other smoke barriers must have a fire-resistance rating $\geq$ 1 hr.

709.4 Continuity

- Smoke barriers must form a membrane continuous between the following points:
  - From exterior wall to exterior wall.
  - From floor slab to floor or roof deck above.
- Smoke barriers must be continuous through the following spaces where applicable:
  - Concealed spaces such as above suspended ceilings.
  - Interstitial structural or mechanical space in the following case:
    - Where ceilings do not resist the passage of fire and smoke to the following degree:
      - To a degree equal that of the smoke barrier walls.
- Construction supporting smoke barriers must have a fire-resistance rating $\geq$ that of the wall or floor supported in the following construction types:
  - Types I, IIA, IIIA, IV, VA.

> **Case study: Fig. 709.4.** The 2nd floor of the hospital's south wing, as shown, is separated into 2 smoke compartments by a wall acting as a smoke barrier. The barrier provides a continuous membrane in the form of a wall across the building and from the 2nd floor to the floor above. It is continuous through the space above the suspended ceiling. Construction supporting the smoke barrier has a fire-resistance rating $\geq$ the barrier as required.

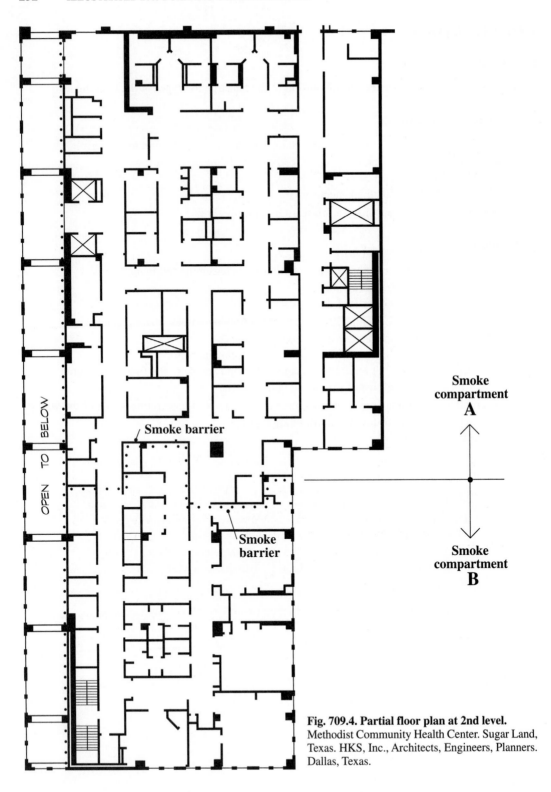

Fig. 709.4. Partial floor plan at 2nd level.
Methodist Community Health Center. Sugar Land, Texas. HKS, Inc., Architects, Engineers, Planners. Dallas, Texas.

709 Smoke Barriers

709.5 Openings

- Doors with all the following characteristics need not meet the requirements indicated below:
  - Characteristics:
    - In occupancy I-2.
    - Located across a corridor.
    - In a smoke barrier.
    - Opposite swinging with no center mullion.
    - With vision panels as follows:
      - Approved fire-resistance-rated glazing and frames.
      - With an area ≤ that tested.
    - Close fitting within operational tolerances.
    - With none of the following:
      - Undercuts.
      - Louvers or grilles.
    - With all the following:
      - Head stops.
      - Jamb stops.
      - Astragals at meeting edges.
      - Rabbets at meeting edges.
      - Automatic-closing devices.
  - Requirements:
    - Doors need not have meet other opening protection requirements.
    - Doors need not have a fire-protection rating of 20 min.
    - Positive-latching devices are not required.
- All other openings in smoke barriers must meet both the following requirements:
  - Openings must comply with opening protective requirements.
  - Openings must have a fire-protection rating ≥ 20 min.

  Note: Section 715, "Opening Protectives," is cited as governing the opening protective requirements for openings in smoke barriers.

710 Smoke Partitions

710.1 General

- This series of sections governs smoke partitions required elsewhere in the code.

710.2 Materials

- Smoke partition materials are governed by the construction type of the building.

710.3 Fire-resistance rating

- The following smoke partitions do not require a fire-resistance rating:
  - Where not required by other sections of the code.

710.4 Continuity

- Smoke partitions must extend to the following termination points:
  - The floor.
  - One of the following:
    Underside of the roof deck overhead.
    Underside of the floor deck overhead.
    Underside of a ceiling built to limit the passage of smoke.

710.5 Openings

- Windows in smoke partitions must comply with one of the following:
  - Sealed to prevent the passage of smoke.
  - Close automatically as follows:
    When smoke is detected.
- Doors are governed in subsequent entries of this section series.

710.5.1 Louvers

- Louvers are prohibited in the following:
  - Doors in smoke partitions.

710.5.2 Smoke and draft-control doors

- Where other sections of the code require doors in smoke partitions to control smoke and drafts, all the following apply:
  - They must be tested for air leakage as per all the following requirements:
    An artificial seal must be in place across the bottom of the door.
    Air leakage may not be > 3 cfm/sf of door opening as follows:
      At 0.10" of water for both the following:
        Ambient temperature test.
        Elevated-temperature exposure test.

Note: UL 1784, "Air Leakage Tests of Door Assemblies," is cited as the applicable test.

710 Smoke Partitions

710.5.3 Self-closing or automatic-closing doors

- Where other sections of the code require any of these doors in smoke partitions, the following applies:
  - Door closing must be activated by any of the following:
    Detection of smoke by a smoke detector as follows:
      Door must start to close within 10 seconds of detector activation.
    Loss of power to smoke detectors.
    Loss of power to mechanism holding door open.

  Note: 715.3.7.3, "Smoke-activated doors," is cited as governing these doors and is partially summarized above.

710.6 Penetrations and joints

- Gaps at the following locations must be filled with a material as indicated below:
  - Locations:
    Around elements penetrating a smoke partition.
    At joints in smoke partitions.
  - Fill material must comply with both the following:
    Must be approved.
    Must retard the transfer of smoke.

710.7 Ducts and air transfer openings

- Openings for the passage of air through smoke partitions are governed as follows:
  - Where a smoke damper will not interfere with a required smoke control system:
    A smoke damper is required.

  Note: 716.3.2, "Smoke damper ratings," is cited as governing the smoke dampers and addresses class and temperature ratings as well as actuation methods.

  - Where a smoke damper would interfere with a required smoke control system:
    An approved protection system as an alternative to a smoke damper is required.

  Note: Section 909, "Smoke Control Systems," is cited as governing the system which must be compatible with air passage openings in smoke partitions.

711 Horizontal Assemblies

711.2 Materials

- Construction for the following must be consistent with the building construction type:
  - Roof and floor assemblies.

711.3 Fire-resistance rating *(part 1 of 2)*

- Floor and roof assemblies must have fire-resistance ratings as follows:
  - ≥ that dictated by the building construction type.
- Floor assemblies separating occupancies are governed as follows:
  - They must have the fire-resistance rating required for mixed occupancy separations.

  Note: 302.3.2, "Separated uses," is cited as the source of fire-resistance ratings required for separating occupancies.

- Floor assemblies dividing an occupancy into fire areas are governed as follows:
  - They must have the following fire-resistance ratings:
    - ≥ 1 hr for the following occupancy:
      - U.
    - ≥ 3 hr for the following occupancies:
      - F-1, H-3, S-1.
    - ≥ 4 hr for the following occupancies:
      - H-1, H-2.
    - ≥ 2 hr for all other occupancies.

  Note: 706.3.7, "Single-occupancy fire areas," is cited as the source of requirements for dividing an occupancy into fire areas. The section is summarized above with data from IBC Table 706.3.7.

- Floor assemblies separating the following units require fire-resistance ratings as indicated below:
  - Units:
    - Dwelling units in the same building.
    - Sleeping units in the following occupancies:
      - R-1 hotels.
      - R-2.
      - I-1.

711 Horizontal Assemblies

711.3 Fire-resistance rating *(part 2 of 2)*

- Fire-resistance ratings required:
  - ≥ ½ hr in any of the following construction types where sprinklers are provided:
    Type IIB.
    Type IIIB.
    Type VB.
  - ≥ 1 hr in the following occupancies which do not qualify for the ½-hr rating specified:
    Dwelling units in the same building.
    Sleeping units in the following occupancies:
      R-1 hotels.
      R-2.
      I-1.

  Note: 903.3.1.1, "NFPA sprinkler systems," is cited as governing the sprinkler system.

711.3.1 Ceiling panels

- Lay-in ceiling panels must resist upward displacement as follows:
  - From a force ≤ 1 psf by one of the following methods:
    Self-weight.
    One of the following restraining systems above the panel:
      Wire system.
      Other approved system.

711.3.1.2 Access doors

- Access doors in a fire-resistance-rated ceiling must have the following characteristics:
  - They must be approved.
  - They must be listed for their purpose.

711.3.3 Unusable space

- The following membranes may be omitted from 1-hr fire-resistance-rated horizontal assemblies:
  - The ceiling membrane as follows:
    At floor construction directly over an unusable crawl space.
  - The floor membrane as follows:
    At ceiling construction directly below unusable attic space.

711 Horizontal Assemblies

711.4 Continuity

- Supporting construction must have a fire-resistance rating as follows:
  - ≥ the horizontal assembly supported.
- Horizontal assemblies must be continuous as follows:
  - Discontinuity is permitted as follows only where indicated by the code:
    Openings.
    Penetrations.
    Joints.
  - Discontinuity is governed as follows:
    Shaft enclosures are required for most openings through a horizontal assembly.
    Penetrations must be detailed to maintain the integrity of the horizontal assembly.
    Joints must be detailed to maintain the integrity of the horizontal assembly.

    Note: The following are cited as sources of applicable requirements:
    707.2, "Shaft enclosure required," governs openings in horizontal assemblies,
    indicating where they are required and where not required.
    712.4, "Horizontal assemblies," governs penetrations.
    Section 713, "Fire-Resistant Joint Systems," governs joints.

  - Skylights and other penetrations in fire-resistance-rated roof construction are governed as follows:
    They must be protected where they would create a fire hazard as follows:
      To a higher wall of an adjacent building on the same lot.
    The structural integrity of the roof construction must be maintained.

    Note: 704.10, "Vertical exposure," is cited as the source of conditions defining a fire
    hazard for adjacent buildings on the same lot.

    Otherwise, skylights need not be protected as follows:
      Where the structural integrity of the fire-resistance-rated roof assembly is
      maintained.

712 Penetrations

712.1 Scope

- This section governs the protection of the following penetrations:
  - Penetrations passing entirely through assemblies.
  - Penetrations passing through membranes of assemblies.

712.2 Installation details

- Sleeves in penetrations are governed as follows:
  - Sleeves must be secured to the assembly penetrated.
  - The following spaces must be protected as per requirements of this section:
    Between a sleeve and the component inside the sleeve.
    Between a sleeve and the opening through which the sleeve passes.
- Insulation or covering as part of a penetrating element is governed as follows:
  - The materials may not penetrate an assembly except for the following case:
    Where they have been tested with the assembly as per requirements of this section.

712.3 Fire-resistance-rated walls

- This section governs penetrations into or through the following:
  - Fire walls.
  - Fire barriers.
  - Smoke barrier walls.
  - Fire partitions.

712.3.1 Through penetrations *(part 1 of 2)*

- This section addresses protection of penetrations through fire-resistive-rated walls.
- The following penetrating items must comply with one of the alternative protection methods indicated in this section or with the other requirements of this section:
  - Penetrating items:
    Steel pipes.
    Steel condiuts.
    Ferrous pipes.
    Copper pipes.

712 Penetrations

712.3.1 Through penetrations *(part 2 of 2)*

- Alternative protection for the metallic penetrating items listed above in this section is as follows:
  - Where concrete or masonry walls are penetrated:
    - Annular space may filled with concrete, mortar, or grout in the following conditions:
      - The penetrating item must be $\leq 6"$ nominal diameter.
      - The opening must be ≤ 144 sq in.
      - Annular space must be filled to one of the following extents:
        - Filled to the full thickness of the wall.
        - Filled to a thickness adequate to maintain the fire-resistance rating of the wall.
  - Where other walls are penetrated:
    - The annular space may be filled with a substance able to perform as follows:
      - Prevents passage of the following fire hazards for the time period indicated below:
        - Fire hazards:
          - Flame.
          - Gases as follows:
            - Hot enough to ignite cotton waste in the following conditions:
              - With a positive pressure differential at penetration $\geq 0.01"$ of water.
        - Time period:
          - For a length of time = the fire-resistance rating of the wall penetrated.

    Note: ASTM E 119, "Standard Test Methods for Fire Tests of Building Construction and Materials," is cited as governing the substance filling the annular space.

- Other through penetrations must meet requirements of the next 2 sections in this series.

    Note: The following are cited as through penetrations of fire-resistance-rated walls:
    712.3.1.1, "Fire-resistance-rated assemblies."
    712.3.1.2, "Through-penetration firestop system."

712.3.1.1 Fire-resistance-rated assemblies

- Penetrations must be installed as follows:
  - In an approved fire-resistance-rated assembly.
  - In the same detailing as tested.

712 Penetrations

712.3.1.2 Through-penetration firestop system

- Through penetrations must be protected as follows:
  - By a penetration fire-stop system with the following conditions:
    Must be approved.
    Must be installed as tested.
    Must be tested with a positive pressure differential ≥ 0.01" of water.
    Must have an F rating ≥ the required fire-resistance rating of the wall penetrated.

  Note: The required test must conform to one of the following cited standards:
  ASTM E 814, "Standard Test Method of Fire Tests of Through-Penetration Fire Stops."
  UL 1479, "Fire Tests of Through-Penetration Firestops."

712.3.2 Membrane penetrations *(part 1 of 2)*

- Steel electrical boxes may penetrate a membrane as follows:
  - The area of the box must be ≤ 16 sq in.
  - The sum of opening areas in any 100 sf of wall must be ≤ 100 sq in.
  - Outlet boxes on opposite faces of a wall must be separated by one of the following:
    By one of the following horizontal distances:
      ≥ the depth of the wall cavity where filled with any of the following insulation:
        Cellulose loose-fill.
        Slag mineral wool.
        Rockwool.
      ≥ 24" in other cases.
    By solid fire-blocking with one of the following materials held securely in place:
      2" nominal lumber.
      2 layers of 1" nominal lumber with staggered joints.
      0.719" wood structural panel with joints backed by the same material.
      0.75" particle board with joints backed by the same material.
      Gypsum board.
      Cement fiber board.
      Batts of mineral wool or glass fiber.
      Blankets of mineral wool or glass fiber.
      Loose-fill insulation only as follows:
        Must be specifically tested in the form and manner of the actual application.
        Ability to remain in place must be demonstrated.
        Ability to retard the spread of fire must be demonstrated.
        Ability to retard the spread of hot gases must be demonstrated.
      Other approved material.
    By using putty pads to protect both outlet boxes as follows:
      Putty pads must be listed.
    By other listed materials and methods.

  Note: 717.2.1, "Fireblocking materials," is cited as applicable.

712 Penetrations

712.3.2 Membrane penetrations *(part 2 of 2)*

- Electrical outlet boxes of any material may penetrate a membrane where they meet all the following conditions:
  ○ Boxes must be listed.
  ○ Boxes must be tested for use in a fire-resistance-rated wall.
  ○ Boxes must be installed according to their listing.
  ○ Outlet boxes located on opposite faces of a wall must be separated by one of the following:
    By a distance ≥ 24" measured horizontally.
    By solid fire-blocking with one of the following materials held securely in place:
      2" nominal lumber.
      2 layers of 1" nominal lumber with staggered joints.
      0.719" wood structural panel with joints backed by the same material.
      0.75" particle board with joints backed by the same material.
      Gypsum board.
      Cement fiber board.
      Batts of mineral wool or glass fiber.
      Blankets of mineral wool or glass fiber.
      Loose-fill insulation only as follows:
        Must be specifically tested in the form and manner of the actual application.
        Ability to remain in place must be demonstrated.
        Ability to retard the spread of fire must be demonstrated.
        Ability to retard the spread of hot gases must be demonstrated.
      Other approved material.
    By using putty pads to protect both outlet boxes as follows:
      Putty pads must be listed.
    By other materials and methods that are listed.

  Note: 717.2.1, "Fireblocking materials," is cited as the source materials that meet the fire-blocking requirement.

- The gap around a fire-sprinkler pipe penetration is governed as follows:
  ○ It must be covered by a metal escutcheon plate.
- Recessed fixtures may not reduce the fire-resistance rating of the following:
  Walls or partitions having a required fire-resistance rating ≥ 1 hr.
- Other membrane penetrations must be protected as are through penetrations.

  Note: 712.3.1, "Through penetrations," is cited as the source for the necessary protection methods for membrane penetrations.

712 Penetrations

712.3.3 Ducts and air transfer openings

- This section governs the penetrations of fire-resistance rated walls by the following components where no fire dampers are provided:
  - Ducts.
  - Air transfer openings.

712.3.4 Dissimilar materials

- The following connection is permitted only with the condition indicated below:
  - Connection:
    Between the following components at a point beyond the fire-stopping:
      Noncombustible penetrating component.
      Combustible component.
  - Condition:
    It must be shown that the required fire resistance of the wall is not diminished.

712.4 Horizontal assemblies *(part 1 of 2)*

- This section addresses penetrations through the following:
  - Floor assembly.
  - Floor/ceiling assembly.
  - Ceiling membrane of a roof/ceiling assembly.
- Penetrations by the following components must comply with selected sections of this series as noted below:
  - Pipes.
  - Tubes.
  - Conduits.
  - Wire.
  - Cable.
  - Vents.
  - Ducts.

  Note: 707.2, "Shaft enclosure required," is cited. Exceptions 3 and 5 are noted as identifying penetrating components (as listed above) which are governed by the following sections:"
  712.4.1, "Through penetrations."
  712.4.2, "Membrane penetrations."
  712.4.3, "Nonfire-resistance-rated assemblies."
  712.4.4, "Ducts and air transfer openings."

712 Penetrations

712.4 Horizontal assemblies *(part 2 of 2)*

- Penetrations in the following locations are not required to have a shaft enclosure:
  - In spaces where floor openings do not require a shaft enclosure.

    Note: 707.2, "Shaft enclosure required," is cited as defining spaces where floor openings do not require a shaft enclosure in Exceptions 1, 2, 5, 7, 8, and 9. Certain of the following spaces are included where they meet specified requirements: dwelling units, nonegress escalators and stairways in sprinklered buildings, covered malls, atriums, certain detailing for limited heights, car ramps in open parking garages, and mezzanines.

- In all other cases, penetrations must meet requirements for shaft and vertical exit enclosures.

    Note: Section 707, "Shaft and Vertical Exit Enclosures," is cited as governing penetrations of the assemblies above.

712.4.1 Through penetrations *(part 1 of 2)*

- This section addresses penetrations passing entirely through fire-resistance-rated horizontal assemblies.
- Requirements for penetrations of single fire-resistance-rated floors are indicated below for the following penetrating items:
  - Penetrating items:
    The following components in the materials indicated below:
    Components:
    Conduits, tubes, and pipes.
    Vents.
    Materials:
    Steel and ferrous metals.
    Copper.
    Concrete and masonry elements.
  - Requirements:
    The annular space must be filled with a substance able to perform as follows:
    Prevents passage of the following fire hazards for the time period indicated below:
    Fire hazards:
    Flame.
    Gases as follows:
    Hot enough to ignite cotton waste in the following condition:
    With a positive pressure differential at penetration $\geq 0.01"$ of water.
    Time period:
    For a length of time = the fire-resistance rating of the wall penetrated.

    Note: ASTM E 119, "Standard Test Methods for Fire Tests of Building Construction and Materials," is cited as governing the substance filling the annular space.

712 Penetrations

712.4.1 Through penetrations *(part 2 of 2)*

- ○ Penetrations are not limited to a single floor where both of the following conditions are met:
  - The penetrating component is ≤ 6" nominal diameter.
  - The area of penetration is ≤ 144 sq in.
- • Electrical outlet boxes of any material may be used as follows:
  - ○ They must be tested for use in such assemblies.
  - ○ They must be installed as tested in such assemblies.
- • Requirements are indicated below for penetrations of a single concrete floor by the following items:
  - ○ Penetrating items:
    - The following components in the materials indicated below:
      - Components:
        - Conduits, tubes, and pipes.
        - Vents.
      - Materials:
        - Steel and ferrous metals.
        - Copper.
  - ○ Requirements:
    - Diameter of penetrating item must be ≤ 6".
    - The annular space must be filled with one of the following:
      - Concrete.
      - Grout.
      - Mortar.
    - The extent of the fill in the annular space must be one of the following:
      - For the full thickness of the floor.
      - ≥ a thickness which does not diminish the required fire-resistance rating.
  - ○ Penetrations are not limited to a single floor where area of the penetration is ≤ 144 sq in.
- • Other penetrations must comply with one of the following:
  - ○ They must be installed as they were tested in the approved fire-resistance-rated assembly.
  - ○ They must be protected by an approved through-penetration fire-stop system.

  Note: The following are cited as sources of requirements for other penetrations, partial summaries of which are provided above:
  712.4.1.1, "Fire-resistance-rated assemblies."
  712.4.1.2, "Through-penetration firestop system."

712.4.1.1 Fire-resistance-rated assemblies

- • Through penetrations of fire-resistance-rated horizontal assemblies are governed as follows:
  - ○ Penetrations must be installed in the manner tested in the approved assembly.

  Note: 711.4.1, "Through penetrations," requires compliance with either this subsection or 711.4.1.2, "Through-penetration firestop system."

712 Penetrations

712.4.1.2 Through-penetration firestop system

- Through penetrations of fire-resistance-rated horizontal assemblies must be protected by an approved through-penetration fire-stop system tested and installed as follows:
  - System must be tested as follows:
    With a positive pressure differential of ≥ 0.01" of water.
  - System must be installed as tested.
- Through penetrations of fire-resistance-rated horizontal assemblies must be protected by a fire-stop system with the following F and T ratings:
  - System must have an F rating ≥ the larger of the following:
    1 hr.
    The rating of the floor penetrated.
  - System T rating is governed as follows:
    No T rating is required for a floor penetration within the cavity of a wall.
    Otherwise, T rating must be ≥ the larger of the following:
    1 hr.
    The rating of the floor penetrated.

    Note: The following as cited as alternative standards for the fire-stop system.
    ASTM E 814, "Standard Test Method of Fire Tests of Through-Penetration Fire Stops."
    UL 1479, "Fire Tests of Through-Penetration Fire Stops."

712.4.2 Membrane penetrations *(part 1 of 2)*

- This section addresses membrane penetrations in horizontal assemblies with a fire-resistance rating.
- Requirements for penetrations by the following elements are listed below:
  - Penetrating elements:
    The following components can be any of the materials listed as appropriate:
    Components:
    Conduits.
    Electrical outlet boxes.
    Tubes.
    Pipes.
    Vents.
    Materials:
    Steel.
    Ferrous metals.
    Copper.
    Concrete elements.
    Masonry elements.

712 Penetrations

712.4.2 Membrane penetrations *(part 2 of 2)*

- ○ Requirements:
     The gap around the penetrating item must comply with one of the following:
         Must be protected as per code requirements.
         Must be protected to prevent the passage of the following:
             Flame.
             Products of combustion.
     Where assemblies were tested without penetrations:
         The sum of penetration areas is limited as follows:
             ≤ 100 sq in in any 100 sf of ceiling area.

   Note: 712.4.1, "Through penetrations," is cited as governing the protection gaps around penetrations.

- Penetrations by electrical outlet boxes of any material are allowed as follows:
  - ○ Boxes must be listed.
  - ○ Boxes must be tested for use in assemblies with fire-resistance ratings.
  - ○ Boxes must be installed as per instructions dictated by their listing.
- A metal escutcheon plate must cover the following:
  - ○ The gap around a fire-sprinkler pipe penetration.
- Other penetrations must comply with one of the following:
  - ○ Must be as tested in the approved fire-resistance-rated assembly.
  - ○ Must be protected by an approved through-penetration fire-stop system.

   Note: The following are cited as governing the requirements for other penetrations, a partial summary of which is provided above:
   711.4.1.1, "Fire-resistance-rated assemblies."
   711.4.1.2, "Through-penetration firestop system."

- Recessed fixtures may not reduce the fire-resistance rating of the following assembly:
  - ○ Floor/ceiling assemblies with a required fire-resistance rating of ≥ 1 hr.

712 Penetrations

712.4.3 Nonfire-resistance-rated assemblies

- This section addresses penetrations of horizontal assemblies that are not required to have a fire-resistance rating.
- Penetrations must meet one of the following requirements:
  - Penetrations as follows must meet the requirements indicated below:
    Penetrations:
      Noncombustible elements.
      Connecting ≤ 3 stories.
    Requirement:
      Annular space must be filled with a material as follows:
        Must be approved.
        Must be noncombustible.
        Must restrict the passage of flame.
        Must restrict the passage combustion products.

    Note: 712.4.3.1, "Noncombustible penetrating items," is cited as an alternative source of requirements and is summarized above.

  - Penetrations connecting ≤ 2 stories are governed as follows:
    Annular space must be filled with a material as follows:
      Must be approved.
      Must restrict the passage of flame.
      Must restrict the passage combustion products.

    Note: 712.4.3.2, "Penetrating items," is cited as an alternative source of requirements and is summarized above.

  - Penetrations must be protected by a shaft enclosure.

    Note: Section 707, "Shaft Enclosures," is cited as governing shaft enclosures and is an alternative source of requirements.

712.4.3.1 Noncombustible penetrating items

- Penetrations as follows must meet the requirements indicated below:
  - Penetrations:
    Noncombustible items.
    Connecting ≤ 3 stories.
  - Requirement:
    Annular space must be filled with an approved noncombustible material as follows:
      Must restrict the passage of flame and combustion products.

712.4.3.2 Penetrating items

- Penetrations connecting ≤ 2 stories are governed as follows:
  - Annular space must be filled with an approved material as follows:
    Must restrict the passage of flame and combustion products.

712 Penetrations

712.4.4 Ducts and air transfer openings

- Penetrations of horizontal assemblies by ducts and air transfer openings must meet the following requirements:
  - Where not required to have dampers:
    Penetrations must comply with this section.
  - Where provided with dampers:
    Penetrations must comply with requirements as follows:
      Those addressing ducts and air-transfer openings elsewhere in the code.

    Note: Section 716, "Ducts and Air Transfer Openings," is cited as governing penetrations by these components with dampers.

712.4.5 Dissimilar materials

- The following connection is permitted only with the condition indicated below:
  - Connection:
    Between the following components at a point beyond the fire-stopping:
      Noncombustible penetrating component.
      Combustible component.
  - Condition:
    It must be shown that the required fire-resistance of the assembly is not diminished.

712.4.6 Floor fire doors

- Fire doors in floors with a fire-resistance rating must comply with the following:
  - Doors must be tested in a horizontal position.
  - Doors must have a fire-resistance rating $\geq$ the assembly penetrated.
  - Doors must be labeled by an approved agency.

    Note: ASTM E 119, "Standard Test Methods for Fire Tests of Building Construction and Materials," is cited as the required test.

715 Opening Protectives

715.2 Fire-resistance-rated glazing

- The following is not governed by this section series:
  - Labeled fire-resistance-rated glazing tested as follows:
    As part of a wall with a fire-resistance rating.

    Note: ASTM E 119, "Test Methods for Fire Tests of Building Construction and Materials."

715.3 Fire door and shutter assemblies *(part 1 of 2)*

- Approved fire door and shutter assemblies are governed as follows:
  - They may be of any material(s) as follows:
    Materials must comply with specified fire tests.
  - They must be installed by the standard cited for fire doors and windows.

    Note: NFPA 80, "Fire Doors and Windows," is cited as governing fire door installation. The following are cited as specifying required tests for doors other than tin-clad fire doors:
    715.3.1, "Side-hinged or pivoted swinging doors."
    715.3.2, "Other types of doors."
    715.3.3, "Door assemblies in corridors and smoke barriers."
    The following are cited as governing tin-clad fire doors:
    UL 10A, "Tin Clad Fire Doors."
    UL 14B, "Sliding Hardware for Standard Horizontally Mounted Tin Clad Fire Doors."
    UL 14C, "Swinging Hardware for Standard Tin Clad Fire Doors Mounted Single and in Pairs."

- Approved fire door and shutter assemblies must have the following fire-protection ratings:*
  - ≥ 20 minutes where located in either of the following where tested as specified:
    ½-hr fire-resistance-rated fire partition corridor wall.
    1-hr fire-resistance-rated fire partition corridor wall.

    Note: 715.3.3, "Door assemblies in corridors and smoke barriers," is cited as identifying tests for the doors and shutter assemblies. Required tests include NFPA 252, "Standard Methods of Fire Tests of Door Assemblies," or UL 10C, "Positive Pressure Tests of Door Assemblies," NFPA 257, "Standard for Fire Test for Window and Glass Block Assemblies," and UL 1784, "Air Leakage Tests of Door Assemblies."

*Source: IBC Table 715.3.

715 Opening Protectives

715.3 Fire door and shutter assemblies *(part 2 of 2)**

- ≥ ¾ hr where located in the following:
    1-hr fire-resistance-rated walls in any of the following applications:
        Exterior walls.
        Fire partitions other than corridor walls.
        Fire barriers other than the following:
            Shaft exit enclosure walls.
            Exit passageway walls.
- ≥ 1 hr where located in the following:
    1-hr fire-resistance-rated fire barriers in either of the following applications:
        Shaft exit enclosure walls.
        Exit passageway walls.
- ≥ 1½ hr where located in one of the following:
    1½-hr fire-resistance-rated walls of either of the following types:
        Fire walls.
        Fire-barriers.
    2-hr fire-resistance-rated walls of any of the following types:
        Fire walls.
        Fire barriers.
        Exterior walls.
- ≥ 1½ hr where located in the following:
    3-hr fire-resistance-rated exterior wall.
- ≥ 1½ hr each where 2 doors or shutters meet all the following conditions:
    Located at the same opening.
    One door is on each side of a wall with all the following characteristics:
        3-hr fire-resistance-rated.
        Wall is one of the following types:
            Fire wall.
            Fire barrier.
- ≥ 3 hr where located in a fire wall or fire barrier with one of the following ratings:
    3-hr fire-resistance rating.
    4-hr fire-resistance rating.

Source: IBC Table 715.3.

715 Opening Protectives

715.3.4.1 Glazing in doors

- Glazing larger than 100 sq in is allowed in fire door assemblies as follows:
  - Glazing must have a fire-protection rating.
  - Glazing must be tested as follows:
    As a component of the door assembly, not as a glass light.
    The transmitted temperature endpoint is governed as follows:
    $\leq 450°F$ above ambient after ½ hr of testing.
    Not limited as follows:
    Where the building is sprinklered as per NFPA 13 or 13R.

  Note: NFPA 252, "Standard Method of Fire Tests of Door Assemblies," is cited as governing the test required above for glazing.

715.3.6 Glazing material

- Fire door assemblies may have glazing that conforms to the following:
  - Glazing must have a fire-protection rating.
  - Glazing must conform to opening protection requirements.

  Note: 714.2, "Fire door and shutter assemblies," is cited as the source of opening protection requirements.

715.3.6.1 Size limitations

- Glazing in fire doors in fire walls is governed as follows:
  - Where doors are serving as a horizontal exit, the following applies:
    A glazed vision panel is permitted as follows:
    Door must be swinging type.
    Door must be self-closing.
    Glazing must have a fire-protection rating.
    Glazing area is limited to ≤ 100 sq in.
    Glazing dimensions are limited to ≤ 10 in.
  - In other cases, glazing is not permitted.
- Glazing in fire doors in fire barriers is governed as follows:
  - Glazing must have a fire-protection rating.
  - Where such doors have a 1½-hr rating:
    Glazing area is limited to ≤ 100 sq in.
- In other cases, glazing in fire doors shall comply with one of the following:
  - Wired glass is limited in size based on its fire-protection rating.
  - Fire-protection-rated glass other than wired glass is governed as follows:
    It must comply with size requirements of the applicable standard.

  Note: The following are cited as governing the glass above:
  NFPA 80, "Fire Doors and Windows," for glass that is not wired glass.
  IBC Table 715.4.3, "Limiting Sizes of Wired Glass Panels," for wired glass.

Case study: Fig. 715.3.6.1. Wired glass is provided in the 1-hr fire door at the exit enclosre. IBC Table 715.4.3 limits the area of such glass to 100 sq in where the fire-protection rating of the opening is 1 hr. The height of the glass is limited to 33", and the maximum width permitted by the table is 10". The 10" × 10" glass meets these requirements.

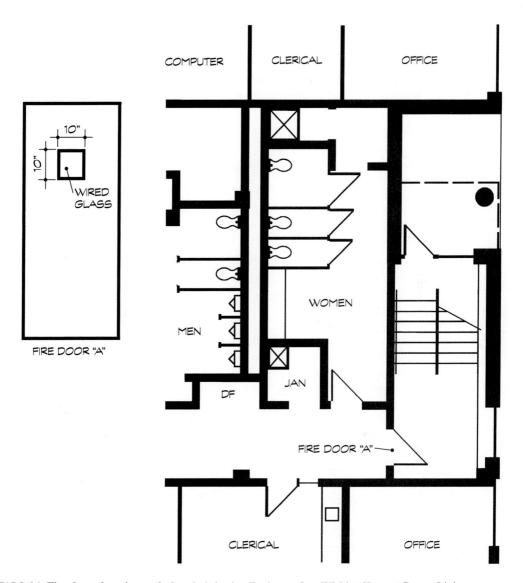

Fig. 715.3.6.1. Fire door elevation and plan. Lubrication Engineers, Inc. Wichita, Kansas. Gossen Livingston Associates, Inc., Architecture. Wichita, Kansas.

715 Opening Protectives

715.4.3 Wired glass

- A ¾-hr fire window assembly has the following characteristics:
  - ○ The window frame is one of the following materials:
    - ≥ 0.125" thick solid steel.
    - ≥ 0.048" thick formed sheet steel.
  - ○ The window frame is fabricated by any of the following methods:
    - Pressing.
    - Mitering.
    - Riveting.
    - Interlocking.
    - Welding.
  - ○ The window frame is able to receive ¼" wired glass.
  - ○ The window frame is secured into the building construction.
  - ○ The glazing is ¼" thick wired glass.
  - ○ The glazing is labeled.
- Wired glass size limitations are as follows:*
  - ○ Where located in openings requiring the following:
    - 3-hr fire-protection rating:
      - Not permitted.
  - ○ Where located in doors of exterior walls requiring the following:
    - 1½-hr fire-protection rating:
      - Not permitted.
  - ○ Where located in openings requiring the following:
    - 1-hr fire-protection rating:
      - Area must be ≤ 100 sq in.
      - Height must be ≤ 33".
      - Width must be ≤ 10".
  - ○ Where located in openings requiring the following:
    - 1½-hr fire-protection rating:
      - Area must be ≤ 100 sq in.
      - Height must be ≤ 33".
      - Width must be ≤ 10".
  - ○ Where located in openings requiring the following:
    - ¾-hr fire-protection rating:
      - Area must be ≤ 1296 sq in.
      - Each dimension must be ≤ 54".
  - ○ Where located in openings requiring the following:
    - 20-minute fire-protection rating:
      - Area not limited.
      - Dimensions not limited.
  - ○ Fire window assemblies:
    - Area must be ≤ 1296 sq in.
    - Each dimension must be ≤ 54".

Source: IBC Table 715.4.3.

715 Opening Protectives

715.4.4 Nonwired glass

- Glazing other than wired glass where used in fire window assemblies is governed as follows:
  - It must be fire-protection-rated.
  - It must comply with standards other than this code for installation and size.

  Note: NFPA 80, "Fire Doors and Windows," is cited as governing glazing other than wired glass used in fire window assemblies.

715.4.5 Installation

- Glazing with a fire-protection rating must comply with the following:
  - Frames must be approved.
  - Glazing must be fixed or automatic-closing.

715.4.6 Window mullions

- The following metal mullions must comply with the requirement indicated below:
  - Mullions:
    Serving glazing with a fire-protection rating.
    > 12' tall.
  - Requirement:
    Mullion fire-resistance rating must be ≥ that of the wall.

715.4.7 Interior fire window assemblies

- This section governs glazing with a fire-protection rating as used in fire window assemblies.
- Such glazing is limited to use of the following components:
  - Fire partitions with a fire-resistance rating ≤ 1 hr.
  - Fire barriers with a fire-resistance rating ≤ 1 hr.

715.4.7.1 Where permitted

- This section governs glazing with a fire-protection rating.
- Such glazing may be used only in the following applications:
  - Fire partitions with a fire-resistance rating of 1 hr.
  - Fire barriers as follows:
    With a fire-resistance rating of 1 hr.
    Separating the following:
    Incidental use areas from the rest of the building.
    Mixed occupancies from each other.
    A single occupancy into different fire areas.

  Note: The following are cited as governing the partitions and barriers indicated above:
  Section 708, "Fire Partitions."
  706.3.5, "Incidental use areas," addresses fire barriers.
  706.3.6, "Separation of mixed occupancies," addresses fire barriers.

715 Opening Protectives

715.4.7.2 Size limitations

- The sum of window areas is limited to ≤ 25% of the following walls between rooms:
  - Fire partitions and fire barriers.

715.4.8 Exterior fire window assemblies *(part 1 of 2)*

- Exterior openings require a fire-protection rating ≥ 1½ hr as follows:
  - Where all the following conditions apply:
    Openings that are not doors.
    Openings that are required to be protected based on the following:
    Size.
    Relationship to other openings above and below.
    Relationship to a lower roof on the same property.
    Openings in walls required to have a fire-resistance rating as follows:
    >1 hr based on fire-separation distance.

  Note: The following are cited as sources of requirements applicable to the openings indicated above:
  704.12, "Opening protection," identifies openings that require protection based on size, relationships to other openings above and below, and to a lower roof on the same property.
  IBC Table 602, "Fire-Resistance Rating Requirements for Exterior Walls Based on Fire Separation Distance."

- Exterior openings require a fire-protection rating ≥ ¾ hr as follows:
  - Where all the following conditions apply:
    Openings that are required to be protected based on size.
    Openings in walls required to have a fire-resistance rating as follows:
    1 hr based on fire-separation distance.

  Note: The following are cited as sources of applicable requirements:
  704.8, "Allowable area of openings," identifies openings that require protection based on size.
  IBC Table 602, "Fire-Resistance Rating Requirements for Exterior Walls Based on Fire Separation Distance."

- Exterior openings require a fire-protection rating ≥ ¾ hr as follows:
  - Where openings are required to be protected based on the following:
    Relationship to other openings above and below.
    Relationship to a lower roof on the same property.

  Note: The following are cited as defining openings addressed above:
  704.9, "Vertical separation of openings," identifies openings that require protection based on relationships to other openings above and below.
  704.10, "Vertical exposure," identifies openings that require protection based on relationships to a lower roof on the same property.

715 Opening Protectives

715.4.8 Exterior fire window assemblies *(part 2 of 2)*

- Exterior openings with the following conditions require a fire-protection rating ≥ ¾ hr:
  - Openings that are in a wall without a fire-resistance rating.
  - Openings that are required to be protected based on the following:
    Size.
    Relationship to other openings above and below.
    Relationship to a lower roof on the same property.

    Note: The following are cited as sources of requirements applicable to openings:
    704.8, "Allowable area of openings," identifies openings that require protection.
    704.9, "Vertical separation of openings," identifies openings that require protection based on relationships to other openings above and below.
    704.10, "Vertical exposure," identifies openings that require protection based on relationships to a lower roof on the same property.

717 Concealed Spaces

717.1 General

- The following are required in combustible concealed spaces:
  - Fire-blocking at the following locations:
    In walls at floor and ceilings.
    In stair construction.
    At penetrations.
    In exterior wall finish systems.
    Between sleepers.
  - Draft-stopping at the following locations:
    Floor/ceiling spaces.
    Attic spaces.
  - Where buildings are required to be noncombustible:
    The use of combustible materials in concealed spaces is limited as follows:
    To locations with conditions specified by the code.

  Note: The following are cited as sources of applicable requirements:
  717.2, "Fireblocking."
  717.3, "Draftstopping in floors."
  717.4, "Draftstopping in attics."
  717.5, "Combustibles in concealed spaces in Type I or II construction."

717.2 Fireblocking

- Fire-blocking is required to seal openings to restrict drafts as follows:
  - In combustible construction in concealed spaces as follows:
    Vertical openings.
    Horizontal openings.
- Fire-blocking is required to form a barrier between the following elements:
  - Between floors.
  - Between the top story and a roof.
  - Between the top story and an attic.

  Note: The following are cited as the source for specific locations requiring fire-blocking:
  717.2.2, "Concealed wall spaces."
  717.2.3, "Connections between horizontal and vertical spaces."
  717.2.4, "Stairways."
  717.2.5, "Ceiling and floor openings."
  717.2.6, "Architectural trim."
  717.2.7, "Concealed sleeper spaces."

717 Concealed Spaces

717.2.1 Fireblocking materials

- Fire-blocking must be one of the following materials:
  - 2" nominal lumber.
  - 2 layers of 1" nominal lumber with staggered joints.
  - 0.719" wood structural panel as follows:
    Joints to be backed by the same material.
  - 0.75" particle board as follows:
    Joints to be backed by the same material.
  - Gypsum board.
  - Cement fiber board.
  - Batts or blankets of either of the following:
    Mineral wool.
    Glass fiber.
  - Loose-fill insulation where all the following apply:
    Must be tested in the form and manner of the actual application.
    Ability to remain in place must be demonstrated.
    Ability to retard the spread of fire must be demonstrated.
    Ability to retard the spread of hot gases must be demonstrated.
  - Other approved material.
- Fire-blocking must be held securely in place.
- The materials listed below are permitted as fire-blocking for the following walls:
  - Walls:
    Where fire-blocking is required at 10' intervals as follows:
    Intervals are measured measured horizontally.
    Includes the following types of construction:
      Parallel rows of studs.
      Staggered studs.
  - Materials:
    Includes any of the following:
      Batts:
        Mineral wool.
        Glass fiber.
      Blankets:
        Mineral wool.
        Glass fiber.
      Other approved nonrigid materials.

717 Concealed Spaces

717.2.1.1 Double stud walls

- The following nonrigid materials may serve as fire-blocking in the walls indicated below:
  - Materials:
    Batts or blankets of mineral fiber.
    Batts of or blankets of glass fiber.
    Other approved nonrigid materials.
  - Walls:
    Double walls with parallel rows of studs.
    Walls with cavity space wider than stud width as follows:
      Alternate studs are flush with opposite sides of the wall.

717.2.2 Concealed wall spaces

- Fire-blocking is required as shown below in the following construction:
  - Construction:
    Stud walls.
    Stud partitions.
    Associated furred spaces.
    Parallel rows of studs.
    Staggered studs.
  - Fire-blocking:
    Required in concealed spaces of the construction as follows:
      At ceiling level.
      At floor level.
      At $\leq 10'$ intervals measured horizontally.

717.2.3 Connections between horizontal and vertical spaces

- Fire-blocking is required to seal through connections as follows:
  - Between the concealed spaces in stud walls or partitions and the following:
    Concealed spaces created by floor joists.
    Concealed spaces created by trusses.
  - Between vertical and horizontal spaces occurring at the following and similar locations:
    Soffits.
    Drop ceilings.
    Cove ceilings.

717 Concealed Spaces

717.2.4 Stairways

- Fire-blocking is required in concealed spaces as follows:
  - Between stair stringers as follows:
    At the top of a stair run.
    At the bottom of a stair run.
  - Enclosed space under a stair requires the greater of the following:
    A fire-resistance rating ≤ 1 hr.
    A fire-resistance rating ≤ the fire-resistance rating of the stairway enclosure.

  Note: 1019.1.5, "Enclosures under stairways," is cited as governing enclosed space under a stair and is partially summarized above. The section includes other requirements and exceptions.

717.2.5 Ceiling and floor openings

- Fire-blocking is required at annular space of the following penetrations at locations indicated:
  - Penetrations:
    Vents.
    Pipes.
    Chimneys.
    Ducts.
    Conduits.
    Fireplaces.
  - Locations:
    Ceilings.
    Floors.

  Note: The following are cited as sources listing penetrations requiring fire-blocking, a partial summary of which is provided above:
  707.2, "Shaft enclosure required," Exception 6.
  712.4.2, "Membrane penetrations," Exception 1.
  712.4.3, "Nonfire-resistance-rated assemblies."

- Fire-blocking must be an approved material.
- Fire-blocking must resist the passage of the following:
  - Flame and combustion products.
- Fire-blocking for prefabricated fireplaces and chimneys is governed by other standards.

  Note: The following are cited as governing prefabricated fireplaces and chimneys:
  UL 103, "Chimneys, Factory-Built, Residential Type and Building Heating Appliance."
  UL 127, "Factory-Built Fireplaces."

717 Concealed Spaces

717.2.6 Architectural trim

- Fire-blocking is required in cornices at the party wall of duplexes.
- Fire-blocking is not required in the following cases:
  - At locations in cornices other than at the party wall of duplexes.
  - In cornices of single-family dwellings.
  - Where both the following conditions are present:
    The architectural trim is installed on noncombustible framing.
    The exterior wall finish exposed to the concealed space is one of the following:
    Aluminum ≥ 0.019" thick.
    Steel as follows:
    Corrosion-resistant.
    Base metal thickness is ≥ 0.016" at thinnest point.
    Other approved noncombustible materials.
- Fire-blocking is required in concealed spaces of the following components as indicated:
  - Components:
    With combustible construction or framing as follows:
    Exterior wall finish.
    Exterior architectural elements.
  - Requirements:
    Continuous concealed spaces must be fire-blocked at a spacing ≤ 20'.
    Noncontinuous concealed spaces must have both the following:
    Closed ends.
    Separation between sections ≥ 4".

  Note: Section 1406, "Combustible Materials on the Exterior Side of Exterior Walls," is cited as governing the combustible materials at exterior walls indicated above.

717.2.7 Concealed sleeper spaces

- Slab-on-grade gymnasium floors do not require fire-blocking:
- Bowling alley lanes require blocking only at the following locations:
  - At the juncture of every other lane.
  - At the ends of each lane.
- In other cases, space between wood sleepers on floors as follows are governed as indicated:
  - Floors:
    Masonry or concrete floors with a fire-resistance rating.
  - Sleeper space:
    Space between flooring and floor slab must be detailed in one of the following ways:
    Fire-blocked to limit the airspace to ≤ 100 sf.
    Filled with an approved material as follows:
    That will prevent passage of the following:
    Flame and combustion products.
    Space between flooring and slab must be completely filled in the following location:
    Under permanent partitions between rooms.

717 Concealed Spaces

717.3 Draftstopping in floors

- This section addresses draft-stopping in the following locations:
  - In combustible construction.
  - In floor/ceiling assemblies.

    Note: The following are cited as sources of specific locations where draft-stopping is required:
    717.3.2, "Groups R-1, R-2, R-3 and R-4."
    717.3.3, "Other groups."

717.3.1 Draftstopping materials

- The following qualify as draft-stopping materials:
  - Gypsum board $\geq$ $^1/_2$" thick.
  - Wood structural panel $\geq$ $^3/_8$" thick.
  - Particle board $\geq$ $^3/_8$" thick.
  - Other approved materials.
- Draft-stopping materials must be adequately supported.

717.3.2 Groups R-1, R-2, R-3 and R-4

- This section applies to draft-stopping in concealed spaces as follows:
  - Combustible floor/ceiling assemblies in the following occupancies:
    R-1.
    R-2 with $\geq$ 3 dwelling units.
    R-3 with 2 dwelling units.
    R-4.
- Draft-stopping is not required as follows:
  - In buildings sprinklered as per NFPA 13.
  - In buildings sprinklered as per NFPA 13R as follows:
    Sprinklers provided in combustible concealed spaces.

  Note: The following are cited as governing the referenced sprinklers:
  903.3.1.1, "NFPA 13 sprinkler systems."
  903.3.1.2, "NFPA 13R sprinkler systems."

- In other cases, draft-stopping is required in the following locations:
  - On the line of separation between dwelling units.
  - On the line of separation between sleeping units.

717 Concealed Spaces

717.3.3 Other groups

- This section applies to draft-stopping in concealed spaces as follows:
  - Combustible floor/ceiling assemblies in the following:
    Occupancies other R.
- Draft-stopping is not required as follows:
  - In buildings sprinklered as per NFPA 13.
- In other buildings, draft-stopping is required as follows:
  - Horizontal airspace must be limited to ≤ 1000 sf of floor area.

717.4 Draftstopping in attics

- This section series addresses draft-stopping in the following locations of combustible construction:
  - In attics.
  - In concealed roof spaces.

  Note: The following sections are cited as sources of specific locations required for draft-stopping:
  717.4.2, "Groups R-1 and R-2."
  717.4.3, "Other groups."

- Ventilation of concealed spaces under the roof must be provided.

  Note: 1203.2, "Attic spaces," is cited as the source for ventilation requirements.

717.4.1 Draftstopping materials

- The following qualify as draft-stopping materials:
  - Gypsum board ≥ $1/2$" thick.
  - Wood structural panel ≥ $3/8$" thick.
  - Particle board ≥ $3/8$" thick.
  - Other approved materials.
- Draft-stopping materials must be adequately supported.

717.4.1.1 Openings

- Openings in draft-stopping attic partitions must be protected as follows:
  - With self-closing doors.
  - Doors must have automatic latches.

717 Concealed Spaces

717.4.2 Groups R-1 and R-2

- This section applies to draft-stopping where required as follows:
  - In combustible concealed spaces of the following occupancies in locations listed below:
    Occupancies:
      R-1.
      R-2 with ≥ 3 dwellings.
    Locations:
      General locations:
        Attics.
        Mansards.
        Overhangs.
        Other concealed roof spaces.
      Specific locations:
        On line with separation walls which do not reach the roof sheathing as follows:
          Between dwelling units.
          Between sleeping units.
- Draft-stopping is required above only one of the two corridor walls in the following case:
  - Where corridor walls provide the following separations:
    Between dwelling units.
    Between sleeping units.
- Draft-stopping is not required as follows:
  - In buildings sprinklered as per NFPA 13.
  - In buildings sprinklered as per NFPA 13R as follows:
    Sprinklers provided in combustible concealed spaces.

  Note: The following are cited as governing the referenced sprinklers:
         903.3.1.1, "NFPA 13 sprinkler systems."
         903.3.1.2, "NFPA 13R sprinkler systems."

- Draft-stopping is required as indicated below in the following occupancy:
  - Occupancy:
    R-2 ≤ 4 stories.
  - Requirement:
    Draft-stops must divide attic space into the smaller of the following areas:
      ≤ 3000 sf.
      ≤ area above every two dwellings.
- Draft-stopping is otherwise required in the general and specific locations specified in this section.

717 Concealed Spaces

717.4.3 Other groups

- This section applies to draft-stopping in the following:
  - Combustible concealed spaces of occupancies other than the following:
    R-1.
    R-2 with ≥ 3 dwellings.
- Draft-stopping is not required in attics and concealed roof spaces as follows:
  - In buildings sprinklered as per NFPA 13.
- Draft-stopping is otherwise required in the following locations as indicated below:
  - Locations:
    Attics.
    Concealed roof spaces.
  - Requirement:
    Horizontal areas must be limited to ≤ 3000 sf.

717.5 Combustibles in concealed spaces in Type I or II construction

- The following combustible materials may be used in concealed spaces of Type I and II construction:
  - Combustible materials permitted in other locations of Type I and II construction.
  - Combustible materials permitted in plenums.
  - Class A finish materials.
  - Combustible piping as follows:
    In the following locations as otherwise governed by this code:
    Partitions.
    Enclosed shafts.
    In concealed spaces where installed as per applicable codes.

  Note: The following are cited as sources of requirements for combustible materials permitted in concealed spaces of Type I and II construction:
  Section 603, "Combustible Material in Type I and II Construction," lists material permitted in other locations in Type I and II construction.
  Section 602 of the International Mechanical Code governs materials in plenums.
  The following provide requirements for combustible piping in concealed spaces:
  International Mechanical Code.
  International Plumbing Code.

- Otherwise combustible materials are not allowed in concealed spaces of the following:
  - Type I construction.
  - Type II construction.

Case study: Fig. 717.4.3. The attic of the occupancy E building is divided by walls providing draftstops. One draftstopping wall separates the new attic (not sprinklered) from the existing attic. A second draftstopping wall separates the new attic into areas of 2780 sf and 1670 sf, both within the 3000 sf limit.

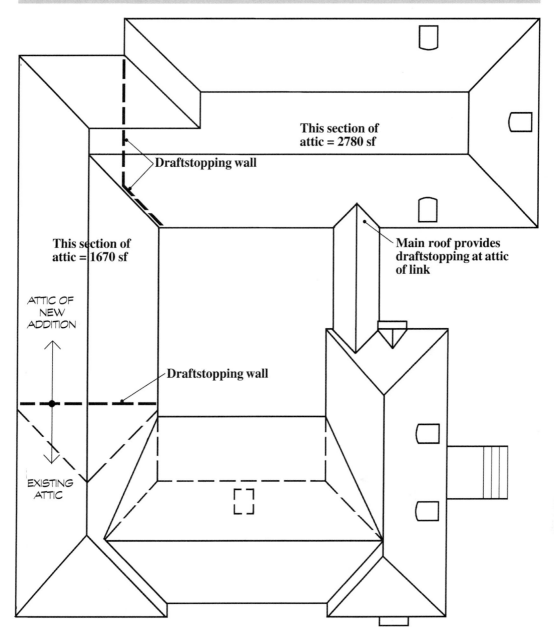

This section of
attic = 2780 sf

Draftstopping wall

This section of
attic = 1670 sf

Main roof provides
draftstopping at attic
of link

ATTIC OF
NEW
ADDITION

Draftstopping wall

EXISTING
ATTIC

Fig. 717.4.3. Roof plan. Multipurpose Building Addition to Children's Home. Wilkes-Barre, Pennsylvania. C. Allen Mullins, Architect. Bear Creek, Pennsylvania.

718 Fire-Resistance Requirements for Plaster

718.1 Thickness of plaster

- The thickness required for the following types of plaster is determined by specified fire tests:
  - Gypsum plaster and portland cement plaster.
- Where applied to the following, plaster thickness is measured to the face of the lath:
  - Gypsum lath and metal lath.

718.2 Plaster equivalents

- The following are considered to have equal fire resistance:
  - 0.5" unsanded gypsum plaster.
  - 0.75" 1:3 gypsum sand plaster.
  - 1" of portland cement sand plaster.

718.3 Noncombustible furring

- In Type I and II construction plaster must be applied directly to one of the following:
  - Concrete or masonry.
  - Approved noncombustible plastering base and furring.

718.4 Double reinforcement

- The following plaster systems do not require supplementary reinforcement:
  - Solid plaster partitions.
  - Assemblies where it is deemed by fire test to be unnecessary.
- Other plaster as follows requires supplementary reinforcement as indicated below:
  - Plaster:
    - With both the following characteristics:
      - Plaster used as fire protection.
      - Plaster > 1" thick.
  - Requirement:
    - An additional layer of approved lath is required as follows:
      - Lath must be embedded ≥ 0.75" from outer surface of plaster.
      - Lath must be fastened securely in place.

718 Fire-Resistance Requirements for Plaster

718.5 Plaster alternatives for concrete

- This section addresses concrete cover protection in reinforced concrete construction.
- The following plaster types may substitute for concrete cover as indicated below:
  - Plaster types:
    Gypsum plaster.
    Portland cement plaster.
  - Substitution:
    Up to ½" of concrete cover may be replaced with plaster as follows:
      Concrete cover may not be reduced below the following:
        $^3/_8$" for poured reinforced concrete floors in addition to the plaster.
        1" for reinforced concrete columns in addition to the plaster.

  Note: 2510.7, "Preparation of masonry and concrete," is cited as the source of requirements for the concrete base.

719 Thermal- and Sound-Insulating Materials

719.1 General

- This section does not apply to the following materials:
  - Fiberboard insulation.

    Note: Chapter 23, "Wood," is cited as governing fiberboard insulation.

  - Foam plastic insulation.

    Note: Chapter 26, "Plastic," is cited as governing foam plastic insulation.

  - Duct insulation.
  - Duct coverings.
  - Pipe insulation.
  - Pipe coverings.
  - Linings in plenums.

    Note: The International Mechanical Code is cited as governing ducts, pipes, and plenums.

- This section governs the following materials:
  - Other insulating materials.
  - Facings such as follows:
    - Vapor retarders.
    - Vapor-permeable membranes.
    - Similar coverings.
  - All layers of the following:
    - Single-layer reflective foil insulation.
    - Multilayer reflective foil insulation.
- Materials are not allowed as follows:
  - Where the following factors increase indexes as indicated below:
    - Factors:
      - Age.
      - Moisture.
      - Other atmospheric conditions.
    - Indexes:
      - Where either of the following increase to surpass prescribed limits:
        - Flame spread index.
        - Smoke-developed index.

    Note: ASTM E 84, "Standard Test Methods for Surface Burning Characteristics of Building Materials," is cited as governing flame spread and smoke-developed indexes where required in this section.

719 Thermal- and Sound-Insulating Materials

719.2 Concealed installation

- Concealed cellulose insulation as follows must have a smoke-developed index ≤ 450:
  ◦ Loose-fill insulation.
  ◦ Insulation that is not spray-applied.
  ◦ Complies with applicable third-party standards.

  Note: 719.6, "Cellulose loose-fill insulation," is cited as the source of required standards.

- Other concealed insulating materials must comply with the following indexes:
  ◦ Flame spread index ≤ 25.
  ◦ Smoke-developed index ≤ 450.

719.2.1 Facings

- This section applies to the following facings installed as indicated below:
  ◦ Facings:
      As follows on insulation installed in concealed spaces governed by this section:
      Facings.
      Coverings.
      Layers of reflective foil insulation.
  ◦ Installation:
      Where installed in the following construction types:
      Types III, IV, and V.
      Where concealed behind and in substantial contact with the following elements:
      Ceiling finish.
      Wall finish.
      Floor finish.
- The following indexes are not limited for facings addressed in this section:
  ◦ Flame spread index.
  ◦ Smoke-developed index.

719.3 Exposed installation

- Exposed cellulose insulation as follows must have a smoke-developed index ≤ 450:
  ◦ Loose-fill insulation.
  ◦ Insulation that is not spray-applied.
  ◦ Complies with applicable third-party standards.

  Note: 719.6, "Cellulose loose-fill insulation," is cited as the source of required standards.

- Other exposed insulating materials must comply with the following indexes:
  ◦ Flame spread index ≤ 25.
  ◦ Smoke-developed index ≤ 450.

719 Thermal- and Sound-Insulating Materials

719.3.1 Attic floors

- Insulation materials exposed on attic floors must have the following property:
  - A critical radiant flux ≥ 0.12 watt/sq cm.

  Note: ASTM E 970, "Standard Test Method for Critical Radiant Flux of Exposed Attic Floor Insulation Using a Radiant Heat Energy Source," is cited as the required test method.

719.4 Loose-fill insulation

- Cellulose loose-fill insulation is not required to comply with the standard surface burning tests specified in this section in the following case:
  - Where it complies with applicable Consumer Product Safety Commission standards.

  Note: 719.6, "Cellulose loose-fill insulation," is cited as listing the applicable Consumer Product Safety Commission standards.

- Other loose-fill insulation that would need the following supplementary devices in the standard test require an alternate test as listed below:
  - Devices:
    A screen to mount the insulation in the test apparatus.
    Artificial supports to mount the insulation in the test apparatus.

  Note: ASTM E 84, "Standard Test Methods for Surface Burning Characteristics of Building Materials," is cited as the standard test applicable to this section.

  - Alternate test:
    The following must be achieved in an alternate test:
    Flame spread index ≤ 25.
    Smoke-developed index ≤ 450.

  Note: CAN/ULC S102, "Surface Burning Characteristics of Building Materials and Assemblies," is cited as the acceptable alternate test.
  The following are cited as listing the required results in the alternate test. The sections are partially summarized above and have other requirements including an exception.
  *   719.2, "Concealed installation."*
  *   719.3, "Exposed Installation."*

719 Thermal- and Sound-Insulating Materials

719.5 Roof insulation

- Combustible roof insulation need not comply with the following standards where the conditions indicated below apply:
  - Standards:
    Flame spread index is not required to be ≤ 25.
    Smoke-developed index is not required to be ≤ 450.
  - Conditions:
    Where insulation is covered with an approved roof covering.
    Where the roof covering is applied directly to the insulation.

  Note: The following are cited as the sources of requirements which are waived for the insulation addressed in this section, a partial summary of which is provided above:
      719.2, "Concealed insulation," which limits flame spread and smoke-developed index.
      719.3, "Exposed insulation," which limits flame spread and smoke-developed index.

719.6 Cellulose loose-fill insulation

- Cellulose loose-fill insulation must comply with the following:
  - Meet standards of the Consumer Product Safety Commission.
  - Have packaging labeled as per the standards.

  Note: The following Consumer Product Safety Commission standards are cited as governing cellulose loose-fill insulation:
      CPSC 16 CFR, 1209, "Interim Safety Standard for Cellulose Insulation."
      CPSC 16 CFR, 1404, "Cellulose Insulation."

719.7 Insulation and covering on pipe and tubing

- Insulation and coverings on pipe and tubing must comply with the following standards:
  - Flame spread index must be ≤ 25.
  - Smoke-developed index must be ≤ 450.

720 Prescriptive Fire Resistance

720.1 General

- This section provides details with assigned fire-resistance ratings.

  Note: The following are cited as sources of details with fire-resistance ratings:
  IBC Table 720.1(1), "Minimum Protection of Structural Parts Based on Time Periods for Various Noncombustible Insulating Materials."
  IBC Table 720.1(2), "Rated Fire-Resistance Periods for Various Walls and Partitions."
  IBC Table 720.1(3), "Minimum Protection for Floor and Roof Systems."

- Where changes are made to the details provided herein, the following applies:
  - Where changes affect the heat dissipation potential of the detail:
    Documentation must be made available as follows:
    Type:
    Fire tests.
    Other data.
    Content:
    Verifying that the fire-resistance period of the detail is not reduced.
    Availability:
    Must be made available to the building official.

720.1.1 Thickness of protective coverings

- Thickness of fire-resistant materials protecting structure must be one of the following:
  - As indicated in details provided in this section.
  - As otherwise indicated in this section.

  Note: IBC Table 720.1(1) ,"Minimum Protection of Structural Parts Based on Time Periods for Various Noncombustible Insulating Materials," is cited as the source of details.

- Protective covering thickness indicated in this section is defined as follows:
  - Net thickness of protecting materials.
  - Thickness does not include air space behind the protecting material.

720.1.2 Unit masonry protection

- Where required, metal ties must be installed as follows:
  - In bed joints of masonry protecting steel columns.
  - Ties must be one of the following:
    As shown in details provided in this section.
    Equivalent to that shown in details of this section.

  Note: IBC Table 720.1(1), "Minimum Protection of Structural Parts Based on Time Periods for Various Noncombustible Insulating Materials," is cited as the source of details.

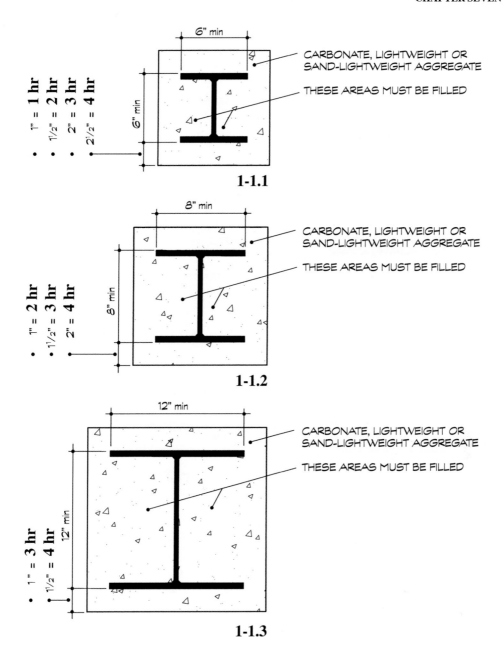

Fig. 720.1(1) 1A. Minimum protection of steel columns and all members of primary trusses. Minimum thicknesses of noncombustible insulating materials are indicated as required for the fire-resistance ratings shown. Such thicknesses are the same on all sides where insulating materials occur. *[Source: IBC Table 720.1(1).]*

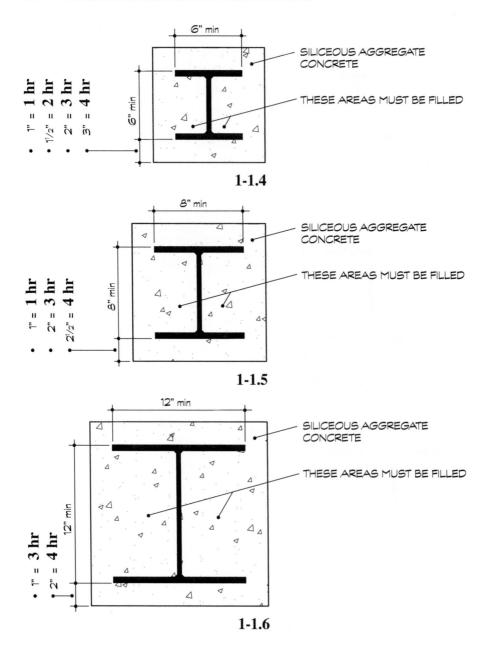

Fig. 720.1(1) 1B. Minimum protection of steel columns and all members of primary trusses. Minimum thicknesses of noncombustible insulating materials are indicated as required for the fire-resistance ratings shown. Such thicknesses are the same on all sides where insulating materials occur. *[Source: IBC Table 720.1(1).]*

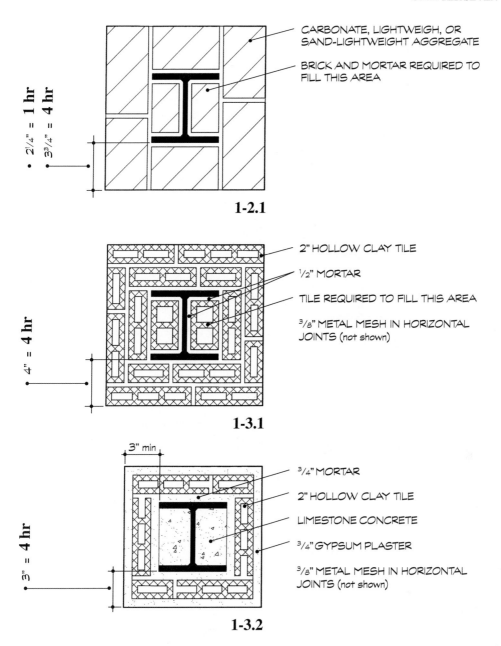

Fig. 720.1(1) 1C. Minimum protection of steel columns and all members of primary trusses. Minimum thicknesses of noncombustible insulating materials are indicated as required for the fire-resistance ratings shown. Such thicknesses are the same on all sides where insulating materials occur. *[Source: IBC Table 720.1(1).]*

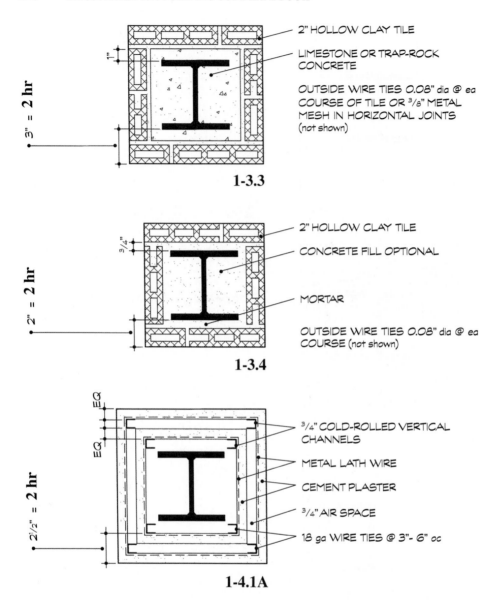

Fig. 720.1(1) 1D. Minimum protection of steel columns and all members of primary trusses. Minimum thicknesses of noncombustible insulating materials are indicated as required for the fire-resistance ratings shown. Such thicknesses are the same on all sides where insulating materials occur. *[Source: IBC Table 720.1(1).]*

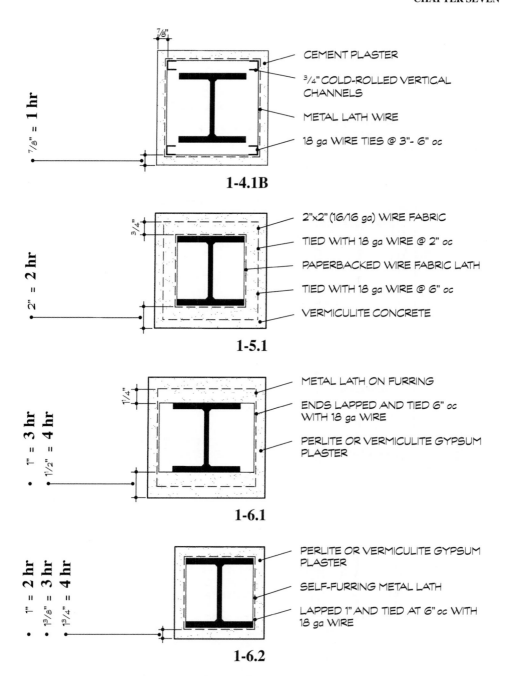

Fig. 720.1(1) 1E. Minimum protection of steel columns and all members of primary trusses. Minimum thicknesses of noncombustible insulating materials are indicated as required for the fire-resistance ratings shown. Such thicknesses are the same on all sides where insulating materials occur. *[Source: IBC Table 720.1(1).]*

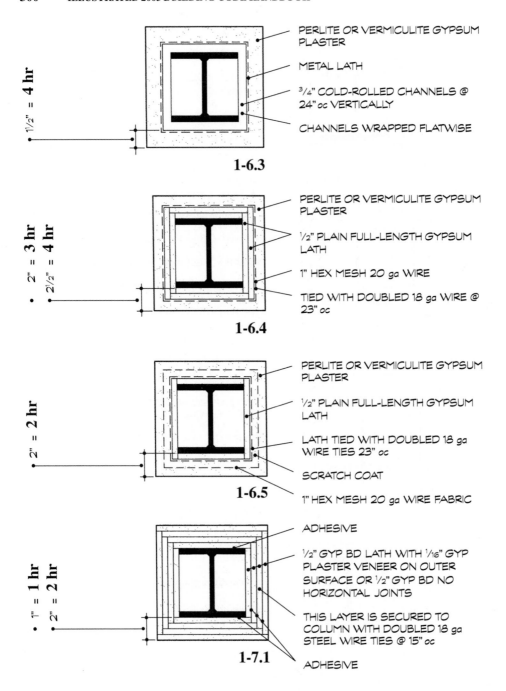

Fig. 720.1(1) 1F. Minimum protection of steel columns and all members of primary trusses. Minimum thicknesses of noncombustible insulating materials are indicated as required for the fire-resistance ratings shown. Such thicknesses are the same on all sides where insulating materials occur. *[Source: IBC Table 720.1(1).]*

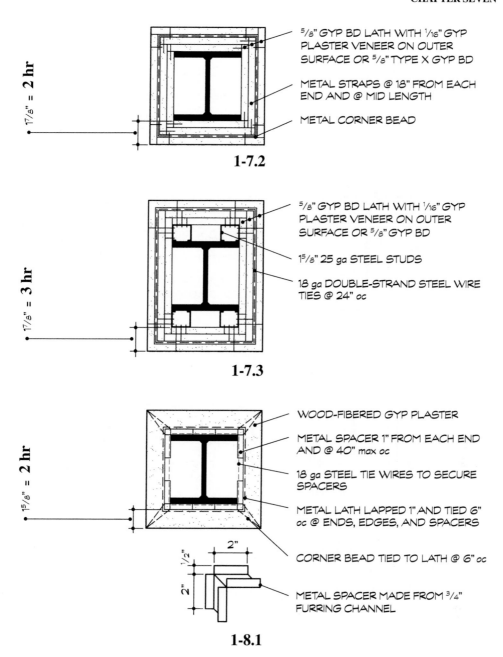

1-7.2

⁵/₈" GYP BD LATH WITH ¹/₁₆" GYP PLASTER VENEER ON OUTER SURFACE OR ⁵/₈" TYPE X GYP BD

METAL STRAPS @ 18" FROM EACH END AND @ MID LENGTH

METAL CORNER BEAD

1⁷/₈" = 2 hr

1-7.3

⁵/₈" GYP BD LATH WITH ¹/₁₆" GYP PLASTER VENEER ON OUTER SURFACE OR ⁵/₈" GYP BD

1⁵/₈" 25 ga STEEL STUDS

18 ga DOUBLE-STRAND STEEL WIRE TIES @ 24" oc

1⁷/₈" = 3 hr

1-8.1

WOOD-FIBERED GYP PLASTER

METAL SPACER 1" FROM EACH END AND @ 40" max oc

18 ga STEEL TIE WIRES TO SECURE SPACERS

METAL LATH LAPPED 1" AND TIED 6" oc @ ENDS, EDGES, AND SPACERS

CORNER BEAD TIED TO LATH @ 6" oc

METAL SPACER MADE FROM ³/₄" FURRING CHANNEL

1⁵/₈" = 2 hr

2"
½"
2"

Fig. 720.1(1) 1G. Minimum protection of steel columns and all members of primary trusses. Minimum thicknesses of noncombustible insulating materials are indicated as required for the fire-resistance ratings shown. Such thicknesses are the same on all sides where insulating materials occur. *[Source: IBC Table 720.1(1).]*

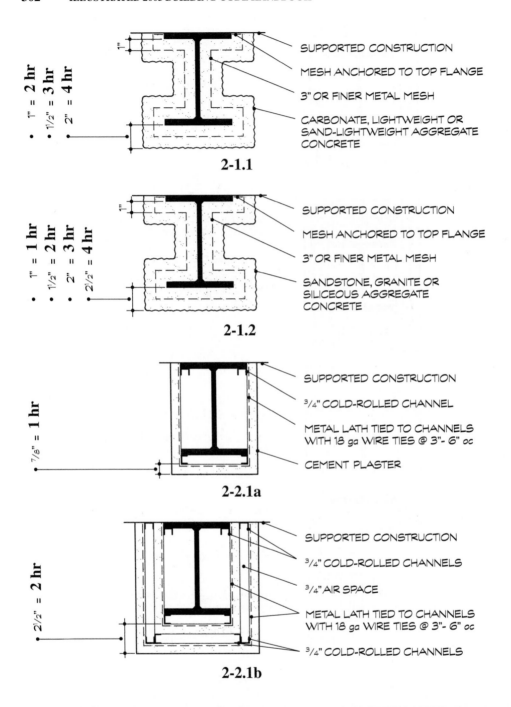

Fig. 720.1(1) 2A. Minimum protection of webs and flanges of steel beams and girders. Minimum thicknesses of noncombustible insulating materials are indicated as required for the fire-resistance ratings shown. Such thicknesses are the same on all sides where insulating materials occur. *[Source: IBC Table 720.1(1).]*

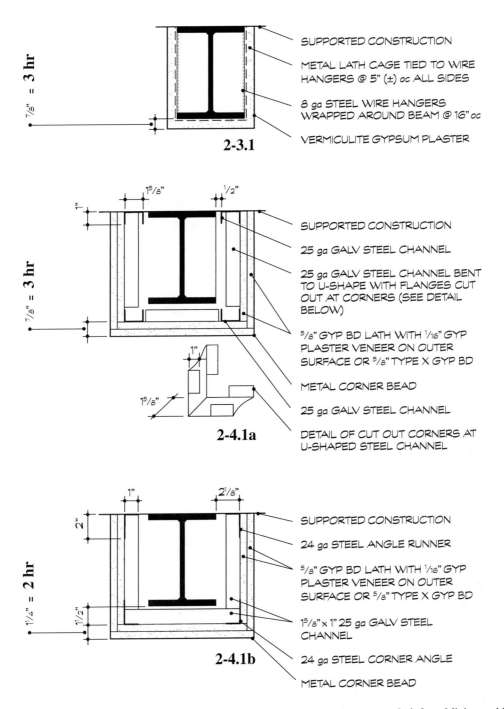

Fig. 720.1(1) 2B. Minimum protection of webs and flanges of steel beams and girders. Minimum thicknesses of noncombustible insulating materials are indicated as required for the fire-resistance ratings shown. Such thicknesses are the same on all sides where insulating materials occur. [*Source: IBC Table 720.1(1).*]

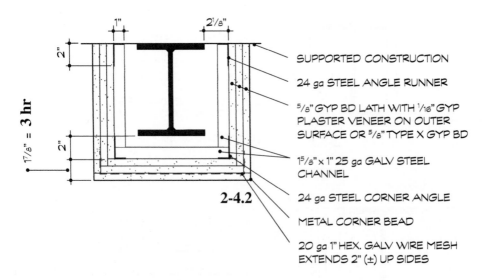

Fig. 720.1(1) 2C. Minimum protection of webs and flanges of steel beams and girders. Minimum thicknesses of noncombustible insulating materials are indicated as required for the fire-resistance ratings shown. Such thicknesses are the same on all sides where insulating materials occur. *[Source: IBC Table 720.1(1).]*

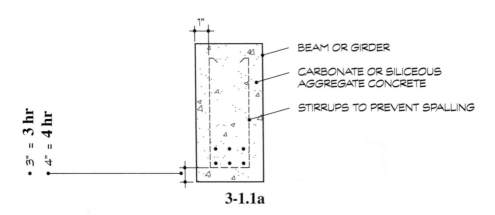

Fig. 720.1(1) 3A. Minimum protection of bonded pretensioned reinforcement in prestressed concrete. Minimum thicknesses of concrete cover are indicated as required for the fire-resistance ratings shown. Such minimum thicknesses are the same on all sides. *[Source: IBC Table 720.1(1).]*

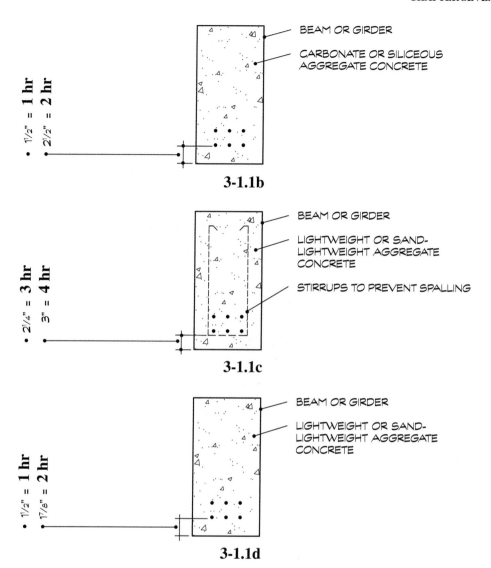

Fig. 720.1(1) 3B. Minimum protection of bonded pretensioned reinforcement in prestressed concrete.
Minimum thicknesses of concrete cover are indicated as required for the fire-resistance ratings shown. Such
minimum thicknesses are the same on all sides. *[Source: IBC Table 720.1(1).]*

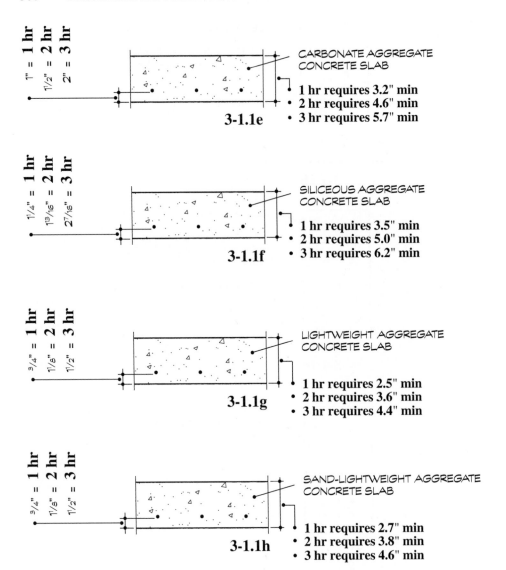

Fig. 720.1(1) 3C. Minimum protection of bonded pretensioned reinforcement in prestressed concrete. Minimum thicknesses of concrete cover are indicated as required for the fire-resistance ratings shown. Such minimum thicknesses are the same on all sides. *[Source: IBC Table 720.1(1).]*

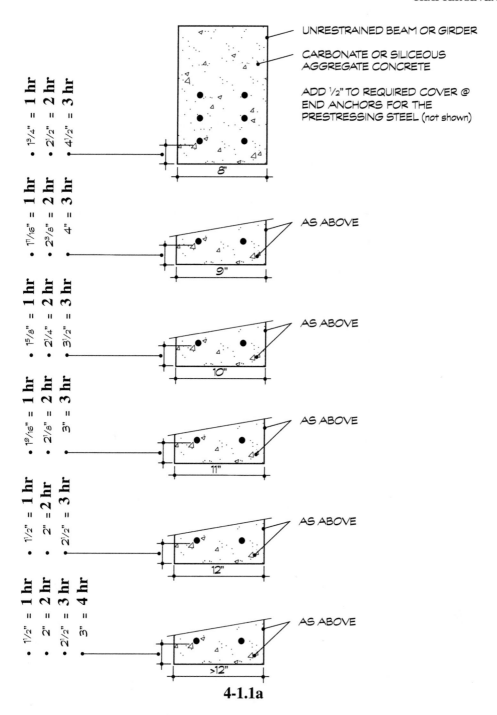

• 1³/₄" = **1 hr**
• 2¹/₂" = **2 hr**
• 4¹/₂" = **3 hr**

UNRESTRAINED BEAM OR GIRDER

CARBONATE OR SILICEOUS
AGGREGATE CONCRETE

ADD ½" TO REQUIRED COVER @
END ANCHORS FOR THE
PRESTRESSING STEEL (not shown)

8"

• 1¹¹/₁₆" = **1 hr**
• 2³/₈" = **2 hr**
• 4" = **3 hr**

AS ABOVE

9"

• 1⁵/₈" = **1 hr**
• 2¹/₄" = **2 hr**
• 3½" = **3 hr**

AS ABOVE

10"

• 1⁹/₁₆" = **1 hr**
• 2⅛" = **2 hr**
• 3" = **3 hr**

AS ABOVE

11"

• 1½" = **1 hr**
• 2" = **2 hr**
• 2½" = **3 hr**

AS ABOVE

12"

• 1½" = **1 hr**
• 2" = **2 hr**
• 2½" = **3 hr**
• 3" = **4 hr**

AS ABOVE

>12"

4-1.1a

Fig. 720.1(1) 4A. Minimum protection of bonded or unbonded post-tensioned tendons in prestressed concrete. Minimum thicknesses of concrete cover are indicated as required for the fire-resistance ratings shown. Such minimum thicknesses are the same on all sides. *[Source: IBC Table 720.1(1).]*

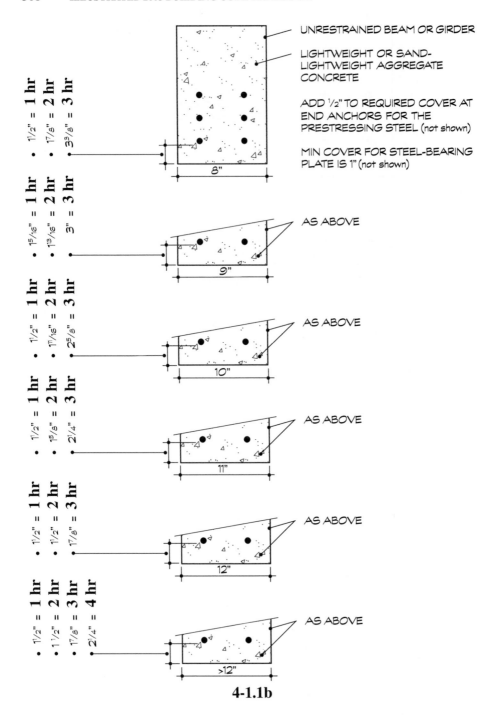

4-1.1b

Fig. 720.1(1) 4B. Minimum protection of bonded or unbonded post-tensioned tendons in prestressed concrete. Minimum thicknesses of concrete cover are indicated as required for the fire-resistance ratings shown. Such minimum thicknesses are the same on all sides. *[Source: IBC Table 720.1(1).]*

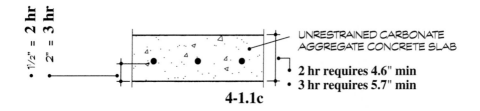

4-1.1c

UNRESTRAINED CARBONATE
AGGREGATE CONCRETE SLAB

• 2 hr requires 4.6" min
• 3 hr requires 5.7" min

• 1/2" = 2 hr
   2" = 3 hr

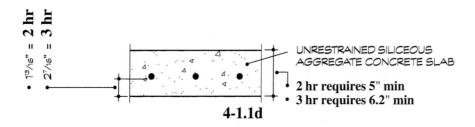

4-1.1d

UNRESTRAINED SILICEOUS
AGGREGATE CONCRETE SLAB

• 2 hr requires 5" min
• 3 hr requires 6.2" min

• 1³/₁₆" = 2 hr
   2⁷/₁₆" = 3 hr

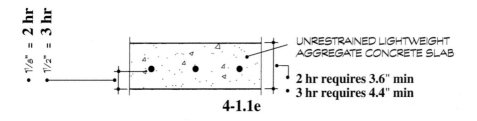

4-1.1e

UNRESTRAINED LIGHTWEIGHT
AGGREGATE CONCRETE SLAB

• 2 hr requires 3.6" min
• 3 hr requires 4.4" min

• 1/8" = 2 hr
   1/2" = 3 hr

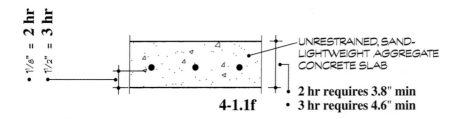

4-1.1f

UNRESTRAINED, SAND-
LIGHTWEIGHT AGGREGATE
CONCRETE SLAB

• 2 hr requires 3.8" min
• 3 hr requires 4.6" min

• 1/8" = 2 hr
   1/2" = 3 hr

Fig. 720.1(1) 4C. Minimum protection of bonded or unbonded post-tensioned tendons in prestressed concrete. Minimum thicknesses of concrete cover are indicated as required for the fire-resistance ratings shown. Such minimum thicknesses are the same on all sides. *[Source: IBC Table 720.1(1).]*

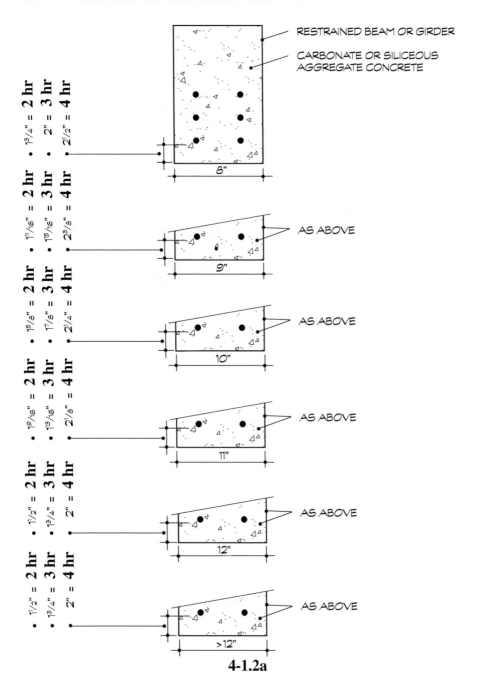

4-1.2a

Fig. 720.1(1) 4D. Minimum protection of bonded or unbonded post-tensioned tendons in prestressed concrete. Minimum thicknesses of concrete cover are indicated as required for the fire-resistance ratings shown. Such minimum thicknesses are the same on all sides. *[Source: IBC Table 720.1(1).]*

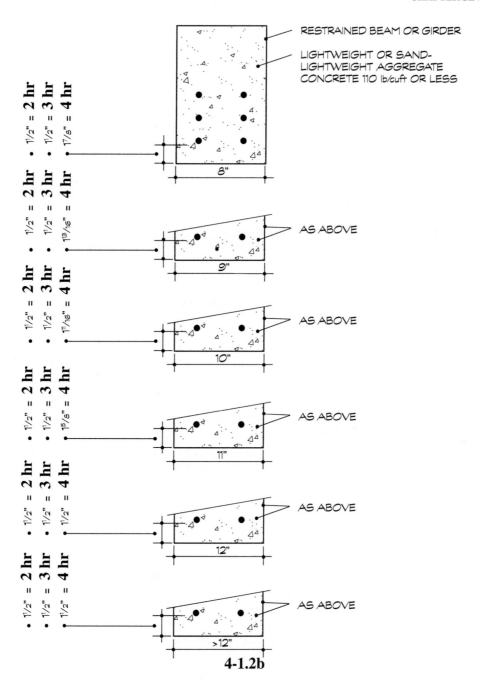

Fig. 720.1(1) 4E. Minimum protection of bonded or unbonded post-tensioned tendons in prestressed concrete. Minimum thicknesses of concrete cover are indicated as required for the fire-resistance ratings shown. Such minimum thicknesses are the same on all sides. *[Source: IBC Table 720.1(1).]*

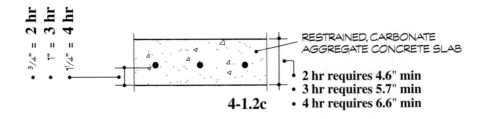

RESTRAINED, CARBONATE
AGGREGATE CONCRETE SLAB

- 2 hr requires 4.6" min
- 3 hr requires 5.7" min
- 4 hr requires 6.6" min

4-1.2c

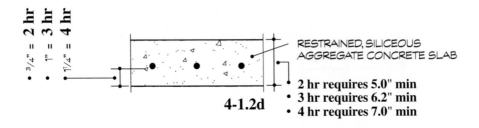

RESTRAINED, SILICEOUS
AGGREGATE CONCRETE SLAB

- 2 hr requires 5.0" min
- 3 hr requires 6.2" min
- 4 hr requires 7.0" min

4-1.2d

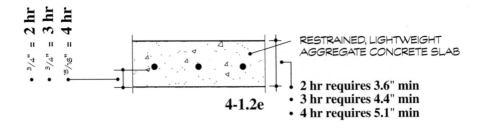

RESTRAINED, LIGHTWEIGHT
AGGREGATE CONCRETE SLAB

- 2 hr requires 3.6" min
- 3 hr requires 4.4" min
- 4 hr requires 5.1" min

4-1.2e

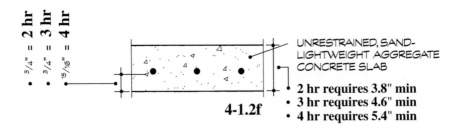

UNRESTRAINED, SAND-
LIGHTWEIGHT AGGREGATE
CONCRETE SLAB

- 2 hr requires 3.8" min
- 3 hr requires 4.6" min
- 4 hr requires 5.4" min

4-1.2f

Fig. 720.1(1) 4F. Minimum protection of bonded or unbonded post-tensioned tendons in prestressed concrete. Minimum thicknesses of concrete cover are indicated as required for the fire-resistance ratings shown. Such minimum thicknesses are the same on all sides. *[Source: IBC Table 720.1(1).]*

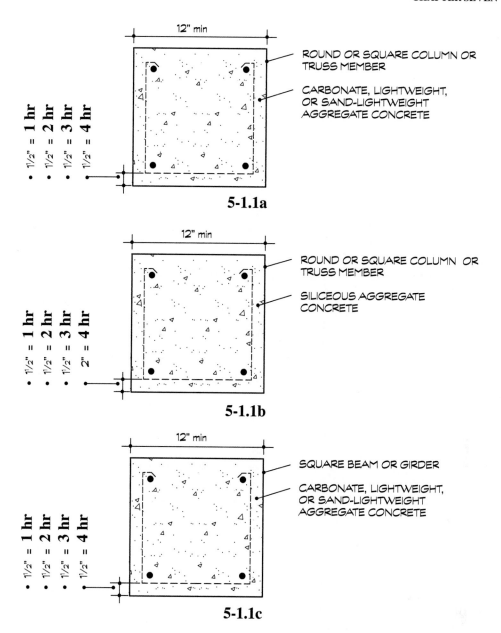

Fig. 720.1(1) 5A. Minimum protection of reinforcing steel in reinforced concrete columns, beams, girders, and trusses. Minimum thicknesses of concrete cover are indicated as required for the fire-resistance ratings shown. Such minimum thicknesses are the same on all sides. *[Source: IBC Table 720.1(1).]*

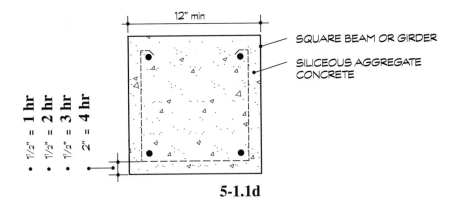

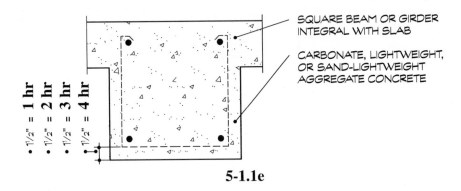

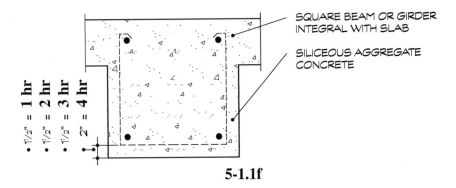

Fig. 720.1(1) 5B. Minimum protection of reinforcing steel in reinforced concrete columns, beams, girders, and trusses. Minimum thicknesses of concrete cover are indicated as required for the fire-resistance ratings shown. Such minimum thicknesses are the same on all sides. *[Source: IBC Table 720.1(1).]*

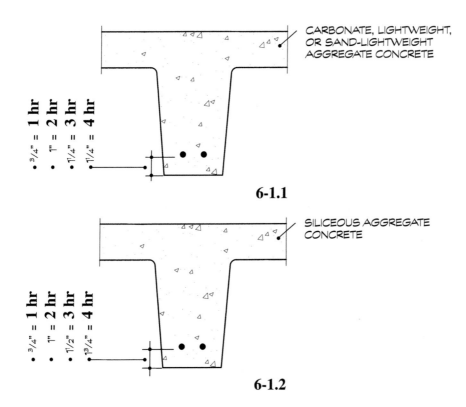

Fig. 720.1(1) 6A. Minimum protection of reinforcing steel in reinforced concrete joists. Minimum thicknesses of concrete cover are indicated as required for the fire-resistance ratings shown. Such minimum thicknesses are the same on all sides. *[Source: IBC Table 720.1(1).]*

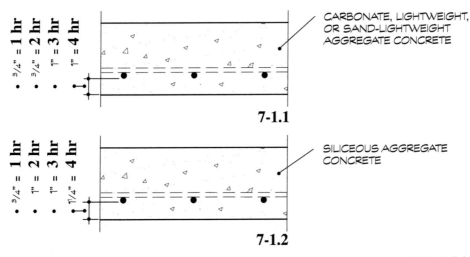

Fig. 720.1(1) 7A. Minimum protection of reinforcing and tie rods in floor and roof slabs. Minimum thicknesses of concrete cover are indicated as required for the fire-resistance ratings shown. Such minimum thicknesses are the same on all sides. *[Source: IBC Table 720.1(1).]*

Note: Acceptable fill materials for voids in details 1-1.1 and 1-1.3 are as follows:

Silicone-treated loose-fill insulation	*Expanded shale lightweight aggregate*
Vermiculite loose-fill insulation	*Expanded lightweight aggregate*
Expanded clay lightweight aggregate	*Grout*

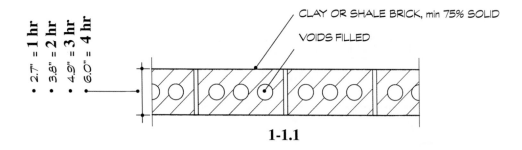

1-1.1

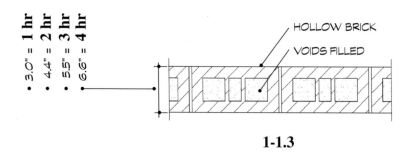

1-1.3

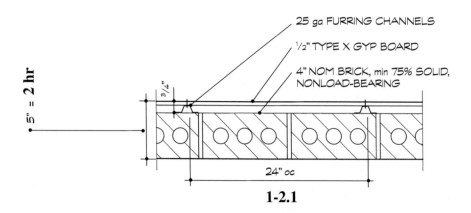

1-2.1

Fig. 720.1(2) 1A. Fire-resistance ratings for clay or shale brick walls and partitions. Minimum thickness of assembly is indicated as required for the fire-resistance rating shown. *[Source: IBC Table 720.1(2).]*

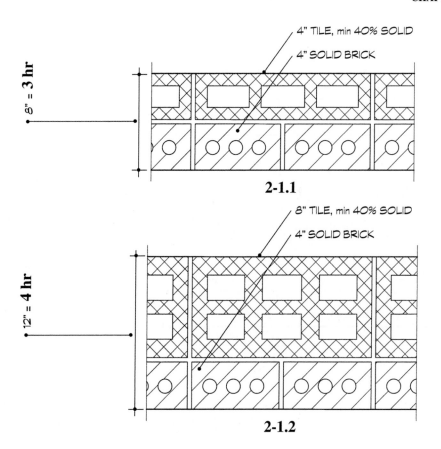

8" = 3 hr

4" TILE, min 40% SOLID

4" SOLID BRICK

2-1.1

12" = 4 hr

8" TILE, min 40% SOLID

4" SOLID BRICK

2-1.2

Note: Acceptable fill materials for voids in details 3-1.1 through 3-1.4 are as follows:

Silicone-treated loose-fill insulation   *Expanded shale lightweight aggregate*
Vermiculite loose-fill insulation   *Expanded lightweight aggregate*
Expanded clay lightweight aggregate   *Grout*

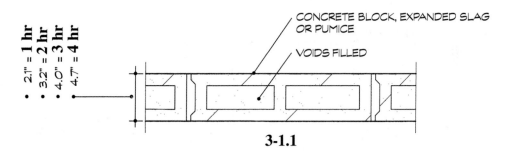

2.1" = 1 hr
3.2" = 2 hr
4.0" = 3 hr
4.7" = 4 hr

CONCRETE BLOCK, EXPANDED SLAG OR PUMICE

VOIDS FILLED

3-1.1

Fig. 720.1(2) 2A. Fire-resistance ratings for clay brick and load-bearing hollow clay tile walls and partitions. Minimum thickness of assembly is indicated as required for the fire-resistance rating shown. *[Source: IBC Table 720.1(2).]*

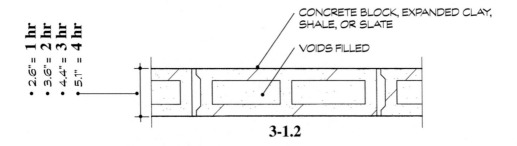

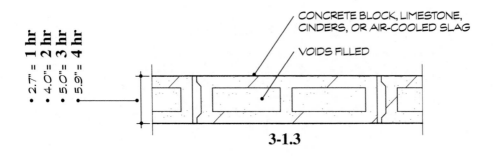

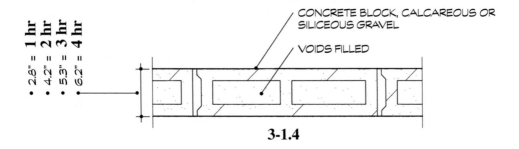

Fig. 720.1(2) 3A. Fire-resistance ratings for concrete masonry walls and partitions. Minimum thickness of assembly is indicated as required for the fire-resistance rating shown. *[Source: IBC Table 720.1(2).]*

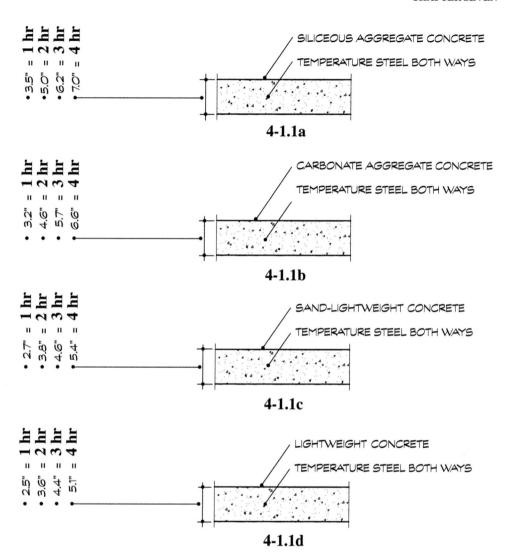

• 3.5" = **1 hr**
• 5.0" = **2 hr**
• 6.2" = **3 hr**
• 7.0" = **4 hr**

SILICEOUS AGGREGATE CONCRETE

TEMPERATURE STEEL BOTH WAYS

4-1.1a

• 3.2" = **1 hr**
• 4.6" = **2 hr**
• 5.7" = **3 hr**
• 6.6" = **4 hr**

CARBONATE AGGREGATE CONCRETE

TEMPERATURE STEEL BOTH WAYS

4-1.1b

• 2.7" = **1 hr**
• 3.8" = **2 hr**
• 4.6" = **3 hr**
• 5.4" = **4 hr**

SAND-LIGHTWEIGHT CONCRETE

TEMPERATURE STEEL BOTH WAYS

4-1.1c

• 2.5" = **1 hr**
• 3.6" = **2 hr**
• 4.4" = **3 hr**
• 5.1" = **4 hr**

LIGHTWEIGHT CONCRETE

TEMPERATURE STEEL BOTH WAYS

4-1.1d

Fig. 720.1(2) 4A. Fire-resistance ratings for solid concrete walls and partitions. Minimum thickness of assembly is indicated as required for the fire-resistance rating shown. *[Source: IBC Table 720.1(2).]*

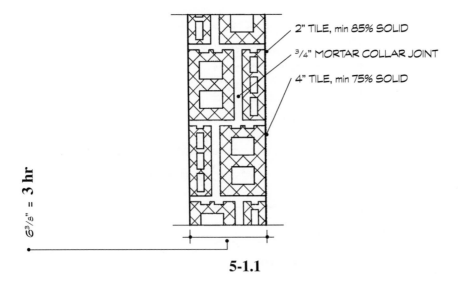

2" TILE, min 85% SOLID

³/₄" MORTAR COLLAR JOINT

4" TILE, min 75% SOLID

$6^{3}/_{8}" = 3$ hr

5-1.1

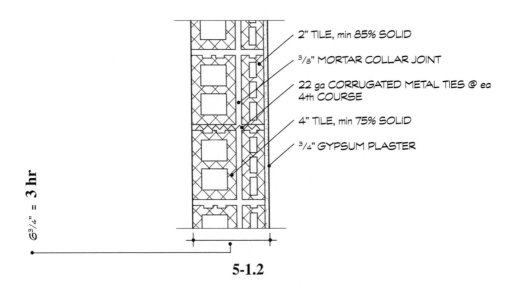

2" TILE, min 85% SOLID

³/₈" MORTAR COLLAR JOINT

22 ga CORRUGATED METAL TIES @ ea 4th COURSE

4" TILE, min 75% SOLID

³/₄" GYPSUM PLASTER

$6^{3}/_{4}" = 3$ hr

5-1.2

Fig. 720.1(2) 5A. Fire-resistance ratings for glazed or unglazed nonload-bearing facing tile walls and partitions. Minimum thickness of assembly is indicated as required for the fire-resistance rating shown. *[Source: IBC Table 720.1(2).]*

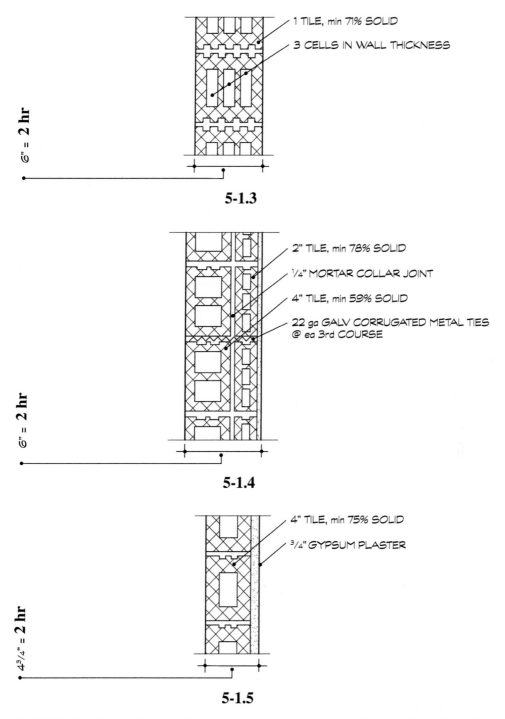

5-1.3

1 TILE, min 71% SOLID

3 CELLS IN WALL THICKNESS

6" = 2 hr

5-1.4

2" TILE, min 78% SOLID

¼" MORTAR COLLAR JOINT

4" TILE, min 59% SOLID

22 ga GALV CORRUGATED METAL TIES @ ea 3rd COURSE

6" = 2 hr

5-1.5

4" TILE, min 75% SOLID

¾" GYPSUM PLASTER

4¾" = 2 hr

Fig. 720.1(2) 5B. Fire-resistance ratings for glazed or unglazed nonload-bearing facing tile walls and partitions. Minimum thickness of assembly is indicated as required for the fire-resistance rating shown. *[Source: IBC Table 720.1(2).]*

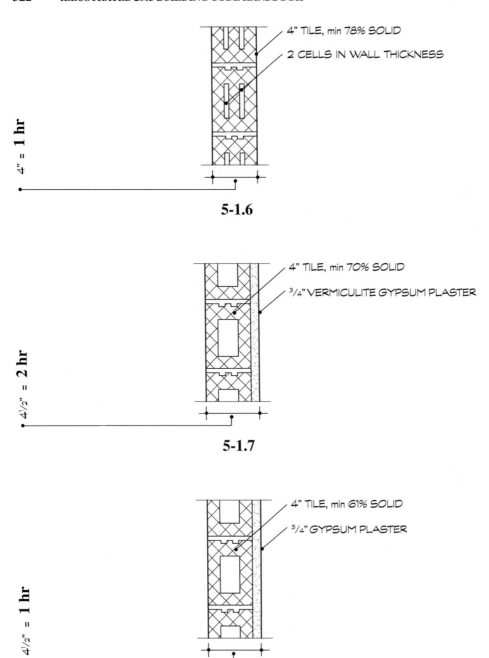

4" = 1 hr

4" TILE, min 78% SOLID

2 CELLS IN WALL THICKNESS

5-1.6

4½" = 2 hr

4" TILE, min 70% SOLID

¾" VERMICULITE GYPSUM PLASTER

5-1.7

4½" = 1 hr

4" TILE, min 61% SOLID

¾" GYPSUM PLASTER

5-1.8

Fig. 720.1(2) 5C. Fire-resistance ratings for glazed or unglazed nonload-bearing facing tile walls and partitions. Minimum thickness of assembly is indicated as required for the fire-resistance rating shown. *[Source: IBC Table 720.1(2).]*

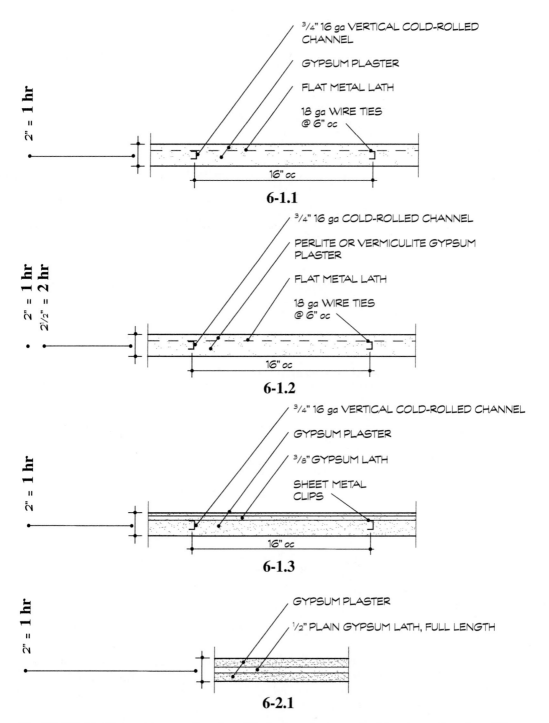

Fig. 720.1(2) 6A. Fire-resistance ratings for solid gypsum plaster nonload-bearing walls and partitions.
Minimum thickness of assembly is indicated as required for the fire-resistance rating shown. *[Source: IBC Table 720.1(2).]*

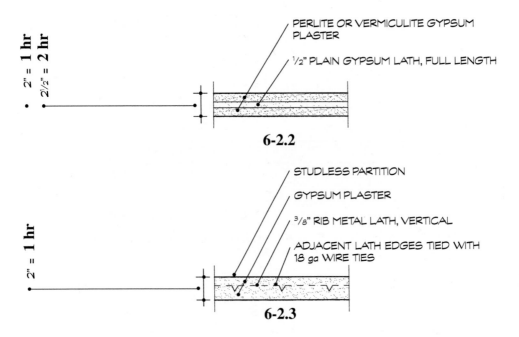

Fig. 720.1(2) 6B. Fire-resistance ratings for solid gypsum plaster nonload-bearing walls and partitions. Minimum thickness of assembly is indicated as required for the fire-resistance rating shown. *[Source: IBC Table 720.1(2).]*

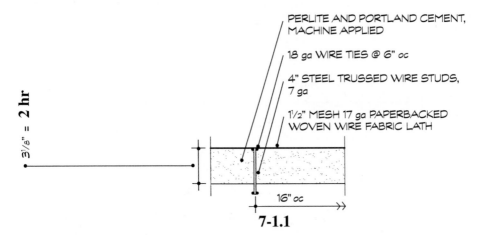

Fig. 720.1(2) 7A. Fire-resistance ratings for solid perlite and portland cement nonload-bearing walls and partitions. Minimum thickness of assembly is indicated as required for the fire-resistance rating shown. *[Source: IBC Table 720.1(2).]*

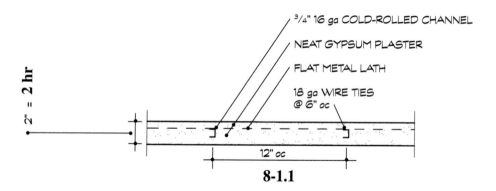

Fig. 720.1(2) 8A. Fire-resistance ratings for solid neat wood fibered gypsum plaster nonload-bearing walls and partitions. Minimum thickness of assembly is indicated as required for the fire-resistance rating shown. *[Source: IBC Table 720.1(2).]*

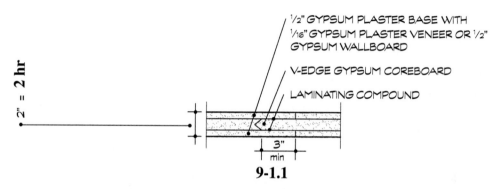

Fig. 720.1(2) 9A. Fire-resistance ratings for solid gypsum wallboard nonload-bearing walls and partitions. Minimum thickness of assembly is indicated as required for the fire-resistance rating shown. *[Source: IBC Table 720.1(2).]*

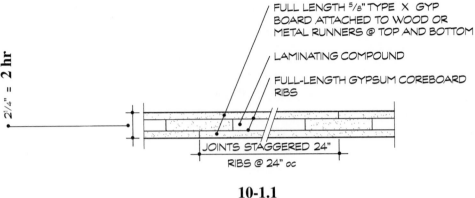

2¼" = 2 hr

FULL LENGTH ⅝" TYPE X GYP BOARD ATTACHED TO WOOD OR METAL RUNNERS @ TOP AND BOTTOM

LAMINATING COMPOUND

FULL-LENGTH GYPSUM COREBOARD RIBS

JOINTS STAGGERED 24"

RIBS @ 24" oc

10-1.1

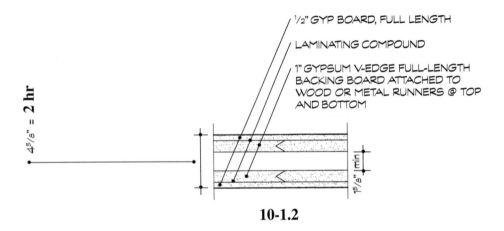

4⅝" = 2 hr

½" GYP BOARD, FULL LENGTH

LAMINATING COMPOUND

1" GYPSUM V-EDGE FULL-LENGTH BACKING BOARD ATTACHED TO WOOD OR METAL RUNNERS @ TOP AND BOTTOM

1⅝" min

10-1.2

Fig. 720.1(2) 10A. Fire-resistance ratings for hollow (studless) gypsum wallboard nonload-bearing walls and partitions. Minimum thickness of assembly is indicated as required for the fire-resistance rating shown. *[Source: IBC Table 720.1(2).]*

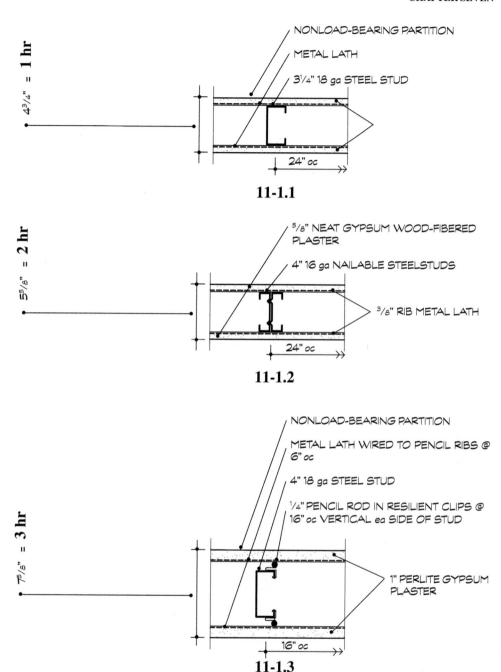

Fig. 720.1(2) 11A. Fire-resistance ratings for interior partitions with noncombustible studs and plaster.
Minimum thickness of assembly is indicated as required for the fire-resistance rating shown. *[Source: IBC Table 720.1(2).]*

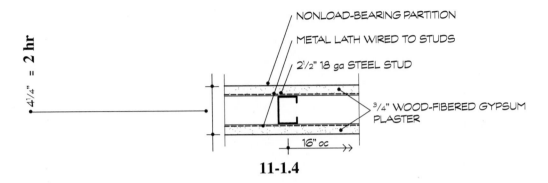

4¼" = 2 hr

NONLOAD-BEARING PARTITION

METAL LATH WIRED TO STUDS

2½" 18 ga STEEL STUD

¾" WOOD-FIBERED GYPSUM PLASTER

16" oc

11-1.4

Fig. 720.1(2) 11B. Fire-resistance ratings for interior partitions with noncombustible studs and plaster. Minimum thickness of assembly is indicated as required for the fire-resistance rating shown. *[Source: IBC Table 720.1(2).]*

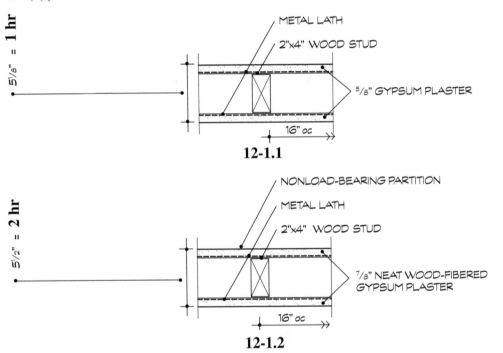

5⅝" = 1 hr

METAL LATH

2"x4" WOOD STUD

⅝" GYPSUM PLASTER

16" oc

12-1.1

5½" = 2 hr

NONLOAD-BEARING PARTITION

METAL LATH

2"x4" WOOD STUD

⅞" NEAT WOOD-FIBERED GYPSUM PLASTER

16" oc

12-1.2

Fig. 720.1(2) 12A. Fire-resistance ratings for interior partitions with wood studs and plaster. Minimum thickness of assembly is indicated as required for the fire-resistance rating shown. *[Source: IBC Table 720.1(2).]*

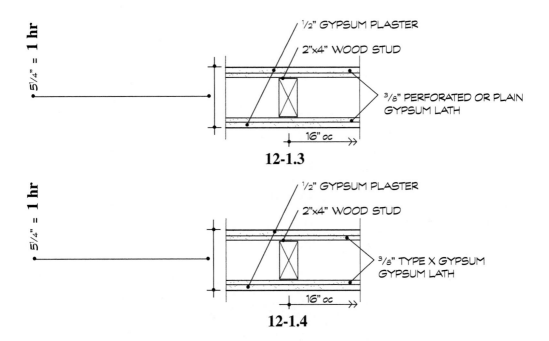

12-1.3

12-1.4

Fig. 720.1(2) 12B. Fire-resistance ratings for interior partitions with wood studs and plaster. Minimum thickness of assembly is indicated as required for the fire-resistance rating shown. *[Source: IBC Table 720.1(2).]*

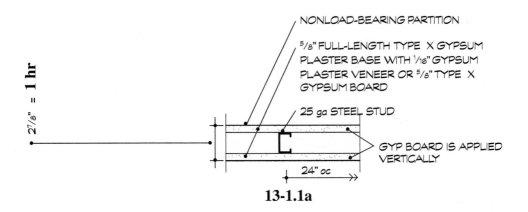

13-1.1a

Fig. 720.1(2) 13A. Fire-resistance ratings for interior partitions with noncombustible studs and gypsum board. Minimum thickness of assembly is indicated as required for the fire-resistance rating shown. *[Source: IBC Table 720.1(2).]*

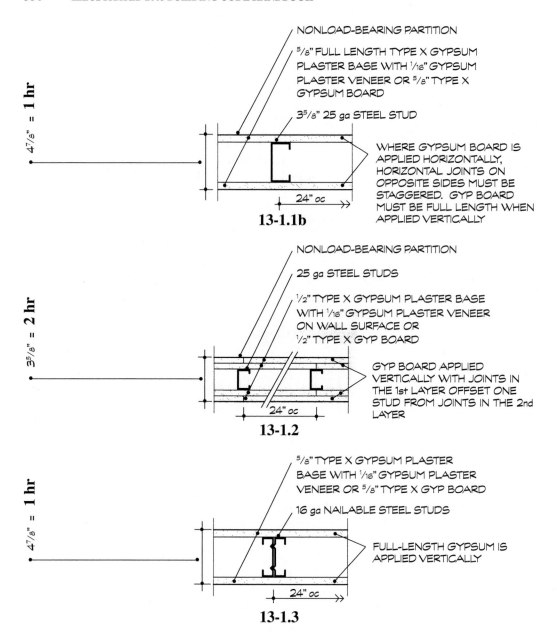

Fig. 720.1(2) 13B. Fire-resistance ratings for interior partitions with noncombustible studs and gypsum board. Minimum thickness of assembly is indicated as required for the fire-resistance rating shown. *[Source: IBC Table 720.1(2).]*

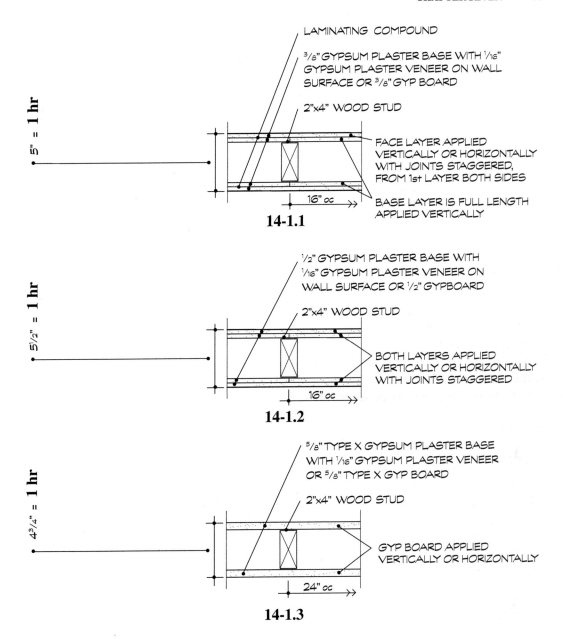

Fig. 720.1(2) 14A. Fire-resistance ratings for interior partitions with wood studs and gypsum board. Minimum thickness of assembly is indicated as required for the fire-resistance rating shown. *[Source: IBC Table 720.1(2).]*

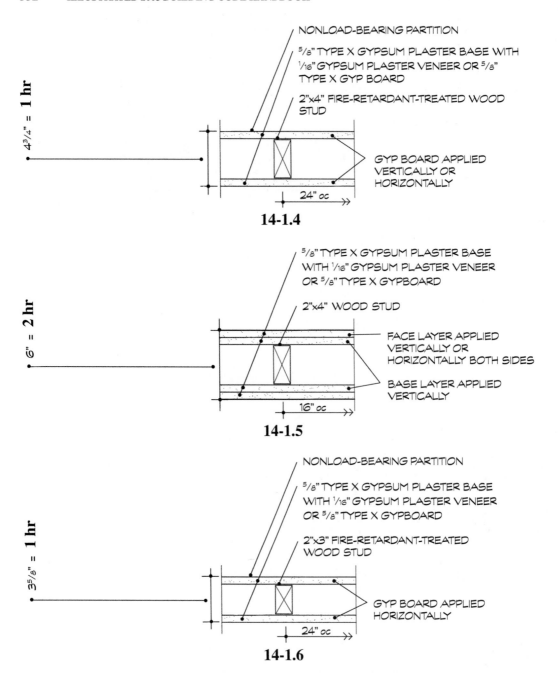

Fig. 720.1(2) 14B. Fire-resistance ratings for interior partitions with wood studs and gypsum board.
Minimum thickness of assembly is indicated as required for the fire-resistance rating shown. *[Source: IBC Table 720.1(2).]*

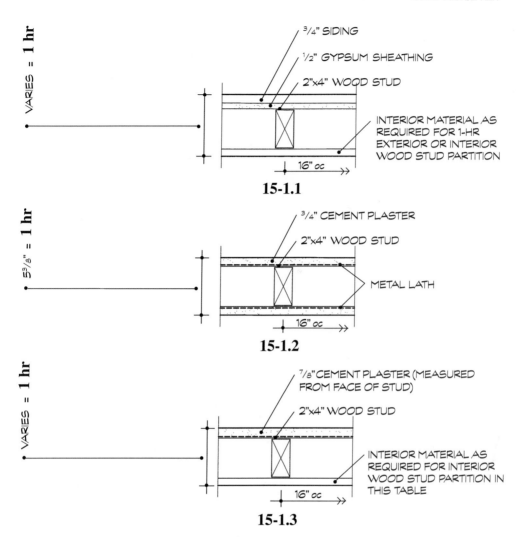

Fig. 720.1(2) 15A. Fire-resistance ratings for exterior or interior walls. Minimum thickness of assembly is indicated as required for the fire-resistance rating shown. *[Source: IBC Table 720.1(2).]*

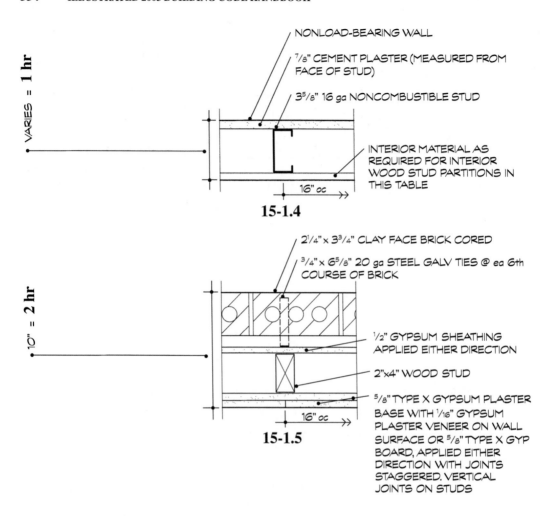

Fig. 720.1(2) 15B. Fire-resistance ratings for exterior or interior walls. Minimum thickness of assembly is indicated as required for the fire-resistance rating shown. *[Source: IBC Table 720.1(2).]*

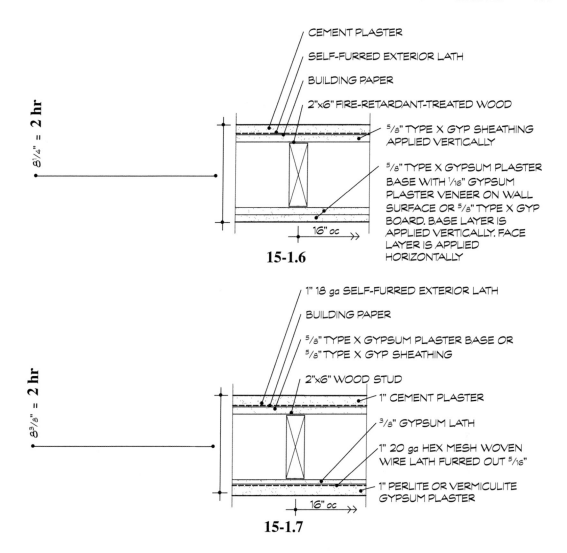

Fig. 720.1(2) 15C. Fire-resistance ratings for exterior or interior walls. Minimum thickness of assembly is indicated as required for the fire-resistance rating shown. *[Source: IBC Table 720.1(2).]*

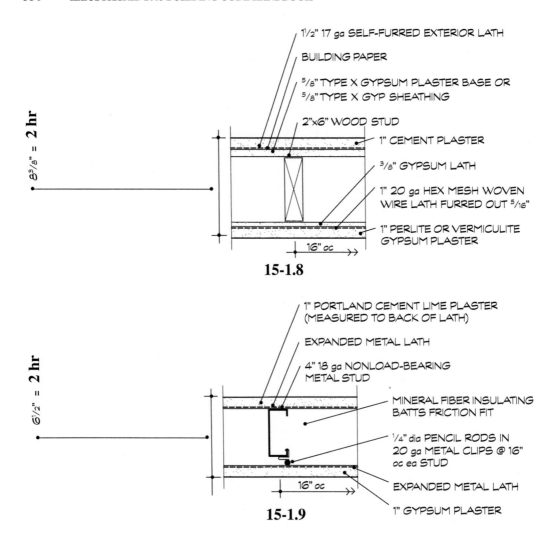

8³/₈" = 2 hr

1¹/₂" 17 ga SELF-FURRED EXTERIOR LATH

BUILDING PAPER

⁵/₈" TYPE X GYPSUM PLASTER BASE OR
⁵/₈" TYPE X GYP SHEATHING

2"x6" WOOD STUD

1" CEMENT PLASTER

³/₈" GYPSUM LATH

1" 20 ga HEX MESH WOVEN
WIRE LATH FURRED OUT ⁵/₁₆"

1" PERLITE OR VERMICULITE
GYPSUM PLASTER

16" oc

15-1.8

6¹/₂" = 2 hr

1" PORTLAND CEMENT LIME PLASTER
(MEASURED TO BACK OF LATH)

EXPANDED METAL LATH

4" 18 ga NONLOAD-BEARING
METAL STUD

MINERAL FIBER INSULATING
BATTS FRICTION FIT

¹/₄" dia PENCIL RODS IN
20 ga METAL CLIPS @ 16"
oc ea STUD

EXPANDED METAL LATH

1" GYPSUM PLASTER

16" oc

15-1.9

Fig. 720.1(2) 15D. Fire-resistance ratings for exterior or interior walls. Minimum thickness of assembly is indicated as required for the fire-resistance rating shown. *[Source: IBC Table 720.1(2).]*

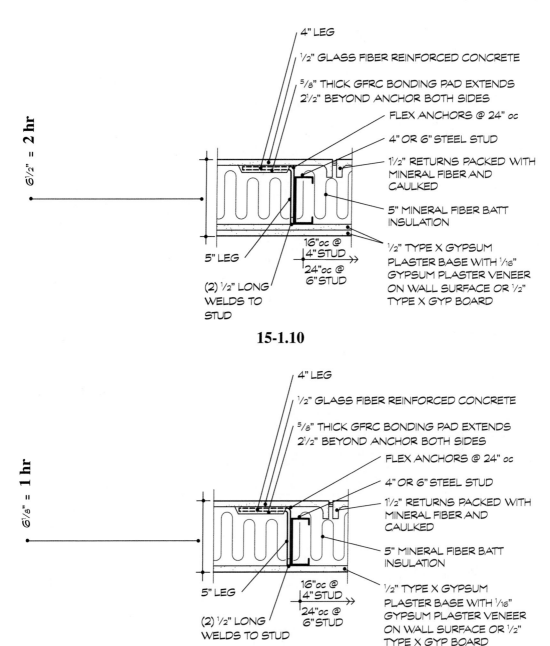

6½" = 2 hr

4" LEG

½" GLASS FIBER REINFORCED CONCRETE

⅝" THICK GFRC BONDING PAD EXTENDS
2½" BEYOND ANCHOR BOTH SIDES

FLEX ANCHORS @ 24" oc

4" OR 6" STEEL STUD

1½" RETURNS PACKED WITH
MINERAL FIBER AND
CAULKED

5" MINERAL FIBER BATT
INSULATION

½" TYPE X GYPSUM
PLASTER BASE WITH ¹⁄₁₆"
GYPSUM PLASTER VENEER
ON WALL SURFACE OR ½"
TYPE X GYP BOARD

5" LEG

16"oc @
4"STUD
24"oc @
6"STUD

(2) ½" LONG
WELDS TO
STUD

15-1.10

6⅛" = 1 hr

4" LEG

½" GLASS FIBER REINFORCED CONCRETE

⅝" THICK GFRC BONDING PAD EXTENDS
2½" BEYOND ANCHOR BOTH SIDES

FLEX ANCHORS @ 24" oc

4" OR 6" STEEL STUD

1½" RETURNS PACKED WITH
MINERAL FIBER AND
CAULKED

5" MINERAL FIBER BATT
INSULATION

½" TYPE X GYPSUM
PLASTER BASE WITH ¹⁄₁₆"
GYPSUM PLASTER VENEER
ON WALL SURFACE OR ½"
TYPE X GYP BOARD

5" LEG

16"oc @
4"STUD
24"oc @
6"STUD

(2) ½" LONG
WELDS TO STUD

15-1.11

Fig. 720.1(2) 15E. Fire-resistance ratings for exterior or interior walls. Minimum thickness of assembly is indicated as required for the fire-resistance rating shown. *[Source: IBC Table 720.1(2).]*

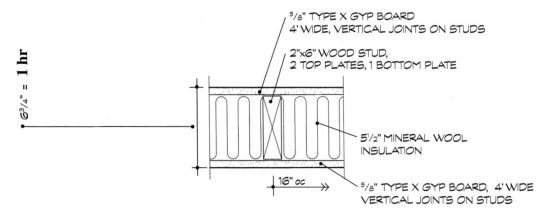

15-1.12

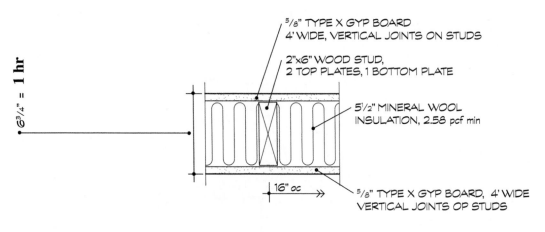

15-1.13

Fig. 720.1(2) 15F. Fire-resistance ratings for exterior or interior walls. Minimum thickness of assembly is indicated as required for the fire-resistance rating shown. These fire-resistance ratings are established for walls loaded to 100% of their design load. *[Source: IBC Table 720.1(2).]*

> Note: Section 2306, "Allowable Stress Design," is cited as the source of requirements for calculating allowable stress.

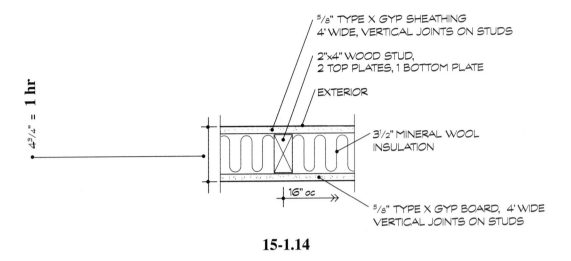

15-1.14

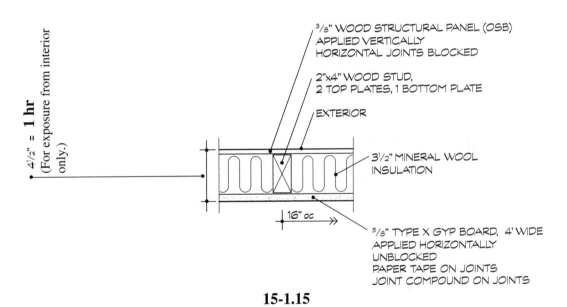

15-1.15

Fig. 720.1(2) 15G. Fire-resistance ratings for exterior or interior walls. Minimum thickness of assembly is indicated as required for the fire-resistance rating shown. These fire-resistance ratings are established for walls loaded to 100% of their design load. *[Source: IBC Table 720.1(2).]*

> *Note: Section 2306, "Allowable Stress Design," is cited as the source of requirements for calculating allowable stress.*

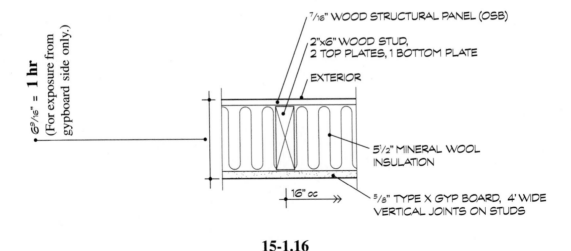

15-1.16

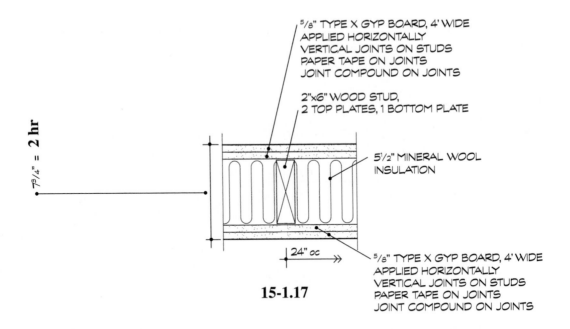

15-1.17

Fig. 720.1(2) 15H. Fire-resistance ratings for exterior or interior walls. Minimum thickness of assembly is indicated as required for the fire-resistance rating shown. These fire-resistance ratings are established for walls loaded to 100% of their design load. *[Source: IBC Table 720.1(2).]*

> *Note: Section 2306, "Allowable Stress Design," is cited as the source of requirements for calculating allowable stress.*

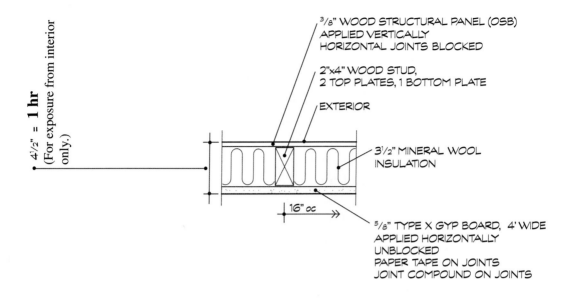

$4^{1}/_{2}" = $ **1 hr**
(For exposure from interior only.)

³/₈" WOOD STRUCTURAL PANEL (OSB)
APPLIED VERTICALLY
HORIZONTAL JOINTS BLOCKED

2"x4" WOOD STUD,
2 TOP PLATES, 1 BOTTOM PLATE

EXTERIOR

3¹/₂" MINERAL WOOL
INSULATION

16" oc

⁵/₈" TYPE X GYP BOARD, 4' WIDE
APPLIED HORIZONTALLY
UNBLOCKED
PAPER TAPE ON JOINTS
JOINT COMPOUND ON JOINTS

Note: 704.5, "Fire-resistance ratings," is cited as addressing, among other issues, exterior walls rated for exposure to fire only from the interior. Such walls must have a fire separation distance ≥ 5'.

16-1.1

Fig. 720.1(2) 15I. Fire-resistance ratings for exterior walls. Minimum thickness of assembly is indicated as required for the fire-resistance rating shown. These fire-resistance ratings are established for walls loaded to 100% of their design load. *[Source: IBC Table 720.1(2).]*

Note: Section 2306, "Allowable Stress Design," is cited as the source of requirements for calculating allowable stress.

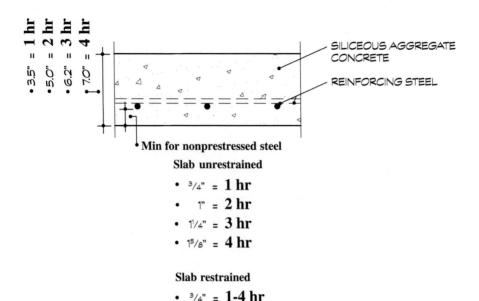

1-1.1

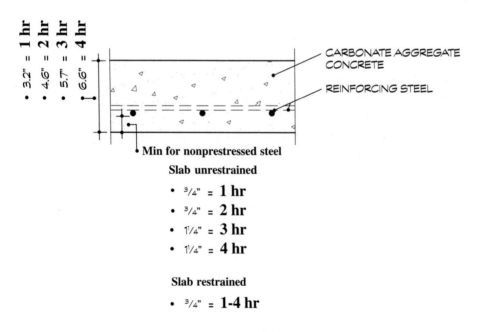

2-1.1

Fig. 720.1(3) 1–5A. Minimum protection for concrete floor and roof systems. Minimum thickness of assembly is indicated as required for the fire-resistance rating shown. *[Source: IBC Table 720.1(3).]*

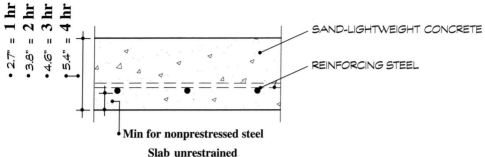

- 2.7" = **1 hr**
- 3.8" = **2 hr**
- 4.6" = **3 hr**
- 5.4" = **4 hr**

SAND-LIGHTWEIGHT CONCRETE

REINFORCING STEEL

•**Min for nonprestressed steel**

Slab unrestrained

- ³/₄" = **1 hr**
- ³/₄" = **2 hr**
- 1¼" = **3 hr**
- 1¼" = **4 hr**

Slab restrained

- ³/₄" = **1-4 hr**

3-1.1

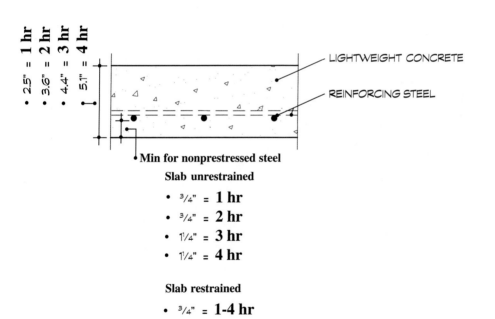

- 2.5" = **1 hr**
- 3.6" = **2 hr**
- 4.4" = **3 hr**
- 5.1" = **4 hr**

LIGHTWEIGHT CONCRETE

REINFORCING STEEL

•**Min for nonprestressed steel**

Slab unrestrained

- ³/₄" = **1 hr**
- ³/₄" = **2 hr**
- 1¼" = **3 hr**
- 1¼" = **4 hr**

Slab restrained

- ³/₄" = **1-4 hr**

4-1.1

Fig. 720.1(3) 1–5B. Minimum protection for concrete floor and roof systems. Minimum thickness of assembly is indicated as required for the fire-resistance rating shown. *[Source: IBC Table 720.1(3).]*

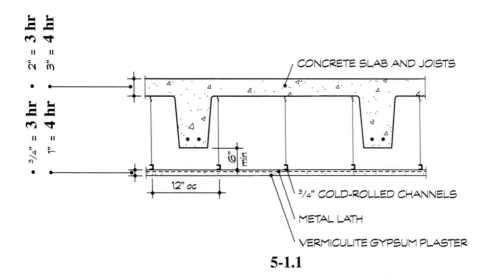

5-1.1

Fig. 720.1(3) 1–5C. Minimum protection for concrete floor and roof systems. Minimum thickness of assembly is indicated as required for the fire-resistance rating shown. *[Source: IBC Table 720.1(3).]*

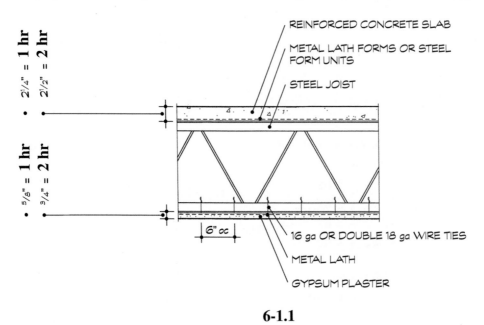

6-1.1

Fig. 720.1(3) 6–12A. Minimum protection for concrete and steel floor and roof systems. Minimum thickness of assembly is indicated as required for the fire-resistance rating shown. *[Source: IBC Table 720.1(3).]*

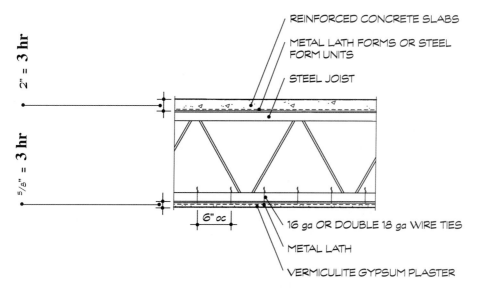

2" = 3 hr

⁵⁄₈" = 3 hr

REINFORCED CONCRETE SLABS

METAL LATH FORMS OR STEEL FORM UNITS

STEEL JOIST

6" oc

16 ga OR DOUBLE 18 ga WIRE TIES

METAL LATH

VERMICULITE GYPSUM PLASTER

6-2.1

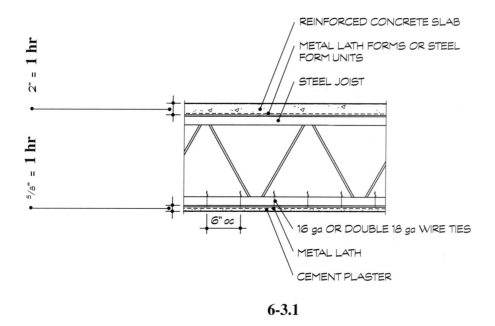

2" = 1 hr

⁵⁄₈" = 1 hr

REINFORCED CONCRETE SLAB

METAL LATH FORMS OR STEEL FORM UNITS

STEEL JOIST

6" oc

16 ga OR DOUBLE 18 ga WIRE TIES

METAL LATH

CEMENT PLASTER

6-3.1

Fig. 720.1(3) 6–12B. Minimum protection for concrete and steel floor and roof systems. Minimum thickness of assembly is indicated as required for the fire-resistance rating shown. *[Source: IBC Table 720.1(3).]*

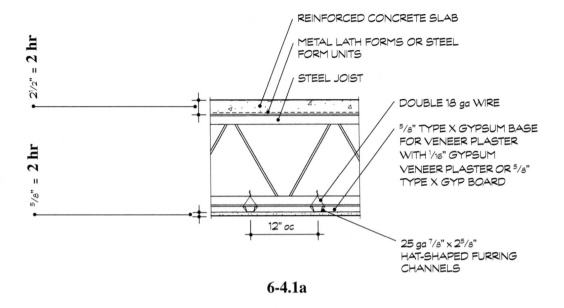

6-4.1a

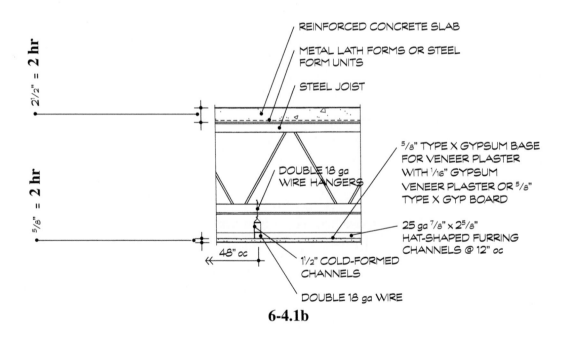

6-4.1b

Fig. 720.1(3) 6–12C. Minimum protection for concrete and steel floor and roof systems. Minimum thickness of assembly is indicated as required for the fire-resistance rating shown. *[Source: IBC Table 720.1(3).]*

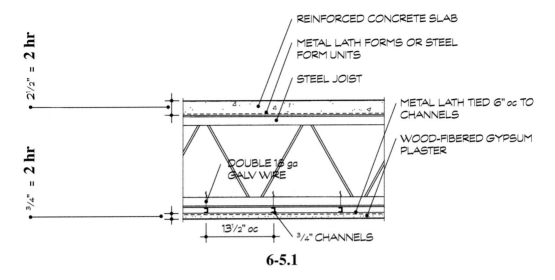

6-5.1

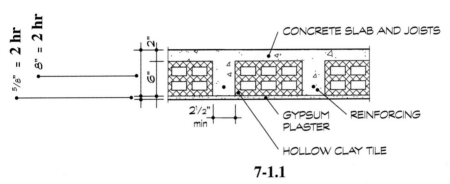

7-1.1

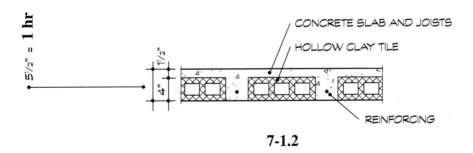

7-1.2

Fig. 720.1(3) 6–12D. Minimum protection for concrete and steel floor and roof systems. Minimum thickness of assembly is indicated as required for the fire-resistance rating shown. *[Source: IBC Table 720.1(3).]*

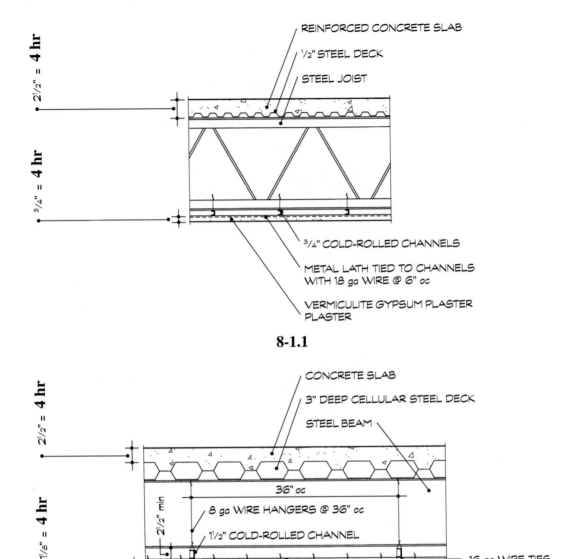

2½" = **4 hr**

¾" = **4 hr**

REINFORCED CONCRETE SLAB

½" STEEL DECK

STEEL JOIST

¾" COLD-ROLLED CHANNELS

METAL LATH TIED TO CHANNELS
WITH 18 ga WIRE @ 6" oc

VERMICULITE GYPSUM PLASTER
PLASTER

8-1.1

2½" = **4 hr**

1⅛" = **4 hr**

CONCRETE SLAB

3" DEEP CELLULAR STEEL DECK

STEEL BEAM

36" oc

2½" min

8 ga WIRE HANGERS @ 36" oc

1½" COLD-ROLLED CHANNEL

16 ga WIRE TIES

6" oc

¾" COLD-ROLLED CHANNELS @ 12" oc

METAL LATH

⅝" VERMICULITE GYPSUM PLASTER BASE
COAT AND ½" VERMICULITE ACOUSTICAL
PLASTER

9-1.1

Fig. 720.1(3) 6–12E. Minimum protection for concrete and steel floor and roof systems. Minimum
thickness of assembly is indicated as required for the fire-resistance rating shown. *[Source: IBC Table 720.1(3).]*

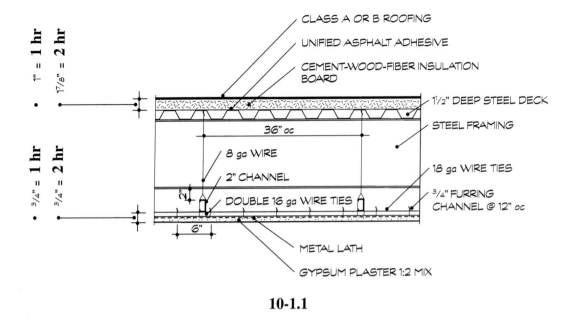

1" = 1 hr
17/8" = 2 hr

3/4" = 1 hr
3/4" = 2 hr

CLASS A OR B ROOFING

UNIFIED ASPHALT ADHESIVE

CEMENT-WOOD-FIBER INSULATION
BOARD

1 1/2" DEEP STEEL DECK

STEEL FRAMING

36" oc

8 ga WIRE

2" CHANNEL

DOUBLE 16 ga WIRE TIES

18 ga WIRE TIES

3/4" FURRING
CHANNEL @ 12" oc

METAL LATH

GYPSUM PLASTER 1:2 MIX

6"

2"

10-1.1

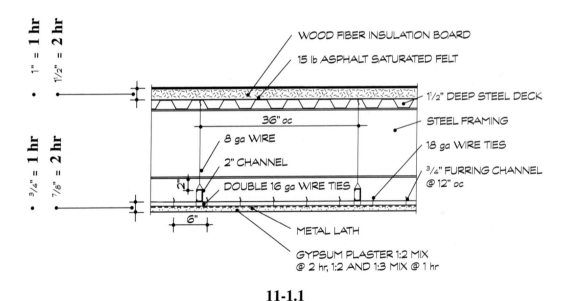

1" = 1 hr
1 1/2" = 2 hr

3/4" = 1 hr
7/8" = 2 hr

WOOD FIBER INSULATION BOARD

15 lb ASPHALT SATURATED FELT

1 1/2" DEEP STEEL DECK

STEEL FRAMING

36" oc

8 ga WIRE

2" CHANNEL

DOUBLE 16 ga WIRE TIES

18 ga WIRE TIES

3/4" FURRING CHANNEL
@ 12" oc

METAL LATH

GYPSUM PLASTER 1:2 MIX
@ 2 hr, 1:2 AND 1:3 MIX @ 1 hr

6"

2"

11-1.1

Fig. 720.1(3) 6–12F. Minimum protection for concrete and steel floor and roof systems. Minimum thickness of assembly is indicated as required for the fire-resistance rating shown. *[Source: IBC Table 720.1(3).]*

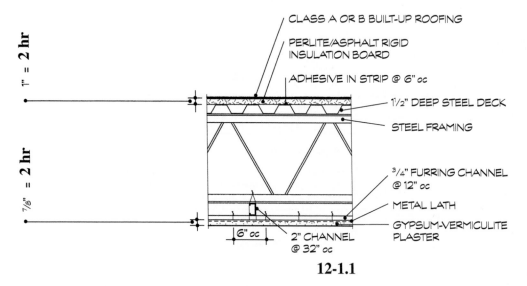

Fig. 720.1(3) 6–12G. Minimum protection for concrete and steel floor and roof systems. Minimum thickness of assembly is indicated as required for the fire-resistance rating shown. *[Source: IBC Table 720.1(3).]*

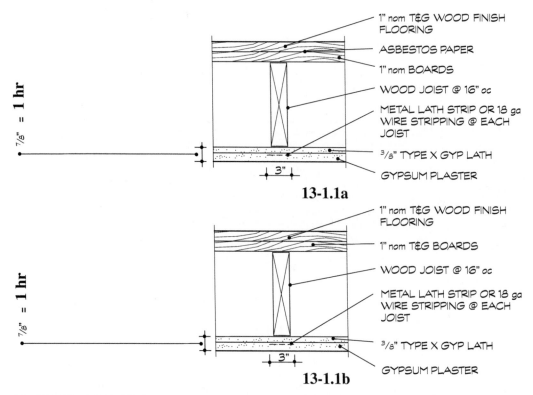

Fig. 720.1(3) 13–14A. Minimum protection for wood floor and roof systems. Minimum thickness of assembly is indicated as required for the fire-resistance rating shown. *[Source: IBC Table 720.1(3).]*

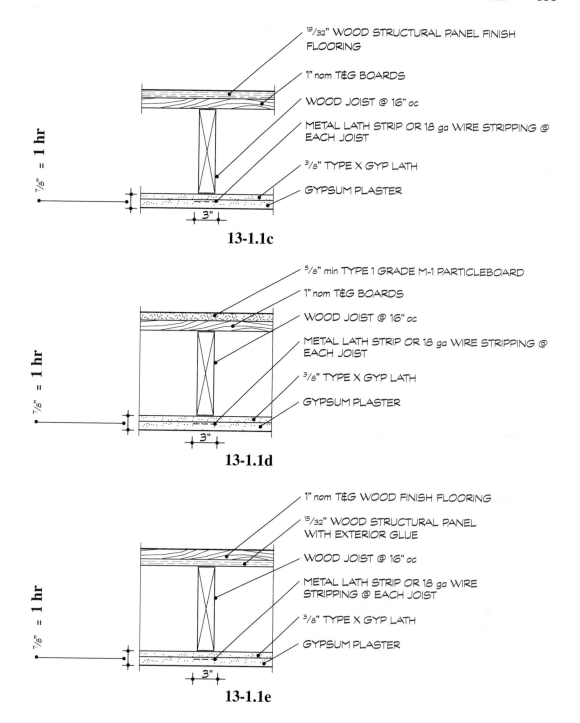

7/8" = 1 hr

¹⁹/₃₂" WOOD STRUCTURAL PANEL FINISH FLOORING

1" nom T&G BOARDS

WOOD JOIST @ 16" oc

METAL LATH STRIP OR 18 ga WIRE STRIPPING @ EACH JOIST

³/₈" TYPE X GYP LATH

GYPSUM PLASTER

3"

13-1.1c

7/8" = 1 hr

⁵/₈" min TYPE 1 GRADE M-1 PARTICLEBOARD

1" nom T&G BOARDS

WOOD JOIST @ 16" oc

METAL LATH STRIP OR 18 ga WIRE STRIPPING @ EACH JOIST

³/₈" TYPE X GYP LATH

GYPSUM PLASTER

3"

13-1.1d

7/8" = 1 hr

1" nom T&G WOOD FINISH FLOORING

¹⁵/₃₂" WOOD STRUCTURAL PANEL WITH EXTERIOR GLUE

WOOD JOIST @ 16" oc

METAL LATH STRIP OR 18 ga WIRE STRIPPING @ EACH JOIST

³/₈" TYPE X GYP LATH

GYPSUM PLASTER

3"

13-1.1e

Fig. 720.1(3) 13–14B. Minimum protection for wood floor and roof systems. Minimum thickness of assembly is indicated as required for the fire-resistance rating shown. *[Source: IBC Table 720.1(3).]*

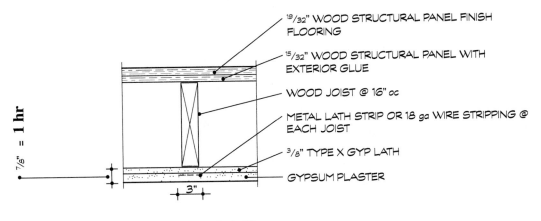

7/8" = 1 hr

¹⁹/₃₂" WOOD STRUCTURAL PANEL FINISH FLOORING

¹⁵/₃₂" WOOD STRUCTURAL PANEL WITH EXTERIOR GLUE

WOOD JOIST @ 16" oc

METAL LATH STRIP OR 18 ga WIRE STRIPPING @ EACH JOIST

³/₈" TYPE X GYP LATH

GYPSUM PLASTER

3"

13-1.1f

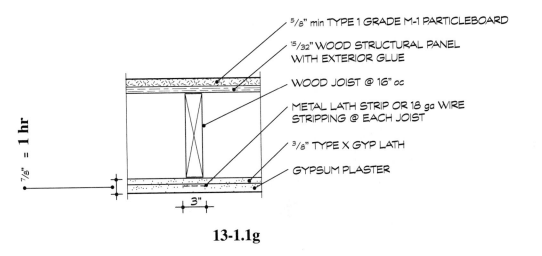

7/8" = 1 hr

⁵/₈" min TYPE 1 GRADE M-1 PARTICLEBOARD

¹⁵/₃₂" WOOD STRUCTURAL PANEL WITH EXTERIOR GLUE

WOOD JOIST @ 16" oc

METAL LATH STRIP OR 18 ga WIRE STRIPPING @ EACH JOIST

³/₈" TYPE X GYP LATH

GYPSUM PLASTER

3"

13-1.1g

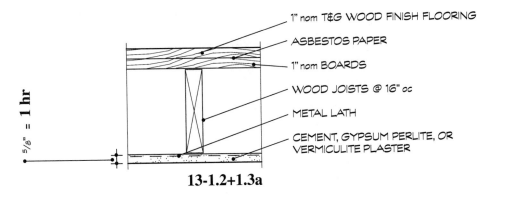

5/8" = 1 hr

1" nom T&G WOOD FINISH FLOORING

ASBESTOS PAPER

1" nom BOARDS

WOOD JOISTS @ 16" oc

METAL LATH

CEMENT, GYPSUM PERLITE, OR VERMICULITE PLASTER

13-1.2+1.3a

Fig. 720.1(3) 13–14C. Minimum protection for wood floor and roof systems. Minimum thickness of assembly is indicated as required for the fire-resistance rating shown. [*Source: IBC Table 720.1(3).*]

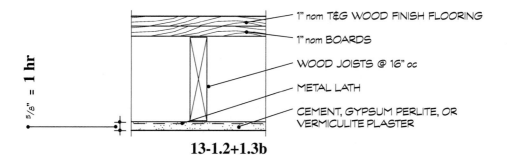

5/8" = 1 hr

1" nom T&G WOOD FINISH FLOORING

1" nom BOARDS

WOOD JOISTS @ 16" oc

METAL LATH

CEMENT, GYPSUM PERLITE, OR VERMICULITE PLASTER

13-1.2+1.3b

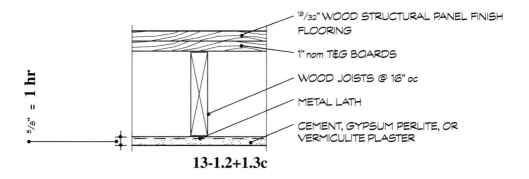

5/8" = 1 hr

19/32" WOOD STRUCTURAL PANEL FINISH FLOORING

1" nom T&G BOARDS

WOOD JOISTS @ 16" oc

METAL LATH

CEMENT, GYPSUM PERLITE, OR VERMICULITE PLASTER

13-1.2+1.3c

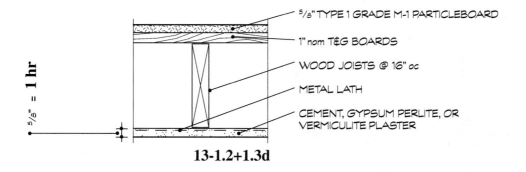

5/8" = 1 hr

5/8" TYPE 1 GRADE M-1 PARTICLEBOARD

1" nom T&G BOARDS

WOOD JOISTS @ 16" oc

METAL LATH

CEMENT, GYPSUM PERLITE, OR VERMICULITE PLASTER

13-1.2+1.3d

Fig. 720.1(3) 13–14D. Minimum protection for wood floor and roof systems. Minimum thickness of assembly is indicated as required for the fire-resistance rating shown. *[Source: IBC Table 720.1(3).]*

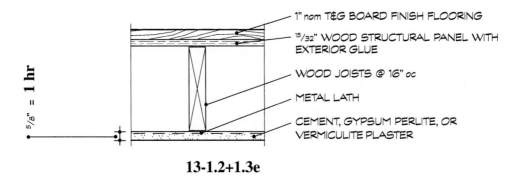

$5/8" = 1$ hr

- 1" nom T&G BOARD FINISH FLOORING
- $^{15}/_{32}"$ WOOD STRUCTURAL PANEL WITH EXTERIOR GLUE
- WOOD JOISTS @ 16" oc
- METAL LATH
- CEMENT, GYPSUM PERLITE, OR VERMICULITE PLASTER

13-1.2+1.3e

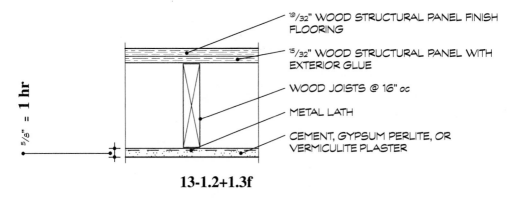

$5/8" = 1$ hr

- $^{19}/_{32}"$ WOOD STRUCTURAL PANEL FINISH FLOORING
- $^{15}/_{32}"$ WOOD STRUCTURAL PANEL WITH EXTERIOR GLUE
- WOOD JOISTS @ 16" oc
- METAL LATH
- CEMENT, GYPSUM PERLITE, OR VERMICULITE PLASTER

13-1.2+1.3f

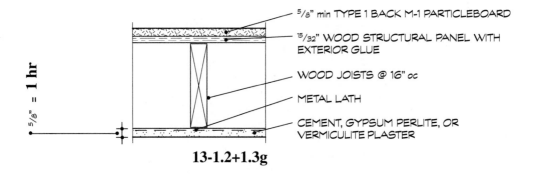

$5/8" = 1$ hr

- $5/8"$ min TYPE 1 BACK M-1 PARTICLEBOARD
- $^{15}/_{32}"$ WOOD STRUCTURAL PANEL WITH EXTERIOR GLUE
- WOOD JOISTS @ 16" oc
- METAL LATH
- CEMENT, GYPSUM PERLITE, OR VERMICULITE PLASTER

13-1.2+1.3g

Fig. 720.1(3) 13–14E. Minimum protection for wood floor and roof systems. Minimum thickness of assembly is indicated as required for the fire-resistance rating shown. *[Source: IBC Table 720.1(3).]*

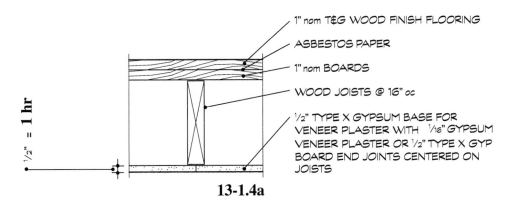

1" nom T&G WOOD FINISH FLOORING

ASBESTOS PAPER

1" nom BOARDS

WOOD JOISTS @ 16" oc

$\frac{1}{2}$" TYPE X GYPSUM BASE FOR VENEER PLASTER WITH $\frac{1}{16}$" GYPSUM VENEER PLASTER OR $\frac{1}{2}$" TYPE X GYP BOARD END JOINTS CENTERED ON JOISTS

$\frac{1}{2}$" = **1 hr**

13-1.4a

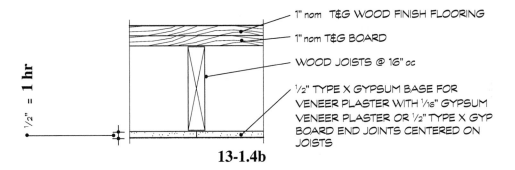

1" nom T&G WOOD FINISH FLOORING

1" nom T&G BOARD

WOOD JOISTS @ 16" oc

$\frac{1}{2}$" TYPE X GYPSUM BASE FOR VENEER PLASTER WITH $\frac{1}{16}$" GYPSUM VENEER PLASTER OR $\frac{1}{2}$" TYPE X GYP BOARD END JOINTS CENTERED ON JOISTS

$\frac{1}{2}$" = **1 hr**

13-1.4b

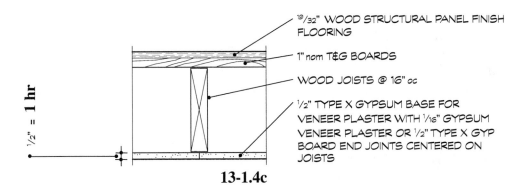

$\frac{19}{32}$" WOOD STRUCTURAL PANEL FINISH FLOORING

1" nom T&G BOARDS

WOOD JOISTS @ 16" oc

$\frac{1}{2}$" TYPE X GYPSUM BASE FOR VENEER PLASTER WITH $\frac{1}{16}$" GYPSUM VENEER PLASTER OR $\frac{1}{2}$" TYPE X GYP BOARD END JOINTS CENTERED ON JOISTS

$\frac{1}{2}$" = **1 hr**

13-1.4c

Fig. 720.1(3) 13–14F. Minimum protection for wood floor and roof systems. Minimum thickness of assembly is indicated as required for the fire-resistance rating shown. *[Source: IBC Table 720.1(3).]*

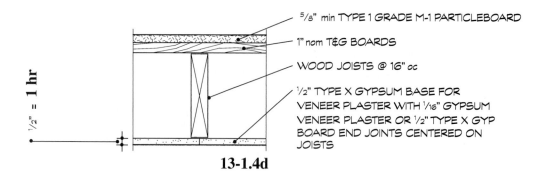

½" = 1 hr

⁵⁄₈" min TYPE 1 GRADE M-1 PARTICLEBOARD

1" nom T&G BOARDS

WOOD JOISTS @ 16" oc

½" TYPE X GYPSUM BASE FOR VENEER PLASTER WITH ¹⁄₁₆" GYPSUM VENEER PLASTER OR ½" TYPE X GYP BOARD END JOINTS CENTERED ON JOISTS

13-1.4d

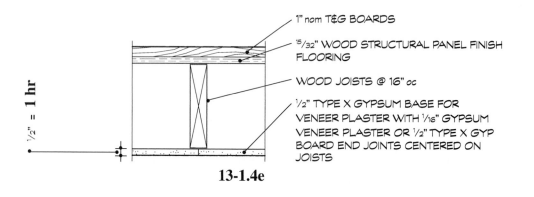

½" = 1 hr

1" nom T&G BOARDS

¹⁵⁄₃₂" WOOD STRUCTURAL PANEL FINISH FLOORING

WOOD JOISTS @ 16" oc

½" TYPE X GYPSUM BASE FOR VENEER PLASTER WITH ¹⁄₁₆" GYPSUM VENEER PLASTER OR ½" TYPE X GYP BOARD END JOINTS CENTERED ON JOISTS

13-1.4e

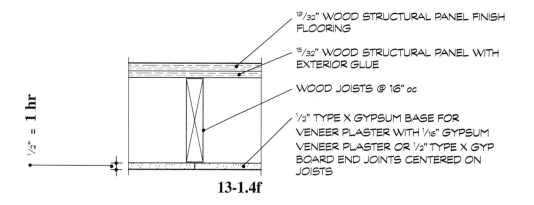

½" = 1 hr

¹⁹⁄₃₂" WOOD STRUCTURAL PANEL FINISH FLOORING

¹⁵⁄₃₂" WOOD STRUCTURAL PANEL WITH EXTERIOR GLUE

WOOD JOISTS @ 16" oc

½" TYPE X GYPSUM BASE FOR VENEER PLASTER WITH ¹⁄₁₆" GYPSUM VENEER PLASTER OR ½" TYPE X GYP BOARD END JOINTS CENTERED ON JOISTS

13-1.4f

Fig. 720.1(3) 13–14G. Minimum protection for wood floor and roof systems. Minimum thickness of assembly is indicated as required for the fire-resistance rating shown. *[Source: IBC Table 720.1(3).]*

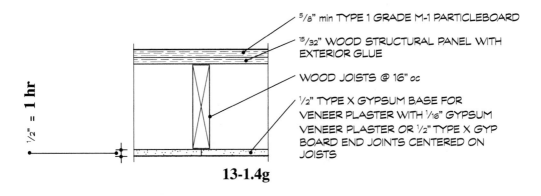

1/2" = 1 hr

⁵/₈" min TYPE 1 GRADE M-1 PARTICLEBOARD

¹⁵/₃₂" WOOD STRUCTURAL PANEL WITH EXTERIOR GLUE

WOOD JOISTS @ 16" oc

1/2" TYPE X GYPSUM BASE FOR VENEER PLASTER WITH 1/16" GYPSUM VENEER PLASTER OR 1/2" TYPE X GYP BOARD END JOINTS CENTERED ON JOISTS

13-1.4g

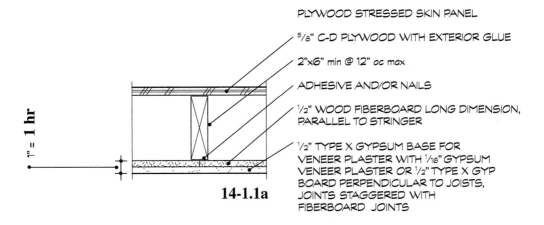

1" = 1 hr

PLYWOOD STRESSED SKIN PANEL

⁵/₈" C-D PLYWOOD WITH EXTERIOR GLUE

2"x6" min @ 12" oc max

ADHESIVE AND/OR NAILS

1/2" WOOD FIBERBOARD LONG DIMENSION, PARALLEL TO STRINGER

1/2" TYPE X GYPSUM BASE FOR VENEER PLASTER WITH 1/16" GYPSUM VENEER PLASTER OR 1/2" TYPE X GYP BOARD PERPENDICULAR TO JOISTS, JOINTS STAGGERED WITH FIBERBOARD JOINTS

14-1.1a

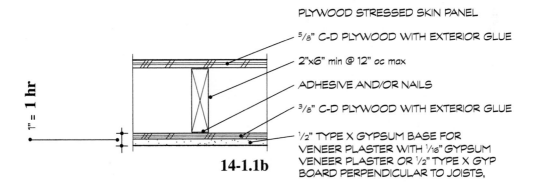

1" = 1 hr

PLYWOOD STRESSED SKIN PANEL

⁵/₈" C-D PLYWOOD WITH EXTERIOR GLUE

2"x6" min @ 12" oc max

ADHESIVE AND/OR NAILS

³/₈" C-D PLYWOOD WITH EXTERIOR GLUE

1/2" TYPE X GYPSUM BASE FOR VENEER PLASTER WITH 1/16" GYPSUM VENEER PLASTER OR 1/2" TYPE X GYP BOARD PERPENDICULAR TO JOISTS,

14-1.1b

Fig. 720.1(3) 13–14H. Minimum protection for wood floor and roof systems. Minimum thickness of assembly is indicated as required for the fire-resistance rating shown. *[Source: IBC Table 720.1(3).]*

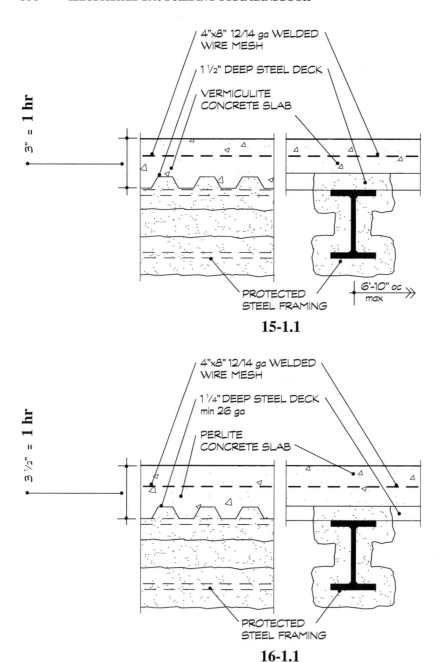

3" = 1 hr

4"x8" 12/14 ga WELDED WIRE MESH

1 1/2" DEEP STEEL DECK

VERMICULITE CONCRETE SLAB

PROTECTED STEEL FRAMING

6'-10" oc max

15-1.1

3 1/2" = 1 hr

4"x8" 12/14 ga WELDED WIRE MESH

1 1/4" DEEP STEEL DECK min 26 ga

PERLITE CONCRETE SLAB

PROTECTED STEEL FRAMING

16-1.1

Fig. 720.1(3) 15–20A. Minimum protection for concrete and steel floor and roof systems. Minimum thickness of assembly is indicated as required for the fire-resistance rating shown. *[Source: IBC Table 720.1(3).]*

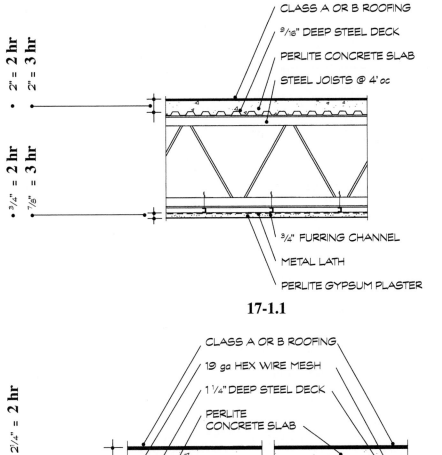

2" = 2 hr
2" = 3 hr

³⁄₄" = 2 hr
⁷⁄₈" = 3 hr

CLASS A OR B ROOFING

⁹⁄₁₆" DEEP STEEL DECK

PERLITE CONCRETE SLAB

STEEL JOISTS @ 4' oc

³⁄₄" FURRING CHANNEL

METAL LATH

PERLITE GYPSUM PLASTER

17-1.1

2¼" = 2 hr

CLASS A OR B ROOFING

19 ga HEX WIRE MESH

1¼" DEEP STEEL DECK

PERLITE
CONCRETE SLAB

PROTECTED
STEEL FRAMING

18-1.1

6'-10" oc max
WHERE DECK IS
< 26 ga

8'-0" oc max
WHERE DECK IS
≥ 26 ga

Fig. 720.1(3) 15–20B. Minimum protection for concrete and steel floor and roof systems. Minimum thickness of assembly is indicated as required for the fire-resistance rating shown. *[Source: IBC Table 720.1(3).]*

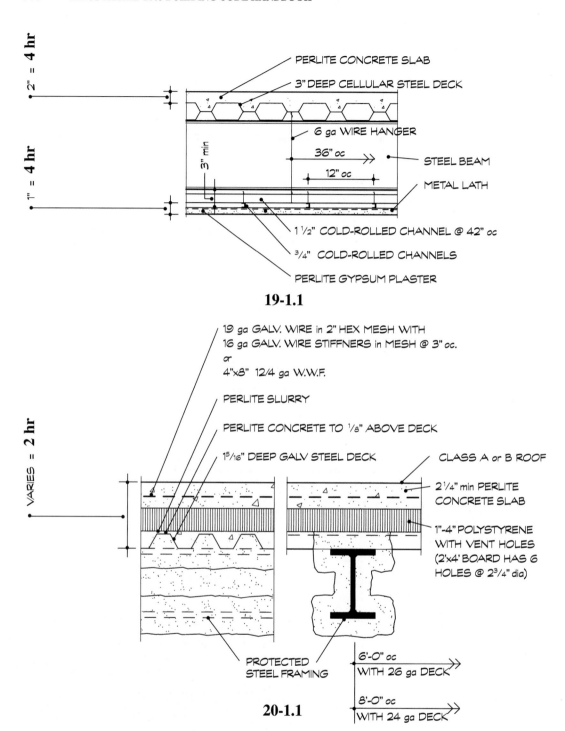

Fig. 720.1(3) 15–20C. Minimum protection for concrete and steel floor and roof systems. Minimum thickness of assembly is indicated as required for the fire-resistance rating shown. *[Source: IBC Table 720.1(3).]*

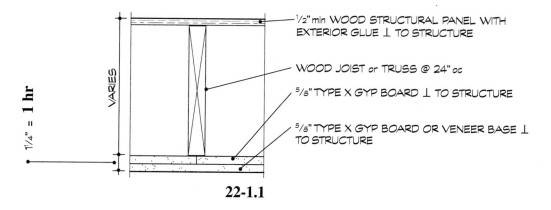

1 hr = 1/4"

22-1.1

Note: Chapter 23, "Wood," is cited as governing the thickness of the wood structural panel. The section might supersede the thickness shown in the drawing in some cases.

Fig. 720.1(3) 22A. Minimum protection for wood floor and roof systems. Minimum thickness of assembly is indicated as required for the fire-resistance rating shown. *[Source: IBC Table 720.1(3).]*

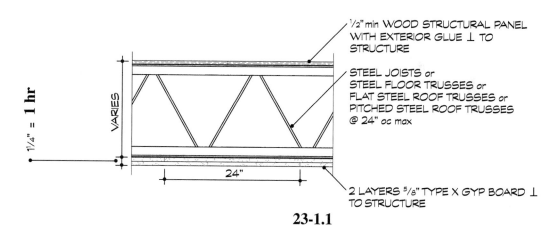

1 hr = 1/4"

23-1.1

Note: Chapter 22, "Steel," is cited as governing the thickness of the wood structural panel. The section might supersede the thickness shown in the drawing in some cases.

Fig. 720.1(3) 23A. Minimum protection for steel and wood floor and roof systems. Minimum thickness of assembly is indicated as required for the fire-resistance rating shown. *[Source: IBC Table 720.1(3).]*

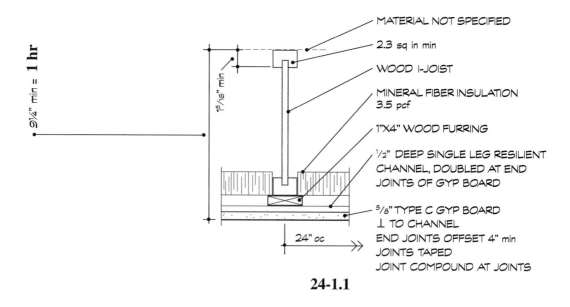

24-1.1

Fig. 720.1(3) 24A. Minimum protection for wood floor and roof systems. Thickness of assembly varies for the fire-resistance rating shown. *[Source: IBC Table 720.1(3).]*

720 Prescriptive Fire Resistance

720.1.3 Reinforcement for cast-in-place concrete column protection

- Cast-in-place concrete protection for steel columns requires the following or equivalent:
  - Wire ties as follows:
    To have a diameter ≥ 0.18".
    To be located a the edges of the column.
    To be wound around the column in a spiral path with a pitch ≤ 8".

720.1.4 Plaster application

- A finish coat of a protective plaster cover is not required in the following case:
  - Where the following meet the requirements of details provided in this section:
    Plaster design mix.
    Total plaster thickness indicated.

  Note: The following tables are cited as listing minimum requirements:
  IBC Table 720.1(1), "Minimum Protection of Structural Parts Based on Time
  Periods for Various Noncombustible Insulating Materials."
  IBC Table 720.1(2), "Rated Fire-Resistance Periods for Various Walls and
  Partitions."
  IBC Table 720.1(3), "Minimum Protection for Floor and Roof Systems."

720.1.5 Bonded prestressed concrete tendons

- The concrete cover for prestressed tendons must be as required by details provided in this section as follows:
  - Where there are single tendons.
    Cover is measured from the nearest surface.
- Multiple tendons with different concrete covers are governed for fire protection as follows:
  - The average cover must be ≥ that required by details provided in this section as follows:
    The average cover is based the following:
      The clear distance from each tendon to the nearest surface.
  - The cover for any tendon may not be less than the following:
    That specified by details provided in this section.
    Required cover for slabs with any type aggregate is ≥ ¾".
    Required cover for beams with any type aggregate is ≥ ¾".
    Tendons with cover less than required are governed as follows:
      They must provide ≤ 50% of the ultimate moment capacity in the following case:
        Where members have a cross-sectional area < 350 sq in.
      They must provide ≤ 65% of the ultimate moment capacity in the following case:
        Where members have a cross-sectional area ≥ 350 sq in.
  - The following assumption is made regarding reduced cover permitted for fire protection:
    Structural integrity is not affected.

  Note: IBC Table 720.1(1), "Minimum Protection of Structural Parts Based on Time
  Periods for Various Noncombustible Insulating Materials," is cited as
  governing the above requirements.

721 Calculated Fire Resistance

721.1.1 Definitions *(part 1 of 2)*

- **Ceramic fiber blanket**
  - Mineral wool insulation as follows:
    Alumina-silica fibers.
    $\geq$ 4 lb/cu ft and $\leq$ 10 lb/cu ft.

- **Concrete, carbonate aggregate**
  - Aggregates are mainly one or both of the following substances:
    Calcium carbonate.
    Magnesium carbonate.
  - Examples of aggregates include the following:
    Limestone.
    Dolomite.
  - Aggregates consist of $\leq$ 40% of the following substances:
    Quartz.
    Chert.
    Flint.

- **Concrete, cellular**
  - Insulating concrete as follows:
    Preformed foam and portland cement slurry mixture.
    Dry weight $\simeq$ 30 pcf.

- **Concrete, lightweight aggregate**
  - Aggregates are one or more of the following:
    Expanded clay.
    Expanded shale.
    Expanded slag.
    Expanded slate.
    Sintered fly ash.
    Natural lightweight aggregates as follows:
      With the same fire-resistive properties as those listed above.
      $\geq$ 85 and $\leq$ 115 pcf.

  *Note: ASTM C 330, "Specifications for Lightweight Aggregates for Structural Concrete,"
  is cited as governing aggregate properties listed above.*

- **Concrete, perlite**
  - Insulating concrete as follows:
    Dry weight $\simeq$ 30 pcf.
    With perlite aggregate as follows:
      From volcanic rock.
      Expanded with heat.
      A glasslike substance.
      Cellular in nature.

721 Calculated Fire Resistance

721.1.1 Definitions *(part 2 of 2)*

- **Concrete, sand-lightweight**
  - Aggregates are one or more of the following mixed with natural sand:
    Expanded clay.
    Expanded shale.
    Expanded slag.
    Expanded slate.
    Sintered fly ash.
    Natural lightweight aggregates as follows:
      With the same fire-resistive properties as those listed above.
      ≥ 105 and ≤ 120 pcf.

  Note: ASTM C 330, "Specifications for Lightweight Aggregates for Structural Concrete," is cited as governing aggregate properties.

- **Concrete, siliceous aggregate**
  - Aggregates are normal weight.
  - Aggregates are mainly in one of the following substances:
    Silica.
    Compounds other than the following:
      Calcium carbonate.
      Magnesium carbonate.
  - Aggregates contain $> 40\%$ of the following substances:
    Quartz.
    Chert.
    Flint.

- **Concrete, vermiculite**
  - Insulating concrete as follows:
    Dry weight $\simeq 30$ pcf.
    With vermiculite aggregate as follows:
      Laminated micaceous substance.
      Ore is expanded with heat.

- **Glass fiberboard**
  - Roof insulation as follows:
    Inorganic glass fibers with binder.
    Formed into rigid boards.
  - Top surface is faced as follows:
    With asphalt and glass fiber reinforced kraft paper.

- **Mineral board**
  - Rigid insulation in flat rectangular boards.
  - One of the following substances:
    Felted mineral fiber.
    Cellular beads of expanded aggregate.

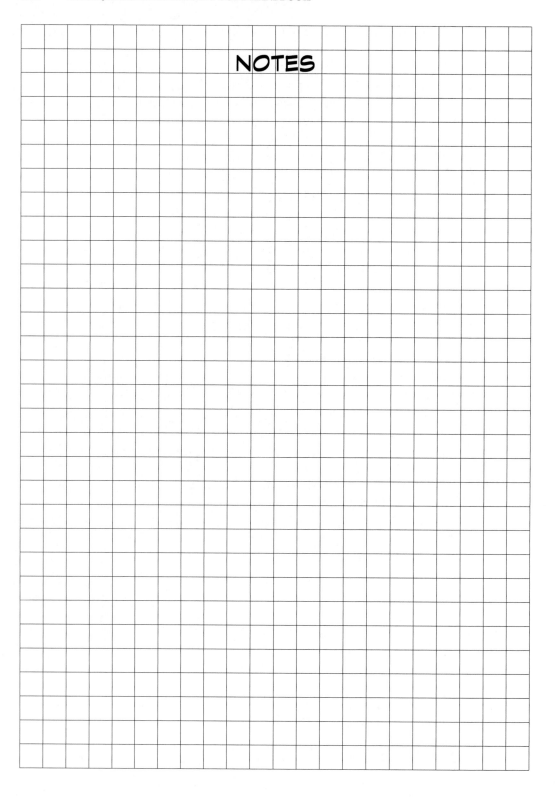

NOTES

8

Interior Finishes

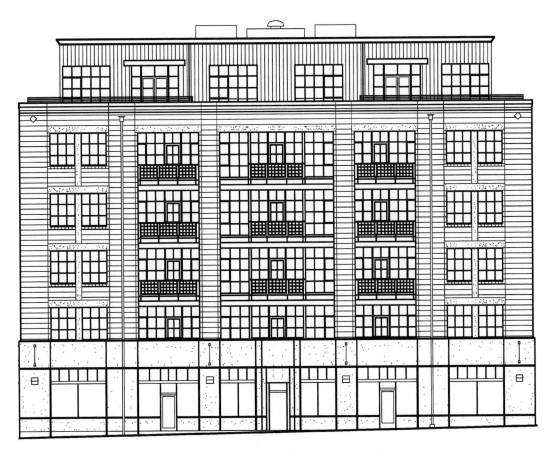

McKenzie Lofts. Portland, Oregon.
Ankrom Moisan Associated Architects. Portland, Oregon.

801 General

801.1 Scope

- This chapter governs materials used for the following:
  - Interior finishes.
  - Interior trim.
  - Interior decorative materials.

801.1.1 Interior finishes

- The following standards required by this chapter do not apply to the materials listed below:
  - Standards not applicable to materials below:
    Flame spread index.
    Smoke-developed index.
  - Materials with the following characteristics are not governed by the standards listed above:
    With a thickness < 0.036".
    Applied directly to the following surfaces:
      Walls.
      Ceilings.
- The following materials are not governed by interior finish requirements:
  - Exposed parts of structural members as follows:
    Those meeting requirements of Type IV construction.

  Note: 602.4, "Type IV," is cited as defining the pertinent requirements of Type IV construction.

- Other interior materials are governed by the following standards based on the criteria listed below:
  - Applicable standards:
    Flame spread index.
    Smoke-developed index.
  - Criteria affecting indexes of above standards:
    Location.
    Occupancy.

801.1.2 Decorative materials and trim

- The following properties are governed by this chapter for the materials listed below:
  - Properties governed:
    Combustibility.
    Flame resistance.
  - Materials governed:
    Decorative materials.
    Trim.

  Note: Section 805, "Decorations and Trim," is cited as governing these materials.

801 General

801.1.3 Applicability

- This section addresses the following materials in a flood hazard area:
  - Interior finishes.
  - Trim.
  - Decorative materials.

  Note: 1612.3, "Establishment of flood hazard areas," is cited as the source of guidelines
  for establishing such an area.
  1612.2, "Definitions," defines a flood hazard area as the greater of the following:
  Area in a floodplain with a chance of flooding ≥ 1% each year.
  One of the following areas:
  Area designated as a flood hazard on the flood hazard map of the community.
  Area otherwise legally designated as a flood hazard.

- Where such materials are below the design flood elevation, they must be resistant to flood damage as follows:
  - They must be able to withstand lengthy contact with floodwaters.
  - They must not sustain damage from floodwaters requiring more than cosmetic repair.

801.2 Application

- Combustible materials may be used as a finish for the following interior surfaces:
  - Walls.
  - Ceilings.
  - Floors.
  - Other interior surfaces.

801.2.1 Windows

- 1st story show windows may be of the following materials:
  - Wood.
  - Unprotected metal framing.

801.2.2 Foam plastics

- Where foam plastics are used as interior finish or trim, they must comply with large-scale tests and other standards and property limitations.

  Note: The following are cited as sources of requirements for foam plastics:
  2603.8, "Special approval."
  Section 2604, "Interior Finish and Trim."

802 Definitions

802.1 General *(part 1 of 2)*

- **Expanded vinyl wall covering**
  - Woven textile backing.
  - Expanded vinyl base coat layer:
    A homogeneous vinyl layer.
    Contains a blowing agent:
      Agent decomposes during processing, causing the layer to expand:
        Closed cells are formed in this process.
  - Nonexpanded vinyl skin coat.
  - Total thickness is $\geq 0.055"(\pm)$, $\leq 0.070"(\pm)$.

- **Flame resistance**
  - The ability of a material or combination thereof to resist the spread of flame.

    Note: NFPA 701, "Methods of Fire Test for Flame-Resistant Textiles and Films," is cited as the measure of this ability.

- **Flame spread**
  - The expansion of flame over a surface.

- **Flame spread index**
  - A number signifying relative speed of the spread of flame on a surface determined by testing.

    Note: ASTM E 84, "Standard Test Methods for Surface Burning Characteristics of Building Materials," is cited as the governing test.

- **Interior finish**
  - Interior wall finish.
  - Interior ceiling finish.
  - Interior floor finish.

- **Interior floor finish**
  - Exposed floor surfaces.
  - Coverings applied over the following:
    A finished floor.
    Stair treads.
    Stair risers.
    Stair landings.

802 Definitions

802.1 General *(part 2 of 2)*

- **Interior wall and ceiling finish**
  - Interior exposed surfaces of a building including but not limited to the following:
    Walls:
    > Fixed.
    > Mobile.
    Partitions:
    > Fixed.
    > Mobile.
    Columns.
    Ceilings.
    Wainscoting.
    Paneling.
    Other finish applied structurally.
    Other finish applied decoratively.
    Acoustical materials.
    Surface insulation.
    Structural fire resistance or similar function.
  - Trim is not included.

- **Smoke-developed index**
  - A number signifying relative speed of the propagation of smoke determined by testing.

  Note: ASTM E 84, "Standard Test Methods for Surface Burning Characteristics of Building Materials," is cited as the governing test.

- **Trim**
  - The following components used in fixed applications:
    Picture molding.
    Chair rails.
    Baseboards.
    Handrails.
    Door frames.
    Window frames.
    Similar decorative materials.
    Similar protective materials.

803 Wall and Ceiling Finishes

803.1 General

- The following interior finishes are classified as indicated below:
  - Interior finishes to be classified:
    Wall finishes.
    Ceiling finishes.
  - Classifications of interior finishes:

Class	Flame spread index	Smoke-developed index
A	0 – 25	0 – 450
B	26 – 75	0 – 450
C	76 – 200	0 – 450

> *Note: ASTM E 84 is cited as the test required for interior finishes and from which the indexes shown above are taken.*
>
> *803.2, "Interior wall or ceiling finishes other than textiles," is cited as specifying an alternative test procedure for materials that are not textiles.*

803.2 Interior wall or ceiling finishes other than textiles

- These materials are permitted to be tested as follows:
  - By a test different from that required for interior materials that include textiles.

> *Note: NFPA 286, "Standard Method of Fire Test for Evaluating Contribution of Wall and Ceiling Interior Finish to Room Fire Growth," is cited as the test that is an alternative to ASTM E 84.*
>
> *803.2.1, "Acceptance criteria," is cited as the source of results required from the NFPA 286 test.*

803.2.1 Acceptance criteria

- This section addresses interior wall and ceiling finish materials that are not textiles.
- The interior finish must perform as follows where the alternative fire test is used:
  - Flames may not spread to the ceiling as follows:
    During the 40 kW exposure.
  - Flames may not spread to the edges of the sample in either of the following cases:
    On the wall during the 160 kW exposure.
    On the ceiling during the 160 kW exposure.
  - Flashover is not permitted as follows:
    During the 160 kW exposure.
  - Total smoke released during the fire test is limited to the following:
    ≤ 1000 sq m.

> *Note: NFPA 286, ""Standard Method of Fire Test for Evaluating Contribution of Wall and Ceiling Interior Finish to Room Fire Growth," is cited as the alternative fire test used and as the standard that defines "flashover."*

803 Wall and Ceiling Finishes

803.3 Stability

- Interior finish materials governed by this chapter must comply with the following:
  - They must remain securely attached under the conditions:
    In room temperatures ≤ 200°F.
    For a time ≥ 30 min.

803.4 Application

- Interior finish materials must comply with this section series as follows:
  - Where applied to any of the following elements with characteristics as indicated:
    Elements:
      Walls.
      Ceilings.
      Structural elements.
    Characteristics:
      Elements have either of the following:
        A required fire-resistance rating.
        A requirement to be noncombustible.

803.4.1 Direct attachment and furred construction

- This section governs the following elements requiring either property listed below:
  - Elements:
    Walls.
    Ceilings.
  - Properties required by other sections of the code:
    A fire-resistance rating.
    To be noncombustible.
- Interior finish materials applied to the elements governed by this section must comply with one of the following:
  - It must be applied directly against the element.
  - It must be applied to furring strips as follows:
    The furring strips must be ≤ 1¾" thick.
    The furring strips must be applied directly to the element.
- Spaces between furring strips must be detailed in one of the following ways:
  - Spaces must be filled with one of the following materials:
    Inorganic.
    Class A.
  - Spaces must be fireblocked so as to isolate air space ≤ 8' in length in any direction.

  Note: Section 717, "Concealed Spaces," is cited as the source of requirements for fire-blocking.

803 Wall and Ceiling Finishes

803.4.2 Set-out construction

- This section governs the following interior elements where they are required to have any of the properties listed below:
  - Building elements:
    Walls where the finished surface is set out from the wall structure > 1¾".
    Ceilings that are dropped >1¾" from the ceiling structure.
  - Properties:
    A fire-resistance rating.
    To be noncombustible.

  Note: 803.4.1, "Direct attachment and furred construction," is cited as specifying the distance for set-out construction to which this section applies. This dimension is shown above.

- Walls and ceilings governed by this section require one of the following:
  - Class A finish materials.
  - Finish materials protected on both sides by sprinklers.
  - Finish materials with all the following characteristics:
    Attached to noncombustible backing or furring strips.
    Any airspace behind finish materials is detailed in one of the following ways:
    Filled with inorganic materials.
    Filled with Class A materials.
    Fire-blocked so as to isolate airspace ≤ 8' in length in any direction.

  Note: 803.4.1, "Direct attachment and furred construction," is cited as specifying the requirements for installation of the finish materials which are summarized above.

- In dropped ceilings the following components are governed as indicated below:
  - Components below the main ceiling line:
    Hangers.
    Assembly members.
  - The components below the main ceiling line must be one of the following:
    Noncombustible materials.
    Fire-retardant-treated wood in the following types of construction only:
    Type III.
    Type V.
- Set-out wall construction must be fire-resistance-rated as per other code requirements.

803 Wall and Ceiling Finishes

803.4.3 Heavy timber construction

- The following wall and ceiling finishes must be fire-blocked as indicated below:
  - Finishes applied in Type IV construction as follows:
    Directly to wood decking or planking.
    To furring strips that are applied directly to wood decking or planking.
  - Any airspace behind the finishes must be detailed in one of the following ways:
    Fill with inorganic material.
    Fill with Class A material.
    Fire-block so as to isolate airspace in ≤ 8' in length in any direction.

  Note: 803.4.1, "Direct attachment and furred construction," is cited as specifying the requirements for installation of the finish materials which are summarized above.

803.4.4 Materials

- This section applies to materials ≤ ¼" thick used as follows:
  - Used as interior wall finish.
  - Used as interior ceiling finish.
- The following materials are not required to be applied directly to a noncombustible backing:
  - Class A materials.
  - Materials successfully tested while set out from the noncombustible backing.
- All other materials must be applied directly to a noncombustible backing.

803.5 Interior finish requirements based on group *(part 1 of 6)**

- This section dictates the minimum flame-spread class of finish materials required for interior walls and ceilings.

  Note: IBC Table 803.5, "Interior Wall and Ceiling Finish Requirements by Occupancy," is cited as the source of flame spread limitations. The table is summarized here and on the following pages.

- Where Class A materials are required, the following applies:
  - Other than textiles, the following materials are acceptable:
    Those tested by the alternative fire test.

  *Note: NFPA 286, "Standard Method of Fire Test for Evaluating Contribution of Wall and Ceiling Interior Finish to Room Fire Growth," is cited as the test that is an alternative to ASTM E 84 which defines Class A materials.
  803.2.1, "Acceptance criteria," is cited as the source of results required from the NFPA 286 test.*

**Source*: IBC Table 803.5.

803 Wall and Ceiling Finishes

803.5 Interior finish requirements based on group *(part 2 of 6)**

- This section does not restrict the flame-spread class for materials in occupancy U.
- Sprinklers cited in this section must comply with NFPA 13 or NFPA 13R.
- Vertical exits and passageways require the following flame-spread class:
  - ≥ Class C finish materials are required for the following conditions:
    Materials are ≤ 1000 sf of surface area of wainscot or paneling.
    Materials are used in the grade-level lobby.
    Materials are applied to one of the following:
      Directly to a noncombustible base.
      To furring on a noncombustible base and fire-blocked by one of the following methods:
        Airspace filled with inorganic materials.
        Airspace filled with Class A materials.
        Airspace fire-blocked so as to isolate airspaces ≤ 8' in length in any direction.
  - Flame-spread class for other conditions are listed with occupancy designations subsequently in this section.
- Vertical exits in other than occupancy I-3 require materials with the following flame spreads:
  - ≥ Class C in buildings ≤ 3 stories in sprinklered buildings.
  - ≥ Class B in buildings ≤ 3 stories in buildings not sprinklered.
  - Flame-spread class for other buildings are reported with occupancy designations subsequently listed in this section.
- Rooms and enclosed spaces are defined by partitions that run from the floor to the ceiling in the following case:
  - Where the structure requires a fire-resistance rating.

  Note: In these cases, a room or enclosed space does not terminate at any partition that does not reach the ceiling, but continues into the adjacent area to a point where a partition reaches the ceiling. Where more than one occupancy occupies such a room or enclosed space, the most restrictive governs flame-spread class.

*Source: IBC Table 803.5.

803 Wall and Ceiling Finishes

803.5 Interior finish requirements based on group *(part 3 of 6)**

Occupancies A-1 and A-2

- Vertical exits and passageways:
  - ○ ≥ Class B finish materials are required where spaces are sprinklered.
  - ○ ≥ Class A finish materials are required where spaces are not sprinklered.
- Exit access corridors and other exitways:
  - ○ ≥ Class B finish materials are required where spaces are sprinklered.
  - ○ Where spaces are not sprinklered:
    - ≥ Class B finish materials are required in lobbies.
    - ≥ Class A finish materials are required in other spaces.
- Rooms and enclosed spaces:
  - ○ ≥ Class C finish materials are required where spaces are sprinklered.
  - ○ Where spaces are not sprinklered:
    - ≥ Class C finish materials are required for occupancy loads ≤ 300.
    - ≥ Class B finish materials are required for occupancy loads > 300.

Occupancies A-3, A-4, and A-5

- The following applies to occupancy A-3:
  - ○ In places of worship, wood may be used for the following:
    - Ornamental purposes.
    - Trusses.
    - Paneling.
    - Chancel furnishing.
  - ○ Other spaces and buildings in A-3 are governed by other requirements of this section.
- Vertical exits and passageways:
  - ○ ≥ Class B finish materials are required where spaces are sprinklered.
  - ○ ≥ Class A finish materials are required where spaces are not sprinklered.
- Exit access corridors and other exitways:
  - ○ ≥ Class B finish materials are required where spaces are sprinklered.
  - ○ Where spaces are not sprinklered:
    - ≥ Class B finish materials are required in lobbies.
    - ≥ Class A finish materials are required in other spaces.
- Rooms and enclosed spaces:
  - ○ ≥ Class C finish materials are required.

*Source: IBC Table 803.5.

803 Wall and Ceiling Finishes

803.5 Interior finish requirements based on group *(part 4 of 6)**

Occupancies B, E, M, R-1, and R-4

- Vertical exits and passageways:
  - ≥ Class B finish materials are required where spaces are sprinklered.
  - ≥ Class A finish materials are required where spaces are not sprinklered.
- Exit access corridors and other exitways:
  - ≥ Class C finish materials are required where spaces are sprinklered.
  - ≥ Class B finish materials are required where spaces are not sprinklered.
- Rooms and enclosed spaces:
  - ≥ Class C finish materials are required.

Occupancy F

- Vertical exits and passageways:
  - ≥ Class C finish materials are required where spaces are sprinklered.
  - ≥ Class B finish materials are required where spaces are not sprinklered.
- Exit access corridors and other exitways:
  - ≥ Class C finish materials are required.
- Rooms and enclosed spaces:
  - ≥ Class C finish materials are required.

Occupancy H

- Vertical exits and passageways:
  - ≥ Class B finish materials are required where spaces are sprinklered.
  - ≥ Class A finish materials are required where spaces are not sprinklered.
- Exit access corridors and other exitways:
  - ≥ Class B finish materials are required where spaces are sprinklered.
  - ≥ Class A finish materials are required where spaces are not sprinklered.
- Rooms and enclosed spaces:
  - ≥ Class C finish materials are required where both of the following conditions are present:
    Where the spaces are sprinklered.
    Where the building is ≤ 2 stories.
  - ≥ Class B finish materials are required in either of the following cases:
    Where the building is not sprinklered.
    Where the building is > 2 stories.

Source: IBC Table 803.5.

803 Wall and Ceiling Finishes

803.5 Interior finish requirements based on group *(part 5 of 6)**

Occupancy I-1

- Vertical exits and passageways:
  - ○ ≥ Class B finish materials are required where spaces are sprinklered.
  - ○ ≥ Class A finish materials are required where spaces are not sprinklered.
- Exit access corridors and other exitways:
  - ○ ≥ Class C finish materials are required where spaces are sprinklered.
  - ○ ≥ Class B finish materials are required where spaces are not sprinklered.
- Rooms and enclosed spaces:
  - ○ ≥ Class C finish materials are required where spaces are sprinklered.
  - ○ ≥ Class B finish materials are required where spaces are not sprinklered.

Occupancy I-2

- Vertical exits and passageways:
  - ○ ≥ Class B finish materials are required where spaces are sprinklered.
  - ○ ≥ Class A finish materials are required where spaces are not sprinklered.
- Exit access corridors and other exitways:
  - ○ ≥ Class B finish materials are required where spaces are sprinklered.
  - ○ ≥ Class A finish materials are required where spaces are not sprinklered.
- Rooms and enclosed spaces:
  - ○ Where spaces are sprinklered:
    - ≥ Class C finish materials are required in administrative spaces.
    - ≥ Class C finish materials are required in rooms having a capacity ≤ 4 persons.
    - ≥ Class B finish materials are required for other conditions.
  - ○ ≥ Class B finish materials are required where spaces are not sprinklered.

Occupancy I-3

- Vertical exits and passageways:
  - ○ ≥ Class A finish materials are required.
- Exit access corridors and other exitways:
  - ○ ≥ Class B finish materials are required in sprinklered spaces as follows:
    - Where used as a wainscot ≤ 48" above the finished floor in exit access corridors.
  - ○ ≥ Class A finish materials are required for all other conditions.
- Rooms and enclosed spaces:
  - ○ ≥ Class C finish materials are required where spaces are sprinklered.
  - ○ ≥ Class B finish materials are required where spaces are not sprinklered.

Source: IBC Table 803.5.

803 Wall and Ceiling Finishes

803.5 Interior finish requirements based on group *(part 6 of 6)**

Occupancy I-4

- Vertical exits and passageways:
  - ≥ Class B finish materials are required where spaces are sprinklered.
  - ≥ Class A finish materials are required where spaces are not sprinklered.
- Exit access corridors and other exitways:
  - ≥ Class B finish materials are required where spaces are sprinklered.
  - ≥ Class A finish materials are required where spaces are not sprinklered.
- Rooms and enclosed spaces:
  - Where spaces are sprinklered:
    - ≥ Class C finish materials are required in administrative spaces.
    - ≥ Class C finish materials are required in rooms having a capacity ≤ 4 persons.
    - ≥ Class B finish materials are required for other conditions.
  - ≥ Class B finish materials are required where spaces are not sprinklered.

Occupancies R-2 and S

- Vertical exits and passageways:
  - ≥ Class C finish materials are required where spaces are sprinklered.
  - ≥ Class B finish materials are required where spaces are not sprinklered.
- Exit access corridors and other exitways:
  - ≥ Class C finish materials are required where spaces are sprinklered.
  - ≥ Class B finish materials are required where spaces are not sprinklered.
- Rooms and enclosed spaces:
  - ≥ Class C finish materials are required.

Occupancy R-3

- Vertical exits and passageways:
  - ≥ Class C finish materials are required.
- Exit access corridors and other exitways:
  - ≥ Class C finish materials are required.
- Rooms and enclosed spaces:
  - ≥ Class C finish materials are required.

*Source: IBC Table 803.5.

803 Wall and Ceiling Finishes

803.6 Textiles

- Textiles, including the following, are governed by this section series where they are used as interior wall or ceiling finishes:
  - Materials with a woven surface.
  - Materials with a surface that is not woven.
  - Materials with a napped surface.
  - Materials with a tufted surface.
  - Materials with a looped surface.
  - Materials with a surface similar to those listed above.

803.6.1 Textile wall coverings

- Textile wall coverings must meet one of the following sets of conditions:
  - Conditions specified by this section include both of the following:
    Coverings must be protected by a sprinkler system as per NFPA 13 or 13R.
    Coverings must have a Class A flame spread index.

    Note: ASTM E 84, "Standard Test Methods for Surface Burning Characteristics of Building Materials," is cited as the standard governing the flame spread index.

  - Conditions specified by other standards and sections.

    Note: The following subsections and standard are cited as governing alternative test methods for textile wall coverings:
    803.6.1.1, "Method A test protocol."
    803.6.1.2, "Method B test protocol."
    NFPA 265, "Standard Methods of Fire Texts for Evaluating Room Fire Growth Contribution of Textile Wall Coverings."

803.6.2 Textile ceiling finish

- This section addresses the following materials used as ceiling finishes:
  - Textiles.
  - Carpet.
  - Similar textile materials.
- Such ceiling finishes must comply with both of the following:
  - The materials must be protected by sprinklers.
  - The materials must have a Class A flame spread index.

  Note: ASTM E 84, "Standard Test Methods for Surface Burning Characteristics of Building Materials," is cited as the standard governing the flame spread index.

803 Wall and Ceiling Finishes

803.7 Expanded vinyl wall coverings

- Expanded vinyl wall coverings must comply with one of the following:
  - Requirements for textile coverings.
  - The alternative fire test.

  Note: Compliance with one of the following cited sections is required:
  > *803.5, "Interior finish requirements based on group," requires that materials be Class A, B, or C as per ASTM E 84.*
  > *803.2, "Interior wall or ceiling finishes other than textiles," provides for the alternative fire test defined by NFPA 286. In this case compliance is not required with 803.1, "General."*

803.9 Acoustical ceiling systems

- The following aspects of the ceiling systems listed below must comply with the requirements indicated:
  - Aspects:
    Quality.
    Design.
    Fabrication.
  - Systems:
    Metal suspension systems for the following:
    Acoustical tile ceiling systems.
    Acoustical lay-in panel ceiling systems.
  - Requirements:
    Generally accepted engineering practice.
    Requirements of this chapter.
    Other applicable requirements of the code.

803.9.1 Materials and installation

- Acoustical materials for ceiling systems must comply with the following:
  - Manufacturer's instructions.
  - Provisions of this section series regarding the application of interior finish.

803.9.1.1 Suspended acoustical ceilings

- Suspended acoustical ceilings must be installed according to the following standards:
  - Standards of the American Society for Testing and Materials.

  Note: The following standards are cited as governing suspended acoustical ceilings:
  > *ASTM C 635, "Specifications for the Manufacture, Performance, and Testing of Metal Suspension Systems for Acoustical Tile and Lay-in Panel Ceilings."*
  > *ASTM C 636, "Standard Practice for Installation of Metal Ceiling Suspension Systems for Acoustical Tile and Lay-in Panels."*

803 Wall and Ceiling Finishes

803.9.1.2 Fire-resistance-rated construction

- The following acoustical ceiling systems must comply with the requirements listed below:
  - Ceiling systems:
    Those that are part of construction which is fire-rated.
  - Requirements:
    Such systems must be installed in the same format as tested.
    Such systems must comply with fire-resistance-rated requirements.

  Note: Chapter 7, "Fire-Resistance-Rated Construction," is cited as the source for requirements for acoustical ceiling systems in fire-rated construction.

804 Interior Floor Finish

804.1 General

- The following traditional floors and coverings are not governed by this section:
  - Wood.
  - Vinyl.
  - Linoleum.
  - Terrazzo.
  - Resilient coverings not composed of fibers.

804.2 Classification

- Materials required by this section to be Class I or Class II must have a heat threshold preventing the advent of flame spread as follows:
  - Class I materials must have a critical radiant flux ≥ 0.45 watts/sq cm.
  - Class II materials must have a critical radiant flux ≥ 0.22 watts/sq cm.

  Note: NFPA 253, "Test for Critical Radiant Flux of Floor Covering Systems Using a Radiant Energy Heat Source," is cited as the applicable standard.
  804.5.1, "Minimum critical radiant flux," is the subsection cited for requiring minimum heat thresholds for interior floor finishes.

804.3 Testing and identification

- Reports of test must be provided to the building official upon request.
- Floor covering materials must be tested as follows:
  - By an approved agency.
  - To determine classification according to critical radiant flux.
  - Carpet-type coverings must be tested in the manner installed, including any underlayment.

  Note: NFPA 253, "Test for Critical Radiant Flux of Floor Covering Systems Using a Radiant Energy Heat Source," is cited as the standard for testing.

- Floor covering materials must be identified in the following manner, providing the information listed below:
  - Methods of identification:
    Hang tag.
    Other suitable method.
  - Information required:
    Manufacturer or supplier.
    Style.
    Classification of critical radiant flux as follows:
      Class I materials must have a critical radiant flux ≥ 0.45 watts/sq cm.
      Class II materials must have a critical radiant flux ≥ 0.22 watts/sq cm.

  Note: 804.2, "Classification," is cited as the applicable classification method which is summarized above.

804 Interior Floor Finish

804.4 Application

- This section does not apply to the following:
  - Stage.
  - Platforms.

  Note: 410.3, "Stages," is cited as the source defining the stages omitted from this section.
  410.4, "Platform construction," is cited as the source defining the platforms omitted from this section.

- This section series governs other combustible floor materials in the following:
  - Type I construction.
  - Type II construction.

804.4.1 Subfloor construction

- This section applies to the following floor components in Type I and II construction:
  - Sleepers.
  - Bucks.
  - Nailing blocks.
- Such floor components must be noncombustible unless the following is provided:
  - The space between the flooring and the floor construction with a fire-resistance rating must be detailed by one of the following methods:
    Space to be filled solid with approved noncombustible materials.
    Space must be fire-blocked.

  Note: Section 717, "Concealed Spaces," is cited as the source for fireblocking requirements.

  - Open space between flooring and floor construction may not pass by the following:
    Permanent partitions.
    Permanent walls.

804.4.2 Wood finish flooring

- Wood finish flooring in Type I and II construction may be attached as follows:
  - Directly to wood sleepers of the following type:
    Embedded wood sleepers.
    Fire-blocked wood sleepers.
  - Cemented directly to the top surface of the floor construction of the following type:
    Approved.
    With a fire-resistance rating.
  - Directly to a wood subfloor that is attached to sleepers.

  Note: 804.4.1, "Subfloor construction," is cited as the source of requirements for sleepers.

804 Interior Floor Finish

804.4.3 Insulating boards

- Combustible insulating boards may be used in flooring of Type I and II construction as follows:
  - Boards must be ≤ 0.5" thick.
  - Boards must be covered with an approved finish flooring.
  - Boards must be attached by one of the following details:
    - Directly to a noncombustible floor assembly.
    - To wood subflooring attached to sleepers.

  Note: 804.4.1, "Subfloor construction," is cited as the source for sleeper requirements.

804.5 Interior floor finish requirements

- This section applies to all occupancies.
- Interior floor finishes in the following locations have the requirement listed below:
  - Locations:
    - Vertical exits.
    - Exit passageways.
    - Exit access corridors.
    - Spaces as follows:
      - That are not separated from exit access corridors by the following:
        - Partitions spanning from the floor to the underside of the ceiling.
  - Requirement:
    - Such finishes must withstand a minimum critical radiant flux.

  Note: 804.5.1, "Minimum critical radiant flux," is cited as specifying the necessary critical radiant flux.

804 Interior Floor Finish

804.5.1 Minimum critical radiant flux

- The minimum critical radiant flux for interior floor finishes in the following locations is required for specific occupancies as shown below:
  - Floor locations:
    - Vertical exits.
    - Exit passageways.
    - Exit access corridors.
    - Rooms or spaces not separated from exit access corridors by the following:
      - Partitions running from the floor to the underside of the ceiling.
  - Buildings not sprinklered:
    - ≥ Class I finish materials are required for the following occupancies:
      - I-2, I-3.
    - ≥ Class II finish materials are required for the following occupancies:
      - A, B, E, H, I-4, M, R-1, R-2, S.
  - Sprinklered buildings:
    - ≥ Class II finish materials are required for the following occupancies:
      - I-2, I-3.
    - ≥ Class II materials and those meeting the "pill test" are permitted in the following:
      - Occupancies A, B, E, H, I-4, M, R-1, R-2, S.

  Note: DOC FF-1, "Pill test" (CPSC 16 CFR 1630), "Standard for the Surface Flammability of Carpets and Rugs," is cited as the required test.

- In all other areas, the interior floor finish must meet the requirements of the "pill test" as noted above.

805 Decorations and Trim

805.1 General

- This section addresses the following materials hung from walls or ceilings:
  - Curtains and draperies.
  - Hangings.
  - Other decorative materials.
- Decorative materials must be flame-resistant or noncombustible in the following locations:
  - Occupancies A, E, I, R-1.
  - Dormitories in occupancy R-2.

  > Note: The following are cited defining flame resistance:
  >   NFPA 701, "Methods of Fire Test for Flame-Resistant Textiles and Films."
  >   805.2, "Acceptance Criteria and Reports."

- Combustible decorations are governed in occupancies I-1 and I-2 as follows:
  - The following decorations are not governed if their quantity is too small to be a hazard:
    Photographs.
    Paintings.
    Similar decorations.
  - Other combustible decorations must be flame retardant.
- Combustible decorations in occupancy I-3 are not permitted.

805.1.1 Noncombustible materials

- Noncombustible decorative materials are not limited in quantity.

805.1.2 Flame-resistant materials

- Flame-resistant decorative material in occupancy A auditoriums in sprinklered buildings is limited as follows:
  - The decorative material is limited to half the sum of wall and ceiling areas as follows:
    Material must compy with wall and ceiling application requirements.

  > Note: 903.3.1.1, "NFPA 13 sprinkler systems," is cited as governing the sprinklers.
  >   803.4, "Application," is cited as the source for application requirements.

- In other locations, flame-resistant decorative material is limited to the following:
  - 10% of the sum of wall and ceiling areas.

805 Decorations and Trim

805.2 Acceptance criteria and reports

- Decorative materials required to be flame-resistant must comply with one of the following:
  - They must be noncombustible.
  - They must pass applicable fire tests for establishing flame resistance:
    Test results are to be available to the code official.

  Note: NFPA 701, "Methods of Fire Test for Flame-Resistant Textiles and Films," is cited as the source for establishing flame resistance. Test 1 or Test 2 of this standard is to be used.

805.3 Foam plastic

- Foam plastic trim must meet the following requirements for interior trim:
  - Minimum density.
  - Maximum thickness.
  - Maximum area.
  - Maximum flame spread.

  Note: 2604.2, "Interior trim," is cited as the source of requirements.

805.4 Pyroxylin plastic

- The following is prohibited in occupancy A:
  - Materials involving pyroxylin plastic such as imitation leather and other materials.
  - Materials involving a substance equally as hazardous as pyroxylin plastic.

805.5 Trim

- Interior trim must have a flame and smoke-developed index $\geq$ Class C.
- Combustible trim is governed as follows:
  - This subsection does not limit the area of handrails or guardrails.
  - Other combustible trim is limited to the following:
    $\leq$ 10% of the sum of wall and ceiling areas in the space where located.

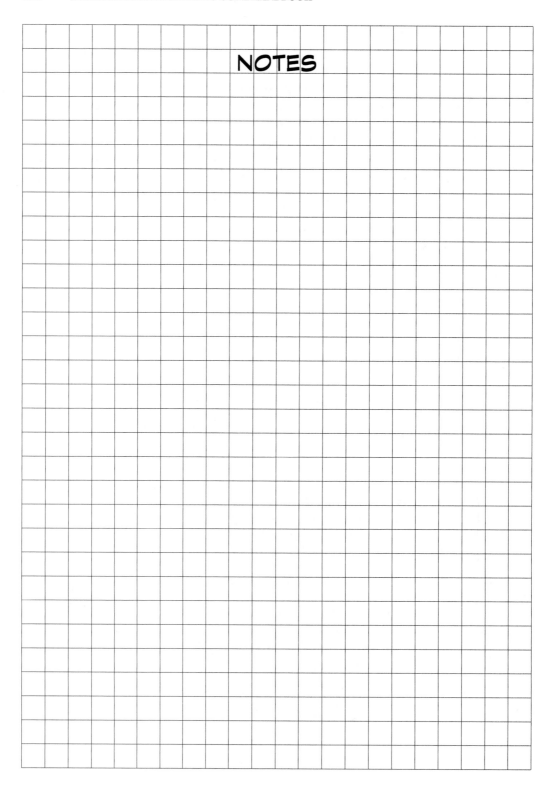

NOTES

9

Fire Protection Systems

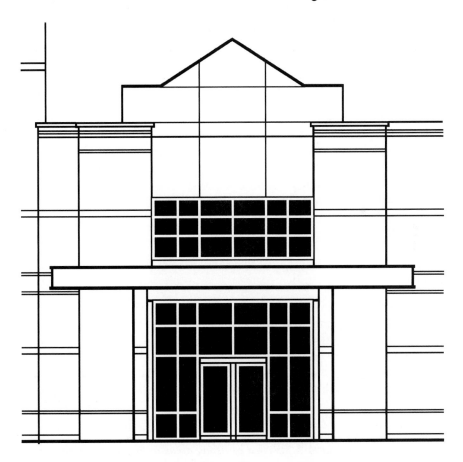

Methodist Community Health Center. Sugar Land, Texas. *(partial elevation)*
HKS, Inc., Architects, Engineers, Planners. Dallas, Texas.

903 Automatic Sprinkler Systems

903.1.1 Alternative protection

- Other automatic fire-protection systems may be substituted for automatic sprinklers where the following apply:
  - Must be approved.
  - Must meet applicable standards.

  > *Note: Section 904, "Alternative Automatic Fire-Extinguishing Systems," is cited as the source of requirements for such systems.*

903.2 Where required

- The following locations with the qualifications listed below do not require sprinklers:
  - Locations:
    - In telecommunciations buildings used only for the following:
      - Telecommunications equipment.
      - Associated electrical power distribution equipment.
      - Batteries.
      - Standby engines.
  - Qualifications:
    - Spaces must have an automatic fire alarm system.
    - Spaces must be isolated from other spaces with both the following:
      - Walls with a fire-resistance rating ≤ 1 hr.
      - Floor/ceiling assemblies with a fire-resistance rating ≤ 2 hr.
- Other locations as follows require the sprinkler systems specified below:
  - Locations:
    - In new buildings as follows:
      - As noted in this section series.
  - Sprinkler systems:
    - Automatic.
    - Approved.

903.2.1 Group A

- Sprinklers are required in occupancy A as specified in this section series.
- Sprinklers are required in the following locations:
  - In occupancies A-1, A-2, A-3, and A-4 as follows:
    - Throughout the floor area.
    - Throughout all floors between these occupancies and the exit discharge level.
  - In occupancy A-5 where any of the following are > 1000 sf:

Concession stands	Retail areas
Press boxes	Other accessory use areas

  > *Note: 903.2.1.2, "Group A-5," is cited as listing areas in A-5 requiring sprinklers and is partially summarized above. The section also includes an exception.*

903 Automatic Sprinkler Systems

903.2.1.1 Group A-1

- Sprinklers are required in an A-1 occupancy fire area with any of the following characteristics:
  - Area is > 12,000 sf.
  - Area occupant load is ≥ 300.
  - Area is not on the exit discharge level.
  - Area contains multiple motion picture theaters.

903.2.1.2 Group A-2

- Sprinklers are required in an A-2 occupancy fire area with any of the following characteristics:
  - Area is > 5000 sf.
  - Area occupant load is ≥ 300.
  - Area is not on the exit discharge level.

903.2.1.3 Group A-3

- This section does not apply to areas used exclusively for participant sports as follows:
  - Main floor and main entrance/exit is on exit discharge level.
- Otherwise, sprinklers are required in an A-3 occupancy fire area with any of the following characteristics:
  - Area is > 12,000 sf.
  - Area occupant load is ≥ 300.
  - Area is not on the exit discharge level.

903.2.1.4 Group A-4

- This section does not apply to areas used exclusively for participant sports as follows:
  - Main floor and main entrance/exit are on exit discharge level.
- Sprinklers are required in an A-4 occupancy fire area with any of the following characteristics:
  - Area is > 12,000 sf.
  - Area occupant load is ≥ 300.
  - Area is not on the exit discharge level.

903.2.1.5 Group A-5

- This section does not apply to areas used exclusively for participant sports as follows:
  - Main floor and main entrance/exit are on exit discharge level.
- Sprinklers are required in the following functions where areas are > 1000 sf:
  - Concession stands.
  - Retail areas.
  - Press boxes.
  - Other accessory use areas.

903 Automatic Sprinkler Systems

903.2.2 Group E

- Sprinklers are not required in the following locations with the characteristics listed below:
  - Locations:
    A fire area.
    An area below the level of exit discharge.
  - Characteristics:
    Every classroom has the following:
      ≥ 1 exterior exit door at ground level.
- Otherwise, sprinklers are required as follows:
  - Throughout all occupancy E fire areas > 20,000 sf.
  - Throughout all parts of occupancy E buildings below exit discharge level.

903.2.3 Group F-1

- Sprinklers are required throughout buildings in all of the following cases:
  - Where a fire area has an F-1 occupancy with any of the following characteristics:
    Fire area is > 12,000 sf.
    Fire area is > 3 stories above grade.
  - Where the sum of all F-1 fire areas in a building including mezzanines is as follows:
    Total area is > 24,000 sf.

903.2.3.1 Woodworking operations

- Sprinklers are required in all F-1 fire areas that have all of the following characteristics:
  - Woodworking operations are present.
  - Woodworking operations are > 2500 sf.
  - Fine combustible particles are present in either of the following formats:
    As waste.
    As materials used in the process.

903.2.4.1 General

- An automatic sprinkler system is required in occupancy H facilities.

903 Automatic Sprinkler Systems

903.2.4.2 Group H-5 occupancies

- Where an H-5 occupancy is present, automatic sprinklers are required throughout the building as follows:
  - System design must comply with both of the following:
    Code requirements according to the following hazard classifications:
      Ordinary Hazard Group 2 applies to the following:
        Fabrication areas.
        Corridors and service corridors.
        Storage rooms without dispensing functions.
      Extra Hazard Group 2 applies to the following:
        Storage rooms with dispensing functions.

    Note: IBC Table 903.2.4.2, "Group H-5 Sprinkler Design Criteria," is cited as the source of requirements based on hazard level, the content of which is summarized above.

  - Corridors with one row of sprinklers are governed as follows:
    ≤ 13 sprinklers are required based on calculations.

903.2.4.3 Pyroxylin plastics

- Sprinklers are required where the following substances are present in amounts > 100 lbs in any of the activities indicated below:
  - Substances:
    Cellulose nitrate film.
    Pyroxylin plastics.
  - Activities:
    The plastics are manufactured.
    The plastics are stored or handled.

903.2.5 Group I

- One of the following sprinkler systems is permitted in occupancy I-1 fire areas:
  - Sprinklers as per NFPA 13R.
  - Sprinklers as per NFPA 13D.

    Note: The following are cited as sources of requirements for the systems listed above.
    903.3.1.2, "NFPA 13R sprinkler systems."
    903.3.1.3, "NFPA 13D sprinkler systems."

- Otherwise, where a building has an occupancy I fire area, the following applies:
  - Sprinklers are required throughout the building.

903 Automatic Sprinkler Systems

903.2.6 Group M

- Sprinklers are required throughout buildings in all of the following cases:
  - Where a fire area has an M occupancy with any of the following characteristics:
    Fire area > 12,000 sf.
    Fire area is > 3 stories above ground level.
  - The sum of all fire areas in a building with M occupancies is as follows:
    Total area including mezzanines is > 24,000 sf.

903.2.6.1 High-piled storage

- Sprinklers are required in occupancy M as follows:
  - Where either of the following storage systems exists:
    High-piled storage.
    Rack storage.

  Note: The International Fire Code is cited as governing such sprinklers.

903.2.7 Group R

- Sprinklers are required throughout the building as follows:
  - In buildings with an occupancy R fire area.

  Note: 903.3, "Installation requirements," is cited as governing such sprinklers.

903.2.8 Group S-1

- Sprinklers are required throughout buildings as follows:
  - Where a fire area has an S-1 occupancy with any of the following characteristics:
    Fire area > 12,000 sf.
    Fire area is > 3 stories above ground level.
    The sum of fire areas in the building is as follows:
    The total area including mezzanines is > 24,000 sf.

903.2.8.1 Repair garages

- Sprinklers are required throughout buildings housing repair garages as follows:
  - Buildings where a repair garage services vehicles in the basement.
  - 1-story buildings with the following:
    A repair garage in a fire area > 12,000 sf.
  - Buildings ≥ 2 stories including basements with the following:
    A repair garage in a fire area > 10,000 sf.

  Note: Section 406, "Motor-Vehicle-Related Occupancies," is cited as the source governing repair garages.

903 Automatic Sprinkler Systems

903.2.8.2 Bulk storage of tires

- Sprinklers must be provided as follows:
  - In buildings where the tire storage area has the following size:
    > 20,000 cu ft.
  - NFPA 13 sprinklers.

  Note: 903.3.1.1, "NFPA 13 sprinkler systems," is cited as governing such sprinklers.

903.2.9 Group S-2

- This section does not govern enclosed parking garages below occupancy R-3.
- Otherwise, sprinklers are required throughout all enclosed parking garages as follows:
  - Those meeting height and area limitations based on occupancy and construction type.
  - Those under other occupancies.

  Note: 406.4, "Enclosed parking garages," is cited as the source of requirements.

903.2.9.1 Commercial parking garages

- Sprinklers are required throughout commercial parking garages as follows:
  - Where fire areas containing the following are > 5000 sf:
    Commercial truck or bus storage.

903.2.10.1 Stories and basements without openings

- This section addresses occupancies other than R-3 and U.
- Sprinklers are required in stories and basements with both of the following characteristics:
  - Where floor area is > 15,000 sf.
  - Where there are no provided openings meeting either of the following conditions:
    Openings totally above adjacent grade:
    Must be located within each segment of wall length ≤ 50':
    Sum of opening areas in each segment must be ≥ 20 sf.
    Must be located on ≥ 1 side of the basement.
    Openings with any part below adjacent grade:
    Must lead directly to grade level as follows:
    Access must be by an exterior stairway or ramp.
    Must be located as follows:
    Within each segment of wall length ≤ 50'.
    On ≥ 1 side of the basement.

  Note: The following are cited as governing the stairways and ramps required above:
  Section 1009, "Stairways and Handrails."
  Section 1010, "Ramps."

903 Automatic Sprinkler Systems

903.2.10.1.1 Opening dimensions and access

- This section addresses stories and basements in occupancies other than R-3 and U.
- Openings provided in lieu of sprinklers must have all of the following characteristics:
  - Dimensions must be ≥ 2'-6".
  - Must comply with one of the following:
    Must provide access from the outside for the fire department.
    Must provide the possibility of the following from the outside:
    Fire fighting.
    Rescue.

903.2.10.1.2 Openings on one side only

- This section addresses stories in occupancies other than R-3 and U.
- Sprinklers are required where openings are not provided as follows:
  - Openings as required in lieu of sprinklers must meet one of the following conditions:
    Openings are on ≥ 2 sides of the story.
    Openings are on 1 side of the story as follows:
    The wall opposite the side with openings is ≤ 75' away.

903.2.10.1.3 Basements

- This section addresses occupancies other than R-3 and U.
- An approved sprinkler system is required in basements as follows:
  - Where any point is > 75' from the following opening:
    An opening qualifying to be provided in lieu of sprinklers.

    Note: 903.2.10.1, "Stories and basements without openings," is cited as the source of requirements for openings qualifying to substitute for sprinklers.

903.2.10.2 Rubbish and linen chutes

- This section addresses rubbish and linen chutes in occupancies other than R-3 and U.
- Sprinklers are required as follows:
  - At the top of chutes.
  - In the terminal rooms of chutes.
  - In chutes through ≥ 3 stories as follows:
    At alternate floors.
    At the top of chutes.
    In the terminal rooms of chutes.
  - Sprinklers must be accessible for servicing.

903 Automatic Sprinkler Systems

903.2.10.3 Buildings over 55 feet in height

- This section addresses occupancies other than R-3 and U.
- The following high-rise occupancies are not governed by this section:
  - Airport control towers.
  - Open parking garages.
  - Occupancy F-2.
- Other buildings as follows require sprinklers throughout:
  - Buildings with a floor level as follows:
    Occupant load $\geq$ 30.
    Located $\geq$ 55' above lowest level of fire department vehicle access.

903.2.11 During construction

- In certain cases sprinklers may be required during the following:
  - Construction.
  - Alteration.
  - Demolition.

  Note: The International Fire Code is cited as governing sprinklers in the above cases.

903.2.12.1 Ducts conveying hazardous exhausts

- The following ducts are not governed by this section:
  - Ducts with a largest diameter of $<$ 10".
- In certain cases sprinklers may be required ducts carrying the following:
  - Hazardous exhaust.
  - Flammable materials.
  - Combustible materials.

  Note: The International Mechanical Code is cited as the standard governing the need for sprinklers in the ducts noted above.

903.2.12.2 Commercial cooking operations

- Sprinklers protecting commerical cooking systems must be as follows:
  - Automatic.
  - Installed in the kitchen exhaust hood and duct system.

  Note: The sprinklers are those specified in order to comply with the following: Section 904, "Alternative Automatic Fire-Extinguishing Systems."

903 Automatic Sprinkler Systems

903.2.13 Other required suppression systems

- In addition to locations requiring sprinklers cited elsewhere in this chapter, the following also require sprinklers in certain cases.

    Note: 903.2, "Where required," is cited as specifying locations requiring sprinklers.

  ○ Covered malls.

    Note: 402.8, "Automatic sprinkler system," is cited as the source of requirements.

  ○ High-rise buildings.

    Note: 403.2, "Automatic sprinkler system," is cited as a source of requirements.
    403.3, "Reduction in fire-resistance rating." is cited as governing also.

  ○ Atriums.

    Note: 404.3, "Automatic sprinkler protection," is cited as the source of requirements.

  ○ Underground structures.

    Note: 405.3, "Automatic sprinkler system," is cited as the source of requirements.

  ○ Occupancy I-2.

    Note: 407.5, "Automatic sprinkler system," is cited as the source of requirements.

  ○ Stages.

    Note: 410.6, "Automatic sprinkler system," is cited as the source of requirements.

  ○ Special amusement buildings.

    Note: 411.4, "Automatic sprinkler system," is cited as the source of requirements.

  ○ Aircraft hangars.

    Note: 412.2.5, "Finishing," is cited as a source of requirements.
    412.2.6, "Fire suppression," is cited as a source of requirements.

  ○ Occupancy H-2.

    Note: 415.7.2.4, "Suppression," is cited as the source of requirements.

  ○ Flammable finishes.

    Note: 416.4, "Fire protection," is cited as the source of requirements.

  ○ Drying rooms.

    Note: 417.4, "Fire protection," is cited as the source of requirements.

  ○ Unlimited area buildings.

    Note: Section 507, "Unlimited Area Buildings," is cited as the source of requirements.

*Source: IBC Table 903.2.13.

903 Automatic Sprinkler Systems

903.3.1.1 NFPA 13 sprinkler systems

- Sprinklers governed by this section must comply with the following:
  - NFPA 13.
- Requirements for buildings to have sprinklers governed by this section do not include the following spaces:
  - Certain spaces with one of the following fire detection systems:
    Detects invisible particles of combustion.
    Detects visible particles of combustion.

    Note: 903.3.1.1.1, "Exempt locations," is cited as listing spaces not required to have a sprinkler system governed by this section where the space is located in a building which does have such a requirement.

903.3.1.1.1 Exempt locations *(part 1 of 2)*

- Sprinklers are not required in any of the following spaces:
  - Where protected by a fire detection system with all the following characteristics:
    Approved.
    Automatic.
    Detects one of the following products of combustion:
    Visible.
    Invisible.

    Note: 907.2, "Where required," is cited as governing the fire detection systems.

  - Where the application of the following substances results in the hazards indicated below:
    Substances:
    Water.
    Flame and water.
    Hazards:
    Hazard to life.
    Fire hazard.
  - Where both of the following conditions apply:
    Nature of contents render sprinklers undesirable.
    Omission of sprinklers is approved.
  - In both of the following rooms where the condition indicated below applies:
    Rooms:
    Generator rooms.
    Transformer rooms.
    Condition:
    Rooms are separated from rest of building as follows:
    By the following assemblies as applicable with a fire-resistance rating $\geq$ 2 hrs:
    Walls.
    Floor/ceiling assemblies.
    Roof/ceiling assemblies.

903 Automatic Sprinkler Systems

903.3.1.1.1 Exempt locations *(part 2 of 2)*

- Sprinklers are not required in any of the following spaces:
  - In spaces of telecommunications buildings as follows with the conditions indicated below:
    - Spaces used only for the following:
      - Telecommunications equipment.
      - Related electrical power distribution equipment.
      - Batteries.
      - Standby engines.
    - Conditions:
      - Spaces have an automatic fire alarm system.
      - Spaces are separated from rest of building as follows:
        - Wall has a fire-resistance rating $\geq$ 1 hr.
        - Floor/ceiling assembly has a fire-resistance rating $\geq$ 2 hr.
  - Where spaces are as follows:
    - Constructed of noncombustible construction.
    - Has noncombustible contents.
- The following conditions do not justify the omission of sprinklers from a space:
  - Space is damp.
  - Space is of construction with a fire-resistance rating.
  - Space contains electrical equipment.

903.3.1.2 NFPA 13R sprinkler systems

- Sprinklers must meet the requirements of NFPA 13R where permitted as follows:
  - In occupancy R buildings $\leq$ 4 stories.

  Note: NFPA 13R, "Installation of Sprinkler Systems in Residential Occupancies up to and Including Four Stories in Height," is cited as the standard for the sprinklers.

903.3.1.2.1 Balconies

- This section governs the following construction as indicated below:
  - Construction:
    - Type V construction as follows:
      - Occupancy R.
  - Requirements:
    - The following elements require sprinkler protection:
      - Ground-floor patios.
      - Exterior balconies as follows:
        - Sidewall sprinklers protecting open wood joist construction may be located as follows:
          - Deflectors may be $\geq$ 1" and $\leq$ 6" below structural members.
          - Deflectors may be $\leq$ 14" below the deck.

903 Automatic Sprinkler Systems

903.3.1.3 NFPA 13D sprinkler systems

- Sprinklers must meet the requirements of NFPA 13D where permitted as follows:
  - In 1- and 2-family dwellings.

    Note: NFPA 13D, "Installation of Sprinkler Systems in One- and Two-Family Dwellings and Manufactured Homes," is cited as the standard for the sprinklers.

903.3.2 Quick-response and residential sprinklers

- Where sprinklers are required one of the following types must be located as indicated:
  - Types:
    Quick-response.
    Residential.
  - Locations required:
    In occupancy I-2 as follows:
    Throughout all spaces within a smoke compartment with sleeping units.
    In the following rooms in the occupancies R and I-1:
    Dwelling units.
    Sleeping units.
    In light-hazard occupancies as follows:
    Buildings with the following characteristics:
    Quantity of combustible material is low.
    Combustibility of contents is low.
    Low rates of heat are anticipated from any fire.
    Typical building types:
    Churches.
    Libraries excluding large stack rooms.
    Clubs.
    Educational buildings.
    Offices.
    Nursing homes, convalescent homes, and hospitals.
    Institutional buildings.
    Restaurant seating.
    Auditoriums and theaters excluding stages and prosceniums.
    Museums.
    Unused attics.
    Residential buildings.

  Note: NFPA 13, "Installation of Sprinkler Systems," is cited as the source of light-hazard occupancies, a partial summary of which is provided above.
  903.3.1, "Standards," is cited as governing the sprinklers addressed in this section.

903 Automatic Sprinkler Systems

903.3.3 Obstructed locations

- Kitchen equipment located under exhaust hoods that are protected by a fire-extinguishing system are not governed by this section.

    Note: Section 904, "Alternative Automatic Fire-Extinguishing Systems," is cited as the source of requirements for the facilities indicated above.

- Sprinklers must be installed so that obstructions will not hinder their function as follows:
    - Water distribution may not be obstructed.
    - Activation may not be delayed.
- Sprinklers must be installed in or under the following covered locations:
    - Kiosks and concession stands.
    - Displays and booths.
    - Equipment > 4' wide.
- Clearance of ≥ 3' is required between sprinklers and the top of stacks of combustible fibers.

903.3.4 Actuation

- Sprinkler systems must be activated automatically unless otherwise specifically permitted.

903.3.5 Water supplies

- Water supplies for sprinklers must comply with the following:
    - This section series.
    - Referenced standards.

    Note: 903.3.1, "Standards," is cited as the source of applicable standards.

    - The potable water supply must be protected as follows:
        Against backflow as per this section.

    Note: The International Plumbing Code is cited as governing backflow protection.

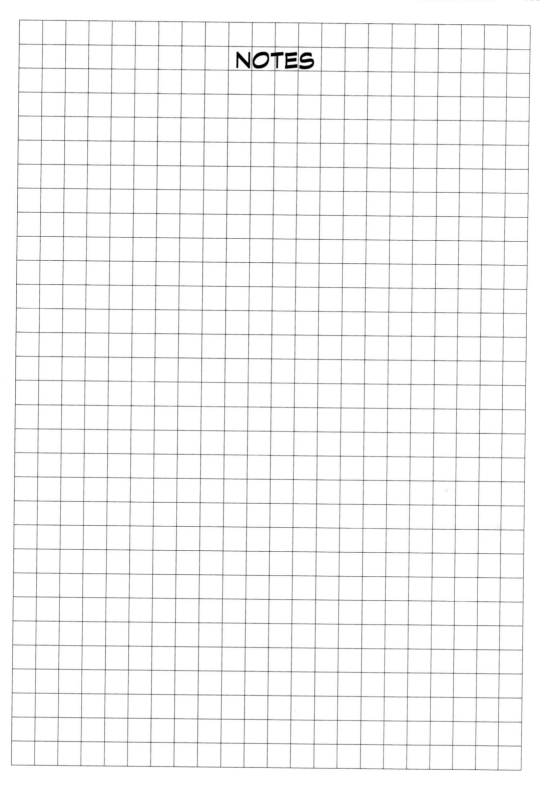

NOTES

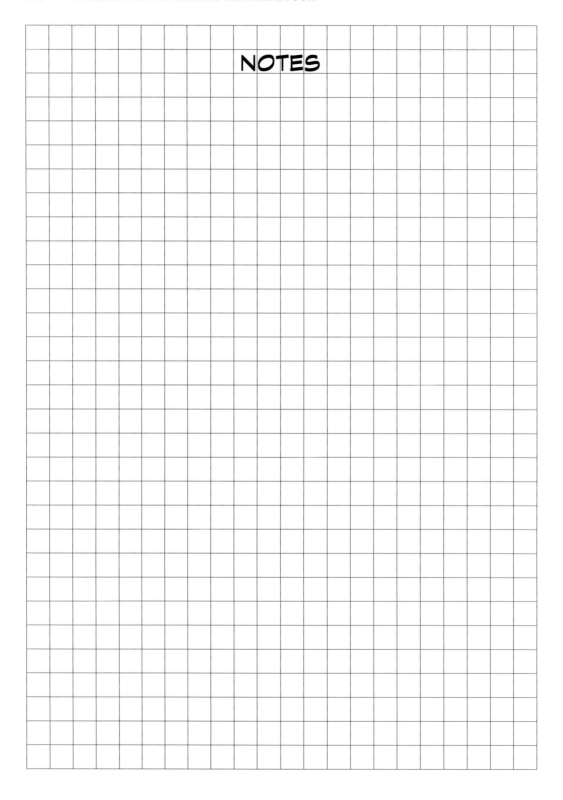

NOTES

10

Means of Egress

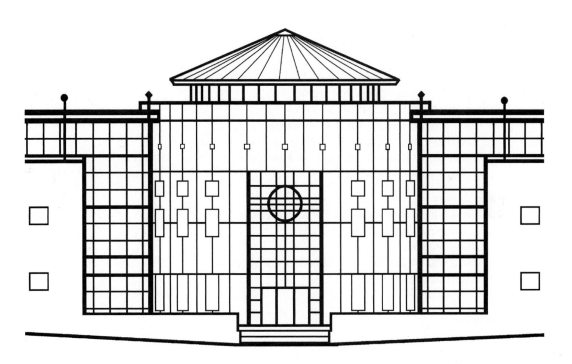

Newman University Sports and Fine Arts Center. Wichita, Kansas. *(partial elevation)*
Gossen Livingston Associates, Inc., Architecture. Wichita, Kansas

1002 Definitions

1002.1 Definitions *(part 1 of 8)*

- **Accessible means of egress**
  - A route of travel as follows:
    - In either of the following:
      - A building.
      - A facility.
    - Route is continuous.
    - Route is unobstructed.
    - Route is from any point in an accessible route to one of the following:
      - An area of refuge.
      - A horizontal exit.
      - A public way.

- **Aisle accessway**
  - A segment of an exit access path as follows:
    - The path leads to an aisle.

- **Alternating tread device**
  - A component with a series of steps as follows:
    - Angle of travel is as follows:
      - $\geq 50°$ and $\leq 70°$.
    - Angle is measured from horizontal.
    - Steps are typically designed as follows:
      - Step width is half the width of the component.
      - Individual steps are provided for each foot of the user.
      - Steps are positioned on the left and right sides of a central support as follows:
        - Steps on one side are halfway between the heights of the steps on the other side.

- **Area of refuge**
  - An area for use during emergency evacuation as follows:
    - For occupants unable to use stairways.
    - Affords temporary protection:
      - Used while waiting for one or both of the following:
        - Instructions.
        - Assistance.

- **Bleachers**
  - Seating in tiers.

1002 Definitions

1002.1 Definitions *(part 2 of 8)*

- **Common path of egress travel**
  - A route of travel as follows:
    Toward an exit.
    Provides the only option for a route of travel.
    Terminates at the following location:
      At the point where more than one option of travel toward an exit is provided.
  - Routes that are initially separate, but which merge at some point, are common paths.

> **Case study: Fig. 1002.1A.** A common path of egress travel is measured on the most direct route available to occupants. The rectangular paths shown in the figure approximate the distance around objects such as furniture and fixtures, the locations of which may vary over time. Some jurisdictions don't require egress paths to follow the rectangular geometry.
>
> **Retail 107:** Path AD is a common path, there being only one choice of travel. Some jurisdictions may not include toilet rooms in common path measurements. Path BDE and BC are not common paths but "exit access travel distance." This is due to the fact that from point B, there are two choices of travel.
>
> **Retail 106A and 106B:** All paths of egress travel in these rooms are common paths since all routes merge at point B and since there is a single choice of path from B to the exit door.
>
> **Storage 108:** All paths in the room are common paths since they must merge at some point prior to leaving the room. The common path extends to point C, which is the first opportunity for more than one choice of travel to an exit. The one diagonal segment is shown since this area is for circulation only, permitting no furnishings to be located there.

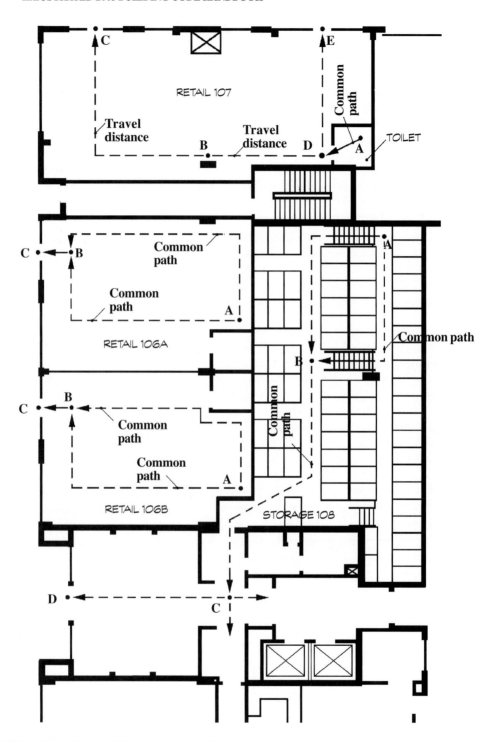

Fig. 1002.1A. Partial ground floor plan, east building. Hoyt Street Properties, Portland, Oregon. Ankrom Moisan Associated Architects. Portland, Oregon.

1002 Definitions

1002.1 Definitions *(part 3 of 8)*

- **Corridor**
  - An exit access component as follows:
    Enclosed.
    Provides a route to an exit.

- **Egress court**
  - One of the following elements providing access to a public way:
    Court.
    Yard.

- **Emergency escape and rescue opening**
  - The following openings providing a means of escape or rescue:
    Operable window.
    Door.
    Other similar element.

- **Exit**
  - A route of travel from an exit access to an exit discharge.
  - Separated from interior building spaces:
    By fire-resistance-rated construction.
    By opening protectives.
  - May include the following elements:
    Exterior exit doors at ground level.
    Exit enclosures.
    Exit passageways.
    Exterior exit stairs.
    Exterior exit ramps.
    Horizontal exits.
  - A part of a means of egress.

- **Exit access**
  - A route of travel from any occupiable place in a building to an exit.
  - A part of a means of egress.

- **Exit discharge**
  - A route between the following:
    The termination of an exit.
    A public way.
  - A part of a means of egress.

- **Exit discharge, level of**
  - A horizontal plane.
  - Located at the termination of an exit.
  - Located at the beginning of an exit discharge.

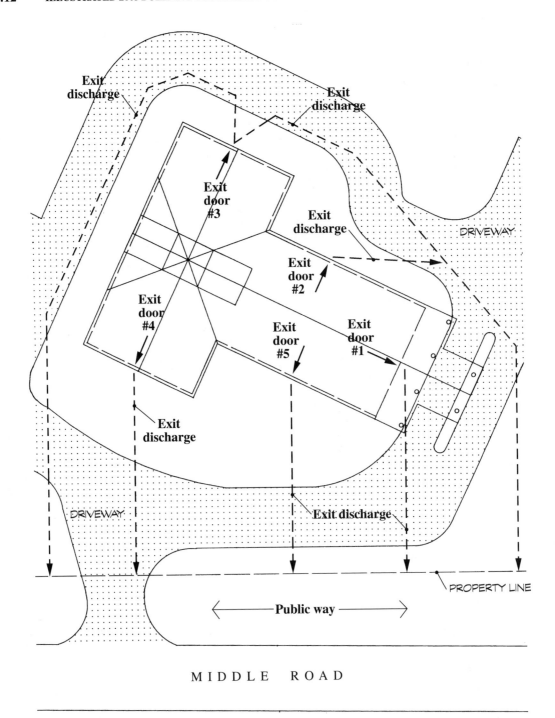

Fig. 1002.1B. Site plan. Glad Tidings Assembly of God Church. Naticoke, Pennsylvania. Mullins and Weida, Architect and Associate. Bear Creek, Pennsylvania.

1002 Definitions

1002.1 Definitions *(part 4 of 8)*

- **Exit enclosure**
  - A component of an exit.
  - Separated from interior building spaces:
    By fire-resistance-rated construction.
    By opening protectives.
  - A protected route of travel to one of the following:
    Exit discharge.
    Public way.
  - May be in either of the following directions:
    Horizontal.
    Vertical.

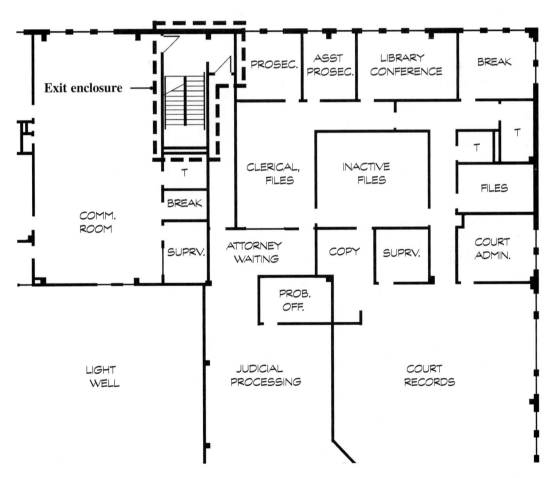

Fig. 1002.1C. Partial floor plan. Lee's Summit Police and Court Facility. Lee's Summit, Missouri. The Hollis and Miller Group, Inc. Lee's Summit, Missouri.

1002 Definitions

1002.1 Definitions *(part 5 of 8)*

- **Exit, horizontal**
  - A route of egress travel.
  - Between either of the following:
    - Two buildings on approximately the same level.
    - Two areas in the same building approximately on the same level.
  - Through an assembly providing protection from fire and smoke.

- **Exit passageway**
  - A component of an exit.
  - Separated from interior building spaces:
    - By fire-resistance-rated construction.
    - By opening protectives.
  - A protected route of travel to one of the following:
    - Exit discharge.
    - Public way.
  - A horizontal route of travel.

- **Fire exit hardware**
  - Panic hardware as follows:
    - Listed for fire door assemblies.

- **Floor area, gross**
  - Area within the inside perimeter of the exterior walls.
  - Does not include the following:
    - Vent shafts.
    - Shafts with no openings.
    - Interior courts.
  - Includes space occupied by the following:
    - Corridors.
    - Stairways.
    - Closets.
    - Interior walls.
    - Columns.
    - Other interior elements.
  - Space not enclosed with exterior walls is included as follows:
    - Usable area under the following horizontal projections:
      - Roof above.
      - Floor above.

1002 Definitions

1002.1 Definitions *(part 6 of 8)*

- **Floor area, net**
  - Occupied area.
  - Unoccupied accessory areas, such as the following, are not included:
    Corridors.
    Stairways.
    Toilet rooms.
    Mechanical rooms.
    Closets.

- **Folding and telescopic seating**
  - A structure for seating as follows:
    Seating is tiered.
    Size can be reduced for the following purposes:
      For moving.
      For storing.

- **Footboards**
  - The walking surface of aisle accessways in the following:
    Reviewing stands.
    Grandstands.
    Bleachers.

- **Grandstand**
  - Seating in tiers.

- **Guard**
  - A barrier as follows:
    Located at the open edge of walking surfaces where there is an elevation change.
    Minimizes chances for falling from the walking surface to the lower level.

- **Handrail**
  - A rail for grasp by the hand as follows:
    Rail can be in either of the following positions:
      Horizontal.
      Sloping.
    For either of the following purposes:
      Guidance.
      Support.

1002 Definitions

1002.1 Definitions *(part 7 of 8)*

- **Means of egress**
  - A route of travel from any occupied place in a building to a public way:
    Route is continuous.
    Route is unobstructed.
  - Consists of 3 separate segments:
    Exit access.
    Exit.
    Exit discharge.

- **Nosing**
  - The leading edge of the following stair components:
    Treads.
    Landings at the top of stair runs.

- **Occupant load**
  - The number of people for which a means of egress is designed.

- **Panic hardware**
  - A door-latching assembly as follows:
    Latch releases upon application of a force in the direction of egress.

- **Public way**
  - Any of the following that leads to a street dedicated to public use:
    Street.
    Alley.
    Parcel of land.
  - Has clear dimensions as follows:
    $\geq 10'$ in height.
    $\geq 10'$ in width.

- **Ramp**
  - A walking surface sloping $> 1:20$ in the direction of travel.

- **Scissor stair**
  - Two stairways with all the following characteristics:
    Interlocking.
    Two separate egress routes.
    Located in the same stairway enclosure.

- **Smoke-protected assembly seating**
  - Seating with all the following characteristics:
    Served by a means of egress.
    Where smoke cannot accumulate.

1002 Definitions

1002.1 Definitions *(part 8 of 8)*

- **Stair**
  - A change in elevation as follows:
    Has ≥ 1 riser.

- **Stairway, exterior**
  - Open to the exterior on at least one side:
    Where required, the following are permitted at open sides:
    Structural columns and beams.
    Guards and handrails.
  - Open to one of the following:
    Yard.
    Court.
    Public way.

- **Winder**
  - A stair tread as follows:
    Long edges are not parallel.

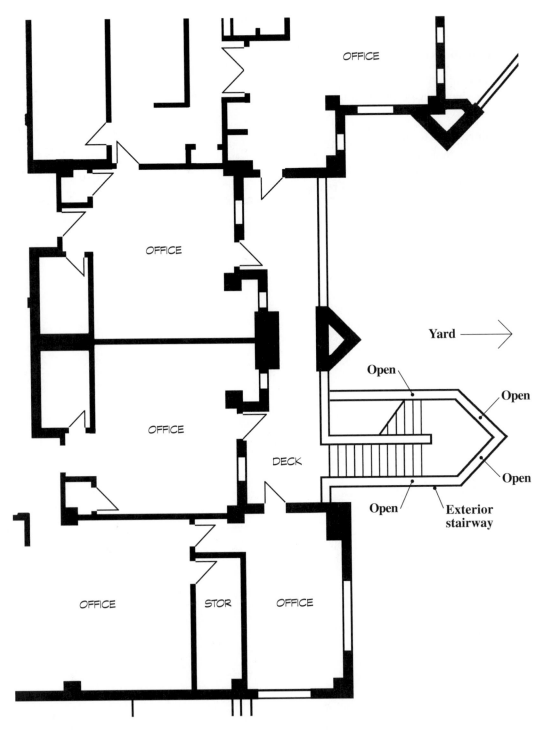

Fig. 1002.1D. Partial second-floor plan showing an exterior stairway. Country Club Park Building One. Wichita, Kansas. Gossen Livingston Associates, Inc., Architecture. Wichita, Kansas.

Case study: Fig. 1003.3.1B. The detailing complies with the requirement to provide a barrier ≤ 2'-3" high to protect a protrusion which reduces headroom to < 6'-8". In this case, the protrusion is the lower flight of the stairway, and the barrier is a rail.

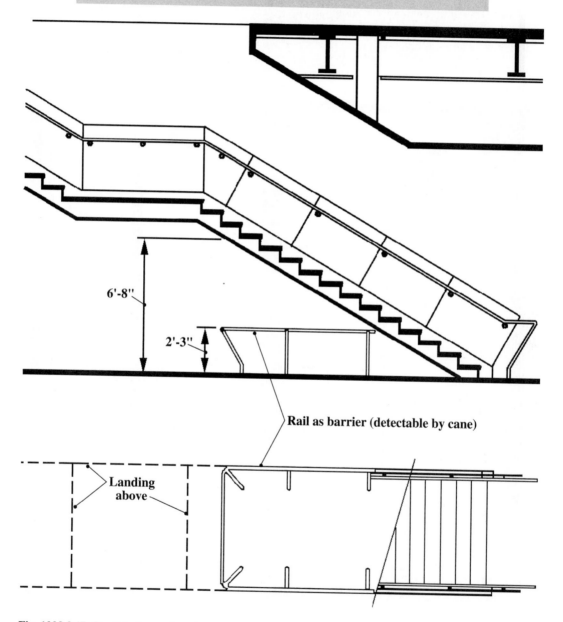

6'-8"

2'-3"

Rail as barrier (detectable by cane)

Landing above

Fig. 1003.3.1B. Partial plan and section of stair in the first-floor concourse. University of Connecticut New Downtown Campus at Stamford, Connecticut. Perkins Eastman Architects, P.C. New York, New York.

Case study: Fig. 1003.3.1C. The ceiling height of the corridor is 11'-4", well over the minimum. The light alcoves at the walls and those spanning across the corridor at the columns have soffits at 7'-4". Thus, the required 6'-8" minimum is maintained for headroom under objects extending below the ceiling.

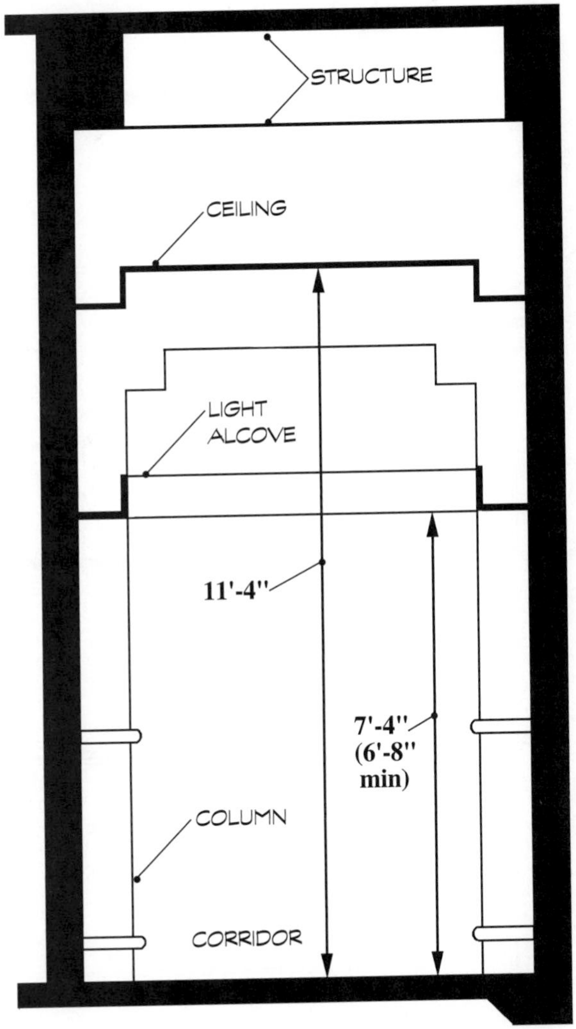

STRUCTURE

CEILING

LIGHT ALCOVE

11'-4"

7'-4" (6'-8" min)

COLUMN

CORRIDOR

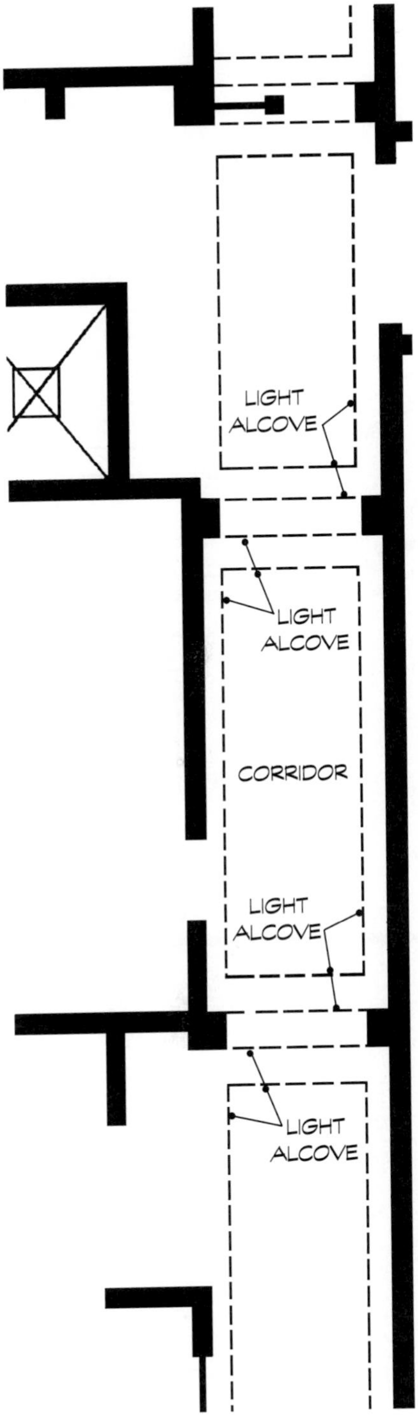

LIGHT ALCOVE

LIGHT ALCOVE

CORRIDOR

LIGHT ALCOVE

LIGHT ALCOVE

Fig. 1003.3.1C. Partial floor plan and section at corridor. Lubrication Engineers, Inc. Wichita, Kansas. Gossen Livingston, Associates, Inc., Architecture. Wichita, Kansas.

1003 General Means of Egress

1003.3.2 Freestanding objects

- This section does not apply to the following:
  - Sloping parts of handrails serving the following:
    - Stairs.
    - Ramps.
- The following freestanding object has the requirement indicated below:
  - Object:
    - Mounted on one of the following:
      - Post.
      - Pylon.
    - Mounted so that its lowest leading edge is between the following heights:
      - > 27" above floor.
      - < 80" above floor.
  - Requirement:
    - May not overhang > 12".
- The following object has the requirements indicated below:
  - Object:
    - Is any of the following:
      - Sign.
      - Other obstruction.
    - Mounted as follows:
      - Betweem any of the following supports:
        - Posts.
        - Pylons.
      - Where supports are spaced as follows:
        - > 12" clear space apart.
  - Requirements:
    - Height of lowest edge cannot be within the following range:
      - > 27" above floor.
      - < 80" above floor.

1003.3.3 Horizontal projections

- Handrails for the following may protrude ≤ 4½" from the wall:
  - Stairs.
  - Ramps.
- The following objects may not project horizontally from either side over a walking surface > 2'-3" or < 6'-8" above the floor:
  - Structural elements.
  - Fixtures.
  - Furnishings.

Case study: Fig. 1003.3.3A. The fire hose cabinet and fire extinguisher cabinet comply with the limit of protrusions to 4" over a walking surface, at a height > 2'-3" and < 6'-8".

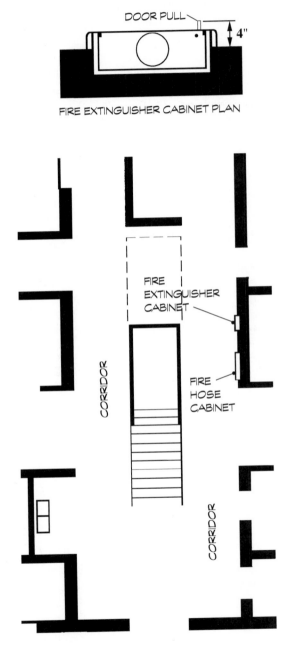

DOOR PULL

4"

FIRE EXTINGUISHER CABINET PLAN

FIRE EXTINGUISHER CABINET

CORRIDOR

FIRE HOSE CABINET

CORRIDOR

Fig. 1003.3.3A. Partial plan and detail. Newman University Sports and Fine Arts Center. Wichita, Kansas. Gossen Livingston Associates, Inc., Architecture. Wichita, Kansas.

Case study: **Fig. 1003.3.3B.** The wall-mounted light fixtures protrude only 4" into the corridor, thus, complying with the 4" limitation for horizontal projections at heights > 2'-3" and < 6'-8". The wall mass projects 6" into the corridor at point A, but since it extends below the 2'-3" height, it is detectable by a cane and complies with the code.

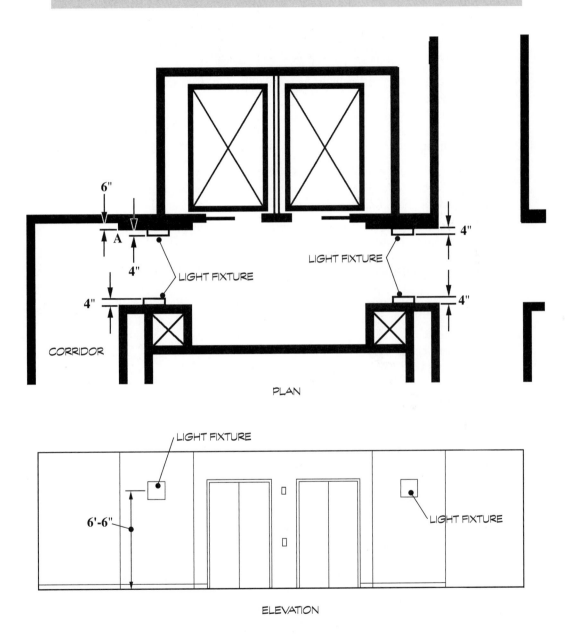

Fig. 1003.3.3B. Partial floor plan and interior elevation at elevators. Methodist Community Health Center. Sugar Land, Texas. HKS, Inc., Architects, Engineers, Planners. Dallas, Texas.

1003 General Means of Egress

1003.3.4 Clear width

- Protruding objects in accessible routes are governed as follows:
  - They may not reduce the minimum required clear width.

  Note: Section 1104, "Accessible Route," is cited as applicable.

1003.4 Floor surface

- Means of egress walking surface must have the following characteristics:
  - Surface must be slip resistant.
  - Surface must be securely attached.

1003.5 Elevation change *(part 1 of 2)*

- A single riser ≤ 7" may be used in a means of egress as follows:
  - At exterior doors not required to be accessible in the following locations:
    In occupancies F, H, R-2, R-3, S, U.

    Note: Chapter 11, "Accessibility," is cited as the source for accessibility requirements throughout this section.

- The following stair has the requirements indicated below:
  - Stair:
    Located in routes not required to be accessible.
    ≤ 2 risers.
  - Requirements:
    Risers must be ≥ 4" and ≤ 7".
    Treads must be ≥ 13".
    ≥ 1 handrail must be provided as follows:
      Located ≤ 2'-6" of the center of anticipated egress travel on the stair.

  Note: The following are cited as sources for other requirements as noted:
  1009.3, "Stair treads and risers," for step requirements.
  1009.11, "Handrails," for handrail requirements.

- Aisles with all the following characteristics may have steps:

  Note:1024.11, "Assembly aisle walking surfaces," is cited as governing the steps.

  - For seating that is not required to be accessible.
  - Where seating has a difference in elevation < 12".
  - Where an aisle handrail is provided.

  Note: 1024.13, "Handrails," is cited as governing the handrails.

1003 General Means of Egress

1003.5 Elevation change *(part 2 of 2)*

- In other locations, a sloped floor with the requirements listed below is required for the following conditions:
  - ○ Conditions:
    - Changes in elevation with both the following characteristics:
      - < 12".
      - Located in a means of egress.
  - ○ Requirements:
    - Where the slope is > 1:20 the following applies:
      - A ramp is required as follows:
        - For elevation changes ≤ 6" one of the following is required for the ramp:
          - Handrails.
          - A surface that contrasts with adjacent floor surfaces.

  Note: Section 1010, "Ramps," is cited as governing required ramps.

- A sloped floor is required in the following cases:
  - ○ For changes in elevation where both of the following apply:
    - In occupancy I-2.
    - In corridors serving nonambulatory occupants.

1003.6 Means of egress continuity

- Continuity of the travel route in a means of egress is required as follows:
  - ○ Only means of egress building components are permitted to interrupt the travel route.
  - ○ The only obstructions permitted in the route are protrusions allowed by this chapter.
- The capacity required for a means of egress may not diminish in the direction of egress.

1003.7 Elevators, escalators, and moving walks

- Elevators may serve as an accessible means of egress.

  Note: 1007.4, "Elevators," is cited as the source of requirements.

- The following may not serve as a required means of egress for persons not already using them at the advent of an emergency:
  - ○ Elevators and escalators.
  - ○ Moving walks.

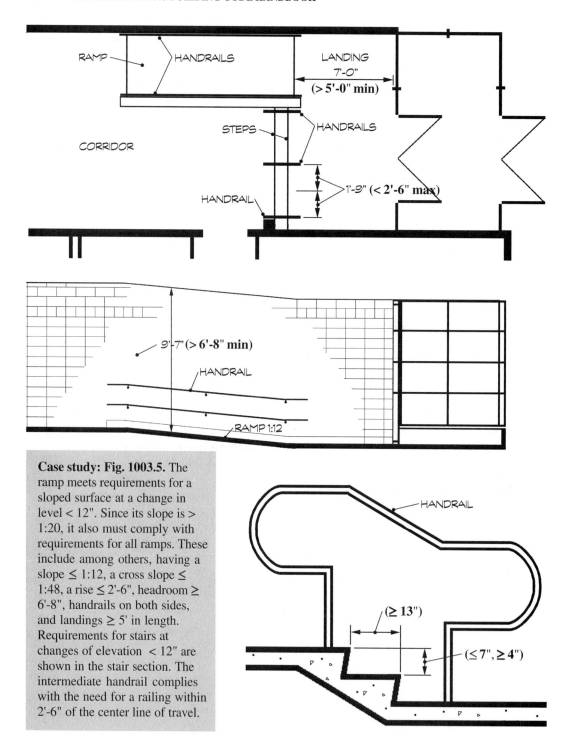

Case study: Fig. 1003.5. The ramp meets requirements for a sloped surface at a change in level < 12". Since its slope is > 1:20, it also must comply with requirements for all ramps. These include among others, having a slope ≤ 1:12, a cross slope ≤ 1:48, a rise ≤ 2'-6", headroom ≥ 6'-8", handrails on both sides, and landings ≥ 5' in length. Requirements for stairs at changes of elevation < 12" are shown in the stair section. The intermediate handrail complies with the need for a railing within 2'-6" of the center line of travel.

Fig. 1003.5. Partial plan and sections at corridor. Montachusett Regional Vocational-Technical High School. Fitchburg, Massachusetts. HKT Architects, Inc. Somerville, Massachusetts.

Case study: Fig. 1003.7. The escalators shown on this hospital floor do not serve as a means of egress as per code limitations. Exits are provided with exit access travel distances in compliance with code requirements. The elevators qualify as an accessible means of egress by virtue of the building being sprinklered and by their size, which meets required standards.

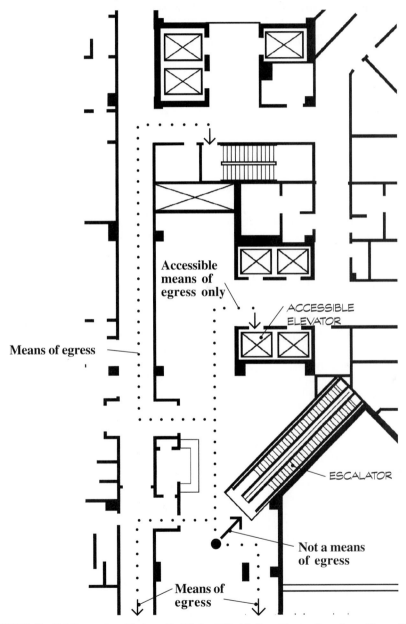

Fig. 1003.7. Partial floor plan. Christus St. Michael Health Care Center. Texarkana, Texas. Watkins Hamilton Ross Architects, Inc. Houston, Texas.

1004 Occupant Load

1004.1 Design occupant load

- The occupant load assigned to a space for purposes of providing adequate egress is the largest of the three methods of determination defined in this section series.

    Note: The following are cited as sources of the three methods of load determination:
    1004.1.1, "Actual number."
    1004.1.2, "Number by Table 1004.1.2."
    1004.1.3, "Number by combination."

1004.1.1 Actual number

- Occupant load used to determine egress requirements is as follows:
  - Use the actual number for which the area is designed.

1004.1.2 Number by Table 1004.1.2 *(part 1 of 2)*

- Occupant load in fixed seating areas is determined in one of the following ways:
  - For individual seats, *occupant load = number of seats.*
  - For continuous seating without arms, *occupant load = length of seating ÷ 18".*
  - For booth seating, *occupant load = length of seating ÷ 24"* as follows:
      Length is measured at the backrest.
- Occupant load used to determine egress requirements is as follows:
  - Divide the floor area served by the following square feet per occupant:

Table 1004.1.2   Maximum Floor Area per Occupant

Function	SF/ occupant	Function	SF/occupant
Agricultural		**Assembly**	
Barns	300 gross	Gambling areas	11 gross
Outbuildings	300 gross	No fixed seats	
Storage	300 gross	Concentrated	
Maintenance	50 gross	(chairs only)	7 net
Aircraft		Standing space	5 net
Hangars	500 gross	Not concentrated	
Fabrication	100 gross	(tables, chairs)	15 net
Office	100 gross	**Bowling centers**	
Airport terminal		5 occupants per	
Concourse	100 gross	lane including 15'	
Waiting area	15 gross	of lane-approach	
Baggage claim	20 gross	Lane service area	300 gross
Baggage handling	300 gross	Other areas	7 net
Newsstand	30 gross	**Business areas**	
Gift shop	30 gross	Offices	100 gross
Lounge	7 net	Computer mainframe	300 gross
Snack bar	7 net	Computer room	100 gross
Ticket area	7 net	Copy room	100 gross
Office	100 gross	Conference room	
Car rental	20 gross	(table, chairs)	15 net

Sources: IBC Table 1004.1.2 and survey data.

1004 Occupant Load

1004.1.2 Number by Table 1004.1.2 *(part 2 of 2)*

Table 1004.1.2 — *Continued*

Function	SF/ occupant	Function	SF/ occupant
Courthouses		**Institutional areas**	
Hearing room		In patient treatment	240 gross
(No fixed seats)	40 net	Outpatient areas	100 gross
Courtroom		Sleeping areas	120 gross
(No fixed seats)	40 net	Admitting	100 gross
Waiting space	15 net	Waiting	15 net
Jury room	15 net	Offices	100 gross
Attorney lounge	15 net	**Kitchens, commercial**	200 gross
Press room	15 net	**Library**	
Witness isolation	100 gross	Reading rooms	50 net
Attorney workspace	100 gross	Stack area	100 gross
Detention cell	120 gross	**Mercantile**	
Dormitories	50 gross	Basement	30 gross
Lounge	7 net	Grade floor	30 gross
Recreation	7 net	Other floors	60 gross
Kitchenette	3 net	Storage, shipping	300 gross
Vending area	3 net	**Parking garages**	200 gross
Dining	15 net	**Residential**	200 gross
Laundry	15 net	**Skating rink**	
Seminar room	15 net	Rink	50 gross
Library reading room	50 net	Deck	15 gross
Mail room	100 gross	**Swimming pool**	
Student rooms	200 gross	Pool	50 gross
Educational		Deck	15 gross
Classroom	20 net	**Stages and platforms**	15 net
Shops	50 net	**Storage** (accessory)	300 gross
Vocational areas	50 net	**Mechanical room**	300 gross
Offices	100 gross	**University center**	
Electrical room	300 gross	Steam room	100 net
Elevator machinery	300 gross	Gymnasium	5 net
Exercise rooms	50 gross	Game room	15 net
H-5 Fabrication and		Dance studio	7 net
manufacturing areas	200 gross	Group study	100 net
Industrial areas	100 gross	Individual study	200 net
		Gymnastics	15 net
		Indoor archery	100 net
		Handball	100 net

Sources: IBC Table 1004.1.2 and survey data.

1004.1.3 Number by combination

• Where occupants in an accessory space egress through a primary area, the calculated occupant load of the primary area is the sum of the following:
  ○ The occupant load of the primary area.
  ○ The occupant load egressing through the primary area from the accessory space.

Case study: Fig. 1004.1.2A. The office area is designated as occupancy B for purposes of determining occupant load. IBC Table 1004.1.2 indicates that the area allowance for occupants is 100 sf (gross) per person. Since the allowance is in gross sf, interior wall thicknesses, toilets, closets, and hall are included in the area computation. The area allowance for the 2 storage rooms is 300 sf (gross) per person. In this example, computing occupants for the storage rooms separately from the business area would result in 1 less occupant for the complex. Since the means of egress serving this occupant load is larger than required, treating the storage rooms separately is not justified. The occupant count for the business area, including storage, is, therefore, determined by the conservative following calculation: *3210 gross sf ÷ 100 sf/ occupant = 33 occupants.*

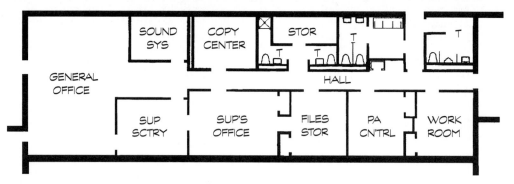

Fig. 1004.1.2A. Partial floor plan. Montachusett Regional Vocational-Technical High School. Fitchburg, Massachusetts. HKT Architects, Inc. Somerville, Massachusetts.

Case study: Fig. 1004.1.2B. Gross (gr) and net square foot (sf) allowances from IBC Table 1004.1.2 are applied to the case study example as follows:

415 Electric room	Mechanical:	985 gr sf	÷ 300 gr sf/occ	=	4 occupants
416 Storage	Storage:	675 gr sf	÷ 300 gr sf/occ	=	3 occupants
417 Utility and storage	Storage:	390 gr sf	÷ 300 gr sf/occ	=	2 occupants
418 Emergency generator	Mechanical:	300 gr sf	÷ 300 gr sf/occ	=	1 occupant
419 Maintenance office	Office:	480 gr sf	÷ 100 gr sf/occ	=	5 occupants
423 Storage	Storage:	1642 gr sf	÷ 300 gr sf/occ	=	6 occupants
424 Incinerator	Mechanical:	350 gr sf	÷ 300 gr sf/occ	=	2 occupants
426 Office	Office:	470 gr sf	÷ 100 gr sf/occ	=	5 occupants
431 Restaurant	Assembly:	2440 net sf	÷ 15 net sf/occ	=	163 occupants
433 Culinary arts	Vocational:	3870 net sf	÷ 50 net sf/occ	=	78 occupants
440 Solarium	Assembly:	184 net sf	÷ 15 net sf/occ	=	13 occupants
448 Nonfood storage	Storage:	144 gr sf	÷ 300 gr sf/occ	=	1 occupant
449 Food storage	Storage:	172 gr sf	÷ 300 gr sf/occ	=	1 occupant
450 Classroom	Classroom:	750 net sf	÷ 20 net sf/occ	=	38 occupants
451 Receiving	Storage:	920 gr sf	÷ 300 gr sf/occ	=	4 occupants

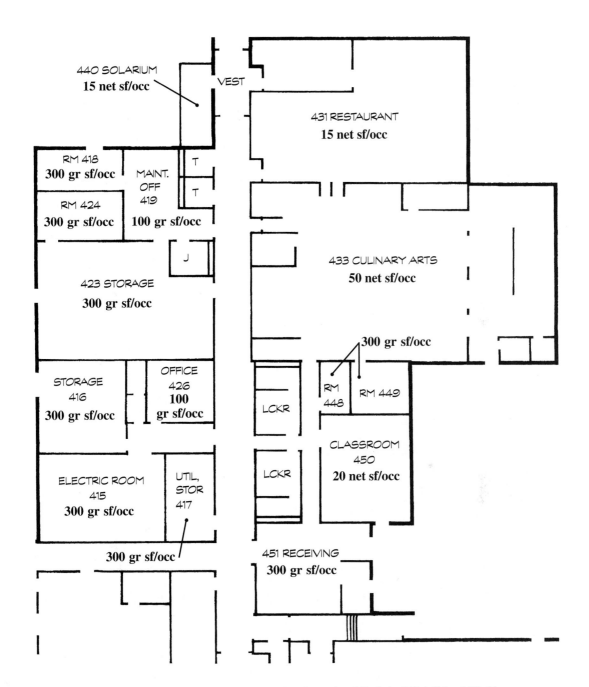

Fig. 1004.1.2B. Partial floor plan. Montachusett Regional Vocational-Technical High School. Fitchburg, Massachusetts. HKT Architects, Inc. Somerville, Massachusetts.

1004 Occupant Load

1004.4 Exiting from multiple levels

- This section addresses exits serving ≥ 1 floor.
- The capacity of the exit at each floor is serves occupants of each floor only.
- Occupant loads are not summed from each floor in the direction of egress.
- The capacity of the exit may not decrease along the route of egress.

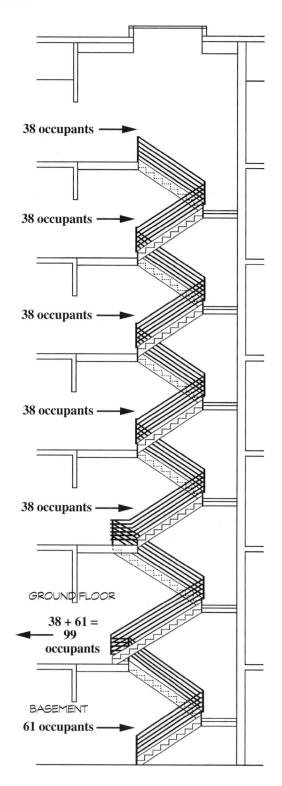

38 occupants →

38 occupants →

38 occupants →

38 occupants →

38 occupants →

GROUND FLOOR

38 + 61 = 99 occupants ←

BASEMENT

61 occupants →

Case study: Fig. 1004.4. The occupant load entering the exit stairway at each floor above grade level is 38. The occupant load used to determine the minimum requirements for the stairway down to the ground floor is, therefore, 38. It is assumed that the occupants from each floor enter the stairway at the same time and vacate each segment of the stairway as the following group enters it behind them. Thus, no segment of the stair has more than 38 occupants in it at any time. Should a larger number have been assigned to any floor, all stairway segments below that floor would have to serve the larger number.

The occupant load entering the stairway from the basement parking area is 61. These occupants merge with the 38 from the 2nd floor, placing both groups in the means of egress at the 1st floor (the intermediate floor) at the same time. The means of egress at the point of convergence must, therefore, serve *38 + 61 = 99 occupants*.

Fig. 1004.4. Stairway section. Hoyt Street Properties, Portland, Oregon. Ankrom Moisan Associated Architects, Portland, Oregon.

1004 Occupant Load

1004.5 Egress convergence

- Where the means of egress from a floor above, converges with that of the floor below, at a level in between, the following applies:
    - Egress capacity in the direction of travel from the point of convergence is as follows:
      Capacity must be ≥ the sum of the capacities of the converging means of egress.

1004.6 Mezzanine levels

- This section governs the exit capacity of a space with mezzanine egress through it.
- The exit capacity of such space is based on the sum of occupant loads of the following:
    - The mezzanine.
    - The space.

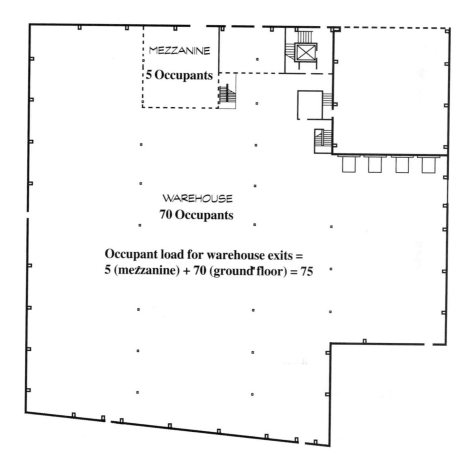

MEZZANINE

5 Occupants

WAREHOUSE

70 Occupants

**Occupant load for warehouse exits =
5 (mezzanine) + 70 (ground floor) = 75**

Fig. 1004.6. Floor plan. New Warehouse Addition. Los Angeles, California. Stephen Wen + Associates, Architects, Inc. Pasadena, California.

1004 Occupant Load

1004.7 Fixed seating

- Occupant load in fixed seating areas is determined in one of the following ways:
  - For individual seats, *occupant load = number of seats.*
  - For continuous seating without arms, *occupant load = length of seating ÷ 18".*
  - For booth seating, *occupant load = length of seating ÷ 24",* as follows:
    Length is measured at the backrest.

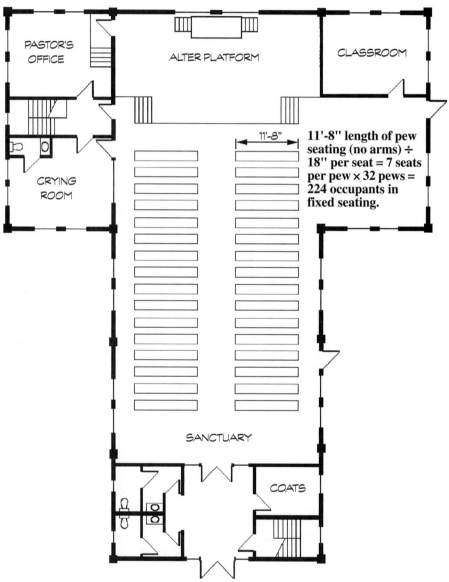

Fig. 1004.7. First-floor plan. Glad Tidings Assembly of God Church. Nanticoke, Pennsylvania. Mullins and Weida, Architect and Associate. Bear Creek, Pennsylvania.

1004 Occupant Load

1004.8 Outdoor areas

- This section does not apply to the following outdoor areas:
    - Outdoor areas of occupancy R-3.
    - Outdoor areas of individual dwelling units of occupancy R-2.
- Outdoor areas used only for building service are required to have only one means of egress.
- Other outdoors areas usable by building occupants, such as the following, must have a means of egress complying with this chapter:
    - Yards.
    - Patios.
    - Courts.
    - Similar outdoor areas.
- The occupant load of outdoor areas is assigned by the building official as per expected use.
- Means of egress of outdoor areas passing through a building are governed as follows:
    - Where an outdoor area serves persons other than building occupants, the following applies:
        Requirements for the means of egress based on the sum of the following occupants:
            Occupant load from the building.
            Occupant load from outside the building.

> **Case study: Fig. 1004.8.** If 102 occupants from adjoining rooms egress through those rooms, 1125 of the courtyard occupant load of 1227 will pass through the auditorium lobby. Total capacity of doors to the lobby is 1440. 566 of the auditorium occupants also egress through the lobby, thus, its means of egress serves 1691. Total capacity of exit doors serving the lobby is 2400. To omit the courtyard load from the lobby means of egress, it would have to be shown that the auditorium and courtyard would not be occupied simultaneously. This scenario reflects one set of assumptions about use of the courtyard.

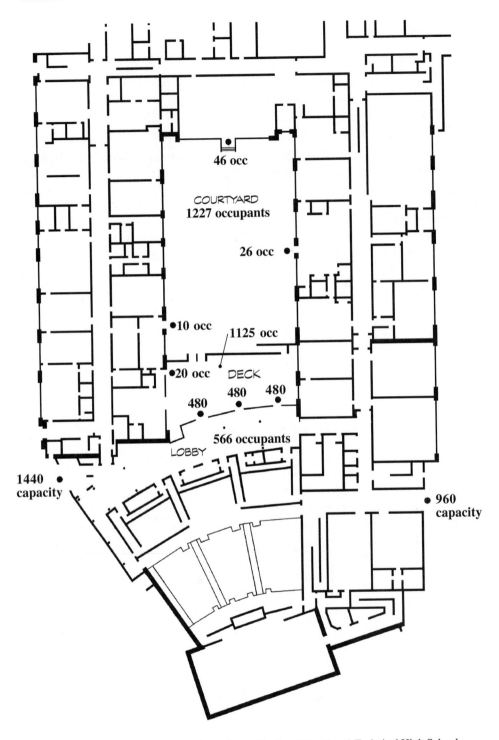

Fig. 1004.8. Partial floor plan at courtyard. Montachusett Regional Vocational-Technical High School. Fitchburg, Massachusetts. HKT Architects, Inc. Somerville, Massachusetts.

1004 Occupant Load

1004.9 Multiple occupancies

- This section applies to buildings containing more than one occupancy.
- Means of egress within an occupancy are governed by the occupancy requirements.
- Where more than one occupancy shares parts of the same means of egress, shared portions are governed by the more restrictive requirements of the occupancies served.

> **Case study: Fig. 1004.9A.** IBC Table 1016.1 requires that corridors serving I-3 occupancies with sprinklers have walls with a fire-resistance rating of 1 hr, although the walls of corridors serving A and B occupancies with sprinklers need have no fire-resistance rating. The corridor between the I-3 and A or B occupancies in the case study serves all these occupancies and, therefore, must have a minimum of 1-hr-rated walls in compliance with the more restrictive I-3 requirement. (In this case, the stair walls and the I-3 corridor wall are rated at 2 hrs, although the other corridor walls are 1 hr.)

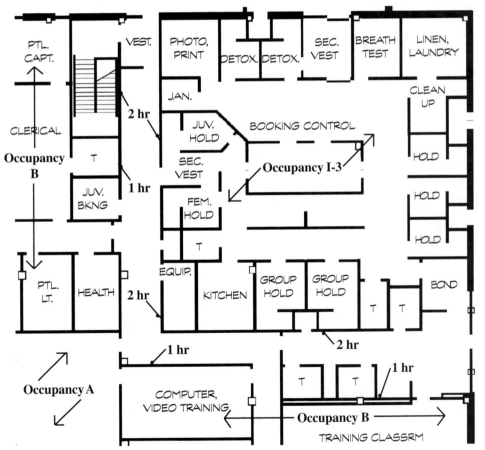

Fig. 1004.9A. Partial floor plan. Lee's Summit Police and Court Facility. Lee's Summit, Missouri. The Hollis and Miller Group, Inc. Lee's Summit, Missouri.

Case study: Fig. 1004.9B. Each exit door in the plan is indicated by a dot with its maximum egress capacity listed in number of occupants. The doors in occupancies B and S have a larger capacity than do doors in the H-2 occupancy for the same width. IBC Table 1003.2.3 indicates that in sprinklered buildings, occupancies B and S require a minimum of 0.15" width per occupant served. In H occupancies the minimum width is 0.2" per occupant. Consequently, the 36" exterior doors have capacities of 240 occupants each in the B and S occupancies, but only 180 occupants in the H occupancy. This is an example of separate means of egress in different occupancies subject to differing occupancy-specific requirements.

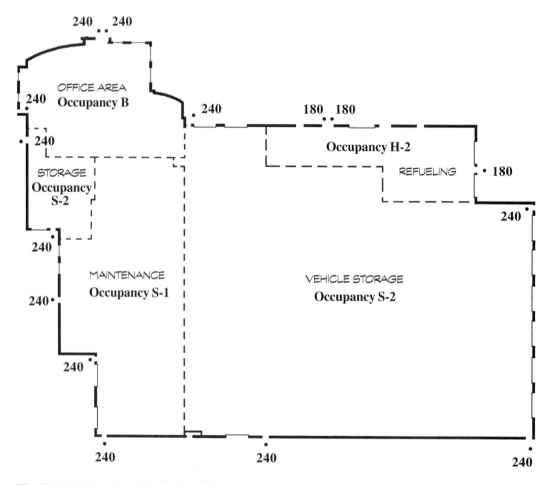

Fig. 1004.9B. Floor plan. Wichita Transit Storage, Administration, and Maintenance Facility. Wichita, Kansas. Wilson Darnell Mann, P.A., Architects. Wichita, Kansas.

1005 Egress Width

1005.1 Egress width

- Requirements for means of egress listed in the assembly section supercede any conflicting requirements of this section.

  Note: Section 1024, "Assembly," is cited as the source governing certain aspects of means of egress for assembly occupancies.

- In other cases, means of egress widths must be ≥ the greater of the following:
  - Minimums required elsewhere in the code.
  - Number of occupants served × the factors below.

Table 1005.1   Means of Egress Width

Minimum width of stairway per occupant served:

Occupancy	Building sprinklered as per NFPA 13 or 13R
A, B, E, F, H-5, I-1, I-3, I-4, M, R, S, U	0.2"
H-1, H-2, H-3, H-4, I-2	0.3"
	Building not sprinklered
A, B, E, F, H-5, I-1, I-3, I-4, M, R, S, U	0.3"
H-1, H-2, H-3, H-4	0.7"
I-2	NA

Minimum width of other egress components per occupant served:

Occupancy	Building sprinklered as per NFPA 13 or 13R
A, B, E, F, H-5, I-1, I-3, I-4, M, R, S, U	0.15"
H-1, H-2, H-3, H-4, I-2	0.2"
	Building not sprinklered
A, B, E, F, H-5, I-1, I-3, I-4, M, R, S, U	0.2"
H-1, H-2, H-3, H-4	0.4"
I-2	NA

Source: IBC Table 1005.1

- A loss of a means of egress may not reduce the total egress capacity by > $1/2$ that required.
- Means of egress capacity must be ≥ the largest required from any point to its termination.

Case study: Fig. 1005.1A. Minimum width per occupant for a stairway in occupancy E with sprinklers = 0.2" from IBC Table 1005.1. Stairway occupant load = 435. Actual width of stairway is 7'-3 ¹/₂". *Minimum width of stairway = 0.2" × 435 = 7'-3".*

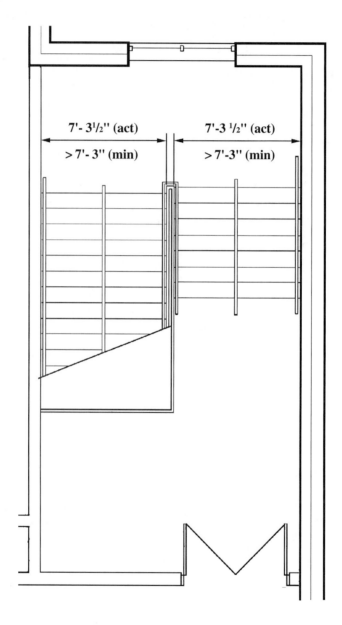

Fig. 1005.1A. Stairway plan. Montachusett Regional Vocational-Technical High School. Fitchburg, Massachusetts. HKT Architects, Inc. Somerville, Massachusetts.

Case study: Fig. 1005.1B. The auditorium requires a total means of egress width ≥ 102", based on IBC Table 1003.2.3. While other requirements are also applicable, this section prohibits a layout wherein the loss of one means of egress would reduce the total width to less than 51". The actual means of egress width available (as limited by exit access doors) is 276". The auditorium meets this requirement because the loss of the largest doorway (72") would leave 204" available. 204" > 51", the minimum permitted to remain upon the loss of a doorway.

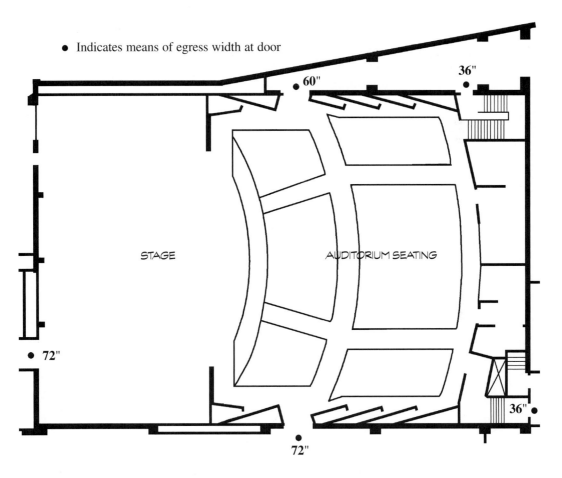

● Indicates means of egress width at door

36"

60"

STAGE   AUDITORIUM SEATING

72"

36"

72"

Fig. 1005.1B. Partial floor plan. Newman University Sports and Fine Arts Center. Wichita, Kansas. Gossen Livingston Associates, Inc., Architecture. Wichita, Kansas.

1005 Egress Width

1005.2 Door encroachment

- Door swing restrictions of this section do not apply to the following doors:
  - In dwelling units of the following occupancies:
    - R-2.
    - R-3.
  - In sleeping units of the following occupancy:
    - R-2.
- In other cases, the following doors have the requirements listed below:
  - Doors:
    - That open into the route of egress travel.
  - Requirements:
    - They may not reduce the required egress width more than the following:
      - ½ the required width as follows:
        - During the process of swinging open.
      - 7" when fully open as follows:
        - Includes door hardware.

Case study: Figure 1005.2. The required egress width of corridor 368 is 6' based on occupant load. The actual width is 8'. It is assumed that the required width is centered in the corridor, although other locations are feasible. When door E05.1 swings 90°, it can open no further. Therefore, the two limitations of its projection into required egress width are applied to the door fully open. When fully open it projects 6" into the required egress width, which is < the 7" maximum and < ½ the required width. The greatest projection of double doors 368.2 into required egress width during their swing is 6", which is < ½ the required width. Although, due to the column, one door is not flush to the wall when fully open, neither door encroaches on the required egress width in the open position.

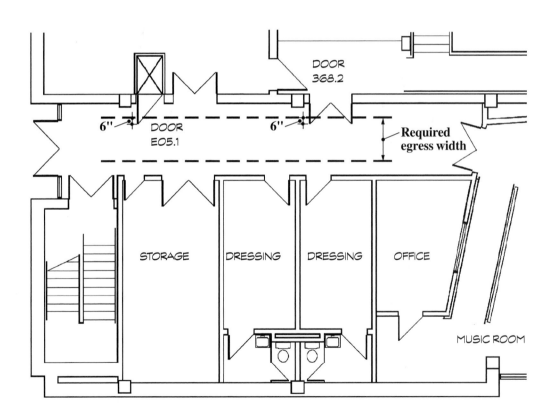

Fig. 1005.2. Partial floor plan. Newman Elementary School Renovations. Needham, Massachusetts. HKT Architects, Inc. Somerville, Massachusetts.

1006 Means of Egress Illumination

1006.1 Means of egress illumination

- Egress illumination requirements during the following time period are shown in the table below:
  - Egress included:
    Means of egress.
    Exit discharge.
  - Time period:
    When the part of the building using the means of egress is occupied:

Table 1006.1   Egress Illumination

Occupancy	Illumination required
U	no
Aisle accessways in A	no
R-1, R-2, R-3 dwelling units	no
R-1, R-2, R-3 sleeping units	no
Sleeping units in I	no
All other	yes

1006.2 Illumination level

- Requirements for illumination at floor level in a means of egress are as follows:

Table 1006.2   Egress Illumination at Floor Level

Location and time	Illumination required if no fire alarm is activated	Illumination required if a fire alarm is activated
During performances in auditoriums, theaters, opera halls, and similar assembly occupancies	≥ 0.2 footcandle	≥ 1.0 footcandle
All other	≥ 1.0 footcandle	≥ 1.0 footcandle

1006 Means of Egress Illumination

1006.3 Illumination emergency power

- Normal power for means of egress illumination is to be the building's electrical source.
- An emergency power system must illuminate the following areas in case of power failure:
  - In areas requiring ≥ 2 means of egress as follows:
    Exit access corridors.
    Exit access passageways.
    Aisles.
  - In buildings requiring ≥ 2 means of egress as follows:
    Exit access corridors.
    Exit stairways.
    Exterior egress elements at the following levels:
      At levels other than the level of exit discharge as follows:
        Continuous to the end of exit discharge.
    Exterior exit discharge elements immediately adjacent to exit discharge doors.
    Exit discharge elements that are within the building interior.

    Note: 1023.1, "General," is cited as governing interior exit discharge elements.

- The emergency power system is governed as follows:
  - It must provide power for ≥ 90 minutes.
  - It must consist of one of the following:
    Storage batteries.
    Unit equipment.
    On-site generator.

    Note: Section 2702, "Emergency and Standby Power Systems," is cited as governing the installation of emergency power systems.

Case study: Fig. 1006.3. The example shows a typical emergency lighting fixture and the symbol used on floor plans to indicate location. The many fixtures available for this purpose are similar in their surface mounting and two adjustble lamps. The battery-powered units meet code performance requirements.

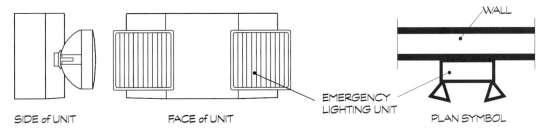

SIDE of UNIT   FACE of UNIT   EMERGENCY LIGHTING UNIT   WALL   PLAN SYMBOL

Fig. 1006.3. Elevations and symbol. Emergency lighting unit. Emergi-Lite. St. Matthews, South Carolina.

1007 Accessible Means of Egress

1007.1 Accessible means of egress required

- Accessible means of egress are not required as follows:
  - In alterations to existing buildings.
- One accessible means of egress is required in the following cases:
  - From an accessible mezzanine.

    Note: One of the following governs this egress as applicable:
    1007.3, "Enclosed exit stairways."
    1007.4, "Elevators."

  - In the following assembly spaces:
    From a space with a sloped floor as follows:
      The common path of travel meets both the following conditions:
        The path provides access to wheelchair spaces.
        The path meets aisle width and other requirements.

    Note: 1024.9, "Assembly aisles required," is cited as governing the aisles.

- In other cases accessible means of egress are governed as follows:
  - They must meet the requirements of this section.
  - ≥ 1 accessible means of egress is required as follows:
    From each accessible space.
  - ≥ 2 accessible means of egress are required as follows:
    From each accessible part of an accessible space where the following is required:
      Where > 1 means of egress is required from the accessible space.

    Note: Either of the following is cited as defining where >1 means of egress is required:
    1014.1, "Exit or exit access doorways required."
    1018.1, "Minimum number of exits."

Case study: Fig. 1007.1 The 1242 occupants of the gymnasium require 4 exits. Therefore, ≥ 2 accessible means of egress are required. The gymnasium is in compliance, as 4 accessible exits are provided.

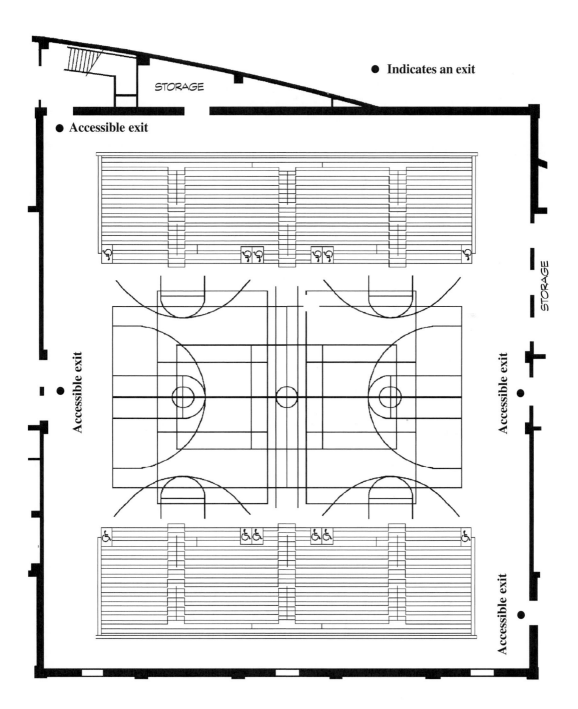

Fig. 1007.1. Gymnasium floor plan. Newman University Sports and Fine Arts Center. Wichita, Kansas. Gossen Livingston, Associates, Inc., Architecture. Wichita, Kansas.

1007 Accessible Means of Egress

1007.2 Continuity and components

- An exterior area for assisted rescue is required in the following case:
  - Where exit discharge is not accessible.

    Note: 1007.8, "Exterior area for assisted rescue," is cited as the source of requirements for this feature.

- Where the exit stairway is open to the exterior, the accessible means of egress must include one of the following:
  - An area of refuge.

    Note: 1007.6, "Areas of refuge," is cited as governing the area.

  - An exterior area for assisted rescue.

    Note: 1007.8, "Exterior area for assisted rescue," is cited as governing the area.

- Otherwise, required accessible means of egress must comply with the following:
  - They must be continuous to a public way.
  - They must consist of ≥ 1 of the following:
    Accessible routes.
    Stairways in exit enclosures.
    Elevators.
    Platform lifts.
    Horizontal exits.
    Smoke barriers.

    Note: The following are cited as governing the above-listed elements as applicable:
    Section 1104, "Accessible Route."
    1007.3, "Enclosed exit stairways," as applicable to stairways.
    1019.1, "Enclosures required," as applicable to stairways.
    1007.4, "Elevators."
    1007.5, "Platform lifts."

1007 Accessible Means of Egress

1007.2.1 Buildings with four or more stories

- This section applies to buildings as follows:
  - In which a required accessible floor has either of the following locations:
    - ≥ 4 stories above the level of exit discharge.
    - ≥ 4 stories below the level of exit discharge.
- An elevator serving as an accessible means of egress is not required where all of the following conditions apply:
  - The building is sprinklered as per NFPA 13 or 13R.
  - The floor has a horizontal exit.
  - The floor is at or above the level of exit discharge.
- An elevator serving as an accessible means of egress is not required where all of the following conditions apply:
  - The building is sprinklered as per NFPA 13 or 13R.
  - The floor has a ramp serving as an accessible means of egress.

  Note: 1010, "Ramps," is cited as governing ramps as means of egress.

- In other cases ≥ 1 accessible means of egress must be an elevator.

  Note: 1007.4, "Elevators," is cited as governing these elevators.

1007.3 Enclosed exit stairways *(part 1 of 2)*

- An accessible means of egress may include the following:
  - An open exit stairway as follows:
    An area of refuge is not required in the following cases:
    Where the building is sprinklered.

  Note: 1019.1, "Enclosures required," is cited as governing locations where an open exit stairway is allowed.
  903.3.1.1, "NFPA 13 sprinkler systems," is cited as governing the sprinklers.

- A clear width between handrails of ≥ 4' is not required in either of the following cases:
  - Where the enclosed exit stairway is accessed as follows:
    From a horizontal exit.
  - Where the building is sprinklered.

  Note: Either of the following is cited as governing the sprinklers:
  903.3.1.1, "NFPA 13 sprinkler systems."
  903.3.1.2, "NFPA 13R sprinkler systems."

1007 Accessible Means of Egress

1007.3 Enclosed exit stairways *(part 2 of 2)*

- An area of refuge is not required in the following case:
  - At exit stairways in the following locations:
    - At opening parking garages.
    - In sprinklered buildings.

    Note: Either of the following is cited as governing the sprinklers:
    903.3.1.1, "NFPA 13 sprinkler systems."
    903.3.1.2, "NFPA 13R sprinkler systems."

- In other cases, stairways serving an accessible means of egress must have the following:
  - A clear width ≥ 4' between handrails.
  - One of the following is required:
    - An area of refuge within a floor-level landing.
    - To be accessed from a horizontal exit.
    - To be accessed from an area of refuge.

    Note: 1007.6, "Areas of refuge," is cited as governing areas of refuge from which the stairway is to be accessed where this option is employed.

1007.4 Elevators

- Accessible elevators need not be accessed from one of the following in open parking garages:
  - Area of refuge.
  - Horizontal exit.
- Accessible elevators need not be accessed from one of the following in buildings sprinklered as per NFPA 13 or 13R:
  - Area of refuge.
  - Horizontal exit.
- In other cases, elevators must comply with the following to serve as an accessible means of egress:
  - They must meet emergency operation and signaling device requirements.

    Note: Section 2.27 of ASME A17.1, "Safety Code for Elevators and Escalators," is cited as governing the emergency systems.

  - They must have standby power.

    Note: The following are cited as governing standby power:
    Section 2702, "Emergency and Standby Power Systems."
    Section 3003, "Emergency Operations."

  - They must be accessed from one of the following:
    - Area of refuge.
    - Horizontal exit.

    Note: 1007.6, "Areas of refuge," is cited as governing these components.

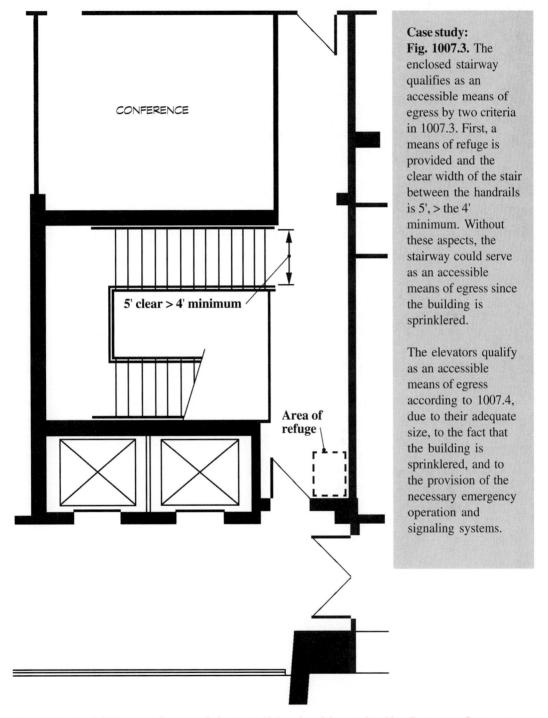

CONFERENCE

5' clear > 4' minimum

Area of refuge

Case study: Fig. 1007.3. The enclosed stairway qualifies as an accessible means of egress by two criteria in 1007.3. First, a means of refuge is provided and the clear width of the stair between the handrails is 5', > the 4' minimum. Without these aspects, the stairway could serve as an accessible means of egress since the building is sprinklered.

The elevators qualify as an accessible means of egress according to 1007.4, due to their adequate size, to the fact that the building is sprinklered, and to the provision of the necessary emergency operation and signaling systems.

Fig. 1007.3. Partial plan at stairway and elevators. University of Connecticut New Downtown Campus at Stamford, Connecticut. Perkins Eastman Architects, P.C. New York, New York.

1007 Accessible Means of Egress

1007.5 Platform lifts

- Platform lifts for wheelchairs may serve as an accessible means of egress as follows:
  - Where permitted as a required accessible route.

    Note: The following are cited as governing these lifts:
    1109.7, "Lifts."
    ASME A18.1, "Safety Standard for Platform Lifts and Stairway Chair Lifts."

  - Where standby power is supplied.

    Note: Section 2702, "Emergency and Standby Power Systems," is cited as governing.

1007.6 Areas of refuge

- A required area of refuge must be accessible from the space it serves as follows:
  - Access must be provided by an accessible means of egress.
  - The length of the following accessible route is limited as indicated below:
    Route:
      Between the following locations:
        An accessible space.
        The nearest area of refuge.
    Limit:
      Route must be ≤ the following travel distance:
        That limited by the occupancy.

    Note: 1015.1, "Travel distance limitations," is cited as governing travel distance.

- A required area of refuge must have direct access to one of the following:
  - An enclosed stairway.

    Note: The following are cited as governing the enclosed stairway:
    1007.3, "Enclosed exit stairways."
    1019.1, "Enclosures required."

  - An elevator.

    Note: 1007.4, "Elevators," is cited as governing.

- An elevator lobby serving as an area of refuge must comply with one of the following:
  - Elevators must be in an area of refuge formed by one of the following:
    Horizontal exit.
    Smoke barrier.
  - Shaft and lobby must meet smokeproof enclosure requirements.

    Note: 1019.1.8, "Smokeproof enclosures," is cited as governing.

Case study: Fig. 1007.6. Access to the area of refuge is provided by an accessible means of egress. The area of refuge has direct access to the elevator. The elevator lobby, including the telephone area, which serves as the area of refuge, meets smokeproof enclosure requirements. The area of refuge is, therefore, in compliance with the code.

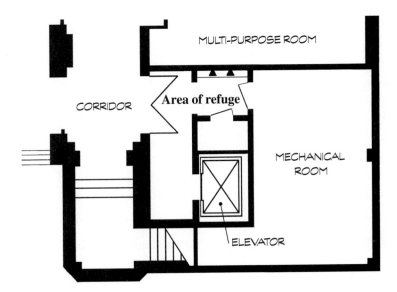

Fig. 1007.6. Plan of elevator with refuge area. Lady Bird Johnson Wildflower Center. Austin, Texas. Overland Partners, Inc. San Antonio, Texas.

1007 Accessible Means of Egress

1007.6.1 Size

- This section addresses wheelchair spaces in an area of refuge.
- Wheelchair spaces may not protrude into the minimum required width of the means of egress.
- Wheelchairs may be positioned no more than two deep from the path of travel.
- Occupant load for determining the number of wheelchairs required is as follows:
  - The sum of the occupant load of the area of refuge plus that of the area served.
- The minimum size of a wheelchair space is 30" × 48".
- Wheelchair spaces required, as listed below, are based on the following equation:

Occupant load ÷ 200 = number of wheelchair spaces required

Table 1007.6.1   Wheelchair Spaces Required

Occupant load	Spaces required	Occupant load	Spaces required
1 – 200	1	1001 – 1200	6
201 – 400	2	1201 – 1400	7
401 – 600	3	1401 – 1600	8
601 – 800	4	1601 – 1800	9
801 – 1000	5	etc.	etc.

1007.6.2 Separation

- The section does not apply to the following areas of refuge:
  - Where located within a stairway enclosure.
  - Where the areas of refuge and areas served are sprinklered as per NFPA 13 or 13R.
- Other areas of refuge must be separated from the rest of the story by a smoke barrier.

  Note: Section 709, "Smoke Barriers," is cited as governing those elements.

- Areas of refuge must be designed to minimize the penetration of smoke.

1007.6.3 Two-way communication

- Areas of refuge must have a communication system as follows:
  - Where a central point is continuously attended, the following is required:
    2-way communication between the area of refuge and the central point.
  - Where a central point is not continuously attended, both of the following are required:
    2-way communication between the area of refuge and the central point.
    A public telephone system available though controlled access.
- The central point for the communication system must be approved by the fire department.
- The 2-way communication system must include audible signals.
- The 2-way communication system must include visual signals.

Case study: Fig. 1007.6.1. The areas of refuge in the enclosed stairway do not encroach on the minimum width required for egress. They are no more than 2 deep from the path of travel. They are 30" × 48", thus, meeting size requirements. The areas of refuge are in compliance.

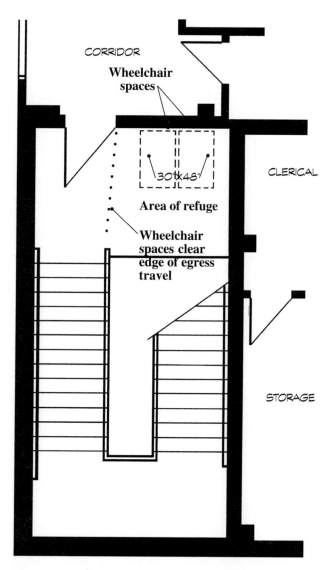

Fig. 1007.6.1. Plan of stair with area of refuge. University of Connecticut New Downtown Campus at Stamford, Connecticut. Perkins Eastman Architects, P.C. New York, New York.

1007 Accessible Means of Egress

1007.6.4 Instructions

- The following instructions for emergencies must be posted as follows:
  - In an area of refuge.
  - Located next to the communications system.
  - Instructions must include the following:
    Directions to other means of egress.
    Instructions to the following ambulatory persons:
      Those who are not assisting others are to be directed as follows:
        To use the exit stairway as soon as possible.
    A description of how assistance will be provided for the following as applicable:
      Use of the stairway.
      Use of the elevator.
    Instructions on how to call for assistance.
    Instructions on how to use the communications system.
    Instructions on how to use the area of refuge.

1007.6.5 Identification

- Doors to areas of refuge from the adjacent floor area must be identified by a sign as follows:
  - Sign must state "AREA OF REFUGE."
  - Sign must have the International Symbol of Accessibility.
  - The area of refuge sign must be illuminated where exit sign illumination is required.

    Note: 1011.2, "Illumination," is cited as identifying locations requiring exit sign illumination.

- Tactile signage is required at doors to areas of refuge.

  Note: ICC A117.1, "Accessible and Usable Buildings and Facilities," is cited as governing the signage required by this section.

1007.7 Signage

- Signage, with directions to accessible means of egress, is required at the following locations:
  - At exits and elevators serving an accessible space but which do not provide an approved accessible means of egress.

1008 Doors, Gates and Turnstiles

1008.1 Doors

- Means of egress doors must be apparent as follows:
  - They must be easily distinguished from adjacent surfaces.
  - They must be readily recognizable as doors.
  - They may not be covered with reflective materials such as mirrors.
  - They may not be concealed by the following:
    Curtains.
    Drapes.
    Decorations.
    Similar materials.

  Note: 1017.2, "Exterior exit doors," is cited as providing additional requirements.

- Doors provided that are in excess of the minimum required must meet the same requirements as those of required doors.

1008.1.1 Size of doors *(part 1 of 2)*

- Clear width for swinging doors is measured as follows:
  - From the stop to the face of the door when it is open at 90°.
- The following doorway must have a width ≥ 32" when only one leaf is open:
  - A door with two leafs.
  - A door required to have a width ≥ 32".
- Minimum door width is the greater of the following:
  - Minimum width established by occupant load.
  - Minimum width listed below:

Table 1008.1.1a   Minimum Width of Doors

Doors	Minimum clear width	Maximum width of swinging door
Serving other than means of egress in R-2 and R-3	none	none
To storage closets < 10 sf other than R-2 and R-3	none	48"
To resident sleeping units in I-3	28"	48"
For moving beds in means of egress in I-2	41½"	48"
Revolving doors	none	none
Interior egress doors in dwelling units and sleeping units not required to be accessible or adaptable	none	none
Doors required to be accessible in Type B dwelling units (units adaptable to accessibility)	31¾"	48"
Other means of egress doors	32"	48"

Note: 1008.1.3.1, "Revolving doors," is cited as governing revolving doors.

1008 Doors, Gates and Turnstiles

1008.1.1 Size of doors *(part 2 of 2)*

- Minimum door heights required are as listed below:

Table 1008.1.1b **Minimum Door Height**

Doors	Minimum height
Doors within dwelling units or sleeping units	6'-6"
Exterior doors in dwelling units and sleeping units other than the required exit	6'-4"
Interior egress doors in dwelling units or sleeping units not required to be accessible or adaptable	none
Other doors	6'-8"

1008.1.1.1 Projections into clear width

- Projections permitted into the clear width of a door opening are as shown below:

Height in door opening	Projection allowed
≥ 2'-10" and ≤ 6'-8"	≤ 4"
< 2'-10"	none

1008.1.2 Door swing *(part 1 of 2)*

- The following means of egress doors are not governed by this subsection:
  - The following locations with an occupant load ≤ 10:
    Private garages.
    Office areas.
    Factory areas.
    Storage areas.
  - In occupancy I-3 used as a place of detention.
  - Within or serving a single dwelling unit in occupancies R-2 and R-3.
  - Revolving doors in occupancies other than H.

    Note: 108.1.3.1, "Revolving doors," is cited as governing these doors.

  - Horizontal sliding doors in occupancies other than H.

    Note: 1008.1.3.3, "Horizontal sliding doors," is cited as governing these doors.

  - Power-operated doors.

    Note: 1008.1.3.2, "Power-operated doors," is cited as governing these doors.

- Other egress doors are required to be side-hinged swinging as follows:
  - Doors must swing in the direction of travel in either of the following cases:
    Where the occupant load ≥ 50.
    In occupancy H.

1008 Doors, Gates and Turnstiles

1008.1.2 Door swing (part 2 of 2)

- At the latch side, the force necessary to open the door is limited as follows:

Table 1008.1.2   Force Required at Door

Door type	Door action	Force necessary for door action
Side-swinging, interior, no closer	To open	≤ 5 lbs
Side-swinging, sliding, folding	Release of latch	≤ 15 lbs
"	Start door in motion	≤ 30 lbs
"	Swing to full-open position	≤ 15 lbs

1008.1.3.1 Revolving doors

- Revolving doors must have all the following characteristics:
  - Be collapsible into a bookfold position as follows:
     Provide parallel paths of travel.
     Travel paths to total 36" in width.
  - Be a minimum distance of 10' from the following:
     Stairs.
     Escalator.
  - Be separated from the following by a dispersal area:
     Stairs.
     Escalator.
  - Be within 10' of a side-swinging door in the same wall.

     Note: 1008.1, "Doors," is cited governing side-swinging doors.

  - Have a maximum speed in revolutions per minute as follows:

Table 1008.1.3.1   Maximum Speed for Revolving Doors

	Inside diameter of door							
Speed control type	6.5'	7.0'	7.5'	8.0'	8.5'	9.0'	9.5'	10'
RPM for power-driven speed control	11	10	9	9	8	8	7	7
RPM for manual speed control	12	11	11	10	9	9	8	8

Source: IBC Table 1008.1.3.1

1008.1.3.1.1 Egress component

- This section addresses revolving doors serving in a means of egress.

  Note: 1008.1.3.1, "Revolving doors," is cited as requiring compliance.

- The doors may not be assigned more than half the required egress capacity.
- The number of occupants assigned to a revolving door must be ≤ 50.
- The doors must be collapsible into a bookfold position as follows:
  - With a force of ≤ 130 lbs.
  - With the force applied ≤ 3" from the outer edge of a door leaf.

1008 Doors, Gates and Turnstiles

1008.1.3.1.2 Other than egress component

- This section addresses revolving doors not serving in a means of egress.
- Such revolving doors must comply with the following:
  - Have collapsible doors of adequate size.
  - Have the necessary relationship to the following:
    Stairs and escalators.
    A swinging door.
  - Have RPM limits as appropriate.

    Note: 1008.1.3.1, "Revolving doors," is cited as requiring compliance. A partial summary of its requirements is shown above.

- The force necessary to collapse the doors may be >180 lbs as follows:
  - Where it is reduced to ≤ 130 lbs in at least one of the following circumstances:
    Loss of power that holds doors in position.
    Activation of sprinklers.
    Activation of smoke detection system as follows:
      System covers the area inside the building within 75' of the revolving doors.
    Activation of manual control switch reducing the necessary force to < 130 lbs:
      The switch must be in an approved location.
      The switch must be clearly defined.

  Note: Section 907, "Fire Alarm and Detection Systems," is cited as governing the smoke detection system indicated above.

- In other cases, the force necessary to collapse a revolving door must be ≤ 180 lbs.

1008.1.3.2 Power-operated doors *(part 1 of 2)*

- Doors in I-3 are not subject to this section.
- Certain horizontal sliding doors are not subject to this section.

  Note: 1008.1.3.3, "Horizontal sliding doors," is cited as defining sliding doors that are not governed by this subsection.

- This section addresses other doors serving in a means of egress as follows:
  - Operated by power.
  - Doors with a photoelectric-actuated mechanism as follows:
    Opens door upon approach of a person.
  - Manual doors with power-assistance.

  Note: The following are cited as governing the types of doors indicated:
    BHMA A156.10, "Power Operated Pedestrian Doors."
    BHMA A156.19, "Power Assist and Low Energy Operated Doors."

- Such doors must have the following capability upon loss of power:
  - Able to be opened or closed manually.

1008 Doors, Gates and Turnstiles

1008.1.3.2 Power-operated doors (*part 2 of 2*)

- The force required to start moving the door manually is limited to the following:
  - ≤ 50 lbs.

    Note: 1008.1.2, "Door Swing," is cited as governing other forces required to open these doors manually.

- Upon application of force in the direction of egress, the door must perform as follows:
  - Swing to full opening width from any position.
- The following applies to biparting doors in the emergency break-out position:
  - The requirement for a 32″ width applies to the opening with both doors open.

    Note: 1008.1.1, "Size of doors," is cited as requiring the 32″ width when one door of a double door is open in other cases.

1008.1.3.3 Horizontal sliding doors

- This section addresses horizontal sliding doors serving in a means of egress.
- Such doors may serve in a means of egress in occupancies other than H.

    Note: 1008.1.2, "Door Swing," exception 5, is cited as permitting this use of sliding doors. The doors are required to meet other code requirements for sliding doors.

- Power requirements are as follows:
  - Doors must be power operated.
  - Doors must have an integrated standby power supply.
  - Door power must be supervised electronically.
- Manual requirements are as follows:
  - Doors must operate manually if power is lost as follows:

    By a simple method from both sides.

    Without special knowledge or effort.
  - The force necessary to operate the doors manually is limited as follows:

    ≤ 30 lbs to set door in motion.

    ≤ 15 lbs to open door to minimum width required for opening.

    ≤ 15 lbs to close door.

    ≤ 15 lbs to open door in the following case:

    When 250-lb force is applied ⊥ to door at a point adjacent to operating device.
- Where fire-protection rating is required, the door is governed as follows:
  - Must have applicable fire-protection rating.
  - Must be automatically closed by smoke detection system.

    Note: NFPA 80, "Fire Doors and Windows," is cited as governing.
    Section 715, "Opening Protectives," is cited as governing.

- Doors must open to required width as follows:
  - Within 10 seconds of activating operating device.

Case study: Fig. 1008.1.3.3. Power-operated sliding doors become manually operated doors upon a loss of power to the doors. As manually operated doors, they are required in many locations by section 1008.1.2, "Door swing," to be side-hinged doors that swing in the direction of egress travel. The horizontal sliding doors in the hospital of the example below are such a case. They comply with the power and force requirements, as well as having the capability to swing from the side in an emergency. They are in compliance with all code requirements.

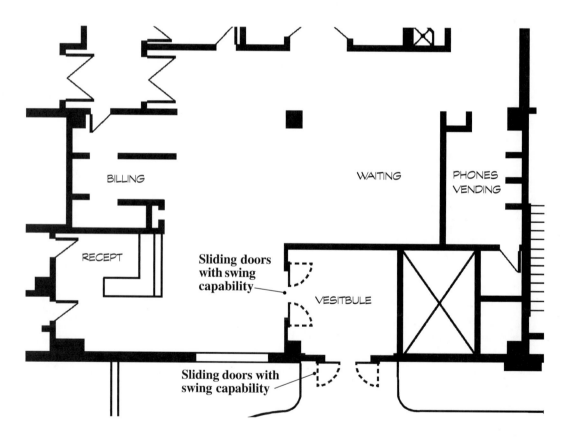

Fig. 1008.1.3.3. Partial floor plan. Christus St. Michael Health Care Center. Texarkana, Texas. Watkins Hamilton Ross Architects, Inc. Houston, Texas.

1008 Doors, Gates and Turnstiles

1008.1.3.4 Access-controlled egress doors

- The section addresses entrance doors in a means of egress.
- The following doors may have an entrance and egress access control system:
  - Doors in occupancy A, B, E, M, R-1, R-2 as follows:
    Entrance doors.
    Entrance doors to tenant spaces.
- Access control systems are governed as follows:
  - They must be approved.
  - A sensor is required on the egress side as follows:
    Sensor detects an approaching person.
    Doors unlock upon a signal from the sensor.
    Doors unlock upon loss of power to the sensor.
  - Doors must unlock upon loss of power to door locks.
  - A manual unlocking device must be provided as follows:
    Located $\geq$ 3'-4" and $\leq$ 4' above floor.
    Located $\leq$ 5' from locked doors.
    Must be readily accessible.
    Must be identified by a sign.
    Device activation must interrupt power to lock.
    Device must operate independently of access control electronics.
    Device activation must leave doors unlocked for $\geq$ 30 seconds.
  - Doors must unlock upon activation of a fire-protection system as follows:
    Building fire alarm system.
    Building sprinkler system.
    Building fire detection system.
    Doors to remain unlocked until the fire alarm system is reset.
- The following applies to occupancies A, B, E, and M:
  - Entrance doors may not be locked as follows:
    From the egress side.
    During times the building is open to the public.

1008.1.3.5 Security grilles

- Security grilles are permitted at the main exit of the following occupancies:
  - B, F, M, S.
- The following types of security grilles are permitted:
  - Horizontal sliding.
  - Vertical.
- Grilles must be operable, as follows, during the time the space is occupied:
  - From inside without the use of a key.
  - Without special knowledge or effort.
- Grilles must remain in full-open position as follows:
  - During times the space is occupied by the general public.

1008 Doors, Gates and Turnstiles

1008.1.4 Floor elevation

- This section addresses floor elevations on each side of a door.
- The following locations have requirements indicated below:
  - Locations:
        Individual units of occupancy R-3 > 3 stories.
        Individual units of occupancy R-2 > 3 stories.
  - Requirements:
        Door at interior stairs:
            Door may open at the top step as follows:
                Door may not swing over the top step.
        Screen doors and storm doors may swing over the following:
            Stairs and landings.
- A single step is permitted at exterior doors where all the following apply:
  - In occupancies F, H, R-2, R-3, S, U.
  - Door is not required to be accessible.
  - Step is ≤ 7" high.

    Note: 1003.5, "Elevation change," exception 1, is cited as governing this circumstance,
    a partial summary of which is provided above.
    1017.2, "Exterior exit doors," is cited as defining the door to which the above
    requirements are applicable.

- Variation in elevation on each side of a door is permitted where both of the following apply:
  - Where caused by differences in finish materials.
  - Where the difference is ≤ ½".
- Variation in elevation on each side of certain doors are limited as indicated below for the following location:
  - In Type B dwelling units (adaptable to accessibility) as follows:
        At exterior decks.
        At exterior patios.
        At exterior balconies.
  - Limitations for exterior surface:
        Must be impervious.
        Must be ≤ 4" below adjacent interior finished floor of the unit.
- The following applies to all other cases:
  - One of the following is required on each side of a door at the same elevation:
        A floor.
        A landing as follows:
            Interior landings must be level.
            Exterior landings may slope ≤ 1:48.

1008 Doors, Gates and Turnstiles

1008.1.5 Landings at doors

- Landing length in the direction of travel is governed as follows:
  - In the following locations such length is not required to be >36":
    Occupancy R-3.
    Occupancy U.
    Within individual units of R-2.
  - Landings in other locations must have a length ≥ 44" in the direction of travel.
- Landings must have a width equal to the larger of the following:
  - Equal to the width of the stairway.
  - Equal to the width of the door.
- A door may protrude ≤ 7" into the required width of a landing as follows:
  - Where the door is fully open.
  - Door hardware is included.
- A door may protrude ≤ ½ the required width of a landing where all the following apply:
  - The occupant load is ≥ 50.
  - With the door in any position.
  - Door hardware is included.

> **Case study: Fig. 1008.1.5.** The landing width at the turn is measured as a radius which must be ≥ the 3'-11" width of the stair. In this case, the landing at the door is 4'-0" wide. The length of the landing in the direction of travel is > than the 44" minimum. The width of the landing is greater than the 3' width of the door. The door (including hardware) protrudes 7" into the landing radius when fully open, thus, complying with the maximum permitted. The door does not protrude into the required landing width more than half the required width, as indicated by the arc in the illustration. The landings comply with the code.

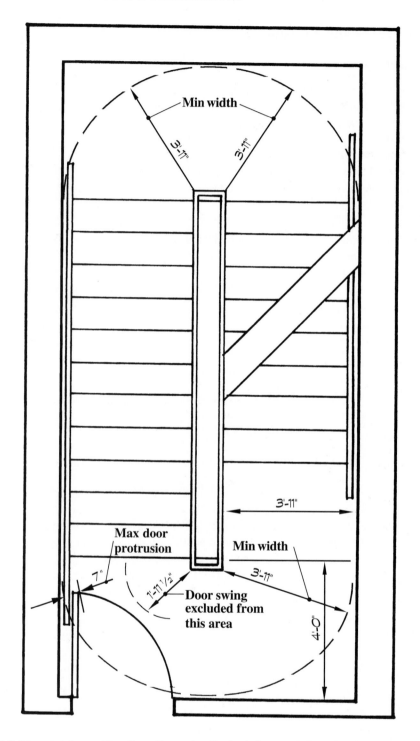

Fig. 1008.1.5. Plan at stairway. Hoyt Street Properties. Portland, Oregon. Ankrom Mosian Associated Architects. Portland, Oregon.

1008 Doors, Gates and Turnstiles

1008.1.6 Thresholds

- Doorway thresholds are limited in height as follows:
    - ≤ 7-¾" where all the following apply:
        Located in occupancy R-2 or R-3.
        Exterior door as follows:
            Not a required means of egress.
            Not on an accessible route.
    - ≤ ¾" for dwelling unit sliding doors.
    - ≤ ½" for other doors.
- Changes in floor level > ¼" have the following requirement:
    - Beveled edge(s) at a slope ≤ 1:2 for the following:
        Thresholds.
        Floor elevation variations.

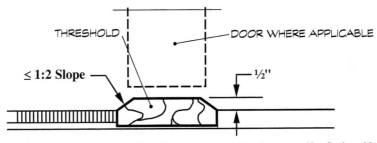

THRESHOLD   DOOR WHERE APPLICABLE

≤ 1:2 Slope   ½"

Fig. 1008.1.6. Threshold detail. Hot Springs Police Department New Headquarters. Hot Springs National Park, Arkansas. Cromwell Architects Engineers. Little Rock, Arkansas.

1008.1.7 Door arrangement

- This section addresses the distance between multiple doors in sequence as encountered in the direction of travel.
- Space required between horizontal sliding power-operated doors in a series is ≥ 4'.
- Spacing of multiple doors in the direction of travel is governed as follows:
    - The following doors are not required to be spaced ≥ 4' apart:
        Exterior doors with storm doors or screen doors for individual dwelling units in the following locations:
            Occupancy R-2.
            Occupancy R-3.
        Doors within dwelling units that are not Type A (accessible) as follows:
            Occupancy R-2.
            Occupancy R-3.
- Other swinging doors in a series must be spaced the following distance apart:
    - 4' + the width of the door swinging into the space.
- Doors in a series must swing in one of the following patterns:
    - In the direction of travel.
    - Away from the space between the doors.

1008 Doors, Gates and Turnstiles

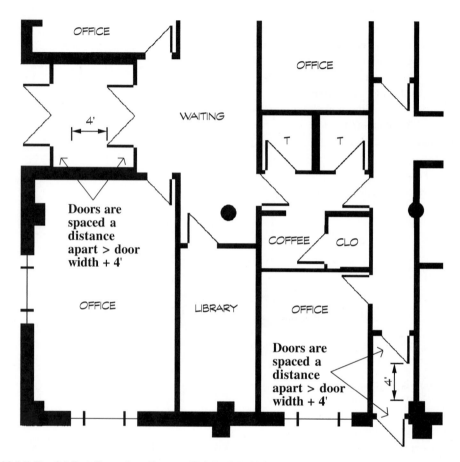

Fig. 1008.1.7. Partial first-floor plan. Country Club Park Building One. Wichita, Kansas. Gossen Livingston Associats, Inc., Architecture. Wichita, Kansas.

1008.1.8 Door operations

- Unless otherwise permitted by this section the following requirement applies to egress doors:
  - Egress doors must be operable as follows:
    - From the egress side.
    - Without the use of a key.
    - Without the requirement of special knowledge.
    - Without special effort.

1008 Doors, Gates and Turnstiles

1008.1.8.1 Hardware

- The following hardware has the requirements listed below:
  - Hardware:
    For doors where required to be accessible as follows:
      Handles.
      Pulls.
      Latches.
      Locks.
      Other operating devices.

    Note: Chapter 11, "Accessibility," is cited as defining doors required to be accessible.

  - Requirements:
    Hardware must not require the following to operate:
      Tight grasping.
      Tight pinching.
      Twisting of the wrist.

1008.1.8.2 Hardware height

- The following locks may be mounted at any height:
  - Locks not used for routine operation but only for security purposes.
- Other door hardware as follows must be positioned at the height indicated below:
  - Door hardware:
      Handles.
      Pulls.
      Latches.
      Locks.
      Other operating devices.
  - Required height:
      $\geq 2'\text{-}10''$ and $\leq 4'$.

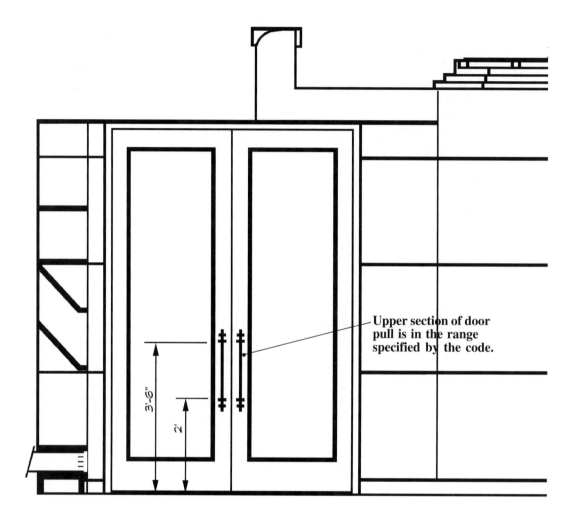

**Upper section of door
pull is in the range
specified by the code.**

3'-6"

2'

Fig. 1008.1.8.2. Door elevation. Christus St. Michael Health Care Center. Texarkana, Texas. Watkins Hamilton
Ross Architects, Inc. Houston, Texas.

1008 Doors, Gates and Turnstiles

1008.1.8.3 Locks and latches *(part 1 of 2)*

- Doors may be secured by locks and latches in any of the following cases:
  - For detention purposes.
  - For restraint purposes.
  - Main exterior door(s) may have the locks specified at the following locations if all the requirements listed below are met:
    - Locks:
      - Key-operated locks.
    - Locations:
      - In occupancy A as follows:
        - Occupant load is ≤ 300.
      - In the following occupancies:
        - B, F, M, S.
      - At churches.
    - Requirements:
      - Keys operate from the egress side.
      - It is obvious that the device is locked.
      - A sign is posted with all the following characteristics:
        - Readily visible.
        - Durable.
        - Posted on egress side of door.
        - Posted in one of the following locations:
          - On the door.
          - Adjacent to the door.
        - Has the following message:
          - THIS DOOR TO REMAIN UNLOCKED WHEN BUILDING IS OCCUPIED.
            - Message is to have all the following characteristics:
              - 1" high letters.
              - Letters to be on a contrasting background.
      - Building official has not disapproved the use of the lock as follows:
        - Based on due cause.
- Pairs of egress doors may have the following devices if all requirements below are met:
  - Devices:
    - Flush bolts.
  - Requirements:
    - Must be approved.
    - Must be automatic.
    - Door has no doorknob.
    - Door has no hardware mounted on its surface.

1008 Doors, Gates and Turnstiles

1008.1.8.3 Locks and latches *(part 2 of 2)*

- Any of the following devices are permitted on the specified doors where requirements as listed below are met:
  - Devices:
    - Night latch.
    - Dead bolt.
    - Security chain.
  - Doors:
    - In occupancy R from any of the following:
      - Individual dwelling units.
      - Individual sleeping units.
  - Requirements:
    - Occupant load must be ≤ 10.
    - Devices must be operable as follows:
      - From the inside.
      - Without a key.
      - Without a tool.

1008.1.8.4 Bolt locks

- The following devices are permitted at the location indicated below:
  - Devices:
    - Manual flush bolts.
    - Manual surface bolts.
  - Locations:
    - On doors not required for egress at either of the following:
      - Individual dwellilng units.
      - Individual sleeping units.
- The following devices are permitted at the location indicated below:
  - Devices:
    - Manual edge-mounted bolt.
    - Manual surface-mounted bolt.
  - Locations:
    - On the inactive door of the following type of doors:
      - Double doors at either of the following rooms:
        - Storage room.
        - Equipment room.
- In other cases the following devices are not permitted:
  - Manual flush bolts.
  - Manual surface bolts.

1008 Doors, Gates and Turnstiles

1008.1.8.5 Unlatching

- Unlatching a door may require more > 1 action in the following cases:
  - At doors for detention.
  - At doors for restraint.
  - At doors which may have the following devices:
    Manual bolt lock.

    Note: 1008.1.8.4, "Bolt locks," is cited as defining locations where these devices are allowed.

  - At doors with automatic flush bolts.

    Note: 1008.1.8.3, "Locks and latches," exception 3, is cited as defining locations where these devices are allowed.

  - At doors in any of the following occupancy R doors:
    From individual dwelling units.
    From individual guest rooms.

    Note: 1008.1.8.3, "Locks and latches," exception 4, is cited as defining locations where these devices are allowed.

1008.1.8.6 Delayed egress locks *(part 1 of 2)*

- Delayed locks may be used on egress doors where the following requirements are met:
  - Locks must be approved.
  - Locks must be listed.
  - Doors are limited to the following occupancies:
    B, F, I, M, R, S, U as follows:
      Where the building has one of the following:
        Sprinklers.
        Smoke detection system.
        Heat detection system.

    Note: 903.3.1.1, "NFPA 13 sprinkler systems," is cited as governing the sprinklers noted above.
    Section 907, "Fire Alarm and Detection Systems," is cited as governing smoke and heat detection systems.

  - Doors with delayed locks may not be located as follows:
    So that travel into an exit requires passing through > 1 door with a delayed lock.
  - Doors must unlock as follows:
    When sprinklers activate.
    When a fire detection system activates.
    By a signal from the fire command center.

1008 Doors, Gates and Turnstiles

1008.1.8.6 Delayed egress locks *(part 2 of 2)*

- ○ Doors must unlock as follows:
    - Within one of the following time periods:
        - 15 seconds.
        - 30 seconds where approved.
    - Due to a force on the release mechanism as follows:
        - ≤ 15 lb.
        - Applied for 1 second.
    - Lock release must activate a signal audible near the door.
    - Lock must require manual relocking.
    - The unlocking process cannot be reversible once initiated.
- ○ The following sign must posted:
    - Located as follows:
        - Above the release device.
        - Within 12" of the release device.
    - Sign must have one of the following messages as applicable:
        - PUSH UNTIL ALARM SOUNDS. DOOR CAN BE OPENED IN 15 SECONDS.
        - PUSH UNTIL ALARM SOUNDS. DOOR CAN BE OPENED IN 30 SECONDS.
- ○ Doors require emergency lighting.

1008.1.8.7 Stairway doors

- • This section governs the following means of egress doors:
    - ○ At interior stairways.
- • This section does not govern the following doors:
    - ○ Stairway doors that are not exit discharge doors.

    Note: 403.12, "Stairway door operations," is cited as governing this type of door.

- • Stairway discharge doors are governed as follows:
    - ○ They must be operable from the egress side.
    - ○ They may be locked only from the side opposite the egress side.
- • Doors in stairways serving ≤ 4 stories are governed as follows:
    - ○ They may be locked from the side opposite the egress side in the following case:
        - Where they are operable from the egress side.
- • In other cases, the stairway doors are governed as follows:
    - ○ They must be operable from both sides without the following:
        - Use of a key.
        - Special knowledge.
        - Special effort.

1008 Doors, Gates and Turnstiles

1008.1.9 Panic and fire exit hardware

- The following hardware must comply with the requirements listed below:
  - Hardware:
    Panic hardware.
    Fire exit hardware.
  - Requirements:
    The component that releases the door latch is governed as follows:
      It must extend ≥ half the door width.
    The force required to release the door latch is limited as follows:
      It must be ≤ 15 lb.
- The following hardware is the only latch type permitted on the doors listed below:
  - Hardware:
    Panic hardware.
    Fire exit hardware.
  - Doors:
    In a means of egress in the following occupancies:
      Occupancy A with an occupant count ≥ 100.
      Occupancy E with an occupant count ≥ 100.
      Occupancies H-1, H-2, H-3, H-5.
- Panic hardware in balanced doors is governed as follows:
  - It must be the push-pad type as follows:
    The pad must be on the latch side of the door.
    The pad may not extend past the center of the door.

1008.2 Gates

- Gates > 4' wide as follows are allowed in fences and walls around a stadium:
  - Horizontal sliding gates.
  - Swinging gates.
- Other gates in a means of egress must comply with applicable requirements for doors.

1008.2.1 Stadiums

- Panic hardware is not required on gates where the following conditions exist:
  - Gates are around stadiums.
  - Gates are continually supervised when the public is present.
  - A dispersal area is provided as follows:
    Area is located between the fence and enclosed space.
    Area is ≥ 50' from enclosed space.
    Area must be ≥ the following size:

    Occupant load × 3 sf (per occupant)

- Dispersal area must meet means of egress requirements.

  Note: Section 1017, "Exits," is cited as governing egress from safe dispersal areas.

1008 Doors, Gates and Turnstiles

1008.3 Turnstiles

- A turnstile may serve in a means of egress as follows:
  - Where assigned ≤ 50 occupants for egress.
  - Turnstile must rotate freely as follows:
    In the direction of egress.
    When released manually by staff.
  - Where assigned ≤ half of the required capacity for egress.
  - Turnstile dimensions must be as follows:
    Height ≤ 39".
    Clear width ≥ 16½" @ ≤ 39" height.
    Clear width ≥ 22" @ > 39" height.
- A turnstile may serve in an accessible route where it meets all the following conditions:
  - Where it does not have a revolving mechanism.
  - Where it has the following dimensions:
    Clear width ≥ 36" @ ≤ 34" height.
    Clear width ≥ 32" @ ≥ 34" and ≤ 80" height.
- In other cases the following may not obstruct a means of egress:
  - Turnstiles.
  - Similar devices as follows:
    That permit travel only in one direction.

1008.3.1 High turnstile

- Turnstiles > 39" in height are governed as follows:
  - They must meet revolving door requirements.

1008.3.2 Additional door

- The following turnstiles have the requirements listed below:
  - Turnstiles:
    Serving an occupant load > 300.
    Other than portable.
  - Requirements:
    Must have a side-hinged swinging door as follows:
      Located ≤ 50' from the turnstile.

  Note: 1008.1, "Doors," is cited as governing these swinging doors.

1009 Stairways and Handrails

1009.1 Stairway width

- Spiral stairways are not governed by this section.

    Note: 1009.9, "Spiral stairways," is cited as the source of requirements for this type of stairway.

- Assembly aisle stairs are not governed by this section.

    Note: Section 1024, "Assembly," is cited as governing aisle stairs.

- A clear passage ≥ 1'-8" is required on stairways where both the following apply:
    - Where a stairway lift is installed as follows:
        Where the lift folds, the clearance is measured as follows:
            To the lift in the folded-up position.
    - In the following occupancies:
        R-3.
        R-2 as follows:
            Within dwelling units.
- In other cases, stairway width must be the larger of the following:
    - ≥ 4' clear width between handrails where required to be accessible.
    - For stairs not required to be accessible, the following widths apply:
        ≥ 3' for occupant loads ≤ 50.
        ≥ 3'-8" for occupant loads > 50.
    - ≥ Number of occupants served × the minimum width per occupant served as follows:

Table 1009.1   Minimum Width of Stairway per Occupant Served

Occupancy	Building sprinklered as per NFPA 13 or 13R
A, B, E, F, H-5, I-1, I-3, I-4, M, R, S, U	0.2"
H-1, H-2, H-3, H-4, I-2	0.3"
	Building not sprinklered
A, B, E, F, H-5, I-1, I-3, I-4, M, R, S, U	0.3"
H-1, H-2, H-3, H-4	0.7"

Source: IBC Table 1005.1.

Note: IBC Table 1005.1, "Egress Width per Occupant Served," is cited as governing stairway width and is summarized above.
1007.3, "Enclosed stairways," is cited as governing stairways in an accessible means of egress.

1009 Stairways and Handrails

1009.2 Headroom

- Spiral stairways may have a headroom clearance of 6'-6".

  Note: 1009.9, "Spiral stairways," is cited as governing these stairs.

- Other stairways require a headroom clearance ≥ 6'-8" as follows:
  - Measured vertically from a line tangent to tread nosings.
  - Required headroom must be continuous to a point directly above the following:
      The point where the line tangent to the nosings intersects the following:
        The landing below the stair run as follows:
          The point is located a distance away from the bottom riser equal to 1 tread depth.
- Minimum headroom clearance is required for the full width of the landing and stairway.

1009.3 Stair treads and risers *(part 1 of 2)*

- The following stairways are not governed by this section:
  - Circular stairways.

    Note: 1009.7, "Circular stairways," is cited as governing these stairs.

  - Winders.

    Note: 1009.8, "Winders," is cited as governing these stairs.

  - Spiral stairways.

    Note: 1009.9, "Spiral stairways," is cited as governing these stairs.

  - Stairways replacing existing stairways.

    Note: International Existing Building Code is cited as governing these stairs.

- In assembly seating areas, the following applies:
  - Where aisle gradient is dictated by sightlines, stair dimensions are required as follows:
      Risers ≥ 4" and ≤ 8".

    Note: 1024.11.2, "Risers," is cited as governing these stairs and is partially summarized above.

- For the following locations and conditions, the requirements indicated below apply:
  - Locations:
      R-3.
      Within dwelling units of R-2.
      U where serving R-3.
  - Conditions:
      Stairs with solid risers.
      Treads < 11" in depth.
  - Requirements:
      A nosing ≥ ¾" and ≤ 1¼".

1009 Stairways and Handrails

1009.3 Stair treads and risers *(part 2 of 2)*

- Winder tread depth is measured as follows:
  - ○ $\perp$ to leading edge.
  - ○ Horizontally between vertical planes as follows:
    - At the leading edges of adjacent treads.
- The requirements indicated below apply to winders in the following locations:
  - ○ Locations:
    - R-3.
    - Within dwelling units of R-2.
    - U where serving R-3.
  - ○ Requirements:
    - Tread depth must be $\geq$ 6" at all points.
    - Tread depth must be $\geq$ 10" as follows:
      - Measured at 12" from the narrow end.
- Other winder treads have the following requirements:
  - ○ Tread depth must be $\geq$ 10" at all points.
  - ○ Tread depth must be $\geq$ 11" measured as follows:
    - At 12" from the narrow end.
  - ○ The difference in depth between the following treads in a flight of stairs must be $\leq$ $^3/_8$":
    - Deepest tread as measured at 12" from the narrow end.
    - Most narrow tread as measured at 12" from the narrow end.
- Other tread and riser sizes requirements are as follows:

Table 1009.3	**Tread and Riser Heights**	
Occupancy	Riser	Tread
R-3	$\geq$ 4" and $\leq$ 7 ¾"	$\geq$ 10"
Within dwelling units of R-2	$\geq$ 4" and $\leq$ 7 ¾"	$\geq$ 10"
U where serving R-3	$\geq$ 4" and $\leq$ 7 ¾"	$\geq$ 10"
All other	$\geq$ 4" and < 7"	$\geq$ 11"

- Riser height is measured vertically between leading edges of adjacent treads.
- Tread depth is measured horizontally as follows:
  - ○ Horizontally between vertical planes as follows:
    - At the leading edges of adjacent treads.
  - ○ $\perp$ to the leading edge of the tread.
- The difference in height between the following risers in a flight of stairs must be $\leq$ $^3/_8$":
  - ○ Largest riser.
  - ○ Smallest riser.
- The difference in depth between following treads in a flight of stairs must be $\leq$ $^3/_8$":
  - ○ Largest tread.
  - ○ Smallest tread.

1009 Stairways and Handrails

1009.3.1 Dimensional uniformity

- Aisle risers serving assembly seating where the gradient is dictated by sightlines are not required to be uniform within certain limits.

  Note: 1024.11.2, "Risers," is cited as the source of requirements for aisle risers.

- Winders may differ from rectangular treads in the same stairway flight as follows:
  - Winders must be consistent in shape with each other.

  Note: 1009.8, "Winders," is cited as governing these stairs.

- Top or bottom stairway risers abutting a sloped surface are governed as follows:
  - Sloped surfaces as follows permitted to serve as landings must have a fixed gradient:
    Public way.
    Walkway.
    Driveway.
  - The abutting riser may follow the slope of the landing to a height < 4" as follows:
    Slope must be ≤ 1:12 across the stairway width.
  - The leading edge of the abutting riser must be identified with a marking stripe as follows:
    Marking stripe to be distinctive.
    Marking stripe to differ from any other nosing marking in the flight.
    Marking stripe to be visible when traveling down the stairs.
    Marking stripe to have a slip-resistant surface.
    Marking stripe to have a width ≥ 1" and ≤ 2".
- Other stair treads and risers are governed as follows:
  - They must be uniform in size and shape.
  - The difference in size between the largest and smallest tread in a flight must be ≤ $^{3}/_{8}$".
  - The difference in size between the largest and smallest riser in a flight must be ≤ $^{3}/_{8}$".

1009 Stairways and Handrails

1009.3.2 Profile

- Solid risers in stairways are governed as follows:
  - Solid risers are not required for stairways in occupancy I-3.
  - Stairways not required to be an enclosed accessible means of egress need not have solid risers as follows:
    Where the opening between treads will not pass a 4" sphere.

    Note: 1007.3, "Enclosed exit stairways," is cited as the source for these and other requirements governing accessible stairways.

- Other stairways must have solid risers in one of the following positions:
  - Vertical.
  - Sloped at ≤ 30° from the vertical as follows:
    Adjoins the underside of the leading edge of the tread above.
- Other aspects of stairways are governed as follows:
  - The leading edge of the treads may not have a radius > ½".
  - Nosings may not be beveled > ½".
  - Nosings may not project > 1¼" over the tread below.
  - Nosings must be uniform in size, including the following:
    The nosing of the floor at the top of a stair run.

1009.4 Stairway landings

- Aisle stairs are not governed by this section where they comply with requirements for aisles in assembly occupancies.

  Note: Section 1024, "Assembly," is cited as the source of requirements for aisle stairs.

- Other stairway landings are governed as follows:
  - One of the following is required at the top and bottom of a stairway:
    Floor.
    Landing.
  - The landing width must be ≥ the stairway width.
  - Landings located in other than straight runs must have the following dimension in the direction of travel:
    A dimension ≥ the stair width.
  - Landings located in straight runs must have the smaller of the following dimensions in the direction of travel:
    A dimension ≥ the stair width.
    ≥ 48".
  - Doors opening onto landings may protrude into the required width as follows:
    A distance ≤ ½ the required width at any point while opening.
    A distance ≤ 7" when the door is fully open.
    The protrusion of a door includes its hardware.

1009 Stairways and Handrails

1009.5 Stairway construction

- Wood handrails are allowed in stairways in all types of building construction.
- Otherwise, stairway materials must conform to the construction-type requirements for the building.

1009.5.1 Stairway walking surface

- The walking surface of the following stairway components must not slope > 1:48 in any direction:
  - Landings.
  - Treads.
- The surfaces of treads and landings are governed as follows:

Table 1009.5.1   Surfaces of Treads and Landings

Locations	Tread and landing surfaces
Occupancies A, B, E, I, M, R, U	Solid surfaces required.
Parking structure public areas	Solid surfaces required.
Occupancies F, H	Openings allowed which cannot pass a $1^1/_8$" sphere.
Occupancy S other than public areas of parking structures	Openings allowed which cannot pass a $1^1/_8$" sphere.

1009.5.2 Outdoor conditions

- The following outdoor walking surfaces must not accumulate water:
  - Outdoor stairways.
  - Outdoor approaches to stairways.
- The following surfaces in locations shown must be protected as indicated below:
  - Surfaces that are a part of exterior stairways:
     Treads.
     Platforms.
     Landings.
  - Locations:
     In the following occupancies:
       A, B, E, F, H, I, M, R-1, R-2, R-4, S.
       U not serving R-3.
     In the following climates:
       Subject to snow or ice.
  - Requirements:
     Surfaces must be protected to prevent the accumulation of snow or ice.

1009 Stairways and Handrails

Case study: Fig. 1009.5.2. The surfaces of the stairway slope 2% to shed water. Snow melting mats are embedded in the landing and the steps, to prevent the accumulation of snow or ice. The stairway meets requirements for exterior conditions as required for a B occupancy.

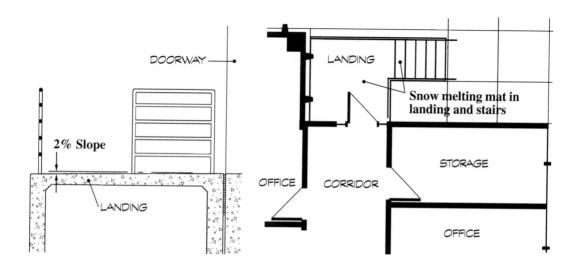

Fig. 1009.5.2. Plan and section at exterior stair. Lubrication Engineers, Inc. Wichita, Kansas. Gossen Livingston, Associates, Inc., Architecture. Wichita, Kansas.

1009.6 Vertical rise

- Aisle stairs are not governed by this section.

  Note: Section 1024, "Assembly," is cited as the source of requirements for aisle stairs.

- Other stairs are limited in their vertical rise to ≤ 12'.

1009 Stairways and Handrails

1009.7 Circular stairways

- The following circular stairs are not governed by this section:
  - In occupancy R-3.
  - In individual dwelling units of R-2.
- Other circular stairs are governed as follows:
  - The smaller stairway radius has the following size requirements:
      It must be ≥ the stairway width.
  - The tread depth must comply with the following:
      ≥ 11" measured as follows:
        At a point 12" from the narrow end of the tread.
      ≥ 10" at the narrow end.

  Note: 1009.3, "Stair treads and risers," is cited as govering circular stair tread width and riser height.

1009.8 Winders

- Winders in a means of egress are governed as follows:
  - Permitted within a dwelling unit.
  - Not permitted in other locations.

1009.9 Spiral stairways

- Use of spiral stairways in a means of egress is governed as follows:
  - Permitted in the following locations:
      Within a dwelling unit:
        From a space with both the following characteristics:
          Area ≤ 250 sf.
          Occupant load ≤ 5 persons.
      For stage-related areas as follows:
        Galleries.
        Catwalks.
        Gridirons.

  Note: 1014.6, "Stage means of egress," is cited as governing galleries, catwalks, and gridirons.

  - Not permitted in other locations.
- Dimensions required of a spiral stairway are as follows:
  - Tread width must be ≥ 7½" measured in the following location:
      At 12" from narrow end.
  - Headroom must be ≥ 6'-6".
  - Riser height must be ≤ 9½".
  - Width of stairway must be ≥ 2'-2".

Case study: Fig. 1009.7. The tower stairway meets requirements for radius as well as tread depth at the narrow end and at a point 12" from the narrow end as indicated in the illustration. The adjacent steps are not circular in the strictest sense, but meet the same requirements.

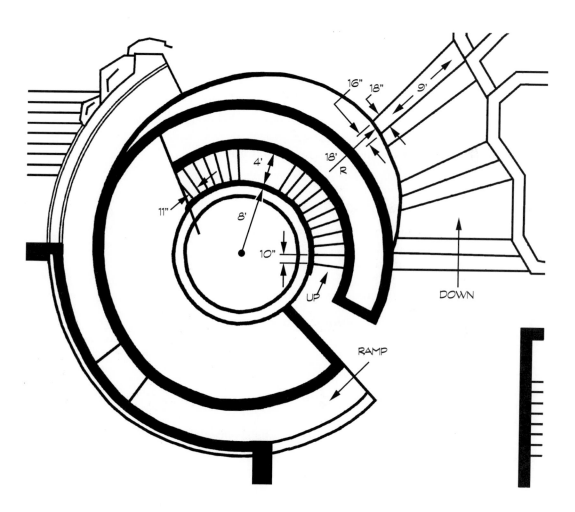

Fig. 1009.7 Plan at tower. Lady Bird Johnson Wildflower Center. Austin, Texas. Overland Partners, Inc. San Antonio, Texas.

1009 Stairways and Handrails

1009.10 Alternating tread devices

- Use of alternating tread devices in a means of egress is governed as follows:
  - Permitted in the following locations:
    - From mezzanines in occupancies F, H, and S as follows:
      - Mezzanine area ≤ 250 sf.
      - Mezzanine occupants ≤ 5.
    - In I-3 areas ≤ 250 sf as follows:
      - Guard towers.
      - Observation stations.
      - Control rooms.
    - For access to unoccupied roofs.
  - Not permitted in other locations.

1009.10.1 Handrails of alternating tread devices

- Handrails for alternating tread devices must meet the following requirements:
  - Must be located on both sides of the stair system.
  - Must meet the same requirements as for stairway handrails.

  Note: 1009.11, "Handrails," is cited as governing stairway handrails.

1009.10.2 Treads of alternating tread devices

- The initial tread of an alternating tread device must be at the same elevation as the following:
  - Landing or floor surface.
  - Platform.
- Alternating tread device dimensions are governed as follows:

Table 1009.10.2   **Alternating Tread Devices**

Device location	Projected tread	Tread depth	Tread width	Rise to next tread
Means of egress from a mezzanine of ≤ 250 sf and ≤ 5 occupants	≥ 8½"	≥ 10½"	≤ 7"	≤ 8"
Other locations	≥ 5"	≥ 8½"	≥ 7"	≤ 9 ½"

Note: "Projected tread" is that visible beyond the tread above in a plan view.

1009 Stairways and Handrails

1009.11 Handrails

- Additional handrails are not required at an aisle stair with a center handrail.

  Note: 1024, "Assembly," is cited as governing aisles noted above.

- The following may have a handrail on one side only:
  - Stairways within dwelling units.
  - Spiral stairways.
  - Aisle stairs with seating only on one side.
- Handrails are not required for the following components where conditions indicated apply:
  - Components:
    Decks and patios.
    Walkways.
  - Conditions:
    At a single change in elevation.
    Landing depth on each side of elevation change is greater than required.
- Handrails are not required at the following:
  - At a single riser at the following occupancy R-3 locations:
    Entrance and egress doors.
  - At a single riser in a room as follows:
    In a dwelling unit of the following occupancies:
    R-2, R-3.
    In a sleeping unit of the following occupancies:
    R-2, R-3.
- Other stairways require a handrail on each side as follows:
  - Handrails must have adequate strength and attachment.

  Note: 1607.7, "Loads on handrails, guards, grab bars and vehicle barriers," is cited as the source for handrail and attachment strength requirements.

- Ramp handrails are governed by this section.

  Note: 1010.8, "Handrails," is cited as identifying ramps requiring handrails.

1009.11.1 Height

- The height of a handrail must be in the following range:
  - $\geq$ 2'-10" and $\leq$ 3'-2" measured as follows:
    Above stair tread nosings.
    Above ramp finished surface.
- Handrail height must be uniform.

1009 Stairways and Handrails

1009.11.2 Intermediate handrails

- Intermediate handrails are required at stairways where necessary as follows:
  - So that all points in the required width are $\leq$ 2'-6" away from a handrail.
  - Intermediate handrails necessary for selected required widths are indicated below:

Table 1009.11.2   Intermediate Handrails Required

Required egress width (less handrail protrusions)	Intermediate handrails required	Required egress width (less handrail protrusions)	Intermediate handrails required
$\leq$ 5'	0	> 15' and $\leq$ 20'	3
> 5' and $\leq$ 10'	1	> 20' and $\leq$ 25'	4
> 10' and $\leq$ 15'	2	> 25' and $\leq$ 30'	5

- Handrails must be located on monumental stairs as follows:
  - Along the most direct path of egress travel.

1009.11.3 Handrail graspability

- Circular handrails meet one of the following requirements:
  - Have an outside diameter $\geq$ 1¼" and $\leq$ 2".
  - Have equivalent graspability to the above diameter range.
- Other handrail shapes must comply with the following:
  - Have a perimeter $\geq$ 4" and $\leq$ 6¼".
  - Have all cross-section dimensions $\leq$ 2¼".
  - Have edges with a radius $\geq$ 0.01".

1009.11.4 Continuity *(part 1 of 2)*

- Handrail-gripping surface continuity is governed as follows:
  - Within a dwelling unit, the following applies:
      A newel post may interrupt a handrail at a stair landing.
      The following details are permitted at the lowest tread:
        Volute.
        Turnout.
        Starting easing.

1009 Stairways and Handrails

1009.11.4 Continuity *(part 2 of 2)*

- ○ The following attachments to handrails are permitted where they comply with the restrictions listed below:
  Attachments:
  Brackets.
  Balusters.
  Restrictions:
  They must be attached to the handrail's bottom surface.
  Clearance below the handrail is required as listed in the following table:

Table 1009.11.4   Clearance Required at Handrail

Circular handrail diameter	Noncircular handrail diameter	Circumference	Clearance below handrail required
1.25"	NA	3.93"	1.5"
1.26" – 1.28"	NA	3.94" – 4"	1.5"
1.29" – 1.44"	NA	4.1" – 4.5"	1.375"
1.45" – 1.60"	NA	4.6" – 5"	1.25"
1.61" – 1.76"	NA	5.1" – 5.5"	1.125"
1.77" – 1.91"	NA	5.6" – 6"	1"
1.92" – 2"	NA	6.1" – 6.28"	1"

- ○ Otherwise, handrails must be continuous as follows:
  Without interruptions by the following:
  Newel posts.
  Other obstructions.

1009.11.5 Handrail extensions

- Handrails serving aisles in occupancy A are not governed by this section.

  Note: 1024.13, "Handrails," is cited as defining the pertinent handrails.

- Handrails in nonaccessible dwelling units are required to extend between the following extremities:
  - ○ Between points above the top and bottom riser.
- Other handrails are governed as follows:
  - ○ They must return to one of the following points:
    A wall.
    A guard.
    The walking surface.
    Be continuous to the handrail of the adjacent stair run.
  - ○ Handrails that are not continuous between stair runs must terminate as follows:
    They must extend horizontally >12" beyond the top riser.
    They must continue to slope beyond the bottom riser equal to a distance of 1 tread.

1009 Stairways and Handrails

1009.11.6 Clearance

- Clear space ≥ 1½" is required between a handrail and the following:
  - Wall.
  - Other surface.
- The following surfaces must be without sharp or abrasive elements:
  - Handrail surfaces.
  - Surfaces adjacent to handrail.

1009.11.7 Stairway projections

- Projections into the required width of a stairway are limited as follows:

Height	Projection permitted
At handrail height	≤ 4½"
Below handrail height	≤ 4½"
Above 6'-8"	Not limited

Note: 1009.2, "Headroom," is cited as specifying minimum headroom which is listed in the above table.

1009.12 Stairway to roof

- A stairway is required to extend to the roof where both of the following apply:
  - In buildings ≥ 4 stories above grade.
  - Where the roof slopes ≤ 4:12.
- Access to unoccupied roof from the top floor may be by the following:
  - An alternating tread device.

1009.12.1 Roof access

- Access to unoccupied roofs may be through a roof hatch as follows:
  - Area of hatch must be ≥ 16 sf.
  - Dimensions of hatch must be ≥ 2'.
- Access provided to other roofs must be by way of a penthouse.

Note: 1509.2, "Penthouses," is cited as the source of applicable requirements.

1010 Ramps

1010.1 Ramps

- This section series does not govern the following ramps:
  - Ramped aisles with both the following characteristics:
    In assembly spaces.
    That do not provide access to wheelchair spaces.

    Note: 1024.11, "Assembly aisle walking surfaces," is cited as governing the ramped aisles that are not addressed in this section series.
      The following sections are cited as defining the wheelchair spaces to which ramp access is covered by this section series:
        1108.2.2, "Wheelchair spaces."
        1108.2.2.1, "General seating."
        1108.2.2.2, "Luxury boxes, club boxes and suites."
        1108.2.2.3, "Other boxes."
        1108.2.3, "Integration."
        1108.2.4, "Dispersion of wheelchair spaces."
        1108.2.4.1, "Multilevel assembly seating areas."

  - Curb ramps.

    Note: ICC A117.1, "Accessible and Usable Buildings and Facilities," is cited as governing curb ramps.

- This section series governs only the following aspects for the ramps listed below:
  - Aspects:
    Running slope.
    Guards.
  - Ramps:
    Vehicle ramps with all the following characteristics:
      In parking garages.
      For pedestrian exit access.
      Not providing an accessible route.
      Not serving accessible parking spaces.
      Not serving other accessible elements.
      Not part of an accessible means of egress.

    Note: 1010.3, "Cross slope," through 1010.9, "Edge protection," are cited as not applicable to the ramps described above. Omitting these sections from the series, therefore, leaves the following which are applicable:
        1010.2, "Slope."
        1010.10, "Guards."

- Other ramps as follows are governed by this section series:
  - Ramps used in a means of egress.

1010 Ramps

1010.2 Slope

- Aisle ramp slope in occupancy A is not governed by this section.

  Note: 1024.11, "Assembly aisle walking surfaces," is cited as governing aisle ramp slope.

- Other ramps are governed as follows:
  - Ramps in a means of egress must have a slope ≤ 1:12.
  - Other ramps must have a slope ≤ 1:8.

1010.3 Cross slope

- The slope of a ramp ⊥ to direction of travel must be ≤ 1:48.

1010.4 Vertical rise

- Rise of any ramp is limited to ≤ 2'-6".

1010.5.1 Width

- The width required for a means of egress ramp is the same as that required for corridors.

  Note: 1016.2, "Corridor width," is cited as the source governing applicable widths.

- ≥ 3' clear width is required for ramps in a means of egress.
- ≥ 3' clear width is required between handrails on ramps in a means of egress.

1010.5.2 Headroom

- Headroom required for all parts of a ramp in a means of egress is ≥ 6'-8".

1010.5.3 Restrictions

- Means of egress ramps are governed as follows:
  - Width may not reduce in direction of egress travel.
  - Projections are not permitted into required width of ramps.
  - Projections are not permitted into required width of landings.
  - Door swing onto a landing must leave ≥ 3'-6" clear width unobstructed.

1010 Ramps

1010.6 Landings

- Landings are required for ramps at the following locations:
  - Bottom of ramp.
  - Top of ramp.
  - At changes of direction.
  - At doors.
  - At entrances.
  - At exits.

    Note: The following sections are cited as governing landings:
    1010.6.1, "Slope."
    1010.6.2, "Width."
    1010.6.3, "Length."
    1010.6.4, "Change in direction."
    1010.6.5, "Doorways."

1010.6.1 Slope

- Changes of level on a ramp landing are not permitted.
- Ramp landings may not slope $\geq$ 1:48 in any direction.

1010.6.2 Width

- The width of a landing must be $\geq$ the width of adjoining ramps.

1010.6.3 Length

- The lengths required for ramp landings are as follows:
  - $\geq$ 3' in the following locations:
    In nonaccessible dwelling units of the following occupancies:
      R-2, R-3.
  - $\geq$ 5' in other locations.

1010.6.4 Change in direction

- Dimensions of ramp landings at changes in direction are required as follows:
  - $\geq$ 3' in all dimensions in the following locations:
    In nonaccessible dwelling units of the following occupancies:
      R-2, R-3.
  - $\geq$ 5' in other locations.

1010.6.5 Doorways

- Clearances required for accessibility at doorways may overlap required landing dimensions.

    Note: ICC A117.1, "Accessible and Usable Buildings and Facilities," is cited as the source of maneuvering requirements at doorways.

1010 Ramps

1010.7 Ramp construction

- Ramp materials are governed as follows:
  - Wood handrails are allowed at ramps in all building construction types.
  - Otherwise, all ramp construction must conform to that required for the building construction type.
- Ramps used as exits must meet the same requirements as do vertical exit enclosures.

  Note: The following are cited as governing requirements for vertical exit enclosures.
  > *1019.1, "Enclosures required."*
  > *1019.1.1, "Openings and penetrations."*
  > *1019.1.2, "Penetrations."*
  > *1019.1.3, "Ventilation."*

1010.7.1 Ramp surface

- Materials on surfaces must comply with the following:
  - Must be slip-resistant.
  - Must be securely attached.

1010.7.2 Outdoor conditions

- Outdoor ramps must not accumulate water.
- Outdoor approaches to ramps must not accumulate water.
- The following surfaces in locations indicated must minimuze accumulation of snow or ice.
  - Exterior ramp surfaces.
  - Exterior ramp landing surfaces.
  - Locations:
    > In the following occupancies:
    > > A, B, E, F, H, I, M, R-1, R-2, R-4, S.
    > > U not serving R-3.
    > In climates subject to snow or ice.

1010.8 Handrails

- Ramps with a rise > 6" must meet the following requirements:
  - Handrails are required on both sides as follows:
    > Handrails must meet the same requirements as do stairways.

  Note: 1009.11, "Handrails," is cited as the source of stairway handrail requirements.

1010 Ramps

1010.9 Edge protection

- Edge protection is not required on the following:
  - At ramps where both of the following conditions apply:
    Handrails are not required.
    Ramps have flared sides meeting curb ramp requirements.

    Note: ICC A117.1, "Accessible and Usable Buildings and Facilities," is cited as governing the pertinent curb ramps.

  - At the sides of ramp landings that meet either of the following:
    A ramp.
    A stairway.
  - At the sides of ramp landings with the following condition:
    Vertical drop at the ramp edge is ≤ ½" over the following distance:
      A 10" distance measured horizontally from the edge of the required landing area.
- Other ramps and landings must have one of the following edge protections:
  - Railing.
  - Curb.
  - Barrier.

    Note: The following are cited as providing the requirements for the edge protection listed above as applicable.
    1010.9.1, "Railings."
    1010.9.2, "Curb or barrier."

1010.9.1 Railings

- The following meets the requirement for ramp or landing edge protection:
  - A rail mounted below the handrail as follows:
    At a distance ≥ 17" and ≤ 19" above the ramp or landing surface.

1010.9.2 Curb or barrier

- The following meets the requirements for ramp or landing edge protection:
  - Curb or barrier that prevents the passage of a 4" sphere as follows:
    Within 8" of the floor or ground surface.

1010.10 Guards

- Guards are required along ramps and landings more than 2'-6" above floor or grade.
- Guards for ramps and landings must comply with the same construction requirements as for stairways.

  Note: Section 1012, "Guards," is cited as the source of requirements for the location and construction of guards for ramps, stairways, and other locations.

1011 Exit Signs

1011.1 Where required

- Exit signs are not required in the following locations:
  - In spaces requiring only one exit or exit access.
  - At main exterior exit doors or gates as follows:
    Where their identity as exits is obvious.
    Where approved by the building official.
  - In the following occupancies and locations:
    I-3 sleeping areas.
    Individual sleeping or dwelling units of the following occupancies:
    R-1, R-2, R-3.
    Occupancy U.
  - On seating side of vomitories or openings to seating areas, where all the following apply:
    In occupancies A-4 and A-5.
    Where there is grandstand seating.
    Where exit signs are provided as follows:
    In the concourse.
    Exit signs are readily apparent from vomitories.
    Where vomitories or openings are identified by emergency egress lighting.
- In other locations, approved exit signs are required as follows:
  - At exits and exit access doors as follows:
    Signs must be readily visible from any direction of egress travel.
  - Where exit access is not readily apparent to occupants.
  - Exit signs must located as follows:
    So that the distance between any position in an exit access corridor and the nearest sign within sight is as follows:
    The distance is to be the shorter of the following:
    $\leq$ 100'.
    $\leq$ the viewing distance listed for the sign.

1011.2 Illumination

- Lighting for tactile signs is not required.

  Note: 1011.3 , "Tactile exit signs," is cited as the source requiring these signs.

- Other exit signs require lighting by one of the following methods:
  - Internal.
  - External.

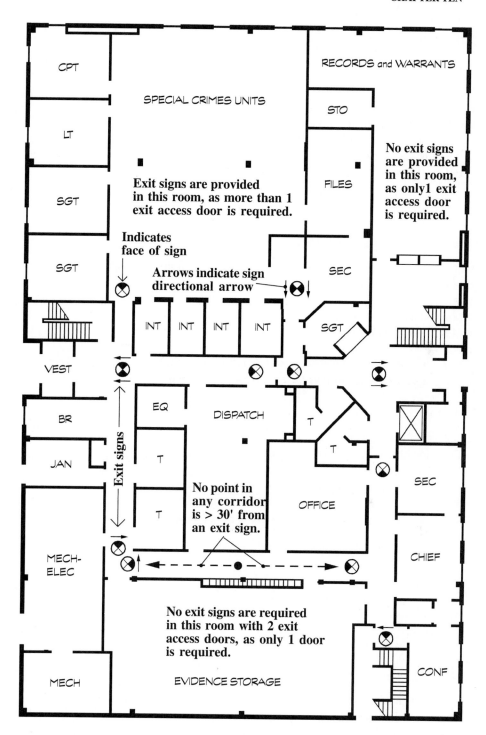

Fig. 1011.1. First-floor plan. Hot Springs Police Department New Headquaraters. Hot Springs National Park, Arkansas. Cromwell Architects Engineers. Little Rock, Arkansas.

1011 Exit Signs

1011.3 Tactile exit signs

- Tactile exit signs are required as follows:
  - Sign must say EXIT.
  - Must be adjacent to each door to the following:
    Egress stairs.
    Exit passageway.
    Exit discharge.

  Note: ICC A117.1, "Accessible and Usable Buildings and Facilities," is cited as governing these signs.

1011.4 Internally illuminated exit signs

- Exit signs that are illuminated from the inside have the following requirements:
  - Must be listed.
  - Must be labeled.
  - Must be installed as per manufacturer's instructions.
  - Must be lit at all times.

  Note: Section 2702, "Emergency and Standby Power Systems," is cited as another source of requirements for these signs.

1011.5.1 Graphics

- Graphics for exit signs is governed as follows:
  - Direction of any arrow must not be readily changeable.
  - Letters in the word "EXIT" must have high contrast with background.
  - Must be clearly discernable when illuminated or not.
  - Proportions of letters larger than minimum must be the same as required for minimum size.
- Required sizes of letters in the word "EXIT" are as follows:

Table 1011.5.1	Exit Sign Graphics
Graphics	Dimension
Height	$\geq 6"$
Width of letter strokes	$\geq \frac{3}{4}"$
Width of letters E, X, and T	$\geq 2"$
Width of letter I	$\geq \frac{3}{4}"$
Spacing between letters	$\geq \frac{3}{8}"$

1011.5.2 Exit sign illumination

- Exit signs that are illuminated from the outside have the following requirements:
  - The face must have the following amount of light:
    ≥ 5 footcandles.

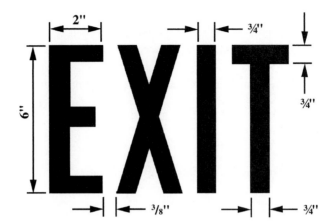

Fig. 1011.5.1A. Exit sign letter dimensions. Required minimums for letter sizes and spacing are shown for exit signs.

Case study: Fig. 1011.5.1B. The signs meet letter size and spacing minimums and other requirements. The arrow direction is not readily changeable, as it is available as a "snap-out" section in the sign face. As required, sign letters (in red) contrast with the sign face (aluminum) when the LED lights are on or off.

Fig. 1011.5.1B. Typical exit signs. Emergi-Lite. St. Matthews, South Carolina.

1011 Exit Signs

1011.5.3 Power source

- Exit signs must be lit at all times.
- Upon power failure signs must remain illuminated $\geq$ 90 minutes.
- Sign lighting that is not dependent on the primary power source need not be connected to an emergency power supply.
- Sign lighting that is dependent on the primary power source must also be connected to one of the following:
  - Storage battery.
  - Unit equipment.
  - On site generator.

  Note: Section 2702, "Emergency and Standby Power Systems," is cited as governing these signs.

1012 Guards

1012.1 Guards

- This section does not govern certain guards in assembly seating as follows:
  - Where guards are providing meeting requirements specific to the occupancy.

    Note: 1024.14, "Assembly guards," is cited as the source of requirements for guards in assembly seating that are not governed by this section.

- Guards are not required in the following locations:
  - On the loading side of loading docks or piers.
  - At stages or raised platforms as follows:
    On the audience side.
    At steps.
    At openings in the floors of performance areas.
    At elevated walkways providing access to the following:
      Special lighting.
      Special equipment.
  - On the following where used for entertainment or presentations:
    Runways.
    Ramps.
    Side stages.
  - Along vehicle service pits as follows:
    Where not accessed by the public.
- Guards are required in other locations as follows:
  - Along the following which are > 2'-6" above an adjacent level:
    Open-sided walking surfaces.
    Mezzanines.
    Industrial equipment platforms.
    Stairways.
    Ramps.
    Landings.
- Guards are required along glazed sides of the following elements where all the conditions indicated below apply:
  - Elements:
    Stairways.
    Ramps.
    Landings.
  - Conditions:
    Where walking surfaces are > 2'-6" above an adjacent level.
    Where glazing does not meet the strength requirements of a guard.
- Guards must meet minimum strength requirements.

  Note: 1607.7, "Loads on handrails, guards, grab bars and vehicle barriers," is cited as the source of applied loading requirements that guards must be able to withstand.

1012 Guards

1012.2 Height

- This section does not govern certain guards in assembly seating as follows:
  - Where guards are providing meeting requirements specific to the occupancy.

    Note: 1024.14, "Assembly guards," is cited as the source of requirements for guards in assembly seating that are not governed by this section.

- Guards serving as handrails in the following locations are governed as listed below:
  - Applicable locations:
    Occupancy R-3.
    Within dwelling units of occupancy R-2.
  - Required heights:
    $\geq$ 38" where adjacent to stairs:
    Measured vertically from the leading edge of the tread nosing.
    $\geq$ 34" where located elsewhere:
    Measured vertically from one of the following:
    Adjacent walking surface.
    Adjacent seatboard.
- Other guards must have a height $\geq$ 42" as follows:
  - Measured vertically from the following lower points as applicable:
    Leading edge of tread.
    Adjacent walking surface.
    Adjacent seatboard.

Case study: Fig. 1012.2. 4", 6", and 8" spheres cannot pass through the guard at heights specified by 1012.3. Circles superimposed on the illustration are to scale and illustrate their relationship to openings. The centerline of the top rail is at 42" above tread nosings, thus, meeting the minimum height requirement of 42" to the top of the rail, as specified in 1012.2. The guard is in full compliance with the code.

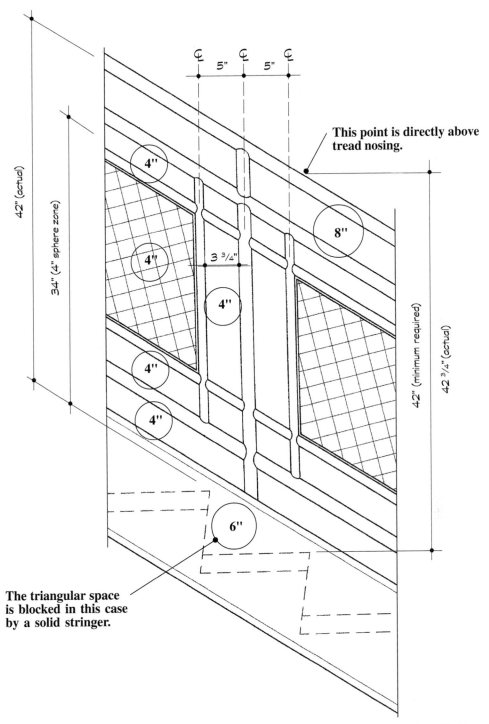

Fig. 1012.2. Elevation of guard at stairs. Montachusett Regional Vocational-Technical High School. Fitchburg, Massachusetts. HKT Architects, Inc. Somerville, Massachusetts.

1012 Guards

1012.3 Opening limitations

- Sizes of openings in guards are limited based on their ability to restrict the passage of spheres of the sizes indicated below.

  Note: This method of measure accounts for space between elements that may not be in a vertical plane.

Table 1012.3	Sizes of Spheres That May Not Pass through a Guard	
Location	Sphere size	Height within guard
Assembly seating at ends of aisles terminating at fascias of boxes, balconies, galleries	4"	To a height of 26"
"	8"	Between heights of 26" and 42"
Other occupancy A areas and occupancy B, E, I-1, I-2, I-4, M, R, U	4"	To a height of 34"
"	6"	In triangular space between bottom rail and treads and risers
"	8"	Between heights of 34" and 42"
In areas nonpublic areas of occupancy I-3, F, H, S	21"	Entire guard area
Access to mechanical electrical, and plumbing in all occupancies	21"	Entire guard area

1012.4 Screen porches

- Screened-in porches or decks are governed as follows:
  - Guards are required in the following case:
    Where the floor is > 2'-6" above the adjacent floor or grade.

1012.5 Mechanical equipment

- The following areas in the location shown have the requirements listed below:
  - Areas:
    With mechanical equipment as follows:
    Appliances.
    Equipment.
    Fans.
    Other devices needing service.
  - Location:
    ≤ 10' from an edge that is > 2'-6" above the surface below.
  - Requirements:
    A guard is required as follows:
    Must not pass a 21" sphere.

1013 Exit Access

1013.2 Egress through intervening spaces

- Egress through a high-hazard space from an adjoining space is governed as follows:
  - Egress is permitted where the spaces involved are the same occupancy.
  - In other cases, egress is not permitted.
- Egress from an adjoining space may not pass through the following spaces:
  - Storage rooms.
  - Closets.
  - Similar spaces.
- Egress though a kitchen from a adjoining space is governed as follows:
  - Egress is permitted in the following locations:
    Within a dwelling unit.
    Within a guest room.
  - In other cases, egress is not permitted.
- Egress may not pass through a room that can be locked to obstruct egress.
- Egress from dwelling units or sleeping areas may not pass through the following:
  - Other sleeping areas.
  - Toilet rooms.
  - Bathrooms.
- In other cases, egress from a space may pass through an adjoining space where both of the following conditions apply:
  - Where the adjoining space is accessory to the initial space.
  - Where adjoining space provides a readily apparent route to an exit.

1013.2.1 Multiple tenants

- Where more than one tenant occupies a floor, the requirements indicated below apply to the following spaces:
  - Spaces:
    Tenant space.
    Dwelling units.
    Sleeping units.
  - Requirements:
    Access to required exits may not pass through the following adjacent spaces:
    Tenant space.
    Dwelling units.
    Sleeping units.

Case study: Fig. 1013.2A – F. Examples on the following pages indicate a variety of intervening rooms in several occupancies though which egress travel may pass or may not pass. Those rooms through which egress travel is not permitted cannot be counted as a required means of egress in order to meet the number required, the total width required, in measuring minimum travel distances, or for other purposes. In all cases illustrated, means of egress requirements are met by the plans with appropriate routes some of which are marked and some of which are not indicated. Arbitrary starting points are marked with a dot, and each means of egress analysis applies only to the room so marked.

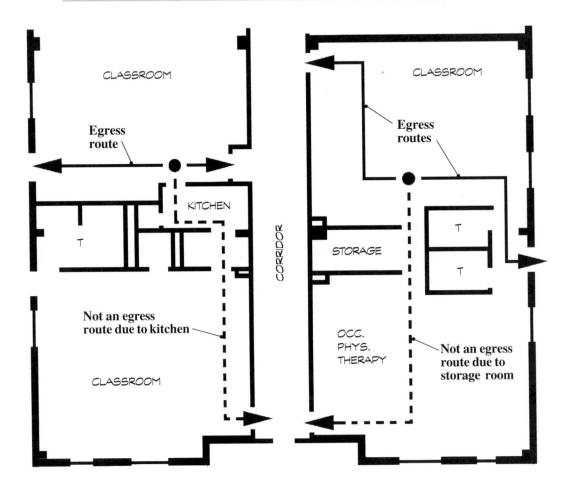

Fig. 1013.2A. Partial floor plan. New Jasper Pre-K – 2nd Grade School. Jasper, Texas. PBK Architects, Inc. Houston, Texas.

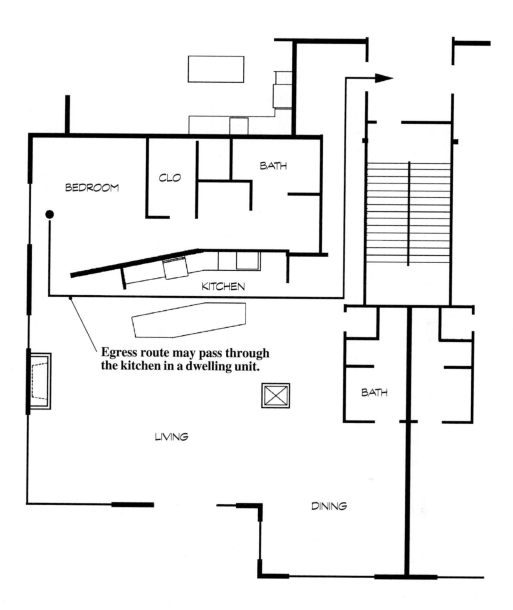

Egress route may pass through the kitchen in a dwelling unit.

Fig. 1013.2B. Apartment floor plan. McKenzie Lofts. Portland, Oregon. Ankrom Moisan Associated Architects. Portland, Oregon.

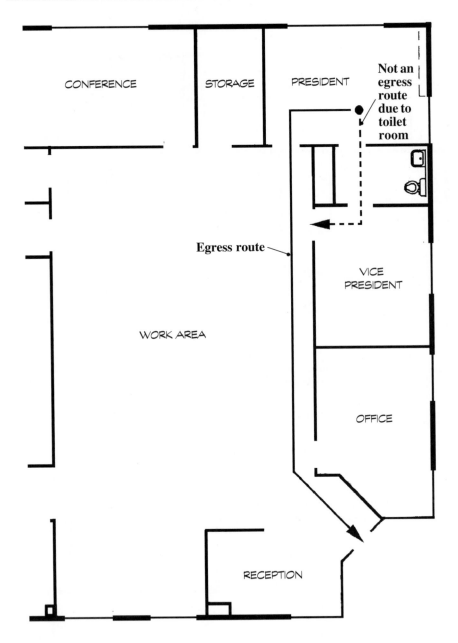

Fig. 1013.2C. Partial floor plan. Garments to Go. Bastrop, Texas. Spencer Godfrey Architects, Round Rock, Texas.

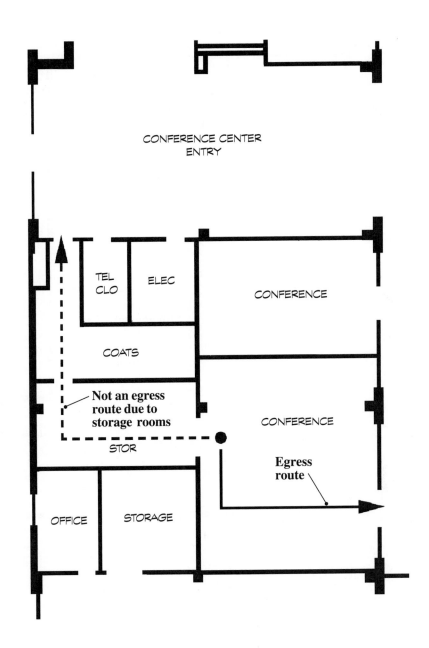

Fig. 1013.2D. Partial floor plan at conference center. University of Connecticut New Downtown Campus at Stamford, Connecticut. Perkins Eastman Architects, New York, New York.

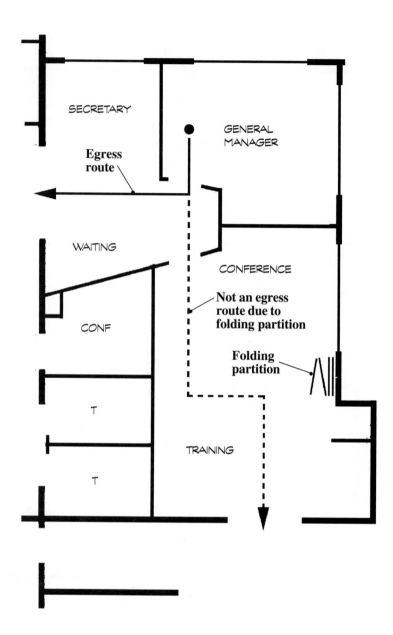

Fig. 1013.2E. Partial floor plan. Wichita Transit Storage Administration, and Maintenance Facility. Wichita, Kansas. Wilson Darnell Mann, P.A., Architects. Wichita, Kansas.

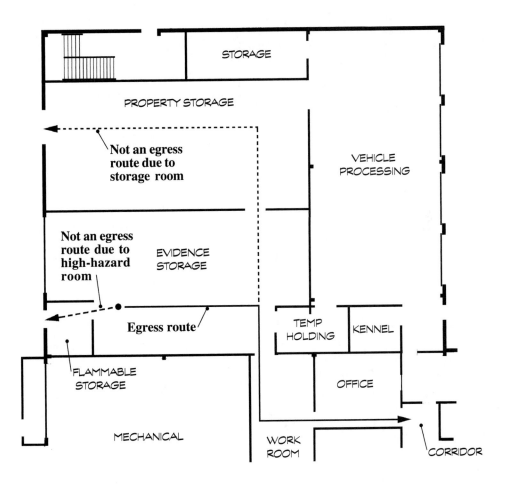

Fig. 1013.2F. Partial floor plan. Lee's Summit Police and Court Facility. Lee's Summit, Missouri. The Hollis and Miller Group, Inc. Lee's Summit, Missouri.

1013 Exit Access

1013.2.2 Group I-2

- Exit access doors leading directly to an exit access corridor are not required as follows:
  - For rooms with exit doors as follows:
    - Opening directly to the exterior.
    - Opening at ground level.
  - Patient sleeping rooms may have 1 intervening room as follows:
    - Intervening room may not serve as exit access for > 8 patient beds.
  - Special nursing suites may have 1 intervening room as follows:
    - Direct continual visual supervision by nursing staff is required.
  - Suites without patient sleeping may have 1 intervening room as follows:
    - Travel distance is ≤ 100' as follows:
      - Within the suite to the exit access door.
  - Suites without patient sleeping may have 2 intervening rooms as follows:
    - Travel distance is ≤ 50' as follows:
      - Within the suite to the exit access door.
- In other habitable rooms or suites in occupancy I-2, the following is required:
  - An exit access door leading directly to an exit access corridor.
- Where ≥ 2 exits or exit access doors are required, they must be remote from each other.
- The following is a summary of requirements for habitable rooms or suites in occupancy I-2:

Table 1013.2.2   **Egress for I-2 Rooms and Suites**

Rooms	Distance to door in room	Exit or exit access doors required based on square footage of room			
		≤ 1000 sf	> 1000 sf	≤ 2500 sf	> 2500 sf
With sleeping	≤ 50'	≥ 1	≥ 2	≥ 2	≥ 2
Other	≤ 50'	≥ 1	≥ 1	≥ 1	≥ 2

Suites	Size	Distance to door in suite	Exit or exit access doors required based on square footage of suite			
			≤ 1000 sf	>1000 sf	≤ 2500 sf	>2500 sf
With sleeping	≤ 5,000 sf	≤ 100'	≥ 1	≥ 2	≥ 2	≥ 2
No sleeping	≤ 10,000 sf	NA	≥ 1	≥ 1	≥ 1	≥ 2

1013 Exit Access

1013.3 Common path of egress travel

- The length of common path egress travel is limited as shown below:
  - Sprinklered buildings are as per NFPA 13.

Table 1013.3   Common Path Distance Limits

Tenant spaces:

Occupancy	Occupant load	Common path distance	
		Buildings sprinklered	Buildings not sprinklered
B, S, U	≤ 30	≤ 100'	≤ 100'
B, S	> 30	≤ 100'	≤ 75'
U	> 30	≤ 75'	≤ 75'

Locations other than tenant spaces:

Occupancy	Common path distance	
	Buildings sprinklered	Buildings not sprinklered
A, E, I-1, I-2, I-4, M, R, U	≤ 75'	≤ 75'
B, F, S	≤ 100'	≤ 75'
H-1, H-2, H-3,	≤ 25'	--
H-4, H-5	≤ 75'	--
I-3	≤ 100'	≤ 100'

Case study: Fig. 1013.3A – B. The shortest common paths of egress travel are shown from remote points in each area. Where a room or area has a single exit door or a single exit access door, all routes in the space are common paths. The termination of a common path arrow indicates the point at which the common path ends. Where this occurs prior to reaching an exit, it indicates the first point encountered in the path at which the occupant has a choice of two routes to separate exits. Diagonal paths are through spaces where no furnishings will block such a route. Otherwise, travel is measured on a rectangular pattern.

Occupancy M sprinklered

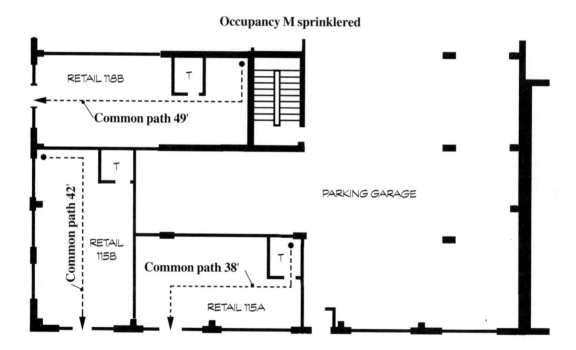

Fig.1013.3A. Partial floor plan at shops. McKenzie Lofts. Portland, Oregon. Ankrom Moisan Associated Architects. Portland, Oregon.

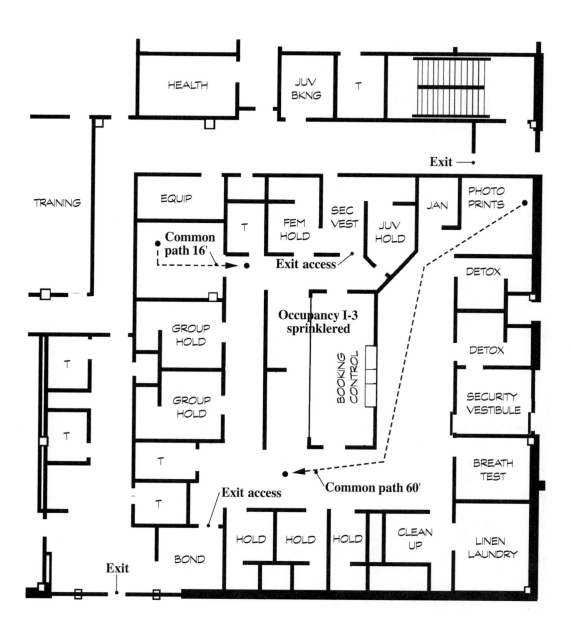

Fig.1013.3B. Partial floor plan. Lee's Summit Police and Court Facility. Lee's Summit, Missouri. The Hollis and Miller Group, Inc. Lee's Summit, Missouri.

1013 Exit Access

1013.4 Aisles

- This section addresses aisles serving in a means of egress.
- The following aisles are not addressed by this section:
    - In assembly other than seating at tables.
    - In reviewing stands.
    - In grandstands.
    - In bleachers.

    Note: Section 1024, "Assembly," is cited as governing these aisles.

- Aisles are required for occupied areas containing the following:
    - Seats.
    - Tables.
    - Furnishing.
    - Displays.
    - Similar fixtures or equipment.
- Obstructions in required aisle width are limited to the following:
    - The following elements may protrude a total ≤ 7" into the required width:
        Fully opened doors.
        Handrails.

    Note: The protrusion limit describes the sum of protrusions where they are directly opposite each other across an aisle. Handrails on each side of an aisle, for example, may each protrude ≤ 3½" so that the total protrusion would be ≤ 7" at point of width measurement in the aisle.

    - Doors in any position may not reduce the required aisle width to < ½.
    - The following nonstructural items may protrude into required width ≤ 1½" from each side:
        Trim.
        Similar decorations.

1013.4.1 Groups B and M

- In occupancies B and M aisle widths are limited as follows:
    - Minimum width varies with occupant load but cannot be less than the following:
        ≥ 28" where all the following conditions exit:
        Aisles are not public.
        Occupant load ≤ 50.
        Aisle is not required to be accessible.
        ≥ 36" for other aisles.

    *Note: 1005.1, "Minimum required egress width," is cited as governing aisle width.
    Chapter 11, "Accessibility," is cited as defining aisles required to be accessible.*

1013 Exit Access

1013.4.2 Seating at tables

- The clear width of an aisle or aisle accessway along the following seating is measured as indicated below:
  - Movable seating:
    At tables.
    At counters.
  - Width measurement:
    Aisle width is measured to a line 19" away from and ‖ to the edge of the following:
    Table.
    Counter.
    The 19" distance is measured ⊥ to the edge of the table or counter.
- The clear width of an aisle or aisle accessway along the following seating is measured as indicated below:
  - Fixed seating:
    At tables.
    At counters.
  - Width measurement is made to the back of the fixed seating.
- Other aisle or aisle accessway width measurements are to bypass any handrails and continue to the bordering element such as follows:
  - Walls.
  - Edges of seating.
  - Tread edges.

1013.4.2.1 Aisle accessway for tables and seating

- An aisle accessway as follows has the requirement listed below:
  - Aisle accessway:
    For seating at tables or counters.
  - Requirement:
    Must have a width ≥ the larger of the following:
    Egress width required for means of egress.

    Note: 1005.1, "Minimum required egress width," is cited as the source of width requirements for means of egress. Minimum width is calculated by an allocation of inches per occupant.

    Accessway width required for seating at tables and counters.

    Note: 1013.4.1, "Groups B and M," is cited as a source of width requirements.

1013 Exit Access

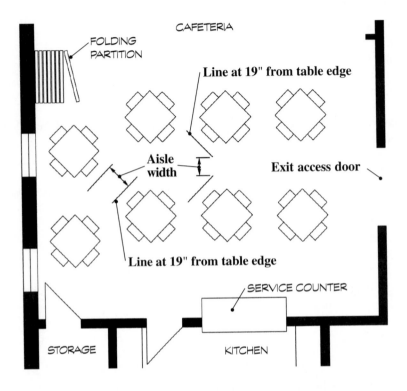

Fig. 1013.4.2.1. Partial floor plan at cafeteria. Multipurpose Building Addition to Children's Home. Wilkes-Barre, Pennsylvania. C. Allen Mullins, Architect. Bear Creek, Pennsylvania.

1013.4.2.2 Table and seating accessway width *(part 1 of 2)*

- Aisle accessway length is measured to the center of the seat most remote from the aisle.
- Segments of an aisle accessway with the both of the following characteristics is not governed by this section:
  - Length ≤ 6'.
  - Occupant load ≤ 4.
- Other aisle accessways must have a width as follows:
  - ≥ 12" where accessways are ≤ 12' in length.
  - The following table lists widths for accessways > 12' and ≤ 30' in length.

1013 Exit Access

1013.4.2.2 Table and seating accessway width *(part 2 of 2)*

Table 1013.4.2.2   Aisle Accessway Widths

Length	Width	Length	Width	Length	Width
> 12' ≤ 13'	≥ 12.5"	> 18' ≤ 19'	≥ 15.5"	> 24' ≤ 25'	≥ 18.5"
> 13' ≤ 14'	≥ 13.0"	> 19' ≤ 20'	≥ 16.0"	> 25' ≤ 26'	≥ 19.0"
> 14' ≤ 15'	≥ 13.5"	> 20' ≤ 21'	≥ 16.5"	> 26' ≤ 27'	≥ 19.5"
> 15' ≤ 16'	≥ 14.0"	> 21' ≤ 22'	≥ 17.0"	> 27' ≤ 28'	≥ 20.0"
> 16' ≤ 17'	≥ 14.5"	> 22' ≤ 23'	≥ 17.5"	> 28' ≤ 29'	≥ 20.5"
> 17' ≤ 18'	≥ 15.0"	> 23' ≤ 24'	≥ 18.0"	> 29' ≤ 30'	≥ 21.0"

Above table is based on the following equation:

Minimum clear width = 12" + 0.5" × [(length in ft − 12') rounded up to next foot]

1013.4.2.3 Table and seating aisle accessway length

- Travel distance in an aisle accessway is limited to ≤ 30' as follows:
  - The distance is measured between the following points:
    From any seat.
    To the point providing a choice of ≥ 2 routes to separate exits.

Case study 1: Fig. 1013.4.2.2. Table group 1: The widths of aisle accessways A and B are not governed as length of travel in these segments is < 6' and occupant load is 4 each. Width E of the aisle accessway between table ends is governed by length of travel. It is assumed that once an occupant enters this accessway, travel continues to an aisle. In this case, longest travel is 10' requiring a width of 12" which is < the 18" provided. Other travel patterns can be assumed which place > 4 occupants in the A or B segments, thus, requiring widths to meet minimums based on length. Such width D is measured between lines that are 19" (dimension C) from the table edges. Width D is 12", which is adequate for travel up to 12'. Travel in this scenario is 10'.

Case study 2: Fig. 1013.4.2.2. Table group 2: Aisle accessways A and B are 7' -6" in length, thus, requiring a minimum width D of 12" which is provided. Width D is measured between lines at 19" (dimension C) from the table edges.

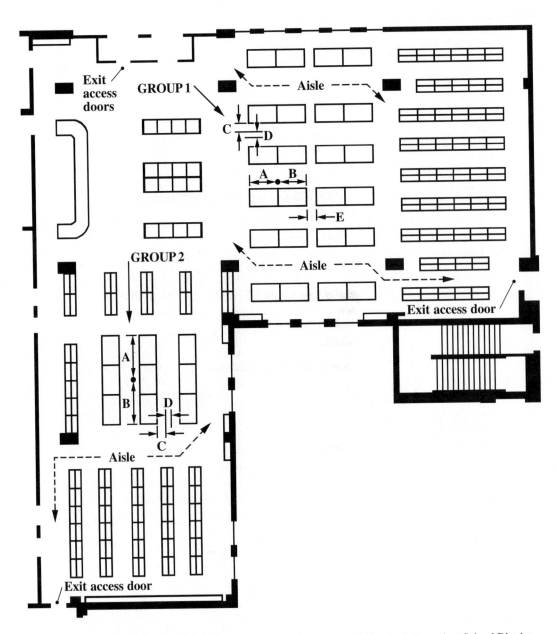

Fig. 1013.4.2.2. Partial floor plan at library. High School 6, Cypress-Fairbanks Independent School District. Harris County, Texas. PBK Architects, Inc. Houston, Texas.

1013 Exit Access

1013.5 Egress balconies

- Balconies in a means of egress must comply with corridor requirements as follows:
  - Width and headroom.
  - Dead ends.
  - Projections.
- Protection against the accumulation of snow or ice is governed as follows:
  - Such protection is not required on exterior balconies and concourses at outdoor stadiums.
  - Such protection is required for all other exterior balconies in a means of egress.

1013.5.1 Wall separation

- This section addresses the separation of a means of egress balcony from the building interior.
- Separation is not required where both of the following conditions apply:
  - The egress balcony is served by ≥ 2 stairs.
  - Travel from a dead end does not pass an unprotected opening en route to a stair.
- Otherwise, such a balcony must be separated from the interior of the building as follows:
  - By the walls as required for corridors.
  - By opening protectives as required for corridors.

1013.5.2 Openness

- The area on the long side of the egress balcony must be open to exterior as follows:
  - ≥ 50% openness is required.
- Open area above guards must be distributed to minimize the collection of smoke and gases.

1014 Exit and Exit Access Doorways

1014.1 Exit or exit access doorways required

- Occupancy I-2 is not governed by this section.

  Note: 1013.2.2, "Group I-2," is cited as the source of requirements for this occupancy.

- Other access doorways are governed as follows:
  - ≥ 2 exit or exit access doorways are required from a space where any of the following conditions apply:
    Where required for the following spaces:
    Boiler rooms.
    Incinerator rooms.
    Furnace rooms.
    Refrigeration machinery rooms.
    Refrigerated rooms or spaces.

  Note: The following are cited as requiring 2 exits or exit access doorways for the above rooms as per specified conditions:
  1014.3, "Boiler, incinerator and furnace rooms."
  1014.4, "Refrigeration machinery rooms."
  1014.5, "Refrigerated rooms or spaces."

  Where the common path of egress travel would otherwise exceed that permitted.

  Note: 1013.3, "Common path of egress travel," is cited as defining limits of common path travel.

  Where the occupant load is as follows:

Table 1014.1	Spaces Requiring ≥ 2 Means of Egress
Occupancy	Occupants
A, B, E, F, M, U	> 50
H-1, H-2, H-3	> 3
H-4, H-5	> 10
I-1, I-3, I-4	> 10
R	> 10
S	> 30

Source: IBC Table 1014.1

1014.1.1 Three or more exits

- Access to ≥ 3 exits per floor is required as follows:
  - Where a floor has an occupant load ≥ 501 and ≤ 1000.*
- Access to ≥ 4 exits per floor is required as follows:
  - Where a floor has an occupant load > 1000.*

  Note: 1018.1, "Minimum number of exits," is cited as governing.

Source: IBC Table 1018.1

Case study: Fig. 1014.1. The church organ loft has an occupant load of 5 based on gross area. Since this is < 50 and the common path distance is < the 75' maximum for the occupancy B space, only 1 exit or exit door is required.

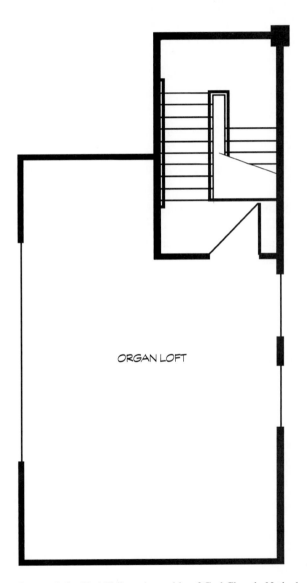

ORGAN LOFT

Fig. 1014.1. Floor plan of organ loft. Glad Tidings Assembly of God Church. Naticoke, Pennsylvania. Mullins and Weida, Architect and Associate. Bear Creek, Pennsylvania.

1014 Exit and Exit Access Doorways

1014.2 Exit or exit access doorway arrangement

- Required exits must be clearly available for their purpose.
- Exits may not be obstructed at any time.
- Exits and exit access doorways must be separated by the following distance:
  - A distance large enough to prevent the loss of more than one in an emergency.

    Note: The following are cited as sources of requirements for separation distances:
    1014.2.1, "Two exits or exit access doorways."
    1014.2.2, "Three or more exits or exit access doorways."

1014.2.1 Two exit or exit access doorways

- Where there are 2 exit enclosures meeting the following conditions, separation is required as indicated below:
  - Exit enclosures connected to each other by the following:
    A corridor with a fire-resistance rating of 1 hr.

    Note: Section 1016, "Corridors," is cited as governing these corridors.

  - Requirements:
    The required distance separating the exits is measured as follows:
    On the shortest line of travel in the corridor.
- In buildings sprinklered as per NFPA 13 or 13R, the following applies:
  - The distance between 2 exits or exit access doors is required to be as follows:
    $\geq \frac{1}{3}$ the greatest overall diagonal dimension of the area served.

    Note: The following are cited as governing the sprinklers as applicable:
    903.3.1.1, "NFPA 13 sprinkler systems."
    903.3.1.2, "NFPA 13R sprinkler systems."

- In other cases, where 2 exits or exit access doorways are required, they must be separated as follows:
  - By a distance $\geq \frac{1}{2}$ the greatest overall diagonal dimension of the building or area served:
    The distance is measured on a straight line between the exits or exit access doorways.
- The following stairways are counted as one exit:
  - Interlocking stairs.
  - Scissor stairs.

Case study: Fig. 1014.2.1. Since the space on each side of the folding partition in the multipurpose room requires an exit access door, the whole space with the open partition will have 2 doors regardless of its occupant load. To determine whether or not the distance between the 2 doors must meet the code minimum, the whole space is analyzed as a single room with the partition open. As an assembly space with chairs and tables, the occupant load would be 98. The storage room adds 1 additional occupant. Consequently, 2 exit access doors are required and must be spaced a minimum distance apart. In this sprinklered building, the minimum distance is ¹/₃ the diagonal of the area or 28'-4". Since double doors are provided and, in this example only a single door is required at each location, an argument could be made for measuring between the most remote doors. The closest doors comply with the code, in any case,

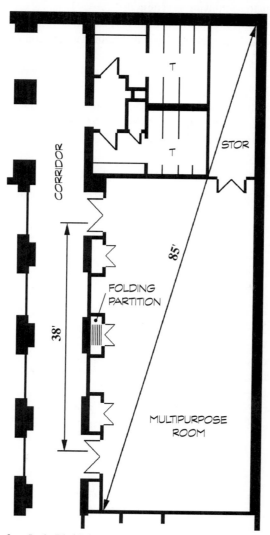

Fig. 1014.2.1. Partial floor plan. Lady Bird Johnson Wildflower Center. Austin, Texas. Overland Partners, Inc. San Antonio, Texas.

1014 Exit and Exit Access Doorways

1014.2.2 Three or more exits or exit access doorways

- The following apply where access is required to ≥ 3 exits:
  - In sprinklered buildings, the following is required:
    ≥ 2 exits or exit access doorways must be separated as follows:
    ≥ ⅓ the greatest overall diagonal dimension of the area served.

    Note: The following are cited as governing the sprinklers as applicable:
    903.3.1.1, "NFPA 13 sprinkler systems."
    903.3.1.2, "NFPA 13R sprinkler systems."

  - In other buildings the following is required:
    ≥ 2 exits or exit access doorways must be separated as follows:
    By a distance ≥ ½ the greatest overall diagonal dimension of the building or area served.
  - The distance between exits is measured on a straight line between the centers of the exits or exit access doorways.
- The separation of additional exits or exit access doorways is required as follows:
  - Separation distance must be adequate to assure the following:
    So that a single emergency will not block > 1 exit or exit access doorway.

1014.3 Boiler, incinerator and furnace rooms

- The following rooms require ≥ 2 exit access doorways where both of the conditions listed below apply:
  - Rooms:
    Boiler.
    Incinerator.
    Furnace.
  - Conditions:
    Area > 500 sf.
    Fuel-fire equipment > 400,000 Btu input capacity.
- Where ≥ 2 exit access doorways are required, the following applies:
  - 1 exit access doorway may be accessed by the following:
    By a fixed ladder.
    By an alternating tread stair.
  - Exit access doorways must be separated by a horizontal distance as follows:
    By a distance ≥ ½ the greatest horizontal dimension of the room.

1014 Exit and Exit Access Doorways

1014.4 Refrigeration machinery rooms

- ≥ 2 exits or exit access doors are required in machinery rooms > 1000 sf.
- Where ≥ 2 exit access doorways are required, the following apply:
  - 1 may be accessed by the following:
    By a fixed ladder.
    By an alternating tread stair.
  - Doorways must be separated by a horizontal distance as follows:
    By a distance $\geq \frac{1}{2}$ the greatest horizontal dimension of the room.
- Travel distance in the room to an exit or exit access doorway is limited as follows:
  - $\leq 150'$.

    Note: Section 1015, "Exit Access Travel Distance," is cited as the source of potential increase to the travel distance limit.

- Doors must swing in the direction of egress travel for any occupant load.
- Doors must fit tightly.
- Doors must be self-closing.

1014.5 Refrigerated rooms or spaces

- Room with limited amounts of refrigerants are not governed by this section.

  Note: The International Mechanical Code is cited as the source of limits on refrigerant volume applicable to the waiver for compliance with this section.

- Otherwise, ≥ 2 exits or exit access doors are required in rooms with all of the following characteristics:
  - ≥ 1000 sf.
  - Contains a refrigerant evaporator.
  - Has a room temperature $< 68°F$.
- Egress travel may pass through adjoining refrigerated spaces.
- Where not sprinklered, travel distance in the room to an exit or exit access doorway must be $\leq$ the smaller of the following:
  - 150'.
  - As required for building occupancy.

    Note: 1015.1, "Travel distance limitations," is cited as governing.

1014.6 Stage means of egress

- A means of egress must be located on each side of a stage as follows:
  - Where ≥ 2 are required based on either of the following:
    Stage size.
    Occupant load.

1014 Exit and Exit Access Doorways

1014.6.1 Gallery, gridiron, and catwalk means of egress

- This section addresses the means of egress from the following:
  - Lighting catwalks.
  - Access catwalks.
  - Galleries.
  - Gridirons.
- Lighting and access catwalks must have a width $\geq$ 22".
- The following are permitted in the means of egress:
  - Spiral stairs.
  - Open stairs.
  - Stairs with width $\geq$ 22".
  - Ladders.
- $>$ 1 means of egress are not required as follows:
  - Where a means of escape is provided to the following locations by the devices indicated below:
    - Locations:
      - To a roof.
      - To a floor.
    - Devices:
      - Ladders.
      - Alternating tread stairs.
      - Spiral stairs.
- Otherwise, means of egress requirements are the same as those for occupancy F-2.

1015 Exit Access Travel Distance

1015.1 Travel distance limitations *(part 1 of 2)*

- Exit access travel distance is measured as follows:
  - Along a normal unobstructed route of circulation.
  - From any occupiable location in a facility to one of the following points:
    - To the nearest riser of an open stair at the following:
      - An open parking garage.
      - An outdoor facility with the following components:
        - Open exit access components.
        - Exterior stair.
    - To the nearest slope of an exterior ramp in the following facility:
      - An outdoor facility with open exit access components.
    - To the nearest exit in other facilities.
  - Where open stairs are on the route, travel is measured as follows:
    - On the centerline along the slope tangent to tread nosings.
  - Where open ramps are on the route, travel is measured as follows:
    - On the centerline along the surface of the slope.
  - Where the exit stair is unenclosed, travel distance is measured between the following points:
    - The most remote location in the building.
    - An exit discharge.

    Note: 1019.1, "Enclosures required," exception 8 or 9, is cited as permitting unenclosed exit stairs subject to specified conditions.

- In the following locations travel distance limitations vary from those specified in this section:
  - Malls.
  - Atriums.
  - Buildings with 1 exit.
  - Assembly seating.
  - Assembly open-air seating.

    Note: The following are cited as governing travel distances in the above areas:
    Section 402, "Covered Mall Buildings."
    Section 404, "Atriums."
    1024.7, "Travel distance," addresses indoor and outddor assembly seating.
    1018.2, "Buildings with one exit."

- In F-1 or S-1 buildings, exit access travel is limited to ≤ 400' where all the following apply:
  - Building is 1 story.
  - Building is sprinklered as per NFPA 13.
  - Building has automatic heat and smoke vents.

    Note: 1015.2, "Roof vent increases," is cited as providing increased travel limits.

1015 Exit Access Travel Distance

1015.1 Travel distance limitations *(part 2 of 2)*

- In temporary structures, exit access travel is limited to ≤ 100'.

    Note: Chapter 31, "Special Construction," is cited as governing temporary structures, including travel distance which is listed above.

- In other locations, exit access travel distance is limited as follows:

Table 1015.1   Exit Access Travel Distance Limits

Buildings sprinklered:

Occupancy	Travel distance	Occupancy	Travel distance
A, E, F-1, I-1, M, R, S-1	≤ 250'	H-2	≤ 100'
B	≤ 300'	H-3	≤ 150'
F-2, S-2, U	≤ 400'	H-4	≤ 175'
H-1	≤ 75'	H-5, I-2, I-3, I-4	≤ 200'

Buildings not sprinklered:

Occupancy	Travel distance	Occupancy	Travel distance
A, B, E, F-1		F-2, S-2, U	≤ 300'
I-1, M, R, S-1	≤ 200'	I-2, I-3, I-4	≤ 150'

Source: IBC Table 1015.1

1015.2 Roof vent increase

- Exit access travel distance must be ≤ 400' where all the following conditions are met:
    - Occupancy is one of the following:
        F-1, S.
    - Building is one story.
    - Building has automatic heat and smoke roof vents.

    Note: Section 910, "Smoke and Heat Vents," is cited as governing these devices.

    - Building is sprinklered.

    Note: 903.3.1.1, "NFPA 13 sprinkler systems," is cited as governing.

1015.3 Exterior egress balcony increase

- Certain travel distance limitations are increased ≤ 100' in the following case:
    - Where the last segment of travel to an exit occurs as follows:
        On an exterior egress balcony.

    Note: 1015.1, "Travel distance limitations," is cited as listing the travel distances that may be increased.
    1013.5, "Egress balconies," is cited as governing these components.

    The increase may not be longer than the egress balcony.

Case study: Fig. 1015.1A – D. Exit accss travel distances are shown in the following examples for various occupancies. Rectangular paths of travel are followed as they simulate actual routes available around possible furnishing or other obstacles. Diagonal paths are followed through areas where no furnishings will occur. The most remote beginning point for travel is indicated in each case by a dot. All examples are in compliance with the code.

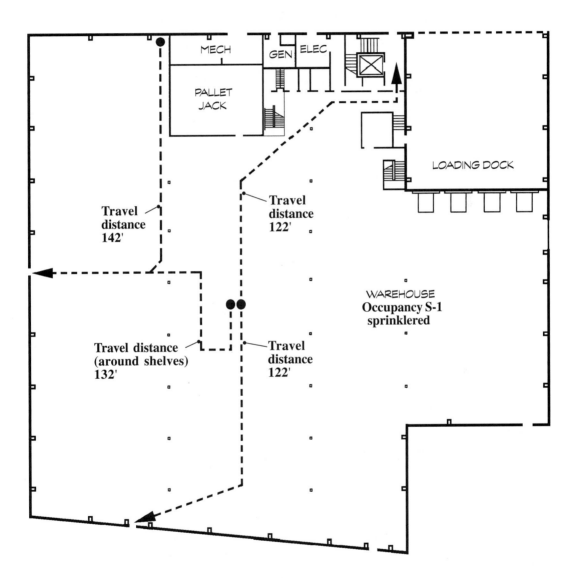

Fig.1015.1A. Floor plan. New Warehouse Addition. Los Angeles, California. Stephen Wen + Associates, Architects, Inc. Pasadena, California.

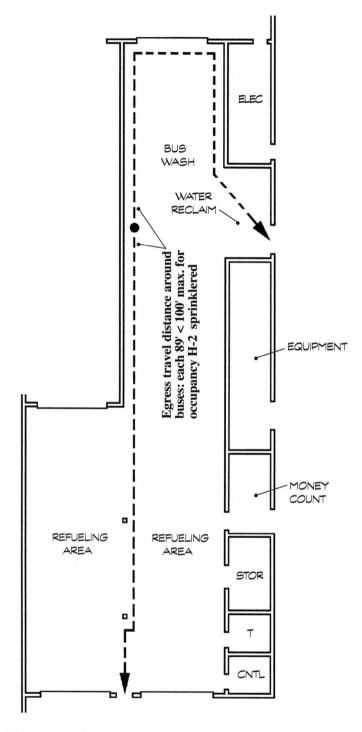

Fig. 1015.1B. Partial floor plan. Wichita Transit Storage, Administration, and Maintenance Facility. Wichita, Kansas. Wilson Darnell Mann, P.A. Wichita, Kansas.

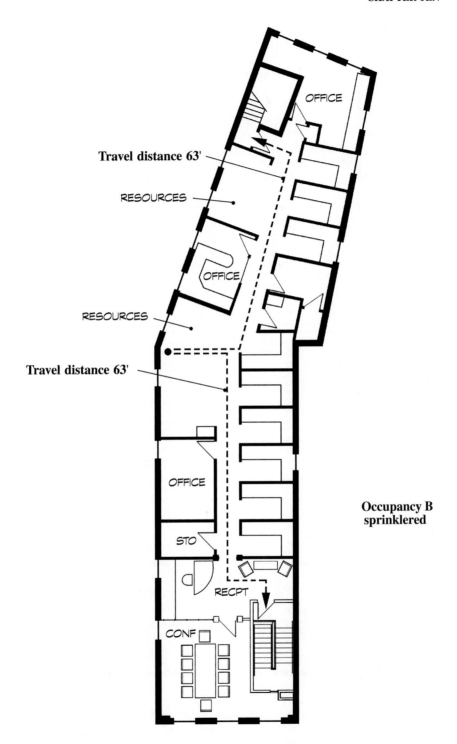

Fig. 1015.1C. 2nd-floor plan. Alterations to 209 Main Street. Annapolis, Maryland. Alt Breeding Schwarz Architects, LLC. Annapolis, Maryland.

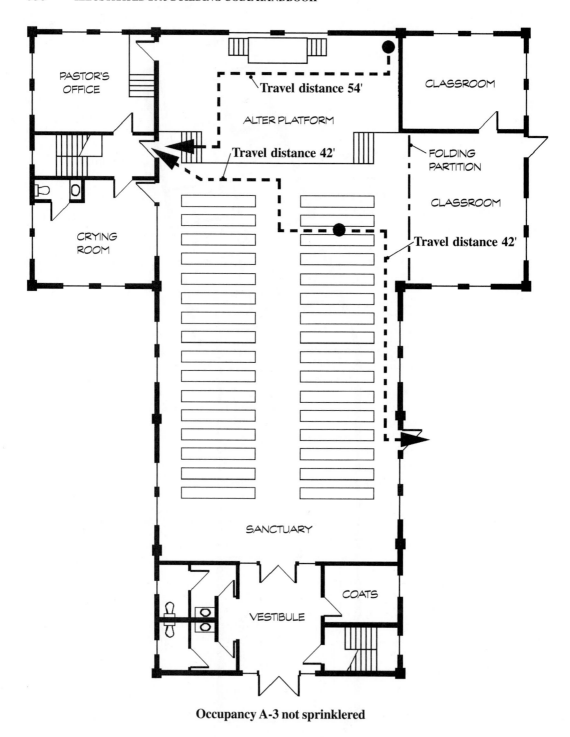

Occupancy A-3 not sprinklered

Fig. 1015.1D. Floor plan. Glad Tidings Assembly of God Church. Naticoke, Pennsylvania. Mullins and Weida, Architect and Associate. Bear Creek, Pennsylvania.

1016 Corridors

1016.1 Construction

- A fire-resistance rating is not required for the following corridors:
  - In occupancy E as follows:
    Each instruction room must have ≥ 1 door meeting the following condition:
      It must discharge directly to the outside at grade level.
    Each assembly room must have the following:
      ≥ half the required means of egress doors must meet the following condition:
        They must discharge directly to the outside at grade level.
  - In occupancy R as follows:
    In a dwelling unit or sleeping unit.
  - In open parking garages.
  - In occupancy B as follows:
    Where only 1 means of egress is required.

    Note: 1014.1, "Exit or exit access doorways required,." is cited as governing.

  - In the following occupancies where sprinklered:*
    A, B, E, F, I-2, I-4, M, S, U.

    Note: 407.3, "Corridor walls," is cited as governing corridors in occupancy I-2.
       The following are cited as governing sprinklers as applicable in this section:
       903.3.1.1, "NFPA 13 sprinkler systems."
       903.3.1.2, "NFPA 13R sprinkler systems."

  - Where the occupant load is ≤ 30 in the following occupancies:*
    A, B, E, F, H-4, H-5, M, S, U.
  - Where the occupant load is ≤ 10 in occupancy R.*
- A corridor fire-resistance rating ≥ 1 hr is required as follows:*
  - In sprinklered buildings of the following occupancies:
    H-1, H-2, H-3, I-1, I-3.

    Note: 408.7. " Subdivision of resident housing areas," is cited as governing I-3.

  - In sprinklered buildings of the following occupancies where the corridor load is > 30:
    H-4, H-5.
  - Where the corridor occupant load is > 30 in the following occupancies:
    A, B, E, F, M, S, U.
  - Where the corridor occupant load is > 10 in occupancy R.
- A corridor fire-resistance rating ≥ ½ hr is required in the following case:*
  - In sprinklered buildings of occupancy R as follows:
    Where the corridor load is > 10.
- Corridor walls required to have a fire-resistance rating must comply with the following:
  - Requirements for fire partitions.

    Note: Section 708, "Fire Partitions," is cited as governing these walls.

*Source: IBC Table 1016.1

1016 Corridors

1016.2 Corridor width

- The following widths are required for corridors serving the locations noted:

Table 1016.2a   Minimum Corridor Widths

Width	Occupants	Location
≥ 24"	Not limited	Access to building service equipment
≥ 36"	≤ 50	All locations
≥ 36"	Not limited	Within a dwelling unit
≥ 72"	≥ 100	Occupancy E
≥ 72"	Not limited	Occupancy I – surgical, health-care centers for ambulatory outpatients incapable of self-preservation
≥ 96"	Not limited	Occupancy I-2 where bed movement is required

- In other locations, corridors must be the larger of the following widths:
  - ≥ 3'-8".
  - ≥ occupant load × the widths per occupant listed below.

Table 1016.2b   Minimum Required Width for Corridors per Occupant Served

Occupancy	Building sprinklered as per NFPA 13 or 13R
A, B, E, F, H-5, I-1, I-3, I-4, M, R, S, U	0.15"
H-1, H-2, H-3, H-4, I-2	0.2"
	Building not sprinklered
A, B, E, F, H-5, I-1, I-3, I-4, M, R, S, U	0.2"
H-1, H-2, H-3, H-4	0.4"

Source: IBC Table 1005.1

Note: 1005.1, "Minimum egress width," is cited as governing these widths.

1016.3 Dead ends

- Where > 1 exit or exit access doorway is required, the following applies:
  - Dead-end corridor length is limited as follows:

Table 1016.3   Dead-End Length Limits

Occupancy	Conditions	Length
B, F	No sprinklers	≤ 20'
B, F	Sprinklered as per NFPA 13	≤ 50'
I-3	Condition 1 or 5	≤ 20'
I-3	Condition 2, 3, or 4	≤ 50'
A, E, H, I-1, I-2, 1-4, M, R, S, U	Width at narrowest point	≤ 20' or < 2.5 × width of dead end, whichever is longer

Note: 308.4 "Group I-3," is cited as the source of characteristics for I-3 conditions.

Case study: Fig. 1016.3A. The dead-end corridor at the storage room in the occupancy E building is 14'-0" long and 7'- 4" wide. The length of a dead end must be < 2.5 × its width or ≤ 20', whichever is greater. Since *2.5 × 7'- 4" = 18'- 4"* which is < 20', maximum length is 20'. The 14'- 0" length is < 20'; thus, the dead end is in compliance with the code.

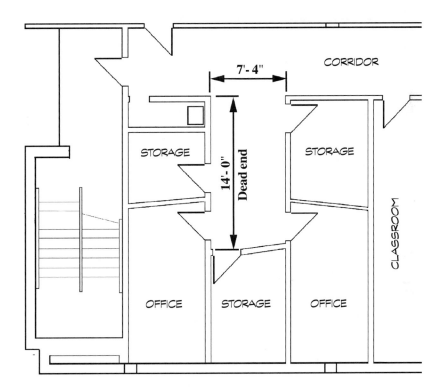

Fig. 1016.3A. Partial floor plan. Newman Elementary School Renovations. Needham, Massachusetts. HKT Architects, Inc. Somerville, Massachusetts.

Case study: Fig. 1016.3B. The elevator lobby of the occupancy B sprinklered building is a dead end 13' in length. This is in compliance with the 50' maximum for sprinklered buildings of this occupancy.

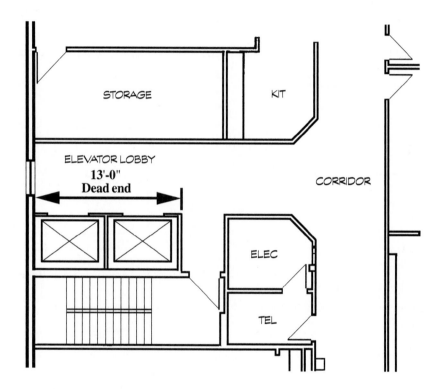

Fig. 1016.3B. Partial floor plan at elevator lobby. South Texas Blood and Tissue Center. San Antonio, Texas. Overland Partners, Inc. San Antonio, Texas.

1016 Corridors

1016.4 Air movement in corridors

- A corridor may be used for exhaust system makeup air for the following rooms where the requirements listed below are met:
  - Rooms:
    Toilet rooms.
    Bathrooms.
    Dressing rooms.
    Smoking lounges.
    Janitor closets.
  - Requirements:
    The rooms must open directly onto the corridor.
    The corridor must receive outside air at the following rate:
    > the rate at which makeup air is taken out.
- Corridors may be used for HVAC return air as follows:
  - In dwelling units.
  - In tenant spaces as follows:
    Of an area $\leq$ 1000 sf.
- In other cases exit access corridors may not convey the following:
  - Supply air.
  - Return air.
  - Exhaust air.
  - Relief air.
  - Ventilation air.

1016.4.1 Corridor ceiling

- The space above a corridor ceiling may be used for HVAC return air in any of the following cases:
  - Where the corridor construction does not have a fire-resistance rating.
  - Where the return air zone is separated from the corridor as follows:
    By fire-resistance-rated construction.
  - Where the fans serving the corridor are shut off in one of the following ways:
    By a sprinkler flow switch where the building is sprinklered.
    By smoke detectors at the fan unit.

    Note: The International Mechanical Code is cited as govering this aspect.

  - Where the space above the corridor ceiling is used as follows:
    As part of a smoke control system with both the following characteristics:
    Approved.
    Engineered.

1016 Corridors

1016.5 Corridor continuity

- This section addresses corridors with a fire-resistant rating.
- Corridors may pass through the following rooms with the condition indicated below:
  - Rooms:
    Foyers
    Lobbies.
    Reception rooms.
  - Condition:
    Rooms to be constructed with fire resistance $\geq$ required for the corridor.
- Otherwise, corridors must comply with both of the following:
  - They must be continuous betweent the following points:
    Their beginning.
    An exit.
  - They may not pass through the following:
    Intervening rooms.

1017 Exits

1017.1 General

- Any use of an exit as follows is prohibited:
  - In any way that interferes with its function.
- The level of protection at any point in an exit may not diminish as follows:
  - Until the exit discharge.

  Note: The following are cited as governing exits:
  Section 1003, "General Means of Egress," through Section 1012, "Guards."
  Section 1017, "Exits," through Section 1022, "Exterior Exit Ramps and Stairways."

1017.2 Exterior exit doors

- ≥ 1 exterior exit door is required as follows:
  - In any building for human occupancy.
  - Must meet size requirements for means of egress doors.

  Note: 1008.1.1, "Size of doors," is cited as the source of size requirements for means of egress doors.

1017.2.1 Detailed requirements

- Exterior exit doors must meet the applicable requirements for means of egress doors.

  Note: 1008.1, "Doors," is cited as the source of requirements for means of egress doors.

1017.2.2 Arrangement

- Exterior exit doors must open directly to one of the following:
  - An exit discharge.
  - A public way.

1018 Number of Exits and Continuity

1018.1 Minimum number of exits

- Occupied roofs have the same requirements for exits as do floors.
- The required number of exits from the following areas must be provided as noted below:
    - Areas:
        A story.
        A basement.
        A space.
    - Requirement:
        The number required at any point must be provided as follows:
            From that point throughout the means of egress to grade or public way.
- The following areas require exits listed below with the characteristics noted:*
    - Areas:
        All rooms in each story.
        All spaces in each story.
    - Characteristics:
        Independent.
        Approved.
    - Exits:
        For < 500 occupants the following is required:
            $\geq$ 2 exits.
        For between > 500 and $\leq$ 1000 occupants, the following is required:
            $\geq$ 3 exits.
        For > 1000 occupants the following is required:
            $\geq$ 4 exits.

    Note: The following are cited as modifying the number of exits required:
        1014.1, "Exit or exit access doorways required."
        1018.2, "Buildings with one exit."

Case study: Fig. 1018.1. The 646 occupants in this occupancy E building require 3 exits. The building complies with the code by providing 8 exits. Exits are numbered in the illustration.

---

* *Source*: IBC Table 1018.1

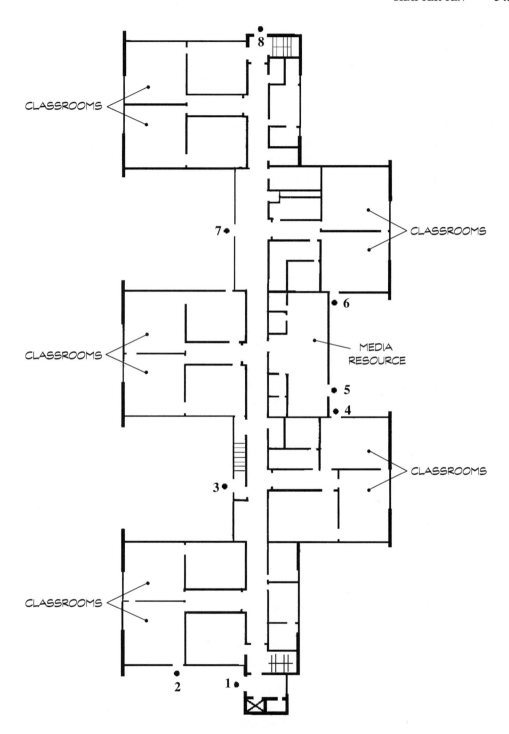

CLASSROOMS

8

CLASSROOMS

7

CLASSROOMS

6

MEDIA
RESOURCE

5

4

CLASSROOMS

3

CLASSROOMS

2   1

Fig. 1018.1. Floor plan of classroom wing. Newman Elementary School Renovations. Needham, Massachusetts. HKT Architects, Inc. Somerville, Massachusetts.

1018 Number of Exits and Continuity

1018.1.1 Open parking structures

- Where vehicles are mechanically parked, exits required are as follows:
  - Only 1 exit is required from each parking level.
- In other parking structures, exits are required as follows:
  - ≥ 2 exits are required from each parking level.
- Open vehicle ramps without pedestrian facilities are not considered exits.
- Open vehicle ramps with pedestrian facilities are considered exits.
- Stairways need not be enclosed.

1018.1.2 Helistops

- Helistops require 2 means of egress as follows:
  - Means of egress must comply with this chapter.
  - One means of egress may be either of the following components where the conditions listed below exist:
    Components:
      A fire escape to the floor below.
      A ladder to the floor below.
    Conditions:
      Where either of the following elements as applicable has the dimensions listed:
      Element:
        Landing platform.
        Roof area.
      Dimensions:
        < 60' in length.
        < 2000 sf.

1018.2 Buildings with one exit *(part 1 of 2)*

- Only 1 exit is required in occupancy R-3.
- Buildings meeting all the following criteria require only 1 exit:
  - The building has only one level.
  - Occupied space is on the level of discharge.
  - Occupant load is under the required limit.
  - Common path egress travel distance is under the required limit.

  Note: 1014.1, "Exit or exit access doorways required," is cited as defining occupant loads and common path distances over which ≥ 2 exits are required.

- Only 1 exit is required from air traffic control towers meeting the following criteria:
  - ≤ 15 occupants.
  - Requirements for the stairway location, construction, and operation.

  Note: 412.1, "Airport traffic control towers," is cited as providing exit requirements for these structures.

1018 Number of Exits and Continuity

1018.2 Buildings with one exit *(part 2 of 2)*

- Exits in open parking garages are required from each parking level as follows:
  - ≥ 1 where vehicles are mechanically parked.
  - > 2 in other cases.

    Note: 1018.1.1, "Open parking structures," is cited as providing requirements for exits from parking garages including the above and other criteria.

- In other cases, only 1 exit is required where the criteria below are met:

Table 1018.2   Conditions Permitting 1 Exit from a Building

Occupancy	Occupants per floor	Travel distance
1-story building with ≤ 1 level below it:		
A, E, F, M, U	≤ 50	≤ 75'
B sprinklered as per NFPA 13	≤ 50	≤ 100'
B not sprinklered	≤ 50	≤ 75'
H-2, H-3	≤ 3	≤ 25'
H-4, H-5, I, R	≤ 10	≤ 75'
S	≤ 30	≤ 75'
2-story buildings with ≤ 1 level below the 1st story:		
B, F, M, S	≤ 30	≤ 75'

Multistory buildings with ≤ 1 level below the 1st story:

Occupancy	Sprinklered as per NFPA 13 and 13R	Escape & rescue openings	Stories permitted	Dwelling units	Travel distance
R-2	no	no	2	≤ 4	≤ 50'
R-2	no	yes	2	≤ 4	≤ 50'
R-2	yes	no	2	≤ 4	≤ 50'
R-2	yes	yes	3	≤ 4	≤ 50'

Source: IBC Table 1018.2

Note: Section 1025, "Emergency Escape and Rescue," is cited as providing requirements for openings necessary to permit 1 exit in 3 stories in occupancy R-2.

Case study: Fig. 1018.2A. The occupancy B pavilion is 1 story with no basement. The space is used by staff only for refreshment preparation. Customers are served at pass-through windows and do not enter the building. With 10 occupants and no sprinklers, the building qualifies for 1 exit since no exit access travel distance is > 54' from any point to either of the 2 exits provided. Since only 1 exit is required, the 2 provided do not have to be located a minimum distance apart. Travel distances shown are those applicable, if either door was omitted. With 2 exits, the distances are shorter.

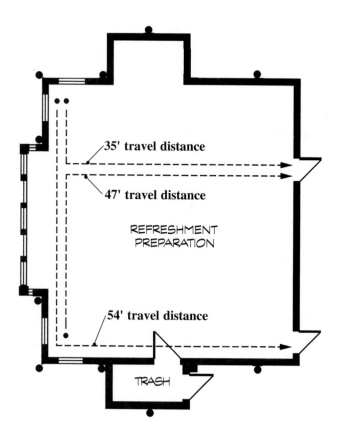

Fig. 1018.2A. Floor plan. Visitor Services Pavilions at Clarence Buckingham Memorial Fountain. Chicago Park District. Chicago, Illinois. David Woodhouse, Architects. Chicago, Illinois.

Case study: Figure 1018.2B. The modular classroom builidng is occupancy E, 1 story, and has no basement. Its 45 occupants and exit access travel distance ≤ 58' require only 1 exit.

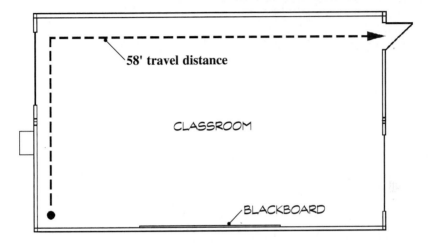

Fig. 1018.2B. Floor plan. Modular Classroom Building, Creston Elementary School. Creston, California. Phillips Metsch Sweeney Moore Architects. Santa Barbara, Calfornia.

1018.3 Exit continuity

- Exits must be continuous between the following points:
  - The beginning of the exit.
  - The exit discharge.

1018.4 Exit door arrangement

- 2 exit doors must be separated by a distance based on the following:
  - In buildings not sprinklered, separation is required as follows:
    ≥ ½ the diagonal dimension of the space served.
  - In sprinklered buildings separation is required as follows:
    ≥ ⅓ the diagonal dimension of the space served.

  Note: The following are cited as governing the separation of the exits, a partial summary of which is provided above:
  1014.2, "Exit or exit access doorway arrangement," through 1014.2.2, "Three or more exits or exit access doorways."

1019 Vertical Exit Enclosures

1019.1 Enclosures required *(part 1 of 2)*

- Exits do not require an enclosure where all of the following conditions are present:
  - In occupancy A-5.
  - Where all parts of the means of egress are essentially open to the exterior.
- Stairways do not require an enclosure in the following cases:
  - Where all of the following conditions are present:
    In occupancies A, B, E, F, M, R, S, U.
    Occupant load < 10.
    Stairway serves ≤ 1 story above the level of exit discharge.
  - In any of the following locations:
    Within a dwelling unit of the following occupancies:
      R-2, R-3.
    Within a sleeping unit of the following occupancies:
      R-2, R-3.
    Sleeping units in occupancy R-1.
  - Where the stairway is not a required means of egress as follows:
    The opening through the floor/ceiling is protected by a shaft enclosure where required.

    Note: 707.2, "Shaft enclosure required," is cited as the source of requirements for shaft protection where floor/ceiling assemblies are penetrated.

  - Where the stairway is in an open parking structure as follows:
    Serves only the parking structure.
  - Where the stairway is serving a stage area.

    Note: 410.5.4, "Stage exits," is cited as identifying stairways associated with a stage.

- Stairway enclosures are not required as follows:
  - For ≤ ½ the egress stairways where all of the following conditions apply:
    In occupancies A, B, E, F, M, R, S, U.
    The stairways serve only 1 adjacent floor.
    ≥ 2 means of egress exist from both floors served by an open stairway.
    The 2 floors connected by the open stairway are not open to other floors.
- Interior egress stairways are not required to be enclosed in the following cases:
  - Where all of the following conditions are present:
    In occupancies A, B, E, F, M, R, S, U.
    Stairs serve only the 1st and 2nd floors.
    The building is sprinklered.
    ≥ 2 means of egress exist as follows:
      From both floors connected by the unenclosed stairs.
    The stories served by these stairs are not open to other stories.

  Note: 903.3.1.1, "NFPA 13 sprinkler systems," is cited as governing the sprinklers.

1019 Vertical Exit Enclosures

1019.1 Enclosures required *(part 2 of 2)*

- 1 required stairway enclosure in a building is not required to meet all the enclosure requirements of this section where both of the following conditions apply:
  - Where located in occupancy I-3.
  - Where complying with requirements permitting glazing in a stairway enclosure.

  Note: 408.3.6, "Vertical exit enclosures," is cited as the source of modifications for egress stairways in occupancy I-3.

- All other interior exit stairways must be enclosed as follows:
  - Enclosures must be constructed as fire barriers.

  Note: Section 706, "Fire Barriers," is cited as the source of requirements for this component.

  - Enclosure fire-resistance ratings are required as follows:

Number of stories: mezzanines are not counted; basements are counted	Fire-resistance rating required
< 4 stories	≥ 1 hr
≥ 4 stories	≥ 2 hr

- Interior exit ramps must meet the requirements of this section.
- An exit enclosure may be used only as a means of egress.

1019.1.1 Openings and penetrations

- Openings into an exit enclosure are limited to the following:
  - Exterior openings not exposed to a possible fire.
  - Openings required for exit access as follows:
    From spaces which usually are occupied.
  - Openings required for egress out of the enclosure.
- The opening between an exit enclosure and an exit passageway is governed as follows:
  - A fire door is required.

  Note: The following are cited as governing openings to exit enclosures:
  Section 715, "Opening Protectives."
  715.3, "Fire door and shutter assemblies."
  715.3.4, "Doors in vertical exit enclosures and exit passageways."

1019 Vertical Exit Enclosures

1019.1.2 Penetrations

- Only the following components are permitted to penetrate an exit enclosure:
  - Standpipes.
  - Exit doors.
  - Components serving the exit enclosure as follows:
      The following components used to pressurize the enclosure:
        Equipment.
        Ductwork.
      Sprinkler piping.
      The following components terminating as noted below:
        Components:
          Electrical raceways as follows:
            Including those for fire department communication.
        Termination:
          Raceways must terminate in a steel box as follows:
            Side facing the enclosure must be ≤ 16 sq in.

    Note: Section 712, "Penetrations," is cited as governing penetrations into an exit enclosure.

- No other penetations or openings through an exit enclosure are permitted.
- None of the following are permitted between adjacent exit enclosures:
  - Penetrations as follows:
      Protected.
      Unprotected.
  - Openings as follows:
      Protected.
      Unprotected.

1019 Vertical Exit Enclosures

1019.1.3 Ventilation

- The following components must comply with at least one of the requirements listed below:
  - Components:
    Equipment for exit enclosure ventilation.
    Ductwork for exit enclosure ventilation.
  - Requirements:
    Where located outside the building, the following applies:
      Must be connected directly to the exit enclosure as follows:
        By construction meeting shaft requirements.
    Where located inside the exit enclosure, the following applies:
      Intake air must be taken directly from outside.
      Exhaust air must be directly to the outside.
    Where located inside the exit enclosure the following applies:
      The following air must be transported through ducts as indicated below:
        Air:
          Intake air.
          Exhaust air.
        Ducts:
          Within construction meeting shaft requirements.
    Where located inside the building the following applies:
      Must be isolated with construction meeting shaft requirements as follows:
        From the building.
        From other equipment.
- Only the following openings into fire-resistance-rated construction are permitted:
  - Openings needed for the following:
    Maintenance.
    Operation.
  - Openings protected by self-closing fire-resistance-rated devices.

    Note: Chapter 7, "Fire-Resistance-Rated Construction," is cited as governing these devices.

- Ventilation systems for exit enclosures are restricted as follows:
  - They must be independent of other ventilating systems.

1019.1.4 Vertical enclosure exterior walls *(part 1 of 2)*

- Vertical exit enclosure walls that are exterior walls must meet fire-resistance requirements for exterior walls.

  Note: Section 704, "Exterior Walls," is cited as the source of fire-resistance requirements for exterior walls.

1019 Vertical Exit Enclosures

1019.1.4 Vertical enclosure exterior walls *(part 2 of 2)*

- In the following circumstances, the conditions listed below are required:
  - Circumstances applying to the exterior wall of a stairway enclosure:
    - The wall has one or both the following characteristics:
      - It does not have a fire-resistance rating.
      - It has unprotected openings.
    - The wall is exposed to another exterior wall of the building at an angle < 180°.
  - Conditions required:
    - The building exterior wall so exposed must be constructed as follows:
      - It must have a fire-resistance rating ≥ 1 hr.
      - It must have opening protectives > ¾ hr.
    - Required fire-resistant construction must cover an area as follows:
      - ≤ 10' horizontally from the stairway wall as defined above.
      - From grade to the lower of the two upper limits described as follows:
        - A level 10' above the highest landing of the stairway.
        - The roof line.

1019.1.5 Enclosures under stairways

- The space under a stairway in a dwelling unit is not governed by this section as follows:
  - In occupancies R-2 and R-3.
- In other cases, space with the characteristics as noted where located under the following stairways is governed by requirements listed below:
  - Stairways:
    - Enclosed.
    - Not enclosed.
  - Characteristics:
    - Space is enclosed and usable.
  - Requirements:
    - Walls and soffits of the space must have the larger of the following:
      - ≥ 1-hr fire-resistance rating.
      - Fire-resistance rating ≥ that of the stairway enclosure.
    - Access to the space must be from outside the stair enclosure.
- The following space under exterior exit stairways is governed as indicated below:
  - Space:
    - Enclosed.
    - Usable.
  - Requirements:
    - Space enclosure must have a fire-resistance rating ≥ 1 hr.
- Open space under exterior stairways is governed as follows:
  - It may not be used for any purpose.

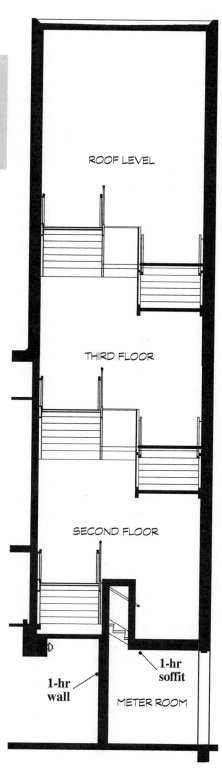

Case study: Fig. 1019.1.5. A meter room is located under an interior stairway as shown in the illustration. The walls of the space and the soffit of the landing above it have a 1-hr fire-resistance rating. The room is accessed from outside the stairway enclosure. The meter room is in compliance with code requirements.

ROOF LEVEL

THIRD FLOOR

SECOND FLOOR

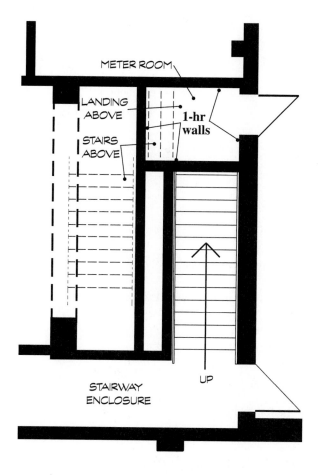

METER ROOM

LANDING ABOVE

1-hr walls

STAIRS ABOVE

STAIRWAY ENCLOSURE

UP

1-hr wall

1-hr soffit

METER ROOM

Fig. 1019.1.5. Plan and section at meter room.
University of Connecticut New Downtown Campus at Stamford, Connecticut. Perkins Eastman Architects, P.C. New York, New York.

1019 Vertical Exit Enclosures

1019.1.6 Discharge identification

- Enclosed exit stairways continuing to below level of exit discharge are governed as follows:
  - An approved barrier is required at the level of exit discharge as follows:
    Barrier must prevent accidental egress travel to below the level of exit discharge.
  - Directional exit signs are required.

    Note: Section 1011, "Exit Signs," is cited as the source of exit sign requirements.

1019.1.7 Stairway floor number signs

- Signs described below are required at floor landings in the following enclosures:
  - Enclosures with both of the following characteristics:
    Interior vertical exit enclosures.
    Enclosure connects > 3 stories.
  - Sign information required:
    Floor level.
    Identifying the termination of the stairway enclosure at the top and bottom.
    Stairway identification.
    Story of the exit discharge.
    Direction to the exit discharge.
    Availability of fire department roof access.
- Required signs are to be positioned as follows:
  - 5' above the floor landing.
  - To be visible when the doors are open or closed.

1019.1.8 Smokeproof enclosures

- This section addresses exits serving the following floor levels:
  - In high-rise buildings as follows:
    Floor surface > 75' above lowest level of fire department vehicle access.
  - In underground buildings as follows:
    Floor surface > 30' below level of exit discharge.

    Note: The following sections are cited as defining the buildings in this subsection:
    Section 403, "High-Rise Buildings."
    Section 405, "Underground Buildings."

- Exits serving such floors must be one of the following:
  - A smokeproof enclosure.
  - A pressurized stairway.

    Note: 909.20, "Smokeproof enclosures," is cited as a source of requirements.

1019 Vertical Exit Enclosures

1019.1.8.1 Enclosure exit

- This section addresses the following enclosures:
  - Smokeproof enclosures.
  - Pressurized stairways.
- Such enclosures must discharge to one of the following:
  - A public way.
  - One of the following with direct access to a public way:
    Exit passageway.
    Yard.
    Open space.
- An exit passageway serving the enclosures is governed as follows:
  - Passageway must be separated from the rest of the building as follows:
    By construction with a 2-hr fire-resistant rating.
  - Openings are permitted only with the following conditions:
    Where passageways serve a smokeproof enclosure:
    Passageway equals the enclosure with regard to the following:
    Fire protection.
    Pressurization.
    Openings are protected at access from other floors.
    Where passageways serve a pressurized stairway:
    Passageway equals the stairway with regard to the following:
    Fire protection.
    Pressurization.

1019.1.8.2 Enclosure access

- Access to stairways in smokeproof enclosures by one of the following components is governed as indicated below:
  - Components:
    Vestibule.
    Open exterior balcony.
  - Requirements:
    Access via the vestibule or balcony is not required where the stairway is pressurized.
    Otherwise, access via the vestibule or balcony is required.

  Note: 909.20.5, "Stair pressurization alternative," is cited as the source of requirements for stairway pressurization.

1020 Exit Passageways

1020.1 Exit passageway

- An exit passageway may be used only for a means of egress.

1020.2 Width

- The width of an exit passageway must be the larger of the following:
  - One of the following dimensions as applicable:
    - $\geq$ 44" for occupant load $\geq$ 50.
    - $\geq$ 36" for occupant load < 50.
  - As calculated by occupant load based on occupancy.

    Note: 1005.1, "Minimum required egress width," is cited as the source of width allocations per occupant and occupancy.

- Protrusions into the required width of an exit passageway are limited as follows:

Table 1020.2   Protrusions into Exit Passageways

Protruding elements	Protrusion permitted
Handrails	$\leq$ 7"
Doors at full open position	$\leq$ 7"
Doors in any position	$\leq$ ½ required width
Nonstructural trim and similar decorative features	$\leq$ 1½" from each side

Note: Where not specified as being from each side, permitted protrusions, as listed above, are the sum of protrusions from both sides at any point of width measurement. For example, the sum of door swing protrusion into the required width from locations directly opposite each other may not be greater than ½ the required width. Thus, at least ½ the required width would remain unobstructed with both doors extended to their fullest protrusion.

1020.3 Construction

- The fire-resistance rating for the following exit passageway enclosure components must be as indicated below:
  - Components:
    - Walls.
    - Floors.
    - Ceilings.
  - Fire-resistance rating must be the larger of the following:
    - 1 hr.
    - The rating required for any connecting exit enclosure.
- An exit passageway must be constructed as a fire barrier.

    Note: Section 706, "Fire Barriers," is cited as the source of requirements for those components.

1020 Exit Passageways

1020.4 Openings and penetrations

- The only openings permitted in exit enclosures include the following:
  - Exterior openings not exposed to a possible fire.
  - Openings to certain building service areas.

    Note: 402.4.6, "Service areas fronting on exit passageways," is cited as permitting these areas to open to an exit passageway where certain fire-resistance-rated construction and opening protectives are in place.

- Other openings into an exit enclosure are limited to the following:
  - Openings required for exit access as follows:
    From spaces which usually are occupied.
  - Openings required for egress out of the enclosure.
- The opening between an exit enclosure and an exit passageway is governed as follows:
  - A fire door is required.

    Note: The following are cited as governing openings to exit enclosures:
    Section 715, "Opening Protectives."
    715.3, "Fire door and shutter assemblies."
    715.3.4, "Doors in vertical exit enclosures and exit passageways."

1020.5 Penetrations

- Only the following components are permitted to penetrate an exit passageway:
  - Standpipes.
  - Exit doors.
  - Components serving the exit passageway as follows:
    The following components used to pressurize the passageway:
      Equipment and ductwork.
    Sprinkler piping.
    The following components terminating as noted below:
      Components:
        Electrical raceways as follows:
          Including those for fire department communication.
      Termination:
        Raceways must terminate in a steel box as follows:
          Side facing the enclosure must be $\leq$ 16 sq in.

  Note: Section 712, "Penetrations," is cited as governing these penetrations.

- No other penetations or openings through an exit passageway are permitted.
- None of the following are permitted between adjacent exit passageways:
  - Protected penetrations.
  - Unprotected penetrations.
  - Protected openings.
  - Unprotected openings.

1021 Horizontal Exits

1021.1 Horizontal exits

- All required exits may be horizontal exits in occupancy I-3 as follows:
  - The space on each side of a horizontal exit must have the following occupant capacity:
    Area ≥ 6 sf × (sum of occupants from both sides of the horizontal exit).
  - A fire compartment defined by a horizontal exit is not required to have the following egress components where the conditions indicated below are present:
    Egress components:
    Stairway leading directly to the exterior.
    Door leading directly to the exterior.
    Conditions:
    An adjoining fire compartment must have one of the egress components listed above.
    Egress does not return to the compartment of origin.
- ≤ ²/₃ of required exits in occupancy I-2 may be horizontal exits as follows:
  - From a building or a floor.
- In other occupancies, horizontal exits are limited as follows:
  - They may not provide the only means of exit from any part of a building.
  - They may provide ≤ ½ the required exits.
  - They may provide ≤ ½ the required exit width.
- Exits serving the area receiving occupants through a horizontal exit are governed as follows:
  - Exit capacity is required for original occupants of the area.
  - Exit capacity is not required for occupants entering the area through a horizontal exit.
  - In other than I-3 ≥ 1 exit must lead to one of the following:
    To the outdoors or to an exit enclosure.

1021 Horizontal Exits

1021.2 Separation

- This section governs separation walls between the following:
  - Buildings connected by a horizontal exit.
  - Areas of refuge connected by a horizontal exit.
- The separation wall must be one of the following types:
  - A fire wall.
  - A fire barrier as follows:
    Walls must completely divide the floor served by the horizontal exit.
    Walls must be continuous between exterior walls.

  Note: Section 705, "Fire Walls," is cited as governing this type wall.
  Section 706, "Fire Barriers," is cited as governing this type wall.

- The separation wall must have a fire-resistance rating ≥ 2 hr.
- Separation wall must extend vertically through entire building in either of the following:
  - Where fire-resistance rating of floor assemblies is < 2 hr.
  - Where floor assemblies have unprotected openings.
- Openings in the separation wall must be protected.

  Note: Section 715, "Opening Protectives," is cited as governing these openings.

- A horizontal exit does not require a fire-resistance rating where all the following conditions are met:
  - Located between the following:
    A building area.
    A pedestrian walkway above grade.
  - The distance between the buildings connected must be as follows:
    > 20'.

  Note: Section 3104, "Pedestrian Walkways and Tunnels," is cited as governing the walkway noted above.

- Horizontal exit walls built as fire barriers have the following requirement:
  - They must run from exterior wall to exterior wall as follows:
    So as to divide the floor completely.

1021.3 Opening protectives

- Opening protectives in horizontal exits must be as per the wall fire-resistance rating.
- Fire doors in horizontal exits must close when activated by a smoke detector.
- Fire doors in a cross-corridor configuration must close when activated by a smoke detector.

  Note: 907.11, "Duct smoke detectors," is cited as a source of smoke detector requirements.

1021 Horizontal Exits

1021.4 Capacity of refuge area

- Refuge areas of a horizontal exit must be one of the following:
  - Areas occupied by the same tenant.
  - Public areas.
- A refuge area must be able to hold the sum of the following:
  - Its original occupants.
  - Occupants expected from the area connected by the horizontal exit.
- The number of occupants expected to travel to an area of refuge through a horizontal exit is based on the following:
  - By the capacity of the horizontal exit doors through which they must pass.
- The space required to house people in a refuge area is governed as follows:
  - Required area $\geq$ floor area per person $\times$ total number of occupants to be accommodated.
  - Area required for housing occupants does not include the following:
    - Stairways.
    - Elevators or other shafts.
    - Courts.
  - Floor areas required per person are based on occupancy as follows:

Table 1021.4   Refuge Area Capacity

Occupancy	Net floor area per person
I-2 housing nonambulatory occupants	30 sf
I-2 housing ambulatory occupants	15 sf
I-3	6 sf
All other occupancies	3 sf

1022 Exterior Exit Ramps and Stairways

1022.1 Exterior exit ramps and stairways

- Exterior exit ramps and stairways at outdoor stadiums as follows are not governed by this section series:
  - Where all portions of the means of egress are essentially open to the exterior.

    Note: 1019.1, "Enclosures required," exception 2, is cited as governing these elements.

- Other ramps and stairways are governed by this section series.

1022.2 Use in a means of egress

- The use of exterior exit ramps and stairways in a required means of egress is governed as follows:
  - Not permitted in occupancy I-2.
  - Permitted in other occupancies where both of the following apply:
    Building is ≤ 6 stories.
    Building is ≤ 75' in height.

1022.3 Open side

- Exterior exit ramps and stairways serving in a means of egress must have ≥ 1 side open as follows in the locations indicated below:
  - A total of ≥ 35 sf must be open.
  - Required open area must be located ≤ 42" above each of the following:
    Each adjacent floor level.
    Each adjacent intermediate landing.

1022.4 Side yards

- The required open side of an exterior exit ramp or stairway must adjoin one of the following:
  - Yard.
  - Court.
  - Public way.
- Closed sides of an exterior exit ramp or stairway may be exterior walls of the building.

1022.5 Location

- Exterior exit ramps and stairways must be positioned as follows:
  - ≥ 10' from lot lines.
  - ≥ 10' from other buildings on the same lot as follows:
    Where adjacent, the exterior building walls and openings are not protected as follows:
    As per exterior wall requirements vs. fire separation distance.

  Note: 1023.3, "Exit discharge location," is cited as the source of requirements for adjacent walls within 10' of the stairway according to fire separation distance.

Case study: Fig. 1022.3. 100% of the exterior stairway is open above the 42" level on both sides of the intermediate landing and on all sides of the 2nd floor landing. The east side of the stairway is 100% open at the first floor landing, thus, providing 38 ½ sf of opening above the 42" level. This is > than the 35 sf minimum. The open sides face yards and are > 10' from lot lines. The stairway serves the power plant and is not part of the I-2 occupancy building. The stairway is in compliance with the code.

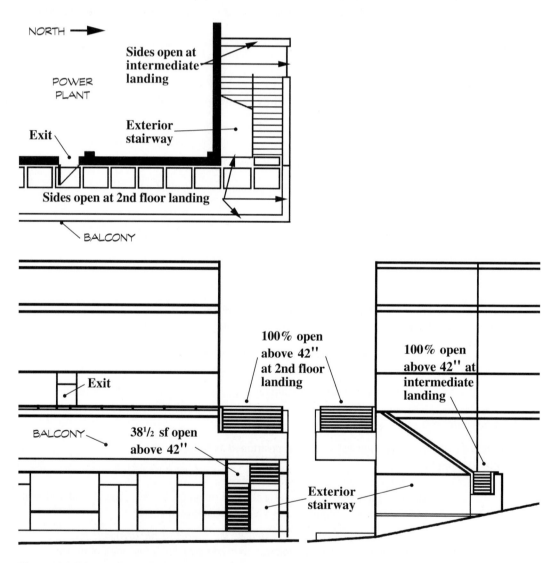

Fig. 1022.3. Plan and elevations of exterior stairway. Christus St. Michael Health Care Center. Texarkana, Texas. Watkins Hamilton Ross Architects, Inc. Houston, Texas.

1022 Exterior Exit Ramps and Stairways

1022.6 Exterior ramps and stairway protection

- This section addresses the separation of an exterior exit ramp or stairway from the building interior.
- Separation is not required where all of the following conditions apply:
  - In occupancies A, B, E, F, H, I, M, R-3, R-4, S, and U.
  - Buildings are ≤ 2 stories above grade.
  - Level of exit discharge is the 1st story above grade.
- Separation is not required where the stairway is served by an exterior balcony meeting all of the following conditions:
  - Balcony connects 2 remote exits that are of the following types:
    Exterior stairways.
    Other approved exits.
  - Balcony has a perimeter that is ≥ 50% open as follows:
    Open area is ≥ half the height of the enclosing wall.
    Top of the open area ≥ 7' above the floor of the balcony.
- Separation is not required at buildings where enclosures are not required for interior stairways.

   Note: 1019.1, "Enclosures required," is cited as the source of requirements permitting open interior stairs.

- Separation is not required where the exterior exit stairway is connected to an open-ended corridor meeting all of the following conditions:
  - Building is sprinklered as per NFPA 13 or 13R, including the following:
    The corridors.
    The stairs.
  - Open-ended corridor complies with requirements for interior corridors.

   Note: Section 1016, "Corridors," is cited as governing interior corridors.

  - Each end of the open-ended corridor connects to an exterior exit ramp or stairway.

   Note: Section 1022, "Exterior exit ramps and stairways," is cited as governing.

  - One of the following is provided at any change of direction > 45°:
    A clear opening to the exterior ≥ 35 sf as follows:
      Opening minimizes accumulation of smoke and toxic gases.
    An exterior exit ramp or stairway.
- For all other cases, the walls separating exterior exit stairways from the interior of the building must comply with the following:
  - They must meet fire-resistance and other requirements for vertical exit enclosures.

   Note: 1019.1, "Enclosures required," is cited as the source of applicable requirements.

  - Only openings necessary for egress are permitted in the separating walls as follows:
    Egress from spaces which are normally occupied.

1023 Exit Discharge

1023.1 General

- Egress from an exit enclosure may pass through an interior space only with all of the following conditions present:
  - The space is at the level of exit discharge.
  - Egress from ≤ 50% of the capacity of enclosures passes through interior space.
  - Egress from ≤ 50% of the number enclosures passes through interior space.
  - The space provides a path to the exterior as follows:
    Path must be unobstructed.
    Path must be readily apparent from the terminal of the exit enclosure.
  - Level of discharge must be separated from areas below as follows:
    Separation construction has a fire-resistance rating = to that of the exit enclosure.
  - The egress path from the exit enclosure is sprinklered.
  - Areas at discharge level with access to the egress path must have one of the following:
    A sprinkler system as per NFPA 13 or 13R.
    Separation from the rest of the building as per exit enclosure requirements.
- Egress from an exit enclosure may pass through a vestibule only with all the following conditions present:
  - Egress from ≤ 50% of the capacity of enclosures passes through interior space.
  - Egress from ≤ 50% of the number of enclosures passes through interior space.
  - The vestibule must have all of the following characteristics:
    It is separated from areas below it as follows:
      Separation construction has a fire-resistance rating = to that of the exit enclosure.
    Depth of vestibule measured from exterior of building is ≤ 10'.
    It is separated from rest of exit discharge level as follows:
      Separation construction is equivalent to the following:
        To that provided by wire glass in steel frames:
          Wire glass must be approved.
    Vestibule is used as a means of egress only.
    Vestibule discharges directly to the exterior.
- Stairways in open parking garages are governed as follows:
  - They may egress through the open parking garage as follows:
    At the exit discharge level.

  Note: 1019.1, "Enclosures required," exception 5, is cited as permitting this condition.

- All other exit discharges must comply with all of the following:
  - Discharge must be directly to the outside.
  - Discharge must occur in one of the following ways:
    At grade.
    At direct access to grade.
  - Discharge may not return to the building.

1023 Exit Discharge

1023.2 Exit discharge capacity

- Exit discharge capacity must be ≥ the required capacity of exits being discharged.

1023.3 Exit discharge location

- The following elements must be located as indicated below:
  - Elements:
    - Exterior balconies.
    - Exterior stairways.
    - Exterior ramps.
  - Location requirements:
    - ≥ 10' from lot lines.
    - ≥ 10' from other buildings on the same lot in the following circumstance:
      - Where adjacent exterior building walls and openings are not protected as follows:
        - As per exterior wall requirements based on fire separation distance.

  Note: Section 704, "Exterior Walls," is cited as the source of requirements for adjacent walls within 10' of the stairway, according to fire separation distance.

> **Case study: Fig. 1023.3.** The 5 exterior stairways are > 10' from lot lines ranging from 160' to 240' away. The 10' minimum distance is indicated at each stairway. The 6 exterior balconies are further from the lot lines. There are no other buildings on the site.

1023.4 Exit discharge components

- Exit discharge components must be open to the exterior as follows:
  - To a degree that minimizes the accumulation of smoke and toxic gases.
- Exit discharge components in a means of egress must meet exit discharge requirements.

  Note: Section 1023, "Exit Discharge," is cited as the source of applicable requirements.

1023.5 Egress courts

- An egress court as follows has the requirement listed below:
  - Egress court:
    - Acting as a component of the exit discharge as follows:
      - In a means of egress.
  - Requirement:
    - The egress court must comply with exit discharge requirements.

  Note: Section 1023, "Exit Discharge," is cited as the source of applicable requirements.

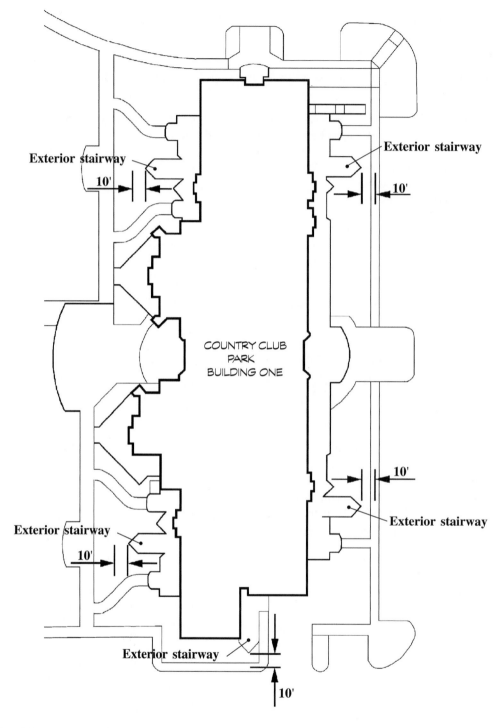

Fig. 1023.3. Partial site plan. Country Club Park Building One. Wichita, Kansas. Gossen Livingston Associates, Inc. Architecture. Wichita, Kansas.

1023 Exit Discharge

1023.5.1 Width

- The width of an egress court must be ≥ the larger of the following:
  - The width required for means of egress.

    Note: 1005.1, "Mininum required egress width," is cited as governing width.

  - Widths as follows:

Occupancy	Width
R-3, U	≥ 3'
Other	≥ 3'-8"

- Unobstructed height of an egress court within required width must be ≥ 7'.

- Only the following protrusions are permitted into the required width of an egress court:

Table 1023.5.1 Protrusions into Egress Courts	
Protruding elements	Protrusion permitted
Handrails	≤ 7"
Doors at full open position	≤ 7"
Doors in any position	≤ ½ required width
Nonstructural trim and similar decorative features	≤ 1½" from each side

    Note: The 7" protrusions listed above are the sum of protrusions on both sides of the court at any point. The ½ width into which doors may protrude is the sum of door protrusions on both sides of a court at any point.

- An egress court may diminish in width in the direction of egress only as follows:
  - Width may not diminish to < the required width.
  - The transition must be gradual.
  - The transition may not form an angle > 30° with the line of travel.
  - The transition must be bordered by a guard ≥ 36" high.

1023.5.2 Construction and openings

- The following egress occupancy R-3 courts are not governed by this subsection:
  - Where the occupant load is < 10.
- In other cases, where an egress court is < 10' wide, the following applies:
  - Egress court walls must comply with both the following:
    Comply with exterior wall requirements.
    Have a fire-resistance rating of ≥ 1 hr as follows:
    Rated construction must extend ≥ 10' above the court floor.
    Openings ≤ 10' high have one of the following:
    Fixed opening protective ≥ ¾ hr.
    Self-closing opening protective ≥ ¾ hr.

    Note: Section 704, "Exterior Walls," is cited as the source of requirements.

1023 Exit Discharge

1023.6 Access to a public way.

- Where access to a public way is not possible the following is permitted:
  - Provision of a safe dispersal area with all the following characteristics:
    - Must provide $\geq$ 5 sf per person.
    - Must be located on the same property as the building served.
    - Must be located $\geq$ 50' from the building served.
    - Must be permanently maintained as a safe dispersal area.
    - Must be identified as a safe dispersal area.
    - Must be accessed from the building served by the following:
      - A safe path as follows:
        - Unobstructed.
- In all other cases the exit discharge must provide the following:
  - Direct access to a public way as follows:
    - Unobstructed.

1024 Assembly

1024.1 General

- This section series governs the following:
  - Space in occupancy A with any of the following:
    Seats.
    Tables.
    Displays.
    Equipment.
    Other material.

1024.1.1 Bleachers

- The following must comply with standards published by the ICC:
  - Bleachers.
  - Grandstands.
  - Folding seating.
  - Telescopic seating.

    Note: ICC 300, "ICC Standard on Bleachers, Folding and Telescopic Seating, and Grandstands," is cited as governing this seating.

1024.2 Assembly main exit

- This section governs buildings and spaces in occupancy A.
- Exits may be distributed on the perimeter of buildings where all of the following conditions apply:
  - Exits have a total egress width ≥ the required width.
  - One of the following cases applies:
    There are no well-defined main exits.
    Multiple main exits are provided.

    Note: Stadiums and arenas are typical of this condition.

- Where the following conditions apply, other buildings and spaces must have a main exit as indicated below:
  - Where the occupant load > 300.
  - Main exit requirement:
    Width must accommodate ≥ ½ the total occupant load.
    Width must accommodate all means of egress served by the exit.
- Where the building is designated as occupancy A, the main exit must face one of the following:
  - A street.
  - An unoccupied space with both the following characteristics:
    ≥ 10' wide.
    Adjoins a street or public way.

1024 Assembly

1024.3 Assembly other exits

- This section governs buildings and spaces in occupancy A.
- Exits may be distributed on the perimeter of buildings where all of the following conditions apply:
  - Exits have a total egress width ≥ the required width.
  - One of the following cases applies:
      There are no well-defined main exits.
      Multiple main exits are provided.

    Note: Stadiums and arenas are typical of this condition.

- Other buildings and spaces with an occupant load > 300 are governed as follows:
  - Exits in addition to the main exit are required for each level of occupancy A as follows:
      Egress capacity must ≥ ½ the total occupant load of the level served.
      Exits must comply with exit access location requirements.

    Note: 1014.2, "Exit or exit access doorway arrangement," is cited as the applicable requirements for exit access location.

1024.4 Foyers and lobbies

- This section addresses the following in occupancy A-1:
  - Lobbies.
  - Similar spaces where people wait for seating.
- Such spaces must comply with the following:
  - Waiting spaces may not overlap into the means of egress required width.
  - Waiting spaces must be separated from the required means of egress by one of the following:
      Substantial permanent partitions.
      Fixed rigid railings ≥ 42" high.
  - Waiting spaces must have one of the following relationships to a public street:
      Be connected directly by all the main entrances or exits.
      Have a corridor or path of travel to every main entrance or exit as follows:
        Travel to be straight.
        Travel to be unobstructed.

1024.5 Interior balcony and gallery means of egress

- This section addresses balcony and gallery seating in occupancy A.
- Where seating is provided for > 50, the following applies:
  - ≥ 2 means of egress are required as follows:
      ≥ 1 means of egress must be located at each side of the seating area.
      ≥ 1 means of egress must lead directly to an exit.

Case study: Fig. 1024.5. The swimming pool balcony seats 86 occupants, thus, requiring ≥ 2 means of egress. The balcony meets the requirement with the provision of a stairway at each side of the seating as stipulated by the code. Both means of egress lead directly to an exit.

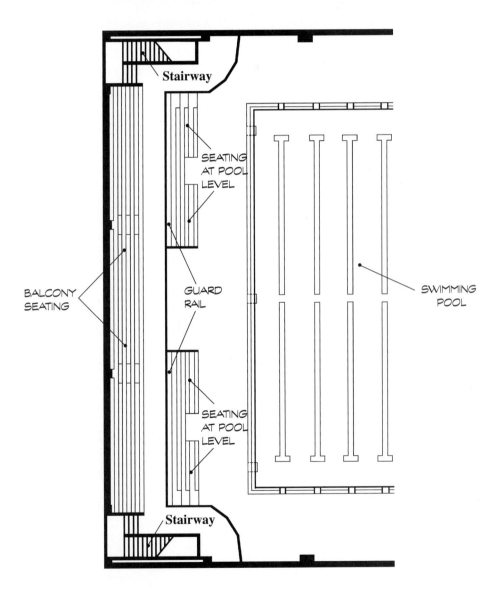

Fig. 1024.5. Partial floor plan at swimming pool. High School 6, Cypress-Fairbanks Independent School District. Harris County, Texas. PBK Architects, Inc. Houston, Texas.

1024 Assembly

1024.5.1 Enclosure of balcony openings

- Stairways may be open between balconies and the main assembly floor in assembly spaces such as the following:
  - Theaters.
  - Churches.
  - Auditoriums.
- In other assembly spaces, the following openings at balconies must be enclosed in vertical exit enclosures:
  - Interior stairways.
  - Other vertical openings.

  Note: 1019.1, "Enclosures required," is cited as the source of applicable requirements.

- ≥ 1 accessible means of egress is required from the following:
  - A balcony with accessible seating.
  - A gallery with accessible seating.

  Note: The following are cited as governing accessible means of egress as noted above:
  1007.3, "Enclosed exit stairways."
  1007.4, "Elevators."

1024.6 Width of means of egress for assembly

- Clear width of aisles and other means of egress is measured to the following:
  - Walls.
  - Edges of seating.
  - Edges of treads.

  Note: 1024.6.1, "Without smoke protection," is cited as governing the widths noted above where seating is not smoke-protected.
  The following are cited as governing widths as noted above where seating is smoke-protected:
  1024.6.2, "Smoke-protected seating."
  1024.6.3, "Smoke control."

- A requirement for a specified clear width does not preclude protrusions into the clear width in certain cases.

1024 Assembly

1024.6.1 Without smoke protection

- This section addresses means of egress clear width with no smoke protection.
- A width per occupant ≥ 0.3" is required on stairways with the following profile:
    - Riser height ≤ 7".
    - Tread depth ≥ 11".
- Where the riser height is > 7", the required width per occupant is as follows:

Width per occupant ≥ {[(riser height – 7") ÷ 0.1] × 0.005"} + 0.3"

This equation yields the following required widths per occupant for riser heights up to 8".

Table 1024.6.1a   Stairway Width Based on Riser Height

Riser height	Width per occupant	Riser height	Width per occupant	Riser height	Width per occupant	Riser height	Width per occupant
7.05"	≥ 0.3025"	7.30"	≥ 0.3150"	7.55"	≥ 0.3275"	7.80"	≥ 0.3400"
7.10"	≥ 0.3050"	7.35"	≥ 0.3175"	7.60"	≥ 0.3300"	7.85"	≥ 0.3425"
7.15"	≥ 0.3075"	7.40"	≥ 0.3200"	7.65"	≥ 0.3325"	7.90"	≥ 0.3450"
7.20"	≥ 0.3100"	7.45"	≥ 0.3225"	7.70"	≥ 0.3350"	7.95"	≥ 0.3475"
7.25"	≥ 0.3125"	7.50"	≥ 0.3250"	7.75"	≥ 0.3375"	8.00"	≥ 0.3500"

- A width per occupant ≥ 0.375" is required as follows:
    - Where egress requires going down stairs.
    - Where risers are ≤ 7".
    - Required for the segment of stairs > 30" from a handrail.
- The width indicated below is required where all of the following conditions apply:
    - Conditions:
        Where egress requires going down stairs.
        Where risers are > 7".
        Required for the segment of stairs > 30" from a handrail.
    - The width required per occupant is defined by the following equation:

Width per occupant ≥ {[(riser height – 7") ÷ 0.1] × 0.005"} + 0.375" required

This equation yields the following required widths per occupant for riser heights up to 8".

Table 1024.6.1b   Descending Egress Stairway Width Based on Riser Height

Riser height	Width per occupant	Riser height	Width per occupant	Riser height	Width per occupant	Riser height	Width per occupant
7.05"	≥ 0.3775"	7.30"	≥ 0.3900"	7.55"	≥ 0.4025"	7.80"	≥ 0.4150"
7.10"	≥ 0.3800"	7.35"	≥ 0.3925"	7.60"	≥ 0.4050"	7.85"	≥ 0.4175"
7.15"	≥ 0.3825"	7.40"	≥ 0.3950"	7.65"	≥ 0.4075"	7.90"	≥ 0.4200"
7.20"	≥ 0.3850"	7.45"	≥ 0.3975"	7.70"	≥ 0.4100"	7.95"	≥ 0.4225"
7.25"	≥ 0.3875"	7.50"	≥ 0.4000"	7.75"	≥ 0.4125"	8.00"	≥ 0.4250"

- Ramped or level means of egress require clear widths per occupant as follows:

Slope	Width per occupant
> 1:12	≥ 0.22"
≤ 1:12	≥ 0.20"

1024 Assembly

1024.6.2 Smoke-protected seating *(part 1 of 3)*

- This section does not address the width of means of egress for the following:
  - Outdoor smoke-protected assembly as follows:
    With an occupant load ≤ 18,000.

    Note: 1024.6.3, "Width of means of egress for outdoor smoke-protected assembly," is cited as governing this seating.

- This section addresses the clear width required for means of egress in smoke-protected assembly seating.
- Width required is calculated as follows:
  - *Total width = (width required per seat served) × (number of seats served)* as follows:
    Seats must be within one assembly space.
    Seats must be exposed to same smoke-protected environment.
  - Factors for inches of width required per seat served, as provided by the code, may be interpolated.
- A Life Safety Evaluation is required for seating utilizing egress widths stipulated by this section.

    Note: NFPA 101, "Code for Safety to Life from Fire in Buildings and Structures," is cited as the source of requirements for the Life Safety Evaluation.

- Required widths for means of egress elements are provided in the tables below as follows:
  - Equations for interpolating factors for width per seat served as required by the code.
  - Tables of required total egress widths for selected quantities of seats.

Table 1024.6.2a	Width of Stairs and Aisle Steps ≤ 30" from a Handrail

Method of calculating inches per seat served for the table of minimum widths below:

Seats	Calculation
1 – 5,000	0.200" – a fixed number
5,001 – 10,000	0.200" – [0.0000140" × (number of seats > 5,000)]
10,001 – 15,000	0.130" – [0.0000068" × (number of seats > 10,000)]
15,001 – 20,000	0.096" – [0.0000040" × (number of seats > 15,000)]
20,001 – 25,000	0.076" – [0.0000032" × (number of seats > 20,000)]
25,000 – up	0.060" – a fixed number

Minimum width per seat served :

Seats	Width	Seats	Width	Seats	Width	Seats	Width
500	≥ 0.200"	7,000	≥ 0.172"	14,000	≥ 0.103"	21,000	≥ 0.073"
1,000	≥ 0.200"	8,000	≥ 0.158"	15,000	≥ 0.096"	22,000	≥ 0.696"
2,000	≥ 0.200"	9,000	≥ 0.144"	16,000	≥ 0.092"	23,000	≥ 0.066"
3,000	≥ 0.200"	10,000	≥ 0.130"	17,000	≥ 0.088"	24,000	≥ 0.063"
4,000	≥ 0.200"	11,000	≥ 0.123"	18,000	≥ 0.084"	25,000	≥ 0.060"
5,000	≥ 0.200"	12,000	≥ 0.116"	19,000	≥ 0.080"	26,000	≥ 0.060"
6,000	≥ 0.186"	13,000	≥ 0.110"	20,000	≥ 0.076"	27,000	≥ 0.060"

Source: IBC Table 1024.6.2

1024 Assembly

1024.6.2 Smoke-protected seating *(part 2 of 3)*

Table 1024.6.2b   Width of Stairs and Aisle Steps > 30" from a Handrail

Method of calculating inches per seat served for the table of minimum widths below:

Seats	Calculation
1 – 5,000	0.250" – a fixed number
5,001 – 10,000	0.250" – [0.0000174" × (number of seats > 5,000)]
10,001 – 15,000	0.163" – [0.0000086" × (number of seats > 10,000)]
15,001 – 20,000	0.120" – [0.0000050" × (number of seats > 15,000)]
20,001 – 25,000	0.095" – [0.0000040" × (number of seats > 20,000)]
25,000 – up	0.075" – a fixed number

Minimum width per seat served:

Seats	Width	Seats	Width	Seats	Width	Seats	Width
500	≥ 0.250"	7,000	≥ 0.215"	14,000	≥ 0.129"	21,000	≥ 0.091"
1,000	≥ 0.250"	8,000	≥ 0.198"	15,000	≥ 0.120"	22,000	≥ 0.087"
2,000	≥ 0.250"	9,000	≥ 0.180"	16,000	≥ 0.115"	23,000	≥ 0.083"
3,000	≥ 0.250"	10,000	≥ 0.163"	17,000	≥ 0.110"	24,000	≥ 0.079"
4,000	≥ 0.250"	11,000	≥ 0.154"	18,000	≥ 0.105"	25,000	≥ 0.075"
5,000	≥ 0.250"	12,000	≥ 0.146"	19,000	≥ 0.100"	26,000	≥ 0.075"
6,000	≥ 0.233"	13,000	≥ 0.137"	20,000	≥ 0.095"	27,000	≥ 0.075"

Source: IBC Table 1024.6.2

Table 1024.6.2c   Width of Passageways, Doorways, and Ramps ≤ 1:10 Slope

Method of calculating inches per seat served for the table of widths below:

Seats	Calculation
1 – 5,000	0.150" – a fixed number
5,001 – 10,000	0.150" – [0.0000100" × (number of seats > 5,000)]
10,001 – 15,000	0.100" – [0.0000060" × (number of seats > 10,000)]
15,001 – 20,000	0.070" – [0.0000028" × (number of seats > 15,000)]
20,001 – 25,000	0.056" – [0.0000024" × (number of seats > 20,000)]
25,000 – up	0.044" – a fixed number

Minimum width per seat served:

Seats	Width	Seats	Width	Seats	Width	Seats	Width
500	≥ 0.150"	7,000	≥ 0.130"	14,000	≥ 0.076"	21,000	≥ 0.054"
1,000	≥ 0.150"	8,000	≥ 0.120"	15,000	≥ 0.070"	22,000	≥ 0.051"
2,000	≥ 0.150"	9,000	≥ 0.110"	16,000	≥ 0.067"	23,000	≥ 0.049"
3,000	≥ 0.150"	10,000	≥ 0.100"	17,000	≥ 0.064"	24,000	≥ 0.046"
4,000	≥ 0.150"	11,000	≥ 0.094"	18,000	≥ 0.062"	25,000	≥ 0.044"
5,000	≥ 0.150"	12,000	≥ 0.088"	19,000	≥ 0.059"	26,000	≥ 0.044"
6,000	≥ 0.140"	13,000	≥ 0.082"	20,000	≥ 0.056"	27,000	≥ 0.044"

Source: IBC Table 1024.6.2.

1024 Assembly

1024.6.2 Smoke-protected seating *(part 3 of 3)*

Table 1024.6.2d   Width of Ramps > 1:10 Slope

Method of calculating inches per seat served for the table of widths below:

Seats	Calculation
1 – 5,000	0.165" – a fixed number
5,001 – 10,000	0.165" – [0.0000110" × (number of seats > 5,000)]
10,001 – 15,000	0.110" – [0.0000066" × (number of seats > 10,000)]
15,001 – 20,000	0.077" – [0.0000030" × (number of seats > 15,000)]
20,001 – 25,000	0.062" – [0.0000028" × (number of seats > 20,000)]
25,000 – up	0.048"– a fixed number

Minimum width per seat served:

Seats	Width	Seats	Width	Seats	Width	Seats	Width
500	≥ 0.165"	7,000	≥ 0.143"	14,000	≥ 0.084"	21,000	≥ 0.059"
1,000	≥ 0.165"	8,000	≥ 0.132"	15,000	≥ 0.077"	22,000	≥ 0.056"
2,000	≥ 0.165"	9,000	≥ 0.121"	16,000	≥ 0.074"	23,000	≥ 0.054"
3,000	≥ 0.165"	10,000	≥ 0.110"	17,000	≥ 0.071"	24,000	≥ 0.051"
4,000	≥ 0.165"	11,000	≥ 0.103"	18,000	≥ 0.068"	25,000	≥ 0.048"
5,000	≥ 0.165"	12,000	≥ 0.097"	19,000	≥ 0.065"	26,000	≥ 0.048"
6,000	≥ 0.154"	13,000	≥ 0.090"	20,000	≥ 0.062"	27,000	≥ 0.048"

Source: IBC Table 1024.6.2

1024.6.2.1 Smoke control

- This section addresses means of egress from smoke-protected seating in an assembly area.
- The means of egress must be protected from smoke by one of the following methods:
  - A smoke control system.

    Note: Section 909, "Smoke Control Systems," is cited as the source of requirements.

  - Natural ventilation as follows:
    Smoke must be held to ≥ 6' above the floor.

1024.6.2.2 Roof height

- This section addresses the roof height in a smoke-protected assembly area.
- In an outdoor stadium, the following applies:
  - A canopy < 15' above the highest aisle or aisle accessway is permitted as follows:
    Where a height < 6'-8" is clear of any object.
- In other locations, the lowest roof deck must be ≥ 15' above the following:
  - The highest aisle.
  - The highest aisle accessway.

1024 Assembly

1024.6.2.3 Automatic sprinklers

- This section addresses smoke-protected assembly seating enclosed with ceiling and walls.
- This section does not apply to outdoor seating facilities as follows:
  - Where seating is essentially open to the exterior.
  - Where means of egress in seating areas are essentially open to the exterior.
- Sprinklers are not required for the following floor areas where the conditions below apply:
  - Floor areas used for the following:
    Competition.
    Performance.
    Entertainment.
  - Conditions:
    Roof construction must be > 50' above the floor level.
    Only low-hazard uses occur.
- Sprinklers are not required for the following where < 1000 sf:
  - Press boxes.
  - Storage.
- In other cases the seating must be protected with sprinklers as per NFPA 13.

  Note: 903.1.1, "NFPA 13 sprinkler systems," is cited as governing the sprinklers.

1024.6.3 Width of means of egress for outdoor smoke-protected assembly

- Means of egress in an outdoor-smoke-protected assembly area must comply with one of the following width requirements:
  - Width required for indoor smoke-protected assembly.

  Note: 1024.6.2, "Smoke-protected seating," is cited as a source of width requirements.

  - Width = (Number of occupants served) × (required width per occupant) as follows:

Table 1024.6.3   Egress Width in Outdoor Smoke-Protected Assembly

Means of egress	Width/occupant	Means of egress	Width/occupant
Aisles	≥ 0.08"	Stairs	≥ 0.08"
Ramps	≥ 0.06"	Corridors	≥ 0.06"
Tunnels	≥ 0.06"	Vomitories	≥ 0.06"

1024 Assembly

1024.7 Travel distance

- Travel distance is measured along aisles and aisle accessways as follows:
  - Without crossing over seats.
- Travel distance is limited in assembly occupancies as indicated below:

Table 1024.7   Travel Distance in Assembly Spaces

Location and description of egress route	Travel distance
From each seat to outside the building:	
In open-air seating on Type I or II construction	not limited
In open-air seating of Type III, IV, and V construction	$\leq 400'$
In smoke-protected seating:	
From each seat to nearest entrance to a vomitory	$\leq 200'$
From vomitory entrance to outside the building:	
To a stair, ramp, or walk	$\leq 200'$
From each seat to nearest entrance to the concourse	$\leq 200'$
From concourse entrance outside the building:	
To a stair, ramp, or walk	$\leq 200'$
In sprinklered buildings to exit door	$\leq 250'$
In unsprinklered buildings to an exit door	$\leq 200'$

1024.8 Common path of travel

- The common path of travel as follows is limited as shown below:
  - Path:
    Between the following locations:
    Any seat.
    A point where the occupant has a choice as follows:
    Between two routes to two exits.
  - Limits:
    The common path is limited as shown in the following table:

Table 1024.8   Common Path of Travel Distance in Assembly Spaces

Conditions	Common path distance
≤ 50 occupants	$\leq 75'$
Smoke-protected seating	$\leq 50'$
Other	$\leq 30'$

1024 Assembly

1024.8.1 Path through adjacent rows *(part 1 of 2)*

- For smoke-protected seating, the following applies:
  - Where 1 of the 2 paths of egress travel is located as follows, the requirements indicated below apply:

    Path:

    Passes across an aisle through a row to the aisle beyond.

    Requirements:

    Seats in the aisle must be ≤ 40.

    Clear width in row must be ≥ 12" + [0.3" × (total number of seats - 7)] as follows:

    The following table lists required clear width based on this requirement:

Table 1024.8.1a   Required Width of Smoke-Protected Row Serving as Means of Egress

Seats in row	Clear width	Seats in row	Clear width	Seats in row	Clear width
1–7	≥ 12"	19	≥ 15.6"	30	≥ 18.9"
8	≥ 12.3"	20	≥ 15.9"	31	≥ 19.2"
9	≥ 12.6"	21	≥ 16.2"	32	≥ 19.5"
10	≥ 12.9"	22	≥ 16.5"	33	≥ 19.8"
11	≥ 13.2"	23	≥ 16.8"	34	≥ 20.1"
12	≥ 13.5"	24	≥ 17.1"	35	≥ 20.4"
13	≥ 13.8"	25	≥ 17.4"	36	≥ 20.7"
14	≥ 14.1"	26	≥ 17.7"	37	≥ 21"
15	≥ 14.4"	27	≥ 18"	38	≥ 21.3"
16	≥ 14.7"	28	≥ 18.3"	39	≥ 21.6"
17	≥ 15"	29	≥ 18.6"	40	≥ 21.9"
18	≥ 15.3"				

1024 Assembly

1024.8.1 Path through adjacent rows *(part 2 of 2)*

- For seating that is not smoke-protected the following applies:
  - Where 1 of the 2 paths of egress travel is located as follows, the requirements indicated below apply:
    Path:
      Passes across an aisle through a row to the aisle beyond.
    Requirements:
      Seats in the aisle must be ≤ 40.
      Clear width in row must be ≥ 12" + [0.6" × (total number of seats - 7)] as follows:
        The following table lists required clear width based on this requirement:

Table 1024.8.1b   Required Width of Smoke-Protected Row Serving as Means of Egress

Seats in row	Clear width	Seats in row	Clear width	Seats in row	Clear width
1–7	≥ 12"	13	≥ 15.6"	19	≥ 19.2"
8	≥ 12.6"	14	≥ 16.2	20	≥ 19.8"
9	≥ 13.2"	15	≥ 16.8"	21	≥ 20.4"
10	≥ 13.8"	16	≥ 17.4"	22	≥ 21"
11	≥ 14.4"	17	≥ 18"	23	≥ 21.6"
12	≥ 15"	18	≥ 18.6"	24	≥ 22.2"

1024.9 Assembly aisles are required

- Occupied areas of occupancy A with the following furnishings must comply with the requirements listed below:
  - Furnishings:
    Seats.
    Tables.
    Displays.
    Similar fixtures.
    Similar equipment.
  - Requirements:
    Aisles must lead to one of the following:
      Exits.
      Exit access doorways.
    Must comply with this section series.
    Aisle accessways must comply with requirements listed elsewhere.

  Note: 1013.4.2, "Seating at tables," is cited governing aisle accessways..

1024 Assembly

1024.9.1 Minimum aisle widths

- Required aisle widths in assembly areas are required as follows:

Table 1024.9.1   Aisle Width in Assembly Spaces

Description	Width
Aisle stairs:	
With seats on both sides totaling > 50	≥ 48"
With seats on both sides totaling ≤ 50	≥ 36"
With seats on one side only	≥ 36"
With ≤ 5 rows of seats on one side	≥ 23" between handrail and seating
Aisle stairs divided by handrail:	≥ 23" between handrail or guard and seating
Level or ramped aisles:	
With seats on both sides totaling > 50	≥ 42"
With seats on both sides totaling >14 and ≤ 50	≥ 36"
With seats on both sides totaling ≤ 14	≥ 30"
With seats on one side only totaling > 14	≥ 36"
With seats on one side only totaling ≤ 14	≥ 30"

1024.9.2 Aisle width

- An aisle must have sufficient width as follows:
  - To serve as egress for its assigned portion of the space.
- Areas served by aisles must be sized as follows:
  - So that the capacity of aisles reflects the following:
    A balanced use of all means of egress.

1024.9.3 Converging aisles

- A means of egress receiving occupant loads of converging aisles must have the following capacity:
  - ≥ the sum of the required capacities of the converging aisles.

1024.9.4 Uniform width

- The the following parts of aisles require a uniform width:
  - Where egress travel is in either direction.

1024 Assembly

1024.9.5 Assembly aisle termination

- A dead-end aisle may be > 20' only as follows:
  - Seats beyond a point 20' into a dead-end must comply with both of the following:
    Seats must be ≤ 24 seats from another aisle counted along the row of seats.
    Required clear width between rows is as follows:

    Width ≥ 12" + [(number of seats − 7) × 0.6"]

    This equation yields the following required clear widths between rows:

Table 1024.9.5a   Row Width at Long Dead-End Aisles

Seats	Width	Seats	Width	Seats	Width	Seats	Width	Seats	Width
1–7	≥ 12.0"	11	≥ 14.4"	15	≥ 16.8"	19	≥ 19.2"	23	≥ 21.6"
8	≥ 12.6"	12	≥ 15.0"	16	≥ 17.4"	20	≥ 19.8"	24	≥ 22.2"
9	≥ 13.2"	13	≥ 15.6"	17	≥ 18.0"	21	≥ 20.4"		
10	≥ 13.8"	14	≥ 16.2"	18	≥ 18.6"	22	≥ 21.0"		

- In smoke-protected seating, a dead-end vertical aisle (⊥ to rows) is governed as follows:
  - It may be > than 21 rows in length only:
    Where seats beyond the 21 rows comply with both of the following:
    Seats must be ≤ 40 seats from another aisle counted along the row of seats.
    Required clear width between rows served by this part of the dead end is:

    Width ≥ 12" + [(number of seats − 7) × 0.3"]

    This equation yields the following required clear widths between rows:

Table 1024.9.5b   Clear Width between Rows of Assembly Seating

Seats	Width	Seats	Width	Seats	Width	Seats	Width	Seats	Width
1–7	≥ 12.0"	14	≥ 14.1"	21	≥ 16.2"	28	≥ 18.3"	35	≥ 20.4"
8	≥ 12.3"	15	≥ 14.4"	22	≥ 16.5"	29	≥ 18.6"	36	≥ 20.7"
9	≥ 12.6"	16	≥ 14.7"	23	≥ 16.8"	30	≥ 18.9"	37	≥ 21.0"
10	≥ 12.9"	17	≥ 15.0"	24	≥ 17.1"	31	≥ 19.2"	38	≥ 21.3"
11	≥ 13.2"	18	≥ 15.3"	25	≥ 17.4"	32	≥ 19.5"	39	≥ 21.6"
12	≥ 13.5"	19	≥ 15.6"	26	≥ 17.7"	33	≥ 19.8"	40	≥ 21.9"
13	≥ 13.8"	20	≥ 15.9"	27	≥ 18.0"	34	≥ 20.1"		

- All other dead-end vertical aisles in smoke-protected seating must be ≤ 21 rows in length.
- All other dead-end aisles must be ≤ 20' in length.
- All other aisles must terminate at both ends as follows:
  - Termination must be at one of the following having access to an exit:
    Cross aisle.
    Vomitory or concourse.
    Doorway.
    Foyer.

1024 Assembly

1024.9.6 Assembly aisle obstructions

- Handrails are the only obstructions permitted within the required aisle width.

  Note: 1024.13, "Handrails," is cited as the source of applicable requirements.

1024.10 Clear width of aisle accessways serving seating

- Clear aisle-accessway width is measured between the following points:
  - From the back of a row of seats to the closest element of the row of seats behind it.
- Width is measured with the seats up where chairs have self-rising seats.
- Width is measured with the seat down for any chair without a self-rising seat.
- Width is measured with the tablet arm down as follows for seats with folding tablet arms.
- For ≤ 14 seats in a row, the the clear aisle-accessway width required is ≥ 12".

> **Case study: Fig. 1024.10.** The central area of the auditorium has 14 seats or fewer seats per row. Since they are self-rising the aisle accessway width is measured with the seat up at 1'-6 ³/₄". This meets the code minimum of 12" for this number of seats.

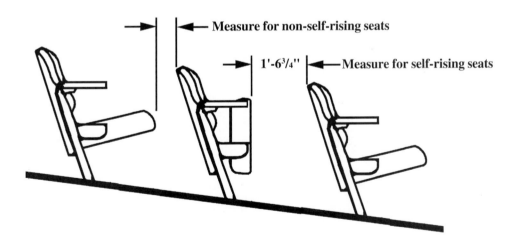

Fig. 1024.10. Elevation of auditorium seating. High School 6, Cypress-Fairbanks Independent School District. Harris County, Texas. PBK Architects, Inc. Houston, Texas.

1024 Assembly

1024.10.1 Dual access *(part 1 of 3)*

- Rows of seating served by aisles or doorways at each side are limited as follows:
  - Limited to ≤ 100 seats per row.
- A clear width of ≥ 12" is required for rows with 1–14 seats.
- Clear width between rows > 22" is not required for rows of any length.
- For rows with > 14 seats, required width is as follows:

  Width ≥ 12" + [(number of seats − 14)] × 0.3"

  This equation yields the following required clear widths up to 22":

Table 1024.10.1a   **Required Width between Rows for Seating Not Smoke-Protected, Access from 2 Sides**

Seats	Width	Seats	Width	Seats	Width	Seats	Width	Seats	Width
1–14	≥ 12.0"	21	≥ 14.1"	28	≥ 16.2"	35	≥ 18.3"	42	≥ 20.4"
15	≥ 12.3"	22	≥ 14.4"	29	≥ 16.5"	36	≥ 18.6"	43	≥ 20.7"
16	≥ 12.6"	23	≥ 14.4"	30	≥ 16.8"	37	≥ 18.9"	44	≥ 21.0"
17	≥ 12.9"	24	≥ 15.0"	31	≥ 17.1"	38	≥ 19.2"	45	≥ 21.3"
18	≥ 13.2"	25	≥ 15.3"	32	≥ 17.4"	39	≥ 19.5"	46	≥ 21.6"
19	≥ 13.5"	26	≥ 15.6"	33	≥ 17.7"	40	≥ 19.8"	47	≥ 21.9"
20	≥ 13.8"	27	≥ 15.9"	34	≥ 18.0"	41	≥ 20.1"	48	≥ 22.0"

Source: IBC Table 1024.10.1

- A clear width of ≥ 12" is required for rows with lengths varying from 14–17 seats and to which 0.3" per seat is added for longer rows as follows:

Table 1024.10.1b   Required Width between Rows for Smoke-Protected Seats, Access from 2 Sides

Seats	Width	Seats	Width	Seats	Width	Seats	Width	Seats	Width
< 4000 smoke-protected seats:									
1–14	≥ 12.0"	21	≥ 14.1"	28	≥ 16.2"	35	≥ 18.3"	42	≥ 20.4"
15	≥ 12.3"	22	≥ 14.4"	29	≥ 16.5"	36	≥ 18.6"	43	≥ 20.7"
16	≥ 12.6"	23	≥ 14.4"	30	≥ 16.8"	37	≥ 18.9"	44	≥ 21.0"
17	≥ 12.9"	24	≥ 15.0"	31	≥ 17.1"	38	≥ 19.2"	45	≥ 21.3"
18	≥ 13.2"	25	≥ 15.3"	32	≥ 17.4"	39	≥ 19.5"	46	≥ 21.6"
19	≥ 13.5"	26	≥ 15.6"	33	≥ 17.7"	40	≥ 19.8"	47	≥ 21.9"
20	≥ 13.8"	27	≥ 15.9"	34	≥ 18.0"	41	≥ 20.1"	48	≥ 22.0"
4000–6999 smoke-protected seats:									
1–15	≥ 12.0"	22	≥ 14.1"	29	≥ 16.2"	36	≥ 18.3"	43	≥ 20.4"
16	≥ 12.3"	23	≥ 14.4"	30	≥ 16.5"	37	≥ 18.6"	44	≥ 20.7"
17	≥ 12.6"	24	≥ 14.4"	31	≥ 16.8"	38	≥ 18.9"	45	≥ 21.0"
18	≥ 12.9"	25	≥ 15.0"	32	≥ 17.1"	39	≥ 19.2"	46	≥ 21.3"
19	≥ 13.2"	26	≥ 15.3"	33	≥ 17.4"	40	≥ 19.5"	47	≥ 21.6"
20	≥ 13.5"	27	≥ 15.6"	34	≥ 17.7"	41	≥ 19.8"	48	≥ 21.9"
21	≥ 13.8"	28	≥ 15.9"	35	≥ 18.0"	42	≥ 20.1"	49	≥ 22.0"

Source: IBC Table 1024.10.1

1024 Assembly

1024.10.1 Dual access *(part 2 of 3)*

Table 1024.10.1 – *Continued*

Seats	Width	Seats	Width	Seats	Width	Seats	Width	Seats	Width
7000–9999 smoke-protected seats:									
1–16	≥ 12.0"	23	≥ 14.1"	30	≥ 16.2"	37	≥ 18.3"	44	≥ 20.4"
17	≥ 12.3"	24	≥ 14.4"	31	≥ 16.5"	38	≥ 18.6"	45	≥ 20.7"
18	≥ 12.6"	25	≥ 14.4"	32	≥ 16.8"	39	≥ 18.9"	46	≥ 21.0"
19	≥ 12.9"	26	≥ 15.0"	33	≥ 17.1"	40	≥ 19.2"	47	≥ 21.3"
20	≥ 13.2"	27	≥ 15.3"''	34	≥ 17.4"	41	≥ 19.5"	48	≥ 21.6"
21	≥ 13.5"	28	≥ 15.6"	35	≥ 17.7"	42	≥ 19.8"	49	≥ 21.9"
22	≥ 13.8"	29	≥ 15.9"	36	≥ 18.0"	43	≥ 20.1"	50	≥ 22.0"
10,000–12,999 smoke-protected seats:									
1–17	≥ 12.0"	24	≥ 14.1"	31	≥ 16.2"	38	≥ 18.3"	45	≥ 20.4"
18	≥ 12.3"	25	≥ 14.4"	32	≥ 16.5"	39	≥ 18.6"	46	≥ 20.7"
19	≥ 12.6"	26	≥ 14.4"	33	≥ 16.8"	40	≥ 18.9"	47	≥ 21.0"
20	≥ 12.9"	27	≥ 15.0"	34	≥ 17.1"	41	≥ 19.2"	48	≥ 21.3"
21	≥ 13.2"	28	≥ 15.3"	35	≥ 17.4"	42	≥ 19.5"	49	≥ 21.6"
22	≥ 13.5"	29	≥ 15.6"	36	≥ 17.7"	43	≥ 19.8"	50	≥ 21.9"
23	≥ 13.8"	30	≥ 15.9"	37	≥ 18.0"	44	≥ 20.1"	51	≥ 22.0"

Source: IBC Table 1024.10.1

- A clear width of ≥ 12" is required for rows with lengths varying from 18–21 seats and to which 0.3" per seat is added for longer rows as follows:

Table 1024.10.1c   Required Width between Rows for Smoke-Protected Seats, Access from 2 Sides

Seats	Width	Seats	Width	Seats	Width	Seats	Width	Seats	Width
13,000–15,999 smoke-protected seats:									
1–18	≥ 12.0"	25	≥ 14.1"	32	≥ 16.2"	39	≥ 18.3"	46	≥ 20.4"
19	≥ 12.3"	26	≥ 14.4"	33	≥ 16.5"	40	≥ 18.6"	47	≥ 20.7"
20	≥ 12.6"	27	≥ 14.4"	34	≥ 16.8"	41	≥ 18.9"	48	≥ 21.0"
21	≥ 12.9"	28	≥ 15.0"	35	≥ 17.1"	42	≥ 19.2"	49	≥ 21.3"
22	≥ 13.2"	29	≥ 15.3"	36	≥ 17.4"	43	≥ 19.5"	50	≥ 21.6"
23	≥ 13.5"	30	≥ 15.6"	37	≥ 17.7"	44	≥ 19.8"	51	≥ 21.9"
24	≥ 13.8"	31	≥ 15.9"	38	≥ 18.0"	45	≥ 20.1"	52	≥ 22.0"
16,000–18,999 smoke-protected seats:									
1–19	≥ 12.0"	26	≥ 14.1"	33	≥ 16.2"	40	≥ 18.3"	47	≥ 20.4"
20	≥ 12.3"	27	≥ 14.4"	34	≥ 16.5"	41	≥ 18.6"	48	≥ 20.7"
21	≥ 12.6"	28	≥ 14.4"	35	≥ 16.8"	42	≥ 18.9"	49	≥ 21.0"
22	≥ 12.9"	29	≥ 15.0"	36	≥ 17.1"	43	≥ 19.2"	50	≥ 21.3"
23	≥ 13.2"	30	≥ 15.3"	37	≥ 17.4"	44	≥ 19.5"	51	≥ 21.6"
24	≥ 13.5"	31	≥ 15.6"	38	≥ 17.7"	45	≥ 19.8"	52	≥ 21.9"
25	≥ 13.8"	32	≥ 15.9"	39	≥ 18.0"	46	≥ 20.1"	53	≥ 22.0"

Source: IBC Table 1024.10.1

1024 Assembly

1024.10.1 Dual access *(part 3 of 3)*

Table 1024.10.1c – *Continued*

Seats	Width	Seats	Width	Seats	Width	Seats	Width	Seats	Width
19,000 –21,999 smoke-protected seats:									
1–20	≥ 12.0"	27	≥ 14.1"	34	≥ 16.2"	41	≥ 18.3"	48	≥ 20.4"
21	≥ 12.3"	28	≥ 14.4"	35	≥ 16.5"	42	≥ 18.6"	49	≥ 20.7"
22	≥ 12.6"	29	≥ 14.4"	36	≥ 16.8"	43	≥ 18.9"	50	≥ 21.0"
23	≥ 12.9"	30	≥ 15.0"	37	≥ 17.1"	44	≥ 19.2"	51	≥ 21.3"
24	≥ 13.2"	31	≥ 15.3"	38	≥ 17.4"	45	≥ 19.5"	52	≥ 21.6"
25	≥ 13.5"	32	≥ 15.6"	39	≥ 17.7"	46	≥ 19.8"	53	≥ 21.9"
26	≥ 13.8"	33	≥ 15.9"	40	≥ 18.0"	47	≥ 20.1"	54	≥ 22.0"
≥ 22,000 smoke-protected seats:									
1–21	≥ 12.0"	28	≥ 14.1"	35	≥ 16.2"	42	≥ 18.3"	49	≥ 20.4"
22	≥ 12.3"	29	≥ 14.4"	36	≥ 16.5"	43	≥ 18.6"	50	≥ 20.7"
23	≥ 12.6"	30	≥ 14.4"	37	≥ 16.8"	44	≥ 18.9"	51	≥ 21.0"
24	≥ 12.9"	31	≥ 15.0"	38	≥ 17.1"	45	≥ 19.2"	52	≥ 21.3"
25	≥ 13.2"	32	≥ 15.3"	39	≥ 17.4"	46	≥ 19.5"	53	≥ 21.6"
26	≥ 13.5"	33	≥ 15.6"	40	≥ 17.7"	47	≥ 19.8"	54	≥ 21.9"
27	≥ 13.8"	34	≥ 15.9"	41	≥ 18.0"	48	≥ 20.1"	55	≥ 22.0"

Source: IBC Table 1024.10.1

1024.10.2 Single access *(part 1 of 2)*

- Clear width required between rows with an aisle or doorway at one side only, where not smoke protected, is as follows:
  - For rows ≤ 7 seats required width is ≥ 12".
  - Clear width between rows of any length is not required to be > 22".
  - For rows > 7 seats, required width is determined by the following equation:

    Width ≥ 12" + [(number of seats – 7) × 0.6"]

    This equation yields the clear widths in the table below:

Table 1024.10.2a   Required Clear Width between Rows for Seating Not Smoke-Protected, Access 1 Side

Seats	Width	Seats	Width	Seats	Width	Seats	Width	Seats	Width
1–7	≥ 12.0"	11	≥ 14.4"	15	≥ 16.8"	19	≥ 19.2"	23	≥ 21.6"
8	≥ 12.6"	12	≥ 15.0"	16	≥ 17.4"	20	≥ 19.8"	24	≥ 22.0"
9	≥ 13.2"	13	≥ 15.6"	17	≥ 18.0"	21	≥ 20.4"	25	≥ 22.0"
10	≥ 13.8"	14	≥ 16.2"	18	≥ 18.6"	22	≥ 21.0"	26	≥ 22.0"

Source: IBC Table 1024.10.1

1024 Assembly

1024.10.2 Single access *(part 2 of 2)*

- A clear width of ≥ 12" is required for rows with lengths varying from 7–11 smoke-protected seats and to which 0.6" per seat is added for longer rows as in the table below:

Table 1024.10.2b   Required Clear Width between Rows for Smoke-Protected Seats, Access 1 Side

Seats	Width	Seats	Width	Seats	Width	Seats	Width	Seats	Width
< 7000 smoke-protected seats:									
1–7	≥ 12.0"	11	≥ 14.4"	15	≥ 16.8"	19	≥ 19.2"	23	≥ 21.6"
8	≥ 12.6"	12	≥ 15.0"	16	≥ 17.4"	20	≥ 19.8"	24	≥ 22.0"
9	≥ 13.2"	13	≥ 15.6"	17	≥ 18.0"	21	≥ 20.4"	25	≥ 22.0"
10	≥ 13.8"	14	≥ 16.2"	18	≥ 18.6"	22	≥ 21.0"	26	≥ 22.0"
7000 – 12,999 smoke-protected seats:									
1–8	≥ 12.0"	12	≥ 14.4"	16	≥ 16.8"	20	≥ 19.2"	24	≥ 21.6"
9	≥ 12.6"	13	≥ 15.0"	17	≥ 17.4"	21	≥ 19.8"	25	≥ 22.0"
10	≥ 13.2"	14	≥ 15.6"	18	≥ 18.0"	22	≥ 20.4"	26	≥ 22.0"
11	≥ 13.8"	15	≥ 16.2"	19	≥ 18.6"	23	≥ 21.0"	27	≥ 22.0"
13,000 – 18,999 smoke-protected seats:									
1–9	≥ 12.0"	13	≥ 14.4"	17	≥ 16.8"	21	≥ 19.2"	25	≥ 21.6"
10	≥ 12.6"	14	≥ 15.0"	18	≥ 17.4"	22	≥ 19.8"	26	≥ 22.0"
11	≥ 13.2"	15	≥ 15.6"	19	≥ 18.0"	23	≥ 20.4"	27	≥ 22.0"
12	≥ 13.8"	16	≥ 16.2"	20	≥ 18.6"	24	≥ 21.0"	28	≥ 22.0"
19,000 – 21,999 smoke-protected seats:									
1–10	≥ 12.0"	14	≥ 14.4"	18	≥ 16.8"	22	≥ 19.2"	26	≥ 21.6"
11	≥ 12.6"	15	≥ 15.0"	19	≥ 17.4"	23	≥ 19.8"	27	≥ 22.0"
12	≥ 13.2"	16	≥ 15.6"	20	≥ 18.0"	24	≥ 20.4"	28	≥ 22.0"
13	≥ 13.8"	17	≥ 16.2"	21	≥ 18.6"	25	≥ 21.0"	29	≥ 22.0"
≥ 22,000 smoke-protected seats:									
1–11	≥ 12.0"	15	≥ 14.4"	19	≥ 16.8"	23	≥ 19.2"	27	≥ 21.6"
12	≥ 12.6"	16	≥ 15.0"	20	≥ 17.4"	24	≥ 19.8"	28	≥ 22.0"
13	≥ 13.2"	17	≥ 15.6"	21	≥ 18.0"	25	≥ 20.4"	29	≥ 22.0"
14	≥ 13.8"	18	≥ 16.2"	22	≥ 18.6"	26	≥ 21.0"	30	≥ 22.0"

Source: IBC Table 1024.10.1

1024 Assembly

1024.11 Assembly aisle walking surfaces

- Aisles with a gradient must have the following configurations:

Aisle Slope	Aisle configuration required
≤ 1:8	Ramp with slip-resistant surface
> 1:8	Treads and risers = to width of aisle

Note: The following are cited as governing the treads and risers cited above:
1024.11.1, "Treads."
1024.11.2, "Risers."
1024.11.3, "Tread contrasting marking stripe."

1024.11.1 Treads

- Treads in aisle steps must comply with the following:
  - Depth required is ≥ 11".
  - Variation in adjacent tread depth is limited to ≤ $^3/_{16}$".

1024.11.2 Risers

- Risers of aisle stairs with the same gradient as adjacent seating are governed as follows:
  - Required riser height is ≥ 4".
  - Required riser height is ≤ 8" where sightlines permit.
  - Required riser height is ≤ 9" where required by sightlines.
- Variations in riser height are limited to those necessary for changes in the slope of seating.
- Riser height is to be uniform in each flight.
- Adjacent riser heights which vary more than $^3/_{16}$" must be identified as follows:
  - A distinctive stripe must be on the nosing of a tread next to a nonuniform riser as follows:
    Width of stripe to be ≥ 1" and ≤ 2".
    Appearance of stripe to be distinctly different from strips marking other tread edges.

1024.11.3 Tread contrasting marking stripe

- Tread edges which are not readily apparent during descent must be marked as follows:
  - A stripe contrasting with the appearance of the tread is required on each nosing as follows:
    Width of marking stripe is to be ≥ 1" and ≤ 2".
    Marking must make treads readily apparent during descent.

1024 Assembly

1024.12 Seat stability

- Seats are not required to be fastened to the floor in the following applications:
  - ≤ 200 seats without ramped or tiered floors for the seating.
  - > 200 seats where both of the following apply:
    Where floors for seating are neither ramped nor tiered.
    Where seats are joined together in groups ≥ 3 seats.
  - Seating at tables without ramped or tiered floors for the seating.
  - ≤ 200 seats where all of the following apply:
    Where flexibility of seating layout is integral with the function of the space.
    Where seating is on tiered levels.
    Where plans for seating, tiers, and aisles are submitted for approval.
  - Groups ≤ 14 seats with both of the following conditions:
    Where the seats are separated from other seating by any of the following:
      Railings or guards.
      Low walls or similar barriers.
    Where floors are level.
  - Seats for musicians or other performers with the following conditions:
    Where the seats are separated from other seating by any of the following:
      Railings or guards.
      Low walls or similar barriers.
- In all other places of assembly, seats must be fastened to the floor.

1024.13 Handrails

- This section addresses the following in places of assembly:
  - Ramped aisles.
  - Stepped aisles.
- Handrails are not required as follows:
  - Where a guard meets handrail, the graspability requirement is as follows:
    The guard is located at the side of the aisle.
- Handrails are not required for ramped aisles where both of the following apply:
  - Where the slope is ≤ 1:8.
  - Where seating is on both sides.
- In other cases, handrails are required as follows:
  - For aisle stairs.
  - For ramped aisles sloping ≥ 1:15.

1024 Assembly

1024.13.1 Discontinuous handrails

- This section addresses aisles where handrails are required.
- The following applies where seating is on both sides of an aisle:
    - Handrails must be discontinuous as follows:
        Gaps in handrails must be spaced as follows:
        At intervals ≤ 5 rows of seating.
        Clear width in handrail gaps is to be as follows:
        ≥ 22" and ≤ 36".
        Measured horizontally.
        The following handrail details are to be rounded:
        Terminations.
        Bends.

1024.13.2 Intermediate handrails

- Where handrails occur in the center of aisle stairs, the following applies:
    - A second handrail is required at 12" (±) below the main handrail.

> **Case study: Fig. 1024.13.2.** The handrail complies with requirements of 1024.13, 1024.13.1, and 1024.13.2. It is provided in the center of stepped aisles where seats are on both sides; it has a 2nd handrail below the top; and it is discontinuous with rounded corners. The intermediate handrail is 12" lower than the main handrail as required.

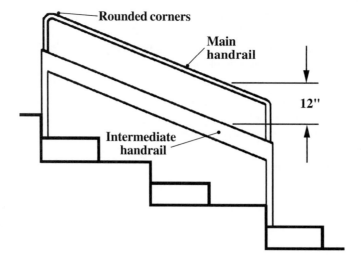

Fig. 1024.13.2. Elevation of handrail. Newman University Sports and Fine Arts Center. Wichita, Kansas. Gossen Livingston Associates, Inc., Architecture. Wichita, Kansas.

1024 Assembly

1024.14.1 Cross aisles

- Cross aisles > 30" above an adjacent level require guards as follows:
  - Guards must be ≥ 42" high.
  - Guards must meet opening and other requirements.
- Cross aisles ≤ 30" above an adjacent lower level are governed as follows:
  - Guards are not required in the following case:
    Where the backs of seats on the lower level extend ≥ 24" above the aisle.
  - In other cases, guards ≥ 26" high are required.

  Note: Section 1012, "Guards," is cited as the source of requirements for guards required by this section.

1024.14.2 Sightline-constrained guard heights

- This section does not apply to the edge of a floor or footboard at the ends of aisles.

  Note: 1024.14.3, "Guards at the end of aisles," is cited as governing the barriers at the end of aisles that are not addressed in this section.

- A guard is required at bleachers as follows:
  - Where the floor or footboard is > 24" above the adjacent level.
  - Guards must be ≥ 26" high in the following location:
    Where a higher barrier would obstruct sightlines of adjacent seating.
- A fascia or guard is required in other locations as follows:
  - Where a floor or foot board is > 30" above the adjacent level.
  - Barriers must be ≥ 26" high in the following location:
    Where a higher barrier would obstruct sightlines of adjacent seating.

  Note: Section 1012, "Guards," is cited as the source of requirements for guards required by this section.

1024.14.3 Guards at the end of aisles

- Where the end of an aisle is > 30" above the adjacent level, a barrier is required as follows:
  - Barrier must meet guard requirements.
  - Barrier must extend the full width of the aisle.
  - Barrier must be ≥ 36" high.
  - The diagonal distance between the following points must be ≥ 42":
    The top of the barrier and the nosing of the nearest tread.

  Note: Section 1012, "Guards," is cited as governing these guards.

1024.15 Bench seating

- The capacity of bench seating is determined as follows:
  - Number of seats = bench length ÷ 18".

Case study: Fig. 1024.14.1. The floor of the balcony cross aisle is 8' -11" above the floor of the adjacent lower level seating, which is greater than the 30" maximum. The edge of the cross aisle, therefore, requires a guard ≥ 3'-6" high as provided.

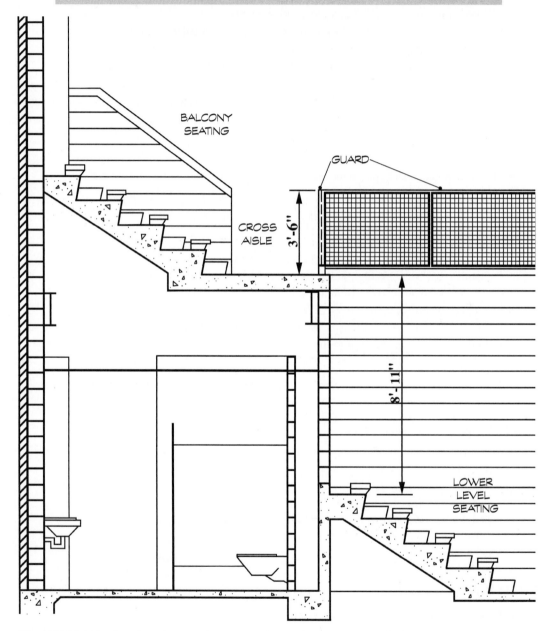

Fig. 1024.14.1. Section of seating at swimming pool. High School 6, Cypress-Fairbanks Independent School District. Harris County, Texas. PBK Architects, Inc. Houston, Texas.

1025 Emergency Escape and Rescue

1025.1 General

- This section series addresses emergency escape and rescue openings as follows:
  - In occupancies R and I-1.
- Such openings are not required in the following cases:
  - In buildings other than R-3, where either of the following conditions apply:
    - Where the building is sprinklered as per NFPA 13 and 13R.
    - Where sleeping rooms have a door to a corridor as follows:
      - Corridor has a fire-resistance rating.
      - Corridor provides access in opposite directions to 2 remote exits.
  - In high-rise buildings.

  Note: Section 403, "High-Rise Buildings," is cited as describing buildings to which this section series does not apply.

  - In basements or sleeping rooms with the following doors:
    - Exit door or exit access door as follows:
      - Opens directly to one of the following:
        - Public street or alley.
        - Yard or egress court.
        - Exterior exit balcony which opens directly to one of the following:
          - Public street or alley.
          - Yard or egress court.
  - In either of the following basements:
    - Where ceiling height is < 6'-8".
    - Where both the following apply:
      - There is no habitable space.
      - The area is ≤ 200 sf.
- Such openings may open to a balcony in an atrium where all of the following apply:
  - Where the balcony serves one of the following:
    - Dwelling unit.
    - Sleeping unit.
  - Where the balcony provides access to an exit.
  - Where a means of egress not open to the atrium is provided.

  Note: Section 404, "Atriums," is cited as governing atriums.

- In other cases ≥ 1 exterior escape and rescue opening is required as follows:
  - In sleeping rooms below the 4th story as follows:
    - Includes 4 stories above the grade plane.
  - In basements as follows:
    - In each sleeping room in a basement.
    - In basement space that does not adjoin a sleeping room.
  - Openings must open directly into one of the following:
    - Public street or alley.
    - Yard or egress court.

1025 Emergency Escape and Rescue

1025.2 Minimum size

- Sizes required for emergency escape and rescue openings are as follows:

Location	Clear area required
At grade floor	$\geq$ 5.0 sf
Other locations	$\geq$ 5.7 sf

1025.2.1 Minimum dimensions

- Dimensions required for emergency escape and rescue openings are as follows:

Clear height required	Clear width required
$\geq$ 2'	$\geq$ 1'-8"

- Normal operation of the opening must yield the required clear dimensions.

1025.3 Maximum height from floor

- Height of emergency escape and rescue openings is limited as follows:
  - The bottom of the clear opening must be $\leq$ 3'-8" from the floor.

1025.4 Operational constraints

- Emergency escape and rescue openings must be operable as follows:
  - From inside the room.
  - Without the use of keys or tools.
- The following devices may cover such openings where the conditions indicated apply:
  - Devices:
    Bars.
    Grilles.
    Grates.
    Similar devices.
  - Required conditions:
    The size requirements for the opening may not be reduced.
    The device must be openable from inside the room as follows:
      Without keys or tools.
      Without a force greater than that required for the opening itself.
    Smoke detectors must be provided in the following case:
      Where devices are installed in existing buildings for all alterations.

Note: The following are cited as the sources of additional requirements:
   1025.2, "Minimum size," governs the size of the opening that must remain available after any covering device is installed.
   907.2.10, "Single- and multiple-station smoke alarms," governs the smoke detector required where covering devices are installed in existing buildings.

1025 Emergency Escape and Rescue

1025.5 Window wells

- This section addresses emergency escape and rescue openings below grade.
- Where the finished sill is below adjacent grade, a window well is required.

   Note: 1025.1, "Minimum size," is cited as a source of requirements for window wells.
   1025.2, "Ladders or steps," is cited as a source of requirements for window wells.

1025.5.1 Minimum size

- Window wells serving emergency escape and rescue openings must have the following size:
  ○ Window well must allow escape and rescue opening to fully open.
  ○ All horizontal dimensions of the window well to be ≥ 3'.
  ○ Window well must be ≥ 9 sf in plan.

1025.5.2 Ladder s or steps

- This section addresses ladders or steps in window wells serving emergency escape and rescue openings.
- Ladders or steps required by this section are not governed by stair requirements.

   Note: Section 1009, "Stairways and Handrails," is cited as the requirements that are waived for ladders and steps required by this section.

- Approved ladders or steps must be provided in window wells ≥ 3'8" in depth as follows:
  ○ Must be permanently affixed.
  ○ Must have an inside width ≥ 12".
  ○ Must project ≥ 3" from the wall.
  ○ Rungs or steps must be spaced ≤ 1'6" center to center vertically.
  ○ Must extend full height of well.
  ○ Must not protrude > 6" into required dimensions of well.
  ○ Must not be obstructed by the escape and rescue opening.

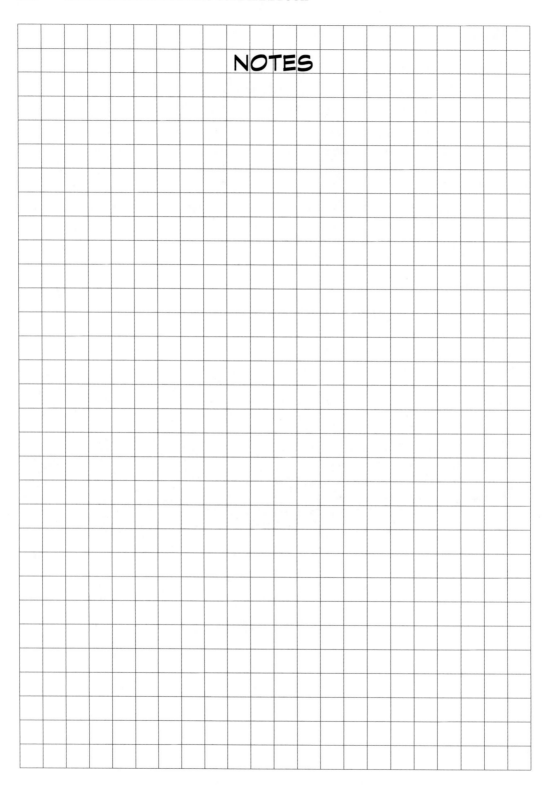

NOTES

11

Accessibility

Hot Springs Police Department New Headquarters.
Hot Springs National Park, Arkansas. *(partial elevation)*
Cromwell Architects Engineers. Little Rock, Arkansas.

1102 Definitions

1102.1 Definitions *(part 1 of 3)*

- **Accessible**
  - A construction that meets the requirements of this chapter as follows:
    Site.
    Building.
    Facility.

- **Accessible route**
  - A path that meets the requirements of this chapter as follows:
    Continuous.
    Unobstructed.

- **Accessible unit**
  - A unit as follows that meets the requirements of this chapter and other standards:
    Dwelling unit.
    Sleeping unit.

  Note: ICC A117.1, "Accessible and Usable Buildings and Facilities," Chapter 1 through Chapter 9, is cited as governing accessible units.

- **Circulation path**
  - A pedestrian route in one of the following locations:
    Outside.
    Inside.

- **Common use**
  - The following items with all the characteristics listed below:
    Items:
      Circulation paths.
      Rooms.
      Spaces.
      Elements.
    Characteristics:
      Exterior or interior.
      Not for the public.
      Used by ≥ two persons.

- **Detectable warning**
  - A standardized feature warning of hazards:
    On a walking surface.
    On other elements.
  - Detectable by visually impaired persons.

1102 Definitions

1102.1 Definitions *(part 2 of 3)*

- **Dwelling unit or sleeping unit, multistory**
  - Has habitable space on > 1 story.

- **Dwelling unit or sleeping unit, Type A**
  - Complies fully with accessibility requirements.

    Note: ICC A117.1, "Accessible and Usable Buildings and Facilities," is cited as the source of accessibility requirements.

- **Dwelling unit or sleeping unit, Type B**
  - Consistent with the Fair Housing Act.
  - Less accessible than a Type A dwelling unit.

    Note: ICC A117.1, "Accessible and Usable Buildings and Facilities," is cited as the source of accessibility requirements.

- **Employee work area**
  - A space with all the following characteristics:
    Used by employees only.
    Used for work only.
  - Does not include the following:
    Corridors.
    Toilet rooms.
    Kitchenettes.
    Break rooms.

- **Facility**
  - The following in whole or part:
    Building.
    Structure.
    Site improvements.
    Elements.
    Pedestrian routes within a site.
    Vehicular routes within a site.

- **Intended to be occupied as a residence**
  - A dwelling unit or sleeping unit as follows:
    Usable as a place to live for either of the following time periods:
    Full time.
    Part time.

1102 Definitions

1102.1 Definitions *(part 3 of 3)*

- **Multilevel assembly seating**
  - Either of the following seating arrangements:
    Groups of multiple rows of seating as follows:
    Where each group is at a level different from the other.
    Box seats accessed as follows:
    From a level different from the level on which the seats set.

- **Public entrance**
  - An entrance other than either of the following:
    Service entrance.
    Restricted entrance.

- **Public-use areas**
  - Space available to the public as follows:
    Interior.
    Exterior.

- **Restricted entrance**
  - An entrance with controlled common use.
  - Includes neither of the following:
    Public entrance.
    Service entrance.

- **Self-service storage facility**
  - A self-service construction for either of the following:
    Rented for storage purposes.
    Leased for storage purposes.

- **Service entrance**
  - An entrance mainly for deliveries.

- **Site**
  - Land defined by any of the following at its edges:
    Property line.
    Public right-of-way.

- **Wheelchair space**
  - A space designed to accommodate the following:
    A wheelchair.
    The occupant of a wheelchair.

1103 Scoping Requirements

1103.1 Where required

- Other constructions in the categories indicated below are required to be accessible to persons with physical disabilities as follows:
    - Constructions:
        Temporary.
        Permanent.
    - Categories:
        Buildings.
        Structures.
        Sites.
        Facilities.

1103.2 General exceptions

- This section series identifies certain facilities not required to be accessible as follows:
    - Sites.
    - Buildings.
    - Facilities.
    - Elements.

1103.2.2 Existing buildings

- Accessibility of existing buildings is governed elsewhere in the code.

    Note: Section 3409, "Accessibility for existing buildings," is cited as governing.

1103.2.3 Employee work areas

- Work areas with all the following characteristics have no accessibility requirements:
    - < 150 sf.
    - Raised above adjacent grade or floor ≥ 7" as follows:
        The height must be necessary for the function of the space.
- Other employee work areas must meet accessibility requirements only as follows:
    - For certain visible fire alarm requirements.

    Note: 907.9.1.2, "Employee work areas," is cited as governing the alarm requirements.

    - For certain accessible means of egress requirements.

    Note: 1007, "Accessible means of egress," is cited as governing egress requirements.

    - For certain circulation routes.

    Note: 1104.3.1, "Employee work areas," is cited as governing circulation routes.

    - Disabled persons must be able to do the following:
        Approach the work area.
        Enter the work area.
        Exit the work area.

1103 Scoping Requirements

1103.2.4 Detached dwellings

- The following dwellings are not required to be accessible:
  - Detached 1-family.
  - Detached 2-family.
  - Accessory structures.
  - Associated sites.
  - Associated facilities.

1103.2.5 Utility buildings

- Agricultural buildings require accessible access to the following areas:
  - Paved work areas.
  - Areas open to the public.
- Private garages are required to meet the requirements of this chapter as follows:
  - Where they are required to have accessible parking.
- Carports are required to meet the requirements of this chapter as follows:
  - Where they are required to have accessible parking.
- Other facilities in occupancy U need not meet the requirements of this chapter.

1103.2.6 Construction sites

- The following elements of construction sites are not required to be accessible:
  - Structures.
  - Sites.
  - Equipment.
  - Materials storage.
  - Scaffolding.
  - Bridging.
  - Materials hoists.
  - Construction trailers.

1103.2.7 Raised areas

- Raised areas similar to the types listed below and used primarily for the following are not required to be accessible or on an accessible route:
  - Uses:
    - Security.
    - Life safety.
    - Fire safety.
  - Types:
    - Observation galleries.
    - Lifeguard stands.
    - Prison guard towers.
    - Fire towers.

1103 Scoping Requirements

1103.2.8 Limited access spaces

- Nonoccupiable spaces with access only by the following need not be accessible:
  - Catwalks.
  - Ladders.
  - Freight elevators.
  - Crawl spaces.
  - Very narrow passageways.

1103.2.9 Equipment spaces

- Spaces such as the types indicated below that are accessed only for the following functions are not required to be accessible:
  - Functions:
    Maintenance.
    Repair.
    Monitoring.
  - Types:
    Communication equipment rooms.
    Electric substations.
    Elevator penthouses.
    Elevator pits.
    Equipment catwalks.
    Highway utility facilities.
    Mechanical equipment rooms.
    Piping catwalks.
    Sewage treatment stations.
    Sewage treatment pump rooms.
    Transformer vaults.
    Tunnel utility facilities.
    Water treatment stations.
    Water treatment pump rooms.

1103.2.10 Single occupant structures

- Facilities occupied by a single person such as the example indicated below and accessed only as follows are not required to be accessible:
  - Access:
    By routes elevated above grade.
    By routes below grade.
  - Example:
    Tollbooths.

1103 Scoping Requirements

1103.2.11 Residential Group R-1

- Buildings in occupancy R-1 meeting both of the following conditions:
  - ≤ 5 sleeping units for rent.
  - Serve as the residence of the proprietor.

1103.2.12 Day care facilities

- Where a residence has a day care component, the following applies:
  - Only the day care component must be accessible.

1103.2.13 Detention and correctional facilities

- Common use areas with all the following characteristics governed as indicated below:
  - Characteristics:
    - Where utilized only by any of the following:
      - Inmates.
      - Detainees.
      - Security personnel.
    - Which are not holding cells.
    - Which are not used for housing as follows:
      - Where required to be accessible.
  - Requirements:
    - The areas are not required to be accessible.
    - The areas are not required to be on an accessible route.

1103.2.14 Fuel-dispensing systems

- Devices of a fuel-dispensing system which are operable are required to meet standards other than this code.

  Note: One of the following sections is cited as governing the devices noted above: ICC A117.1, "Accessible and Usable Buildings and Facilities," section 308.2.1 or 308.3.1.

1104 Accessible Route

1104.1 Site arrival points

- No accessible route is required between the following locations in the circumstance noted:
  - Locations:
    Site arrival point.
    Facility entrance.
  - Circumstance:
    Where only one access between the two locations is as follows:
    A vehicle route with no pedestrian accommodation.
- Otherwise, accessible routes to an accessible entrance are required from the following:
  - Accessible passenger loading areas.
  - Accessible parking.
  - Public streets.
  - Public transportation stops.
  - Public sidewalks.

Case study: Fig. 1104.1. An accessible route is provided as required from accessible parking to an accessible building entrance. Included is a ramp meeting slope requirements.

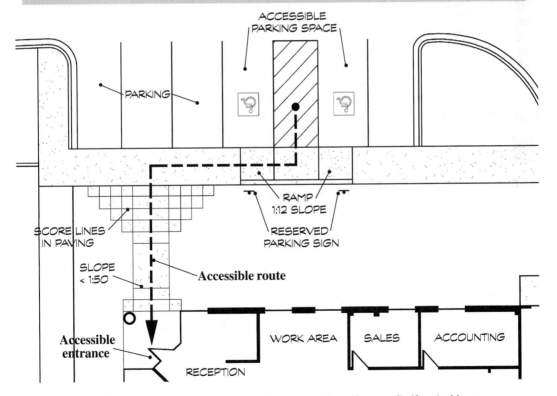

Fig. 1104.1. Partial site plan at entry. Garments to Go. Bastrop, Texas. Spencer Godfrey Architects. Round Rock, Texas.

1104 Accessible Route

1104.2 Within a site

- Accessible routes are not required between accessible facilities in the following case:
  - Where the only means of access between facilities is vehicular as follows:
    No pedestrian access is provided.
- Otherwise, ≥ 1 accessible route is required connecting the following within a site:
  - Accessible buildings.
  - Accessible facilities.
  - Accessible elements.
  - Accessible spaces.

1104.3 Connected spaces

- Fixed seating in assembly areas as follows is governed as noted below:
  - Fixed seating:
    Which is required to be accessible.
    Which does not have the following:
      Wheelchair spaces required to be on an accessible route.
      Designated aisle seats required to be on an accessible route.
  - Requirements:
    This seating is not required to be on an accessible route.
- Mezzanines are not required to be on an accessible route in either of the following cases:
  - In facilities of only 1 story.
  - In facilities > one story as follows:
    Where the stories are not connected by an accessible route.

  Note: 1104.4, "Multilevel buildings and facilities," is cited as governing accessible routes in multilevel facilities.

- In other cases an accessible route is required to connect the following:
  - Each part of a building required to be accessible.
  - Building entrances required to be accessible.
  - Pedestrian walkways required to be accessible.
  - The public way.
- The following applies where only 1 accessible route is provided:
  - In an accessible dwelling unit the route may pass through the following:
    A kitchen.
    A storage room.
  - Otherwise, the route may not pass through the following or similar spaces:
    A kitchen.
    A storage room.
    A closet.
    A restroom.

Case study: Fig. 1104.2. All buildings on the site are accessible and all are on accessible routes as indicated. The site plan complies with the code regarding accessibility.

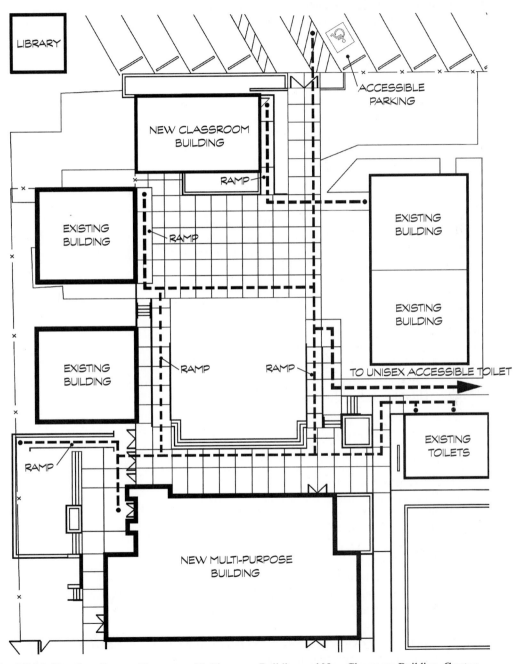

Fig. 1104.2. Site plan. Creston Elementary Multipurpose Building and New Classroom Building. Creston, California. Phillips Metsch Sweeney Moore Architects. Santa Barbara, California.

1104 Accessible Route

1104.3.1 Employee work areas

- The following common use routes need not be accessible routes:
  - Where the work area is < 300 sf as follows:
    - Perimeter is bounded by any of the following permanent fixtures:
      - Partitions.
      - Counters.
      - Casework.
      - Furnishings.
  - Where the work area is integral to equipment.
  - Where the work area is unprotected from the weather.
- In other cases common use routes are governed as follows:
  - They must be accessible routes.

1104.3.2 Press boxes

- This section addresses press boxes in assembly areas.
- The following press boxes need not be on accessible routes:
  - Those in bleachers with both the following chacteristics:
    - With points of entry at 1 level only.
    - Total area of all press boxes must be ≤ 500 sf.
  - Where freestanding with both the following characteristics:
    - Raised ≥ 12'.
    - Total area of all press boxes must be ≤ 500 sf.
- In other cases press boxes are governed as follows:
  - They must be on accessible routes.

1104.4 Multilevel buildings and facilities *(part 1 of 2)*

- Accessible routes are required for the following:
  - Occupancy M tenant spaces as follows:
    - ≥ 5 tenants.
  - Occupancy B or I as follows:
    - Health care provider offices.
  - Occupancy A-3 or B passenger facilities as follows:
    - Airports.
    - Other transportation.
- Otherwise, accessible routes are not required for the following:
  - For floors above and below accessible levels as follows:
    - Not required in the following case:
      - Total area of floors above and below an accessible level is ≤ 3000 sf as follows:
        - Includes mezzanines.
  - In a 2-story building:
    - Not required between stories where 1 story has all the following characteristics:
      - Occupant load is ≤ 5 people.
      - With no public space.

1104 Accessible Route

1104.4 Multilevel buildings and facilities *(part 2 of 2)*

- ○ In occupancies A, I, R, S as follows:
    Not required from an accessible level to a level with none of the following:
    Accessible elements.
    Accessible spaces required elsewhere in this chapter.

    Note: The following are cited as requiring accessible spaces in the occupancies above:
        Section 1107, "Dwelling Units and Sleeping Units."
        Section 1108, "Special Occupancies."

- ○ Not required for an airport control tower control room.
- ○ Not required on the floor directly below an airport control tower control room.
- ● In other cases the following applies to multiple levels including mezzanines:
    - ○ ≥ 1 accessible route is required to connect each accessible level.

1104.5 Location

- ● Accessible routes must have one of the following relationships to general circulation:
    - ○ Accessible routes must coincide with general circulation routes.
    - ○ Accessible routes must be located in the same area as general circulation routes.
- ● The location of accessible routes is governed as follows:
    - ○ Accessible routes are not required to be interior in the following case:
        From parking garages contained within and serving Type B dwelling units.
    - ○ In other locations, the accessible route must be interior as follows:
        Where the general circulation path is interior.

1104.6 Security barriers

- ● The following security barriers must not obstruct the routes listed below:
    - ○ Barriers:
        Bollards.
        Checkpoints.
        Others.
    - ○ Routes:
        Accessible routes.
        Accessible means of egress.
- ● An accessible route must bypass the following obstructions as noted below:
    - ○ Obstructions:
        Security screening devices such as the following:
            Metal detectors.
            Fluoroscopes.
            Similar devices.
    - ○ Requirements:
        Accessible route must provide users visual contact with personal items as follows:
            To the same degree as provided to persons passing through the screening devices.

1105 Accessible Entrances

1105.1 Required

- Entrances are not required to be accessible in the following cases:
  - To spaces not required to be accessible.
  - Loading and service entrances that are not the sole entrance to the following:
    A building.
    A tenant space.
- In other locations, accessible entrances are required as follows:
  - As required by subsequent sections in this series.

    Note: The following are cited as requiring accessible entrances:
    1105.1.1, "Parking garage entrances."
    1105.1.2, "Entrances from tunnels or elevated walkways."
    1105.1.3, "Restricted entrances."
    1105.1.4, "Entrances for inmates or detainees."
    1105.1.5, "Service entrances."
    1105.1.6, "Tenant spaces, dwelling units and sleeping units."

  - $\geq$ half of the public entrances provided in addition to those noted above.

1105.1.1 Parking garage entrances

- The following building entrances are required to be accessible:
  - Any access provided directly from a parking structure.

1105.1.2 Entrances from tunnels or elevated walkways

- $\geq$ 1 accesible entrance to a building is required as follows:
  - From any of the following elements that provide access directly to a building:
    Pedestrian tunnels.
    Elevated walkways.

1105.1.3 Restricted entrances

- $\geq$ 1 accessible restricted entrance to a building is required as follows:
  - Where $\geq$ 1 restricted entrance is provided.

1105 Accessible Entrances

1105.1.4 Entrances for inmates or detainees

- The following buildings used by any of the personnel listed have the requirement indicated below:
  - Buildings:
    Judicial facilities.
    Detention facilities.
    Correctional facilities.
  - Personnel:
    Inmates.
    Detainees.
    Security personnel.
  - Requirements:
    ≥ 1 accessible entrance is required at each building as follows:
    Among any entrances used only by the personnel listed above.

1105.1.5 Service entrances

- The service entrance must be accessible in the following case:
  - Where it is the only entrance to either of the following:
    A building.
    A tenant space.

1105.1.6 Tenant spaces, dwelling units and sleeping units

- Accessible entrances are not required for the following:
  - Tenant spaces that are not required to be accessible.
  - Dwelling units or sleeping units that are not required to be one of the following:
    Accessible Type A unit.
    Accessible Type B unit.
- In other cases:
  - ≥ 1 accessible entrance is required for the following:
    Each tenant.
    Each dwelling unit.
    Each sleeping unit in a facility.

1106 Parking and Passenger Loading Facilities

1106.1 Required

- This section does not govern accessible parking in the following:
  - Where accessible dwelling units are required in the following occupancies: R-2, R-3.

    Note: 1106.2, "Groups R-2 and R-3," is cited as governing accessible parking in these occupancies.

  - Rehabilitation facilities.

    Note: 1106.3, "Rehabilitation facilities and outpatient physical therapy facilities," is cited as governing accessible parking in these facilities.

  - Parking used exclusively for the following:
    Buses.
    Trucks.
    Other delivery vehicles.
    Law enforcement vehicles.
    Vehicular impound.
    Motors pools as follows:
       Where parking accessed by the public has an accessible passenger loading zone.
- In other parking, the number required to be accessible is as follows:

Table 1106.1   Accessible Parking Spaces Required

Total spaces	Accessible required	Total spaces	Accessible required	Total spaces	Accessible required
1–25	≥ 1	651–700	≥ 14	1501–1600	≥ 26
26–50	≥ 2	701–750	≥ 15	1601–1700	≥ 27
51–75	≥ 3	751–800	≥ 16	1701–1800	≥ 28
76–100	≥ 4	801–850	≥ 17	1801–1900	≥ 29
101–150	≥ 5	851–900	≥ 18	1901–2000	≥ 30
151–200	≥ 6	901–950	≥ 19	2001–2100	≥ 31
201–300	≥ 7	951–1000	≥ 20	2101–2200	≥ 32
301–400	≥ 8	1001–1100	≥ 21	2201–2300	≥ 33
401–500	≥ 9	1101–1200	≥ 22	2301–2400	≥ 34
501–550	≥ 11	1201–1300	≥ 23	2401–2500	≥ 35
551–600	≥ 12	1301–1400	≥ 24	2501–2600	≥ 36
601–650	≥ 13	1401–1500	≥ 25	2601–2700	≥ 37

Source: IBC Table 1106.1.

- The number of accessible parking places required in parking > 2700 total spaces is determined indicated below:
  - Fractions of accessible spaces required are rounded up to the next higher whole number.

  Number of accessible parking spaces = [(Total spaces – 2700) ÷ 100] + 37

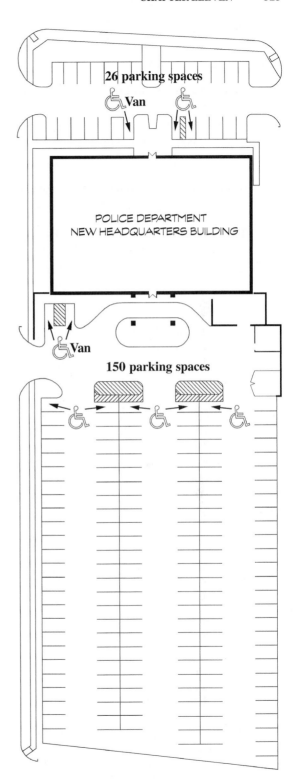

Case study: Fig. 1106.1. The parking lot in front of the occupancy B building has 26 parking spaces. IBC Table 1106.1 requires 2 spaces to be accessible where 26 to 50 regular spaces are provided. 3 accessible spaces are provided, which meets the code requirement. Section 1106.5 requires that 1 of every 6 accessible spaces be van-accessible. 1 van-accessible space is provided in the front parking lot as required.

The parking lot in back of the building has 150 parking spaces. IBC Table 1106.1 requires that 5 spaces be accessible where 101 to 150 regular spaces are provided. 6 accessible parking spaces are provided, which supercede the minimum requirement. 1 van-accessible space is needed since 6 accessible spaces are provided. 2 van-accessible spaces are provided, which is > the minimum requirement.

Fig. 1106.1. Site plan. Hot Springs Police Department New Headquarters. Hot Springs National Park, Arkansas. Cromwell Architects Engineers. Little Rock, Arkansas.

1106 Parking and Passenger Loading Facilities

1106.2 Groups R-2 and R-3

- Accessible parking as listed below is required in the following location:
  - Location:
    Where either of the following dwelling or sleeping units are required:
    Accessible Type A.
    Accessible Type B.
  - Requirements:
    ≥ 1 accessible parking place is required.
    ≥ 2% of the total parking spaces are required to be accessible as listed below:

Table 1106.2   Accessible Parking Required in R-2 and R-3

Total spaces	Accessible required	Total spaces	Accessible required	Total spaces	Accessible required
1–50	≥ 1	451–500	≥ 10	901–950	≥ 19
51–100	≥ 2	501–550	≥ 11	951–1000	≥ 20
101–150	≥ 3	551–600	≥ 12	1001–1050	≥ 21
151–200	≥ 4	601–650	≥ 13	1051–1100	≥ 22
201–250	≥ 5	651–700	≥ 14	1101–1150	≥ 23
251–300	≥ 6	701–750	≥ 15	1151–1200	≥ 24
301–350	≥ 7	751–800	≥ 16	1201–1250	≥ 25
351–400	≥ 8	801–850	≥ 17	1251–1300	≥ 26
401–450	≥ 9	851–900	≥ 18	etc.	

- Accessible parking is required to be within or beneath a building in the following case:
  - Where general parking is provided within or beneath a building.

1106.3 Hospital outpatient facilities

- 10% of the following types of parking must be accessible:
  - Patient and visitor.
- A partial table of parking spaces required to be accessible is provided below:

Table 1106.3   Accessible Parking Required for Hospital Outpatient Facilities

Total spaces	Accessible required	Total spaces	Accessible required	Total spaces	Accessible required
1–10	≥ 1	81–90	≥ 9	161–170	≥ 17
11–20	≥ 2	91–100	≥ 10	171–180	≥ 18
21–30	≥ 3	101–110	≥ 11	181–190	≥ 19
31–40	≥ 4	111–120	≥ 12	191–200	≥ 20
41–50	≥ 5	121–130	≥ 13	201–210	≥ 21
51–60	≥ 6	131–140	≥ 14	211–220	≥ 22
61–70	≥ 7	141–150	≥ 15	221–230	≥ 23
71–80	≥ 8	151–160	≥ 16	etc.	

Case study: Fig. Fig. 1106.2. This occupancy R-2 building provides 136 parking spaces in the parking plan shown. At least 2% of these must be accessible. 4 accessible parking spaces are provided, thus, meeting the minimum requirement of 3. Section 1106.5 requires at least 1 van- accessible space for every 6 or fraction of 6 accessible spaces. 2 van-accessible spaces are provided, thus, meeting the minimum of 1 required. Since parking is provided beneath the building, accessible parking must be provided there as well. The parking garage also meets this requirement and is, therefore, in compliance with the code in all respects.

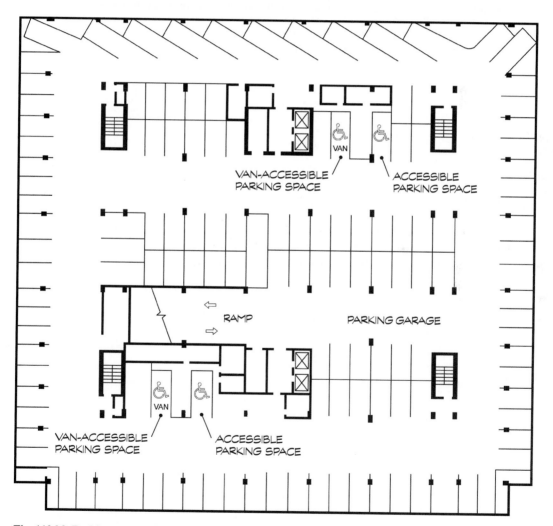

Fig. 1106.2. Parking garage floor plan. Hoyt Street Properties. Portland, Oregon. Ankrom Moisan Associated Architects. Portland, Oregon.

1106 Parking and Passenger Loading Facilities

1106.4 Rehabilitation facilities and outpatient physical therapy facilities

- The requirement listed below applies to the following types of parking:
  - Parking:
    Patients of rehabilitation and physical therapy facilities.
    Visitors to rehabilitation and physical therapy facilities.
  - Requirement:
    The larger of the following numbers of parking places must be accessible:
    1.
    $\geq$ 20% of the parking as noted above.
- A partial table of parking spaces required to be accessible is provided below:

Table 1106.4 Accessible Parking at Rehabilitation and Outpatient Physical Therapy Facilities

Total spaces	Accessible required	Total spaces	Accessible required	Total spaces	Accessible required
1–5	$\geq$ 1	31–35	$\geq$ 7	61–65	$\geq$ 13
6–10	$\geq$ 2	36–40	$\geq$ 8	66–70	$\geq$ 14
11–15	$\geq$ 3	41–45	$\geq$ 9	71–75	$\geq$ 15
16–20	$\geq$ 4	46–50	$\geq$ 10	76–80	$\geq$ 16
21–25	$\geq$ 5	51–55	$\geq$ 11	81–85	$\geq$ 17
26–30	$\geq$ 6	56–60	$\geq$ 12	etc.	

1106.5 Van spaces

- The larger of the following numbers of parking spaces must be van-accessible:
  - 1.
  - $\geq 16^{2}/_{3}$% of accessible parking spaces.
- The required number of van-accessible spaces is also listed below:

Accessible spaces	Accessible van spaces required
1–6	$\geq$ 1
7–12	$\geq$ 2
13–18	$\geq$ 3
19–24	$\geq$ 4
etc.	

1106 Parking and Passenger Loading Facilities

1106.6 Location

- Where parking serves a particular building, the following applies:
  - Accessible parking spaces must be located as follows:
      On the shortest accessible route to the following:
          An accessible building entrance.
- Where parking does not serve a particular building, the following apply:
  - Accessible parking must be located as follows:
      On the shortest accessible route to the following:
          An accessible pedestrian entrance to the parking facility.
- Accessible parking must have the following distribution:
  - Among all the types of parking facilities provided as follows:
      All van-accessible spaces may be located on 1 level.
      Other accessible spaces must be distributed near all accessible entrances.

1106.7 Passenger loading zones

- These facilities are governed by other standards.

    Note: ICC A117.1, "Accessible and Usable Buildings and Facilities," is cited as governing passenger loading zones.

1106.7.1 Continuous loading zones

- Where passenger loading zones are provided, the following applies:
  - An accessible loading zone must be provided as follows:
      In every continuous length of loading zone = 100'.

1106.7.2 Medical facilities

- An accessible passenger loading zone is required as follows:
  - At an accessible entrance to the following facilities with the functions listed below:
      Facilities:
          Licensed medical facilities.
          Licensed long-term care facilities.
      Functions:
          Where people stay > 24 hours per visit.
          Where people receive the following care:
              Physical.
              Medical.

1106.7.3 Valet parking

- An accessible passenger loading zone is required as follows:
  - Where valet parking is provided.

1107 Dwelling Units and Sleeping Units

1107.3 Accessible spaces

- Recreational facilities are not governed by this section.

    Note: 1109.14, "Recreational facilities," is cited as governing these areas.

- Other spaces with all the following characteristics are required to be accessible:
    - Used by following people:
        Public.
        Residents.
    - Serving the following units:
        Accessible.
        Type A units.
        Type B units.
    - Including the following:
        Toilet rooms.
        Bathing rooms.
        Kitchens.
        Living areas.
        Dining areas.
        Patios.
        Terraces.
        Balconies.

1107.4 Accessible Route *(part 1 of 2)*

- For either of the following conditions an accessible route may be omitted in lieu of the substitution listed below:
    - Conditions:
        Where the finished grade slopes > 1:12 between accessible facilities.
        Where physical barriers prevent installation of an accessible route.
    - Substitution:
        A vehicular route as follows:
            With parking at each accessible facility or building.

    Note: Section 1106, "Parking and Passenger Loading Facilities," is cited as governing the parking as required above.

- The following facilities may have a floor surface ≤ 4" below the adjacent interior floor where the conditions below apply:
    - Facilities:
        Exterior decks.
        Patios.
        Balconies.
    - Conditions:
        At Type B dwelling units.
        The facility must have an impervious surface.

1107 Dwelling Units and Sleeping Units

1107.4 Accessible Route (*part 2 of 2*)

- In all other cases, ≥ 1 accessible route is required as follows:
  - Between accessible building entrances and the following elements of the units in the building as noted below:
    Elements:
      Primary entrances.
      Exterior spaces serving the units.
      Interior spaces serving the units.
    Units:
      Accessible dwelling units.
      Type A units.
      Type B units.

1107.5.1.1 Accessible units

- The following occupancy I-1 facilities must be accessible in the quantity indicated below:
  - Facilities:
    Dwelling units and sleeping units.
  - Quantity:
    The greater of the following quantities:
      1 unit.
      ≥ 4% of the units as follows:
        A partial list of units required to be accessible is listed in the table below:

Table 1107.5.1.1   Accessible Occupancy I-1 Dwelling Units and Sleeping Units

Total number of units	Units to be accessible	Total number of units	Units to be accessible
1–25	≥ 1	151–175	≥ 7
26–50	≥ 2	176–200	≥ 8
51–75	≥ 3	201–225	≥ 9
76–100	≥ 4	226–250	≥ 10
101–125	≥ 5	251–275	≥ 11
126–150	≥ 6	276–300	≥ 12

1107.5.1.2 Type B units

- The requirements listed below apply to occupancy I-1 buildings as follows:
  - Buildings:
    Where there are ≥ 4 units used as residences as follows:
      Dwelling units and sleeping units.
  - Requirements:
    Units must be Type B.

  Note: 1107.7, "General exceptions," is cited as permitting the number of Type B units to be reduced based on the absence of elevators and other access problems.

1107 Dwelling Units and Sleeping Units

1107.5.2.1 Accessible units

- The following units in occupancy I-2 nursing homes must be accessible in the quantity indicated below:
  - o Units:
    Dwelling units.
    Sleeping units.
  - o Quantity:
    The number of units that must be accessible is the larger of the following:
    1 unit.
    ≥ half of the total number of units.

1107.5.2.2 Type B units

- The requirements listed below apply to occupancy I-2 nursing homes as follows:
  - o Nursing homes:
    Where there are ≥ 4 of either or both of the following units used as residences:
    Dwelling units.
    Sleeping units.
  - o Requirements:
    Units must be Type B.

    Note: 1107.7, "General exceptions," is cited as permitting the number of Type B units to be reduced based on the absence of elevators and other access problems.

1107.5.3.1 Accessible units *(part 1 of 2)*

- The following units of the facilities in occupancy I-2 listed below must be accessible in the quantity indicated:
  - o Units:
    Dwelling units.
    Sleeping units.
  - o Facilities:
    General-purpose hospitals.
    Psychiatric facilities.
    Detoxification facilities.
    Residential care/assisted living facilities.
  - o Quantity:
    The number of units that must be accessible is the larger of the following:
    1 unit.
    ≥ 10% of the total number of units.

1107 Dwelling Units and Sleeping Units

1107.5.3.1 Accessible units *(part 2 of 2)*

- The following is a partial table showing the number of accessible units required by this section based on the total number of units.

Table 1107.5.3.1   Accessible Dwelling or Sleeping Units Required

Total units	Accessible required	Total units	Accessible required	Total units	Accessible required
1–10	≥ 1	81–90	≥ 9	161–170	≥ 17
11–20	≥ 2	91–100	≥ 10	171–180	≥ 18
21–30	≥ 3	101–110	≥ 11	181–190	≥ 19
31–40	≥ 4	111–120	≥ 12	191–200	≥ 20
41–50	≥ 5	121–130	≥ 13	201–210	≥ 21
51–60	≥ 6	131–140	≥ 14	211–220	≥ 22
61–70	≥ 7	141–150	≥ 15	221–230	≥ 23
71–80	≥ 8	151–160	≥ 16	etc.	

1107.5.3.2 Type B units

- The following units of the facilities in occupancy I-2 listed below have the requirements indicated:
  - Units:
    Dwelling units.
    Sleeping units.
  - Facilities:
    General-purpose hospitals.
    Psychiatric facilities.
    Detoxification facilities.
    Residential care/assisted living facilities.
  - Requirements:
    Units must be Type B.

    Note: 1107.7, "General exceptions," is cited as permitting the number of Type B units to be reduced based on the absence of elevators and other access problems.

1107.5.4 Group I-2 Rehabilitation facilities

- All the following units must be accessible where they are in any of the occupancy I-2 facilities listed below having any of the functions indicated:
  - Units:
    Dwelling units or sleeping units.
  - Facilities:
    Hospitals.
    Rehabilitation facilities.
  - Functions:
    Treatment of mobility problems.

1107 Dwelling Units and Sleeping Units

1107.5.5.1 Group I-3 sleeping units

- The following units must be accessible in the quantity indicated below:
  - Units:
    Dwelling units.
    Sleeping units.
  - Quantity:
    The number of units required to be accessible is the larger of the following:
    1 unit.
    $\geq$ 2% of the total number of units as follows:
    The partial table below lists number of accessible units required.

Table 1107.5.5.1   Accessible Dwelling Units and Sleeping Units in Occupancy I-3

Total units	Accessible required	Total units	Accessible required	Total units	Accessible required
1–50	≥ 1	451–500	≥ 10	901–950	≥ 19
51–100	≥ 2	501–550	≥ 11	951–1000	≥ 20
101–150	≥ 3	551–600	≥ 12	1001–1050	≥ 21
151–200	≥ 4	601–650	≥ 13	1051–1100	≥ 22
201–250	≥ 5	651–700	≥ 14	1101–1150	≥ 23
251–300	≥ 6	701–750	≥ 15	1151–1200	≥ 24
301–350	≥ 7	751–800	≥ 16	1201–1250	≥ 25
351–400	≥ 8	801–850	≥ 17	1251–1300	≥ 26
401–450	≥ 9	851–900	≥ 18	etc.	

1107.5.5.2 Special holding cells and special housing cells or rooms

- The following occupancy I-3 spaces are not required to have grab bars:
  - Spaces designed to prevent suicide as follows:
    Without protrusions.
- In other cases, one of each kind of the following I-3 spaces such as those used as listed below must be accessible where provided:
  - Spaces:
    Special holding cells.
    Special housing cells or rooms.
  - Uses:

    Orientation   Protective custody
    Administrative detention   Disciplinary detention
    Segregation   Detoxification
    Medical isolation

Note: 1107.5.5.1, "Group I-3 sleeping units," is cited as identifying required accessible spaces that are in addition to those listed in this section.

1107 Dwelling Units and Sleeping Units

1107.5.5.3 Medical care facilities

- Where the following occupancy I-3 spaces are required, the following applies:
  - They are in addition to the cells listed below where also required:
    Spaces:
    Accessible patient sleeping units.
    Accessible cells.
    Cells:
    Medical isolation cells.

    Note: 1107.5.5.2, "Special holding cells and special housing cells or rooms," is cited as requiring medical isolation cells.

1107.6.1 Accessible units *(part 1 of 2)*

- In occupancy R-1 the following units must be provided as required below:
  - Units:
    Accessible dwelling units.
    Accessible sleeping units.
  - Requirements:
    The number of accessible units required is based on the following:
    The total numer of units on the site.
    Accessible units must be distributed as follows:
    Among the various classes of units.
    Roll-in showers in accessible units must have the following:
    A permanent folding seat.
    Where > 2500 units are on a site, the number of accessible units required is determined as follows:
    Units to be accessible and requiring a roll-in shower:

    [(Total accommodations on site – 2500) ÷100] + 25

    Units to be accessible and not requiring a roll-in shower:

    [(Total accommodations on site – 2500) ÷ 100] + 35

    Total accessible units required:

    {[(Total accommodations on site – 2500) ÷ 100] × 2} + 60

    Where ≤ 2500 units are on a site, the number of accessible units required is listed in the following table:

1107 Dwelling Units and Sleeping Units

1107.6.1 Accessible units *(part 2 of 2)*

Table 1107.6.1   Accessible Dwelling Units and Sleeping Units Required

Total number of units on site	Required accessible units with roll-in shower	Required accessible units, no roll-in shower	Total accessible units required
1–25	≥ 0	≥ 1	≥ 1
26–50	≥ 0	≥ 2	≥ 2
51–75	≥ 1	≥ 3	≥ 4
76–100	≥ 1	≥ 4	≥ 5
101–150	≥ 2	≥ 5	≥ 7
151–200	≥ 2	≥ 6	≥ 8
201–300	≥ 3	≥ 7	≥ 10
301–400	≥ 4	≥ 8	≥ 12
401–500	≥ 4	≥ 9	≥ 13
501–533	≥ 6	≥ 10	≥ 16
534–566	≥ 6	≥ 11	≥ 17
567–600	≥ 6	≥ 12	≥ 18
601–633	≥ 7	≥ 12	≥ 19
634–666	≥ 7	≥ 13	≥ 20
667–700	≥ 7	≥ 14	≥ 21
701–733	≥ 8	≥ 14	≥ 22
734–766	≥ 8	≥ 15	≥ 23
767–800	≥ 8	≥ 16	≥ 24
801–833	≥ 9	≥ 16	≥ 25
834–866	≥ 9	≥ 17	≥ 26
867–900	≥ 9	≥ 18	≥ 27
901–933	≥ 10	≥ 18	≥ 28
934–966	≥ 10	≥ 19	≥ 29
967–1000	≥ 10	≥ 20	≥ 30
1001–1100	≥ 11	≥ 21	≥ 32
1101–1200	≥ 12	≥ 22	≥ 34
1201–1300	≥ 13	≥ 23	≥ 36
1301–1400	≥ 14	≥ 24	≥ 38
1401–1500	≥ 15	≥ 25	≥ 40
1501–1600	≥ 16	≥ 26	≥ 42
1601–1700	≥ 17	≥ 27	≥ 44
1701–1800	≥ 18	≥ 28	≥ 46
1801–1900	≥ 19	≥ 29	≥ 48
1901–2000	≥ 20	≥ 30	≥ 50
2001–2100	≥ 21	≥ 31	≥ 52
2101–2200	≥ 22	≥ 32	≥ 54
2201–2300	≥ 23	≥ 33	≥ 56
2301–2400	≥ 24	≥ 34	≥ 58
2401–2500	≥ 25	≥ 35	≥ 60

Source: IBC Table 1107.6.1.1.

1107 Dwelling Units and Sleeping Units

1107.6.1.2 Type B units

- The requirements listed below apply to occupancy R-1 buildings as follows:
    - Buildings:
      Where there are ≥ 4 of either or both of the following units used as residences:
      Dwelling and sleeping units.
    - Requirements:
      Units must be Type B.

    Note: 1107.7, "General exceptions," is cited as permitting the number of Type B units to be reduced based on the absence of elevators and other access problems.

1107.6.2.1.1 Type A units

- This section governs the following buildings in occupancy R-2:
    - Apartment buildings.
    - Monasteries.
    - Convents.
- The requirements below apply where > 20 of any of the following units are provided:
    - Units:
      Dwelling and sleeping units.
    - Requirements:
      Type A units must be distributed among the following:
        All classes of units provided.
      The number of Type A units required is the greater of the following:
        1 unit.
        2% of the total units on the site as follows:
          Existing units on the site are not counted in the total units.
          All other units on the site are counted in the total number of units.
      The following table is a partial listing of the number of Type A units required:

Table 1107.6.2.1.1   Type A Units Required in Apt. Bldgs., Monasteries, and Convents

Total units	Type A required	Total units	Type A required	Total units	Type A required
1–50	≥ 1	451–500	≥ 10	901–950	≥ 19
51–100	≥ 2	501–550	≥ 11	951–1000	≥ 20
101–150	≥ 3	551–600	≥ 12	1001–1050	≥ 21
151–200	≥ 4	601–650	≥ 13	1051–1100	≥ 22
201–250	≥ 5	651–700	≥ 14	1101–1150	≥ 23
251–300	≥ 6	701–750	≥ 15	1151–1200	≥ 24
301–350	≥ 7	751–800	≥ 16	1201–1250	≥ 25
351–400	≥ 8	801–850	≥ 17	1251–1300	≥ 26
401–450	≥ 9	851–900	≥ 18	etc.	

Note: 1107.7, "General exceptions," is cited as permitting the number of Type A units to be reduced based on the absence of elevators and other access problems.

1107 Dwelling Units and Sleeping Units

1107.6.2.1.2 Type B units

- This section governs the following buildings in occupancy R-2:
  - Apartment buildings.
  - Monasteries.
  - Convents.
- The requirements below apply where there are ≥ 4 of any of the following units used as residences:
  - Units:
    - Dwelling units.
    - Sleeping units.
  - Requirements:
    - Units must be Type B.

  Note: 1107.7, "General exceptions," is cited as permitting the number of Type B units to be reduced based on the absence of elevators and other access problems.

1107.6.2.2.1 Accessible units

- The following buildings are governed by the requirements listed below:
  - Buildings:
    - Boarding houses.
    - Dormitories.
    - Fraternity houses.
    - Sorority houses.
  - Requirements:
    - These buildings require the following accessible units as noted below:
      - Units:
        - Dwelling units.
        - Sleeping units.
      - Requirements:
        - The number of accessible units required is as follows:
          - The same number as required for occupancy R-1.

  Note: IBC Table 1107.6.1.1, "Accessible Dwelling and Sleeping Units," is cited as listing the number of accessible units required.
  Table 1107.6.1, "Accessible Dwelling Units and Sleeping Units Required," of this handbook provides an expanded version of the IBC table.

1107 Dwelling Units and Sleeping Units

1107.6.2.2.2 Type B units

- The requirements listed below apply to occupancy R-2 buildings as follows:
  - Buildings:
    Boarding houses.
    Dormitories.
    Fraternity houses.
    Sorority houses.
  - Requirements:
    Where there are ≥ 4 of either or both of the following units used as residences, the requirement indicated applies:
    Units:
    Dwelling units.
    Sleeping units.
    Requirement:
    Units must be Type B.

    Note: 1107.7, "General exceptions," is cited as permitting the number of Type B units to be reduced based on the absence of elevators and other access problems.

1107.6.3 Group R-3

- This section applies to occupancy R-3 buildings.
- Where there are ≥ 4 of either or both of the following units used as residences, the requirement listed below applies:
  - Units:
    Dwelling units.
    Sleeping units.
  - Requirement:
    Units must be Type B.

    Note: 1107.7, "General exceptions," is cited as permitting the number of Type B units to be reduced based on the absence of elevators and other access problems.

1107.6.4.1 Accessible units

- The following is required in an occupancy R-4 building:
  - ≥ 1 of either of the following units must be accessible:
    Dwelling unit.
    Sleeping unit.

1107 Dwelling Units and Sleeping Units

1107.6.4.1.2 Type B units

- This section applies to occupancy R-4 buildings.
- Where there are ≥ 4 of either or both of the following units used as residences, the requirement listed below applies:
  ○ Units:
  Dwelling units.
  Sleeping units.
  ○ Requirement:
  Units must be Type B.

> *Note: 1107.7, "General exceptions," is cited as permitting the number of Type B units to be reduced based on the absence of elevators and other access problems.*

1107.7 General exceptions

- This section series provides for reductions in required numbers of the following units where permitted elsewhere in the code:
  ○ Type A units.
  ○ Type B units.

> *Note: The following sections are cited as permitting reductions described by this section series:*
> *1107.5, "Group I."*
> *1107.6, "Group R."*
> *The following are cited as constituting this section series:*
> *1107.7.1, "Buildings without elevator service," through 1107.7.5, "Design flood elevation."*

1107.7.1 Buildings without elevator service

- Only certain stories of the following buildings are required to have the types of units indicated below:
  ○ Buildings:
  Buildings without an elevator.
  ○ Units:
  Type A units.
  Type B units.

> *Note: The following sections are cited as specifying which stories are required to have Type A and Type B units:*
> *1107.7.1.1, "One story with Type B units required."*
> *1107.7.1.2, "Additional stories with Type B units."*
> *1107.6.2.1.1,"Type A units," is cited as specifying the number of Type A units required.*

1107 Dwelling Units and Sleeping Units

1107.7.1.1 One story with Type B units required

- Where a building with any of the following units has no elevator, the requirement listed below applies:
  - Units:
    Dwelling units to be used as residences.
    Sleeping units to be used as residences.
  - Requirements:
    ≥ 1 story with such units must have the following:
    An accessible exterior entrance.
    All Type B units as follows:
    Where units are intended to be used as a residence.

1107.7.1.2 Additional stories with Type B units

- Building stories governed by this section are required to have all Type B units.
- This section governs each building story with the following characteristics:
  - The story does not have elevator service.
  - The story is not governed in the previous section of the code.
  - The story has any of the the following units:
    Dwelling units to be used as residences.
    Sleeping units to be used as residences.
  - The story is served by a building entrance as follows:
    Entrance is near the arrival point serving the story.
    Entrance is served by the following grades in the locations listed below:
    Grades:
    Original site grade that slopes ≤ 1:10.
    Design finished grade that slopes ≤ 1:10.
    Locations:
    Between the building entrance and the following points:
    All vehicular arrival points ≤ 50' from the entrance.
    All pedestrian arrival points ≤ 50' from the entrance.
    Nearest arrival point to the entrance > 50' from it in the following case:
    Where the nearest arrival point has both the following characteristics:
    It is > 50' from the entrance.
    It does not serve a story required to be all Type B units as follows:
    As required by the previous section.

Note: 1107.7.1.1, "One story with Type B units required," is cited as the section requiring all units on one story to be Type B units.

1107 Dwelling Units and Sleeping Units

1107.7.2 Multistory units

- A multistory unit as follows has the requirements listed below:
  - Unit:
    Dwelling unit.
    Sleeping unit.
  - Requirements:
    The unit need not be a Type B unit in the following case:
    Where the unit does not have its own internal elevator serving all levels.
    Where an external elevator serves only 1 floor, the following applies:
    The main entry floor is governed as follows:
    It must be served by the elevator.
    It must meet Type B unit requirements.
    It must have a toilet.

1107.7.3 Elevator service to the lowest story with units

- The lowest story with the following units has the requirements listed below:
  - Units:
    Dwelling units to be used as residences.
    Sleeping units to be used as residences.
  - Requirements:
    Such units are required to be Type B units in the following case:
    Where an elevator provides an accessible route to only that story.

1107 Dwelling Units and Sleeping Units

1107.7.4 Site impracticality

- This section applies to sites with > 1 building without an elevator.
- The following number of required Type B units may be reduced in certain cases:
  - The number required for buildings without elevators.

    Note: 1107.7.1, "Buildings without elevator service," is cited as the section requiring a minimum quantity of Type B units.

- The number of Type B units required may be reduced as follows where the conditions listed below are met:
  - Reduction:
    The smaller number of units required is specified as a % of the following:
    The number of units required without a reduction.
    The % of units required is equal to the following:
    The % of the site having original grade < 10% slope.
  - Conditions:
    The number of Type B units on the site must total the following:
    ≥ 20% of the number required without a reduction.
    The following units with either circumstance listed below must be Type B units:
    Units:
    Dwelling units to be used as residences.
    Sleeping units to be used as residences.
    Circumstance 1:
    Grade serving the building entrance for the units noted above slopes as follows:
    It slopes ≤ 1:12 between the entrance and either of the following locations:
    A pedestrian arrival point.
    A vehicular arrival point.
    Circumstance 2:
    Grade serving the building entrance for the units noted above slopes as follows:
    It slopes ≤ 1:10 between the entrance and either of the following locations:
    A pedestrian arrival point.
    A vehicular arrival point.
    An elevated walkway is provided between the entrance and either of the arrival points noted above.

    Note: 1107.7.1, "Buildings without elevator service," is cited as defining the units addressed by this requirement.

    The following units where served by an elevator must be Type B units:
    Dwelling units to be used as residences.
    Sleeping units to be used as residences.

    Note: 1107.7.1, "Buildings without elevator service," is cited as defining the units addressed by this requirement.

1107 Dwelling Units and Sleeping Units

1107.7.5 Design flood elevation

- This section applies to buildings without elevators on sites described herein.
- Sites addressed by this section do not require the following:
  The number of Type A and Type B units otherwise required.
- This section applies to sites where all the following conditions apply:
  - The following are required to be at a level ≥ the design flood elevation:
    Lowest floor.
    Lowest structural member.
  - The floor is at a height measured as follows with the grade conditions listed below:
    Height measurement:
       Height is measured between the following two points:
          Minimum floor elevation required at primary entrances.
          One of the following elevations:
             Elevation of any of the following arrival points ≤ 50' away where they exist:
                Vehicular arrival points.
                Pedestrian arrival points.
             Elevation at the closet arrival point in the following case:
                Where no arrival point is within 50' of a primary entrance.
    Grade conditions:
       Floor height is >30" above grade as specified above.
       Slope of grade is > 1:10 between the following two locations:
          Arrival point.
          Floor at primary entrance.

1108 Special Occupancies

1108.1 General

- This section series governs certain occupancies as follows:
  - Other requirements in this chapter also apply to these occupancies.

  Note: 1108.2, "Assembly area seating," through 1108.4, "Dispersion of wheelchair spaces," are cited as constituting this section series.

1108.2.1 Services

- The following functions and locations listed below have the requirements indicated:
  - Functions:
    Services in areas not required to be accessible.
    Facilities in areas not required to be accessible.
  - Location:
    In assembly areas with fixed seating.
  - Requirements:
    Such functions must also be provided on an accessible level.
    Such functions must be accessible.

1108.2.2 Wheelchair spaces

- This section series addresses the following assembly areas with fixed seating:
  - Theaters.
  - Bleachers.
  - Grandstands.
  - Stadiums.
  - Arenas.
  - Other fixed seating.

  Note: ICC A117.1, "Accessible and Usable Buildings and Facilities," is cited as governing the wheelchair spaces of this section series.
  1108.2.2.1, "General seating," through 1108.2.2.5, "Companion seats," are cited as the section series governing wheelchair spaces.

1108 Special Occupancies

1108.2.2.1 General seating

- A partial listing of wheelchair spaces required in fixed seating assembly areas is provided in the following table:

Table 1108.2.2.1   Wheelchair Spaces Required in Fixed Seating Assembly Areas

Total seats	Wheelchair spaces required	Total seats	Wheelchair spaces required	Total seats	Wheelchair spaces required
4–25	≥ 1	1551–1700	≥ 14	3351–3500	≥ 26
26–50	≥ 2	1701–1850	≥ 15	3501–3650	≥ 27
51–100	≥ 4	1851–2000	≥ 16	3651–3800	≥ 28
101–300	≥ 5	2001–2150	≥ 17	3801–3950	≥ 29
301–500	≥ 6	2151–2300	≥ 18	3951–4100	≥ 30
501–650	≥ 7	2301–2450	≥ 19	4101–4250	≥ 31
651–800	≥ 8	2451–2600	≥ 20	4251–4400	≥ 32
801–950	≥ 9	2601–2750	≥ 21	4401–4550	≥ 33
951–1100	≥ 10	2751–2900	≥ 22	4551–4700	≥ 34
1101–1250	≥ 11	2901–3050	≥ 23	4701–4850	≥ 35
1251–1400	≥ 12	3051–3200	≥ 24	4851–5000	≥ 36
1401–1550	≥ 13	3201–3350	≥ 25	5001–5200	≥ 37

Source: IBC Table 1108.2.2.1

- Number of wheelchair spaces required where total seats are > 5000 is determined by the following equation:

$$\text{Wheelchair spaces} = [(\text{Total seats} - 5000) \div 200] + 36$$

  - Fractions of wheelchair spaces required are rounded up to the next higher whole number.

1108.2.2.2 Luxury boxes, club boxes and suites

- This section governs the following box seating in assembly areas having fixed seating:
  - Luxury boxes.
  - Club boxes.
  - Suites.
- Seating governed by this section requires wheelchair spaces as follows:
  - As per the table in the previous section.
    Note: IBC Table 1108.2.2.1, "Accessible Wheelchair Spaces," is cited as governing the number of wheelchair spaces required by this section.

- Wheelchair spaces must be provided in ≥ 20% of all boxes.

STOR

AUDITORIUM

4 wheelchair spaces

4 wheelchair spaces

PROJECTION

LOBBY

T   T

Case study: Fig. 1108.2.2.1. The auditorium seats 120. IBC Table 1108.2.2.1 indicates that 5 wheelchair spaces are required where seating totals 101 through 300. The auditorium provides 8 wheelchair spaces, thus, meeting this requirement. The 4 wheelchair spaces in the front of the auditorium are provided by way of removable standard seats. As required, a companion seat is provided by every wheelchair space.

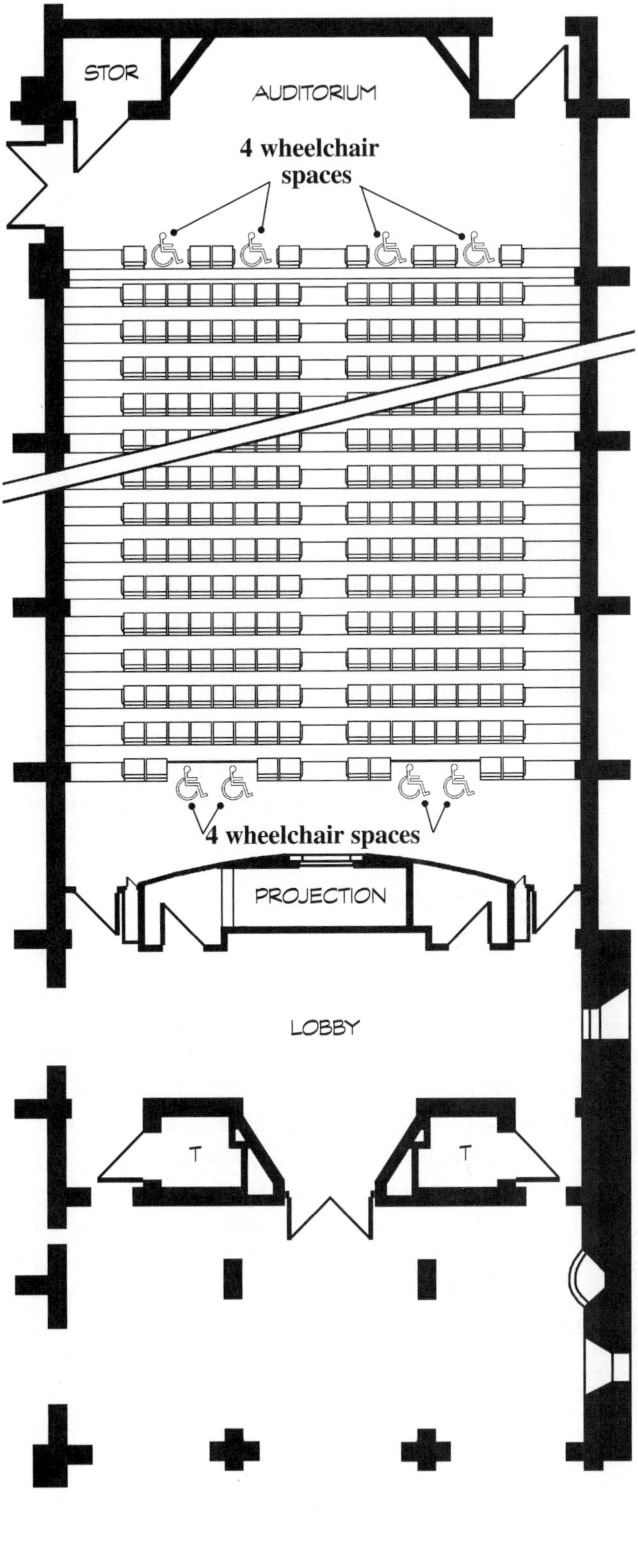

Fig. 1108.2.2.1. Partial floor plan at auditorium. Lady Bird Johnson Wildflower Center. Austin, Texas. Overland Partners, Inc. San Antonio, Texas.

1108 Special Occupancies

1108.2.2.3 Other boxes

- Wheelchair spaces must be provided in ≥ 20% of all boxes.
- This section governs the number of wheelchair spaces in assembly box seating other than the following:
  - Luxury boxes.
  - Club boxes.
  - Suites.
- Seating governed by this section requires wheelchair spaces as follows:
  - As per the previous table specifying required wheelchair spaces for fixed assembly seating.

    Note: IBC Table 1108.2.2.1, "Accessible Wheelchair Spaces," is cited as governing the number of wheelchair spaces required by this section.

1108.2.3 Integration

- Wheelchair spaces must planned as follows:
  - As an integral part of the seating arrangement.

1108.2.4 Dispersion of wheelchair spaces

- Dispersion of wheelchair spaces is to be based on the following:
  - Availability of accessible routes as follows:
    To different seating areas including the following:
      That on different levels where > 1 level is provided.

1108.2.4.1 Multilevel assembly seating areas

- Wheelchair spaces are required on the main floor level of all multilevel facilities.
- All wheelchair spaces may be on the main floor where both of the following apply:
  - The space is used for worship services.
  - The upper level contains ≤ 25% of the total seating capacity.
- All wheelchair spaces may be on the main floor where both of the following apply:
  - The upper level contains ≤ 25% of the total seating capacity.
  - The upper level contains ≤ 300 seats.
- For other conditions of multilevel assembly seating, the following applies:
  - Wheelchair spaces are required on upper levels as follows:
    For every pair of upper levels the following applies:
      Wheelchair spaces are required on one level of the pair.
- Wheelchair spaces are required in each of the following:
  - Luxury box.
  - Club box.
  - Suite.

1108 Special Occupancies

1108.2.5 Companion seats

- $\geq$ 1 seat for a companion is required for each wheelchair space.

  Note: ICC A117.1, "Accessible and Usable Buildings and Facilities," is cited as governing the seat for a companion.
  1108.2.2, "Wheelchair spaces," is cited as requiring the wheelchair spaces for which a companion seat is also required.

1108.2.6 Designated aisle seats

- The larger of the following numbers in fixed seating assembly areas must be designated aisle seats:
  - 1 aisle seat.
  - $\geq$ 5% of the total number of aisle seats.

  Note: Designated aisle seats have removable armrests, folding armrests, or no armrests on the aisle side. Such seats are provided for people who have difficulty walking.

1108.2.7 Assistive listening systems

- An assistive listening system is required in both the following types of courtrooms:
  - Where an audio amplification system is provided.
  - Where an audio amplification system is not provided.
- In other locations with no audio amplification system, the following applies:
  - An assistive listening system is not required.
- In areas with all the following characteristics, an assistive listening system is required:
  - An assembly area with fixed seating.
  - An audio amplification system is provided.
  - Hearing is integral to the function of the space.

1108.2.7.1 Receivers *(part 1 of 2)*

- Receivers are required for assistive listening systems as indicated in the partial table provided in this section.
- Where there is more than one assembly area in a building requiring receivers, the following applies:
  - The total number of receivers required may be based on the following:
    The sum of the seats in all the assembly areas where all the following apply:
    All receivers must be usable in all assembly areas.
    All areas required to have receivers must be under the same management.

1108 Special Occupancies

1108.2.7.1 Receivers *(part 2 of 2)*

Table 1108.2.7.1   Number of Receivers Required for Assistive Listening

Total seats	Receivers required	Hearing-aid-compatible required	Total seats	Receivers required	Hearing-aid-compatible required
1–50	≥ 2	≥ 2	864–896	≥ 32	≥ 8
51–75	≥ 3	≥ 2	897–929	≥ 33	≥ 9
76–100	≥ 4	≥ 2	930–962	≥ 34	≥ 9
101–125	≥ 5	≥ 2	963–995	≥ 35	≥ 9
126–150	≥ 6	≥ 2	996–1050	≥ 36	≥ 9
151–175	≥ 7	≥ 2	1051–1100	≥ 37	≥ 10
176–200	≥ 8	≥ 2	1101–1150	≥ 38	≥ 10
201–225	≥ 9	≥ 3	1151–1200	≥ 39	≥ 10
226–250	≥ 10	≥ 3	1201–1250	≥ 40	≥ 10
251–275	≥ 11	≥ 3	1251–1300	≥ 41	≥ 11
276–300	≥ 12	≥ 3	1301–1350	≥ 42	≥ 11
301–325	≥ 13	≥ 4	1351–1400	≥ 43	≥ 11
326–350	≥ 14	≥ 4	1401–1450	≥ 44	≥ 11
351–375	≥ 15	≥ 4	1451–1500	≥ 45	≥ 12
376–400	≥ 16	≥ 4	1501–1550	≥ 46	≥ 12
401–425	≥ 17	≥ 5	1551–1600	≥ 47	≥ 12
426–450	≥ 18	≥ 5	1601–1650	≥ 48	≥ 12
451–475	≥ 19	≥ 5	1651–1700	≥ 49	≥ 13
476–500	≥ 20	≥ 5	1701–1750	≥ 50	≥ 13
501–533	≥ 21	≥ 6	1751–1800	≥ 51	≥ 13
534–566	≥ 22	≥ 6	1801–1850	≥ 52	≥ 13
567–599	≥ 23	≥ 6	1851–1900	≥ 53	≥ 14
600–632	≥ 24	≥ 6	1901–1950	≥ 54	≥ 14
633–665	≥ 25	≥ 7	1951–2000	≥ 55	≥ 14
666–698	≥ 26	≥ 7	2001–2100	≥ 56	≥ 14
699–731	≥ 27	≥ 7	2101–2200	≥ 57	≥ 15
732–764	≥ 28	≥ 7	2201–2300	≥ 58	≥ 15
765–797	≥ 29	≥ 8	2301–2400	≥ 59	≥ 15
798–830	≥ 30	≥ 8	2401–2500	≥ 60	≥ 15
831–863	≥ 31	≥ 8	2501–2600	≥ 61	≥ 16

Source: IBC Table 1108.2.7.1

- The number of receivers required for > 2000 seats is determined as follows:

  Receivers required = [(Total seats – 2000) ÷ 100] + 55

- The number of receivers that must be hearing-aid-compatible for > 200 seats is determined as follows:
  - ≥ 25% of the standard receivers required.
- Fractions of receivers required are rounded up to the next whole number.

1108 Special Occupancies

1108.2.7.2 Public address systems

- The requirements below apply to the following facilities:
  - Facilities:
    Stadiums.
    Arenas.
    Grandstands.
  - Requirements:
    Where such facilities provide verbal public announcements, the following applies:
    They must also provide equivalent messages in written form.

  Note: The following are cited as providing specific requirements for required text messages:
  1108.2.7.2.1, "Prerecorded text messages."
  1108.2.7.2.2, "Real-time messages."

1108.2.7.2.1 Prerecorded text messages

- This section addresses announcements in assembly areas as follows:
  - Stadiums.
  - Arenas.
  - Grandstands.
- Verbal announcements that cannot be recorded prior to an event are governed as follows:
  - Such announcements are not required to be displayed in written form.
- Verbal announcements that are recorded prior to an event are governed as follows:
  - The equivalent of such announcements must be displayed as written messages in the following case:
    Where electronic signs are available that can display such messages.

1108.2.7.2.2 Real-time messages

- Real-time verbal announcements at the following facilities are governed as indicated below:
  - Facilities:
    Stadiums.
    Arenas.
    Grandstands.
  - Requirement:
    The equivalent of such announcements must be displayed as written messages in the following case:
    Where electronic signs are available that can display such messages.

1108 Special Occupancies

1108.2.8 Performance areas

- A direct accessible route must connect the following terminals in the circumstance indicated below:
  - Terminals:
    - Performance area.
    - Assembly seating.
  - Circumstance:
    - Where a circulation path connects the same terminals.
- An accessible route must connect the following:
  - Performance areas.
  - Related areas used by performers.

1108.2.9 Dining areas

- An accessible route (typically an elevator) to a mezzanine is not required where both of the following apply:
  - The mezzanine has $< \frac{1}{4}$ of the total dining area.
  - The building has no accessible route (typically an elevator) between levels.
  - The same services provided on the mezzanine are provided in the accessible area.
- Tiered dining spaces in sports facilities are governed as follows:
  - Where the dining spaces are required to have accessible seating, the following applies:
    - Accessible routes are required to serve $\geq \frac{1}{4}$ of the dining area as follows:
      - Where both the following conditions are present:
        - Accessible routes are provided for accessible seating.
        - All tiers have the same services.
- In other cases the total dining area for tables and seating must be accessible.

1108.2.9.1 Dining surfaces

- This section addresses seating or standing spaces adjacent to dining surfaces (typically counters) as follows:
  - For eating.
  - For drinking.
- The greater number of the following adjacent spaces must comply with the requirements listed below:
  - Spaces:
    - 1 standing or seating space.
    - $\geq 5\%$ of all standing or seating spaces.
  - Requirements:
    - They must be accessible.
    - They must be dispersed throughout the dining area.

1108 Special Occupancies

1108.3 Self-service storage facilities

- The numbers of self-storage units required to be accessible are listed below:

Table 1108.3   Accessible Self-Storage Units

Total number of units provided	Number to be accessible	Total number of units provided	Number to be accessible
1–20	≥ 1	301–350	≥ 13
21–40	≥ 2	351–400	≥ 14
41–60	≥ 3	401–450	≥ 15
61–80	≥ 4	451–500	≥ 16
81–100	≥ 5	501–550	≥ 17
101–120	≥ 6	551–600	≥ 18
121–140	≥ 7	601–650	≥ 19
141–160	≥ 8	651–700	≥ 20
161–180	≥ 9	701–750	≥ 21
181–200	≥ 10	751–800	≥ 22
201–250	≥ 11	801–850	≥ 23
251–300	≥ 12	851–900	≥ 24

Source: IBC Table 1108.3

- The number of self-storage units required to be accessible in a facility with > 900 units is determined as indicated below:

   Required accessible units = [(Total number of units – 900) × 0.02] + 24

1108.3.1 Dispersion

- Where there are fewer accessible self-storage units required than there are classes of storage, the following applies:
   ○ The number of accessible units provided need not be > the number otherwise required for the following purpose:
      To distribute accessible units among all classes of storage.
- Otherwise, accessible self-storage units must be distributed among all classes of storage spaces provided.
- In a multibuilding storage facility, accessible self-storage units may be distributed in a single building.

1108 Special Occupancies

1108.4.1 Courtrooms

- All courtrooms must be accessible.

1108.4.2.1 Central holding cells

- The following central holding cells must comply with the requirement listed below:
  - Cells:
    Multipurpose cells not separated by the following categories:
    Age.
    Gender.
  - Requirement:
    ≥ 1 cell must be accessible.
- The following central holding cells must comply with the requirement listed below:
  - Cells:
    Separate cells assigned to any of the following categories:
    Adult males.
    Juvenile males.
    Adult females.
    Juvenile females.
  - Requirement:
    ≥ 1 cell of each category must be accessible.

1108.4.2.2 Court-floor holding cells

- The following holding cells serving courtrooms must comply with the requirement listed below:
  - Cells:
    Multipurpose cells at the court-floor level not separated by the following categories:
    Age.
    Gender.
  - Requirement:
    ≥ 1 accessible cell must serve the courtrooms.
- The following holding cells serving courtrooms must comply with the requirements listed below:
  - Cells:
    Separate cells at the court-floor level assigned to any of the following categories:
    Adult males.
    Juvenile males.
    Adult females.
    Juvenile females.
  - Requirement:
    ≥ 1 accessible cell of each category must serve each courtroom.
- More than one courtroom may be served by an accessible cell.

1108 Special Occupancies

1108.4.3.1 Cubicles and counters

- This section addresses the following elements in the visiting area of a judicial facility:
  - Detainee visiting cubicles.
  - Detainee visiting counters.
- This section does not govern the following elements in the visiting area of a judicial facility:
  - The detainee side of visiting cubicles where both the following apply:
    Where no contact between detainee and visitors is permitted.
    Where the visiting area does not serve an accessible holding cell.
- In other cases, the following applies:
  - The greater number of the following visiting cubicles must meet the requirement listed below:
    Cubicles:
      1 visitor cubicle.
      $\geq$ 5% of all visitor cubicles.
    Requirement:
      The cubicles must be accessible on both sides.
  - Any visiting counters provided are governed as follows:
    $\geq$ 1 must be accessible on both sides.

1108.4.3.2 Partitions

- The following elements in the visiting area of a judicial facility must meet the requirements listed below:
  - Elements:
    Visiting cubicles with any of the following separating visitors from detainees:
      Solid partitions.
      Security glazing.
    Visiting counters with any of the following separating visitors from detainees:
      Solid partitions.
      Security glazing.
  - Requirement:
    $\geq$ 1 of each type of the following must be accessible:
    Counter partition.
    Cubicle partition.

1109 Other Features and Facilities

1109.1 General

- Type A and Type B dwelling units are not governed by this section series.

    Note: ICC A117.1, "Accessible and Usable Buildings and Facilities," is cited as governing Type A and Type B dwelling units.

1109.2 Toilet and bathing facilities *(part 1 of 2)*

- Alternatives to the accessibility requirements of this section for the following facilities are provided below:
  - Facilities:

    Toilet rooms or bathing facilities where all the following conditions apply:

    Facilities accessed only through a private office.

    Facilities not for public use.

    Facilities intended for use by a single occupant.
  - Alternatives:

    Doors may swing into the clear floor space in the following case:

    Where it can be reversed to meet other accessibility standards.

    Height requirements of other accessibility standards do not apply for the water closet.

    Toilet room grab bars not required in the following case:

    Where backing is provided in walls suitable for their installation.

    The following requirements at the lavatory do not apply:

    Height minimum.

    Knee clearance.

    Toe clearance.

    Note: ICC A117.1, "Accessible and Usable Buildings and Facilities," is cited as the accessibility standard that applies to the above alternatives or which is waived as indicated.

- This section does not apply to the following facilities:
  - Those serving the following units where not required to be accessible:

    Dwelling units.

    Sleeping units.

    Note: Section 1107, "Dwelling Units and Sleeping Units," is cited as the source that does not require certain facilities to be accessible as indicated above.

1109 Other Features and Facilities

1109.2 Toilet and bathing facilities *(part 2 of 2)*

- Where there is a group of ≥ 2 toilet rooms or bathing facilities as follows, the requirements listed below apply:
  - Facilities:
    - Each is designed for use by a single occupant.
    - Where such facilities combined have more fixtures than the total required.
  - Requirement:
    - The larger of the following number of rooms or bathing facilities must be accessible:
      - For men's facilities:
        - 1 room.
        - ≥ 5% of the rooms.
      - For women's facilities:
        - 1 room.
        - ≥ 5% of the rooms.
      - For unisex facilities:
        - 1 room.
        - ≥ 5% of the rooms.
- This section does not apply to the following facilities:
  - Where toilet room fixtures have all the following characteristics:
    - They are in excess of those required by the plumbing code.
    - They are for use by children in either of the following:
      - Day care.
      - Primary school.

  Note: The International Plumbing Code is cited as the code which requires a minimum number of toilet room fixtures.

- Other toilet rooms and bathing facilities are governed as follows:
  - Such rooms and facilities are required to be accessible.
  - ≥ 1 of the following in each accessible room or facility must be accessible:
    - Fixture.
    - Element.
    - Control.
    - Dispenser.
  - Where such rooms or facilities are the only ones in a building, the following applies:
    - They may not be located on a floor without an accessible route.
- A urinal is not required to be accessible in the following cases:
  - Where it is the only one as follows:
    - In a toilet room.
    - In a bathing facility.
- The following toilet rooms are not required to be accessible:
  - Where in a critical-care patient sleeping room.
  - Where in an intensive-care patient sleeping room.

1109 Other Features and Facilities

1109.2.1 Unisex toilet and bathing rooms

- A unisex bathing room is not required in the following case:
  - Where fixtures in each separate-sex bathing room are limited as follows:
    Where a bathtub is provided, there is only 1.
    Where a shower is provided, there is only 1.
- In other cases, the following requirements apply:
  - An accessible unisex toilet room is required where all the following conditions apply:
    In occupancies A and M.
    Where the sum of male and female water closets required is ≥ 6.
  - Where A or M occupancies are mixed with others, the following applies:
    An accessible unisex toilet room is required for the following condition:
    Where the sum of male and female water closets required is ≥ 6 as follows:
    In the A or M occupancy only.
- An accessible unisex toilet room is required in recreational facilities as follows:
  - Where separate-sex bathing rooms are provided.
- Fixtures in unisex toilet and bathing rooms count toward the following minimum:
  - The total number of fixtures required.

1109.2.1.1 Standard

- Unisex toilet rooms and bathing facilities must comply with this section and other standards.

  Note: ICC A117.1, "Accessible and Usable Buildings and Facilities," is cited as the other standard governing unisex facilities as indicated above.

1109.2.1.2 Unisex toilet rooms

- A unisex toilet room must have one of the following combinations of fixtures:
  - Combination 1:
    1 lavatory.
    1 water closet.
  - Combination 2:
    1 lavatory.
    1 water closet.
    1 urinal.

  Note: 1109.2.1.3, "Unisex bathing rooms," is cited as the source of bathing rooms that qualify as unisex toilets.

1109 Other Features and Facilities

1109.2.1.3 Unisex bathing rooms

- Unisex bathing rooms must include no more and no fewer of the following plumbing fixtures:
  - One bathtub or shower.
  - One water closet.
  - One lavatory.
- Accessible storage facilities are required for unisex bathing rooms in the following case:
  - Where storage is provided for separate-sex bathing rooms.

1109.2.1.4 Location

- Unisex toilet and bathing rooms must be on an accessible route.
- Unisex toilet rooms must be placed in one of the following locations:
  - $\leq$ 1 story above separate-sex toilet rooms.
  - $\leq$ 1 story below separate-sex toilet rooms.
- The accessible route between the following points is limited to $\leq$ 500':
  - Any separate-sex toilet room.
  - A unisex toilet room.

1109.2.1.5 Prohibited location

- This section addresses passenger transportation facilities and airports.
- The accessible route between the following facilities is governed as indicated below:
  - Facilities:
    Separate-sex toilet rooms.
    A unisex to toilet room.
  - Requirement:
    The route may not pass through a security checkpoint.

1109.2.1.6 Clear floor space

- Where doors swing into the following rooms, the following clear space is required:
  - Rooms:
    Unisex toilet room.
    Unisex bathing rooms.
  - Requirement:
    Clear floor space must be available in the room beyond the door swing as follows: $\geq 30" \times \geq 48"$.

1109.2.1.7 Privacy

- Doors to the following rooms must be securable from inside the rooms:
  - Unisex toilet rooms.
  - Unisex bathing rooms.

1109 Other Features and Facilities

1109.2.2 Water closet compartment

- This section addresses toilet rooms and bathing rooms.
- Where water closet compartments are provided, the following is required:
  - ≥ 1 wheelchair-accessible water closet compartment.
- Where the sum of the following facilities is ≥ 6, the requirement indicated below applies:
  - Facilities:
      Water closet compartments.
      Urinals.
  - Requirement:
      ≥ 1 wheelchair-accessible water closet compartment is required.
      ≥ 1 ambulatory-accessible water closet compartment is required.

  Note: ICC A117.1, "Accessible and Usable Buildings and Facilities," is cited as governing wheelchair-accessible and ambulatory-accessible compartments.

1109.3 Sinks

- The following sinks are not governed by this section:
  - Mop sinks.
  - Service sinks.
  - Children's sinks in the following locations:
      Day care.
      Primary school.
- In other cases where other sinks are provided, the number required to comply with accessibility requirements are listed below:

Total number of sinks provided	Sinks required to meet accessibility requirements
1–20	≥ 1
21–40	≥ 2
41–60	≥ 3

- Where > 60 sinks are provided, ≥ 5% must meet accessibility requirements.

  Note: ICC A117.1, "Accessible and Usable Buildings and Facilities," is cited as governing the sinks indicated above.

Case study: Fig. 1109.3. Where 1–20 sinks are provided, ≥ 1 must meet accessibility requirements. In this classroom laboratory, 4 sinks are provided. 1 meets accessibility requirements; thus, the sinks are in compliance with the code.

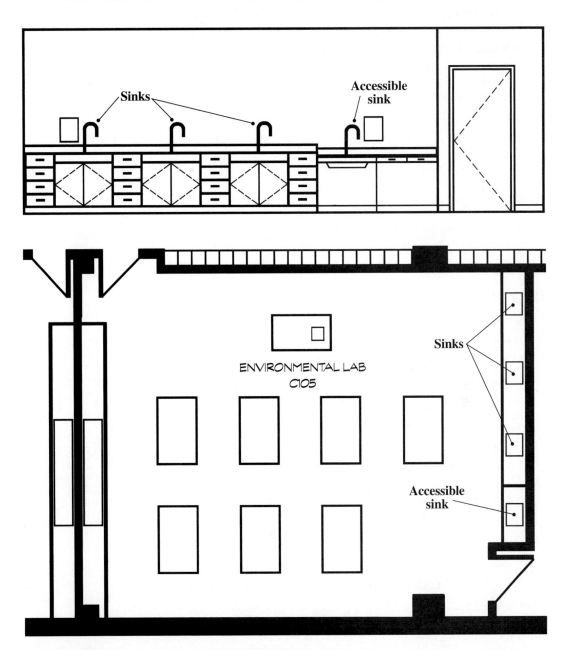

Fig. 1109.3. Plan and elevation at environmental lab C105. High School 6, Cypress-Fairbanks Independent School District. Harris County, Texas. PBK Architects, Inc. Houston, Texas.

1109 Other Features and Facilities

1109.4 Kitchens and kitchenettes

- Where provided in accessible spaces, the following must be accessible:
  - Kitchens.
  - Kitchenettes.

    Note: ICC A117.1, "Accessible and Usable Buildings and Facilities," is cited as governing the facilities indicated above.

1109.5 Drinking fountains

- Where drinking fountains are provided, the following applies:
  - The larger of the following numbers of drinking fountains must be accessible:
    1 drinking fountain.
    $\geq 50\%$ of the drinking fountains provided.

1109.6 Elevators

- The following passenger elevators must be accessible:
  - Where on an accessible route.

    Note: 3001.3, "Accessibility," is cited as governing these elevators.

1109.7 Lifts *(part 1 of 2)*

- Platform (wheelchair) lifts are permitted in the following accessible routes in new construction:
  - To a performing area in occupancy A.
  - To a speaker's platform in occupancy A.
  - To spaces meeting both of the following conditions:
    Not open to the general public.
    Having an occupant load ≤ 5.
  - Within a dwelling unit.
  - Within a sleeping unit.
  - In occupancy A-5, with all of the following conditions:
    Route is to wheelchair seating spaces.
    Route is to outdoor dining.
    Means of egress as follows is open to the outdoors:
      From the outdoor dining to a public way.
  - To any of the following areas in a courtroom:

Judge's bench	Clerks' station	Other raised areas
Witness stand	Jury box	Other depressed areas

  - Where the following are not feasible due to existing exterior site constraints:
    Ramp or elevator.

    Note: ASME A18.1, "Safety Standards for Platform Lifts and Stairway Chairlifts," is cited as governing the installation of platform lifts.

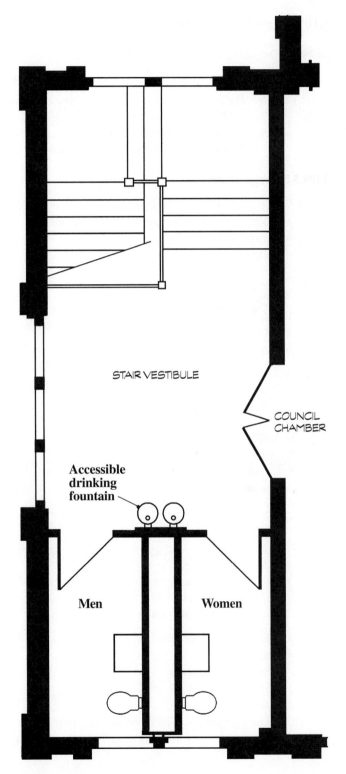

Case study: Fig. 1109.5.
Two drinking fountains are provided on the 2nd floor of the building. Half of those provided or a minimum of 1 is required to be accessible. The drinking fountains meet this requirement.

STAIR VESTIBULE

COUNCIL CHAMBER

Accessible drinking fountain

Men   **Women**

Fig. 1109.5. Plan at south stair. Lake Forest City Hall Renovation and Addition. Lake Forest, Illinois. David Woodhouse Architects. Chicago, Illinois.

1109 Other Features and Facilities

1109.7 Lifts *(part 2 of 2)*

> ○ In an accessible route to wheelchair spaces which are distributed according to code.
>
> *Note: The following are cited as requiring distribution of wheelchair spaces:*
> *1108.2.2, "Wheelchair spaces."*
> *1108.2.3, "Integration."*
> *1108.2.4, "Dispersion of wheelchair spaces."*

1109.8 Storage

- Where fixed or built-in storage units such as the following are provided in a required accessible space, the requirement below applies:
  - ○ Storage units:
    - Cabinets.
    - Shelves.
    - Medicine cabinets.
    - Closets.
    - Drawers.
    - Similar storage components
  - ○ Requirement:
    - ≥ 1 of each type must comply with accessibility requirements.

  > *Note: ICC A117.1, "Accessible and Usable Buildings and Facilities," is cited as the source of accessibility requirements for the units indicated above.*

1109.8.1 Lockers

- Where lockers are provided in accessible spaces, the following numbers must be accessible:

Total number of lockers provided	Lockers required to be accessible	Total number of lockers provided	Lockers required to be accessible
1–20	≥ 1	61–80	≥ 4
21–40	≥ 2	81–100	≥ 5
41– 60	≥ 3	101–120	≥ 6

- Where > 120 lockers are provided, ≥ 5% are required to be accessible.

1109.8.2 Shelving and display units

- The following components are governed as indicated below:
  - ○ Components:
    - Self-service shelves.
    - Self-service display units.
  - ○ Requirements:
    - The components must be on an accessible route.
    - The components need not comply with reach-range requirements.

1109 Other Features and Facilities

1109.8.3 Coat hooks and folding shelves

- Where the following devices are provided in the spaces listed below, the requirements indicated apply:
  - Devices:
    - Coat hooks.
    - Folding shelves.
  - Spaces:
    - Toilet rooms.
    - Toilet compartments.
    - Dressing rooms.
    - Fitting rooms.
    - Locker rooms.
  - Requirements:
    - ≥ 1 accessible version of each device is required as follows:
      - They must be provided for the following spaces:
        - Accessible toilet rooms without compartments.
        - Accessible toilet compartments.
        - Accessible dressing rooms.
        - Accessible fitting rooms.
        - Accessible locker rooms.

1109.9 Detectable warnings

- Detectable warnings are not required in the following locations:
  - At bus stops.
- Other passenger transit platforms as follows must have a detectable warning for the following hazard:
  - Any platform edge with a drop-off hazard as follows:
    - Where neither of the following is provided:
      - Protective screens.
      - Guards.

1109.10 Assembly area seating

- All occupancies with the following seating must meet the requirements listed below:
  - Seating:
    - Fixed assembly seating.
  - Requirements:
    - Seating must meet wheelchair requirements.
    - Seating must meet assistive listening device requirements.

  Note: 1108.2, "Assembly area seating," is cited as having the requirements that must be met by seating governed by this section.

1109 Other Features and Facilities

1109.11 Seating at tables, counters and work surfaces

- This section does not apply to the following:
  - Where a checkout aisle is not accessible, the following applies:
    Check-writing surfaces are not required to be accessible.
  - The following elements must meet the requirements listed below:
    Elements:
    Visiting cubicles in occupancy I-3.
    Visiting counters in occupancy I-3.
    Requirements:
    They are not required to be accessible on the detainee side as follows:
    In either of the following cases:
    Where the visiting area does not permit contact.
    Where the visiting area does not serve either of the following:
    Accessible holding cells.
    Accessible sleeping units.
- In other cases the requirements listed below apply where there is seating and/or standing space at the following locations:
  - Locations:
    At fixed or built-in tables.
    At fixed or built-in counters.
    At fixed or built-in work surfaces.
  - Requirements:
    The larger of the following is required to be accessible:
    1 seat and standing space.
    $\geq$ 5% of the seats and standing spaces as indicated in the partial table below:

Total seats and spaces	Seats and spaces to be accessible	Total seats and spaces	Seats and spaces to be accessible
1–20	≥ 1	61–80	≥ 4
21–40	≥ 2	81–100	≥ 5
41–60	≥ 3	101–120	≥ 6

- Where the number of seats and standing spaces > 120, the following applies:
  - The number required to be accessible is $\geq$ 5% of the total provided.

1109.11.1 Dispersion

- Where accessible seating provided at the following locations, it must be distributed throughout the seating area:
  - At fixed or built-in tables.
  - At fixed or built-in counters.
  - At fixed or built-in work surfaces.

1109 Other Features and Facilities

1109.12.1 Dressing, fitting and locker rooms

- Where the following facilities are provided, the number required to be accessible in each group is as listed below:
  - Dressing rooms.
  - Fitting rooms.
  - Locker rooms.

Total of each facility type	Number of each to be accessible
1–20	≥ 1
21–40	≥ 2
41–60	≥ 3

- Where the number of such facilities is > 60, the following applies:
  - The number required to be accessible is ≥ 5% of the total number provided.

1109.12.2 Check-out aisles

- Where the area of selling space is < 5000 sf, the following applies:
  - Only 1 checkout aisle must be accessible.
- For selling space ≥ 5000 sf, the following applies:
  - Accessible checkout aisles must be distributed throughout a facility in the following case:
    Where inaccessible checkout aisles are distributed throughout the facility.
  - The following devices located in accessible checkout aisles must be accessible:
    Traffic control devices.
    Security devices.
    Turnstiles.
  - Where checkout aisles serve different functions, the following applies:
    ≥ 1 accessible checkout aisle must be provided for each function.
  - Where checkout aisles are provided the following number for each sales function must be accessible:

Table 1109.12.2   Accessible Checkout Aisles

Checkout aisles at each function	Checkout aisles at each function to be accessible	Checkout aisles at each function	Checkout aisles at each function to be accessible
1–4	≥ 1	16–20	≥ 4
5–8	≥ 2	21–25	≥ 5
9–15	≥ 3	26–30	≥ 6

Source: IBC Table 1109.12.2.

  - Where checkout aisles are > 30, the number to be accessible is determined as follows:

Number to be accessible = [(Checkout aisles provided – 30) × 0.2] + 6

1109 Other Features and Facilities

1109.12.3 Point of sales and service counters

- Counters for sales and distribution of goods and services are governed as follows:
  - Where such counters are provided the following applies:
    - ≥ 1 of each type must be accessible.
  - Where such counters are distributed throughout the facility, the following applies:
    The accessible counters must be distributed throughout the facility.

1109.12.4 Food service lines

- Food service lines must be accessible.
- Where self-service shelves are provided, the following applies:
  - The greater of the following numbers of shelves must be accessible:
    - ≥ 1 of each type.
    - ≥ 50% of each type.

1109.12.5 Queue and waiting lines

- Queue and waiting lines for the following facilities must be accessible:
  - Accessible counters.
  - Accessible checkout aisles.

1109.13 Controls, operating mechanisms and hardware *(part 1 of 2)*

- The following are not required to be accessible:
  - Devices designed for use by the following:
    Service personnel.
    Maintenance personnel.
  - The following receptacles with a dedicated function:
    Electrical.
    Communication.
  - One of the following electrical outlets:
    Where ≥ 2 outlets are over the following kitchen counter:
    A counter without interruptions by either of the following:
    Sink.
    Appliance.
  - Electrical outlets located on the floor.
  - One of the following controls in each space:
    Where redundant controls serve a single component as follows:
    Where the controls are not light switches.

1109 Other Features and Facilities

1109.13 Controls, operating mechanisms and hardware *(part 1 of 2)*

- In other cases devices used by occupants such as the following must be accessible where located as shown below:
  - Devices:
    - Controls.
    - Operating mechanisms.
    - Operating hardware.
    - Light switches.
    - Ventilation switches.
    - Switches for electrical convenience outlets.
  - Locations:
    - In accessible spaces.
    - Along accessible routes.
    - As parts of accessible elements.

1109.13.1 Operable windows

- Accessible windows are not required in the following rooms:
  - Bathrooms.
  - Kitchens.
- In other rooms required to be accessible in the locations listed below, the following operable windows must be accessible:
  - Windows:
    - ≥ 1 operable window in each room where operable windows are provided.
    - Every required operable window.
  - Locations:
    - In accessible dwelling units and sleeping units as follows:
      - Occupancy I-3.
      - Occupancy I-2 nusring homes.
      - Occupancy I-2 hospitals.
      - Occupancy I-2 rehabilitation facilities.
      - Occupancy R-1.
      - Occupancy R-2.
      - Occupancy R-4.

> *Note: The following are cited as sources listing rooms that must be accessible, a partial summary of which is provided above:*
> *1107.5.1.1, "Accessible units."*
> *1107.5.2.1, "Accessible units."*
> *1107.5.3.1, "Accessible units."*
> *1107.5.4, "Group I-2 Rehabilitation facilities."*
> *1107.6.1.1, "Accessible units."*
> *1107.6.2.2.1, "Accessible units."*
> *1107.6.4.1, "Accessible units."*

1109 Other Features and Facilities

1109.14.1 Facilities serving a single building

- Recreational facilities where provided in the following locations have requirements as listed below:
  - Locations:
    Occupancies R-2 and R-3 as follows:
    Where recreational facilities serve 1 building with the following units:
    Type A units and Type B units.
  - Requirements:
    The larger of the following number must be accessible:
    1 facility of each type provided.
    ≥ 25% of each type of facility provided.
  - The required accessible number of facilities is based on the following:
    All facilities of every type on the site.

1109.14.2 Facilities serving multiple buildings

- Recreational facilities where provided in the following locations have requirements as listed below:
  - Locations:
    Occupancies R-2 and R-3 as follows:
    Where recreational facilities serve > 1 building with the following units:
    Type A units and Type B units.
  - Requirements:
    The larger of the following numbers serving each building must be accessible:
    1 facility of each type provided.
    ≥ 25% of each type of facility provided.
  - The required accessible number of facilities is based on the following:
    All facilities of all types serving every building on the site.

1109.14.3 Other occupancies

- All the following recreation facilities must be accessible:
  - Those not governed by the previous two sections.

  Note: The following are cited as governing the excluded recreational facilities:
  1109.14.1, "Facilities serving a single building."
  1109.14.2, "Facilities serving multiple buildings."

1109.15 Stairways

- Stairways on accessible routes must comply with following:
  - They must meet egress and accessibility requirements.

  Note: The following are cited as providing the requirements for the stairways:
  ICC A117.1, "Accessible and Usable Buildings and Facilities."
  Chapter 10, "Means of Egress."

1110 Signage

1110.1 Signs

- Required accessible elements require the International Symbol of Accessibility as follows:
  - For accessible parking spaces where > 5 total parking spaces are provided.
  - For accessible loading zones for passengers.
  - For accessible areas of refuge.
  - For accessible toilet and bathing rooms as follows:
    Single-user rooms grouped at a single location.
  - For accessible entrances where not all entrances are accessible.
  - For accessible checkout aisles where not all aisles are accessible as follows:
    Signage must be located above the aisle as is other checkout aisle identification.
  - For unisex toilet and bathing rooms.
  - For the following facilities where not all similar facilities are accessible:
    Dressing rooms.
    Fitting rooms.
    Locker rooms.

  Note: The following are cited as sources of applicable requirements as indicated:
      1106.1, "Required," requires accessible parking spaces as indicated above.
      1007.6, "Areas of refuge," provides requirements for areas of refuge.

1110.2 Directional signage

- Signage with the following information is required at the locations indicated below:
  - Information:
    Indicates route to nearest similar facility that is accessible.
    Exhibits the International Symbol of Accessibility.
  - Locations:
    At inaccessible building entrances.
    At inaccessible public toilets and bathing facilities.
    At elevators not serving an accessible route.
    At each separate-sex toilet and bathing room indicating the following:
      The location of nearest unisex toilet or bathing room.
    At the following locations which serve a required accessible space:
      Exits which are not an accessible means of egress.
      Elevators which are not an accessible means of egress.

  Note: 1109.2.1, "Unisex toilet and bathing rooms," is cited as the source providing
      requirements for such rooms.

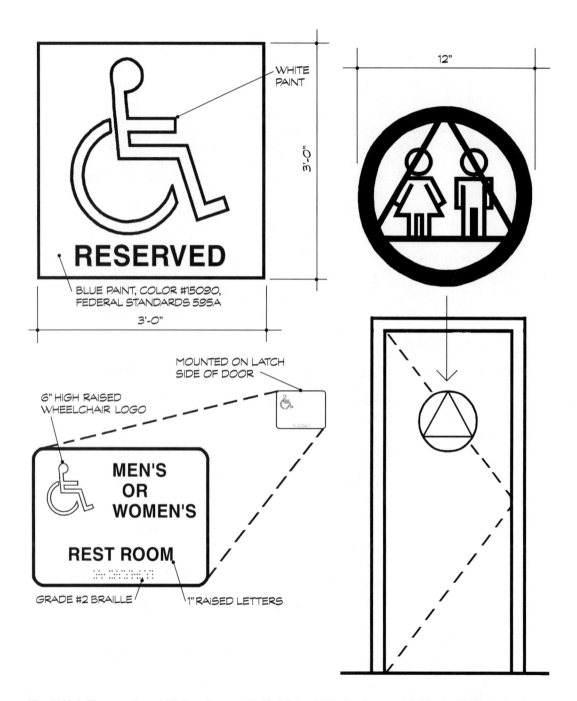

Fig. 1110.1. Signage. Central Kitchen. Lompoc Unified School District. Lompoc, California. Phillips Metsch Sweeney Moore Architects. Santa Barbara, California.

1110 Signage

> **Case study: Fig. 1110.1.** The International symbol for accessibility, as shown in the illustration, is painted on the pavement at each accessible parking space in this project and is applied to signs reserving the spaces. The symbol is also used on the sign beside the door of the unisex toilet room. In addition, the toilet room is identified as being unisex by the symbol on the door and by the wording on the accessibility sign, which includes Braille. The signs at the toilet room are mounted 5' above the floor. The signage complies with code requirements.

1110.3 Other signs

- Signage reporting assistive listening system availability to patrons is required as follows:
  - Where assistive listening systems are required in assembly spaces.
  - Signage is to be placed in any of the following locations:
        At ticket offices.
        At ticket windows.
        At the assembly area.

    Note: 1108.2.7, "Assistive listing systems," is cited as the source requiring such systems.

- Tactile exit signage is required at each door to the following:
  - Egress stairways.
  - Exit passageways.
  - Exit discharges.

    Note: 1011.3, "Tactile exit signs," is cited as the source governing these signs.

- Signage of the following nature is required at areas of refuge:
  - Instructional.
  - Directional.
  - Identification.

    *Note: The following sections are cited as governing the signs required at areas of
        refuge:*
        1007.6.3, "Two-way communication."
        1007.6.4, "Instructions."
        1007.6.5, "Identification."

- Areas designated for assisted rescue must have identifying signage.

    Note: 1007.8.3, "Identification," is cited as governing the signage for these areas.

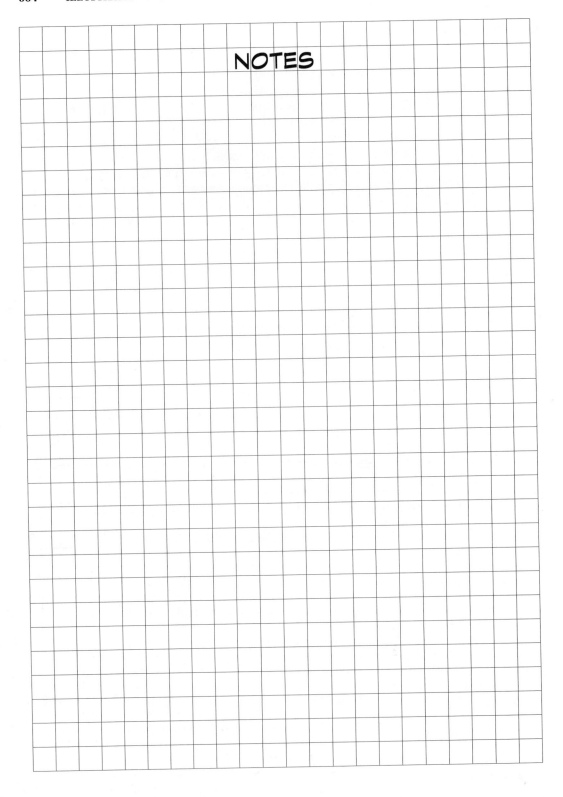

NOTES

12

Interior Environment

Multipurpose Building Addition to Children's Home. Wilkes-Barre, Pennsylvania. *(partial elevation)*
C. Allen Mullins, Architects. Bear Creek, Pennsylvania.

1202 Definitions

1202.1 General

- **Sunroom addition**
  - A structure added to a building as follows:
    One story.
    Glazing > 40% of the enclosure surface of the addition as follows:
      Walls.
      Roof.

- **Thermal isolation**
  - A separation between the following spaces by the elements listed below:
    Spaces:
      Sunroom addition.
      Dwelling unit.
    Elements:
      Existing or new elements among the following:
        Walls.
        Doors.
        Windows.

1203 Ventilation

1203.1 General

- One of the following types of ventilation is required for buildings:
  - Natural ventilation as governed by this chapter.
  - Mechanical ventilation.

  Note: International Mechanical Code is cited as governing mechanical ventilation.

1203.2 Attic spaces

- Spaces between rafters enclosed as follows must be ventilated as indicated below:
  - Rafter spaces:
    Enclosed by attaching a ceiling directly to the underside of rafters.
  - Requirements:
    Each separate rafter space must be ventilated.
    Air space required for ventilation is $\geq 1"$ as follows:
      Between the insulation and roof sheathing.
    Area of rafter space is measured on the plane of rafter slope.
- Enclosed attics and enclosed rafter spaces must be ventilated as follows:
  - Net clear open area for ventilation must be the following size:
    $\geq 1/300$ of the area ventilated:
      Where a vapor retarder is provided as follows:
        Retarder must have a transmission rate ≤ 1 perm.
        Retarder is placed on the warm side of the attic insulation.
    $\geq 1/150$ of the area ventilated:
      Where a vapor retarder is not provided as required.
  - $1/2$ the required vents must be located as follows:
    In the upper part of the ventilated space.
    $\geq 3'$ above the eave or cornice vents.
  - $1/2$ the required vents must be at the eave or cornice.

  Note: ASTM E 96, "Standard Test Method for Water Vapor Transmission of Materials," is cited as governing vapor retarders.

- Openings ventilation may not permit penetration by the following:
  - Rain.
  - Snow.
- The following may not interfere with ventilation airflow:
  - Blocking.
  - Bridging.

Case study: Fig. 1203.2. Spaces, between rafters enclosed by the attachment of a ceiling to the bottom of the rafters, are ventilated. Metal soffit vents are provided under the eave and blocking is cut to permit the through-flow of air. A 1" airspace is provided between the top of the insulation and the bottom of the roof sheathing for airflow as required. Ventilation of the rafter spaces is in compliance with the code.

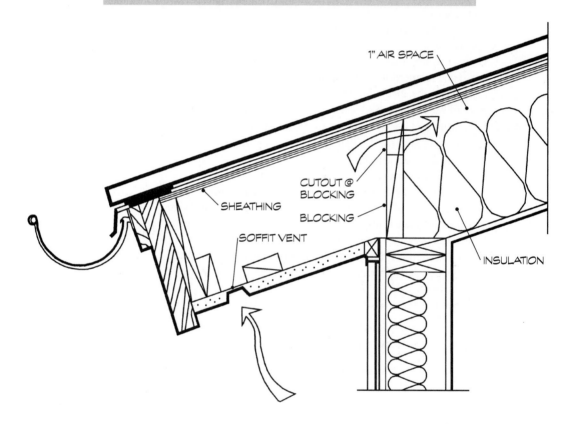

Fig. 1203.2. Detail at eave. Central Kitchen. Lompoc Unified School District. Lompoc, California. Phillips Metsch Sweeney Moore Architects. Santa Barbara, California.

1203 Ventilation

1203.2.1 Openings into attic

- This section addresses attics in buildings for human occupancy.
- Openings into attics from the outside must be covered as follows:
    - Corrosion resistant materials such as the following are required:
        Wire cloth screening.
        Hardware cloth.
        Perforated vinyl.
        Similar material.
    - Coverings must prevent entry of the following and similar creatures:
        Birds.
        Squirrels.
        Rodents.
        Snakes.
    - Openings in the coverings to be $\geq$ $\frac{1}{8}$" and $\leq$ $\frac{1}{4}$".
- Combustion air taken from the attic is not governed by this section.

    Note: International Mechanical Code, Chapter 7, is cited governing combustion air taken from the attic.

Case study: Fig. 1203.2.1. A corrosion-resistant screen is provided at the attic opening to prevent the entry of birds and other creatures. Openings in the screen are between $\frac{1}{8}$" and $\frac{1}{4}$" as required. The sleeve surrounding the passage to the mechanical louvers is lined with sheet metal, and the bottom surface slopes to the exterior for drainage. Protection of the opening into the attic is in compliance with the code.

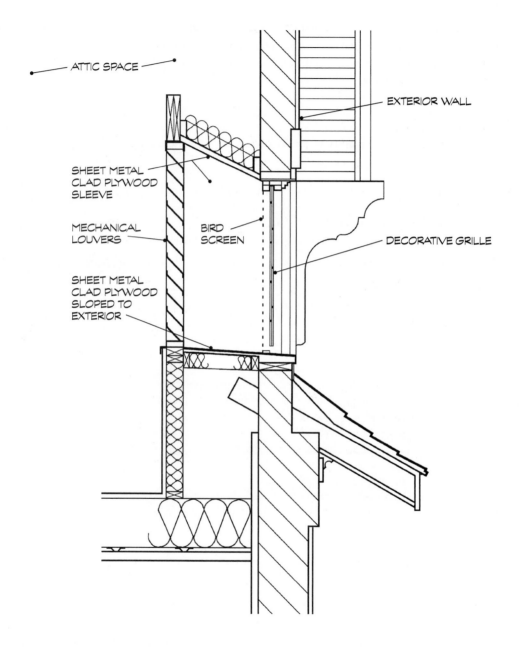

Fig. 1203.2.1. Detail at attic vent. Lake Forest City Hall Renovation and Addition. Lake Forest, Illinois. David Woodhouse Architects. Chicago, Illinois.

1203 Ventilation

1203.3 Under-floor ventilation

- This section addresses crawl spaces for which conditions require natural ventilation.
- Space between the earth and floor joists, other than the following, must be ventilated as indicated below:
  - Spaces not governed by this section:
    - Basements.
    - Cellars.
  - Requirements:
    - Spaces must be ventilated by openings through the following as applicable:
      - Foundation walls.
      - Exterior walls.
    - Ventilation openings must be located to provide cross-ventilation of the space.

  Note: 1203.3.2, "Exceptions," lists conditions which warrant variations on these requirements.

1203.3.1 Openings for under-floor ventilation

- This section addresses ventilation of crawl spaces where no vapor retarder is used.
- The net clear open area required for ventilating crawl spaces is as follows:
  - $\geq \frac{1}{150}$ of the crawl space area.
- Openings providing ventilation must be covered with one of the following:
  - Materials with openings $\leq \frac{1}{4}$" are as follows:
    - Perforated sheet metal ≥ 0.070" thick.
    - Expanded sheet metal ≥ 0.047" thick.
    - Cast iron grille or grating.
    - Extruded load bearing vents.
    - Hardware cloth:
      - Wire diameter ≥ 0.035".
  - Corrosion resistant wire mesh:
    - Openings $\leq \frac{1}{8}$".

Note: 1203.3.2, "Exceptions," lists conditions which warrant variations on these requirements.

1203 Ventilation

1203.3.2 Exceptions

- This section includes exceptions to the previous two sections, which addressed crawl-space ventilation.
- Openings providing ventilation are not required to the exterior in the following case:
  ○ Where the climate warrants vent openings to the interior of the building.
- The required net area of ventilation openings is as follows:
  ○ $\geq$ $^1/_{1500}$ of the crawl-space area where the following are provided:
     The ground is covered with an approved vapor retarder.
     Openings must be positioned to provide cross-ventilation of the space:
        Openings with operable louvers are permitted.
- Openings providing ventilation are not required in the following case:
  ○ Where mechanical ventilation is provided as follows:
     Mechanical ventilation must be continuous.
     1.0 cfm per 50 sf of crawl-space area must be provided.
     The ground must be covered as follows:
        With an approved vapor retarder.
- Openings providing ventilation are not required where both of the following apply:
  ○ Where the ground in the crawl space is covered as follows:
     With an approved vapor retarder.
  ○ Where the surrounding walls are insulated.
  ○ Where the space is conditioned.

     Note: International Energy Conservation Code is cited as governing conditioning of the insulated crawl space.

- Openings providing ventilation in flood hazard areas are governed as follows:
  ○ They may be designed according to flood resistance principles.

     Note: 1612.3, "Establishment of flood hazard areas," is cited as the source of requirements for establishing such areas.
     ASCE 24, "Flood Resistance Design and Construction," is cited as governing the design of openings in flood hazard areas.

1203.4 Natural ventilation

- Where natural ventilation is provided to occupied space, it must be through one or more of the following openings to the exterior:
  ○ Windows.
  ○ Doors.
  ○ Louvers.
  ○ Other openings.

1203 Ventilation

1203.4.2 Contaminants exhausted

- This section addresses spaces that are naturally ventilated.
- The removal of contaminants from such spaces is outside the scope of this code.

  Note: The following are cited as governing the removal of such contaminants:
  International Mechanical Code.
  International Fire Code.

1203.4.2.1 Bathrooms

- Spaces with the following fixtures must be mechanically ventilated:
  ○ Bathtubs.
  ○ Showers.
  ○ Spas.
  ○ Similar bathing fixtures.

  Note: International Mechanical Code is cited as governing such ventilation.

1203.4.3 Openings on yards or courts

- The following may provide natural ventilation to an interior space where they meet size and other requirements:
  ○ Yards.
  ○ Courts.

  Note: Section 1206, "Yards or Courts," is cited as providing requirements for these areas.

1203.5 Other ventilation and exhaust systems

- Ventilation for spaces with the following hazards is beyond the scope of this code:
  ○ Flammable hazards.
  ○ Combustible hazards.
  ○ Other contaminant sources.

  Note: The following are cited as governing the removal of such hazards:
  International Mechanical Code.
  International Fire Code.

1204 Temperature Control

1204.1 Equipment and systems

- This section does not govern the following interior spaces:
  - ○ Where human comfort is not required.
- In other spaces occupied by people the following applies:
  - ○ Either of the following heating systems is required with the capability listed below:
    Systems:
      Passive systems.
      Active systems.
    Capability:
      The system must be able to maintain a temperature in the space as follows:
        ≥ 68°F as follows:
          At 3' above floor level.
          On the design heating day.

1205 Lighting

1205.1 General

- All spaces designed for people must have lighting by one of the following means:
  - Artificial.

  Note: 1205.3, "Artificial light," is cited as governing this type of light.

  - Natural as follows:
    Openings providing light must be as follows:
    Exterior.
    Glazed.
    Open to one of the following:
    Public way.
    Yard.
    Court.

  Note: The following are cited as sources of applicable requirements:
  1205.2, "Natural light."
  Section 1206, "Yards or Courts."

1205.2 Natural light

- Net glazed area providing natural light must be the following size:
  - ≥ 8% of floor area served.

1205.2.1 Adjoining spaces

- Required exterior light openings may open to the following spaces where the requirements listed below are met:
  - Spaces:
    Thermally isolated sunroom addition.
    Thermally isolated patio cover.
  - Requirements:
    The opening in the common wall must have the characteristic listed below:
    Spaces:
    Sunroom space.
    Patio cover.
    Characteristic:
    The opening area must be equal to the greater of the following:
    ≥ 10% of the area of the interior space.
    20 sf.
- In other cases a space may receive required natural light through an adjoining space as follows:
  - ≥ 50% the common wall must be open.
  - The opening in the common wall must be the larger of the following:
    ≥ 10% of the interior space floor area.
    ≥ 25 sf.

1205 Lighting

1205.2.2 Exterior openings

- Exterior openings providing required natural light must comply with any of the following:
  - Openings must open directly to one of the following:
    Public way.
    Yard or court.
    A roofed porch with all the following characteristics:
      Porch abuts one of the following:
        Public way.
        Yard or court.
      Porch ceiling is ≥ 7' high.
      Longer side of porch is ≥ 65% open.

    Note: The following are cited as sources of applicable requirements:
    1205.2, "Natural light."
    Section 1206, "Yards or Courts."

  - Openings must be skylights.

1205.3 Artificial light

- Artificial light must provide the following illumination:
  - An average intensity ≥ 10 footcandles is required as follows:
    At a level 2'-6" high across the room.

1205.4 Stairway illumination

- Treads on the following stairways must be illuminated at a level ≥ 1 footcandle:
  - Within dwelling units.
  - Exterior dwelling unit stairways
- Other stairways are not governed by this section.

  Note: Chapter 10, "Means of Egress," is cited as governing other stairways.

1205.4.1 Controls

- The means for controlling stairway lighting is not governed by this code.

  Note: ICC Electrical Code is cited as governing these controls.

1205.4.5 Emergency egress lighting

- Means of egress illumination is not governed by this section.

  Note: 1006.1, "Illumination required," is cited as governing means of egress lighting.

1206 Yards or Courts

1206.1 General

- This section addresses yards and courts as follows:
  - ○ Next to openings for any of the following purposes:
    - Ventilation.
    - Natural light.
  - ○ They must be located on the same property as the building served.

1206.2 Yards

- The width of a yard measured ⊥ to the building façade is required as indicated below:

Table 1206.2   Minimum Yard Width

Building height	Yard width	Building height	Yard width	Building height	Yard width
1 story	≥ 3'	6 stories	≥ 7'	11 stories	≥ 12'
2 stories	≥ 3'	7 stories	≥ 8'	12 stories	≥ 13'
3 stories	≥ 4'	8 stories	≥ 9'	13 stories	≥ 14'
4 stories	≥ 5'	9 stories	≥ 10'	14 stories	≥ 15'
5 stories	≥ 6'	10 stories	≥ 11'	>14 stories	≥ 15'

1206.3 Courts *(part 1 of 2)*

- Courts with windows on any two opposite sides require widths as listed below:
  - ○ Width is measured between walls with facing windows.
  - ○ Where all walls have facing windows:
    - Either dimension is designated as width:
      - The other dimension is designated as length:
        - Length is governed by Table 1206.3c.

Table 1206.3a   Courts with Windows on Opposite Sides

Building height	Court width	Building height	Court width	Building height	Court width
1 story	≥ 6'	6 stories	≥ 10'	11 stories	≥ 15'
2 stories	≥ 6'	7 stories	≥ 11'	12 stories	≥ 16'
3 stories	≥ 7'	8 stories	≥ 12'	13 stories	≥ 17'
4 stories	≥ 8'	9 stories	≥ 13'	14 stories	≥ 18'
5 stories	≥ 9'	10 stories	≥ 14'	>14 stories	≥ 18'

- Courts without windows on opposite sides require widths as listed below:
  - ○ Where courts are open on one end to a public way or yard:
    - Width is measured between facing walls.
  - ○ Where courts are not open on one side to a public way or yard:
    - Either dimension is designated as width:
      - The other dimension is designated as length:
        - Length is governed by Table 1206.3c.

1206 Yards or Courts

1206.3 Courts *(part 2 of 2)*

Table 1206.3b   Courts without Windows on Opposite Sides

Building height	Court width	Building height	Court width	Building height	Court width
1 story	≥ 3'	6 stories	≥ 7'	11 stories	≥ 12'
2 stories	≥ 3'	7 stories	≥ 8'	12 stories	≥ 13'
3 stories	≥ 4'	8 stories	≥ 9'	13 stories	≥ 14'
4 stories	≥ 5'	9 stories	≥ 10'	14 stories	≥ 15'
5 stories	≥ 6'	10 stories	≥ 11	>14 stories	≥ 15'

- Courts not open on one end to a public way or yard require lengths as listed below:
  ○ Length is ⊥ to the required widths governed by Table 1206.3a and 1206.3b.

Table 1206.3c   Minimum Length of Courts

Building height	Court length	Building height	Court length	Building height	Court length
1 story	≥ 10'	6 stories	≥ 18'	11 stories	≥ 28'
2 stories	≥ 10'	7 stories	≥ 20'	12 stories	≥ 30'
3 stories	≥ 12'	8 stories	≥ 22'	13 stories	≥ 32'
4 stories	≥ 14'	9 stories	≥ 24'	14 stories	≥ 34'
5 stories	≥ 16'	10 stories	≥ 26'	>14 stories	≥ 34'

1206.3.1 Court access

- Access is required to the bottom of a court for cleaning.

1206.3.2 Air intake

- Courts require a way to bring in air at the bottom as follows:
  ○ Air intake is required for the following courts:
    Courts which do not abut a yard or public way.
    Courts > 2 stories high.
  ○ Air intake requires the following characteristics:
    Must be horizontal.
    Must be located at the bottom of the court.
    Must be ≥ 10 sf in area.
    Must lead to the exterior.

1206.3.3 Court drainage

- The following is required for drainage of a court:
  ○ Court must be graded for adequate drainage.
  ○ Court must be drained to one of the following:
    A public sewer.
    Other approved disposal system.

  Note: International Plumbing Code is cited as the source governing drainage disposal systems as required above.

Case study: Fig. 1206.3. All walls facing the courtyard of this 2-story building have windows. One corner of the courtyard is open to the public way on the ground level only. The minimum width of the courtyard is 6'. The minimum length of the courtyard between walls is 10'. The courtyard is 27'-9" wide and 33' long, thus, meeting size minimums. The courtyard is graded and drained as required by the code. The courtyard is in compliance with code requirements.

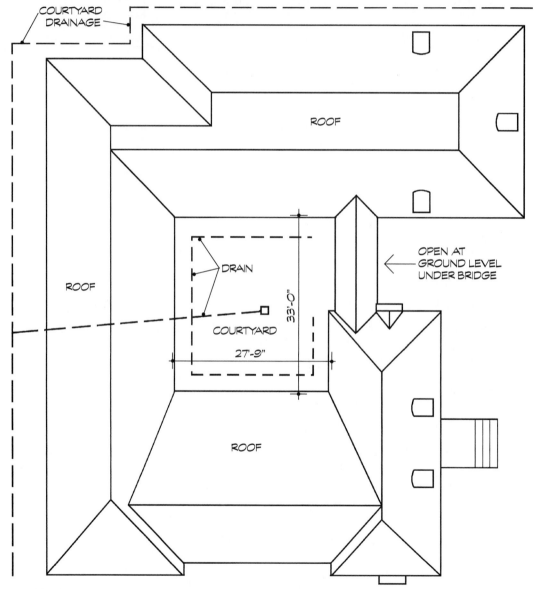

Fig. 1206.3. Courtyard plan. Multipurpose Building Addition to Children's Home. Wilkes-Barre, Pennsylvania. C. Allen Mullins, Architect. Bear Creek, Pennsylvania.

1207 Sound Transmission

1207.1 Scope

- This section provides sound transmission requirements indicated below as applicable to elements of dwelling units as follows:
  - Elements:
    Common interior walls between adjacent units.
    Interior walls between units and adjacent public areas:
      Halls.
      Corridors.
      Stairs.
      Service areas.
    Floor/ceiling assemblies between adjacent units.
    Floor/ceiling assemblies between units and adjacent public areas:
      Halls.
      Corridors.
      Stairs.
      Service areas.

1207.2 Air-borne sound

- Dwelling unit entrance doors are governed for airborne sound as follows:
  - Tight fit to the frame and sill are required.
  - A required Sound Transmission Class (STC) rating is not specified.
- One of the following STC ratings is required for walls and floors governed by this section:
  - STC $\geq$ 50 is required where not verified by field test.
  - STC $\geq$ 45 is required where verified by field test.

  Note: ASTM E90, "Test Method for Laboratory Measurement of Airborne Sound Transmission Loss of Building Partitions and Elements," is cited as governing the method for determining STC ratings.

1207.3 Structure-borne sound

- One of the following Impact Insulation Class (IIC) ratings is required for floor/ceiling assemblies governed by this section:
  - IIC $\geq$ 50 is required where not verified by field test.
  - IIC $\geq$ 45 is required where verified by field test.

  Note: ASTM E492, "Test Method for Laboratory Measurement of Impact Sound Transmission Through Floor-ceiling Assemblies Using the Tapping Machine," is cited as governing the method for determining IIC ratings.

1208 Interior Space Dimensions

1208.1 Minimum room widths

- Habitable spaces other than kitchens require the following size:
  - ○ ≥ 7' for any room dimension in plan.
- Kitchens require ≥ 3' clear space as follows:
  - ○ Between counter fronts and any of the following:
    - Appliances.
    - Other counter fronts.
    - Walls.

1208.2 Minimum ceiling heights

- Mezzanines are not governed by this section.

  Note: 505.1, "General," is cited as governing mezzanines.

- In 1- and 2-family dwellings, the following applies:
  - ○ Beams and girders may project below the required the ceiling height as follows:
    - Where spaced ≥ 4' on center.
    - Where projecting ≤ 6" below required ceiling height.
- In all occupancies, the following applies:
  - ○ ≥ 7'-0" is the required ceiling height in the following spaces:
    - Bathrooms.
    - Toilet rooms.
    - Kitchens.
    - Storage rooms.
    - Laundry rooms.
  - ○ ≥ 7'-6" is the required ceiling height for other spaces as follows:
    - Habitable space.
    - Occupiable space.
    - Corridors.
- The following applies to sloped ceilings:
  - ○ The required ceiling height must be provided for ≥ $\frac{1}{2}$ the area.
  - ○ Floor area counted in minimum area requirements must have the following height:
    - Ceiling height ≥ 5'.

Case study: Fig. 1208.1. The kitchen complies with the requirement that at least 3' of space be provided between counters and other objects and walls as indicated in the plan.

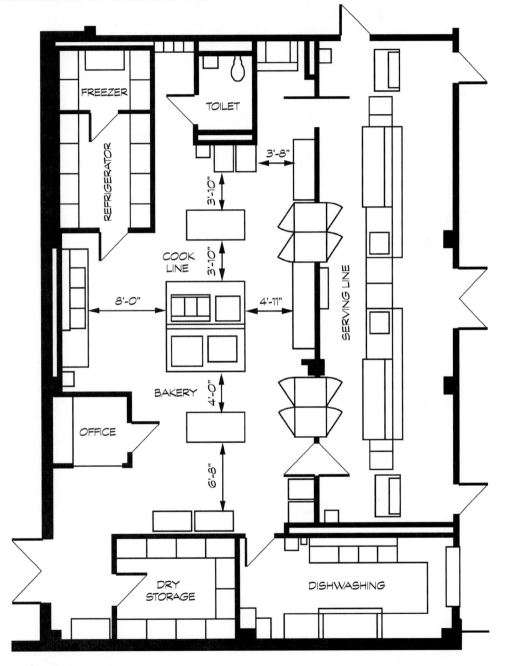

Fig. 1208.1. Partial floor plan at kitchen. New Jasper Pre-K–2nd Grade School. Jasper, Texas. PBK Architects, Inc. Houston, Texas.

1208 Interior Space Dimensions

1208.2.1 Furred ceiling

- Furred ceilings are governed as follows:
  - A furred ceiling must have the required ceiling height as follows:
    In ²/₃ the room area.
  - Otherwise, a furred ceiling may not have a height < 7'.

1208.3 Room area

- Rooms in dwelling units are governed as follows:
  - Kitchens in 1- and 2-family units must have the following size:
    ≥ 50 sf of gross floor area.
  - A net floor area ≥ 120 sf is required in ≥ 1 room.
  - Other habitable rooms require a net floor area ≥ 70 sf.

1208.4 Efficiency dwelling units

- A living room ≥ 220 sf is required for units with ≤ 2 occupants:
  - 100 sf is added to this requirement for each additional occupant.
- A separate closet is required.
- The following appliances and clearances are required:

Appliance	Clearance in front of appliance
Cooking	≥ 2'-6"
Refrigerator	≥ 2'-6"

- A separate bathroom is required with the following:
  - Water closet.
  - Lavatory.
  - Bathtub or shower.
- Units must conform to the requirements of the code as follows:
  - For light.
  - For ventilation.
  - All other requirements as applicable.

1209 Access to Unoccupied Spaces

1209.1 Crawl spaces

- Crawl spaces required ≥ 1 access opening as follows:
  - Dimensions must be as follows:
    Width ≥ 1'-6".
    Length ≥ 2'.

1209.2 Attic spaces

- Attic space with a clear height ≥ 2'-6" has the following access requirements:
  - Dimensions of an access opening must be as follows:
    Width ≥ 1'-8".
    Length ≥ 2'-6".
  - Headroom ≥ 2'-6" is required at the access opening.

> **Case study: Fig. 1209.2.** The clear height of the attic is > 2'-6"; thus, it must meet minimum access requirements. The headroom at the attic access is 4'-3", which is > than the 2'-6" minimum required. The access opening is 3' × 3', which complies with the minimum size requirements of 1'-8" × 2'-6". Access to the attic is in compliance with code requirements.

1209.3 Mechanical appliances

- Access to mechanical appliances in the following locations is not governed by this code:
  - In crawl spaces.
  - In attic spaces.
  - On roofs.
  - On elevated structures.

Note: International Mechanical Code is cited as governing such access.

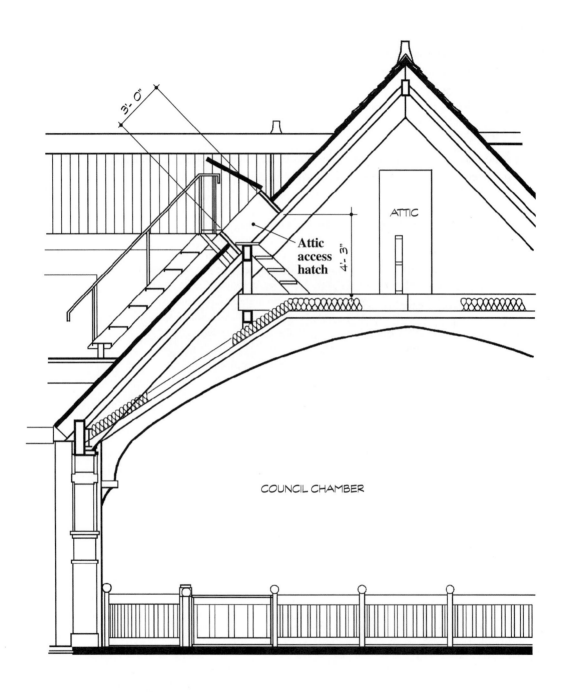

3'- 0"

ATTIC

Attic
access
hatch

4'- 3"

COUNCIL CHAMBER

Fig. 1209.2. Partial section at attic. Lake Forest City Hall Renovation and Addition. Lake Forest, Illinois. David Woodhouse Architects. Chicago, Illinois.

1210 Surrounding Materials

1210.1 Floors

- The following applies to other than dwelling units:
  - ○ Floors of the following rooms are governed as indicated below:
    Rooms:
    Toilets.
    Bathing rooms.
    Floors:
    Smooth surface required.
    Hard nonabsorbent surface required.
    Floor surface material must extend up walls ≥ 6".

1210.2 Walls

- Requirements indicated below do not apply to the following:
  - ○ Toilet rooms in dwelling units and sleeping units.
  - ○ Toilet rooms with both of the following characteristics:
    Rooms not accessible to the public.
    Rooms with < 2 water closets.
- Other toilet rooms are governed as follows:
  - ○ Walls ≤ 2' of urinals and water closets have the following requirements:
    Surface to a height ≥ 4' must have the following characteristics:
    Smooth.
    Hard.
    Nonabsorbent.
    Materials other than structure are governed as follows:
    Must not be affected by moisture.
  - ○ Accessories as follows must be installed as indicated below:
    Accessories:
    Grab bars.
    Towel bars.
    Paper dispensers.
    Soap dishes.
    Similar accessories.
    Requirement:
    Installed and sealed to protect structure from moisture.

Case study: Fig. 1210.2. The wall of the toilet room within 2' of the water closet is covered with tile to a height of 7'. The floor is tile, and tile is provided as a base at the wall. These surfaces meet the minimum requirement wherein a smooth, hard, and non-absorbent material must reach a height ≥ 4' on the wall, cover the floor, and reach ≥ 6" up the wall from the floor. As required, accessories such as grab bars and toilet paper holder are sealed where they connect to the wall to prohibit the penetration of moisture. This toilet room complies with all code requirements.

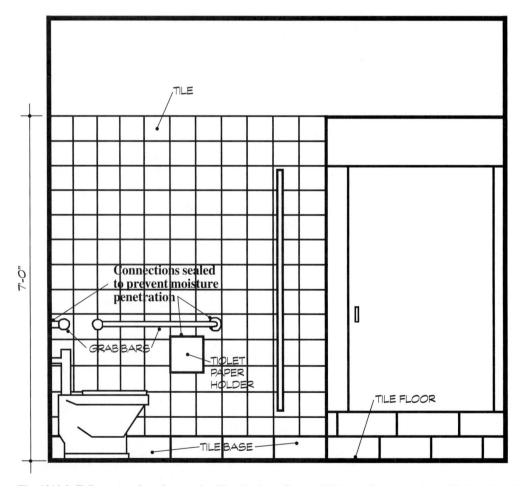

Fig. 1210.2. Toilet room elevation. AmberGlen Business Center. Hillsboro, Oregon. Ankrom Moisan Associated Architects. Portland, Oregon.

1210 Surrounding Materials

1210.3 Showers

- Finish materials in the following shower areas are governed as indicated below:
  - Shower areas:
    Shower stalls.
    Showers in bathtubs.
  - A surface as follows is required to a height $\geq$ 5'-10" above the drain inlet:
    Smooth.
    Hard.
    Nonabsorbent.

1210.4 Waterproof joints

- The joint between the following components must be waterproof:
  - A built-in bathtub with a shower.
  - The adjacent wall.

1210.5 Toilet rooms

- Toilet rooms may not open directly to the following space:
  - A space where food for service to the public is prepared.

Case study: Fig. 1210.5. Toilet rooms are prohibited from opening into a space where food is prepared for the public. The staff toilet room for this kitchen opens into an alcove, thus, complying with this code restriction.

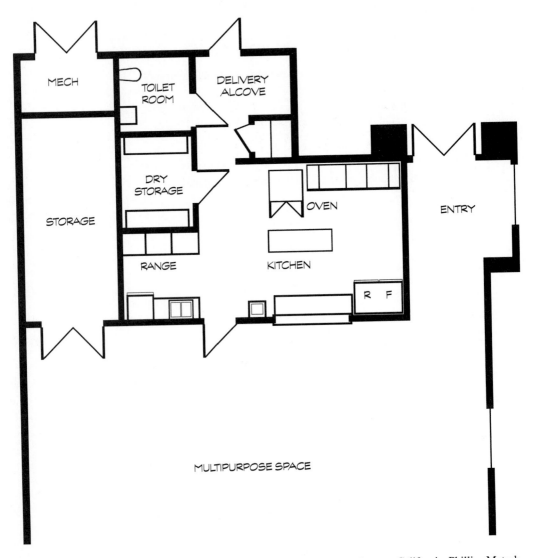

Fig. 1210.5. Partial floor plan. Creston Elementary Multipurpose Building. Creston, California. Phillips Metsch Sweeney Moore Architects. Santa Barbara, California.

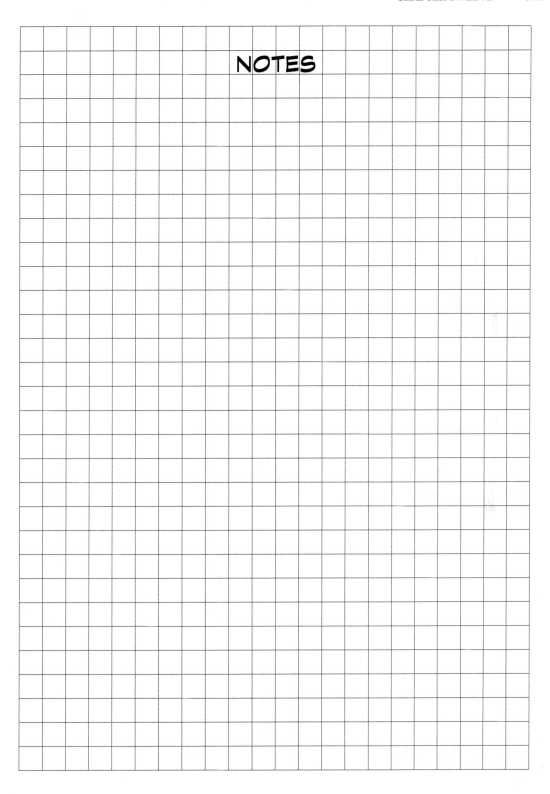

NOTES

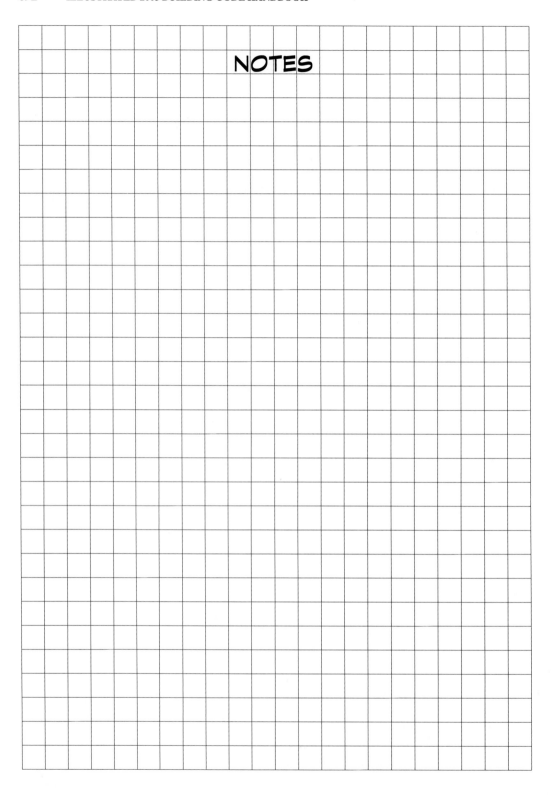

NOTES

13

Energy Efficiency

Alterations to 209 Main Street. Annapolis, Maryland.
Alt Breeding Schwarz Architects, LLC. Annapolis, Maryland.

1301 General

1301.1.1 Criteria

- For purposes of energy efficiency, buildings must comply with the following code:
  - *International Energy Conservation Code.*

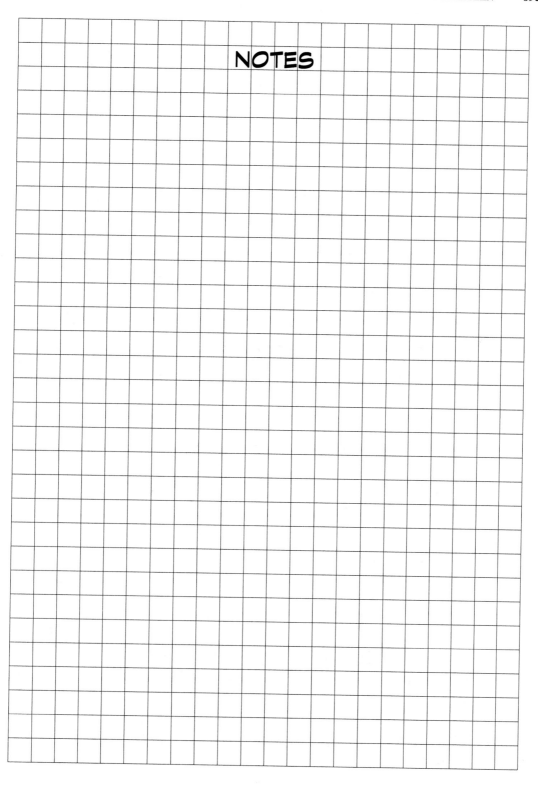

NOTES

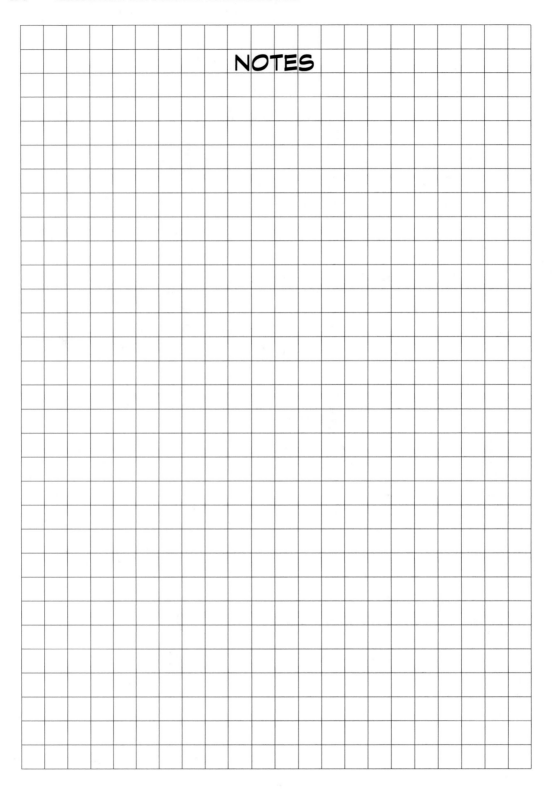

NOTES

14

Exterior Walls

New Warehouse Addition. Los Angeles, California. *(partial elevation)*
Stephen Wen + Associates, Architects, Inc. Pasadena, California.

1403 Performance Requirements

1403.1 General

- This section applies to the following:
  - Exterior walls.
  - Exterior wall coverings.
  - Components of exterior walls.

1403.2 Weather protection *(part 1 of 2)*

- This section addresses detailing of the exterior wall.
- A weather-resistant exterior wall envelope is not required on the following:
  - Concrete walls.
  - Masonry walls.

  Note: The following are cited as governing the walls indicated above:
  Chapter 19, "Concrete."
  Chapter 21, "Masonry."

- Otherwise, the following is required for exterior walls:
  - A weather-resistant exterior wall envelope including the following:
    Flashing.

  Note: 1405.3, "Flashing," is cited as governing required flashing.

- The following detailing may be omitted in lieu of testing the exterior wall envelope as indicated below:
  - Details:
    The following details as specified in this chapter may be omitted:
    Drainage.
    Weather protection.
    Flashing.
  - Testing:
    Test must demonstrate the following:
    Ability of alternative detailing to resist wind-driven rain.

  Note: The following are cited as governing the detailing that may be omitted in lieu of testing:
  1405.2, "Weather protection."
  1405.3, "Flashing."
  ASTM E 331, "Test Method for Water Penetration of Exterior Windows, Skylights, Doors, and Curtain Wall by Uniform Static Air Pressure Difference," is cited as governing the required testing.

1403 Performance Requirements

1403.2 Weather protection *(part 2 of 2)*

- Where water penetration would compromise building performance:
  - The following detailing must be provided to perform as indicated below:
    Detailing:
    A water-resistant barrier behind the exterior veneer.
    A method for drainage.
    Flashing.
    Performance:
    Must prevent collection of water within the assembly.

    Note: 1404.2, "Water-resistive barrier," is cited as governing such components.

- The wall must be protected against condensation.

    Note: International Energy Conservation Code is cited as providing requirements applicable to condensation.

1403.3 Vapor retarder

- A vapor retarder as specified in this section is not required in an exterior wall in the following cases:
  - Where other approved methods are provided to prevent the following:
    Condensation.
    Moisture leakage.
  - In exterior concrete walls.
  - In exterior masonry walls.

    Note: The following are cited as governing concrete and masonry walls in lieu of this section:
    Chapter 19, "Concrete."
    Chapter 21, "Masonry."

- Otherwise, an interior vapor retarder must be provided in exterior walls as follows:
  - Must be approved.

1403 Performance Requirements

1403.6 Flood resistance

- The following applies to buildings in flood hazard areas:
  - Exterior walls below design flood elevation are governed as follows:
    They must resist water damage.
    Wood must be one of the following:
      Pressure-treated with preservative.
      Decay-resistant heartwood of any of the following:
        Redwood.
        Black locust.
        Cedar.

    Note: 1612.3, "Establishment of flood hazard areas," is cited as establishing such
    areas to which this section applies.
    The following are cited as governing pressure-treated wood as required above:
      AWPA C1, "All Timber Products—Preservative Treatment by Pressure
        Processes."
      AWPA C2, "Lumber, Timber, Bridge Ties and Mine Ties—Preservative Treatment
        by Pressure Processes."
      AWPA C3, "Piles—Preservative Treatment by Pressure Processes."
      AWPA C4, "Poles-—Preservative Treatment by Pressure Processes."
      AWPA C9, "Plywood—Preservative Treatment by Pressure Processes."
      AWPA C15, "Wood for Commercial-Residential Construction Preservative
        Treatment by Pressure Processes."
      AWPA C18, "Standard for Pressure Treated Material in Marine Construction."
      AWPA C22, "Lumber and Plywood for Permanent Wood Foundations—
        Preservative Treatment by Pressure Processes."
      AWPA C24, "Sawn Timber Piles Used to Support Residential and Commercial
        Structures."
      AWPA C28, "Standard for Preservative Treatment by Pressure Process of
        Structural Glued Laminated Members and Lamination before Gluing."
      AWPA P1, "Standard Creosote Preservative."
      AWPA P2, "Standard for Creosote Solutions."
      AWPA P3, "Standard for Creosote-Petroleum Oil Solutions."

1403.7 Flood resistance for high-velocity wave action areas

- Buildings in flood zones with high-velocity wave potential are governed as follows:
  - The following elements have the requirements listed below:
    Elements:
      Electrical, mechanical, and plumbing system elements.
    Requirements:
      Such elements may not be secured to or penetrate the following exterior walls:
        Those designed to collapse with wave impact.

  Note: 1612.3, "Establishment of flood hazard areas," is cited as governing these zones.

1405 Installation of Wall Coverings

1405.2 Weather protection

- Exterior walls must provide the following for a building:
  - Protection from the weather.
- The following materials are acceptable as weather coverings on exterior walls:
  - Materials with the nominal thickness shown in details provided with this section as follows:

    Figs. 1405.2A through Fig. 1405.2G.

    Note: IBC Table 1405.2, "Minimum Thickness of Weather Coverings," is cited as the source of acceptable materials as required above and is the source for the data with the details provided by this section.

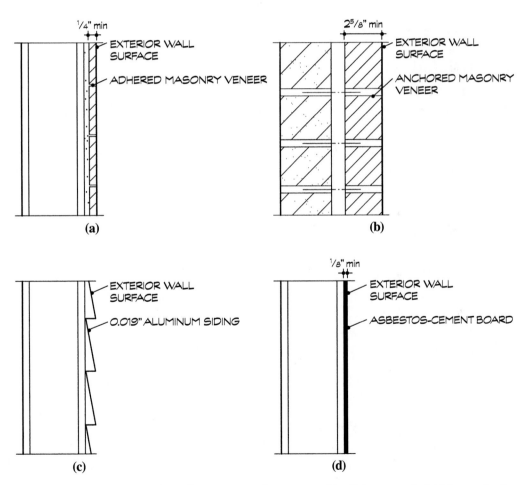

Fig. 1405.2A. Minimum thickness of weather coverings. Acceptable minimum nominal thickness of various types of cladding are shown in the wall sections.

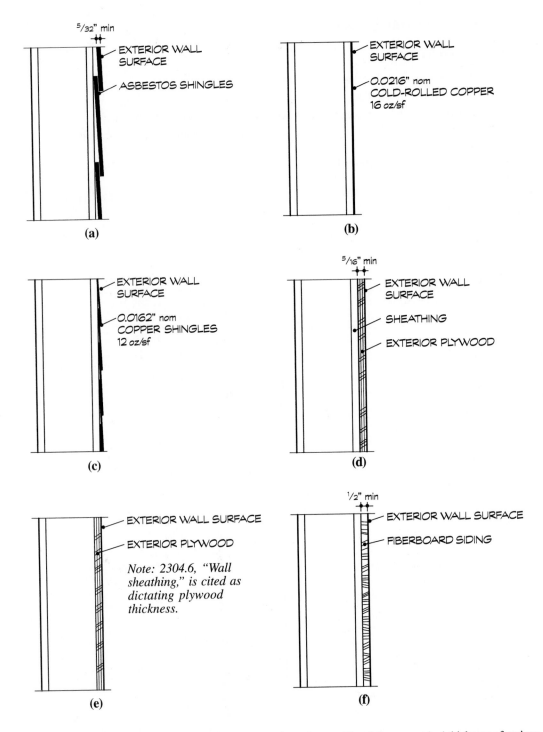

Fig. 1405.2B. Minimum thickness of weather coverings. Acceptable minimum nominal thickness of various types of cladding are shown in the wall sections.

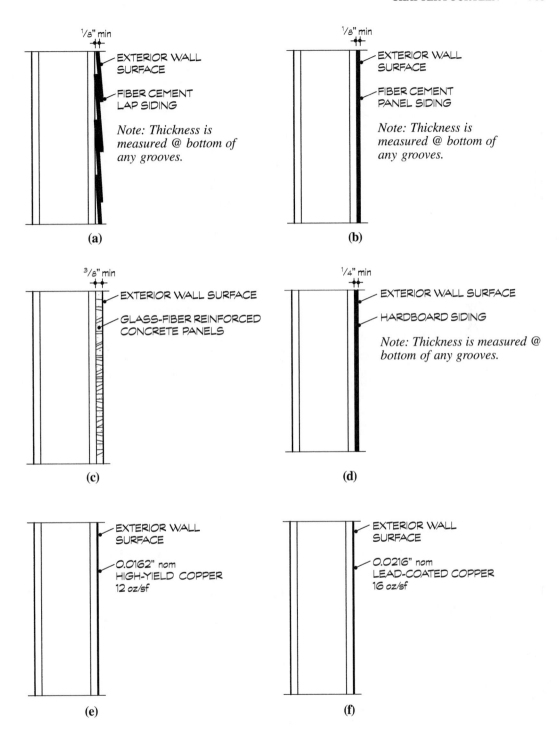

Fig. 1405.2C. Minimum thickness of weather coverings. Acceptable minimum nominal thickness of various types of cladding are shown in the wall sections.

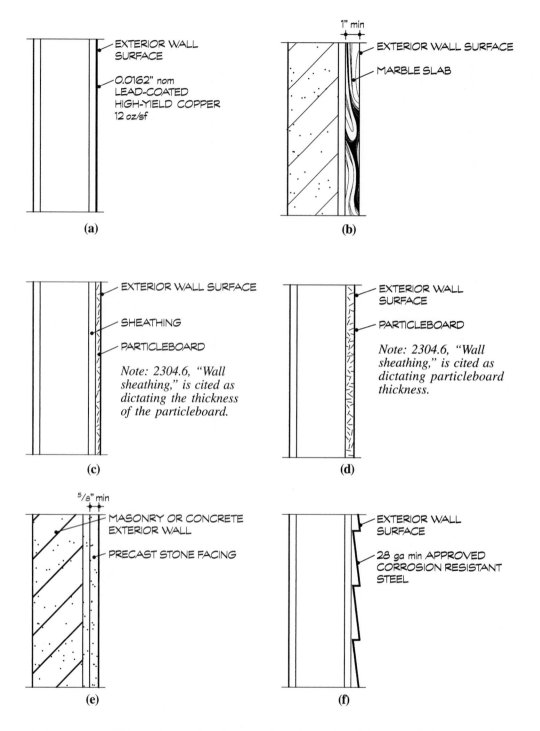

Fig. 1405.2D. Minimum thickness of weather coverings. Acceptable minimum nominal thickness of various types of cladding are shown in the wall sections.

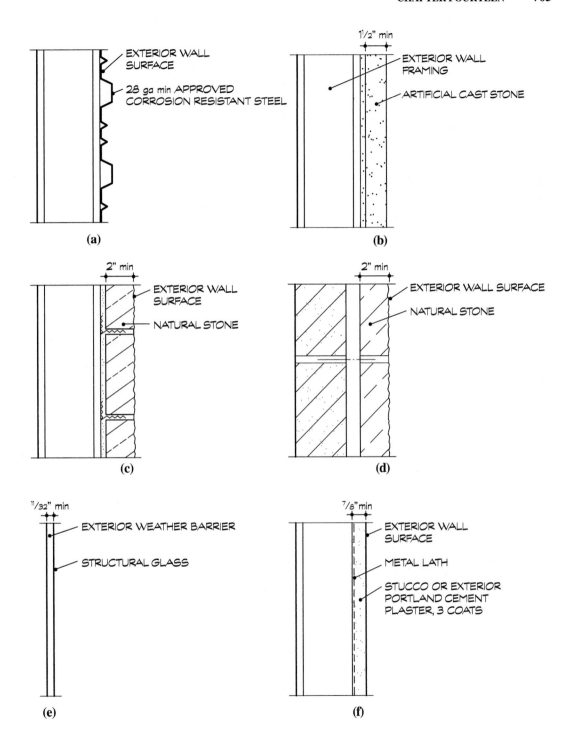

Fig. 1405.2E. Minimum thickness of weather coverings. Acceptable minimum nominal thickness of various types of cladding are shown in the wall sections.

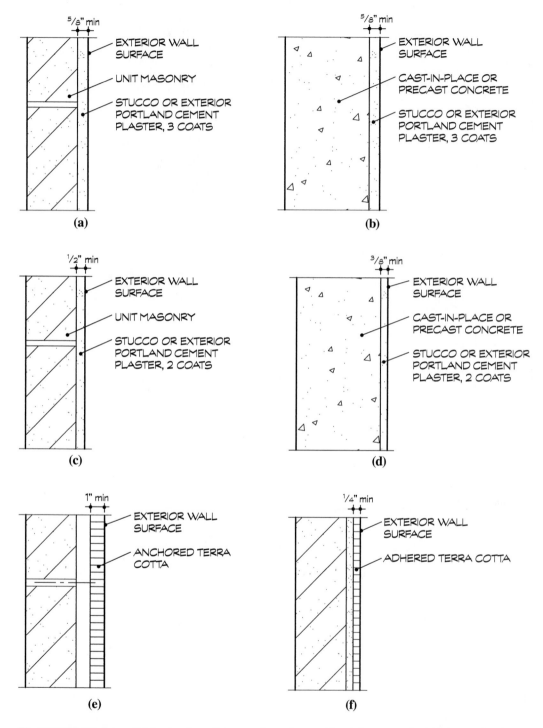

Fig. 1405.2F. Minimum thickness of weather coverings. Acceptable minimum nominal thickness of various types of cladding are shown in the wall sections.

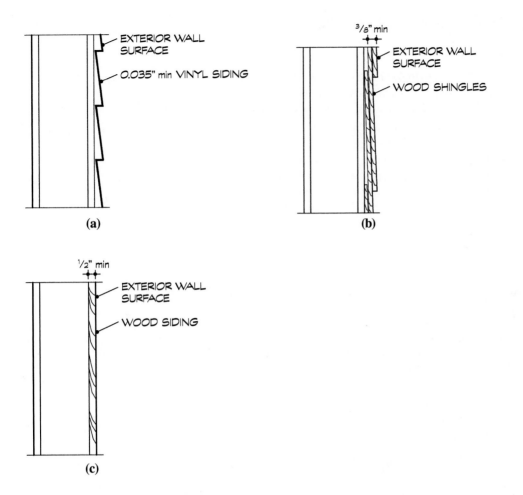

Fig. 1405.2G. Minimum thickness of weather coverings. Acceptable minimum nominal thickness of various types of cladding are shown in the wall sections.

1405 Installation of Wall Coverings

1405.3 Flashing

- Flashing must perform in one or both of the following ways:
  - Prevent water from penetrating a wall.
  - Deliver water from inside a wall to the exterior.
- Flashing is required at the following locations:
  - At the perimeters of door assemblies.
  - At the perimeters of window assemblies.
  - At penetrations of exterior wall assemblies.
  - At terminations of exterior wall assemblies.
  - At exterior wall intersections with the following:
    Roofs.
    Chimneys.
    Porches.
    Decks.
    Balconies.
    Projections similar to balconies.
  - At built-in gutters.
  - At locations similar to built-in gutters as follows:
    Where water might penetrate a wall.
- Flashing with flanges is required in the following locations:
  - At copings as follows:
    On both sides.
    On ends.
  - Under sills.
  - Above projecting trim as follows:
    As continuous flashing.

1405.3.1 Exterior wall pockets

- Detailing at exterior walls that permits moisture to collect is governed as follows:
  - Such is not permitted without the following protection:
    Devices to prevent water damage as follows:
    Caps.
    Drips.
    Other approved protection.

Case study: Fig. 1405.3. The intersection of the entry canopy roof and the building wall is required to have flashing in the step-configuration. Such flashing is provided; thus, the detailing is in compliance with the code.

Fig. 1405.3. Partial elevation at east entry. Hot Springs Police Department New Headquarters. Hot Springs National Park, Arkansas. Cromwell Architects Engineers. Little Rock, Arkansas.

1405 Installation of Wall Coverings

1405.3.2 Masonry

- The following detailing is required in anchored masonry veneers at the locations indicated:
  - Detailing:
    - Flashing.
    - Weep holes.
  - Locations:
    - Above grade and in the first course of masonry above the following:
      - Foundation wall.
      - Slab.
      - Points of masonry support such as the following:
        - Structural floors.
        - Shelf angles.
        - Lintels.

  Note: 1405.5, "Anchored masonry veneer," is cited as a source of requirements.

1405.4 Wood veneers

- This section addresses exterior wood veneers in construction other than Type V.
- The following materials are required for such veneers:
  - ≥ 1" wood.
  - $\geq \frac{7}{16}$" exterior hardboard siding.
  - $\geq \frac{3}{8}$" exterior wood structural panels.
  - $\geq \frac{3}{8}$" exterior particleboard.
- Such wood veneers must comply with all of the following:
  - The height of the veneer measured from grade is limited as follows:
    - Fire-retardant-treated wood must be ≤ 4 stories.
    - Other wood must be ≤ 3 stories.
  - The veneer must be attached as follows to a backing as indicated below:
    - Attachment:
      - To a noncombustible backing.
      - To furring on a noncombustible backing.
    - Backing:
      - Must have the fire-resistance rating as required elsewhere in the code.
  - Open or spaced veneers without concealed spaces are governed as follows:
    - Veneer not projecting $> 2'$ from the building wall.

1405.6 Stone veneer *(part 1 of 2)*

- Stone veneer ≤ 10" thick must be anchored directly to one of the following types of construction:
  - Masonry.
  - Concrete.
  - Stud.

1405 Installation of Wall Coverings

1405.6 Stone veneer *(part 2 of 2)*

- Where backed by concrete or masonry the following applies:
  - One of the following anchor ties is required:
    - ≥ 0.1055" diameter (12 gage) corrosion-resistant wire.
    - Approved equal.
  - Anchor ties are to be formed in loops as follows:
    - Legs ≥ 6" are to be bent at right angles for embedding in the backing wall.
    - Loop must extend beyond the face of the backing wall.
    - Loops must be spaced ≤ 12" on center in both directions.
  - One of the following masonry ties is required as follows:
    - ≥ 0.1055" diameter (12 gage) corrosion-resistant wire.
    - Approved equal.
  - Masonry ties are to be formed into loops as follows:
    - They are to be threaded through anchor tie loops in the following manner:
      - ≥ 1 masonry tie is required for every ≤ 2 sf of stone.
      - Legs ≥ 15" bent are to lie in joint of stone veneer as follows:
        - The last 2" of each leg must be bent at a right angle.
  - ≥ 1" cement grout must be placed as follows:
    - Between stone and backing.
- Where backed by stud construction the following apply:
  - Wood studs to be spaced ≤ 16" on center.
  - 2 layers of waterproof paper backing are applied to the studs.

  Note: 1403.3, "Vapor retarder," is cited as governing the waterproof paper.

  - Wire mesh is attached to the studs over the paper backing as follows:
    - Mesh to be corrosion-resistant wire ≥ 0.0625" diameter (16 gage).
    - Mesh to be 2" × 2".
    - Mesh is attached to studs as follows:
      - With 2" steel wire furring nails at 4" on center.
      - Nails to penetrate studs ≥ 1$^{1}/_{8}$".
    - Mesh is attached to top and bottom plates as follows:
      - With the following 8d common nails or equivalent wire ties:
        - Nails at 8" on center.
  - One of the following masonry ties is required as follows:
    - Corrosion-resistant wire ≥ 0.1055" diameter (12 gage).
    - Approved equal.
  - Masonry ties to be formed into loops in the following manner:
    - Threaded through the wire mesh as follows:
      - ≥ 1 masonry tie is required for every ≤ 2 sf of stone.
      - Legs ≥ 15" bent to lie in joint of stone veneer as follows:
        - Last 2" of each leg must be bent at a right angle.
  - ≥ 1" cement grout must be placed as follows:
    - Between stone and backing.

1405 Installation of Wall Coverings

1405.7 Slab-type veneer

- Slab-shaped masonry veneer units must be anchored directly to the following construction:
  - Masonry.
  - Concrete.
  - Stud.
- Slab-shaped masonry veneer units must comply with the following size limits:
  - Thickness must be ≤ 2".
  - Face area must be ≤ 20 sf.
- The requirements indicated below apply to the following veneer units:
  - Units:
    Marble.
    Travertine.
    Granite.
    Other slab-shaped stone.
  - Requirements:
    Corrosion-resistant dowels are required to secure ties to slabs.
    ≥ 4 dowels and ties for each veneer unit are required.
    Dowels are to be located as follows:
    In holes drilled in the middle $^1/_3$ of the edge thickness:
    Holes to be spaced around the perimeter of the unit as follows:
    At ≤ 2' on center.
    Holes to be one of the following:
    Tight-fitting around dowel.
    With a diameter ≤ $^1/_{16}$" > dowel diameter as follows:
    Hole is countersunk as follows:
    With a diameter 2 × that of the dowel.
    To a depth 2 × that of the dowel diameter.
    Hole is grouted with cement mortar around dowel.
    Ties are to be as follows:
    Corrosion-resistant metal.
    Able to resist tensile or compressive forces as follows:
    ≥ 2 × the weight of the veneer unit attached.
    In one of the following shapes:
    Sheet metal ≥ 0.0336" (22 gage) × 1" in cross section.
    Wire ≥ 0.1483" diameter (9 gage).

1405 Installation of Wall Coverings

1405.8 Terra cotta

- This section addresses terra cotta or ceramic units anchored directly to backing walls.
- Veneer units specified in this section must be anchored directly to the following construction:
  - Masonry.
  - Concrete.
  - Stud.
- Veneer units must have the following physical properties:
  - Ribbed profile as follows:

    Dovetail ribs at 8"(±) on center.
  - $\geq 1^5/_8$" thick including the ribs.
- Veneer units are tied to the backing as follows:
  - Ties are corrosion-resistant wire as follows:

    Diameter ≥ 0.162" (8 gage).
  - Ties are installed into the top of each unit:

    In horizontal bed joints as follows:

    ≥ 12" and ≤ 18" on center.
  - Ties are connected to ¼" diameter steel rods as follows:

    Rods are vertical.

    Rods pass through loops of anchors secured in the backing wall.
  - Ties must have the following strength:

    To support the full weight of the veneer in tension.
- Veneer units must be installed as follows:
  - With ≥ 2" space behind the units as follows:

    Between the face of the ribs and the backing wall.
  - Space must be grouted solid with the following:

    Portland cement grout.

    Pea gravel.
  - Just prior to setting, the following must be thoroughly wetted with clean water:

    Veneer units.

    Backing wall.
  - The following must be visibly damp when the veneer units are set:

    Veneer units.

    Backing wall.

1405 Installation of Wall Coverings

1405.9.1 Adhesion

- The adhesion between the following layers must be as required below:
  - Layers:
    Veneer masonry units.
    Backing construction.
  - Requirement:
    Shear strength developed must be $\geq$ 50 psi as follows:
    Based on gross unit surface area.

  Note: Compliance Article 3.3C of the following is provided as an alternative method of adhering the masonry to backing as specified in this section:
  ACI 530.1, "Buildng Code Requirements for Masonry Structures."
  ASCE 6, "Specifications for Masonry Structures."
  TMS 602, "Specifications for Masonry Structures."

1405.9.1.1 Interior masonry veneers

- Veneer weight is limited to $\leq$ 20 lbs/sf.
  - Where supported by wood construction, the following applies:
    Supporting members which have a span must be designed as follows:
    Deflection is limited to $\leq$ $^1/_{600}$ of the span.

  Note: 1405.9, "Adhered masonry veneer," is cited as the source of requirements for the installation of such components.

1405.10 Metal veneers

- Metal veneers must be one of the following:
  - Of approved corrosion-resistant materials.
  - Be protected with porcelain enamel as follows:
    On the front.
    On the back.
  - Be processed to provided corrosion resistance.
- Metal veneers must be as follows:
  - $\geq$ 0.0149" thick (28 gage) sheet steel.
  - Mounted on one of the following:
    Wood furring strips.
    Metal furring strips.
    Approved sheathing on wood construction.

1405 Installation of Wall Coverings

1405.10.1 Attachment

- Metal veneers must be attached to the following construction as indicated below:
  - ○ Construction:
    - Masonry.
    - Framing.
  - ○ Attachment:
    - One of the following attachment methods is required:
      - Corrosion-resistant fastenings.
      - Metal ties.
      - Other approved methods.
    - Spacing of attachments must be ≤ 2' as follows:
      - Vertically and horizontally.
    - Where units are > 4 sf:
      - ≥ 4 attachments per unit are required.
    - Attachment devices must have the following cross-sectional area:
      - ≥ that provided by W 1.7 wire (0.017 sq in).
    - Attachments and their supports must have strength as per the larger of the following:
      - They must be able to resist applicable wind loads.
      - They must be able to resist a horizontal load ≥ 20 lbs/sf.

Note: Section 1609, "Wind Loads," is cited as the source governing wind loading.

1405.10.2 Weather protection

- Metal supports for exterior metal veneer must be protected by one of the following:
  - ○ Painting or galvanizing.
  - ○ Other equivalent method.
- The following wood supports must be protected from moisture as indicated below:
  - ○ Supports:
    - Studs and furring strips.
    - Other wood supports.
  - ○ Moisture protection:
    - One of the following is required:
      - Supports must be approved pressure-treated wood.
      - Must be protected from moisture contact.
    - The following details must be protected as indicated below:
      - Details:
        - Joints and edges exposed to the weather.
      - Protection:
        - Must be caulked by one of the following to prevent moisture penetration:
          - With a durable waterproofing material.
          - Other approved material.

Note: 1403.2, "Weather protection," is cited as the source of methods to protect wood supports from moisture contact.

1405 Installation of Wall Coverings

1405.11 Glass veneer

- The area limitations of exterior glass veneer panels as follows is indicated below:
  - Structural glass veneer as follows:

    Single sections of thin glass:

Height above grade	Glass area
≤ 15'	≤ 10 sf
> 15'	≤ 6 sf

1405.11.1 Length and height

- Thin exterior structural glass veneer dimensions are governed as follows:
  - All dimensions are limited to ≤ 4'.

1405.11.2 Thickness

- Thin exterior structural glass veneer thickness is governed as follows:
  - Thickness must be ≥ 0.344".

1405.11.3 Application

- Thin exterior structural glass veneer must be set in the following conditions:
  - Backing must be dry.
  - An approved bond coat applied to the backing as follows:

    Bond coat must be evenly distributed.

    Backing surface must be completely sealed.
  - Glass panels must be installed as follows:

    With an approved mastic cement.

    So that ≥ 50% of each glass panel is bonded to the backing as follows:

    By mastic ≥ ¼" and ≤ ⅝" thick.

    Compatibility of mastic with bond coat must be verified.

    Mastic must adhere securely to backing.

1405.11.4 Installation at sidewalk level

- Glass veneer at sidewalk level must be detailed as follows:
  - Glass panels must set in a metal molding as follows:

    Must be approved.

    Space between molding and sidewalk must be treated as follows:

    Caulked for watertightness.
  - Glass panels must be set ≥ ¼" above the following:

    The highest point of the sidewalk.

1405 Installation of Wall Coverings

1405.11.4.1 Installation above sidewalk level

- This section applies to thin exterior structural glass veneer as follows:
  - Where installed ≥ higher than one of the following levels:
    - The level of the top of a bulkhead facing.
    - A level > 36" above the sidewalk.
- In such cases the following are required in addition to mastic behind the glass:
  - Shelf angles:
    - With all of the following characteristics:
      - Approved.
      - Nonferrous metal.
      - ≥ 0.0478" thick.
      - ≥ 2" long ‖ to the glass.
    - Installed as follows:
      - Spaced at approved intervals.
      - ≥ 2 angles per glass panel.
      - Secured to the backing by one of the following:
        - Expansion bolts.
        - Toggle bolts.
        - Other approved means.

1405.11.5 Joints

- This section applies to thin exterior structural glass veneer.
- The abutting edges of such glass panels must be square as follows:
  - Miters are not permitted as follows:
    - Where not specifically approved for obtuse-angled surfaces.
  - Other shapes are not permitted unless approved.
- An approved jointing compound must be applied uniformly to joints.
- Horizontal joints must be ≥ $^1/_{16}$" as follows:
    - Spaced by approved nonrigid materials.
- Where glass panels abut rigid materials the following is required:
    - Expansion joints ≥ ¼" as follows:
      - At the sides of the glass.
      - At the top of the glass.

1405 Installation of Wall Coverings

1405.11.6 Mechanical fastenings

- This section applies to thin exterior structural glass veneer.
- Glass veneer panels installed at the following heights is governed as indicated below:
  - Heights:
    - Above the level of heads of show windows.
    - > 12' above the sidewalk.
  - Requirements:
    - Fastenings required include all the following:
      - Mastic as required at lower levels.
      - Shelf angles as required at lower levels.
      - Mechanical fasteners are required as follows:
        - At one of the following locations of each glass panel:
          - At each horizontal edge.
          - At each vertical edge.
          - At each corner.
        - Fasteners must be fixed to the backing by one of the following:
          - Expansion bolts.
          - Toggle bolts.
          - Other methods.
        - Fasteners must support the glass as follows:
          - In a vertical plane without assistance from the mastic.
        - Shelf angles that also serve as mechanical fasteners are acceptable.

1405.11.7 Flashing

- This section applies to thin exterior structural glass veneer.
- Exposed edges of the glass veneer panels must be detailed as follows:
  - Covered with overlapping flashing of the following material:
    - Corrosion-resistant metal.
  - Made moisture tight as follows:
    - By caulking with a waterproof substance.

1405.12.1 Installation

- The following components must meet the requirements listed below:
  - Components:
    - Windows.
    - Doors.
  - Requirements:
    - Components must be installed according to the manufacturer's instructions as follows:
      - Instructions must be approved.
      - Instructions must include fastener size and spacing as follows:
        - These must be calculated based on results where the following were tested:
          - Maximum loading.
          - Maximum fastener spacing.

1405 Installation of Wall Coverings

1405.13 Vinyl siding

- Vinyl siding is permitted on exterior walls as follows:

  Note: ASTM D 3679, "Specification for Rigid Poly [Vinyl Chloried (PVC) Siding]," is cited as the standard with which the vinyl siding must comply.

  ○ In Type V construction.
  ○ Where basic wind speed is ≤ 100 mph as follows:
    In Exposure C.

  Note: Chapter 16, "Structural Design," is cited as providing the criteria for wind speed.

  ○ Where the building is < 40' tall.
  ○ Where test results or calculations are submitted as follows:
    Verifying compliance with structural requirements in either of the following cases:
      Where the building is > 40' tall.
      Where the wind speed is > 100 mph.
  ○ Vinyl siding must be installed so as to provide the following:
    Weather protection to exterior walls.

1405.13.1 Application

- Vinyl siding must be installed as follows:
  ○ Over sheathing or other materials.

  Note: 2304.6, "Wall sheathing," is cited as the source of materials over which sheathing must be applied.

  ○ So as to meet weather-resistant barrier requirements.

  Note: Section 1403, "Performance Requirements," is cited as governing.

  ○ In compliance with manufacturer's instructions as follows:
    Including accessories.
    Instructions must be approved.
  ○ Using one of the following types of nails:
    Nails specified in the manufacturer's instructions.
    Nails as follows where not specified in manufacturer's instructions:
      Head diameter = 0.313".
      Shank diameter = 0.125".
      Nails are to be corrosion-resistant.
      Nails must penetrate the nailing substrate ≥ $^3/_4$".
      Nails are spaced as follows where siding is horizontal:
        ≤ 16" horizontally.
        ≤ 12" vertically.
      Nails are spaced as follows where siding is vertical:
        ≤ 12" horizontally.
        ≤ 12" vertically.

1405 Installation of Wall Coverings

1405.15 Fiber cement siding

- Fiber cement siding is permitted on exterior walls as follows:

    Note: 1404.10, "Fiber cement siding," is cited as governing this material.

    - On all construction types.
    - For wind conditions cited by the following:
        The manufacturer's compliance report.
        Manufacturer's instructions as follows:
            Where approved.
    - Where installed over sheathing or other materials.

        Note: 2304.6, "Wall sheathing," is cited as listing appropriate materials over which the siding may be installed.

    - Where meeting weather-resistant barrier requirements.

        Note: Section 1403, "Performance Requirements," is cited as governing these requirements.

    - Where installed according to manufacturer's instructions as follows:
        Including accessories.
        Instructions must be approved.
    - Using nails as follows where fastening to wood studs:
        Nails specified in the manufacturer's instructions.
        Nails as follows where not specified in manufacturer's instructions:
            Nails are to be corrosion-resistant.
            Nails are to have round heads.
            Nails are to have smooth shanks.
            Nails must penetrate the studs $\geq 1"$.
    - Using screws as follows where fastening to metal framing:
        All-weather screws.
        Screws must penetrate the metal framing ≥ 3 threads.

1405 Installation of Wall Coverings

1405.16 Fastening

- The following exterior wall materials must fastened as indicated below:
  - ○ Materials:
    Weather boarding.
    Wall coverings.
  - ○ Fastening:
    Any of the following fasteners must be used:
    Aluminum.
    Copper.
    Zinc.
    Zinc-coated.
    Other corrosion-resistant fasteners as follows:
      Where approved.
    As per one of the following:
    The manufacturer's installation instructions.
    The nailing schedule provided by the code.

  Note: Table 2304.9.1, "Fastening Schedule," is cited as the required schedule.

- The following exterior wall materials must be fastened as indicated below:
  - ○ Materials:
    Shingles.
    Similar weather coverings.
  - ○ Fastening:
    One of the following fasteners is required:
    Standard-shingle nails.
    Mechanically bonded nails where approved.
    Weather coverings are to be attached to one of the following:
    Furring strips nailed to studs.
    Wood sheathing ≥ 1" nominal thickness.
    Wood structural panels as listed elsewhere in the code.

  Note: IBC Table 2308.9.3(3), "Size, Height and Spacing of Wood Studs," is cited as the source of appropriate wood structural panels.

1405 Installation of Wall Coverings

1405.17.1 Panel siding

- Fiber cement panel siding is to be installed as follows:
  - Long dimension ‖ to framing.
  - Vertical joints must be as follows:
    On framing members.
    Sealed by one of the following methods:
      Caulking.
      Battens.
  - Horizontal joints must be as follows:
    Protected with Z-flashing.
    Blocked with solid wood.

1405.17.2 Horizontal lap siding

- Fiber cement lap siding is to be installed as follows:
  - With an overlap ≥ 1¼".
  - Ends must be sealed by one of the following methods:
    Caulked.
    Protected by an H-section joint cover.
    Installed over flashing.
  - With the following fasteners:
    One of the following as per manufacturer's instructions where approved:
      Exposed heads.
      Concealed heads.

1406 Combustible Materials on the Exterior Side of Exterior Walls

1406.1 General

- This section series governs the following, where constructed of combustible materials:
  - Exterior wall coverings.
  - Balconies.
  - Attachments similar to balconies.
  - Bay windows.
  - Oriel windows.

1406.2 Combustible exterior wall coverings

- This section series does not govern plastics.
- This section series governs other exterior wall coverings as follows:
  - Where they are combustible.

1406.2.1 Ignition resistance

- The following exterior wall coverings need not be tested for ignition by radiant heat:
  - Wood.
  - Wood products.
  - Products that are covered with an exterior material other than vinyl siding.
  - $\geq 0.019"$ thick aluminum.
  - Materials on Type V construction.
- Other exterior wall coverings must be tested for ignition by radiant heat.

  Note: NFPA 268, "Standard Test Method for Determining Ignitibility of Exterior Wall Assemblies Using a Radiant Heat Energy Source," is cited as the required test.

1406.2.1.1 Fire separation of 5 feet or less

- Exterior wall materials installed where the fire separation distance is $\leq 5'$ must resist ignition as follows:
  - When subjected to a radiant heat level of 12.5 kW/m². *

  Note: NFPA 268, "Standard Test Method for Determining Ignitibility of Exterior Wall Assemblies Using a Radiant Heat Energy Source," is cited as governing.

* Source: IBC Table 1406.2.1.2

1406.2.1.2 Fire separation greater than 5 feet

- Exterior wall materials must resist ignition from radiant heat as follows:
  - Required resistance to radiant heat decreases with increased fire separation distance.

  Note: NFPA 268, "Standard Test Method for Determining Ignitibility of Exterior Wall Assemblies Using a Radiant Heat Energy Source," is cited as governing.
  IBC Table 1406.2.1.2, "Minimum Fire Separation for Combustible Veneers," is cited as listing radiant heat tolerance required vs. fire separation distance.

1406 Combustible Materials on the Exterior Side of Exterior Walls

1406.2.2 Architectural trim

- This section applies to the following construction types:
    Types I, II, III, and IV.
- Exterior wall coverings may be of the following materials where the conditions indicated below apply:
    ○ Materials:
        Wood.
        Materials of equivalent combustibility.
    ○ Conditions:
        Building ≤ 3 stories.
        Such wall coverings other than fire-retardant treated wood are governed as follows:
            Limited to ≤ 10% of the exterior wall surface in the following case:
                Where the fire separation distance is ≤ 5'.
- Architectural trim ≥ 40' above the grade plane is governed as follows:
    ○ Approved noncombustible materials are required.
    ○ Must be fastened to the wall with one of the following:
        Metal brackets.
        Other approved noncombustible brackets.

    Note: The following are cited as sources of applicable requirements:
        1405.4, "Wood veneers," provides requirements for exterior wall coverings that are permitted to be constructed of wood.
        2303.2, "Fire-retardant-treated wood," governs such material.

1406.2.3 Location

- Combustible wall covering may not extend above the exterior wall.
- Combustible wall covering may not extend over the top of the exterior wall.
- Combustible wall covering at the top of an exterior wall is governed as follows:
    ○ The wall must be behind the combustible covering at every point.

1406 Combustible Materials on the Exterior Side of Exterior Walls

1406.2.4 Fireblocking

- Fire-blocking is not required in the following locations:
  - In cornices of single-family dwellings.
  - Where the following two conditions are present:
    The architectural trim is installed on noncombustible framing.
    The exterior wall finish exposed to the concealed space is one of the following:
    Aluminum ≥ 0.019" thick.
    Corrosion-resistant steel as follows:
    Base metal thickness is ≥ 0.016" at thinnest point.
    Other approved noncombustible materials.
- In other cases, the following applies:
  - Concealed furred space thus formed by combustible wall coverings is governed as follows:
    The dimension between the back of the wall covering and the wall must be ≤ $1^5/8$".
    The furred space must be fire-blocked as follows:
    So that no airspace will be > 100 square feet in area.
    Wood furring must be one of the following:
    Approved wood of natural decay resistance.
    Preservative-treated wood.

  Note: Section 717, "Concealed Spaces," is cited as the source of requirements for fire-blocking in the furred spaces indicated above.

1406 Combustible Materials on the Exterior Side of Exterior Walls

1406.3 Balconies and similar projections

- This subsection addresses the following elements where they are of combustible construction:
  - Balconies.
  - Similar projections from buildings.
- Fire-retardant-treated wood may be used as follows:
  - For the following elements in construction Types I and II where the conditions below apply:
    Elements:
      Balconies.
      Porches.
      Decks.
      Exterior stairways.
    Conditions:
      Building must be ≤ 3 stories.
      Elements may not be required exits.
- Wood that is not fire-retardant treated may be used in guardrail systems that are ≤ 42" in height as follows:
  - As pickets.
  - As rails.
  - For similar components.
- Balconies and similar projections on the following construction types are governed as indicated below:
  - Construction Types:
    II, III and IV.
  - Requirements:
    They may be Type V construction.
    They are not required to have a fire-resistance rating as follows:
      Where the element is protected by sprinklers.
- In other cases, balconies and similar projections are governed as follows:
  - They must comply with one of the following:
    Must have the fire-resistance rating required floors in the building construction type.
    Must be Type IV construction.
  - The total length of these on a building is limited as follows:
    Must be ≤ ½ the building perimeter at each floor.

  Note: IBC Table 601, "Fire-Resistance Rating Requirements for Building Elements," is cited as the source of such requirements for the floor construction noted above. 602.4, "Type IV," is cited as the source of requirements for Type IV construction.

1406 Combustible Materials on the Exterior Side of Exterior Walls

> **Case study: Fig. 1406.3.** Type V construction is permitted for the balcony of the Type IIIB building. The balcony must meet the fire-resistance requirements for floor construction as specified in IBC Table 601 for Type IIIB construction for which there is no fire-resistance-rating required. Wood that is not fire-retardant treated is permitted for the guardrail system. The balcony length is 8% of the building perimeter, which is less than the 50% maximum. The balcony is in compliance with the code.

1406.4 Bay windows and oriel windows

- The following windows are governed as indicated below:
  - Windows:
    Bay windows.
    Oriel windows.
  - Requirements:
    Window assemblies may be fire-retardent-treated wood as follows:
    In buildings ≤ 3 stories in the following types of construction:
    Type I.
    Type II.
    Type III.
    Type IV.
    In other cases the window assemblies must conform to the following:
    The type of construction in which they are installed.

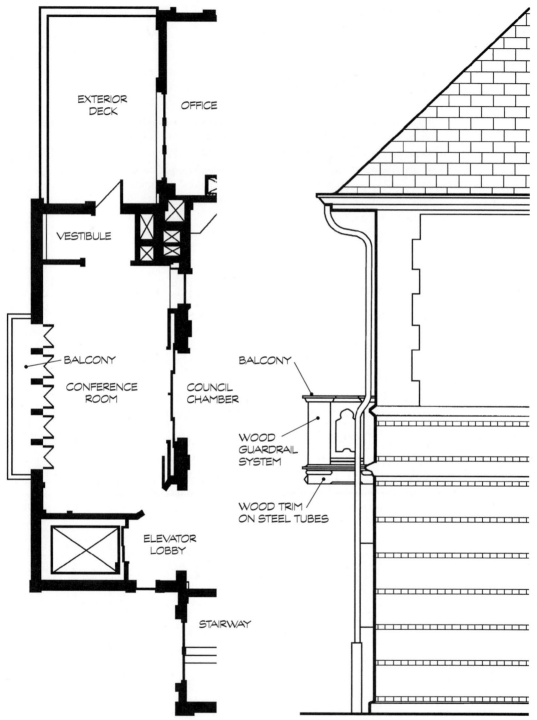

Fig. 1406.3. Partial elevation and plan at balcony. Lake Forest City Hall Renovation and Addition. Lake Forest, Illinois. David Woodhouse Architects. Chicago, Illinois.

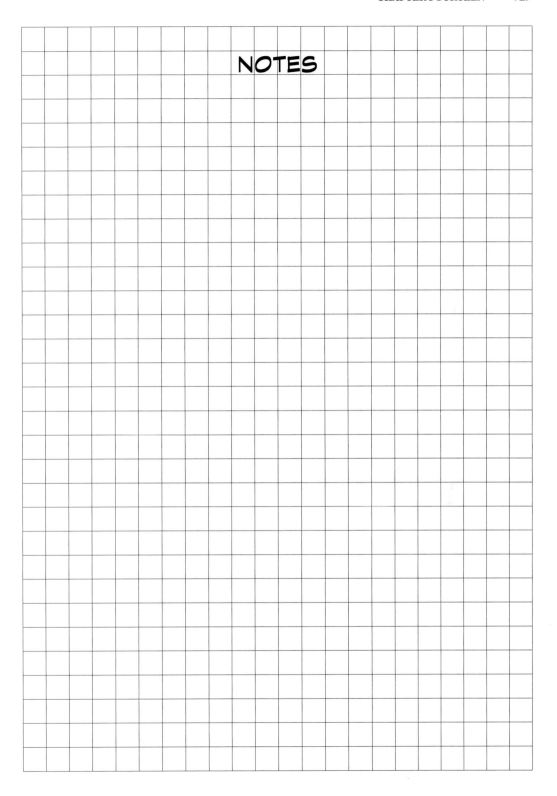

NOTES

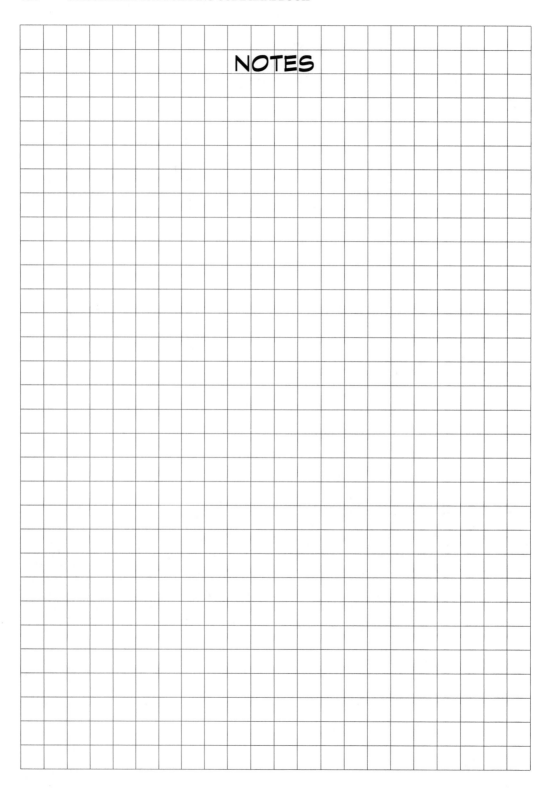

NOTES

15

Roof Assemblies and Rooftop Structures

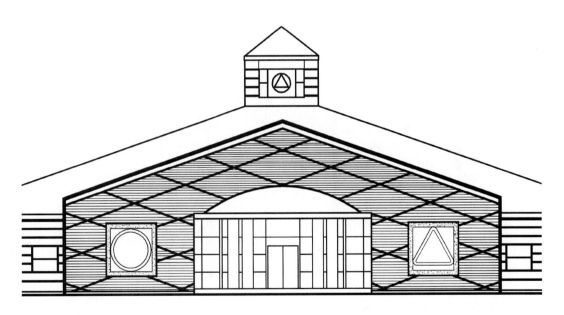

New Jasper Pre-K–2nd Grade School. Jasper, Texas. *(partial elevation)*
PBK Architects, Inc. Houston, Texas.

1503 Weather Protection

1503.2 Flashing

- Flashing is required to stop water penetration as follows:
  - Through the wall and roof at the following locations:
    Joints in copings.
    Through materials permeable to moisture.
    At parapet intersections with the roof.
    At other penetrations through the roof.

1503.2.1 Locations

- Flashing must be installed at the following locations:
  - At intersections of walls and roofs.
  - At gutters.
  - At changes in roof slope.
  - At changes in roof direction.
  - Around openings in the roof.
- Where flashing is metal, it must be as follows:
  - Corrosion resistant.
  - ≥ 0.019" thick.

> **Case study: Fig. 1503.2.1.**
> Flashing is installed at the intersection of the wall and the roof as required by the code. It meets corrosion resistance and thickness requirements.

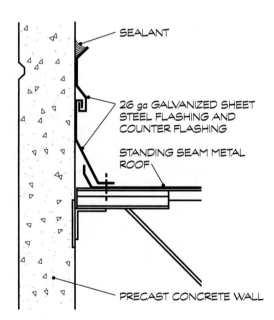

Fig. 1503.2.1. Wall detail. Garments to Go. Bastrop, Texas. Spencer Godfrey Architects. Round Rock, Texas.

1503.3 Coping

- Parapet walls must be coped with materials as follows:
  - Noncombustible.
  - Weatherproof.
  - With a width ≥ the thickness of the parapet.

1503 Weather Protection

1503.4.1 Gutters

- This section does not apply to the following:
  - Occupancy R-3.
  - Private garages.
  - Buildings of Type IV construction.
- The following devices are governed as indicated below:
  - Devices:
    Gutters.
    Leaders.
  - Requirement:
    Devices must be one of the following materials:
    Noncombustible.
    Schedule 40 plastic pipe.

Case study: Fig. 1503.4.1. The gutters and leaders on this building are metal and, thus, meet the code requirements for these components by being noncombustible.

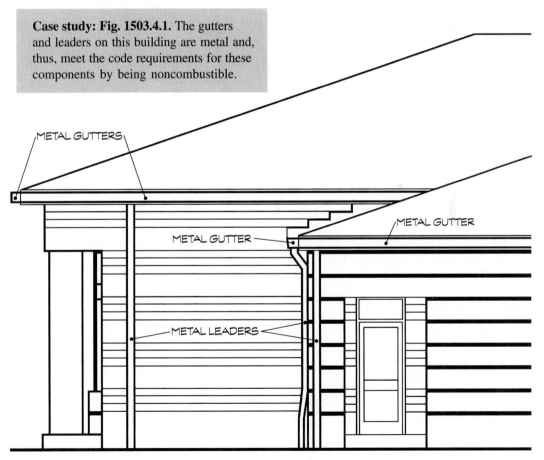

Fig. 1503.4.1. Partial elevation. New Jasper Pre-K–2nd Grade School. Jasper, Texas. PBK Architects, Inc. Houston, Texas.

1505 Fire Classification

1505.2 Class A roof assemblies

- Class A roofs may be used in all types of construction.
- Class A roofs include the following materials:

○ Brick	○ Masonry
○ Slate	○ Clay roof tile
○ Concrete roof tile	○ Exposed concrete roof deck
○ Ferrous shingles	○ Copper shingles
○ Ferrous sheet material	○ Copper sheet material

- ○ Other materials which perform as follows:
  They must be listed by an approved testing agency.
  They must be identified as Class A by an approved testing agency.
  They must be effective against severe fire testing.

  Note: Class A roof assemblies must have been tested by one of the following:
  ASTM E 108, "Test Methods for Fire Tests of Roof Coverings."
  UL 790, "Tests for Fire Resistance of Roof Covering Materials."

1505.3 Class B roof assemblies

- Class B roof assemblies perform as follows:
- ○ Effective against moderate fire testing.

  Note: Class B roof assemblies must have been tested by one of the following:
  ASTM E 108, "Test Methods for Fire Tests of Roof Coverings."
  UL 790, "Tests for Fire Resistance of Roof Covering Materials."

- Class B roof assemblies include the following:
- ○ Metal sheets.
- ○ Metal shingles.
- Other Class B assemblies and roof coverings must have the following characteristics:
  - ○ They must be listed by an approved testing agency.
  - ○ They must be identified as Class B by an approved testing agency.

1505.4 Class C roof assemblies

- Class C roof assemblies perform as follows:
- ○ Effective against light fire testing.
- Such assemblies and roof coverings must have the following characteristics:
  - ○ They must be listed by an approved testing agency.
  - ○ They must be identified as Class C by an approved testing agency.

  Note: Class B roof assemblies must have been tested by one of the following:
  ASTM E 108, "Test Methods for Fire Tests of Roof Coverings."
  UL 790, "Tests for Fire Resistance of Roof Covering Materials."

1505 Fire Classification

1505.5 Nonclassified roofing

- Materials with all the following characteristics are designated as nonclassified roofing:
  - Roofing materials that are approved.
  - Roofing materials that are not classified as one of the following:
    Class A.
    Class B.
    Class C.

1505.6 Fire-retardant-treated wood shingles and shakes

- The following is required for fire-retardant-treated wood shingles and shakes:
  - They must be treated as follows:
    By impregnation with chemicals using the following method:
      Full-cell vacuum-pressure process.
      As specified in the applicable standard.

  Note: AWPA C1, "All Timber Products—Preservative Treatment by Pressure Processes," is cited as the standard governing the process.

  - Bundles of the products must be labeled with the following information:
    The product identification.
    The manufacturer.
    The company that treated the product.
    The quality control agency.
    The classification of the product as follows:
      As established by fire tests.

  Note: 1505.1, "General," is cited as listing the necessary testing.

1505.7 Special purpose roofs

- The following special-purpose roofing is governed as indicated below:
  - Roofing:
    Wood shingles.
    Wood shakes.
  - Requirements:
    One of the following sheathings is required under the roofing:
      $\geq \frac{1}{2}"$ wood structural panel solid sheathing.
      $\geq$ Nominal 1" boards spaced sheathing.
    Gypsum backing board or sheathing is required under the wood sheathing as follows:
      $\geq \frac{5}{8}"$ Type X.
      Water resistant.

  Note: The following are cited as sources of requirements for special purpose roofing:
      1507.8, "Wood shingles."
      1507.9, "Wood shakes."

1507 Requirements for Roof Coverings

1507.2.1 Deck requirements

- Asphalt shingles must be secured to the following:
  - Solidly sheathed deck.

Case study: Fig. 1507.2.1. A solid deck is required for the asphalt shingles on the roof of the example below. Such a deck is provided. The minimum slope of the shingles is 2:12. This roof slopes 3:12 and, thus, meets this code requirement. Since the slope is < 4:12, double underlayment is provided as required.

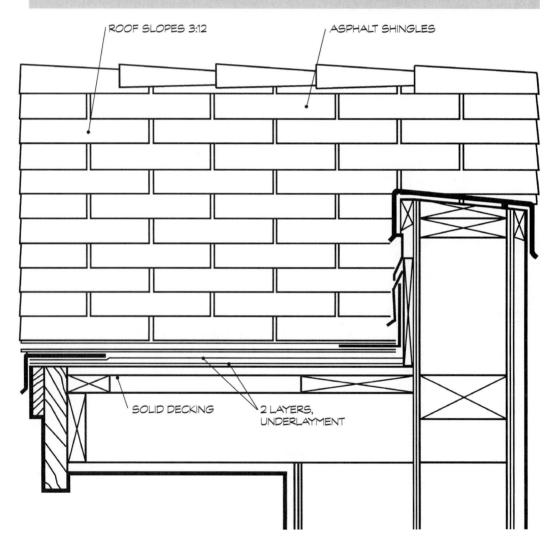

ROOF SLOPES 3:12

ASPHALT SHINGLES

SOLID DECKING

2 LAYERS, UNDERLAYMENT

Fig. 1507.2.1. Detail at roof. Creston Elementary Multipurpose Building. Creston, California. Phillips Metsch Sweeney Moore Architects. Santa Barbara, California.

1507 Requirements for Roof Coverings

1507.2.2 Slope

- The slope required for asphalt shingles is as follows:
  - ○ ≥ 2:12 slope.
- Double underlayment is required for asphalt shingles at the following range of slopes:
  - ○ slopes ≥ 2:12 and < 4:12.

    Note: 1507.2.8, "Underlayment application," is cited as governing the application of two layers of underlayment.

1507.2.8 Underlayment application

- This section applies to asphalt shingles.
- For roof slopes ≥ 2:12 and < 4:12 underlayment is required as indicated below:
  - ○ 2 layers must be applied as follows:
    Apply ≥ 19" wide underlayment felt strip in the following way:
      At the eaves.
      ‖ to the eaves.
    Apply sheets of underlayment as follows:
      36" wide sheets in the following manner:
        Starting at the eaves.
        With 19" overlaps.
- For roof slopes ≥ 4:12 underlayment is required as indicated below:
  - ○ Apply one layer in shingle format as follows:
    Starting at the eaves.
    With 2" overlaps.

1507.2.8.2 Ice dam membrane

- This section applies to asphalt shingles.
- This section does not apply to accessory buildings without conditioned space.
- For any of the following conditions, the underlayment indicated below is required:
  - ○ Conditions:
    Average daily temperature in January is ≤ 25°F.
    Ice can form along the eaves that accumulate water.
  - ○ Underlayment:
    One of the following ice barriers is required in lieu of standard underlayment:
      ≥ 2 layers of underlayment cemented together.
      Self-adhering polymer modified bitumen sheet.
    Ice barriers must be applied as follows:
      Barrier meets the eave.
      Barrier extends over the interior of the building as follows:
        ≥ 2' inside the exterior wall.

1507 Requirements for Roof Coverings

1507.2.9.1 Base and cap flashing

- This section applies to asphalt shingles.
- Base and cap flashing are required as follows:
  - Installed as per manufacturer's instructions.
  - Base flashing must be one of the following:
      Corrosion-resistant metal ≥ nominal 0.019" thick.
      Mineral-surfaced roll roofing ≥ 77 lbs/100 sf.
  - Cap flashing must be the following:
      Corrosion-resistant metal ≥ nominal 0.019" thick.

1507.2.9.2 Valleys

- Valley linings for asphalt shingles are required as follows:
  - Installed as per manufacturer's instructions.
  - The following materials are acceptable for the valley types indicated below:
    Materials:
      Metal as follows:
        ≥ 1'-4" wide.
        Any of the following are permitted:
          Copper.
          Aluminum.
          Stainless steel.
          Painted terne.
          Lead.
          Zinc alloy.
          Galvanized steel.
      Two plies of mineral surface roll roofing as follows:
        Bottom layer to be ≥ 1'-6" wide.
        Top layer to be ≥ 3' wide.
  - Valleys:
    Where valley lining is exposed (open valleys).
    Where valley lining is covered with shingles (closed valleys).
- The following material may be used where valley lining is covered with shingles:
    1-ply smooth roll roofing ≥ 3' wide.

  Note: The following are cited as sources of applicable requirements:
  IBC Table 1507.2.9.2, "Valley Lining Material," lists acceptable valley lining metals and metal thickness.
  ASTM D 224, "Specification for Smooth-Surfaced Asphalt Roll Roofing (Organic Felt)," addresses lining for closed valleys.
  ASTM D 1970, "Specification for Self-Adhering Polymer Modified Bituminous Sheet Materials Used as Steep Roof Underlayment for Ice Dam Protection," addresses underlayment for closed valley linings.

1507 Requirements for Roof Coverings

1507.2.9.3 Drip edge

- A drip edge for asphalt shingles is required on shingled roofs at the following locations:
  - Eaves.
  - Gables.
- A drip edge must be detailed as follows:
  - Extend ≥ 2" onto the roof under the shingles.
  - Extend downward past the bottom edge of sheathing ≥ ¼".
  - Attached with mechanical fasteners ≤ 12" on center.
- A chimney requires a cricket or saddle as follows:
  - On the side of the chimney where the roof is higher in the following case:
    Where water will drain toward an ≥ 2'-6" width of chimney.
  - Coverings must be one of the following:
    Sheet metal.
    Same material as roofing.

1507.3.1 Deck requirements

- The following roofing must be installed on one of the sheathing materials listed below:
  - Roofing:
    Concrete tile.
    Clay tile.
  - Sheathing:
    Solid sheathing.
    Spaced structural sheathing boards.

1507.3.2 Deck slope

- Clay and concrete roof tile must be installed on slopes as follows:
  - ≥ 2½:12 slope.
- Slopes < 4:12 require the following:
  - Double underlayment.

    Note: 1507.3.3, "Underlayment," is cited as the source providing requirements applicable to double underlayment.

1507 Requirements for Roof Coverings

1507.3.3.1 Low slope roofs

- This section addresses clay and concrete tile roofing.
- $\geq$ 2 layers of underlayment are required for roofs as follows:
  - Where the slope is 2½:12 $\leq$ slope < 4:12 the following is required:
    First strip of underlayment:
      $\geq$ 1'-7" wide.
      Applied ‖ to and meeting the eave.
    Second strip of underlayment:
      $\geq$ 3' wide.
      Applied over the 1ˢᵗ strip meeting the eave.
    Subsequent strips of underlayment:
      Applied overlapping previous strips as follows:
        $\geq$ 1'-7" overlap.

1507.3.3.2 High slope roofs

- This section addresses clay and concrete tile roofing.
- Roof slopes $\geq$ 4:12 require the following underlayment:
  - 1 layer of underlayment felt as follows:
    First strip applied ‖ to and meeting the eaves.
    Subsequent strips lap previous strips $\geq$ 2".

1507.3.9 Flashing *(part 1of 2)*

- This section addresses flashing for clay and concrete tile roofing.
- Flashing and counterflashing is required as follows:
  - At the intersection of the roof with vertical surfaces.
- Where flashing is metal, the following is required:
  - Corrosion-resistant metal $\geq$ 0.019" thick.
- Flashing must be installed according to manufacturer's instructions.
- Valley flashing is governed as follows:
  - It must extend $\geq$ 11" in to each side of the valley centerline.
  - It must have a splash diverter rib $\geq$ 1" high as follows:
    At the centerline of the valley.
    Integrally formed with the flashing.
- Flashing sections must overlap each other $\geq$ 4" where ends meet.
- For roof slopes $\geq$ 3:12, valley flashing is governed as follows:
  - The following valley underlayment is required:
    $\geq$ 3' wide.
    Type I underlayment.
    Extending the full length of the valley.
    Provided in addition to other underlayment required for the roof.

1507 Requirements for Roof Coverings

1507.3.9 Flashing *(part 2 of 2)*

- Where all of the following conditions apply, the detailing indicated below is required:
  - ○ Conditions:
    Roof slope is < 7:12.
    Where one of the following applies:
      Average daily January temperature is ≤ 25°F.
      Where ice can form to accumulate water along the eaves.
  - ○ Requirement:
    The underlayment for the metal valley flashing is detailed as follows:
      In one of the following ways:
        It is cemented across its entire surface to the roofing underlayment.
        It consists of self-adhering polymer modified bitumen sheet.

1507.4.1 Deck requirements

- Metal roof panels must be applied to one of the following types of decks:
  - ○ Solid deck.
  - ○ Closely fitted deck.
  - ○ Spaced decking as follows:
    Where the metal roofing is specifically designed for such application.

1507.4.2 Deck slope

- The following metal roofing requires the slope indicated below:
  - ○ Roofing:
    Nonsoldered seam metal roofing.
    Lapped sections.
    No lap sealant.
  - ○ Slope:
    Required slope is ≥ 3:12.
- The following metal roofing requires the slope indicated below:
  - ○ Roofing:
    Nonsoldered seam metal roofing.
    Lapped sections.
    With lap sealant.
  - ○ Slope:
    Required slope is ≥ 1½:12.
- Standing seam metal roofing requires the following slope:
  - ○ ¼:12.

Case study: Fig. 1507.4.2A. The batten seam metal roofing requires a minimum slope of 3:12 according to manufacturer's recommendations and code requirements. The actual slope of the roofs is 4:12; thus, the roofing is in compliance with the code.

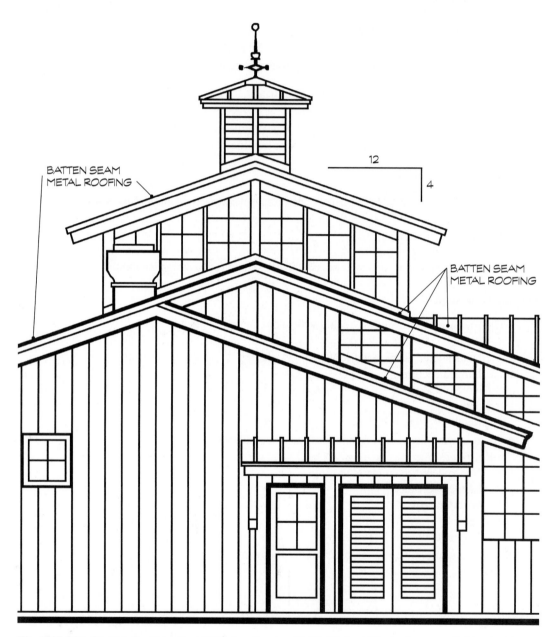

Fig. 1507.4.2A. Partial elevation. Central Kitchen. Lompoc Unified School District. Lompoc, California. Phillips Metsch Sweeney Moore Architects. Santa Barbara, California.

Case study: Fig. 1507.4.2B. The standing seam roof on the cupola of the tower slopes 2:12, which is > $^1/_4$:12, the minimum required slope. The standing seam roof is, therefore, in compliance with code requirements for slope.

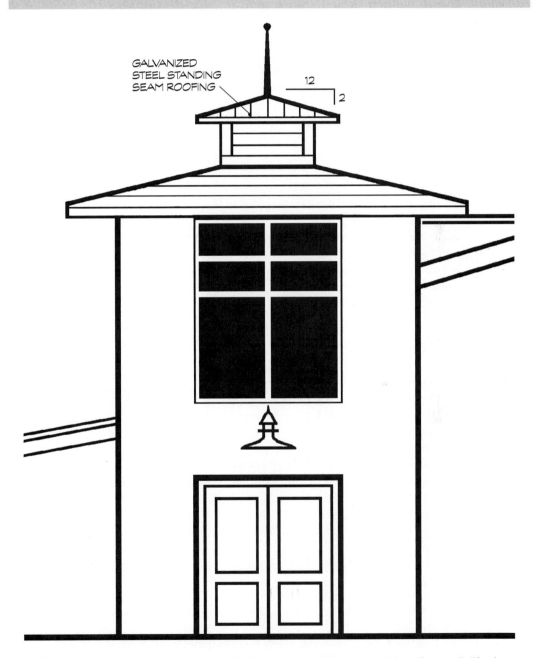

GALVANIZED
STEEL STANDING
SEAM ROOFING

12

2

Fig. 1507.4.2B. Partial elevation at tower. Creston Elementary Multipurpose Building. Creston, California. Phillips Metsch Sweeney Moore Architects. Santa Barbara, California.

1507 Requirements for Roof Coverings

1507.5.1 Deck requirements

- Metal roof shingles must be applied to one of the following types of decks:
  - Solid deck.
  - Closely fitted deck.
  - Spaced decking as follows:
    Where the metal shingles are specifically designed for such application.

1507.5.2 Deck slope

- Metal roof shingles must slope ≥ 3:12.

1507.5.6 Flashing

- This section addresses metal roof shingles.
- Valley flashing must be one of the following materials:
  - Galvanized steel.
  - Corrosion-resistant metal matching the roof shingle material.
  - Prepainted steel.
  - Aluminum-zinc alloy coated steel.
  - Copper.
  - Lead-coated copper.
  - Hard or soft lead.
  - Terne (tin).
  - Terne-coated stainless steel.
  - Aluminum.
- Valley flashing must be detailed as follows:
  - Extend ≥ 8" on both sides of the valley center line.
  - Have a splash diverter rib ≥ ¾" high as follows:
    At the center line of the valley.
    Formed as an integral part of the flashing.
  - Flashing sections must lap ≥ 4" where ends meet.
- Where either of the following conditions apply, the detailing indicated below is required:
  - Conditions:
    Average daily January temperature is ≤ 25°F.
    Where ice can form to accumulate water along the eaves.
  - Requirement:
    The following valley underlayment is required:
      ≥ 3' wide.
      Extending the full length of the valley.
      Provided in addition to other underlayment required for the roof shingles.
    Where the roof slope is < 7:12, the following is required:
      The underlayment for the metal valley flashing must be one of the following:
        Cemented across its entire surface to the roofing underlayment.
        It must be self-adhering polymer modified bitumen sheet.

1507 Requirements for Roof Coverings

1507.6.1 Deck requirements

- Mineral-surfaced roll roofing must be applied to a solidly sheathed surface.

1507.6.2 Deck slope

- Mineral-surface roll roofing must be applied to a slope $\geq$ 1:12.

1507.6.3 Underlayment

- This section does not apply to accessory buildings with no conditioned space.
- Where one of the following conditions applies, the detailing indicated below is required:
  - Conditions:
    Average daily January temperature is $\leq 25°F$.
    Where ice can form to accumulate water along the eaves.
  - Requirement:
    An ice barrier is required as follows:
    One of the following is required:
    $\geq$ 2 layers of underlayment cemented together.
    A self-adhering polymer modified bitumen sheet.
    Ice barrier must extend from the eave to the following point above the interior:
    $\geq$ 2' inside the exterior wall.

  Note: ASTM D 226, "Specification for Asphalt-Saturated Organic Felt Used in Roofing and Waterproofing, Type I," is cited as governing the underlayment.

1507.7.1 Deck requirements

- Slate shingles must be applied to the following:
  - A solidly sheathed surface.

1507.7.2 Deck slope

- Slate shingles must be applied to the following slope:
  - $\geq$ 4:12.

1507 Requirements for Roof Coverings

1507.7.3 Underlayment

- This section does not apply to accessory buildings with no conditioned space.
- Underlayment for slate shingles is Type II.
- Where one of the following conditions applies, underlayment for slate shingles is detailed as indicated below:
  - Conditions:
    Average daily January temperature is $\leq 25°F$.
    Where ice can form to accumulate water along the eaves.
  - Requirement:
    An ice barrier is required as follows:
    One of the following is required:
    ≥ 2 layers of underlayment cemented together.
    A self-adhering polymer modified bitumen sheet.
    Ice barrier must extend from the eave to the following point above the interior:
    $\geq 2'$ inside the exterior wall.

  Note: ASTM D 226, "Specification for Asphalt-Saturated Organic Felt Used in Roofing and Waterproofing, Type II," is cited as governing the underlayment.

1507.7.5 Application

- Slate shingles must be applied to the roof as follows:
  - With 2 fasteners for each piece.
- Slate shingles must have the headlap shown in the details provided for this section.

  Note: IBC Table 1507.5, "Slate Shingle Headlap," is cited as listing headlap requirements and is the source of data provided in Fig. 1507.7.5.

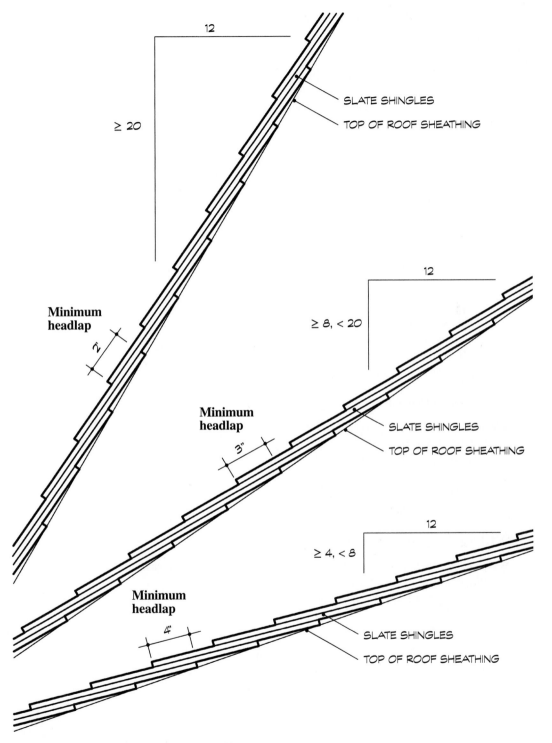

Fig. 1507.7.5. Minimum headlap for slate shingles.

1507 Requirements for Roof Coverings

1507.7.6 Flashing

- Flashing and counterflashing for slate shingles must be of the following material:
  - Sheet metal as follows:
    ≥ 0.0179" uncoated thickness zinc coated G90.
- Valley flashing is governed as follows:
  - Sheet metal as follows:
    ≥ 0.0179" uncoated thickness zinc coated G90.
  - Must be ≥ 1'-3" wide.
- Intersections between the roof and the following vertical surfaces require the cap flashing indicated below:
  - Vertical surfaces:
    Chimneys.
    Stucco walls.
    Brick walls.
  - Cap flashing:
    Two plies of felt are required as follows:
      4" wide strips of felt set in plastic cement.
      Top felt extends 1" above the bottom felt.
      Top coating of plastic cement.
      Felts overlaps the base flashing 2".

1507.8.1 Deck requirements

- Wood shingles must be applied to one of the following:
  - Solidly sheathed surface.
  - Spaced sheathing as follows:
    ≥ nominal 1"×4" boards are required.
    Spacing must = the following:
      Length of shingle exposed to the weather.

1507.8.1.1 Solid sheathing required

- Wood shingles require solid sheathing in either of the following cases:
  - Where average daily temperature in January is ≤ 25°F.
  - Where ice can form to accumulate water along the eaves.

1507.8.2 Deck slope

- Wood shingles must be applied to the following slope:
  - ≥ 3:12.

1507 Requirements for Roof Coverings

1507.8.3 Underlayment

- This section does not apply to accessory buildings with no conditioned space.
- Wood shingles require underlayment as indicated below, where either of the following conditions apply:
  - Conditions:
    Where average daily temperature in January is $\leq 25°F$.
    Where ice can form to accumulate water along the eaves.
  - Underlayment:
    ≥ 2 layers of underlayment are adhered in one of the following ways:
    Layers must be cemented together.
    Layers must be self-adhering polymer modified bitumen sheet.
    Underlayment must extend from eave edge to a point over the interior space as follows:
    To a point $\geq 24"$ inside the exterior wall.

1507.8.6 Application

- Naturally durable wood shingles must be installed as follows:
  - With a lap between side joints in adjacent courses as follows:
    $\geq 1\frac{1}{2}"$ lap is required.
  - Shingles in alternate courses may not align.
  - Spacing between adjacent shingles in the same course must be as follows:
    $\geq \frac{1}{2}"$ and $\leq \frac{3}{8}"$.
  - The length of shingles that may be exposed to the weather is as follows:
    As indicated in the details provided for this section.

  Note: IBC Table 1507.8.6, "Wood Shingle Weather Exposure and Roof Slope," is cited as governing weather exposure for shingles.

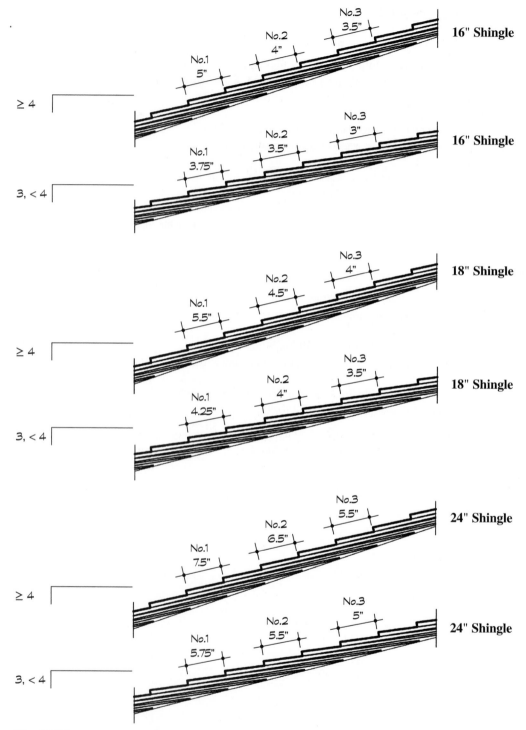

Fig. 1507.8.6. Maximum permitted exposure of wood shingles. *[Source: IBC Table 1507.8.6.]*

1507 Requirements for Roof Coverings

1507.8.7 Flashing

- Wood shingles require flashing and counterflashing as follows:
  - At the intersection of the roof and vertical surfaces.
  - Installed as per manufacturer's instructions.
  - Where flashing is metal, the following is required:
    Must be corrosion-resistant.
    Must be ≥ 0.019" thick (26 galvanized sheet gage).
- Valley flashing is governed as follows:
  - It must extend ≥ 11" on either side of the centerline of the valley.
  - It must have a splash diverter rib as follows:
    ≥ 1" high.
    Located at the centerline of the valley.
    Formed as part of the valley flashing.
  - Flashing sections must lap ≥ 4" where ends meet.
  - Valley flashing requires Type I underlayment as follows:
    ≥ 3' wide.
    Extending the full length of the valley.
    Provided in addition to other underlayment required for the roof shingles.
  - Where either of the following conditions apply, the detailing indicated below is required:
    Conditions:
      Average daily January temperature is ≤ 25°F.
      Where ice can form to accumulate water along the eaves.
    Requirement:
      Where the roof slope is < 7:12, the following is required:
        The underlayment for the metal valley flashing must be detailed as follows:
          It is cemented across its entire surface to the roofing underlayment.

1507.9.1 Deck requirements

- Wood shakes must be applied to one of the following:
  - Solidly sheathed surface.
  - Spaced sheathing as follows:
    ≥ nominal 1" × 4" boards are required.
    Spacing must = the following:
      Length of shingle exposed to the weather.
- Where 1" × 4" sheathing is spaced 10" on center, the following applies:
  - 1" × 4" boards must be added between them.

1507.9.1.1 Solid sheathing required

- Wood shakes require solid sheathing in either of the following cases:
  - Where average daily temperature in January is ≤ 25°F.
  - Where ice can form to accumulate water along the eaves.

1507 Requirements for Roof Coverings

1507.9.2 Deck slope

- Wood shakes must be applied to the following slopes:
  - ○ ≥ 4:12.

1507.9.3 Underlayment

- This section does not apply to accessory buildings with no conditioned space.
- Wood shakes require underlayment as indicated for either of the following conditions:
  - ○ Conditions:
    - Where average daily temperature in January is ≤ 25°F.
    - Where ice can form to accumulate water along the eaves.
  - ○ Underlayment:
    - ≥ 2 layers of underlayment are required in one of the following details:
      - Layers must be cemented together.
      - Layers must be self-adhering polymer modified bitumen sheet.
    - Underlayment must extend from eave edge to a point over the interior space as follows:
      - To a point ≥ 24" inside the exterior wall.
- Wood shakes require Type 1 underlayment.

  Note: ASTM D 226, Type I, "Specifications for Asphalt-Saturated Organic Felt Used in Roofing and Waterproofing," is cited as governing the underlayment as required above.

1507.9.7 Application

- Wood shakes must be installed as follows:
  - ○ With a lap ≥ 1½" between side joints in adjacent courses.
  - ○ Shakes in alternate courses may not align.
  - ○ Spacing between adjacent shakes in the same course must be as follows:
    - ≥ ³⁄₈" and ≤ ⁵⁄₈" for the following:
      - Shakes.
      - Taper-sawn shakes of naturally durable wood.
    - ≥ ¼" and ≤ ³⁄₈" for the following:
      - Taper-sawn shakes that are preservative treated.
  - ○ The length of shakes that may be exposed to the weather is as shown in the details provided for this section.

  Note: IBC Table 1507.9.7, "Wood Shake Weather Exposure and Roof Slope," is cited as governing weather exposure and is the source of data shown in Fig. 1507.9.7.

1507 Requirements for Roof Coverings

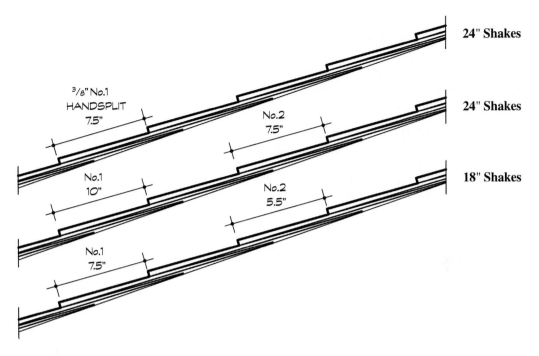

Fig. 1507.9.7. Maximum permitted exposure of wood shakes.

1507.9.8 Flashing *(part 1 of 2)*

- Wood shakes require flashing and counterflashing as follows:
    - At the intersection of the roof and vertical surfaces.
    - Installed as per manufacturer's instructions.
    - Where flashing is metal, the following is required:
        Must be corrosion-resistant.
        Must be ≥ 0.019" thick (26 galvanized sheet gage).
- Valley flashing for wood shakes is governed as follows:
    - It must extend ≥ 11" on either side of the centerline of the valley.
    - It must have a splash diverter rib as follows:
        ≥ 1" high.
        Located at the centerline of the valley.
        Formed as part of the valley flashing.
    - Flashing sections must lap ≥ 4" where ends meet.
    - Valley flashing requires Type I underlayment as follows:
        ≥ 3' wide.
        Extending the full length of the valley.
        Provided in addition to other underlayment required for the roof shingles.

1507 Requirements for Roof Coverings

1507.9.8 Flashing *(part 2 of 2)*

> ○ Where either of the following conditions apply, the detailing indicated below is required:
>   Conditions:
>   Average daily January temperature is ≤ 25°F.
>   Where ice can form to accumulate water along the eaves.
>   Requirement:
>   Where the roof slope is < 7:12, the following is required:
>   The underlayment for the metal valley flashing must be detailed as follows:
>   It is cemented across its entire surface to the roofing underlayment.

1507.10.1 Slope

- Coal-tar built-up roofs must have a slope as follows:
  ○ ≥ ⅛:12.
- Other built-up roofs must have a slope as follows:
  ○ ≥ ¼:12.

1507.12.1 Slope

- Thermoset single-ply membrane roofs must have a slope as follows:
  ○ ≥ ¼:12.

1507.13.1 Slope

- Thermoplastic single-ply membrane roofs must have a slope as follows:
  ○ ≥ ¼:12.

1507.14.1 Slope

- Sprayed polyurethane foam roofs must have the following slope:
  ○ ≥ ¼:12.

1507.15.1 Slope

- Liquid-applied roofs must have the following slope:
  ○ ≥ ¼:12.

1509 Rooftop Structures

1509.2 Penthouses

- This section addresses the following roof structures on buildings of Type I construction:
  - Penthouses.
  - Other projections above the roof.
- The following constructions may project above the roof a height as indicated below:
  - Constructions:
    Housing the following:
    Tanks.
    Elevators stopping at roof level.
  - Height:
    Required height is $\leq 28'$.
- Other constructions may project above the roof the following height:
  - Required height is $\leq 18'$.
- The following constructions above the roof are limited to the uses noted and the detailing indicated below:
  - Constructions:
    Penthouses.
    Bulkheads.
    Similar constructions.
  - Uses:
    Shelter of mechanical equipment.
    Shelter of vertical shaft openings in the roof.
  - Detailing:
    Such constructions require the following as applicable to protect equipment and the building interior:
    Louvers.
    Louver blades.
    Flashing.
    Similar provisions.
- The following constructions above the roof used for purposes other than allowed by this section are governed indicated below:
  - Constructions:
    Penthouses.
    Bulkheads.
  - Requirement:
    Such constructions must meet code requirements for an additional story.
- The following devices are permitted above the roof:
  - Wood flagpoles.
  - Similar structures.

1509 Rooftop Structures

1509.2.1 Type of construction

- The following applies to penthouses on buildings of Type I and II construction:
  - Where exterior walls and roofs have a fire separation distance > 5' and < 20':
    - They require the following:
      - A fire-resistance rating of ≥ 1 hr is required.
      - Noncombustible construction is required.
  - Where exterior walls and roofs are > 20' from a common property line:
    - Noncombustible construction is required.
  - The following must be noncombustible construction:
    - Interior framing.
    - Interior walls.
- The following apply to penthouses on buildings of Type III, IV, and V construction:
  - Where exterior walls have a fire separation distance > 5' and < 20':
    - They must have a fire-resistance rating of ≥ 1 hr.
  - Where exterior walls have a fire separation distance > 20':
    - They must be ≥ one of the following:
      - Type IV construction.
      - Noncombustible construction.
  - Interior walls are required to be ≥ one of the following:
    - Type IV construction.
    - Noncombustible construction.
  - Roofs must have materials as required for the construction type.
  - Roofs must have fire-resistance ratings as required for the construction type.

  Note: IBC Table 601, "Fire-Resistance Rating Requirements for Building Elements," is cited as the source of requirements for roofs as indicated above.

- Unprotected noncombustible enclosures on the roof are permitted where both the following conditions exist:
  - Where containing only mechanical equipment.
  - With a fire separation distance ≥ 20'.
- Mechanical equipment screens on the roof may be combustible where all of the following apply:
  - Building must be 1 story.
  - No roof may be present on the screens.
  - Screens must have a fire separation distance ≥ 20'.
  - Screens must be ≤ 4' in height above the roof surface.
- Dormers must be the same type construction as one of the following:
  - The roof of which they are a part.
  - The exterior walls of the building.
- Other penthouses must have the following constructed as required for the building:
  - Walls.
  - Floors.
  - Roof.

1509 Rooftop Structures

1509.3 Tanks

- Tanks > 500 gal in any of the following locations are governed as indicated below:
  - Located in or on a building.
  - Requirements:
    Such tanks must be supported by one of the following:
    Masonry.
    Reinforced concrete.
    Steel.
    Type IV construction.
    Where tank supports in a building are above the lowest story, the following applies:
    Support construction must meet fire-resistance ratings for Type IA construction.

1509.4 Cooling towers

- The following components of a cooling tower are permitted to be wood where all the conditions listed below apply:
  - Components:
    Drip boards.
    Enclosing construction.
  - Requirements:
    The wood must have a nominal thickness ≥ 1".
    Wood must be covered on the outside of the tower with the following:
    Noncombustible material.
- Otherwise cooling towers must be of noncombustible construction in the follow cases:
  - Where either of the following applies to a location > 50' high:
    Where a tower is > 250 sf at its base.
    Where a tower is > 15' high.

1509.5 Towers, spires, domes and cupolas

- The following is required where the roof elements of this section are ≤ 85' above grade:
  - They must have a fire-resistance rating ≥ that of the building.
- Where roof elements addressed in this section have the following characteristics, the construction indicated below is required:
  - Characteristics:
    Height is > 85' above grade and either of the following also applies:
    Area at any horizontal section is > 200 sf.
    Where the elements are used for anything other than the following:
    A belfry.
    An architectural embellishment.
  - Requirements:
    The following must be Type I or II construction:
    Roof elements addressed in this section.
    The construction on which such elements are supported.

1509 Rooftop Structures

1509.5.1 Noncombustible construction required

- This section addresses the following elements:
  - Towers.
  - Spires.
  - Domes.
  - Cupolas.
- Where such elements have any of the following characteristics, the requirements below apply:
  - Characteristics:
    - \> 60' high above the following point:
      - Highest point of contact with the roof.
    - \> 200 sf at any horizontal section.
    - To be used for any purpose other than the following:
      - A belfry.
      - An architectural embellishment.
  - Requirements:
    - Constructed entirely of noncombustible materials.
    - Supported by noncombustible materials.
    - Separated from the building below by construction as follows:
      - With a fire-resistance rating ≥ 1½ hrs.
      - With openings having a fire-protection rating ≥ 1½ hrs.
- The requirements listed below apply to elements on the roofs of buildings that are > 50' high other than the following:
  - Elements:
    - The following elements are not included in the requirements below:
      - Aerial supports ≤ 12' high.
      - Flagpoles.
      - Water tanks.
      - Cooling towers.
  - Requirements:
    - Other types of elements must comply with the following:
      - Elements must be noncombustible.
      - Construction supporting the elements must be noncombustible.

1509.5.2 Towers and spires

- Where such structures are enclosed, the following applies:
  - The exterior walls must be constructed as required for the building.
- The roof covering of spires is governed as follows:
  - It must be the class of roofing required for the main roof of the building.

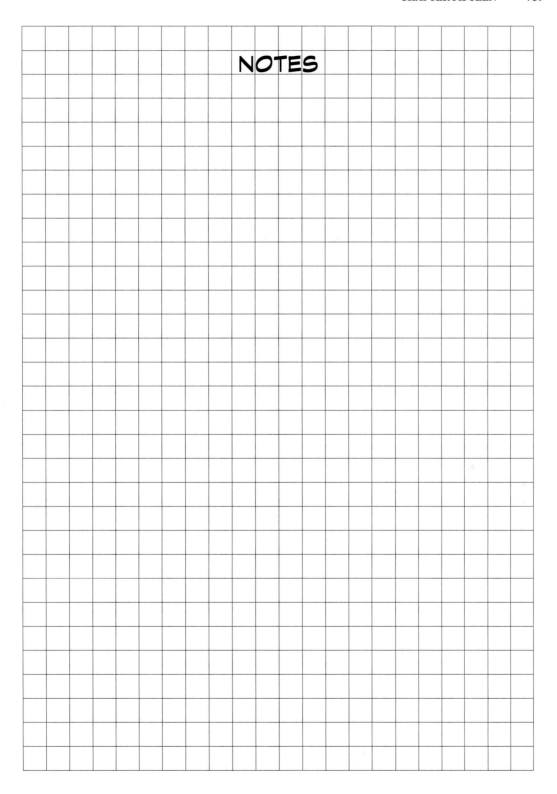

NOTES

NOTES

16

Structural Design

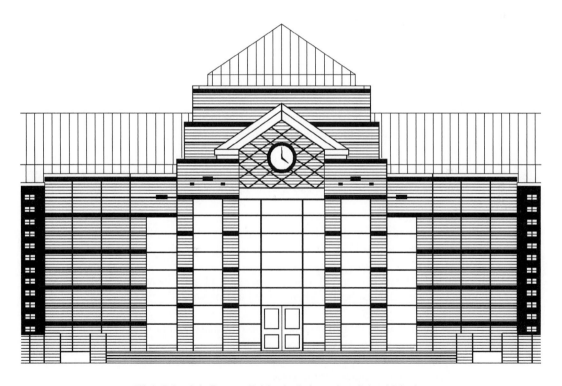

High School 6, Cypress-Fairbanks Independent School District.
Harris County, Texas. *(partial elevlation)*
PBK Architects, Inc. Houston, Texas.

1604 General Design Requirements

1604.3.6 Limits *(part 1 of 3)*

- Deflection in metal building components is governed as follows:
  - Total load deflection of the following cladding is limited as indicated below:
    Structural roofing of formed metal sheets:
    Deflection must be ≤ span ÷ 60.
    Structural siding of formed metal sheets:
    Deflection must be ≤ span ÷ 60.
  - Live load deflection of the following roof structure is limited as indicated below:
    Secondary roof structure supporting the following:
    Formed metal roofing with no roof covering:
    Deflection must be ≤ span ÷ 150.
  - Wind load deflection of the following wall structure is limited as indicated below:
    Secondary roof structure supporting formed metal siding:
    Deflection must be ≤ span ÷ 90.
- Interior partitions are governed as follows:
  - The following interior partitions are not regulated by this section:
    Partitions ≤ 6' high.
    Flexible partitions.
    Folding partitions.
    Portable partitions.
  - Interior partitions > 6' high are governed as follows:
    Actual deflection is based on the greater of the following lateral loads:
    Actual loads to which the partition is subjected.
    5 psf.

    Note: 1607.13, "Interior walls and partitions," is cited as the source of requirements for partition loading, a summary of which is provided above.

- Deflection of glass is limited as follows:
  - Deflection of the edge of a glass sheet is limited to the smaller of the following:
    Length of glass edge ÷ 175.
    ¾".
  - Differential deflection of adjacent unsupported edges of glass located by a walking surface is limited to that indicated below, where loaded as follows:
    Loading:
    50 lbs/linear foot is applied horizontally to one sheet as follows:
    At any point ≤ 3'-6" above the walking surface.
    Deflection:
    Limited to ≤ the thickness of the glass.

    Note: Section 2403, "General Requirements for Glass," is cited as governing glass deflection, a partial summary of which is provided above.

1604 General Design Requirements

1604.3.6 Limits *(part 2 of 3)*

- Wood structural members with all of the following characteristics are governed as indicated below:
  - Characteristics:
    Moisture content < 16% at time of installation.
    Used in dry conditions.
  - Deflection:
    Actual total deflection is permitted to be based on the following:
    Live load + half the dead load.
- Where roof drainage is not assured, the possibility of ponding must be investigated for the following reason:
  - The deflection limits of this section do not necessarily prevent ponding.

    Note: The following sections are cited as sources of applicable requirements:
    Section 1611, "Rain Loads."
    Section 1503.4, "Roof drainage."

- In computing actual deflection, wind load may be taken as the following:
  - 0.7 × "component and cladding" loads.
- In computing actual total load deflection, dead load of steel structural members is taken as zero.
- The following aluminum members, where used in locations and applications listed below, have the requirements indicated:
  - Members:
    Structural members.
    Panels.
  - Locations:
    Roofs.
    Walls.
  - Applications:
    Sunroom additions.
    Patio covers.
  - Requirements:
    Where not supporting either of the following members, the deflection is limited as indicated below:
    Members:
    Edge of glass.
    Aluminum sandwich panel.
    Deflection:
    Total load deflection must be ≤ span ÷ 160.

1604 General Design Requirements

1604.3.6 Limits *(part 3 of 3)*

- The deflection of aluminum sandwich panels used in the following locations and applications is limited as indicated below:
    - Locations:
        Walls.
        Roofs.
    - Applications:
        Sunroom additions.
        Patio covers.
    - Deflection:
        Total load deflection must be $\leq$ span $\div$ 120.
- The following applies where determining deflection limits for cantilevers:
    - Span is taken as 2 $\times$ the length of the cantilever as follows:
        Where dividing span by the given denominator.
- Otherwise, deflection of structural members is limited to a fraction of span as indicated below:

Table 1604.3.6   Deflection Limit for Structural Members

Deflection of structural members	Fraction of span
Deflection based on live load:	
Roof members:	
Supporting a plaster ceiling	Span $\div$ 360
Supporting a ceiling not plaster	Span $\div$ 240
Not supporting a ceiling	Span $\div$ 180
Floor members	Span $\div$ 360
Deflection based on snow or wind load:	
Roof members:	
Supporting a plaster ceiling	Span $\div$ 360
Supporting a ceiling not plaster	Span $\div$ 240
Not supporting a ceiling	Span $\div$ 180
Exterior walls and interior partitions:	
With brittle finishes	Span $\div$ 240
With flexible finishes	Span $\div$ 120
Deflection based on total load (dead load + live load):	
Roof members:	
Supporting a plaster ceiling	Span $\div$ 240
Supporting a ceiling not plaster	Span $\div$ 180
Not supporting a ceiling	Span $\div$ 120
Floor members	Span $\div$ 240
Farm buildings	Span $\div$ 180
Greenhouses	Span $\div$ 120

Source: IBC Table 1604.3.

1607 Live Loads

1607.3 Uniform live loads *(part 1 of 4)*

- Lives loads for structural design are to be the larger of the following:
  - The maximum loads anticipated.
  - The minimum uniformly distributed loads listed in this section.
- Passenger vehicle garage floors are to be designed for the greater of the following loads:
  - The minimum uniformly distributed load listed in this section.
  - The concentrated load described in the next section.

  Note: IBC Table 1607.1, "Minimum Uniformly Distributed Live Loads and Minimum Concentrated Live Loads," is cited as listing the applicable uniform load. The uniform loads of the table are summarized in this section.

- The library book stack loading minimum provided in this section is for the following:
  - A floor that supports book stacks as follows:
    Nonmobile stacks.
    Double-sided stacks.
    Book-stack units with a nominal height ≤ 90".
    Shelf depth on each side must have a nominal depth ≤ 12".
    ‖ rows of double-sided stacks must be separated by aisles with a width ≥ 36".
- Loading for the following seating is not governed by this section:
  - Reviewing stands.
  - Grandstands.
  - Bleachers.

  Note: ICC 300, "ICC Standard on Bleachers, Folding and Telescopic Seating, and Grandstands," is cited as governing these types of seating.

- Loading for the following seating is governed as indicated below:
  - Seating:
    Stadium bleachers.
    Arena bleachers.
    Stadium fixed seats.
    Arena fixed seats.
  - Loading requirements provided by this section must be verified by other standards:

  Note: ICC 300, "ICC Standard on Bleachers, Folding and Telescopic Seating, and Grandstands," is cited as governing these types of seating.

1607 Live Loads

1607.3 Uniform live loads *(part 2 of 4)*

- Loading for the following elements is determined by one of the methods listed below:
  - Elements:
    - The following where subject to truck loading:
      - Sidewalks.
      - Driveways.
      - Vehicular yards.
  - Methods:
    - Using loads specified in this section.
    - Using loads derived by other approved methods where appropriate.
- Snow loading greater than that listed in this section must be accommodated as follows:
  - Where loads are elevated due to drifting.
  - Where required by the building official.

  Note: Section 1608, "Snow Loads," is cited as governing these loads.

- Roofs used for the following special purposes must be designed for the loads indicated:
  - For promenades, ≥ 60 psf.
  - For gardens, ≥ 100 psf.
  - For assembly, ≥ 100 psf.
  - Other special purposes, as directed by the building official.

  Note: 1607.11.2.2, "Special purpose roofs," is cited as governing these roofs, a summary of which is provided above.

- Decks:
  - Live load to be the same as the occupancy served.

  Note: 1604.8.3, "Decks," is cited as a source of related requirements where decks are attached to exterior walls.

- Loading for the following is not provided in this section:
  - Trucks and buses.

  Note: 1607.6, "Trucks and bus garages," is cited as governing this loading.

  - All of the following:
    - Handrails.
    - Guards.
    - Grab bars.
    - Vehicle barriers.

  Note: 1607.7, "Loads on handrails, guards, grab bars and vehicle barriers," is cited as governing this loading.

  - Roofs:

  Note: 1607.11, "Roof loads," is cited as governing this loading.

1607 Live Loads

1607.3 Uniform live loads *(part 3 of 4)*

• For other than special cases, minimum uniformly distributed live loads are to be as follows:

Table 1607.3   Minimum Uniformly Distributed Live Loads

Use	psf	Use	psf
Access floors		**Corridors**—*continued*	
Computer	100	Libraries:	
Office	50	1st floor	100
		Upper floors	80
Apartments		Office buildings:	
Corridors serving public rooms	100	1st floor	100
Private rooms	40	Upper floors	80
Public rooms	100	Penal institutions	100
		Schools:	
Arenas		1st floor	100
Bleachers	100	Upper floors	80
Fixed seats	60	Other locations	100
Armories and drill rooms	150	**Dance halls**	100
		Dining rooms	100
Assembly		**Driveways subject to trucks**	250
Catwalks	40		
Control rooms	50	**Fire escapes**	
Fixed seat area	60	1-family dwellings	40
Follow-spot floors	50	Other locations	100
Lobbies	100		
Movable seat area	100	**Garages, passenger cars**	40
Platforms (similar to stage)	125	**Grandstands**	100
Projection rooms	50		
Stages	125	**Gymnasiums**	
		Main floor	100
Balconies, exterior		Balconies	100
Other than 1- & 2-family dwelling	100		
		Hospitals	
Ballrooms	100	Corridors:	
		1st floor	100
Bowling alleys	75	Upper floors	80
		Laboratories	60
Canopies	75	Operating rooms	60
		Private rooms	40
Corridors		Wards	40
Hospitals:			
1st floor	100	**Hotels**	
Upper floors	80	Corridors serving private rooms	40
Hotels, serving public rooms	100	Corridors serving public rooms	100
Hotels, serving private rooms	40	Private rooms	40
		Public rooms	100

Source: IBC Table 1607.1.

1607 Live Loads

1607.3 Uniform live loads *(part 4 of 4)*

- For other than special cases, minimum uniformly distributed live loads are to be as follows:

Table 1607.3—*Continued*

Use	psf	Use	psf
Libraries		**Residential** – *Continued*	
Corridors:		Multifamily dwellings:	
Upper floors	80	Corridors serving public rooms	100
Reading rooms	60	Private rooms	40
Stacks	150	Public rooms	100
		Stairs and exits	100
Manufacturing		Corridors serving private rooms	40
Light	125		
Heavy	250	**Restaurants**	100
Marquees	75	**Schools**	
		Classrooms	40
Office buildings		Corridors:	
Corridors:		1st floor	100
1st floor	100	Upper floors	80
Upper floors	80		
Lobbies	100	**Sidewalks subject to trucks**	250
Offices	50	**Skating rinks**	100
Penal institutions		**Stadium bleachers**	100
Cell blocks	40	**Stadium fixed seats**	60
Corridors	100		
		Stairs and exits	
Platforms, elevated	60	Other than 1- & 2-family dwellings	40
(not an exitway, not similar to stage)			
		Storage warehouses	
Residential		Light	125
1-family dwellings:		Heavy	250
Fire escapes	40		
1- & 2-family dwellings:		**Stores**	
Stairs and exits	40	Retail:	
Balconies, exterior ≤ 100 sf	60	1st floor	100
Balconies, exterior > 100 sf	100	Upper floors	75
Habitable attics	30	Wholesale, all floors	125
Sleeping areas	30		
Uninhabitable attics:		**Terraces, pedestrian**	100
No storage	10	**Walkways** (not exitways)	60
With storage	20		
Other areas not including decks	40	**Yards**	
		Pedestrian	100
		Subject to trucks	250

Source: IBC Table 1607.1.

1607 Live Loads

1607.4 Concentrated loads *(part 1 of 2)*

- Floors and similar surfaces must be designed to support the live loads indicated below:
  - The following load that produces greater stresses in the structure is required:
    Uniformly distributed loads as specified in the previous section.
    The following concentrated loads:
      To be evenly distributed over 2½ sf.
      To be located to yield the greatest stresses in the structure.

    Note: IBC Table 1607.1, "Minimum Uniformly Distributed Live Loads and Minimum Concentrated Live Loads," is cited as listing the applicable loads. The concentrated loads of the table are summarized in this section.

- Passenger vehicle garages are to be designed for the greater of the following loads:
  - The minimum uniformly distributed floor load listed in the previous section.
  - A concentrated floor load as follows:
    Where a garage is limited to vehicles carrying ≤ 9 people, the following applies:
      Concentrated design live load must be ≥ 3000 lb as follows:
        Applied to an area 4½" × 4½".
    For the following garages the load listed below is required:
      Garages:
        Using only mechanical parking devices.
        Without slab.
        Without a deck.
      Load:
        The design load is to be ≥ 2250 lb/wheel.
- The live load at each wheel for the following surfaces is to be distributed over 20 sq in:
  - Sidewalks subject to truck traffic.
  - Driveways subject to truck traffic.
  - Yards subject to truck traffic.
- The live load on a stair tread is to be ≥ 300 lb as follows:
  - Distributed over 4 sq in.
- Loading for the following is not provided in this section:
  - Trucks and buses.

    Note: 1607.6, "Trucks and bus garages," is cited as governing this loading.

  - All of the following:
    Handrails and guards.
    Grab bars.
    Vehicle barriers.

    Note: 1607.7, "Loads on handrails, guards, grab bars and vehicle barriers," is cited as governing this loading.

  - Roofs.

    Note: 1607.11, "Roof loads," is cited as governing this loading.

1607 Live Loads

1607.4 Concentrated loads *(part 2 of 2)*

- For other than special cases, minimum concentrated live loads are to be as follows:

Table 1607.4   Minimum Concentrated Live Loads

Use	Concentrated load in lbs	Use	Concentrated load in lbs
Access floors		**Office buildings**	
Computer	2000	Corridors	2000
Office	2000	Lobbies	2000
		Offices	2000
Ceilings			
Able to be accessed	200	**Schools**	
		Classrooms	1000
Driveways		Corridors	1000
Subject to trucks	8000		
		Scuttles	200
Hospitals			
Corridors, upper floors	1000	**Sidewalks**	
Laboratories	1000	Subject to trucks	8000
Operating rooms	1000		
Private rooms	1000	**Skylight ribs**	200
Wards	1000		
		Stores	
Libraries		Retail	1000
Corridors, upper floors	1000	Wholesale	1000
Reading rooms	1000		
Stacks	1000	**Yards**	
		Subject to trucks	8000
Manufacturing			
Light	2000		
Heavy	2000		

Source: IBC Table 1607.1.

1607.5 Partition loads

- In the following buildings, the additional live load must be added as indicated below:
  - Buildings:
      Office buildings.
      Buildings where partition locations change.
  - Load:
      Where the required live load is ≤ 80 psf:
        20 psf must be added to the required live load.

1607 Live Loads

1607.7.1 Handrails and guards

- This section does not apply to 1- and 2-family dwellings.
- In other locations, the following components and their supports must resist the loading indicated below:
  ○ Components:
    Handrail assemblies.
    Guards.
  ○ ≥ 50 lb/linear foot as follows:
    Applied in any direction at the top.
    Load is not applied simultaneously with other loads.

1607.7.1.1 Concentrated load

- The following components and their supports must resist the loading indicated below:
  ○ Components:
    Handrail assemblies.
    Guards.
  ○ A single concentrated load ≥ 200 lb as follows:
    Applied in any direction at any point at the top.
    Load is not applied simultaneously with other loads.

1607.7.1.2 Components

- Components of a handrail assembly or guard as follows must resist the load indicated:
  ○ Components:
    All rails other than the top handrail.
    Balusters.
    Panel fillers.
  ○ ≥ 50 lb as follows:
    Applied horizontally ⊥ to the component.
    Applied to an area of 1 sf including the following:
      Openings.
      Space between rails.
    Load is not applied simultaneously with loads specified in the previous 2 sections.

  Note: The following sections are cited as specifying the loads which are not to be applied simultaneously with the load specified in this section:
  1607.7.1, "Handrails and guards."
  1607.7.1.1, "Concentrated load."

1607.7.2 Grab bars, shower seats and dressing room bench seats

- Such components must resist 250 lb as follows:
  ○ Applied at any point.
  ○ Applied in any direction.

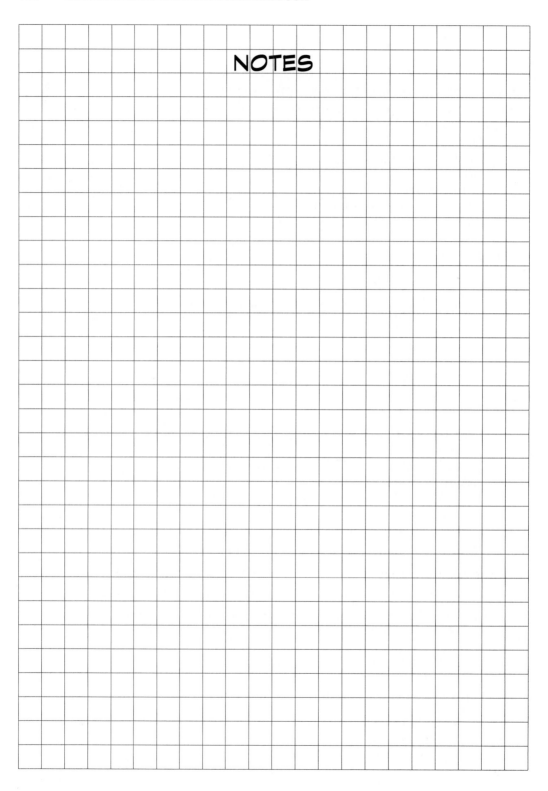

17

Structural Tests and Special Inspections

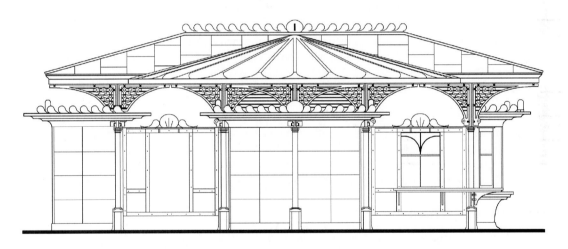

Visitor Services Pavilions at Clarence Buckingham Memorial Fountain.
Chicago Park District. Chicago, Illinois
David Woodhouse Architects. Chicago, Illinois.

1703 Approvals

1703.5 Labeling

- Where the following components are to be labeled, the requirements indicated below apply:
  - Components:
    Materials.
    Assemblies.
  - Requirements:
    Such components must be labeled by an approved agency.
    Such components must be labeled according to the requirements of this section.

  Note: Section 1703, "Approvals," is cited as governing the approved agency indicated.
  The following are cited as governing the labeling of components indicated above:
  1703.5.1, "Testing."
  1703.5.2," Inspection and identification."
  1703.5.3, "Label information."

1703.5.1 Testing

- This section addresses a part of the labeling process.
- An approved agency must test an example of the component to be labeled as follows:
  - Tests must be based on relevant standards.
  - The agency must maintain a record of tests performed as follows:
    Adequate information must be recorded to verify compliance with the relevant standards.

1703.5.2 Inspection and identification

- This section addresses a part of the labeling process.
- The approved agency must inspect the components subsequently labeled as follows:
  - Inspections must be periodic.
  - Inspections of the component fabrication must be done where necessary.
  - Inspections must verify that the labeled component is representative of that tested.

1703.5.3 Label information

- Labels must include the following information:
  - Identification of one of the following:
    Manufacturer.
    Distributor.
  - One of the following types of information:
    Description of the components performance properties.
    Both identification numbers as follows:
      Model number.
      Serial number.
  - Identification of the approved agency issuing the label.

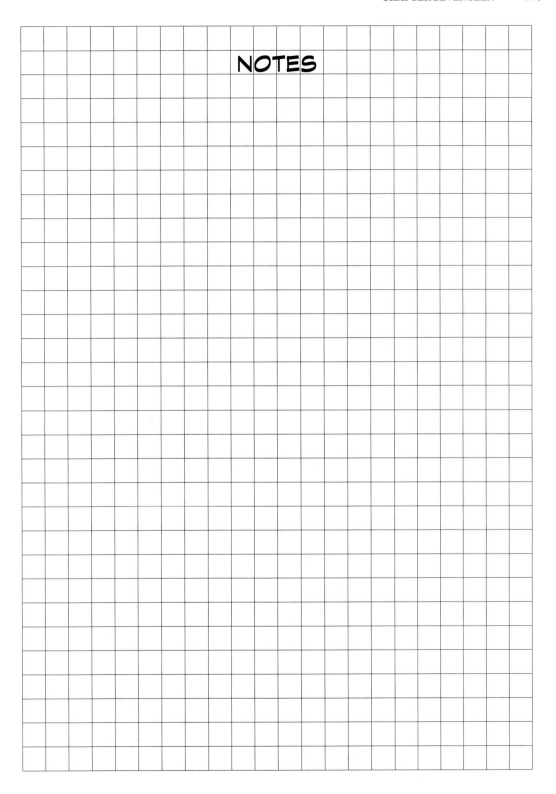

NOTES

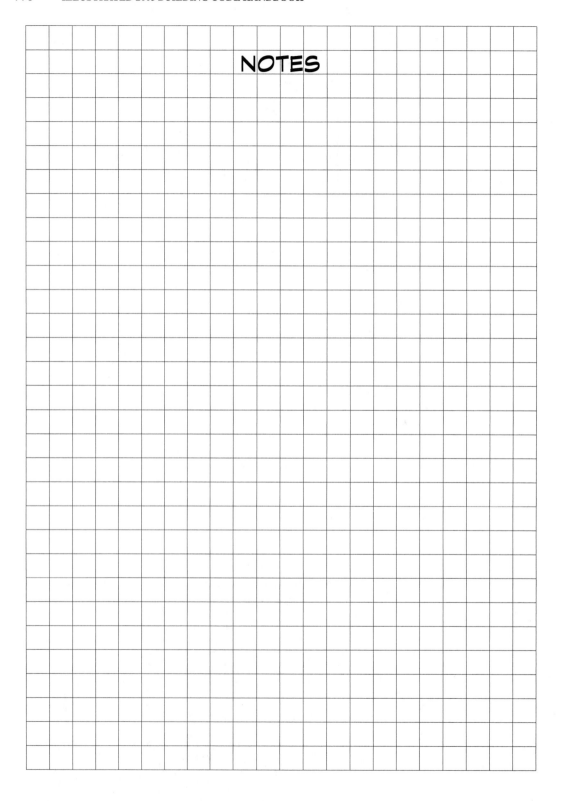

NOTES

18

Soil and Foundations

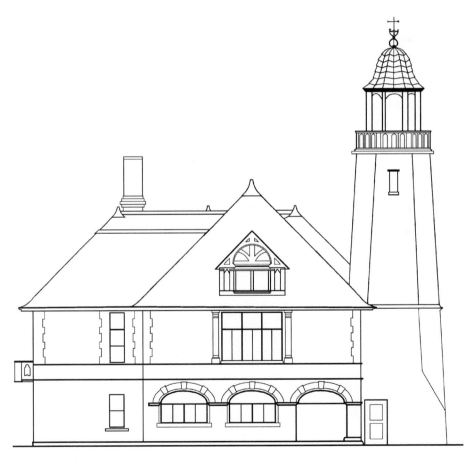

Lake Forest City Hall Renovation and Addition. Lake Forest, Illinois.
David Woodhouse Architects. Chicago, Illinois.

1803 Excavation, Grading and Fill

1803.1 Excavations near footings or foundations

- Where excavations are done the following is required:
  - The following elements must be protected from the movement listed below:
    Elements:
      Where existing lateral support is to be removed from the following:
        Footing.
        Foundation.
    Movement:
      Settlement.
      Lateral translation.

1803.2 Placement of backfill

- This section addresses excavation outside the foundation.
- Excavation must be backfilled with one of the following:
  - Soil free of any of the following substances:
    Organic material.
    Construction debris.
    Cobbles.
    Boulders.
  - Controlled low-strength material (CLSM).
- Backfill excluding CLSM must be placed as follows:
  - In lifts with the following process:
    Compacted without damage to the following:
      Foundation.
      Waterproofing.
      Dampproofing.

1803.3 Site grading

- Water is to be directed away from the foundation by one of the following methods:
  - Grade must slope away from the foundation as per one of the following:
    At a slope ≥ 1:20 as follows:
      For a distance ≥ 10' from the foundation.
    At a slope ≥ 1:48 as follows:
      For a distance ≥ 10' from the foundation.
      Where this slope is adequate based on the following:
        Limited precipitation.
        Highly efficient draining soil.
  - Another approved method.
- Settlement of backfill must be considered in determining final grade.

1805 Footings and Foundations

1805.1 General

- The top of a footing must be level.
- The bottom of a footing may slope ≤ 1:10.
- Footing surfaces must be stepped as follows:
  ○ At the top where required for to change level.
  ○ At the bottom where grade slopes > 1:10.
- The following components must be constructed on the soil indicated below:
  ○ Components:
    Foundations.
    Footings.
  ○ Soil:
    Undisturbed.
    Compacted.
    Controlled low-strength material (CLSM).

*Note: 1805.1, "General," through 1805.9, "Seismic requirements," are cited as governing
    footings and foundations.
    1803.5, "Compacted fill material," is cited as governing that material.
    1803.6, "Controlled low-strength material," is cited as governing CLSM.*

1805.2 Depth of footings

- Footing depth is required to be one or more of the following as applicable:
  ○ ≥ 12".
  ○ Adequate depth to be protected from frost.

    Note: 1805.2.1, "Frost protection," is cited as governing this aspect of footings.

  ○ At a depth that does not destabilize adjacent footings as follows:
    Where footings are the isolated type.

    Note: 1805.2.2, "Isolated footings," is cited as governing these footings.

  ○ Adequate depth to assure stability as follows:
    Where located near unstable soil.

    Note: 1805.2.3, "Shifting or moving soils," is cited as governing unstable soils.

1805 Footings and Foundations

1805.2.1 Frost protection

- Buildings that have all the following characteristics are not governed by this section:
  - Freestanding.
  - Where a building failure presents a low risk to human life such as the following:
    Agricultural facilities.
    Certain temporary facilites.
    Certain storage facilities.
  - ≤ 400 sf.
  - ≤ 10' eave height.
- Other building foundations as follows must be protected from frost by one of the methods listed below:
  - Foundations:
    Foundation walls.
    Piers.
    Other permanent foundations.
  - Methods:
    Setting the foundation at a level below the local frost line.
    Setting foundations on solid rock.
    By special methods designed for shallow foundations.
    Other methods.

    Note: ASCE-32, "Design and Construction of Frost Protected Shallow Foundations," is cited as governing this type of foundation.

- Footings may bear on frozen soil only in the following case:
  - Where soil is always frozen.

1805.2.2 Isolated footings

- Isolated footings on granular soil are governed as follows:
  - The slope of a line between the bottom edges of adjacent isolated footings must comply with one of the following:
    ≤ 30° with the horizontal.
    As needed where the higher footing is laterally supported as follows:
      By an approved method.
    As permitted by engineering analysis of soil stability.

1805.2.3 Shifting or moving soils

- Where the soil is unstable the following applies:
  - Footing depth must be adequate to provide stability.

1805 Footings and Foundations

1805.3.1 Building clearance from ascending slopes

- Buildings near the bottom of a slope with a gradient > 1:3 are governed as follows:
  - Buildings must be located far enough from such a slope to be protected from the following:
    Drainage.
    Erosion.
    Sloughing.
  - The distance required between building face and toe of slope is to be one of the following:
    That verified to be adequate by engineering analysis.
    ≥ the smaller of the following distances as defined below:
    Distance:
    ½ the rise of the slope.
    15'.
    Definitions:
    Where the slope is > 1:1, the toe is defined as follows:
    The toe is located at the intersection of the following lines:
    A 45° line tangent to the top of the slope.
    A horizontal line at the top of the foundation.
    Rise of slope is measured vertically between the following points:
    Top of the slope.
    Toe of slope if there is no retaining wall.
    Top of any retaining wall at the toe of the slope.

    Note: The following are cited as sources of pertinent requirements:
    1805.3.5, "Alternate setback and clearance," addresses requirements pertaining to the engineering analysis as indicated above.
    Figure 1805.3.1, "Foundation clearances from slopes," includes setback requirements, a summary of which is provided above.

1805 Footings and Foundations

1805.3.2 Footing setback from descending slope surface

- This section applies to buildings on or near a slope with a gradient > 1:3.
- Footings of such buildings are governed as follows:
  - They must be embedded in firm material.
  - They must be set back from the sloped surface as follows:
    - So as to avoid damaging settlement by the following:
      - Adequate vertical support.
      - Adequate lateral support.
  - They must be set back equal to one of the following distances:
    - That verified to be adequate by engineering analysis.
    - ≥ the smaller of the following distances measured as defined below:
      - Distance:
        - $\frac{1}{3}$ the rise.
        - 40'.
      - Measurement:
        - The setback distance is measured from the near face of the footing as follows:
          - From the footing at bearing level on a horizontal line to one of the following:
            - Where the slope is ≤ 1:1:
              - To a point on the surface of the slope.
            - Where the slope is > 1:1:
              - To a point on a line as follows:
                - A 45° line connecting to the bottom of the slope.
        - Rise of slope is measured vertically between the following points:
          - Top of the slope.
          - Bottom of slope.

  Note: The following are cited as sources of pertinent requirements:
  1805.3.5, "Alternate setback and clearance," addresses requirements pertaining to the engineering analysis as indicated above.
  IBC Figure 1805.3.1, "Foundation clearances from slopes," includes setback requirements, a summary of which is provided above.

1805.3.3 Pools

- This section addresses pools near a slope with a gradient > 1:3 as follows:
  - Pools regulated by the code.
- The required setback between pools and slopes is as follows:
  - ½ the setback required for building footings.
- Any part of a pool wall which is ≤ 7' from the top of a slope is governed as follows:
  - The wall must be able to support the water contained without the following:
    - Assistance from the soil.

1805 Footings and Foundations

1805.3.4 Foundation elevation

- On all sites, the top of the foundation wall must be at one of the following heights:
  - ≥ a height equal to the sum of the following dimensions:
    12".
    2% of the distance between the building and either of the following:
    The surface of the street gutter as follows:
    At the point where the site drains into it.
    An approved drainage device as follows:
    At the inlet where the site drains into it.
  - A height as follows:
    Approved by the building official.
    Where the following drainage is verified at all points on the site:
    Site drainage is to the point of discharge.
    Site drainage is away from the structure.

1805.3.5 Alternate setback and clearance

- The following dimensional requirements for construction near slopes may vary from those specified in this section as indicated below:
  - Requirements:
    Setbacks.
    Clearances.
  - Variations:
    Building official approval is required.
    Building official may require the following:
    Investigation and recommendation as follows:
    By a registered design professional verifying the following:
    That the intent of the setbacks and clearances is met.
    Investigation must include consideration of the following:
    Slope material.
    Slope height.
    Slope gradient.
    Loading.
    Erosion characteristics of slope material.

1805.4.1 Design

- Footings must be sized as follows:
  - So that the soil bearing capacity is not surpassed.
- A width ≥ 12" is required for footings.
- Footings in expansive soils must be designed as follows:
  - To accommodate the expansive soil.

  Note: 1805.8, "Design for expansive soils," is cited as governing such footing design.

1805 Footings and Foundations

1805.4.2 Concrete footings

- Light-frame construction is governed as follows:
  - Concrete footings may be designed according to details provided in this section on the following pages.

    Note: IBC Table 1805.4.2, "Footings Supporting Walls of Light-Frame Construction," is cited as listing design parameters for masonry unit footings supporting light-frame construction. The data of this table is summarized in the details provided in this section in Fig. 1805.4.2 A–G on the following pages.

  - Footing depth is governed elsewhere in the code.

    Note: 1805.2, "Depth of Footings," is cited in the footnotes of IBC Table 1805.4.2 as governing this aspect of footings.

  - Grade below the floor may be excavated to the following level:
    The top of the footing.
  - Seismic requirements for the following are governed elsewhere in the code:
    Seismic Design Category C, D, E, or F.

    Note: Section 1910, "Seismic Design Provisions," is cited in the footnotes of IBC Table 1805.4.2 as governing this aspect of footings.

- For other construction, the following aspects of concrete footings must comply with this section series and the concrete design requirements of the code:
  - Design.
  - Materials.
  - Construction.

    Note: 1805.4.2.1, "Concrete strength," through 1805.4.2.6, "Forming concrete,"and Chapter 19, "Concrete," are cited as governing concrete footing design.
    IBC Table 1805.4.2, "Footings Supporting Walls of Light-Frame Construction," is cited as a source of footing sizes where a design is not otherwise provided.

1805.4.2.3 Plain concrete footings

- An edge thickness ≥ 6" is required for plain concrete footings as follows:
  - In occupancy R-3 where both the following apply:
    Where the footing extends beyond the foundation wall as follows:
      A distance ≤ wall thickness.
    Where bearing on soil.
- Plain concrete footings in the following locations have the requirement listed below:
  - Locations:
    Other than R-3.
    Other than in light-frame construction.
  - Requirement:
    Must have an edge thickness ≥ 8" where bearing on soil.

1805 Footings and Foundations

1805.4.3 Masonry-unit footings

- Light-frame construction is governed as follows:
  - Masonry unit footings may be designed according to details provided in this section on the following pages.

    Note: IBC Table 1805.4.2, "Footings Supporting Walls of Light-Frame Construction," is cited as listing design parameters for masonry unit footings supporting light-frame construction. The data of this table is summarized in the details provided in this section in Fig. 1805.4.2A–G on the following pages.

  - Footing depth is governed elsewhere in the code.

    Note: 1805.2, "Depth of footings," is cited in the footnotes of IBC Table 1805.4.2 as governing this aspect of footings.

  - Grade below the floor may be excavated to the following level:
    The top of the footing.
  - Seismic requirements for the following are governed elsewhere in the code:
    Seismic Design Category C, D, E, or F.

    Note: Section 1910, "Seismic Design Provisions," is cited in the footnotes of IBC Table 1805.4.2 as governing this aspect of footings.

- For other construction, the following aspects of masonry unit footings must comply with this section series and the masonry design requirements of the code:
  - Design.
  - Materials.
  - Construction.

    Note: The following are cited as governing masonry-unit footings:
    1805.4.3.1, "Dimensions."
    1805.4.3.2, "Offsets."
    Chapter 21, "Masonry."

1805.4.3.1 Dimensions

- Masonry unit footings are governed as follows:
  - Footing depth (thickness) required is as follows:
    $\geq 2 \times$ footing projection beyond the following:
    Wall.
    Pier.
    Column.
  - Footing width required is as follows:
    $\geq 8"$ wider than the foundation wall supported.
  - Masonry must be set in one of the following mortar types:
    M, S.

  Note: 2103.7, "Mortar," is cited as governing this material as indicated above.

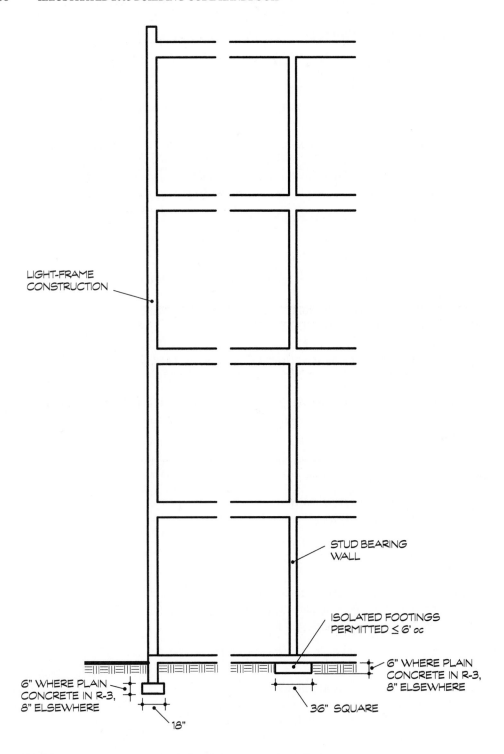

LIGHT-FRAME
CONSTRUCTION

STUD BEARING
WALL

ISOLATED FOOTINGS
PERMITTED ≤ 6' oc

6" WHERE PLAIN
CONCRETE IN R-3,
8" ELSEWHERE

6" WHERE PLAIN
CONCRETE IN R-3,
8" ELSEWHERE

36" SQUARE

18"

Fig. 1805.4.2A. Concrete or masonry unit foundations supporting 3 floors.

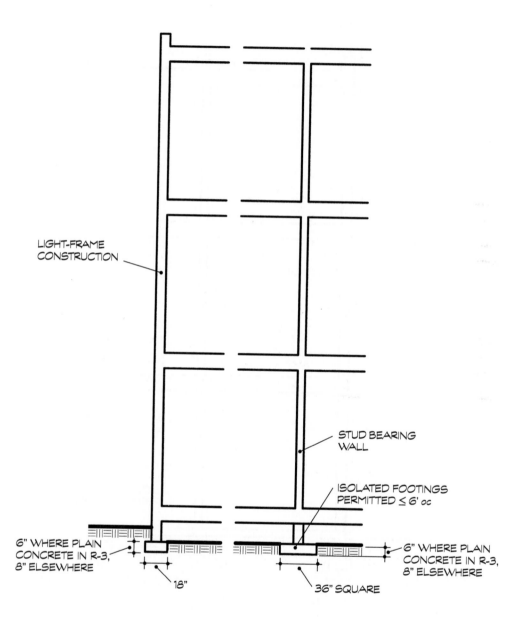

LIGHT-FRAME
CONSTRUCTION

STUD BEARING
WALL

ISOLATED FOOTINGS
PERMITTED ≤ 6' oc

6" WHERE PLAIN
CONCRETE IN R-3,
8" ELSEWHERE

6" WHERE PLAIN
CONCRETE IN R-3,
8" ELSEWHERE

18"

36" SQUARE

Fig. 1805.4.2B. Concrete or masonry unit foundations supporting 3 floors.

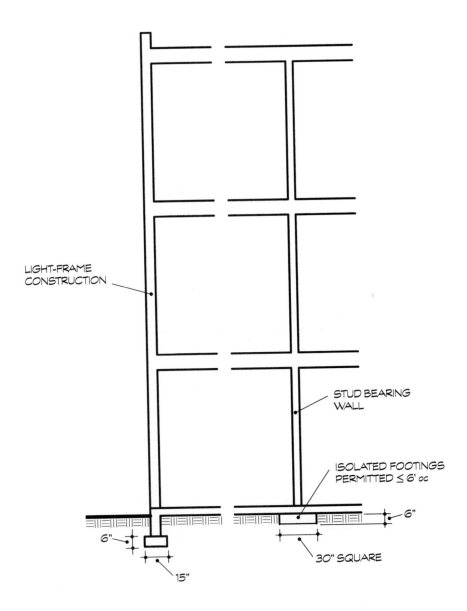

LIGHT-FRAME
CONSTRUCTION

STUD BEARING
WALL

ISOLATED FOOTINGS
PERMITTED ≤ 6' oc

6"

6"

15"

30" SQUARE

Fig. 1805.4.2C. Concrete or masonry unit foundations supporting 2 floors.

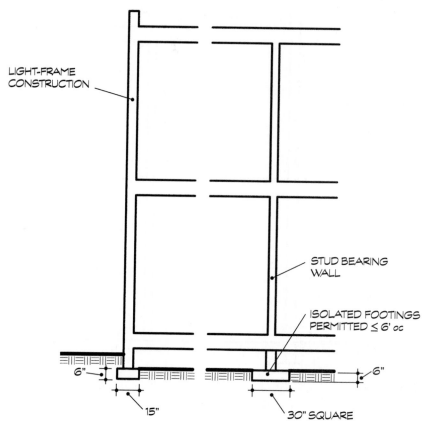

Fig. 1805.4.2D. Concrete or masonry unit foundations supporting 2 floors.

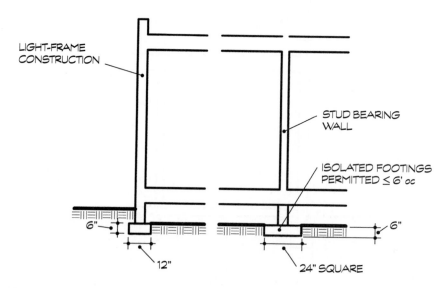

Fig. 1805.4.2E. Concrete or masonry unit foundations supporting 1 floor.

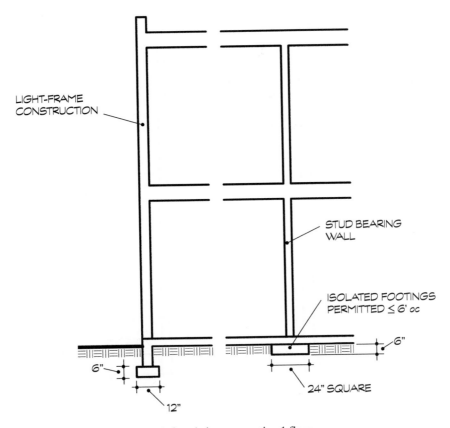

Fig. 1805.4.2F. Concrete or masonry unit foundations supporting 1 floor.

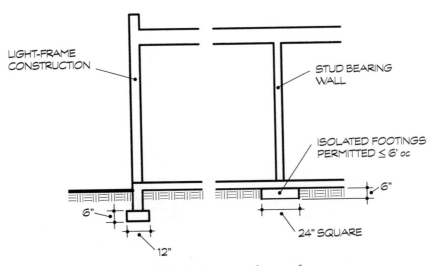

Fig. 1805.4.2G. Concrete or masonry unit foundations supporting a roof.

1805 Footings and Foundations

1805.4.3.2 Offsets

- This section governs brick foundations as follows:
  - Where successive brick courses step back from a wider footing to approach the thickness of the foundation wall.
- Where such foundations step back with each course, the following applies:
  - Courses must be set back ≤ 1½" from the course below.
- Where each step back is a pair of courses flush with each other, the following applies:
  - Pairs of flush courses must be set back ≤ 3" from the pair of courses below.

1805.4.4 Steel grillage footings

- Structural steel sections in grillage footings are governed as follows:
  - Components must be separated by approved steel spacers.
  - Components must be completely encased in concrete as follows:
    ≥ 6" thick on the bottom.
    ≥ 4" elsewhere.
  - Space between components must be filled with one of the following:
    Concrete.
    Cement grout.

1805.4.5 Timber footings

- Timber footings are permitted as follows:
  - In Type V construction.
  - As approved by the building official.
- Treatment of timber footings is governed as follows:
  - The timber is not required to be treated in the following locations:
    Where located completely below the water table permanently.
    Where used as caps for wood piling as follows:
      Where above the water level in the following locations:
        Over marsh-type lands.
  - In other locations the timber must be treated.

  Note: The following are cited as standards governing the treatment of timber footings:
      AWPA C2, "Lumber, Timber, Bridge Ties, and Mine Ties."
      AWPA C3, "Piles."

- Stress is limited in the following footings as indicated below:
  - Footings:
    Untreated timber footings supported on piling.
  - Limitation:
    Compressive stress ⊥ to the grain is limited as follows:
      To ≤ 70% of the otherwise allowable stress.

  Note: AFPA NDS, "National Design Specifications for Wood Construction," is cited as governing the allowable stress of the timber.

1805 Footings and Foundations

1805.5 Foundation walls

- This section series addresses concrete and masonry foundation walls.
- Walls meeting the following conditions may be constructed according to this section:
  - Walls laterally supported at top and bottom.
  - Walls conforming to the details provided in this section on the following pages.

    Note: The following 4 tables are cited as an option for design of walls qualified as noted above:
    IBC Table 1805.5 (1), "Plain Masonry and Plain Concrete Foundation Walls," through IBC Table 1805.5 (4), "12-Inch Concrete and Masonry Foundation Walls with Reinforcing Where d ≥ 8.75 Inches." The guidelines of these tables are summarized in Fig. 1805.5.1.2A-1 through Fig. 1805.5.1.2D-7.
    The following 5 sections are cited as governing foundation walls which are within the parameters of the tables noted above:
    1805.5.1, "Foundation wall thickness," through 1805.5.5, "Seismic requirements."

- Other foundation walls must meet design requirements of this code.

    Note: The following are cited as governing foundation walls as indicated above:
    Chapter 19, "Concrete."
    Chapter 21, "Masonry."

1805.5.1.1 Thickness based on walls supported

- This section addresses concrete and masonry foundation walls.
- Foundation walls ≥ 8" nominal thickness may support the following walls where meeting requirements indicated below:
  - Walls:
    Frame walls with brick veneers.
    10"-wide cavity walls.
  - Requirements:
    A corbeled 8" wall is governed as follows:
    The top corbel must be the following:
    A full course of headers ≥ 6" long.
    Height of the wall is limited as follows:
    ≤ that of the bottom of the floor framing.

    Note: The following are cited as sources of applicable requirements:
    1805.5.1.2, "Thickness based on soil loads, unbalanced backfill height and wall height," provides requirements for the 8" walls indicated above.
    2104.2, "Corbeled masonry," governs such detailing.

- Otherwise, foundation wall thickness is governed as follows:
  - It must be ≥ the thickness of the wall it supports.

1805 Footings and Foundations

1805.5.1.2 Thickness based on soil loads, unbalanced backfill height and wall height

- The following applies to the details of foundation walls provided for this section:
  - Where the walls are masonry, they are based on the following:
    Masonry set in the following type M or S mortar.
  - The height of unbalanced backfill is measured as follows:
    Between the following two levels:
    The finished exterior grade.
    One of the following interior levels:
    Interior grade where there is no concrete slab.
    Top of concrete slab where provided.
  - Foundation wall thickness must comply with the details provided in Figs. 1805.5.1.2A–D.

  Note: The following are cited as sources of required wall thickness:
  IBC Table 1805.5 (1), "Plain Masonry and Plain Concrete Foundation Walls."
  IBC Table 1805.5 (2), "8-Inch Concrete and Masonry Foundation Walls with Reinforcing Where d ≥ 5 Inches."
  IBC Table 1805.5 (3), "10-Inch Concrete and Masonry Foundation Walls with Reinforcing Where d ≥ 6.75 Inches."
  IBC Table 1805.5 (4), "12-Inch Concrete and Masonry Foundation Walls with Reinforcing Where d ≥ 8.75 Inches."

1805.5.1.3 Rubble stone

- Foundation walls of random rubble stone are governed as follows:
  - Thickness must be ≥ 1'-4".
  - Such walls may not be used in the following Seismic Design Categories:
    C, D, E, and F.

1805.5.3 Alternative foundation wall reinforcement

- Reinforcement indicated in details provided in this section may be varied as follows:
  - Bar sizes and spacing may be adjusted providing the following is met:
    Cross-sectional area of steel per linear foot of wall must remain the same.
  - Bar spacing must be ≤ 6'.
  - Bar size must be ≤ #11.

  Note: The following are cited as sources of required wall reinforcing:
  IBC Table 1805.5 (2), "8-Inch Concrete and Masonry Foundation Walls with Reinforcing Where d ≥ 5 Inches."
  IBC Table 1805.5 (3), "10-Inch Concrete and Masonry Foundation Walls with Reinforcing Where d ≥ 6.75 Inches."
  IBC Table 1805.5 (4), "12-Inch Concrete and Masonry Foundation Walls with Reinforcing Where d ≥ 8.75 Inches."

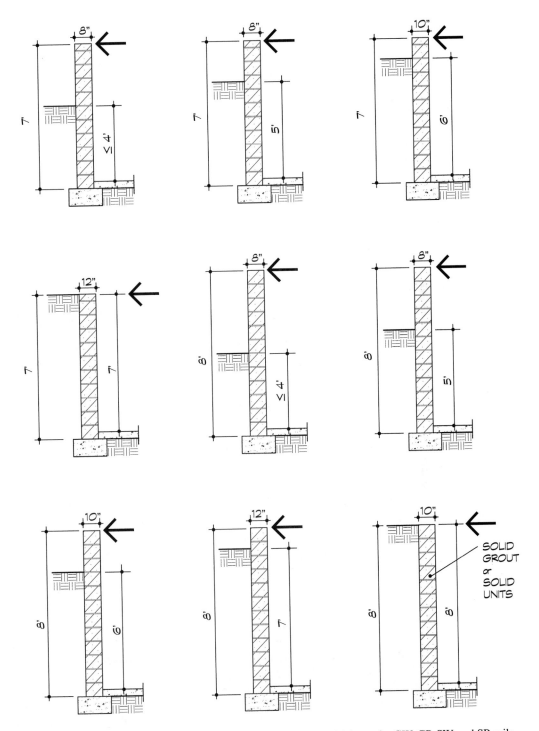

Fig. 1805.5.1.2A-1. Plain masonry foundation wall minimum, nominal thickness for GW, GP, SW, and SP soils. *[IBC Table 1805.5(1)]*

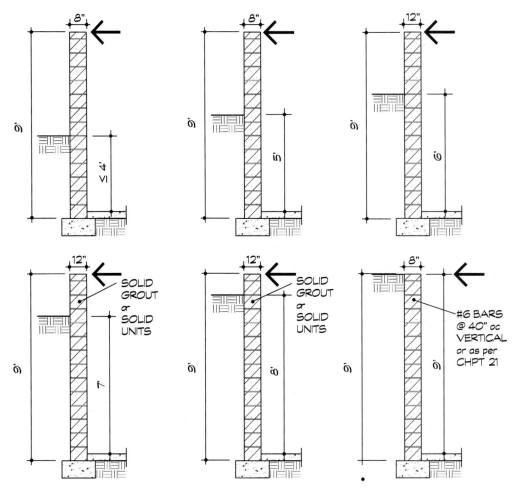

Fig. 1805.5.1.2A-2. Plain masonry foundation wall minimum, nominal thickness for GW, GP, SW, and SP soils. *[IBC Table 1805.5(1)]*

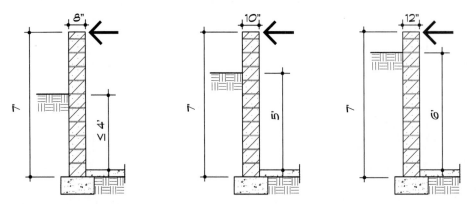

Fig. 1805.5.1.2A-3. Plain masonry foundation wall minimum, nominal thickness for GM, GC, SM-SC, and ML soils. *[IBC Table 1805.5(1)]*

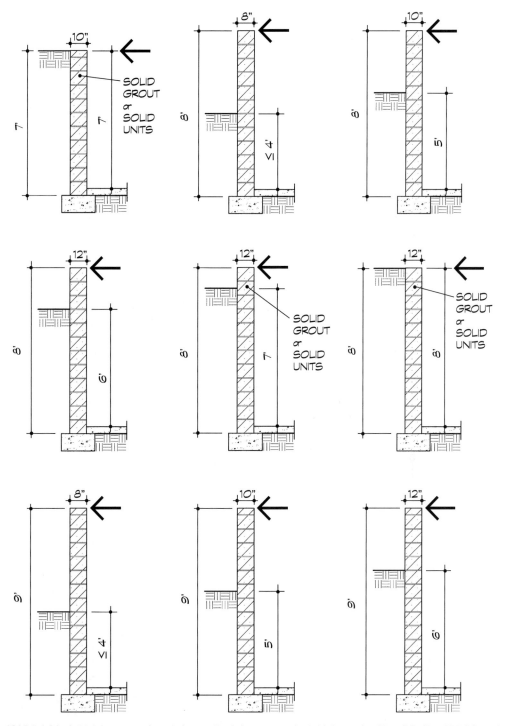

Fig. 1805.5.1.2A-4. Plain masonry foundation wall minimum, nominal thickness for GM, GC, SM, SM-SC, and ML soils. *[IBC Table 1805.5(1)]*

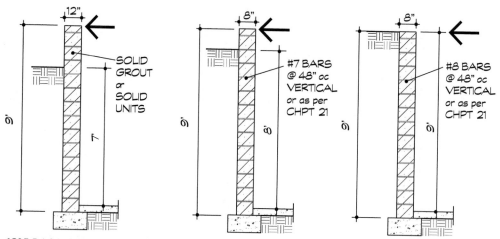

Fig. 1805.5.1.2A-5. Plain masonry foundation wall minimum, nominal thickness for GM, GC, SM, SM–SC, and ML soils. *[IBC Table 1805.5(1)]*

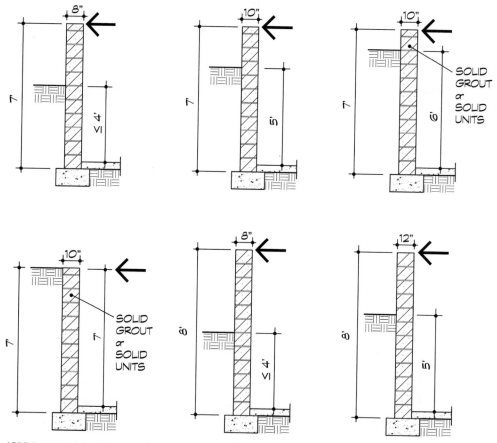

Fig. 1805.5.1.2A-6. Plain masonry foundation wall minimum, nominal thickness for SC, MH, ML–CL, and inorganic CL soils. *[IBC Table 1805.5(1)]*

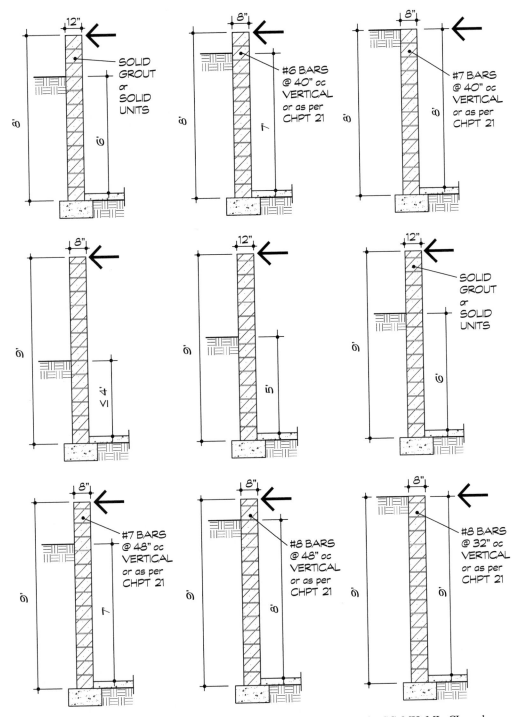

Fig. 1805.5.1.2A-7. Plain masonry foundation wall minimum, nominal thickness for SC, MH, ML–CL, and inorganic CL soils. *[IBC Table 1805.5(1)]*

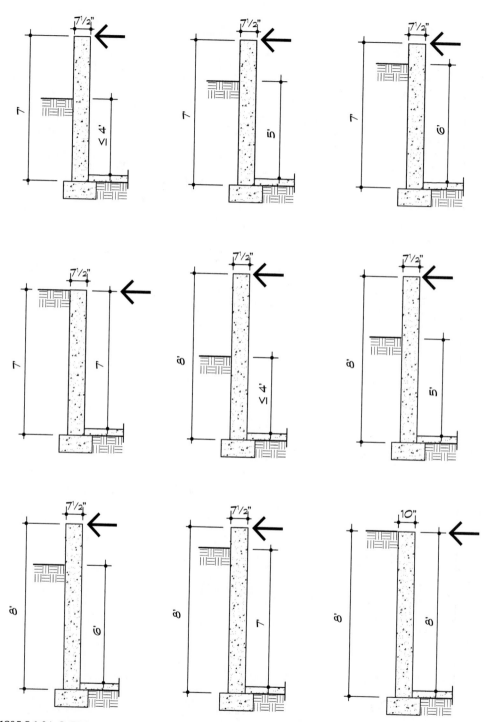

Fig. 1805.5.1.2A-8. Plain masonry foundation wall minimum, nominal thickness for GW, GP, SW, and SP soils.
[IBC Table 1805.5(1)]

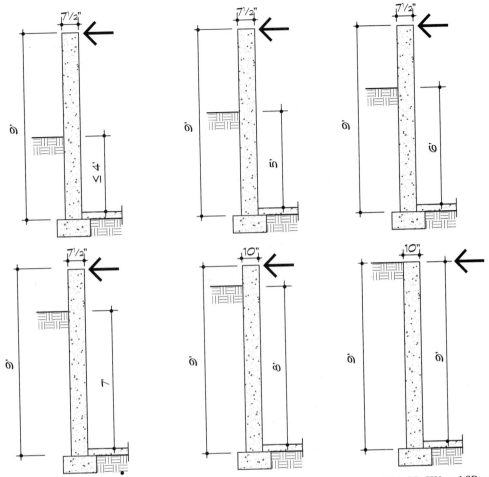

Fig. 1805.5.1.2A-9. Plain concrete foundation wall minimum, nominal thickness for GW, GP, SW, and SP soils. *[IBC Table 1805.5(1)]*

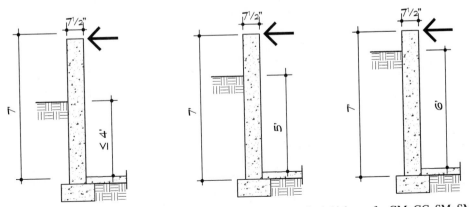

Fig. 1805.5.1.2A-10. Plain masonry foundation wall minimum, nominal thickness for GM, GC, SM, SM–SC, and ML soils. *[IBC Table 1805.5(1)]*

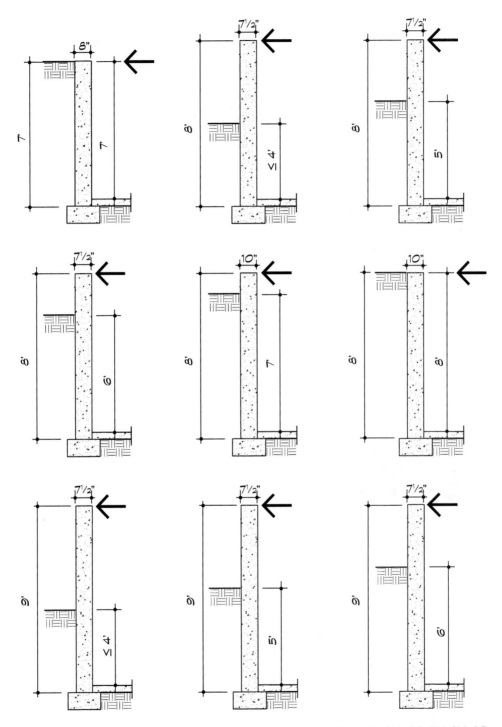

Fig. 1805.5.1.2A-11. Plain concrete foundation wall minimum, nominal thickness for GM, GC, SM, SM–SC, and ML soils. *[IBC Table 1805.5(1)]*

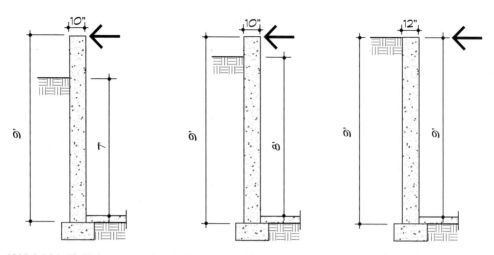

Fig. 1805.5.1.2A-12. Plain concrete foundation wall minimum, nominal thickness for GM, GC, SM, SM–SC, and ML soils. *[IBC Table 1805.5(1)]*

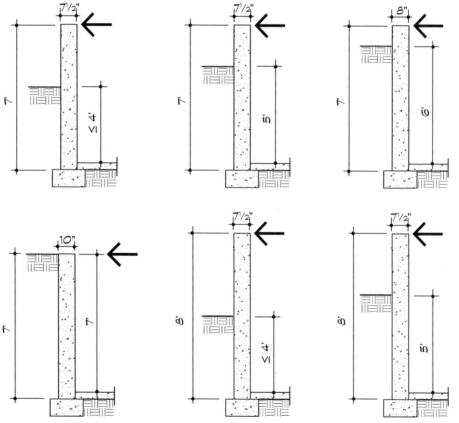

Fig. 1805.5.1.2A-13. Plain concrete foundation wall minimum, nominal thickness for SC, MH, ML–CL, and inorganic CL soils. *[IBC Table 1805.5(1)]*

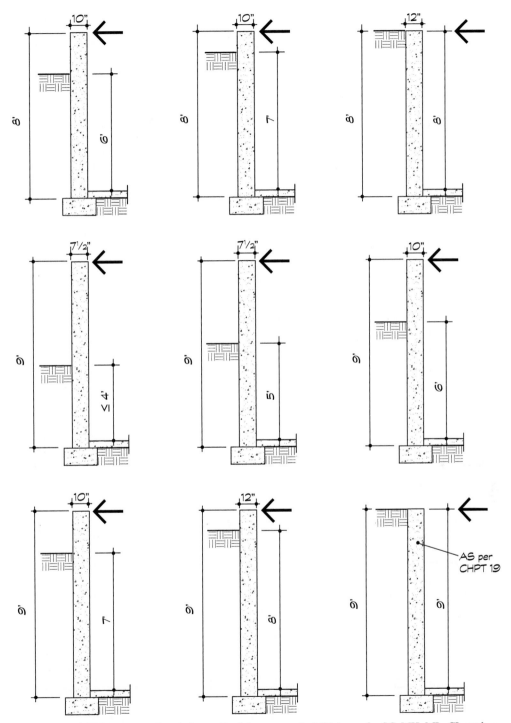

Fig. 1805.5.1.2A-14. Plain concrete foundation wall minimum, nominal thickness for SC, MH, ML–CL, and inorganic CL soils. *[IBC Table 1805.5(1)]*

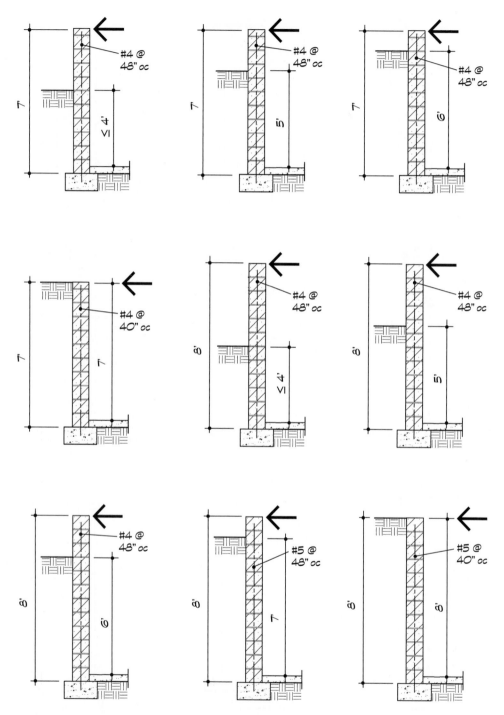

Fig. 1805.5.1.2B-1. Vertical reinforcement for 8" concrete and masonry foundation walls with $d \geq 5$". Soil is GW, GP, SW, or SP. *[IBC Table 1805.5(2)]*

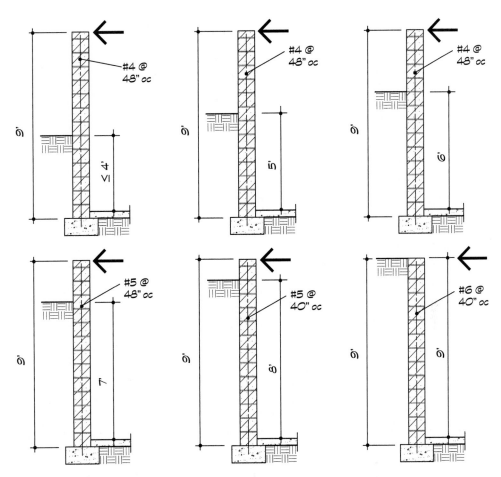

Fig. 1805.5.1.2B-2. Vertical reinforcing for 8" concrete and masonry foundation walls with $d \geq 5$". Soil is GW, GP, SW, or SP. *[IBC Table 1805.5(2)]*

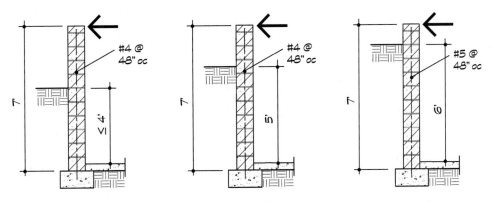

Fig. 1805.5.1.2B-3. Vertical reinforcing for 8" concrete and masonry foundation walls with $d \geq 5$". Soil is GM, GC, SM, SM–SC, or ML. *[IBC Table 1805.5(2)]*

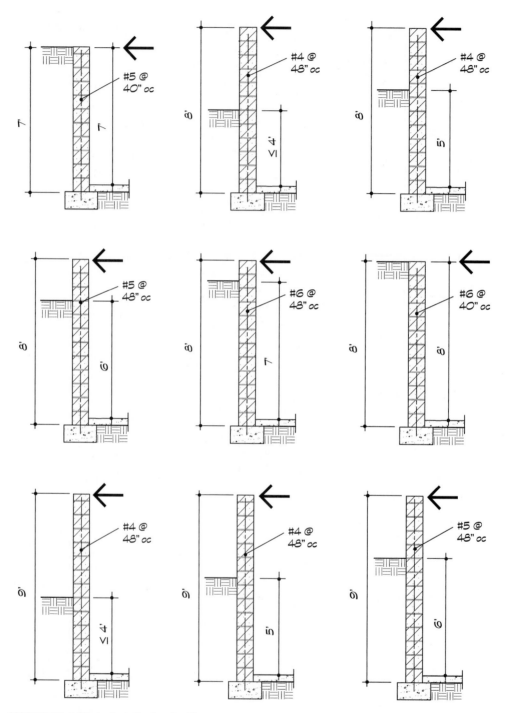

Fig. 1805.5.1.2B-4. Vertical reinforcing for 8" concrete and masonry foundation walls with $d \geq 5$". Soil is GM, GC, SM, SM–SC, or ML. *[IBC Table 1805.5(2)]*

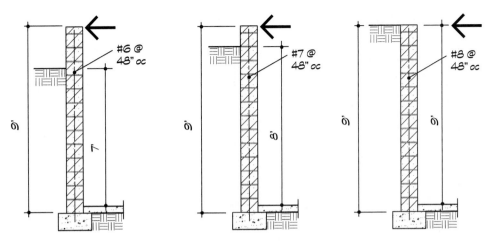

Fig. 1805.5.1.2B-5. Vertical reinforcing for 8" concrete and masonry foundation walls with $d \geq 5$". Soil is GM, GC, SM, SM–SC, or ML. *[IBC Table 1805.5(2)]*

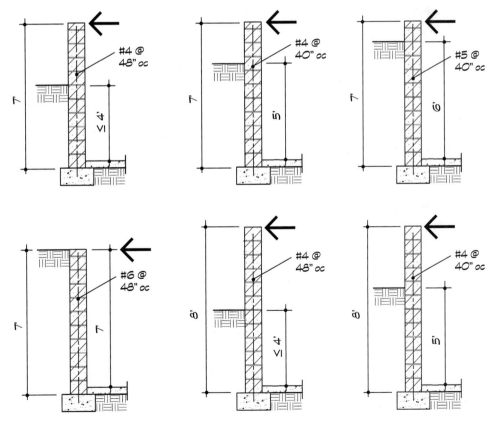

Fig. 1805.5.1.2B-6. Vertical reinforcing for 8" concrete and masonry foundation walls with $d \geq 5$". Soil is SC, MH, ML–CL, or inorganic CL. *[IBC Table 1805.5(2)]*

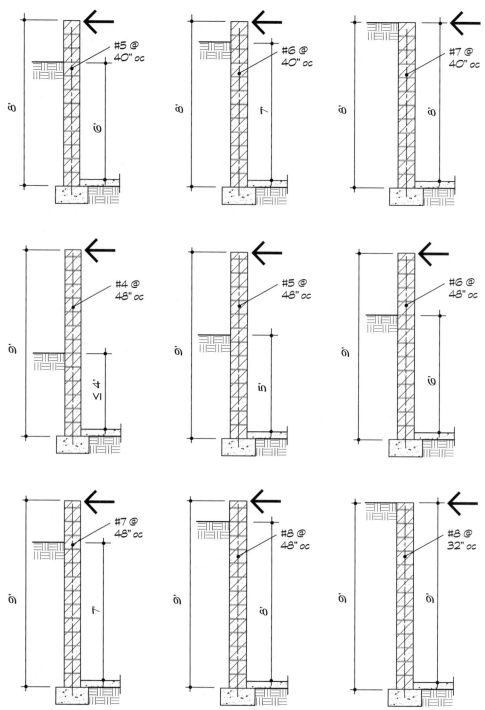

Fig. 1805.5.1.2B-7. Vertical reinforcing for 8" concrete and masonry foundation walls with $d \geq 5$". Soil is SC, MH, ML–CL, or inorganic CL. *[IBC Table 1805.5(2)]*

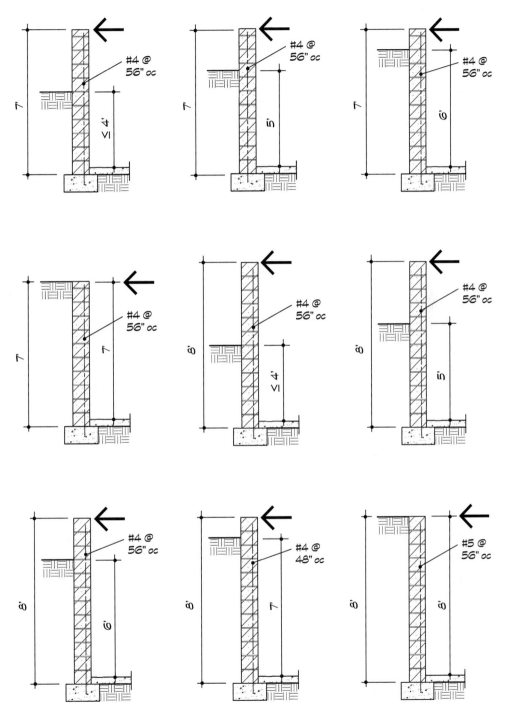

Fig. 1805.5.1.2C-1. Vertical reinforcing for 10" concrete and masonry foundation walls with $d \geq 6.75$". Soil is GW, GP, SW, or SP. *[IBC Table 1805.5(3)]*

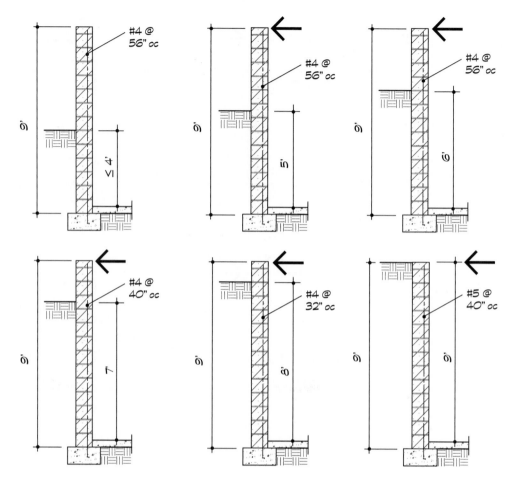

Fig. 1805.5.1.2C-2. Vertical reinforcing for 10" concrete and masonry foundation walls with $d \geq 6.75$". Soil is GW, GP, SW, or SP. *[IBC Table 1805.5(3)]*

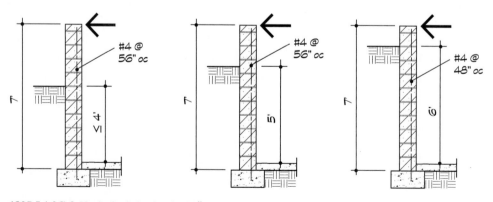

Fig. 1805.5.1.2C-3. Vertical reinforcing for 10" concrete and masonry foundation walls with $d \geq 6.75$". Soil is GM, GC, SM, SM–SC, and ML. *[IBC Table 1805.5(3)]*

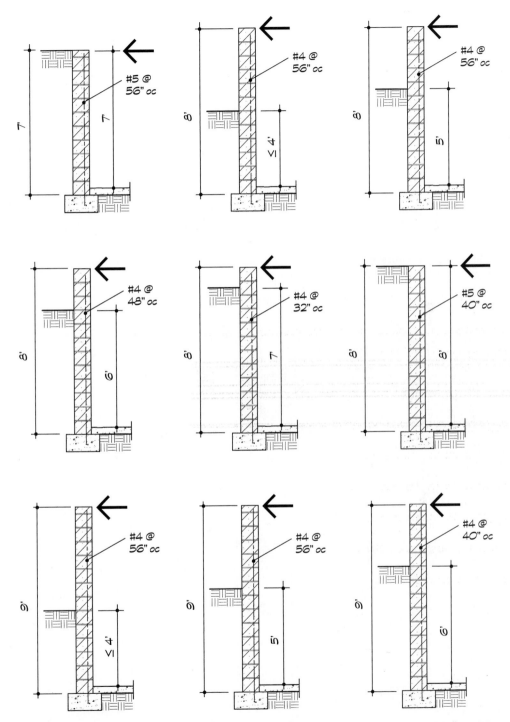

Fig. 1805.5.1.2C-4. Vertical reinforcing for 10" concrete and masonry foundation walls with $d \geq 6.75$". Soil is GM, GC, SM, SM–SC, and ML. *[IBC Table 1805.5(3)]*

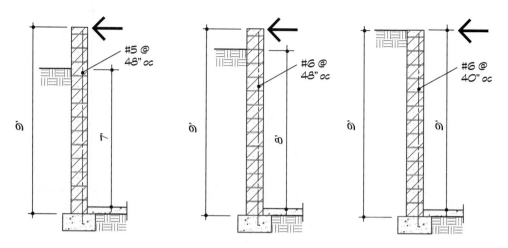

Fig. 1805.5.1.2C-5. Vertical reinforcing for 10" concrete and masonry foundation walls with $d \geq 6.75$". Soil is GM, GC, SM, SM–SC, and ML. *[IBC Table 1805.5(3)]*

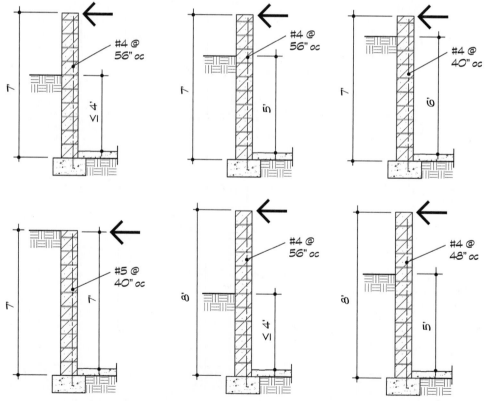

Fig. 1805.5.1.2C-6. Vertical reinforcing for 10" concrete and masonry foundation walls with $d \geq 6.75$". Soil is SC, MH, ML–CL, or inorganic CL. *[IBC Table 1805.5(3)]*

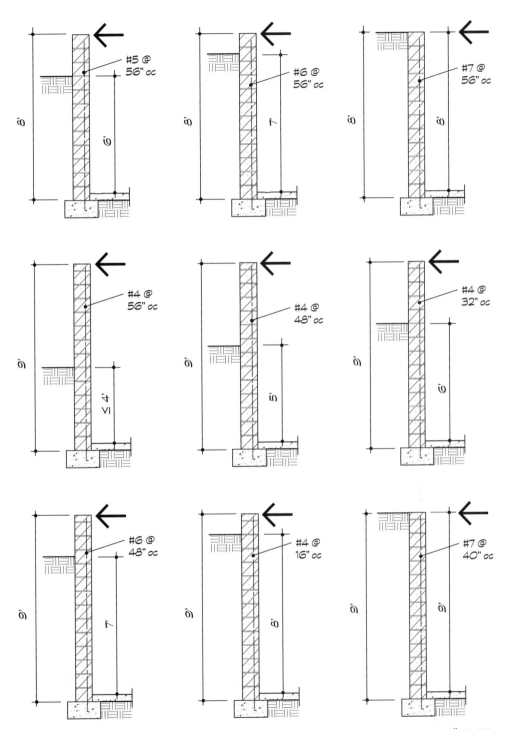

Fig. 1805.5.1.2C-7. Vertical reinforcing for 10" concrete and masonry foundation walls with $d \geq 6.75$". Soil is SC, MH, ML–CL, or inorganic CL. *[IBC Table 1805.5(3)]*

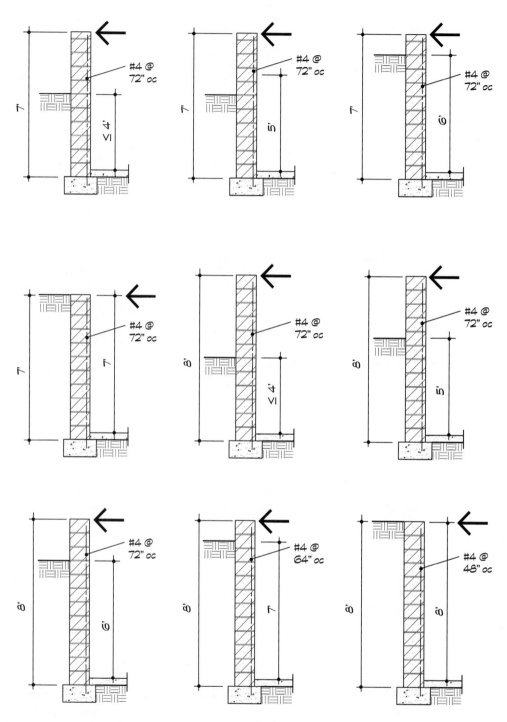

Fig. 1805.5.1.2D-1. Vertical reinforcing for 12" concrete and masonry foundation walls with $d \geq 8.75"$. Soil is GW, GP, SW, or SP. *[IBC Table 1805.5(4)]*

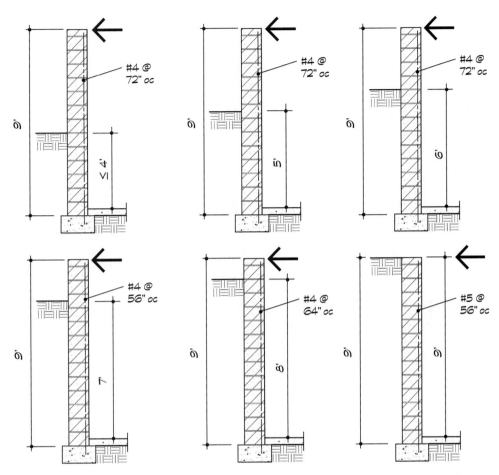

Fig. 1805.5.1.2D-2. Vertical reinforcing for 12" concrete and masonry foundation walls with $d \geq 8.75$". Soil is GW, GP, SW, or SP. *[IBC Table 1805.5(4)]*

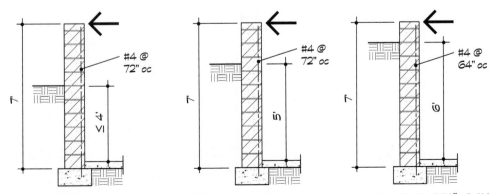

Fig. 1805.5.1.2D-3. Vertical reinforcing for 12" concrete and masonry foundation walls with $d \geq 8.75$". Soil is GM, GC, SM, SM–SC, or ML. *[IBC Table 1805.5(4)]*

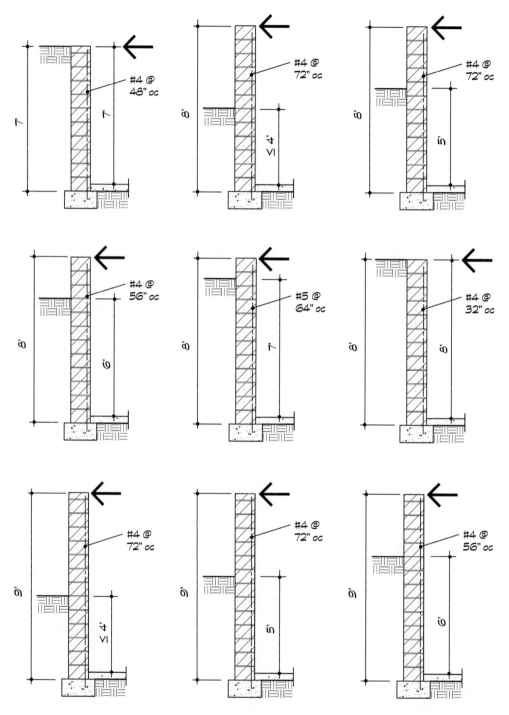

Fig. 1805.5.1.2D-4. Vertical reinforcing for 12" concrete and masonry foundation walls with $d \geq 8.75$". Soil is GM, GC, SM, SM–SC, or ML. *[IBC Table 1805.5(4)]*

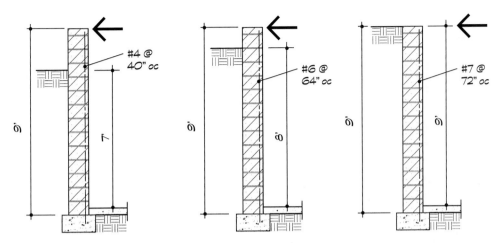

Fig. 1805.5.1.2D-5. Vertical reinforcing for 12" concrete and masonry foundation walls with $d \geq 8.75$". Soil is GM, GC, SM, SM–SC, or ML. *[IBC Table 1805.5(4)]*

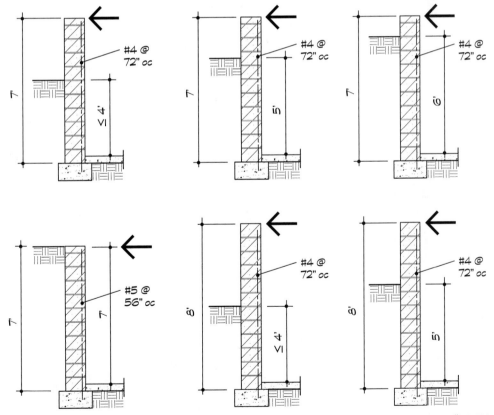

Fig. 1805.5.1.2D-6. Vertical reinforcing for 12" concrete and masonry foundation walls with $d \geq 8.75$". Soil is SC, MH, ML–CL, or inorganic CL. *[IBC Table 1805.5(4)]*

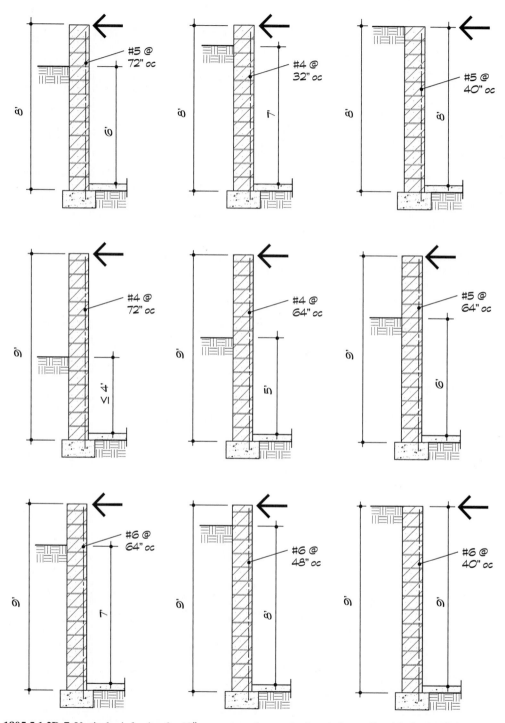

Fig. 1805.5.1.2D-7. Vertical reinforcing for 12" concrete and masonry foundation walls with $d \geq 8.75$". Soil is SC, MH, ML–CL, or inorganic CL. *[IBC Table 1805.5(4)]*

1805 Footings and Foundations

1805.5.4 Hollow masonry walls

- The following is required for foundation walls of hollow masonry units:
  - ○ ≥ 4" of solid masonry as follows:
    - At the tops of walls.
    - At girder supports.

1805.5.7 Pier and curtain wall foundations *(part 1 of 2)*

- Pier and curtain wall foundations may be used as follows where the conditions indicated in this section apply:
  - ○ In locations other than the following Seismic Design Categories:
    - D, E, F.
  - ○ For light-frame construction as follows:
    - ≤ 2 stories.
- Load-bearing walls must meet the following requirements:
  - ○ They must bear on continuous footings with the following detail:
    - Footings must tie into exterior wall footings.
  - ○ Thickness must be one of the following:
    - ≥ 4" nominal.
    - ≥ 3⁵/₈" actual.
  - ○ They must be integral with piers as follows:
    - Spaced ≤ 6' on center.
- Piers must meet the following requirements:
  - ○ Unsupported height of masonry piers is limited as follows:
    - Height must be ≤ 10 × the least pier dimension.
  - ○ The following units supporting beams and girders must meet requirements shown below:
    - Units:
      - Structural clay tile.
      - Hollow concrete masonry.
    - Requirements:
      - Where unsupported height of piers is > 4 × least dimension:
        - Cellular spaces must be filled with the following:
          - Type M or S mortar.
      - Where unsupported height of piers is ≤ 4 × least dimension:
        - Cellular spaces need not be filled.
      - Hollow piers must be capped by one of the following methods:
        - With ≥ 4" of solid masonry.
        - With ≥ 4" of concrete.
        - By filling the cells of the top course with concrete or grout.

1805 Footings and Foundations

1805.5.7 Pier and curtain wall foundations *(part 2 of 2)*

- The height of a 4" load-bearing masonry wall is limited as follows:
  - To ≤ 4' where supporting the following:
    Wood-framed walls.
    Wood-framed floors.
- The height of unbalanced fill for 4" foundation walls is limited as follows:
  - To ≤ 2' for solid masonry.
  - To ≤ 1' for hollow masonry.

1805.7 Designs employing lateral bracing

- This section series governs the following design using the columns listed below:
  - Design:
    Design to resist the following loads:
    Axial.
    Lateral.
  - Columns:
    Posts.
    Poles.
- Design governed by this section series is subject to the following:
  - The following elements where located on the soils listed below have requirements indicated:
    Elements:
    Walls and slabs.
    Soils:
    Silts and clays.
    Requirements:
    Frictional resistance for these elements is taken as ≤ 50% of the following:
    The force normal to the soil as follows:
    From the weight of the elements.
  - Bracing is required to meet deflection limits as follows:
    Where lateral support for the following elements is provided by the method indicated below:
    Elements:
    Structural or nonstructural materials such as the following:
    Plaster.
    Masonry and concrete.
    Method:
    Posts embedded in soil.
- Wood poles must be treated.

  Note: The following are cited as governing the treatment of the poles:
  AWPA C2, "Lumber, Timber, Bridge Ties, and Mine Ties."
  AWPA C4, "Poles."

1807 Dampproofing and Waterproofing

1807.1 Where required

- The following components must be detailed as indicated below:
  - ○ Components:
    Walls or parts of walls with both the characteristics:
      In contact with earth.
      Enclose interior space.
    Floors below grade.
  - ○ Detailing:
    Components in locations indicated below must be treated with one of following systems:
      Systems:
        Dampproofing as per requirements of this section.
        Waterproofing as per requirements of this section.
      Locations:
        Occupancies R, I.
        Other occupancies where omission of the systems would be detrimental as follows:
          To the building.
          To the occupancy.

  Note: 1203.3, "Under-floor ventilation," is cited as the source governing ventilation for crawl spaces.

1807.1.1 Story above grade

- This section applies to a basement that qualifies as a story above grade.
- Where finished grade is as follows, the requirements below apply:
  - ○ Grade:
    Located below the basement floor for $\geq$ ¼ of the perimeter.
  - ○ Requirements:
    The walls below grade must be dampproofed.
    The floor must be dampproofed.
    A foundation drain is required around the walls below grade.
- A subsurface soil investigation is not required as follows:
  - ○ To determine the height of the water table.
- Such a basement need not be waterproofed.
- A base course is not required under such a basement floor.

  Note: The following are cited as not applicable to basements governed by this section.
      1802.2.3, "Ground-water table."
      1807.3, "Waterproofing required."
      1807.4.1, "Floor base course."
  The following are cited as sources of requirements applicable to this section:
      1807.2, "Dampproofing required."
      1807.4.2, "Foundation drain."

1807 Dampproofing and Waterproofing

1807.1.2 Under-floor space

- Ground surface in a crawl space is governed as follows:
  - It may not be below footing bearing level.
- One of the following details must be provided where either condition indicated applies:
  - Details:
      Ground surface in a crawl space must be at the following height:
        ≥ the height of exterior finished grade.
      An approved drainage system must be provided.
  Conditions:
      Groundwater table rises to ≤ 6" of finished grade at building perimeter.
      Surface groundwater does not readily drain from the site.
- Where a crawl space is as follows, the conditions listed below may be omitted:
  - Crawl space:
      Where ground surface is ≥ the height of exterior finished grade.
  - Conditions:
      The following requirements may be omitted:
        A subsurface soil investigation to determine the height of the water table.
        Dampproofing.
        Waterproofing.
        A subsoil drainage system.

  *Note: The following are cited as sources of requirements which do not apply to
           under-floor space governed by this section:
           1802.2.3, "Ground-water table."
           1807.2, "Dampproofing required."
           1807.3, "Waterproofing required."
           1807.4, "Subsoil drainage system."*

1807.1.2.1 Flood hazard areas

- Where located in a flood hazard area, the following applies:
  - Ground surface in a crawl space must be as follows:
      ≥ the height of exterior finished grade.

  *Note: 1612.3, "Establishment of flood hazard areas," is cited as the source defining the
           conditions that establish the area indicated above.*

1807 Dampproofing and Waterproofing

1807.1.3 Ground-water control

- This section addresses the following components:
  - ○ Walls or parts of walls with both the following characteristics:
       In contact with earth.
       Enclose interior space.
  - ○ Floors below grade.
- Such walls and floors must be dampproofed in the following case:
  - ○ Where the groundwater table is lowered as follows:
       Lowered and maintained at < 6" below the bottom of lowest floor.
- Systems utilized to lower the groundwater table must be in consideration of the following:
  - ○ Accepted principles of engineering.
  - ○ Permeability of the soil.
  - ○ Rate of water flow into the drainage system.
  - ○ Capacity of pumps.
  - ○ Pressure against which pumps must perform.
  - ○ Capacity of disposal area for the system.
  - ○ Other applicable conditions.

    Note: 1807.2, "Dampproofing required," is cited as the source of requirements for dampproofing.

1807.2 Dampproofing required

- This section does not apply to wood foundations.
- This section applies to walls and floors qualifying for one of the following:
  - ○ Waterproofing.
  - ○ Dampproofing.
- Such walls and floors must be dampproofed in the following case:
  - ○ Where there is no hydrostatic pressure.

    Note: The following are cited as sources of applicable requirements:
       1802.2.3, "Ground-water table," describes conditions where no hydrostatic pressure will occur.
       AFPA TR7, "Basic Requirements for Permanent Wood Foundation System," provides requirements by which such foundations must be designed.

1807 Dampproofing and Waterproofing

1807.2.1 Floors

- This section applies to floors requiring dampproofing.
- Where there is no separate floor above a slab, dampproofing is installed as follows:
  - Dampproofing must be installed between the floor and base course.

    Note: 1807.4.1, "Floor base course," is cited as the source of requirements for the base course indicated above.

- Where located below a slab, dampproofing is governed as follows:
  - One of the following systems is required:
    - ≥ 6-mil polyethylene as follows:
      With joints lapped ≥ 6".
    - Other approved materials and methods.
- Where located on top a slab, dampproofing is governed as follows:
  - One of the following systems is required:
    - Dampproofing is to be mopped-on-bitumen.
    - ≥ 4-mil polyethylene.
    - Other approved materials and methods.
  - Joints in the dampproofing membrane are governed as follows:
    To be lapped and sealed as per manufacturer's instructions.

1807.2.2 Walls

- This section applies to walls requiring dampproofing.
- Dampproofing must be installed as follows:
  - On the exterior surface of the wall.
  - From the top of footing to above grade.
- Dampproofing must be one of the following materials:
  - Bituminous material.
  - Acrylic modified cement at 3 lbs/square yard.
  - $1/8$" coat of surface-bonding mortar.
  - Any waterproofing material as follows:
    Two-ply hot mopped felts.
    ≥ 6-mil polyvinyl chloride.
    ≥ 40-mil polymer-modified asphalt.
    ≥ 6-mil polyethylene.
    Other approved materials and methods.

    Note: The following are cited as sources of applicable requirements:
    ASTM C 887, "Specification for Packaged, Dry Combined Materials for Surface Bonding Mortar," governs surface bonding mortar as indicated above.
    1807.3.2, "Walls," lists waterproofing materials as summarized above.

1807 Dampproofing and Waterproofing

1807.2.2.1 Surface preparation of walls

- Walls to receive dampproofing must be prepared as follows:
  - Concrete walls:
    Form tie holes and recesses must be sealed with one of the following:
      Bituminous material.
      Other approved material or method.
  - Unit masonry:
    Where dampproofing is not approved for direct application:
      Walls must be parged as follows:
        On the exterior surface below grade.
        With $\geq \, ^3/_8$" portland cement mortar.
        Parging is to be coved at the footing.
    Where dampproofing is approved for direct application:
      Parging is not required.

1807.3 Waterproofing required

- This section applies to walls and floors qualifying for one of the following:
  - Waterproofing.
  - Dampproofing.
- Such walls and floors must be waterproofed as follows:
  - Where both of the following conditions apply:
    Where there is hydrostatic pressure.
    Where a groundwater control system is not provided.

  Note: The following are cited as sources of applicable requirements:
    1802.2.3, "Groundwater table," describes the conditions where hydrostatic pressure will occur.
    1806.1.3, "Groundwater control," provides requirements for the control system indicated above.

1807.3.1 Floors

- Concrete floors required to be waterproofed must use the following material:
  - Material designed to resist the hydrostatic pressure against it.
- One of the following or other approved waterproofing material must be placed under the slab:
  - Rubberized asphalt membrane.
  - Butyl rubber membrane.
  - $\geq$ 60-mil polyvinyl chloride as follows:
    Joints lapped $\geq$ 6".
  - Membrane joints must be lapped and sealed as per manufacturer's instructions.

1807 Dampproofing and Waterproofing

1807.3.2 Walls

- Walls and parts of walls required to be waterproofed are governed as follows:
  - They must be one of the following:
    Concrete.
    Masonry.
  - They must be designed to resist the following:
    Hydrostatic pressure applied.
    Lateral loads applied.
  - They must have waterproofing between the following points:
    The bottom of the wall.
    A point $\geq$ 12" above the highest groundwater table level.
  - They must have dampproofing as follows:
    On the remainder of the wall below grade.
  - Waterproofing must consist of one of the following:
    Two-ply hot mopped felts.
    $\geq$ 6-mil polyvinyl chloride.
    $\geq$ 40-mil polymer-modified asphalt.
    $\geq$ 6-mil polyethylene.
    Other approved materials and methods.
  - Joints in the waterproofing membrane must be detailed as follows:
    Lapped and sealed as per manufacturer's instructions.

    Note: 1807.2.2, "Walls," is cited as the source of requirements for dampproofing as required above.

1807.3.2.1 Surface preparation of walls

- Walls to receive waterproofing must be prepared as follows:
  - Concrete walls:
    Form tie holes and recesses must be sealed with one of the following:
      Bituminous material.
      Other approved material or method.
  - Unit masonry:
    Where waterproofing is not approved for direct application:
      Walls must be parged as follows:
        On the exterior surface below grade.
        With $\geq$ $^3/_8$" portland cement mortar.
        Parging is to be coved at the footing.
    Where waterproofing is approved for direct application:
      Parging is not required.

    Note: 1807.2.2.1, "Surface preparation of walls," is cited as the source of requirements for wall preparation, a summary of which is provided above.

1807 Dampproofing and Waterproofing

1807.4 Subsoil drainage system

- This section addresses floors below grade and walls enclosing space and contacting earth.
- Where hydrostatic pressure is not present, the following applies:
  - Dampproofing is required.
  - A base is required under the floor.
  - A drain is required at the perimeter of the foundation.
  - The water table may be lowered by the subsoil drainage system described in this section.

    Note: 1807.1.3, "Ground-water control," is cited as the source of requirements for the subsoil drainage system indicated above.

1807.4.1 Floor base course

- The following basement floors are not subject to the requirements indicated below:
  - Excluded floors:
    Basements with both the following characteristics:
    The basement qualifies as a story above grade.
    The finished grade is below ≥ ¼ of the basement wall perimeter.
    Where the site has either of the following conditions:
    Site soil is well-drained gravel mixture.
    Site soil is well-drained sand/gravel mixture.
  - Requirements:
    Other basement floors must be on a base course as follows:
    ≥ 4" of gravel crushed stone.
    Base must have ≤ 10% material passing a #4 sieve.

1807.4.2 Foundation drain

- This section addresses foundation drains where required.
- One of the following foundation drains is required at the perimeter of the foundation:
  - Gravel or crushed stone as follows:
    With ≤ 10% material passing a #4 sieve.
    Drain must extend horizontally ≥ 12" beyond the outside edge of the footing.
    Bottom of drain must be ≤ the height of the bottom of the base under floor.
    Top of drain must be ≥ 6" above top of footing.
    Top of drain must be covered with an approved membrane filter.
  - Drain tile or perforated pipe as follows:
    Drain invert elevation must be ≤ that of the floor.
    Top of joints or perforations must be covered with an approved membrane filter.
    Drain must be placed on ≥ 2" of gravel or crushed stone.
    Drain must be covered with ≥ 6" of gravel or crushed stone.

    Note: 1807.4.1, "Floor base course," is cited as governing the gravel or crushed stone required for the drain tile or pipe above.

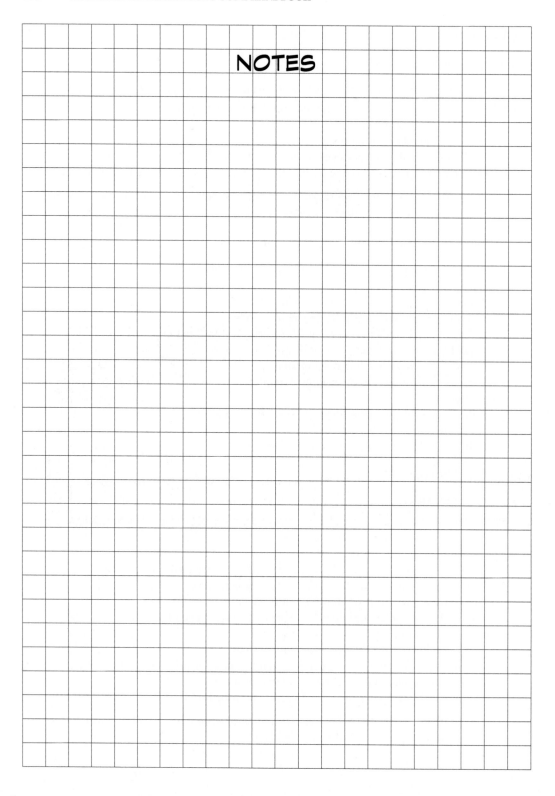

NOTES

19

Concrete

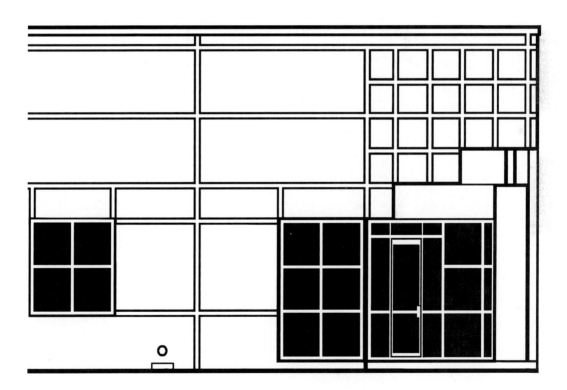

Garments to Go. Bastrop, Texas. *(partial elevlation)*
Spencer Godfrey Architects. Round Rock, Texas.

1907 Details of Reinforcement

1907.5.2.1 Depth and cover

- Tolerances permitted for the following are as shown in the details provided in this section:
  - Placement of reinforcing in the following concrete components:
    Flexural members.
    Walls.
    Compression members.

    Note: IBC Table 1907.5.2.1, "Tolerances," is cited as listing tolerances for d and concrete cover and is summarized in the illustrations below:

- Tolerance may not reduce cover > $^1/_3$ that required by construction documents.

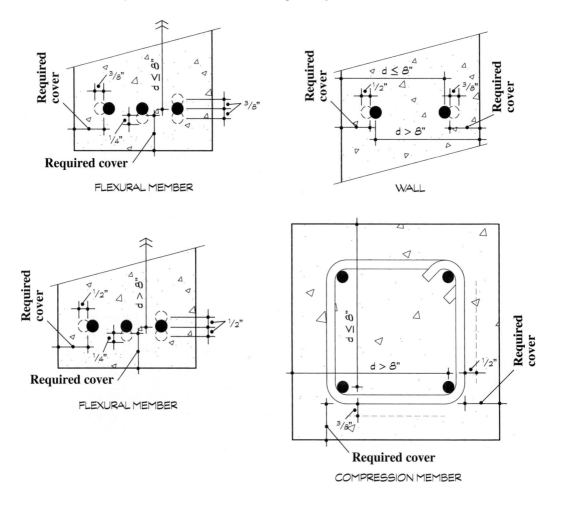

Fig. 1907.5.2.1. Tolerances for steel in concrete. Maximum tolerances for placing reinforcement, prestressing tendons, and prestressing ducts in concrete are shown.

1907 Details of Reinforcement

1907.5.2.2 Bends and ends

- Tolerances permitted for locations of the following are as shown in the detail provided below:
  - Bends in reinforcement.
  - Ends of reinforcement.
  - Concrete cover.

    Note: IBC Table 1907.5.2.1, "Tolerances," is cited as listing the permitted tolerances which are summarized in the illustration below.

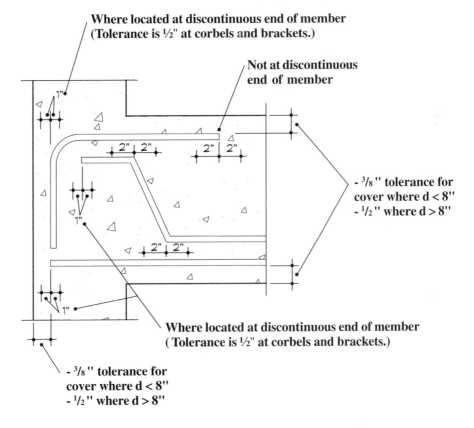

Fig. 1907.5.2.2. Tolerances for location of bends and ends of concrete reinforcing and concrete cover.

1907 Details of Reinforcement

1907.7.1 Cast-in-place concrete (nonprestressed)

- Details provided in this section show the concrete cover required for reinforcement in the following:
  - Nonprestressed, cast-in-place concrete.

    Note: IBC Table 1907.7.1, "Minimum Concrete Cover," is cited as listing such minimums which are summarized in Fig. 1907.7.1A through Fig. 1907.7.1C.

- Required concrete cover may be greater than that specified by this section for the following purposes:
  - Protection in corrosive environments.

    Note: 1907.7.5, "Corrosive environments," is cited as governing concrete cover in such conditions.

  - Fire protection.

    Note: 1907.7.7, "Fire protection," is cited as governing concrete cover for this purpose.

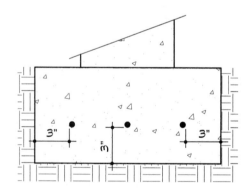

Cast against earth, permanent contact to earth

Fig. 1907.7.1A. Minimum concrete cover for nonprestressed steel in cast-in-place concrete.

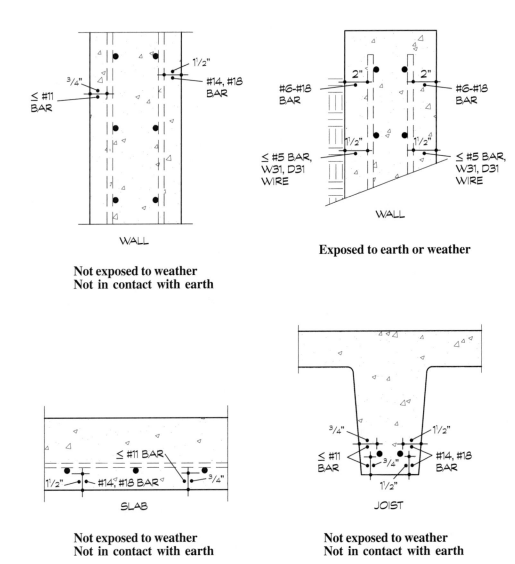

Fig. 1907.7.1B. Minimum concrete cover for nonprestressed steel in cast-in-place concrete.

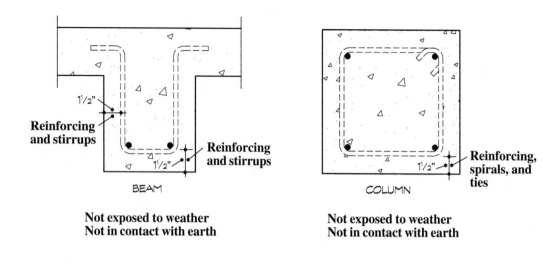

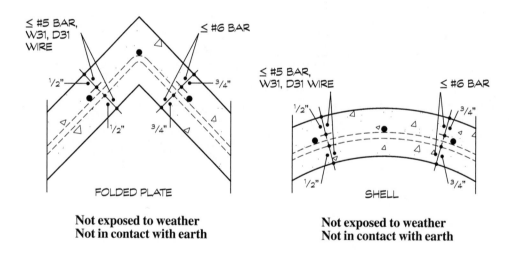

Fig. 1907.7.1C. Minimum concrete cover for nonprestressed steel in cast-in-place concrete.

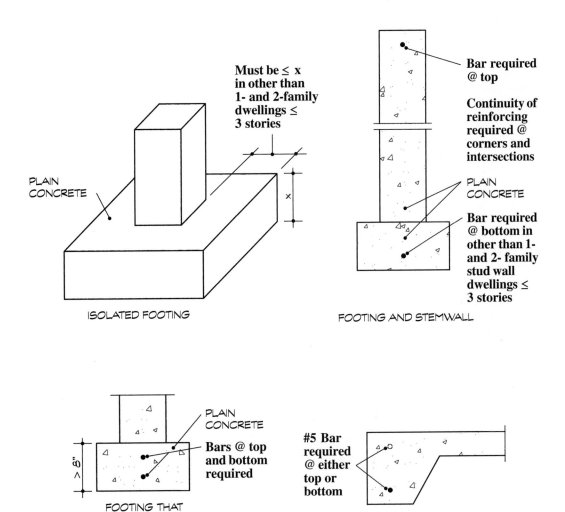

Fig. 1910.4.3.2. Plain concrete footings in Seismic Design Category C.

1911 Minimum Slab Provisions

1911.1 General

- Requirements for concrete floor slabs-on-grade are shown in the detail provided in this section.
- A vapor retarder is not required under a slab in the following locations:
  - In detached buildings which are accessory to occupancy R-3 such as follows:
    Garages.
    Utility buildings.
    Other unheated facilities.
  - In unheated storage rooms as follows:
    < 70 sf in area.
  - In unheated carports attached to occupancy R-3 buildings.
  - In buildings of occupancies other than R-3 as follows:
    Where moisture migrating to the surface of the slab will not be detrimental.
  - Where the following slabs will remain unenclosed:
    Driveways.
    Walks.
    Patios.
    Other similar slabs.
  - Where local site conditions permit as follows:
    Must be approved.

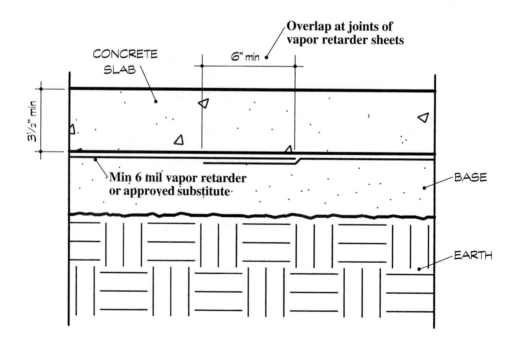

Fig. 1911.1A. Detail at concrete slab. The detail shows code requirements for concrete slabs on grade.

Case study: Fig. 1911.1B. The concrete slab is 4" thick, which is > than the 3¹/₂" required minimum. The 8 mil vapor retarder is thicker than the minimum 6 mils required. The concrete slab is in compliance with code requirements.

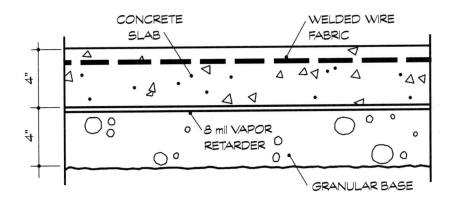

Fig. 1911.1B. Detail at concrete slab. Multipurpose Building Addition to Children's Home. Wilkes-Barre, Pennsylvania. C. Allen Mullins, Architect. Bear Creek, Pennsylvania.

1914 Shotcrete

1914.4.1 Size

- Required reinforcing for shotcrete construction is one of the following:
  - ○ ≤ #5 bars.
  - ○ Any size for which preconstruction tests verify that adequate encasement will be provided.

1914.4.2 Clearance

- Required clearances between reinforcing bars are shown in the details provided in this section as follows:
  - ○ Required clearances may be reduced where both of the following apply:
    Where preconstruction tests verify that adequate encasement will be provided.
    Where approved by the building official.

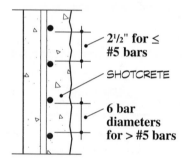

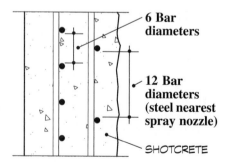

Fig. 1914.4.2. Minimum clearance required between reinforcing for shotcrete.

1915 Reinforced Gypsum Concrete

1915.2 Minimum thickness

- The thickness required for reinforced gypsum concrete is shown in the details provided in this section as follows:
  - Requirements for the reduced thickness include those indicated on the detail and the following:

    Diaphragm action must not be required of the assembly.

    The live load may not > 40 psf.

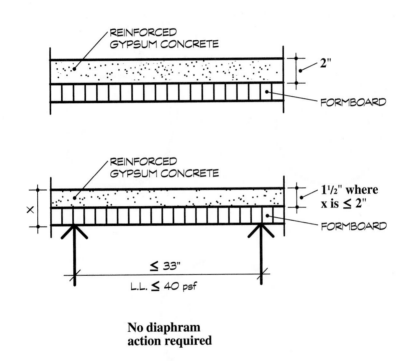

**No diaphram
action required**

Fig. 1915.2. Minimum thickness of reinforced gypsum concrete.

1916 Concrete-Filled Pipe Columns

1916.4 Reinforcement

- Reinforcing in concrete-filled pipe columns is governed as follows:
  - Reinforcing is to be one of the following:
    Rods.
    Structural shapes.
    Pipe.
  - Structural shapes must be milled to provide bearing on the following:
    Cap plate.
    Baseplate.
  - Adequate clearance between pipe wall and reinforcing is required for composite action.
  - Minimum clearance between pipe wall and reinforcing is shown in the details provided.

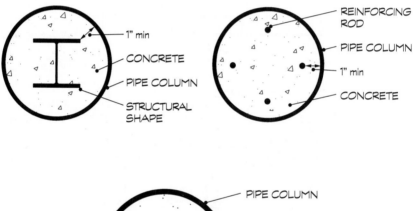

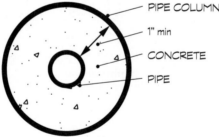

Fig. 1916.4. Clearance for reinforcement in concrete-filled pipe columns.

1916 Concrete-Filled Pipe Columns

1916.5 Fire-resistance-rating protection

- Pipe columns must have the fire-resistance rating required for the building type.
- Where a steel shell surrounds the fire-resistive covering, it may not be assumed to carry a structural load.
- Required sizes are shown in the details provided.

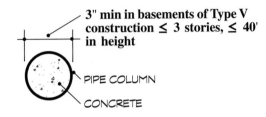

3" min in basements of Type V construction ≤ 3 stories, ≤ 40' in height

PIPE COLUMN

CONCRETE

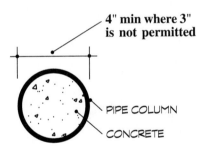

4" min where 3" is not permitted

PIPE COLUMN

CONCRETE

Fig. 1916.5. Minimum diameter of concrete-filled pipe columns.

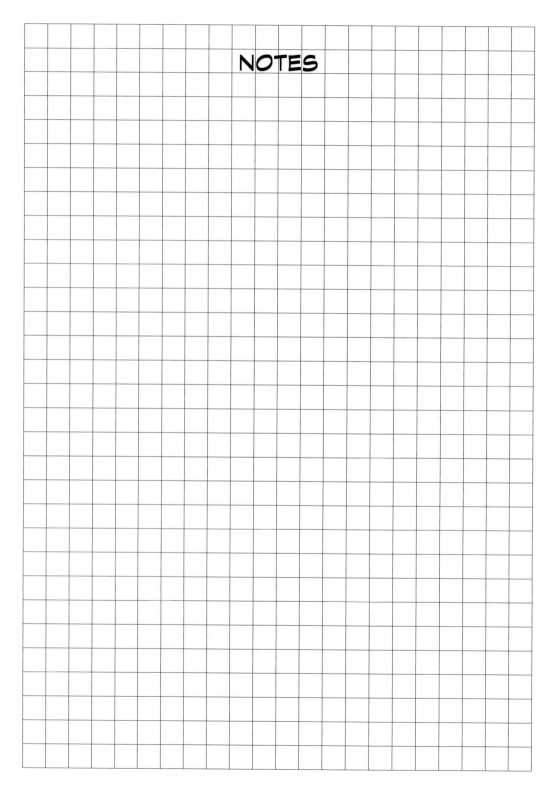

NOTES

20

Aluminum

Multipurpose Building Addition to Children's Home. Wilkes-Barre, Pennsylvania. *(partial elevation)*
C. Allen Mullins, Architects. Bear Creek, Pennsylvania.

2002 Materials

2002.1 General

- Design of aluminum components for structural application is governed as follows:
  - Design must comply with structural load requirements of the code.
  - Design must comply with industry standards.

  Note: The following are cited as governing the design of aluminum components:
  Chapter 16, "Structural Design."
  AA ASM 35, "Aluminum Sheet Metal Work in Building Construction."
  AA ADM 1 Aluminum Design Manual, Part 1-A, "Aluminum Structures, Allowable Stress Design."
  AA ADM 1 Aluminum Design Manual, Part 1-B, "Aluminum Structures, Load and Resistance Factor Design of Buildings and Similar Type Structures."

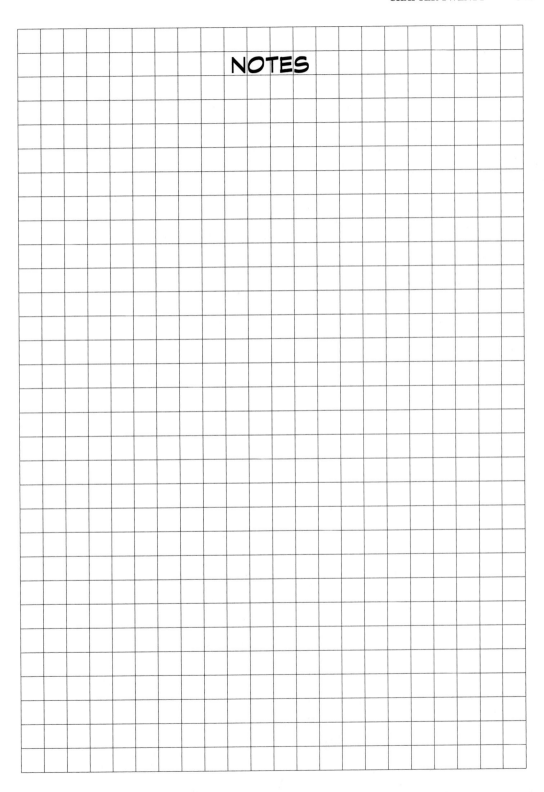

NOTES

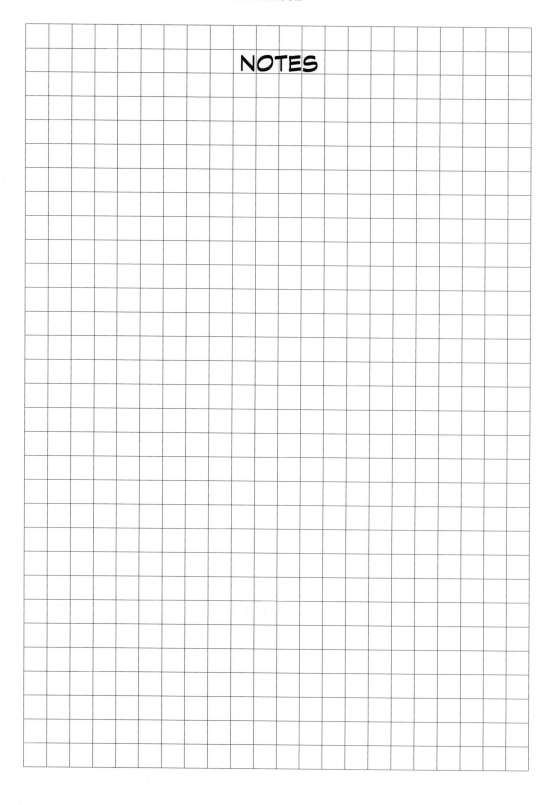

NOTES

21

Masonry

Country Club Park Building One. Wichita, Kansas. *(partial elevation)*
Gossen Livingston Associates, Inc., Architecture. Wichita, Kansas.

2103 Masonry Construction Materials

2103.5 Glass unit masonry

- Requirements for hollow glass blocks are as follows:
  - Reclaimed units may not be used.
  - Other requirements are shown on the detail provided.

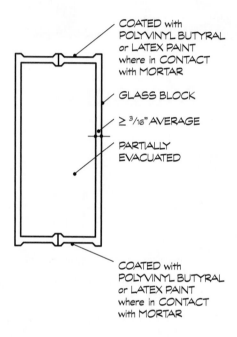

Fig. 2103.5. Section through hollow glass block.

2104 Construction

2104.1.2.1 Bed and head joints

- Unless superceded by other requirements, sizes required for the following masonry joints are shown in the detail provided:
  - Head joints.
  - Bed joints.

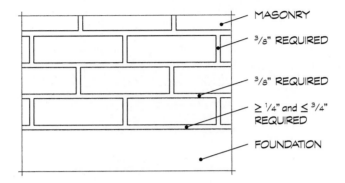

Fig. 2104.1.2.1. Masonry joint sizes.

2104.1.2.1.1 Open-end units

- Grout requirements for open-end masonry units are shown in the detail provided.

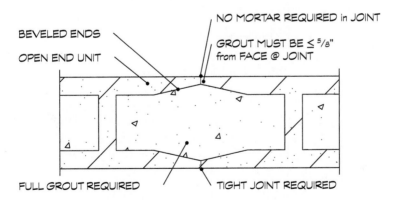

Fig. 2104.1.2.1.1. Grouted open-end masonry units.

2104 Construction

2104.1.2.2 Hollow units

- Fill requirements for head and bed joints of hollow masonry units are shown in the details provided.

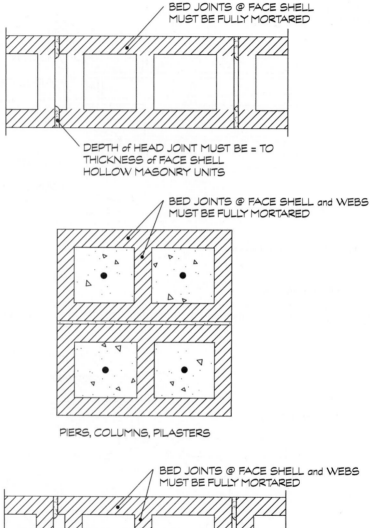

Fig. 2104.1.2.2A. Mortar joint requirements for hollow masonry.

2104 Construction

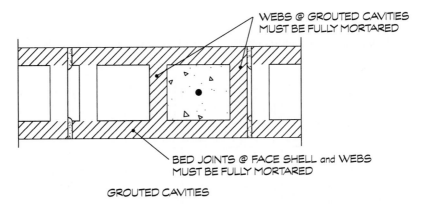

WEBS @ GROUTED CAVITIES
MUST BE FULLY MORTARED

BED JOINTS @ FACE SHELL and WEBS
MUST BE FULLY MORTARED

GROUTED CAVITIES

Fig. 2104.1.2.2B. Mortar joint requirements for hollow masonry.

2104.1.2.3 Solid units

- Joint requirements for head and bed joints of solid masonry units are shown in the detail provided, where not superceded by the following:
  - Directions in construction documents.
  - Other requirements.
- Head joints must be fully buttered.
- "Slushing" mortar to fill head joints is not permitted.
- Head joints must be formed by pushing mortar against the adjacent unit.

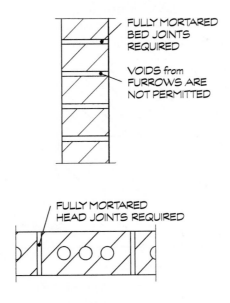

FULLY MORTARED
BED JOINTS
REQUIRED

VOIDS from
FURROWS ARE
NOT PERMITTED

FULLY MORTARED
HEAD JOINTS REQUIRED

Fig. 2104.1.2.3. Mortar joint requirements for solid masonry.

2104 Construction

2104.1.2.4 Glass unit masonry

- Size and other joint requirements for glass block are shown in the detail provided.

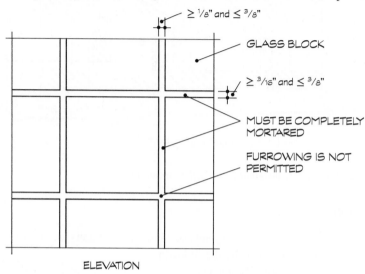

Fig. 2104.1.2.4. Mortar joint requirements for glass unit masonry.

2104.1.3 Installation of wall ties

- Requirements for embedding wall ties in masonry are as follows:
  - Wall ties must be embedded in mortar joint.
  - Wall ties may not be bent once they are embedded in grout or mortar.
  - Other requirements are shown in the details provided.

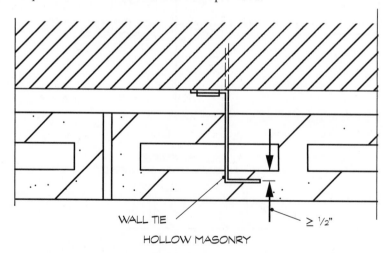

Fig. 2104.1.3A. Requirements for embedment of wall ties in masonry.

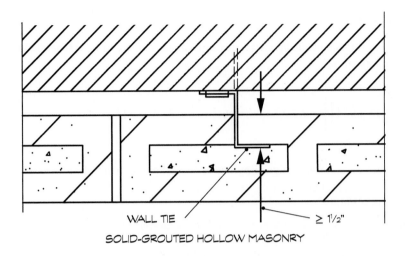

WALL TIE   ≥ 1½"

SOLID-GROUTED HOLLOW MASONRY

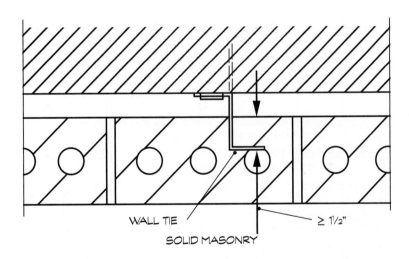

WALL TIE   ≥ 1½"

SOLID MASONRY

Fig. 2104.1.3B. Requirements for embedment of wall ties in masonry.

2104 Construction

2104.1.4 Chases and recesses

- Where the following occur in masonry construction, they are to be constructed as the masonry units are set:
  - Chases.
  - Recesses.
- A lintel is required for masonry above chases or recesses > 12".

2104.1.5 Lintels

- Masonry lintels are to be designed by one of the following methods:
  - Working stress design.
  - Strength design.

    Note: The following are cited as governing the design of masonry lintels:
    Section 2107, "Working Stress Design."
    Section 2108, "Strength Design of Masonry."

- The bearing requirement for lintels in masonry construction is shown in the detail provided.

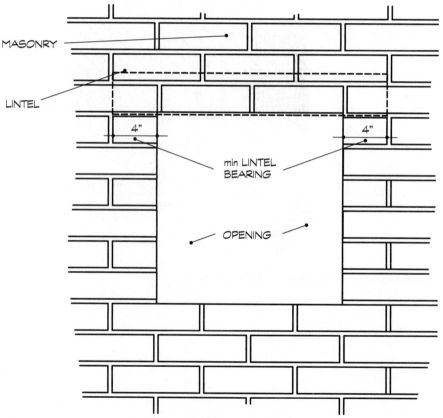

Fig. 2104.1.5. Minimum bearing length of lintels for masonry.

2104 Construction

2104.1.8 Weep holes

- Requirements for weep holes in masonry are shown in the detail provided.

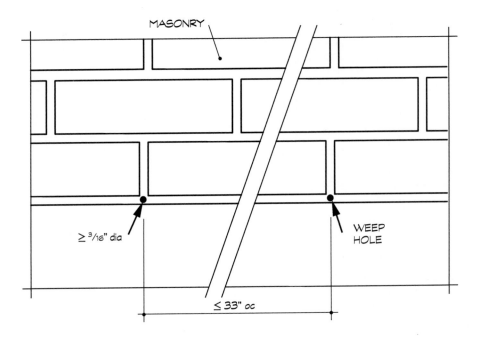

Fig. 2104.1.8. Weep hole size and spacing for masonry.

2104 Construction

2104.2 Corbeled masonry

- Projection limitations for corbeled masonry are shown in the details provided.

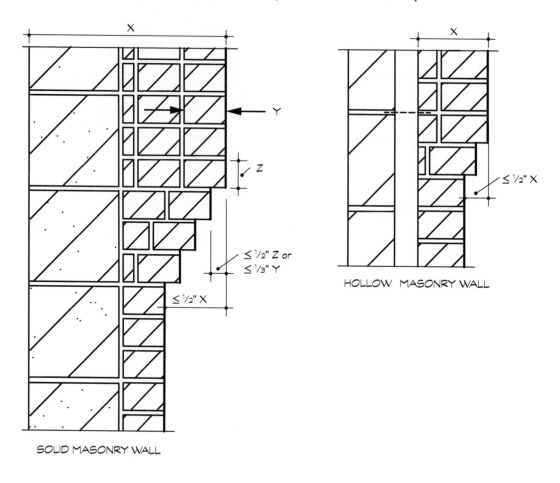

Fig. 2104.2. Projection limitations for corbeled masonry.

2106 Seismic Design

2106.3.1 Masonry walls not part of the lateral-force-resisting system

- This section addresses masonry walls in Seismic Design Category B.
- This section governs the following walls with the characteristics indicated below:
    - Walls:
        Partitions.
        Screen walls.
        Other similar elements.
    - Characteristics:
        Walls do not resist loads other than those due to their own mass as follows:
            Vertical loads.
            Lateral loads.
- Requirements for isolation from the structure are shown in the detail provided.

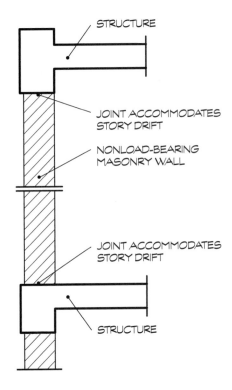

Fig. 2106.3.1 Isolation of nonload-bearing masonry walls.

2107 Working Stress Design

2107.2.2 ACI 530/ASCE 5/TMS 402, Section 2.1.6

- This section addresses masonry columns with all the following characteristics:
  - Located in the following Seismic Design Categories:
    Category A.
    Category B.
    Category C.
  - Supporting light-frame roofs ≤ 400 sf of the following:
    Carports.
    Porches.
    Sheds.
    Similar structures.
  - With a height ≤ 12'.
- Masonry materials must meet minimum specification of this chapter.

  Note: The following are cited as sources of applicable material specifications:
  2103.1, "Concrete masonry units."
  2103.2, "Clay or shale masonry units."

- Where columns must resist uplift, the following applies:
  - The sum of the following must ≥ 1.5 × uplift load:
    Weight of column.
    Weight of footing.

  Note: Chapter 16, "Structural Design," is cited as the source of requirements for loading
  that the anchorage must resist including anchorage of the roof.

- Other requirements are indicated in the details provided.

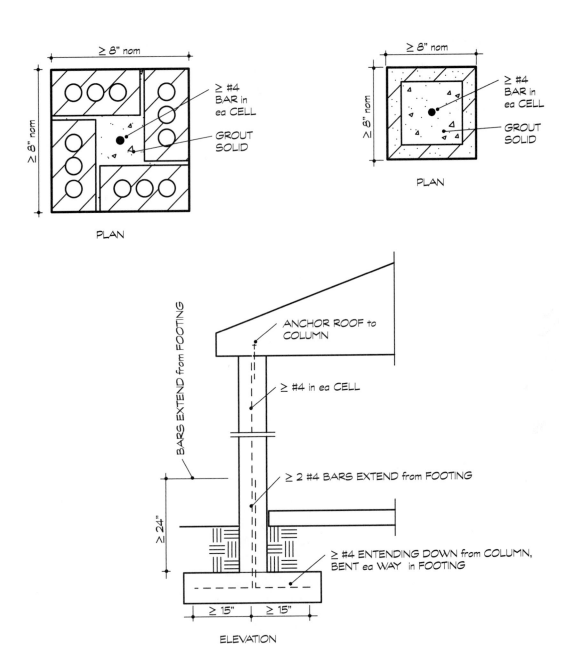

Fig. 2107.2.2. Masonry columns supporting light structures in Seismic Design Categories A, B, and C.

2109 Empirical Design of Masonry

2109.2.1.1 Shear wall thickness

- Minimum thickness of masonry shear walls is shown in the detail below.

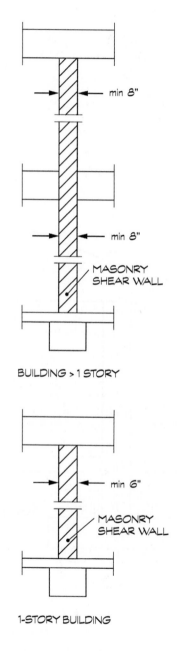

Fig. 2109.2.1.1. Minimum thickness of masonry shear walls.

2109 Empirical Design of Masonry

2109.2.1.2 Cumulative length of shear walls

- The length of shear walls where required is governed as follows:
  - Shear walls must be located as follows:
    - In 2 separate planes as follows:
      - In each direction where shear walls are required.
  - The sum of individual shear wall lengths does not include the following:
    - A wall where length < ½ height.
    - Openings.
  - The sum of individual shear wall lengths in any direction must total the following:
    - ≥ 0.4 × the long dimension of the building as follows:
      - Illustrated in Fig. 2109.2.1.2 on the next page.

Case study: Fig. 2109.2.1.2. The illustration shows a shear wall system in each direction. The minimum length in each direction where a shear wall is required is indicated in the summation of the segments as shown below: Dimension "x" indicates the long dimension of the building.

Where shear walls are required in the long dimension of the building:

$$A + B + C + D + E + F + G + H + I + J + K + L \geq 0.4x.$$

Where shear walls are required in the short direction of the building:

$$M + N + O + P + Q + R + S \geq 0.4x.$$

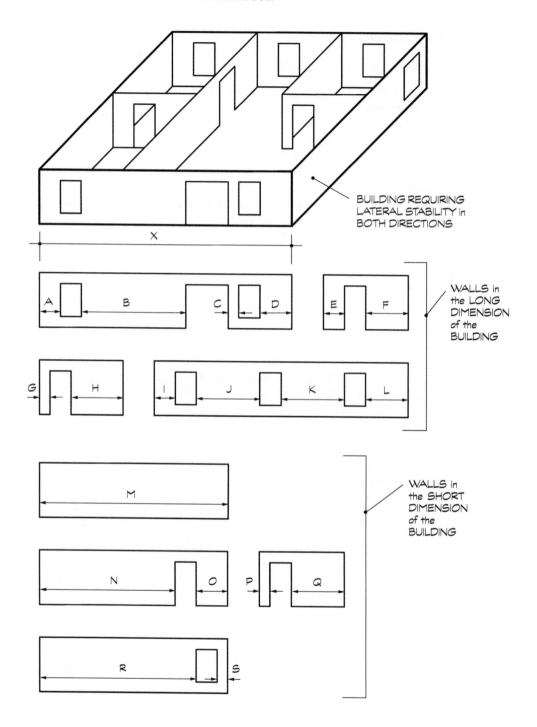

Fig. 2109.2.1.2. Cumulative length of shear walls.

2109 Empirical Design of Masonry

2109.2.1.3 Maximum diaphragm ratio

- Masonry shear walls are required in locations as follows:
  - That will establish length-to-width ratios of diaphragms as follows:
    - As shown in the details below for the following building elements:
      - Roof diaphragms.
      - Floor diaphragms.

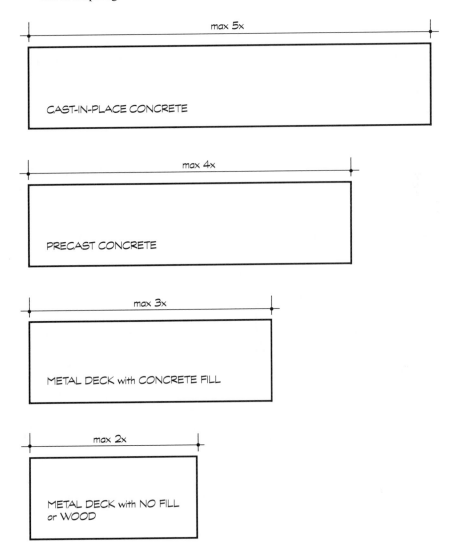

Fig. 2109.2.1.3. Plan views. Maximum diaphragm ratios of various floor and roof systems as defined by shear wall locations.

2109 Empirical Design of Masonry

2109.4.1 Intervals *(part 1 of 2)*

- A partial list of maximum dimensions between lateral support is provided below for the following walls:
  - Load-bearing masonry walls with solid units or fully grouted as follows:
    Length must be ≤ 20 × thickness.
    Width must be ≤ 20 × thickness.

  Note: IBC Table 2109.4.1, "Wall Lateral Support Requirements," is cited as the source of ratios governing wall dimensions.

Table 2109.4.1a   Maximum Distance between Lateral Supports for Masonry Walls

Wall thickness	Max. length Max. height	Wall thickness	Max. length Max. height	Wall thickness	Max. length Max. height
4"	6'-8"	12"	20'-0"	18"	30'-0"
6"	10'-0"	13"	21'-8"	19"	31'-8"
8"	13'-4"	14"	23'-4"	20"	33'-4"
9"	15'-0"	15"	25'-0"	21"	35'-0"
10"	16'-8"	16"	26'-8"	22"	36'-8"
11"	18'-4"	17"	28'-4"	23"	38'-4"

- A partial list of maximum dimensions between lateral support is provided below for the following walls:
  - Load-bearing walls other than solid units or fully grouted:
    Length must be ≤ 18 × thickness.
    Width must be ≤ 18 × thickness.

  Note: IBC Table 2109.4.1, "Wall Lateral Support Requirements," is cited as the source of ratios governing wall dimensions.

Table 2109.4.1b   Maximum Distance between Lateral Supports for Masonry Walls

Wall thickness	Max. length Max. height	Wall thickness	Max. length Max. height	Wall thickness	Max. length Max. height
4"	6'-0"	12"	18'-0"	18"	27'-0"
6"	9'-0"	13"	19'-6"	19"	28'-6"
8"	12'-0"	14"	21'-0"	20"	30'-0"
9"	13'-6"	15"	22'-6"	21"	31'-6"
10"	15'-0"	16"	24'-0"	22"	33'-0"
11"	16'-6"	17"	25'-6"	23"	34'-6"

2109 Empirical Design of Masonry

2109.4.1 Intervals *(part 2 of 2)*

- A partial list of maximum dimensions between lateral support is provided below for the following walls:
  - Exterior nonload-bearing walls:
    Length must be $\leq 18 \times$ thickness.
    Width must be $\leq 18 \times$ thickness.

  Note: IBC Table 2109.4.1, "Wall Lateral Support Requirements," is cited as the source of ratios governing wall dimensions.

Table 2109.4.1c   Maximum Distance between Lateral Supports for Masonry Walls

Wall thickness	Max. length Max. height	Wall thickness	Max. length Max. height	Wall thickness	Max. length Max. height
4"	6'-0"	12"	18'-0"	18"	27'-0"
6"	9'-0"	13"	19'-6"	19"	28'-6"
8"	12'-0"	14"	21'-0"	20"	30'-0"
9"	13'-6"	15"	22'-6"	21"	31'-6"
10"	15'-0"	16"	24'-0"	22"	33'-0"
11"	16'-6"	17"	25'-6"	23"	34'-6"

- A partial list of maximum dimensions between lateral support is provided below for the following walls:
  - Interior nonload-bearing walls:
    Length must be $\leq 36 \times$ thickness.
    Width must be $\leq 36 \times$ thickness.

  Note: IBC Table 2109.4.1, "Wall Lateral Support Requirements," is cited as the source of ratios governing wall dimensions.

Table 2109.4.1d   Maximum Distance between Lateral Support for Masonry Walls

Wall thickness	Max. length Max. height	Wall thickness	Max. length Max. height	Wall thickness	Max. length Max. height
4"	12'-0"	12"	36'-0"	18"	54'-0"
6"	18'-0"	13"	39'-0"	19"	57'-0"
8"	24'-0"	14"	42'-0"	20"	60'-0"
9"	27'-0"	15"	45'-0"	21"	63'-0"
10"	30'-0"	16"	48'-0"	22"	66'-0"
11"	33'-0"	17"	51'-0"	23"	69'-0"

2109 Empirical Design of Masonry

2109.4.2 Thickness

- Wall thickness is measured as shown in the details provided.
- The ratio of height to thickness for cantilever walls is as indicated in the details provided.

  Note: 2109.5.5, "Parapet walls," is cited as the source of thickness requirements for such walls in lieu of those in this section.

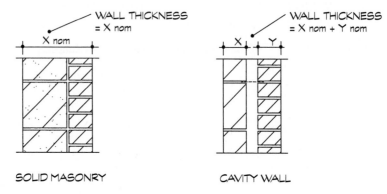

Fig. 2109.4.2A. Measurement of masonry wall thickness.

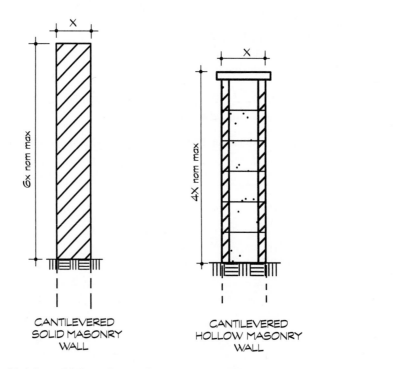

Fig. 2109.4.2B. Ratio of height to thickness for cantilever masonry walls.

2109 Empirical Design of Masonry

2109.4.3 Support elements

- Lateral support must be provided to masonry walls as follows and as indicated in the details provided:
  - Where the horizontal dimension is limited by thickness:
    Lateral support is to be provided by the following elements:
    Cross walls.
    Pilasters.
    Buttresses.
    Structural frame members.
  - Where the vertical dimension is limited by thickness:
    Lateral support is to be provided by the following elements:
    Floors acting as diaphragms.
    Roofs acting as diaphragms.
    Structural frame members.

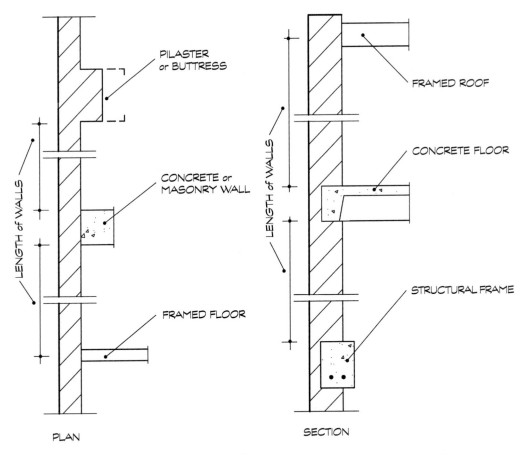

Fig. 2109.4.3. Lateral support for masonry walls.

2109 Empirical Design of Masonry

2109.5.2 Minimum thickness

- The required thickness of masonry bearing walls is shown in the details provided below.

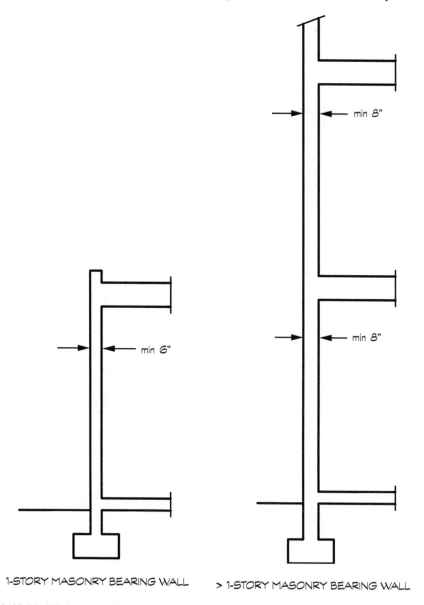

1-STORY MASONRY BEARING WALL   > 1-STORY MASONRY BEARING WALL

Fig. 2109.5.2. Minimum thickness of masonry bearing walls.

2109.5.3 Rubble stone walls

- The required thickness of rubble stone walls is ≥ 16".

2109 Empirical Design of Masonry

2109.5.4 Change in thickness

- Where a higher part of a masonry wall with the following units is thinner than a lower part, the requirement indicated below applies:
  - ○ Walls:
    Hollow units.
    Bonded hollow walls.
  - ○ Requirement:
    One of the following is required at the transition to transfer loads:
    One or more courses of solid masonry as required.
    Special units as shown in the detail provided.
    Special construction.

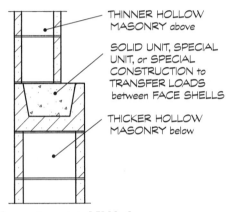

Fig. 2109.5.4. Change in masonry wall thickness at a grouted U-block.

2109.5.5.1 Minimum thickness

- The thickness required for unreinforced masonry parapet walls is shown in details provided.

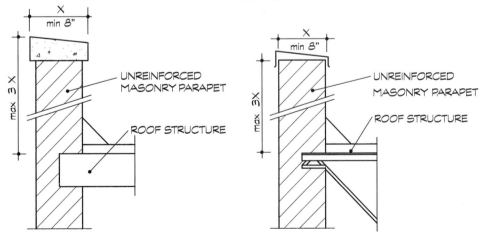

Fig. 2109.5.5.1. Minimum thickness required for unreinforced masonry parapet walls.

2109 Empirical Design of Masonry

2109.6.2.1 Solid units

- This section addresses solid masonry units.
- Where adjacent wythes are bonded with masonry headers, the following is required:
  - Vertical and horizontal distance between headers must be ≤ 24".
  - ≥ 4% of the wall surface must be headers, acceptable examples of which are shown in the elevations provided.
  - Other requirements are shown in the details provided.

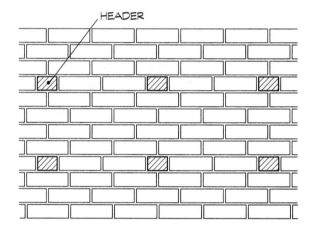

Fig. 2109.6.2.1A. Bond pattern providing headers at the minimum 4% of wall surface.

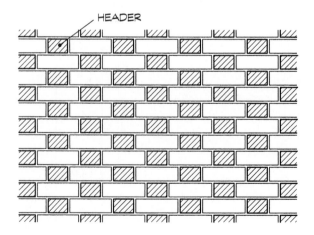

Fig. 2109.6.2.1B. Flemish bond providing headers at 33% of the wall surface.

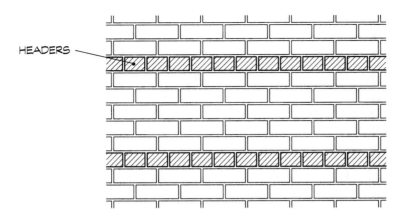

Fig. 2109.6.2.1C. Common bond with 6th course headers providing headers at 16% of the wall surface.

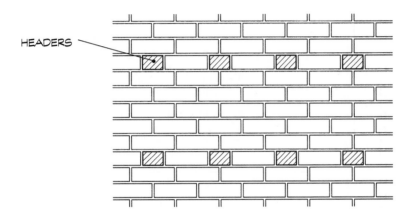

Fig. 2109.6.2.1D. Common bond with 6th course Flemish headers providing headers @ 5% of the wall surface.

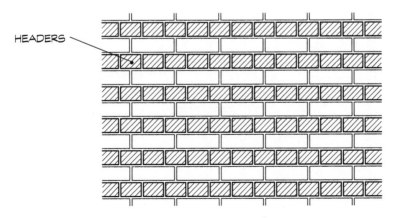

Fig. 2109.6.2.1E. English bond providing headers at 50% of the wall surface.

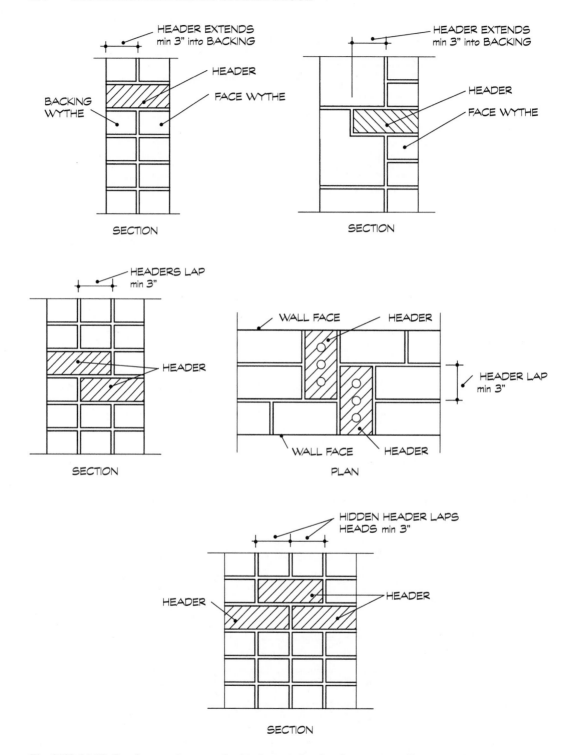

Fig. 2109.6.2.1F. Overlap requirements for headers used to bond masonry walls.

2109 Empirical Design of Masonry

2109.6.2.2 Hollow units

- This section addresses hollow masonry units.
- Where adjacent wythes are bonded with masonry headers, the requirements shown in the following details apply:

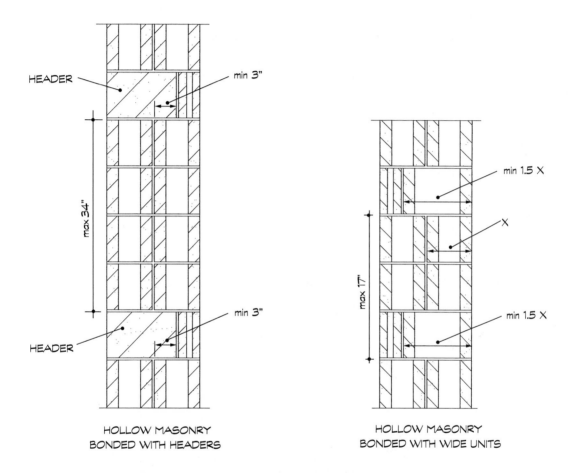

HOLLOW MASONRY
BONDED WITH HEADERS

HOLLOW MASONRY
BONDED WITH WIDE UNITS

Fig. 2109.6.2.2. Requirements for bonding masonry walls with hollow units.

2109.6.2.3 Masonry bonded hollow walls

- This section addresses hollow masonry walls.
- Where adjacent wythes are bonded with masonry headers, the requirements are as follows:
  - Headers must constitute $\geq 4\%$ of the wall surface.
  - Other requirements are as shown in the details provided.

2109 Empirical Design of Masonry

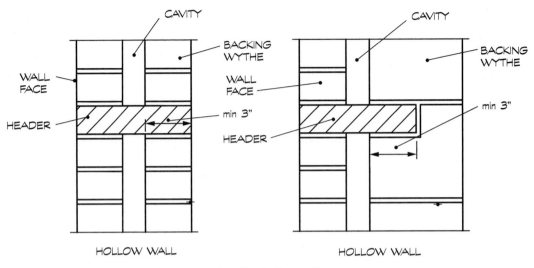

Fig. 2109.6.2.3. Requirements for masonry bonding hollow walls.

2109.6.3.1 Bonding with wall ties

- This section addresses rigid metal ties for masonry walls as follows:
  - Adjustable wall ties are not included.
- Requirements are shown in the following details.

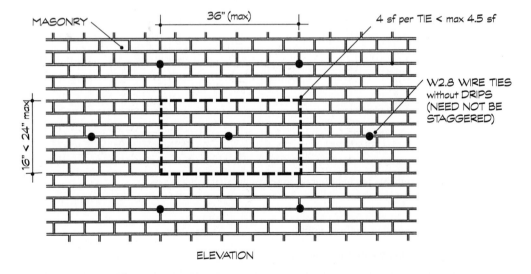

Fig. 2109.6.3.1A. Bonding masonry walls with metal ties. Wire ties at the maximum horizontal spacing of 36" and at 16" vertical spacing results in ties at each 4 sf of wall surface, which is less than the maximum permitted 4½ sf. 24" vertical spacing (max permitted) and 24" horizontal spacing also yield 4 sf of wall surface per tie.

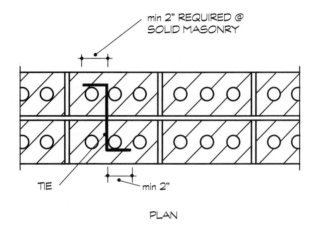

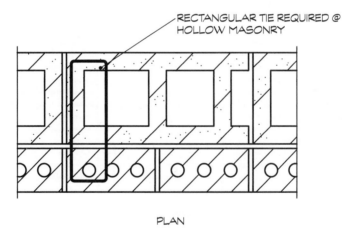

Fig. 2109.6.3.1B. Bonding masonry walls with metal ties.

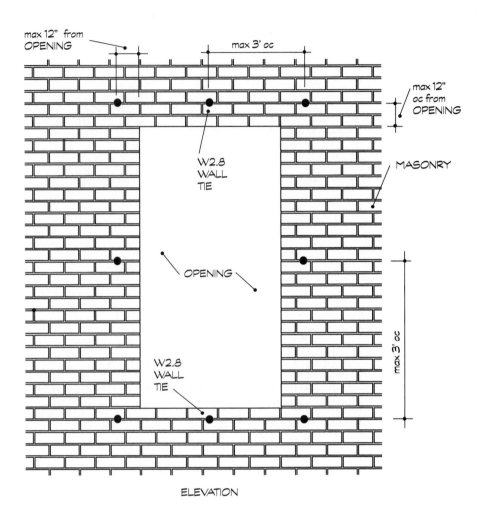

Fig. 2109.6.3.1C. Bonding masonry walls with metal ties.

2109 Empirical Design of Masonry

2109.6.3.1.1 Bonding with adjustable wall ties

- This section addresses adjustable wall ties where used to bond masonry walls as follows:
  - Where pintle legs are used:
    Ties must have $\geq$ 2 legs $\geq$ W2.8 wire.
- Other requirements are shown on the following details.

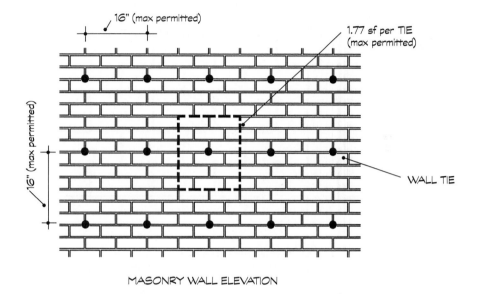

MASONRY WALL ELEVATION

Fig. 2109.6.3.1.1A. Bonding with adjustable wall ties. Adjustable wall ties @ 16" oc in both directions limits the area of wall face served by a tie to 1.77 sf, which is the maximum permitted.

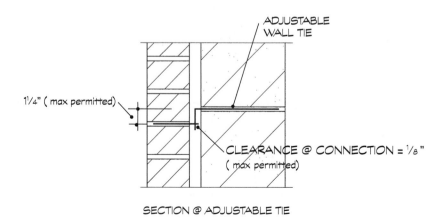

SECTION @ ADJUSTABLE TIE

Fig. 2109.6.3.1.1B. Bonding with adjustable wall ties.

2109 Empirical Design of Masonry

2109.6.3.2 Bonding with prefabricated joint reinforcement

- Requirements for masonry walls bonded with prefabricated joint reinforcement are shown in the following details.

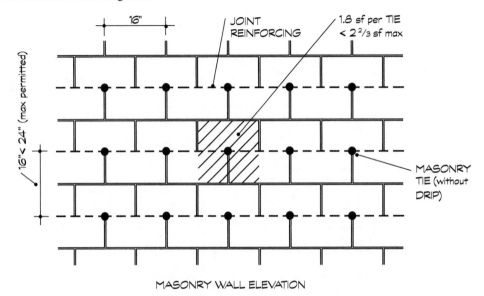

MASONRY WALL ELEVATION

Fig. 2109.6.3.2A. Bonding with prefabricated joint reinforcement. Cross wires @ 16" oc horizontally and joint reinforcement @ 16" oc vertically yield 1.8 sf of wall surface per cross wire. This is $< 2^2/_3$ sf per cross wire, the maximum permitted.

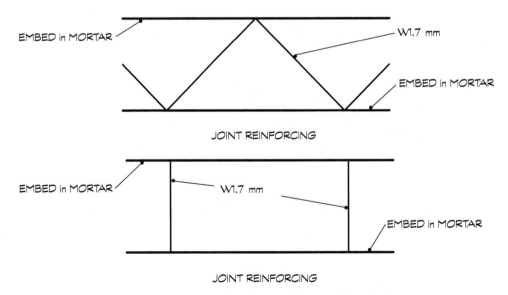

JOINT REINFORCING

JOINT REINFORCING

Fig. 2109.6.3.2B. Minimum wire sizes for bonding with prefabricated joint reinforcement.

2109 Empirical Design of Masonry

2109.6.4.1 Ashlar masonry

- Requirements for bonding ashlar natural or cast stone masonry are shown in the following details.

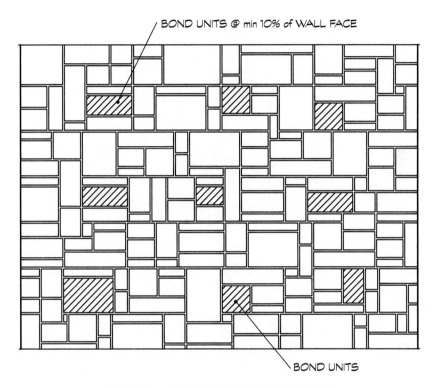

NATURAL or CAST STONE WALL ELEVATION

Fig. 2109.6.4.1A. Bonding ashlar masonry with masonry units. Units used to bond ashlar masonry must = 10% minimum of the wall face and be uniformly distributed.

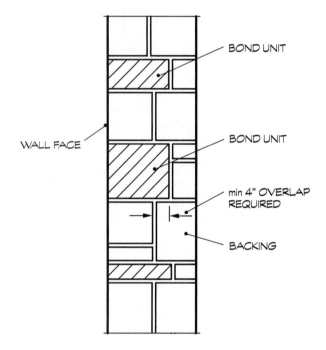

BOND UNIT

BOND UNIT

WALL FACE

min 4" OVERLAP
REQUIRED

BACKING

NATURAL or CAST STONE WALL ELEVATION

Fig. 2109.6.4.1B. Required overlap for bonding ashlar masonry with masonry units.

2109 Empirical Design of Masonry

2109.6.4.2 Rubble stone masonry

• Requirements for bonding with rubble stone masonry are shown in the following details.

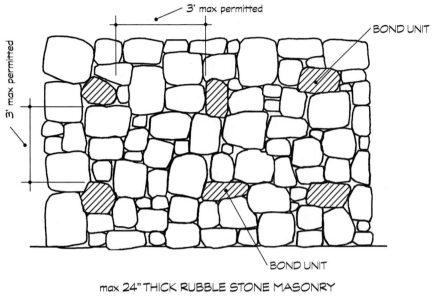

max 24" THICK RUBBLE STONE MASONRY

ELEVATION

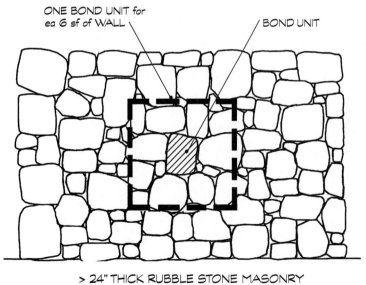

> 24" THICK RUBBLE STONE MASONRY

ELEVATION

Fig. 2109.6.4.2. Bonding with rubble stone masonry.

2109 Empirical Design of Masonry

2109.6.5.1 Masonry laid in running bond

- Masonry laid in running bond must meet the unit overlap requirements shown in the detail below.
- Masonry with overlaps < ¼ unit length must be reinforced longitudinally.

  Note: 2109.6.5.2, "Masonry laid in stack bond," is cited as the source of requirements for units laid with less than ¼ unit length overlap.

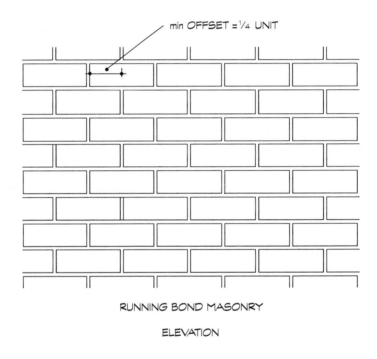

RUNNING BOND MASONRY

ELEVATION

Fig. 2109.6.5.1. Masonry laid in running bond.

2109 Empirical Design of Masonry

2109.6.5.2 Masonry laid in stack bond

- Masonry laid with units overlapping < ¼ unit length are governed as follows:
  - Area of reinforcing must ≥ 0.0003 × the vertical cross-sectional area of the wall.
  - Reinforcing is required in bed joints or bond beams.
- Horizontal reinforcing may not be spaced vertically > 4'.
- The tables below provide partial lists of reinforcing that meet the requirements of this section:
  - Table for wire reinforcing includes allowance for cross-wires.

Table 2109.6.5.2a   Maximum Vertical Spacing of Wire Joint Reinforcing

Longitudinal wire size	Nominal wall thickness					
	4"	6"	8"	10"	12"	16"
Truss-type wire joint reinforcing:						
2 - W1.7	42.50"	27.77"	20.00"	15.66"	12.50"	8.95"
2 - W2.8	48.00"	39.44"	28.75"	22.66"	18.33"	13.33"
3 - W1.7	na	na	27.50"	21.33"	17.50"	12.50"
3 - W2.8	na	na	40.41"	31.66"	26.11"	19.16"
4 - W1.7	na	na	na	27.00"	22.22"	16.25"
4 - W2.8	na	na	na	41.00"	33.88"	24.79"
Ladder-type wire joint reinforcing:						
2 - W1.7	28.33"	18.89"	14.17"	11.33"	9.44"	7.08"
2 - W2.8	46.67"	31.11"	23.33"	18.67"	15.56"	11.67"
3 - W1.7	na	na	21.25"	17.00"	14.17"	10.63"
3 - W2.8	na	na	35.00"	28.00"	23.33"	17.50"
4 - W1.7	na	na	na	22.67"	18.89"	14.17"
4 - W2.8	na	na	na	37.33"	31.11"	23.33"

Table 2109.6.5.2b   Maximum Vertical Spacing of Deformed Reinforcing Bars in Bond Beams

Bar	Nominal wall thickness					
	4"	6"	8"	10"	12"	16"
#3	48.00"	48.00"	45.83"	36.67"	30.56"	22.92"
#4	48.00"	48.00"	48.00"	48.00"	48.00"	41.67"
#5	48.00"	48.00"	48.00"	48.00"	48.00"	48.00"
#6	48.00"	48.00"	48.00"	48.00"	48.00"	48.00"
#7	48.00"	48.00"	48.00"	48.00"	48.00"	48.00"
#8	48.00"	48.00"	48.00"	48.00"	48.00"	48.00"

2109 Empirical Design of Masonry

2109.7.2.1 Bonding pattern

- This section addresses the intersection of masonry walls that provide lateral support to each other.
- Such walls must be anchored to each other as follows:
  - 2 acceptable methods with masonry bond anchorage are shown in the following details.

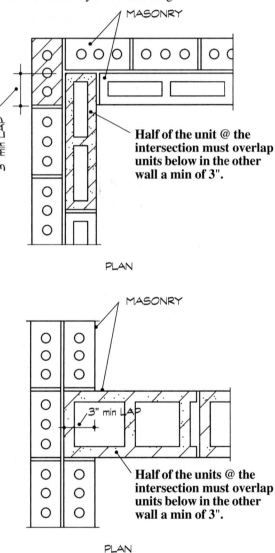

Fig. 2109.7.2.1. Bonding requirements at intersection of masonry walls.

2109 Empirical Design of Masonry

2109.7.2.2 Steel connectors

- This section addresses the intersection of masonry walls that provide lateral support to each other.
- Such walls must be anchored to each other as follows:
  - One acceptable method with steel connectors is shown in the following detail.

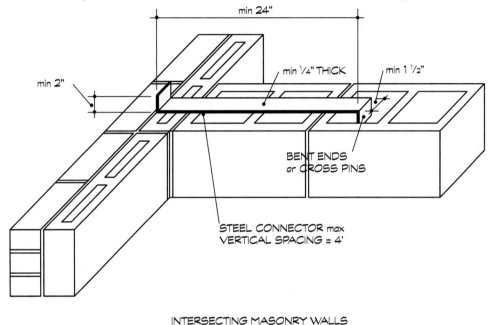

Fig. 2109.7.2.2. Steel connectors at intersections of masonry walls.

2109.7.2.3 Joint reinforcement

- This section addresses the intersection of masonry walls that provide lateral support to each other.
- Such walls must be anchored to each other as follows:
  - Acceptable methods with joint reinforcement are shown in the following details.

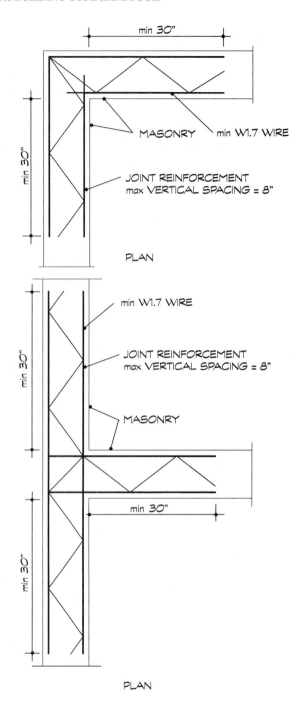

Fig. 2109.7.2.3. Joint reinforcement at intersection masonry walls.

2109 Empirical Design of Masonry

2109.7.2.4 Interior nonload-bearing walls

- This section addresses the intersection of masonry walls that provide lateral support to each other.
- Such walls must be anchored to each other as follows:
  - One acceptable method for walls with both the following characteristics is shown in the following detail:
    Interior.
    Nonload-bearing.

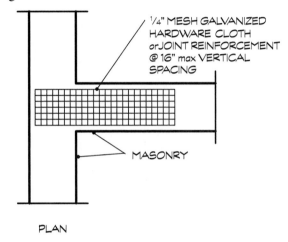

PLAN

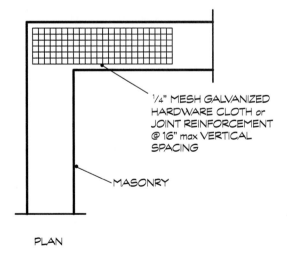

PLAN

Fig. 2109.7.2.4. Anchorage at intersections of interior nonload-bearing walls.

2109 Empirical Design of Masonry

2109.7.3.1 Wood floor joists

- This section addresses wood floor diaphragms providing lateral stability to masonry walls.
- The floor joists must be anchored to the wall as shown in the following details.

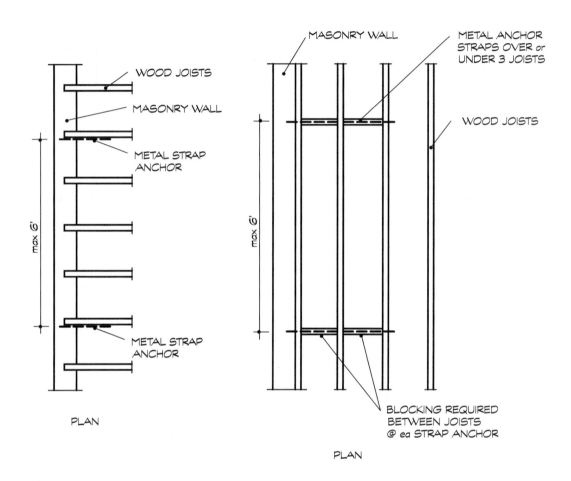

Fig. 2109.7.3.1. Anchorage of wood floor diaphragms providing lateral stability to masonry walls.

2109 Empirical Design of Masonry

2109.7.3.2 Steel floor joists

- This section addresses steel floor joist diaphragms providing lateral stability to masonry walls.
- The floor joists must be anchored to the wall as shown in the following details.

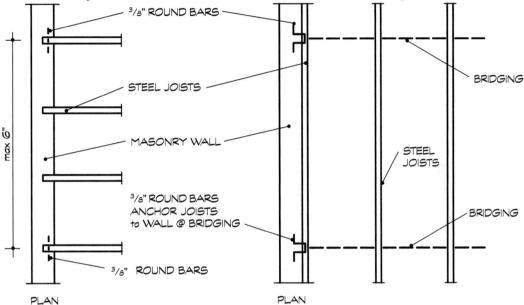

Fig. 2109.7.3.2. Anchorage of steel floor joist diaphragms providing lateral stability to masonry walls.

2109.7.3.3 Roof diaphragms

- This section addresses roof diaphragms providing lateral stability to masonry walls.
- The roof must be anchored to the wall as shown in the details provided.

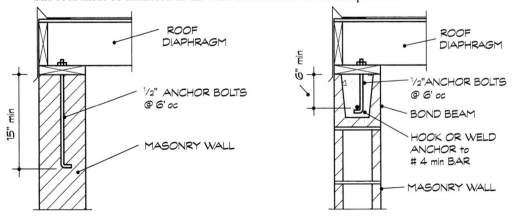

Fig. 2109.7.3.3. Anchorage of roof diaphragms providing lateral stability to masonry walls.

2109 Empirical Design of Masonry

2109.7.4 Walls adjoining structural framing

- Walls dependent on the structural frame for lateral support must be anchored to the frame as shown in the following details.

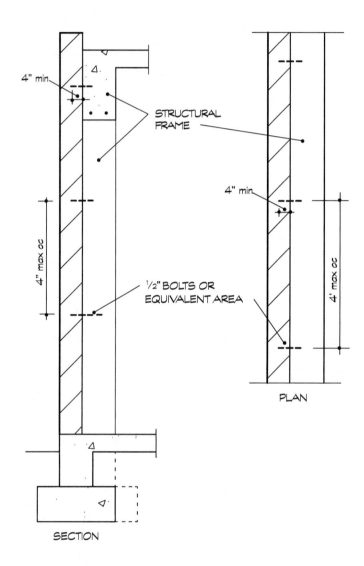

Fig. 2109.7.4. Anchorage of masonry walls adjoining structural framing.

2110 Glass Unit Masonry

2110.2.1 Standard units

- The thickness of standard units is shown in the following detail.

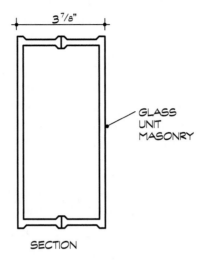

SECTION

Fig. 2110.2.1. Minimum thickness of standard glass masonry units.

2110.2.2 Thin units

- The thickness of thin units is shown in the following details.

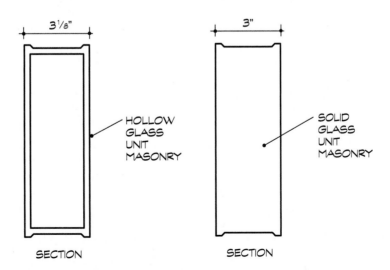

Fig. 2110.2.2. Minimum thickness of thin glass masonry units.

2110 Glass Unit Masonry

2110.3.1 Exterior standard-unit panels *(part 1 of 4)*

- This section addresses exterior glass block panels with standard units.
- Maximum panel height between structural supports is 20'.
- Maximum panel width between structural supports is 25'.
- Maximum panel area varies with wind load as follows:
  - The tables below provide a partial list of width and height combinations that yield an area within the maximum permitted for the wind pressure indicated:

    Width and height are multiples of standard glass block dimensions.

    Either or both dimensions in any combination may be smaller than those listed.

  Note: IBC *Figure 2110.3.1, "Glass Masonry Design Wind Load Resistance," is cited as the source of glass block panel area limits. The following tables are based on this graph.*

Table 2110.3.1   Maximum Dimensions of Glass Block Panels

Width	Height	Width	Height	Width	Height	Width	Height
Widths and heights ≤ 57 sf as permitted by a wind pressure of 60 psf:							
24'-8"	2'-0"	18'-8"	2'-8"	12'-8"	4'-0"	7'-4"	7'-4"
24'-0"	2'-0"	18'-0"	2'-8"	12'-0"	4'-8"	6'-8"	8'-0"
23'-4"	2'-0"	17'-4"	2'-8"	11'-4"	4'-8"	6'-0"	9'-4"
22'-8"	2'-0"	16'-8"	3'-4"	10'-8"	5'-4"	5'-4"	10'-8"
22'-0"	2'-0"	16'-0"	3'-4"	10'-0"	5'-4"	4'-8"	12'-0"
21'-4"	2'-8"	15'-4"	3'-4"	9'-4"	6'-0"	4'-0"	14'-0"
20'-8"	2'-8"	14'-8"	3'-4"	8'-8"	6'-0"	3'-4"	16'-8"
20'-0"	2'-8"	14'-0"	4'-0"	8'-0"	6'-8"	2'-8"	20'-0"
19'-4"	2'-8"	13'-4"	4'-0"				
Widths and heights ≤ 62 sf as permitted by a wind pressure of 55 psf:							
24'-8"	2'-0"	18'-8"	2'-8"	12'-8"	4'-8"	7'-4"	8'-0"
24'-0"	2'-0"	18'-0"	3'-4"	12'-0"	4'-8"	6'-8"	8'-8"
23'-4"	2'-0"	17' 4"	3'-4"	11'-4"	5'-4"	6'-0"	10'-0"
22'-8"	2'-8"	16'-8"	3'-4"	10'-8"	5'-4"	5'-4"	11'-4"
22'-0"	2'-8"	16'-0"	3'-4"	10'-0"	6'-0"	4'-8"	12'-8"
21' 4"	2'-8"	15'-4"	4'-0"	9'-4"	6'-0"	4'-0"	15'-4"
20'-8"	2'-8"	14'-8"	4'-0"	8'-8"	6'-8"	3'-4"	18'-0"
20'-0"	2'-8"	14'-0"	4'-0"	8'-0"	7'-4"	2'-8"	20'-0"
19'-4"	2'-8"	13'-4"	4'-0"				

2110 Glass Unit Masonry

2110.3.1 Exterior standard-unit panels *(part 2 of 4)*

Table 2110.3.1—*Continued.*

Width	Height	Width	Height	Width	Height	Width	Height
Widths and heights ≤ 70 sf as permitted by a wind pressure of 50 psf:							
24'-8"	2'-8"	18'-8"	3'-4"	13'-4"	4'-8"	8'-0"	8'-8"
24'-0"	2'-8"	18'-0"	3'-4"	12'-8"	5'-4"	7'-4"	9'-4"
23'-4"	2'-8"	17'-4"	4'-0"	12'-0"	5'-4"	6'-8"	10'-0"
22'-8"	2'-8"	16'-8"	4'-0"	11'-4"	6'-0"	6'-0"	11'-4"
22'-0"	2'-8"	16'-0"	4'-0"	10'-8"	6'-0"	5'-4"	12'-8"
21'-4"	2'-8"	15'-4"	4'-0"	10'-0"	6'-8"	4'-8"	14'-8"
20'-8"	3'-4"	14'-8"	4'-8"	9'-4"	7'-4"	4'-0"	17'-4"
20'-0"	3'-4"	14'-0"	4'-8"	8'-8"	8'-0"	3'-4"	20'-0"
19'-4"	3'-4"						

Widths and heights ≤ 77 sf as permitted by a wind pressure of 45 psf:

Width	Height	Width	Height	Width	Height	Width	Height
24'-8"	2'-8"	18'-8"	4'-0"	13'-4"	5'-4"	8'-0"	9'-4"
24'-0"	2'-8"	18'-0"	4'-0"	12'-8"	6'-0"	7'-4"	10'-0"
23'-4"	2'-8"	17'-4"	4'-0"	12'-0"	6'-0"	6'-8"	11' 4"
22'-8"	3'-4"	16'-8"	4'-0"	11'-4"	6'-8"	6'-0"	12'-8"
22'-0"	3'-4"	16'-0"	4'-8"	10'-8"	6'-8"	5'-4"	14'-0"
21'-4"	3'-4"	15'-4"	4'-8"	10'-0"	7'-4"	4'-8"	16'-0"
20'-8"	3'-4"	14'-8"	4'-8"	9'-4"	8'-0"	4'-0"	18'-8"
20'-0"	3'-4"	14'-0"	5'-4"	8'-8"	8'-8"	3'-4"	20'-0"
19'-4"	3'-4"						

Widths and heights ≤ 84 sf as permitted by a wind pressure of 40 psf:

Width	Height	Width	Height	Width	Height	Width	Height
24'-8"	3'-4"	19'-4"	4'-0"	14'-0"	6'-0"	8'-8"	9- 4"
24'-0"	3'-4"	18'-8"	4'-0"	13' 4"	6'-0"	8'-0"	10'-0"
23'-4"	3'-4"	18'-0"	4'-8"	12'-8"	6'-0"	7'-4"	11'-4"
22'-8"	3'-4"	17'-4"	4'-8"	12'-0"	6'-8"	6'-8"	12'-0"
22'-0"	3'-4"	16'-8"	4'-8"	11'-4"	7'-4"	6'-0"	14'-0"
21'-4"	3'-4"	16'-0"	4'-8"	10'-8"	7'-4"	5'-4"	15'-4"
20'-8"	4'-0"	15'-4"	5'-4"	10'-0"	8'-0"	4'-8"	17'-4"
20'-0"	4'-0"	14'-8"	5'-4"	9'-4"	8'-8"	4'-0"	20'-0"

2110 Glass Unit Masonry

2110.3.1 Exterior standard-unit panels *(part 3 of 4)*

Table 2110.3.1—*Continued.*

Width	Height	Width	Height	Width	Height	Width	Height
Widths and heights ≤ 94 sf as permitted by a wind pressure of 35 psf:							
24'-8"	3'-4"	19'-4"	4'-8"	14'-0"	6'-8"	8'-8"	10'-8"
24'-0"	3'-4"	18'-8"	4'-8"	13'-4"	6'-8"	8'-0"	11'-4"
23'-4"	4'-0"	18'-0"	4'-8"	12'-8"	7'-4"	7'-4"	12'-8"
22'-8"	4'-0"	17'-4"	5'-4"	12'-0"	7'-4"	6'-8"	14'-0"
22'-0"	4'-0"	16'-8"	5'-4"	11'-4"	8'-0"	6'-0"	15'-4"
21'-4"	4'-0"	16'-0"	5'-4"	10'-8"	8'-8"	5'-4"	17'-4"
20'-8"	4'-0"	15'-4"	6'-0"	10'-0"	9'-4"	4'-8"	20'-0"
20'-0"	4'-8"	14'-8"	6'-0"	9'-4"	10'-0"		
Widths and heights ≤ 104 sf as permitted by a wind pressure of 30 psf:							
24'-8"	4'-0"	19'-4"	5'-4"	14'-0"	7'-4"	8'-8"	11'-4"
24'-0"	4'-0"	18'-8"	5'-4"	13'-4"	7'-4"	8'-0"	12'-8"
23'-4"	4'-0"	18'-0"	5'-4"	12'-8"	8'-0"	7'-4"	14'-0"
22'-8"	4'-0"	17'-4"	6'-0"	12'-0"	8'-8"	6'-8"	15'-4"
22'-0"	4'-8"	16'-8"	6'-0"	11'-4"	8'-8"	6'-0"	17'-4"
21'-4"	4'-8"	16'-0"	6'-0"	10'-8"	9'-4"	5'-4"	19'-4"
20'-8"	4'-8"	15'-4"	6'-8"	10'-0"	10'-0"	4'-8"	20'-0"
20'-0"	4'-8"	14'-8"	6'-8"	9'-4"	10'-8"		
Widths and heights ≤ 119 sf as permitted by a wind pressure of 25 psf:							
24'-8"	4'-8"	18'-8"	6'-0"	12'-8"	9'-4"	8'-8"	13'-4"
24'-0"	4'-8"	18'-0"	6'-0"	12'-0"	9'-4"	8'-0"	14'-8"
23'-4"	4'-8"	17'-4"	6'-8"	11' 4"	10'-0"	7'-4"	16'-0"
22'-8"	4'-8"	16'-8"	6'-8"	10'-8"	10'-8"	6'-8"	17'-4"
22'-0"	5'-4"	16'-0"	7'-4"	10'-0"	11'-4"	6'-0"	19'-4"
21'-4"	5'-4"	15'-4"	7'-4"	9'-4"	12'-8"	5'-4"	20'-0"
20'-8"	5'-4"	14' 8"	8'-0"				
20'-0"	5'-4"	14'-0"	8'-0"				
19'-4"	6'-0"	13'-4"	8' 8"				

2110 Glass Unit Masonry

2110.3.1 Exterior standard-unit panels *(part 4 of 4)*

Table 2110.3.1—*Continued.*

Width	Height	Width	Height	Width	Height	Width	Height
Widths and heights ≤ 144 sf as permitted by a wind pressure of 20 psf.							
24-8"	5'-4"	20'-0"	6'-8"	15'-4"	9'-4"	10'-8"	13'-4"
24'-0"	6'-0"	19' 4"	7'-4"	14'-8"	9'-4"	10'-0"	14'-0"
23'-4"	6'-0"	18'-8"	7'-4"	14'-0"	10'-0"	9'-4"	15' 4"
22'-8"	6'-0"	18'-0"	8'-0"	13'-4"	10'-8"	8'-8"	16'-0"
22'-0"	6'-0"	17'-4"	8'-0"	12'-8"	11'-4"	8'-0"	18'-0"
21' 4"	6'-8"	16'-8"	8'-0"	12'-0"	12'-0"	7'-4"	19'-4"
20'-8"	6'-8"	16'-0"	8'-8"	11' 4"	12'-8"	6'-8"	20'-0"
Widths and heights ≤ 182 sf as permitted by a wind pressure of 15 psf:							
24'-8"	7'-4"	20'-0"	8'-8"	16'-0"	11'-4"	12'-0"	14'-8"
24'-0"	7'-4"	19'-4"	9'-4"	15'-4"	11'-4"	11'-4"	16'-0"
23'-4"	7'-4"	18'-8"	9'-4"	14'-8"	12'-0"	10'-8"	16'-8"
22'-8"	8'-0"	18'-0"	10'-0"	14'-0"	12'-8"	10'-0"	18'-0"
22'-0"	8'-0"	17'-4"	10'-0"	13'-4"	13'-4"	9'-4"	19'-4"
21'-4"	8'-0"	16'-8"	10'-8"	12'-8"	14'-0"	8'-8"	20'-0"
20'-8"	8'-8"						
Widths and heights ≤ 235 sf as permitted by a wind pressure of 10 psf:							
24'-8"	9'-4"	20'-8"	11'-4"	17'-4"	13'-4"	14'-0"	16'-8"
24'-0"	9'-4"	20'-0"	11'-4"	16'-8"	14'-0"	13'-4"	17'-4"
23'-4"	10'-0"	19'-4"	12'-0"	16'-0"	14'-8"	12'-8"	18'-0"
22'-8"	10'-0"	18'-8"	12'-0"	15'-4"	14'-8"	12'-0"	19'-4"
22'-0"	10'-8"	18'-0"	12'-8"	14'-8"	16'-0"	11'-4"	20'-0"
21'-4"	10'-8"						

2110 Glass Unit Masonry

2110.3.2 Exterior thin-unit panels

- This section addresses exterior glass block panels with standard units.
- Panels may not be subjected to wind pressure > 20 psf.
- Maximum panel height between structural supports is 10'.
- Maximum panel width between structural supports is 15'.
- Maximum panel area between structural supports is 85 sf.
- The table below provides a partial list of widths and heights which yield an area within the maximum permitted as follows:
  - Width and height are multiples of standard glass block dimensions.
  - Either or both dimensions in any combination may be smaller than those listed.

Table 2110.3.2   **Thin Glass Block Units: Widths × Heights ≤ 85 sf**

Width	Height		Width	Height
14'-8"	5'-4"		11'-4"	7'-4"
14'-0"	6'-0"		10'-6"	7'-4"
13'-4"	6'-0"		10'-0"	8'-0"
12'-8"	6'-8"		9'-4"	8'-8"
12'-0"	6'-8"		8'-8"	9'-4"

2110 Glass Unit Masonry

2110.3.3 Interior panels

- This section addresses interior glass block panels.
- Maximum panel height between structural supports is 20'.
- Maximum panel width between structural supports is 25'.
- Standard units are governed as follows:
  - Maximum panel area between structural supports is 250 sf.
- Thin units are governed as follows:
  - Maximum panel area between structural supports is 150 sf.
- The tables below provide a partial list of widths and heights which yield an area within the maximum permitted as follows:
  - Width and height are multiples of standard glass block dimensions.
  - Either or both dimensions in any combination may be smaller than those listed.

Table 2110.3.3a   **Standard Glass Block Units: Width × Height ≤ 250 sf**

Width	Height	Width	Height	Width	Height	Width	Height
24-'8"	10'-0"	21'-4"	11'-4"	18'-0"	13'-4"	14'-8"	16'-8"
24'-0"	10'-0"	20'-8"	12'-0"	17'-4"	14'-0"	14'-0"	17'-4"
23'-4"	10'-8"	20'-0"	12'-0"	16'-8"	14'-8"	13'-4"	18'-8"
22'-8"	10'-8"	19'-4"	12'-8"	16'-0"	15'-4"	12'-8"	19'-4"
22'-0"	11'-4"	18'-8"	13'-4"	15'-4"	16'-0"	12'-0"	20'-0"

Table 2110.3.3b   **Thin Glass Block Units: Width × Height ≤ 150 sf**

Width	Height	Width	Height	Width	Height
24-'8"	6'-0"	18'-8"	8'-0"	12'-8"	11'-4"
24'-0"	6'-0"	18'-0"	8'-0"	12'-0"	12'-0"
23'-4"	6'-0"	17'-4"	8'-0"	11'-4"	12'-8"
22'-8"	6'-0"	16'-8"	8'-8"	10'-8"	14'-0"
22'-0"	6'-8"	16'-0"	9'-4"	10'-0"	14'-8"
21'-4"	6'-8"	15'-4"	9'-4"	9'-4"	16'-0"
20'-8"	6'-8"	14'-8"	10'-0"	8'-8"	16'-8"
20'-0"	7'-4"	14'-0"	10'-8"	8'-0"	18'-8"
19'-4"	7'-4"	13'-4"	10'-8"	7'-4"	20'-0"

2110.3.4 Solid units

- Solid glass-block wall panels are governed as follows:
  - Maximum area is ≤ 100 sf in the following locations:
    Outside.
    Inside.

2110 Glass Unit Masonry

2110.3.5 Curved panels

- The width of curved glass-block panels must comply with the same dimensional limitations that govern straight panels.

    Note: The following are cited as sources of width requirements governing curved-block panels:
    2110.3.1, "Exterior standard-unit panels."
    2110.3.2, "Exterior thin-unit panels."
    2110.3.3, "Interior panels."

- Additional structural supports are required at the following locations as shown in the details provided:
    - At the connection of a curved panel to a straight panel.
    - At inflection points of serpentine curves.

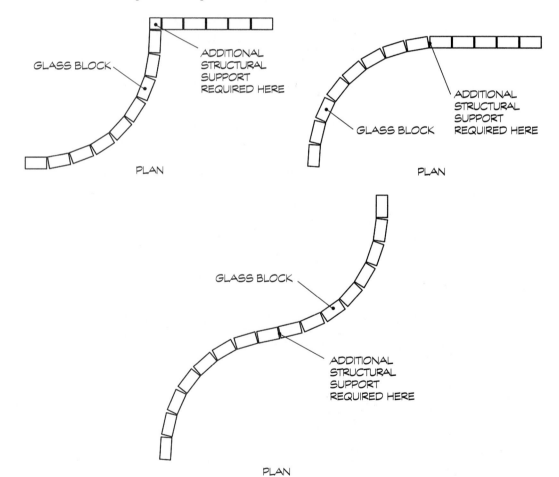

Fig. 2110.3.5. Additional structural support in curved glass block panels.

2110 Glass Unit Masonry

2110.4.3 Lateral

- Lateral support for glass block is required as follows.
  - At the top of a panel as follows:
    Where the panel is more than one block wide.
    Lateral support is not required where the panel is only 1 block wide.
  - At the sides of a panel as follows:
    Where the panel is more than one block high.
    Lateral support is not required where the panel is only 1 block high.
- Lateral supports must resist the greater of the following loads:
  - Actual loads applied.
  - 200 lbs/lineal foot.
- Dimensional requirements for lateral support are shown in the following details.

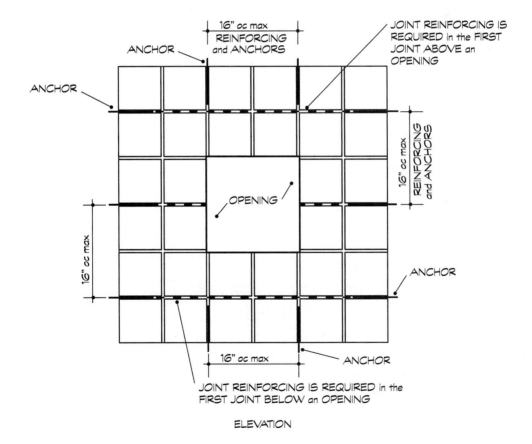

Fig. 2110.4.3A. Lateral support for glass block.

2110 Glass Unit Masonry

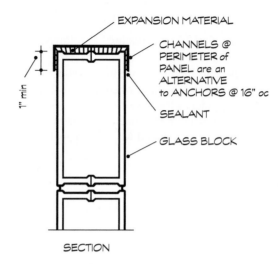

Fig. 2110.4.3B. Lateral support for glass block.

2110.7 Reinforcement

- Glass block panels require joint reinforcing as follows and as shown in the following detail:
  - Reinforcing does not cross expansion joints.

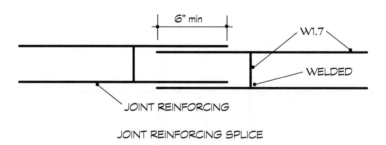

Fig. 2110.7. Size and splice requirements for joint reinforcement.

NOTES

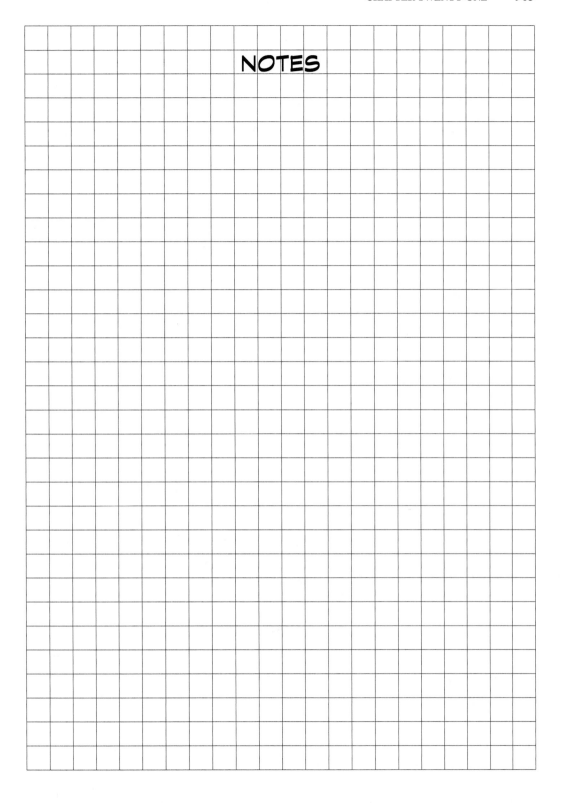

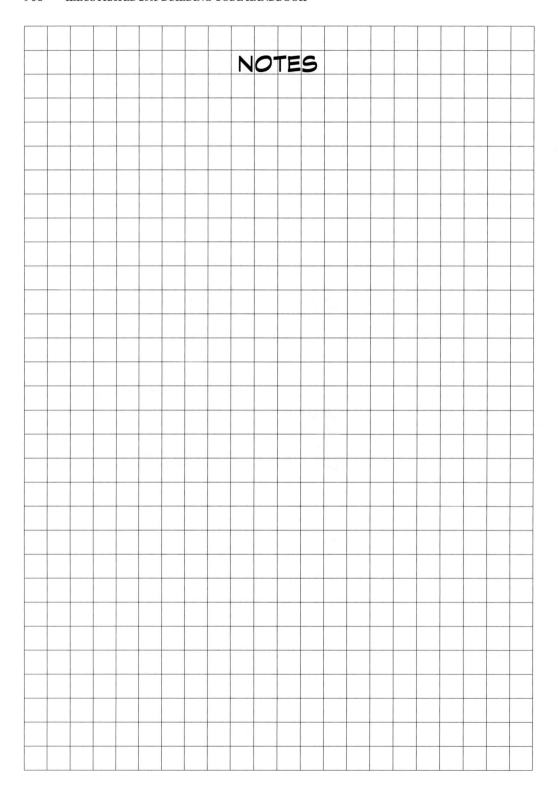

22

Steel

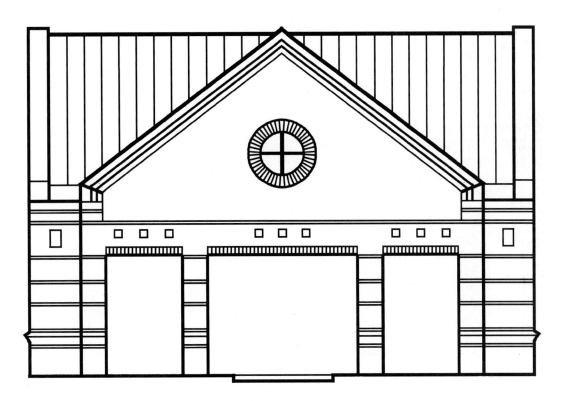

Christus St. Michael Health Care Center. Texarkana, Texas. *(partial elevation)*
Watkins Hamilton Ross Architects, Inc. Houston, Texas.

2202 Definitions and Nomenclature

2202.1 Definitions *(part 1 of 2)*

- **Adjusted shear resistance**
  - A term used regarding Type II shear walls.
  - Unadjusted shear reisstance × shear resistance adjustment factors.

    Note: IBC Table 2211.3, "Shear Resistance Adjustment Factor—Co," is cited as the source of the adjustment factors.

- **Steel construction, cold-formed**
  - Steel construction with products such as listed below produced from the following materials by cold-forming processes:
    Materials:
      Steel strip.
      Steel sheet.
    Products:
      Roof deck.
      Floor panels.
      Wall panels.
      Studs.
      Floor joists.
      Roof joists.
      Other products.

- **Steel joist**
  - A steel structural member with characteristics as follows:
    Formed by one of the following processes:
      Hot-rolled.
      Cold-formed.
    With one of the following web conditions:
      Closed.
      Open.
    Fabricated from any of the following components:
      Riveted bars.
      Welded bars.
      Strip steel.
      Sheet steel.
      Slotted and expanded sections.
      Other deformed rolled sections.

- **Steel member, structural**
  - Any rolled steel structural shape other than the following:
    Cold-formed shapes.
    Steel joists.

2202 Definitions and Nomenclature

2202.1 Definitions *(part 2 of 2)*

- **Type I shear wall**
  - Resists in-plane lateral forces.
  - Fully sheathed.
  - May have openings in the following case:
    Where detailed to transfer force around openings.
  - Equipped with hold-down anchors at ends of wall segments.

    Note: IBC Fig. 2202.1, "Type I and Type II Shear Walls," is cited as illustrating positions for hold-down anchors.

- **Type II shear wall**
  - Resists in-plane lateral forces.
  - Sheathed in one of the following:
    Wood.
    Sheet steel.
  - Has openings as follows:
    Not specifically detailed to transfer force around openings.
  - Has hold-down anchors at each end of wall.

    Note: IBC Fig. 2202.1, "Type I and Type II Shear Walls," is cited as illustrating positions for hold-down anchors.

- **Type II shear wall segment**
  - A section of shear wall.
  - Sheathed for full height.
  - Meets proportion requirements.

    Note: 2211.3.2(3), "Type II shear wall resistance," is cited as listing the proportions required.

- **Unadjusted shear resistance**
  - The design shear of Type II shear walls.

    Note: 2211.3.1. "Limitations," is cited as specifying the necessary characteristics of Type II shear walls.

2211 Cold-Formed Steel Light-Framed Shear Walls

2211.2 Type I shear walls

- This section governs Type I shear walls as follows:
  - Constructed with the following framing:
    Cold-formed light-gage steel.
  - Designed to resist the following forces:
    Wind.
    Seismic.
- This section provides nominal shear values as follows:
  - Used to determine allowable shear values.
  - Used to determine design shear values.
  - As shown in details on the following pages.

    Note: The following tables are cited as listing nominal shear values for Type I shear walls, which are summarized in the details provided on the following pages:
    IBC Table 2211.2(1), "Nominal Shear Values for Wind Forces in Pounds per Foot for Shear Walls Framed with Cold-Formed Steel Studs."
    IBC Table 2211.2(2), "Nominal Shear Values for Wind Forces in Pounds per Foot for Shear Walls Framed with Cold-Formed Steel Studs Faced with Gypsum Board."
    IBC Table 2211.2(3), "Nominal Shear Values for Seismic Forces in Pounds per Foot for Shear Walls Framed with Cold-Formed Steel Studs."

  - The following elements must be designed to transmit applied forces:
    Boundary members.
    Chords.
    Collectors.
    Connections.
  - Calculations using the following may be used in lieu of tables:
    Approved fastener values.
    Approved shear values for the sheathing.
  - Type I shear walls may have windows as follows:
    In segments of the shear wall with hold-down anchors in the following locations:
      At ends of each segment.
  - The proportions of the following are limited by this section:
    Wall segments.
    Wall piers on each side of openings as follows:
      Pier height (*h*) is clear height at the side of the opening.
      Pier width (*w*) is the width of the sheathed pier as follows:
        Width must be ≥ 24".

    Note: 2211.2.2, "Limitations for systems," Item 5, is cited as governing proportions.

  - At each end of a Type I shear wall the following is required:
    Hold-down anchors adequate to resist design forces.

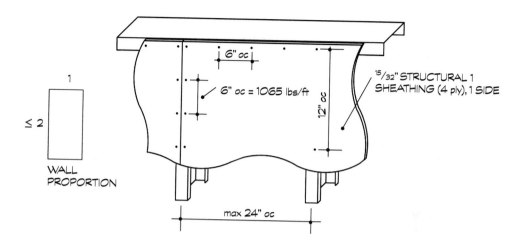

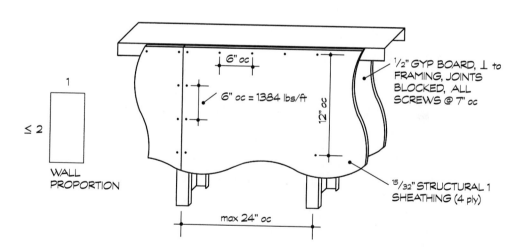

Fig. 2211.2(1)A. Nominal shear value of shear walls framed with cold-formed steel studs and subject to wind. *[IBC Table 2211.2(1)]*

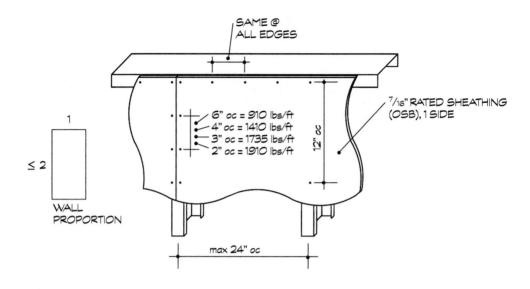

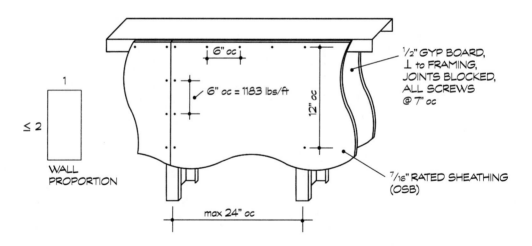

Fig. 2211.2(1)B. Nominal shear value of shear walls framed with cold-formed steel studs and subject to wind. *[IBC Table 2211.2.(1)]*

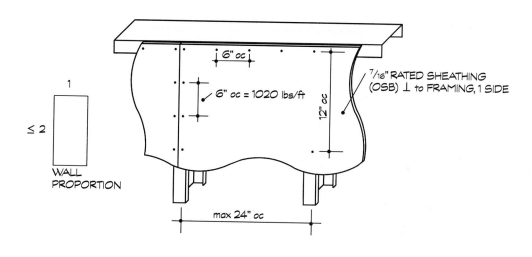

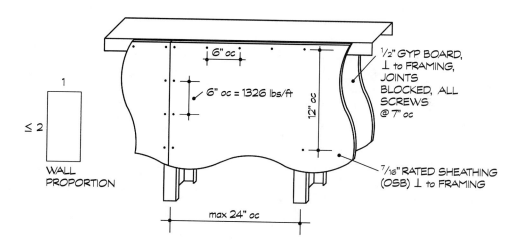

Fig. 2211.2(1)C. Nominal shear value of shear walls framed with cold-formed steel studs and subject to wind. *[IBC Table 2211.2(1)]*

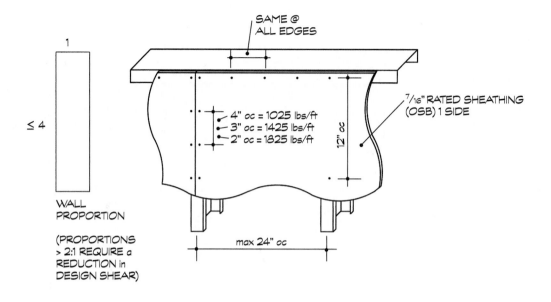

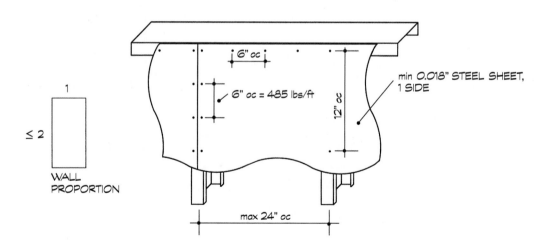

Fig. 2211.2(1)D. Nominal shear value of shear walls framed with cold-formed steel studs and subject to wind. *[IBC Table 2211.2(1)]*

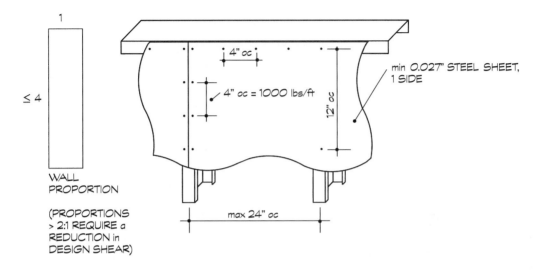

Fig. 2211.2(1)E. Nominal shear value of shear walls framed with cold-formed steel studs and subject to wind. *[IBC Table 2211.2(1)]*

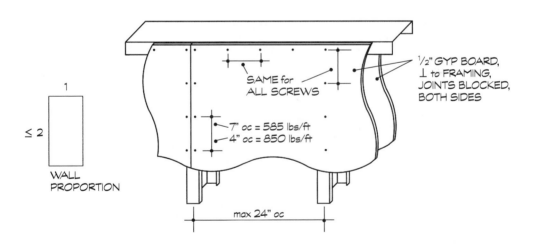

Fig. 2211.2(2). Nominal shear value of shear walls framed with cold-formed steel studs and gypsum board and subject to wind. *[IBC Table 2211.2(2)]*

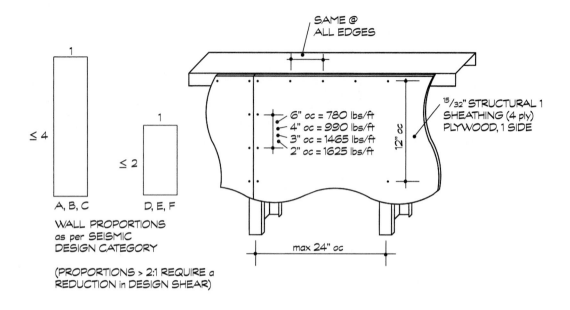

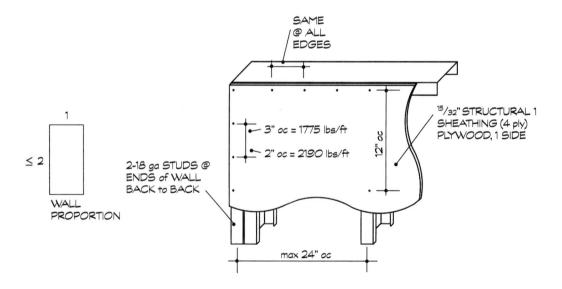

Fig. 2211.2(3)A. Nominal shear value of shear walls framed with cold-formed steel studs and subject to seismic forces. *[IBC Table 2211.2(3)]*

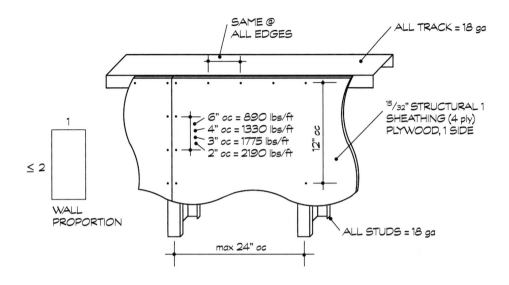

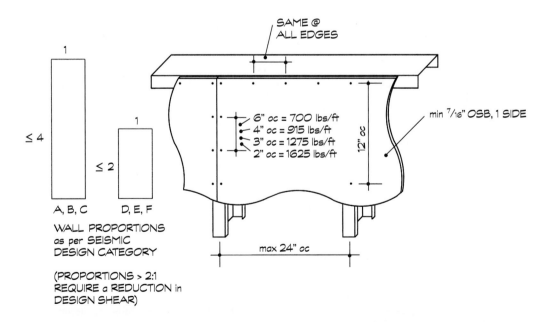

Fig. 2211.2(3)B. Nominal shear value of shear walls framed with cold-formed steel studs and subject to seismic forces. *[IBC Table 2211.2(3)]*

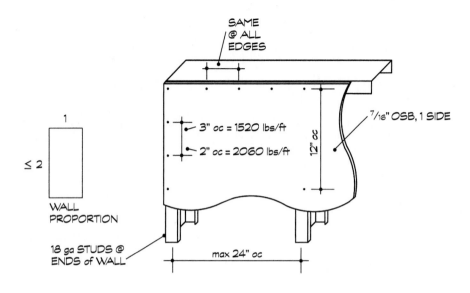

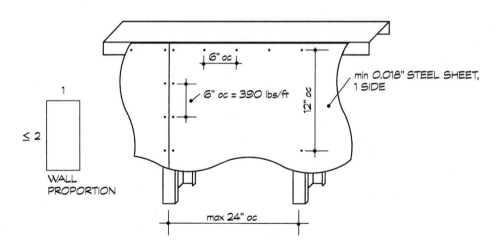

Fig. 2211.2(3)C. Nominal shear value of shear walls framed with cold-formed steel studs and subject to seismic forces. *[IBC Table 2211.2(3)]*

2211 Cold-Formed Steel Light-Framed Shear Walls

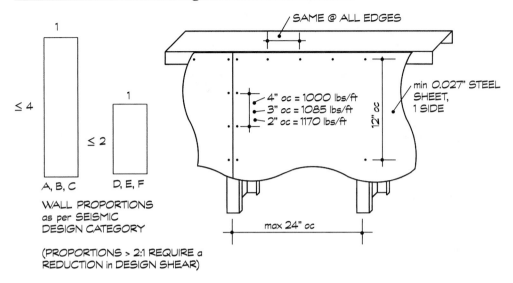

Fig. 2211.2(3)D. Nominal shear value of shear walls framed with cold-formed steel studs and subject to seismic forces. *[IBC Table 2211.2(3)]*

2211.2.1 Design shear determination

- The previous section provides nominal shear values for Type I shear walls as follows:
  - Used to determine allowable shear values.
  - Used to determine design shear values.

    Note: The following tables are cited as listing the nominal shear values:
    IBC Table 2211.2(1), "Nominal Shear Values for Wind Forces in Pounds per
    Foot for Shear Walls Framed with Cold-Formed Steel Studs."
    IBC Table 2211.2(2), "Nominal Shear Values for Wind Forces in Pounds per
    Foot for Shear Walls Framed with Cold-Formed Steel Studs Faced with
    Gypsum Board."
    IBC Table 2211.2(3), "Nominal Shear Values for Seismic Forces in Pounds per
    Foot for Shear Walls Framed with Cold-Formed Steel Studs."

- For allowable stress design (ASD) the following applies:
  - Design shear values are determined as follows:
    Nominal shear values ÷ 2.5 (a safety factor).
  - Design shear values as computed above are shown in the following illustrations.
- For load and resistance factor design (LRFD) the following applies:
  - Design shear values are determined as follows:
    Nominal shear values × 0.55 (a resistance factor).
  - Design shear values as computed above are shown in the following illustrations.

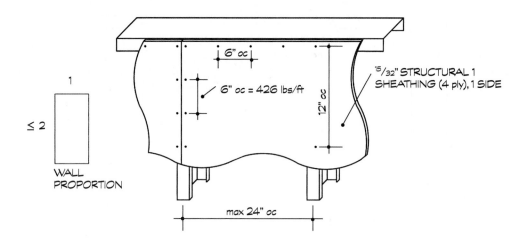

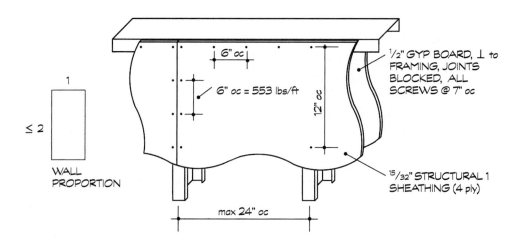

Fig. 2211.2.1(1)A. Shear values for allowable stress design (ASD) of shear walls framed with cold-formed steel studs and subject to wind. *[IBC Table 2211.2(1)]*

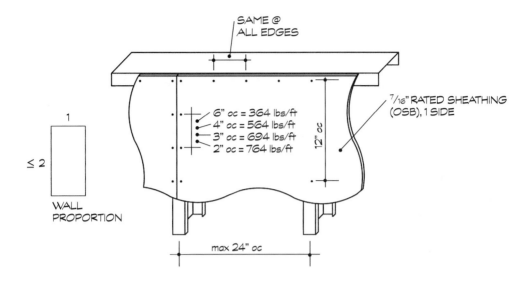

SAME @
ALL EDGES

1

≤ 2

WALL
PROPORTION

6" oc = 364 lbs/ft
4" oc = 564 lbs/ft
3" oc = 694 lbs/ft
2" oc = 764 lbs/ft

12" oc

max 24" oc

$^{7}/_{16}$" RATED SHEATHING
(OSB), 1 SIDE

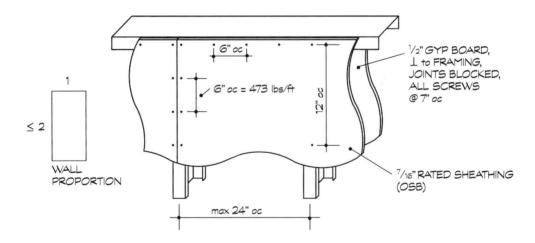

1

≤ 2

WALL
PROPORTION

6" oc

6" oc = 473 lbs/ft

12" oc

max 24" oc

$^{1}/_{2}$" GYP BOARD,
⊥ to FRAMING,
JOINTS BLOCKED,
ALL SCREWS
@ 7" oc

$^{7}/_{16}$" RATED SHEATHING
(OSB)

Fig. 2211.2.1(1)B. Shear values for allowable stress design (ASD) of shear walls framed with cold-formed steel studs and subject to wind. *[IBC Table 2211.2.(1)]*

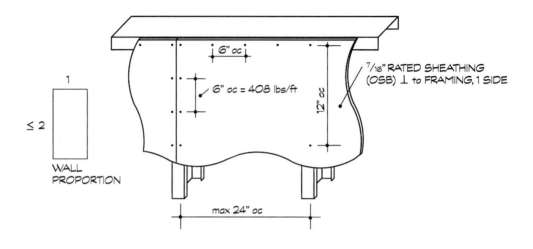

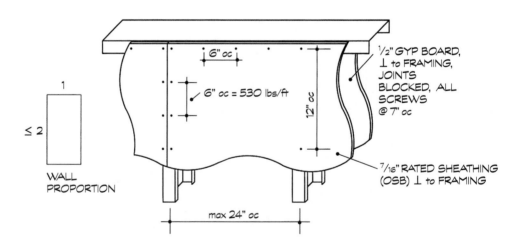

Fig. 2211.2.1(1)C. Shear values for allowable stress design (ASD) of shear walls framed with cold-formed steel studs and subject to wind. *[IBC Table 2211.2(1)]*

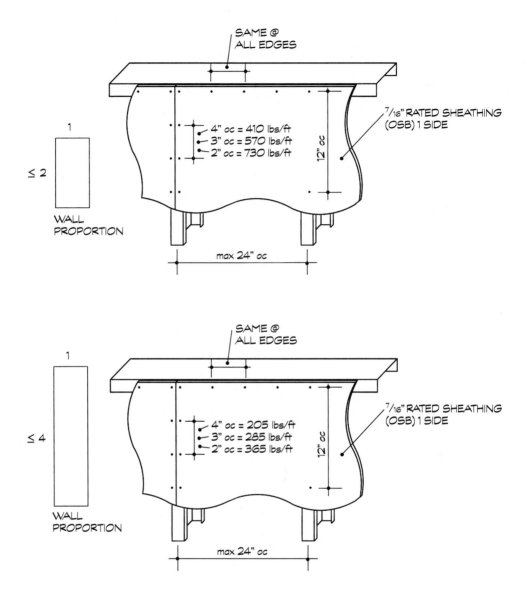

Fig. 2211.2.1(1)D. Shear values for allowable stress design (ASD) of shear walls framed with cold-formed steel studs and subject to wind. Shear values vary with wall proportions between 2:1 and 4:1. *[IBC Table 2211.2(1)]*

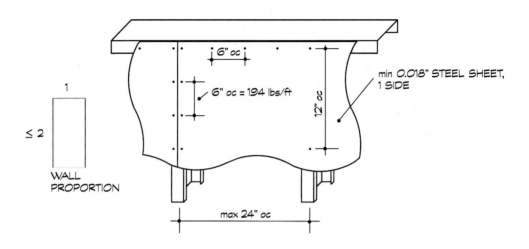

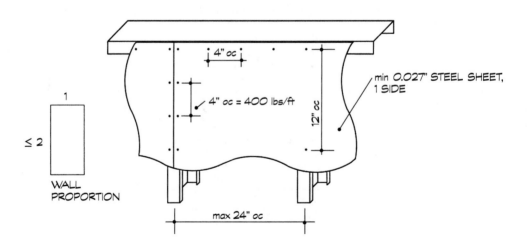

Fig. 2211.2.1(1)E. Shear values for allowable stress design (ASD) of shear walls framed with cold-formed steel studs and subject to wind. *[IBC Table 2211.2(1)]*

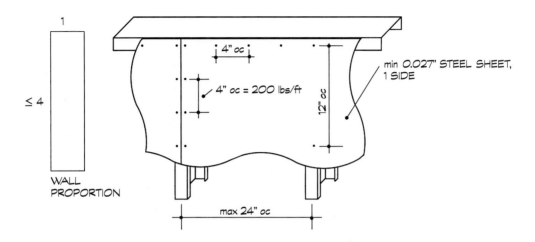

Fig. 2211.2.1(1)F. Shear values for allowable stress design (ASD) of shear walls framed with cold-formed steel studs and subject to wind. Shear values vary with wall proportions between 2:1 and 4:1. *[IBC Table 2211.2(1)]*

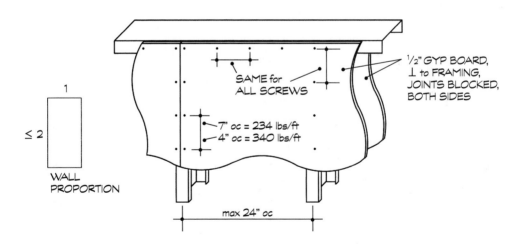

Fig. 2211.2.1(2). Shear values for allowable stress design (ASD) of shear walls framed with cold-formed steel studs and gypsum board and subject to wind. *[IBC Table 2211.2(2)]*

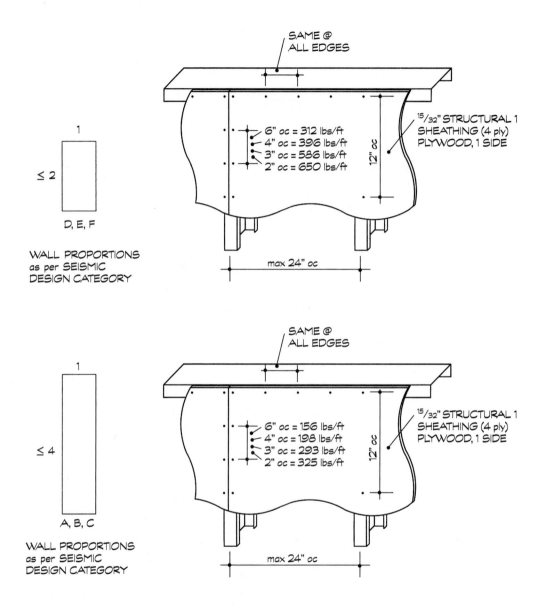

Fig. 2211.2.1(3)A. Shear values for allowable stress design (ASD) of shear walls framed with cold-formed steel studs and subject to seismic forces. Shear values vary with wall proportions between 2:1 and 4:1. *[IBC Table 2211.2(3)]*

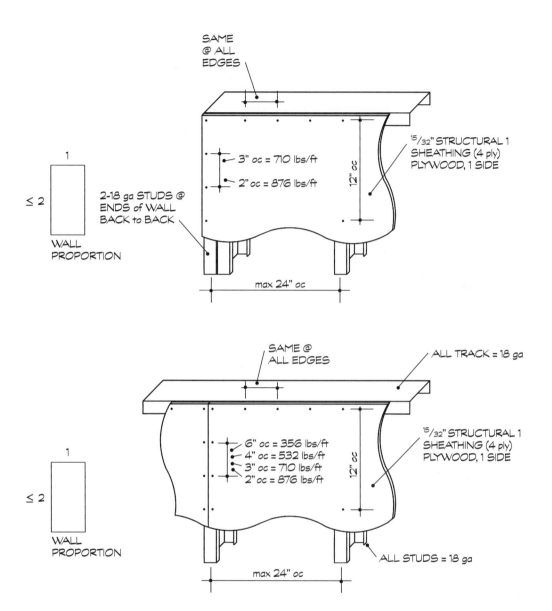

Fig. 2211.2.1(3)B. Shear values for allowable stress design (ASD) of shear walls framed with cold-formed steel studs and subject to seismic forces. *[IBC Table 2211.2(3)]*

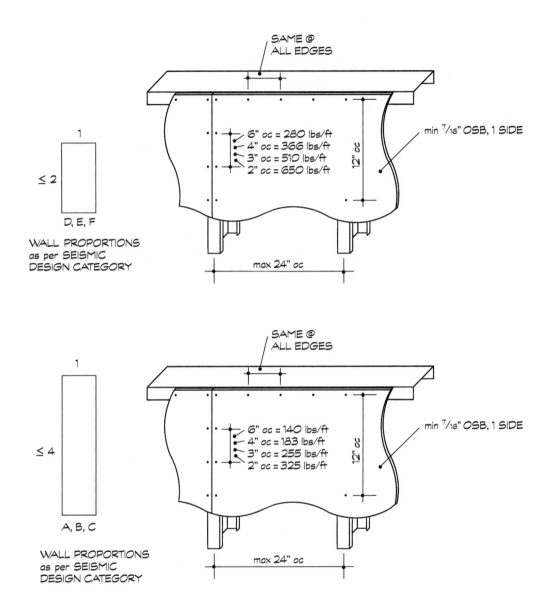

SAME @
ALL EDGES

1

≤ 2

D, E, F

WALL PROPORTIONS
as per SEISMIC
DESIGN CATEGORY

6" oc = 280 lbs/ft
4" oc = 366 lbs/ft
3" oc = 510 lbs/ft
2" oc = 650 lbs/ft

12" oc

min ⁷/₁₆" OSB, 1 SIDE

max 24" oc

SAME @
ALL EDGES

1

≤ 4

A, B, C

WALL PROPORTIONS
as per SEISMIC
DESIGN CATEGORY

6" oc = 140 lbs/ft
4" oc = 183 lbs/ft
3" oc = 255 lbs/ft
2" oc = 325 lbs/ft

12" oc

min ⁷/₁₆" OSB, 1 SIDE

max 24" oc

Fig. 2211.2.1(3)C. Shear values for allowable stress design (ASD) of shear walls framed with cold-formed steel studs and subject to seismic forces. Shear values vary with wall proportions between 2:1 and 4:1. *[IBC Table 2211.2(3)]*

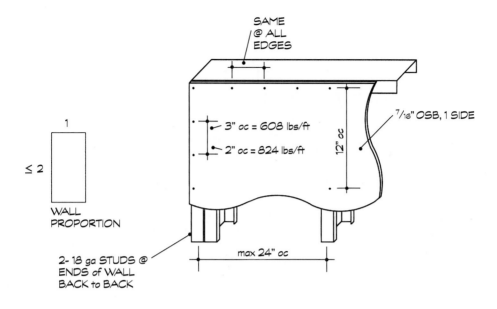

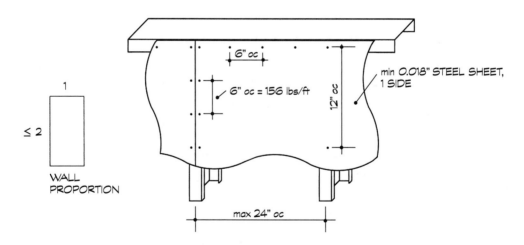

Fig. 2211.2.1(3)D. Shear values for allowable stress design (ASD) of shear walls framed with cold-formed steel studs and subject to seismic forces. *[IBC Table 2211.2(3)]*

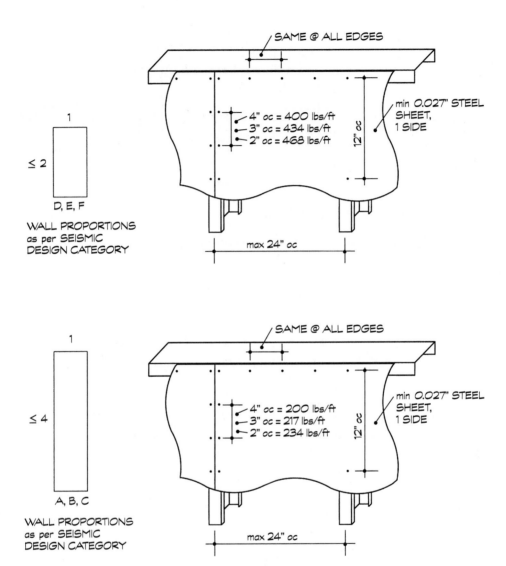

Fig. 2211.2.1(3)E. Shear values for allowable stress design (ASD) of shear walls framed with cold-formed steel studs and subject to seismic forces. Shear values vary with wall proportions between 2:1 and 4:1. *[IBC Table 2211.2(3)]*

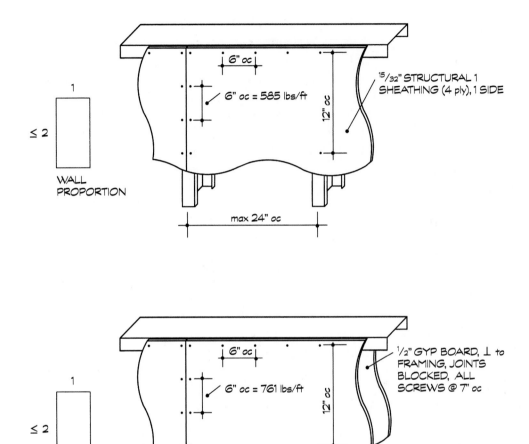

Fig. 2211.2.1(1)2A. Shear values for load and resistance factor design (LRFD) of shear walls framed with cold-formed steel studs and subject to wind. *[IBC Table 2211.2(1)]*

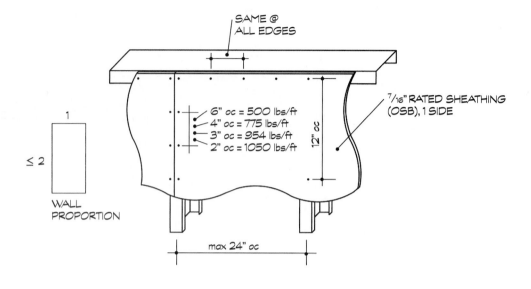

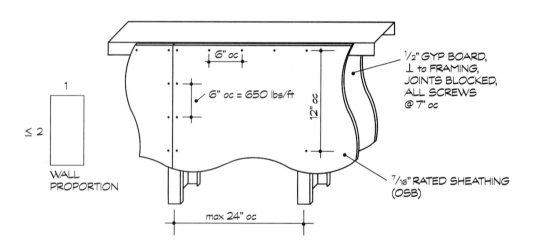

Fig. 2211.2.1(1)2B. Shear values for load and resistance factor design (LRFD) of shear walls framed with cold-formed steel studs and subject to wind. *[IBC Table 2211.2(1)]*

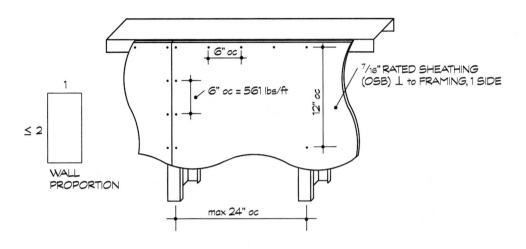

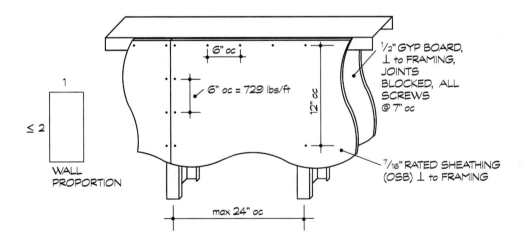

Fig. 2211.2.1(1)2C. Shear values for load and resistance factor design (LRFD) of shear walls framed with cold-formed steel studs and subject to wind. *[IBC Table 2211.2(1)]*

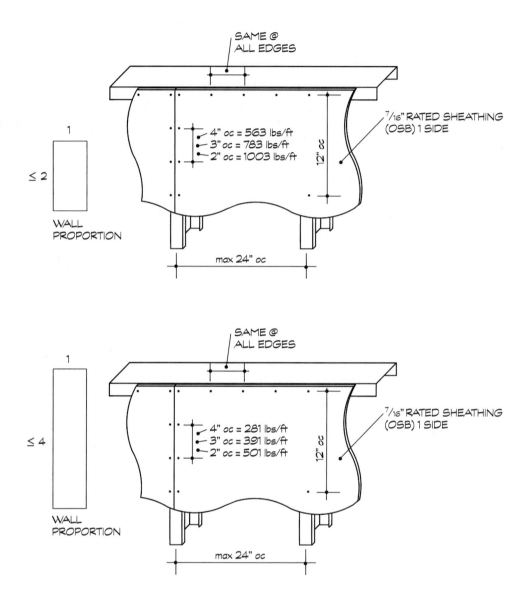

Fig. 2211.2.1(1)2D. Shear values for load and resistance factor design (LRFD) of shear walls framed with cold-formed steel studs and subject to wind. Shear values vary with wall proportions between 2:1 and 4:1. *[IBC Table 2211.2(1)]*

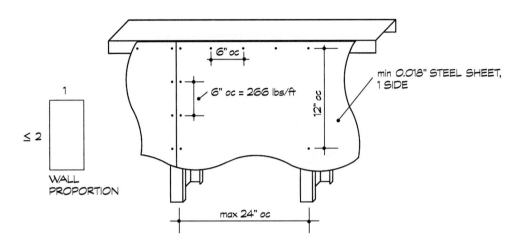

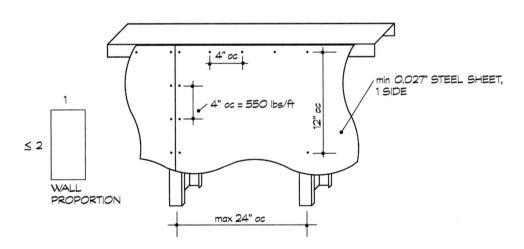

Fig. 2211.2.1(1)2E. Shear values for load and resistance factor design (LRFD) of shear walls framed with cold-formed steel studs and subject to wind. *[IBC Table 2211.2(1)]*

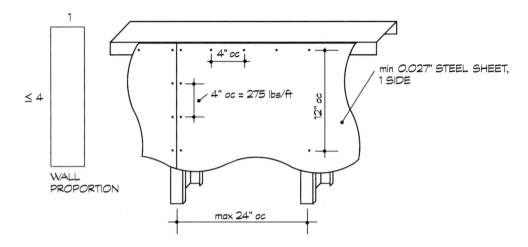

Fig. 2211.2.1(1)2F. Shear values for load and resistance factor design (LRFD) of shear walls framed with cold-formed steel studs and subject to wind. Shear values vary with wall proportions between 2:1 and 4:1. *[IBC Table 2211.2(1)]*

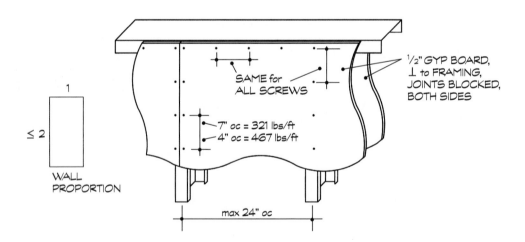

Fig. 2211.2.1(2)2. Shear values for load and resistance factor design (LRFD) of shear walls framed with cold-formed steel studs and gypsum board and subject to wind. *[IBC Table 2211.2(2)]*

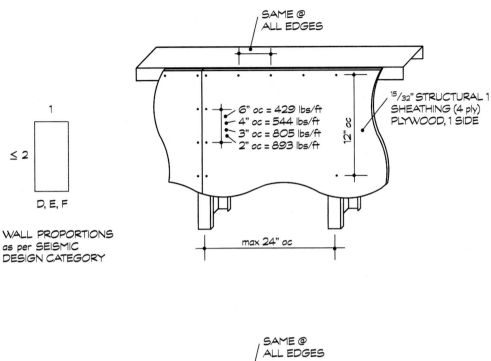

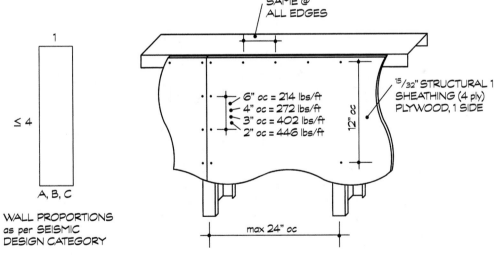

Fig. 2211.2.1(3)2A. Shear values for load and resistance factor design (LRFD) of shear walls framed with cold-formed steel studs and subject to seismic forces. Shear values vary with wall proportions between 2:1 and 4:1. *[IBC Table 2211.2(3)]*

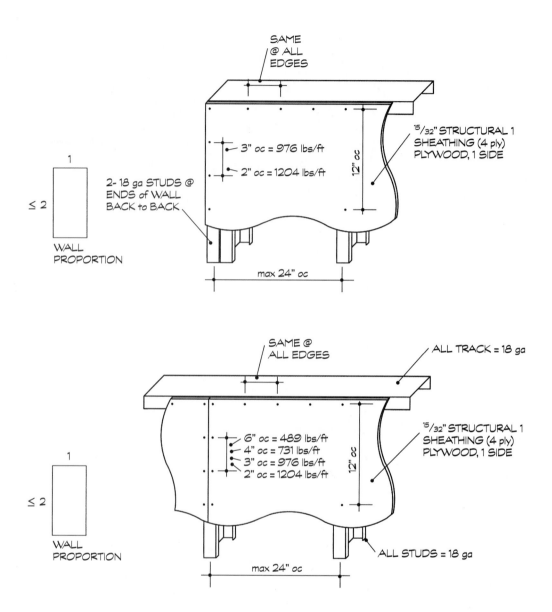

Fig. 2211.2.1(3)2B. Shear values for load and resistance factor design (LRFD) of shear walls framed with cold-formed steel studs and subject to seismic forces. *[IBC Table 2211.2(3)]*

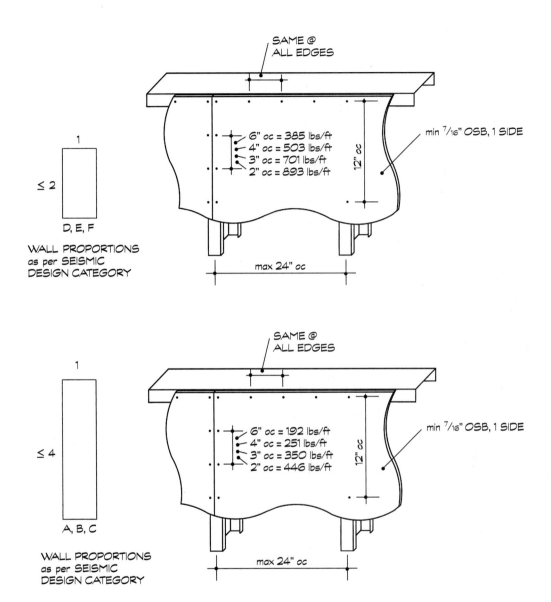

SAME @
ALL EDGES

6" oc = 385 lbs/ft
4" oc = 503 lbs/ft
3" oc = 701 lbs/ft
2" oc = 893 lbs/ft

12" oc

min $^7/_{16}$" OSB, 1 SIDE

1

≤ 2

D, E, F

WALL PROPORTIONS
as per SEISMIC
DESIGN CATEGORY

max 24" oc

SAME @
ALL EDGES

6" oc = 192 lbs/ft
4" oc = 251 lbs/ft
3" oc = 350 lbs/ft
2" oc = 446 lbs/ft

12" oc

min $^7/_{16}$" OSB, 1 SIDE

1

≤ 4

A, B, C

WALL PROPORTIONS
as per SEISMIC
DESIGN CATEGORY

max 24" oc

Fig. 2211.2.1(3)2C. Shear values for load and resistance factor design (LRFD) of shear walls framed with cold-formed steel studs and subject to seismic forces. Shear values vary with wall proportions between 2:1 and 4:1. *[IBC Table 2211.2(3)]*

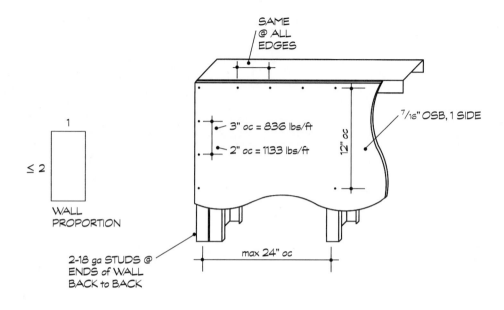

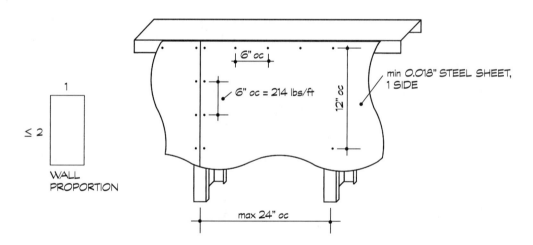

Fig. 2211.2.1(3)2D. Shear values for load and resistance factor design (LRFD) of shear walls framed with cold-formed steel studs and subject to seismic forces. *[IBC Table 2211.2(3)]*

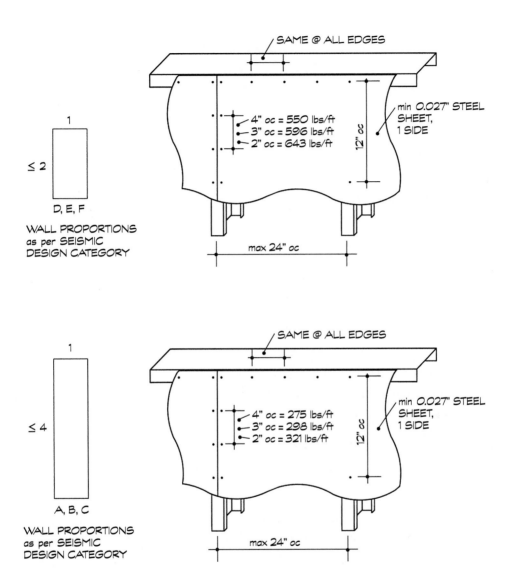

Fig. 2211.2.1(3)2E. Shear values for load and resistance factor design (LRFD) of shear walls framed with cold-formed steel studs and subject to seismic forces. Shear values vary with wall proportions between 2:1 and 4:1. *[IBC Table 2211.2(3)]*

2211 Cold-Formed Steel Light-Framed Shear Walls

2211.2.2 Limitations for systems

- Shear walls described in the previous 2 sections must meet the requirements shown in the illustrations on the following page.

    Note: The following tables are cited as describing shear walls that are governed by this section:

    IBC Table 2211.2(1), "Nominal Shear Values for Wind Forces in Pounds per Foot for Shear Walls Framed with Cold-Formed Steel Studs."

    IBC Table 2211.2(2), "Nominal Shear Values for Wind Forces in Pounds per Foot for Shear Walls Framed with Cold-Formed Steel Studs Faced with Gypsum Board."

    IBC Table 2211.2(3), "Nominal Shear Values for Seismic Forces in Pounds per Foot for Shear Walls Framed with Cold-Formed Steel Studs."

    The following are cited as alternative grades required for the studs and track:

    ASTM A 653 SS Grade 33, "Specification for Steel Sheet, Zinc-Coated Galvanized or Zinc-Iron Hot-Dip Process."

    ASTM A 792 SS Grade 33, "Specification for Steel Sheet, 55% Aluminum -Zinc Alloy-Coated by the Hot-Dip Process.

    ASTM A 875 SS Grade 33, "Specification for Steel Sheet Zinc-54% Aluminum Alloy-Coated by the Hot-Dip Process."

- Where the height-to-width ratio of a shear wall is > 2:1, the following applies:
  - Shear values must be reduced based on the following:

    2 × shear value × width ÷ height

  - Shear values as reduced by the expression above are reported as follows:
    In illustrations of the previous section where height-to-width ratios are 4:1.
- Thicknesses of panels shown in the illustrations of the previous two sections are minimums.
- Horizontal strap used as edge blocking for panels must comply with the following:
  - ≥ 1½" wide.
  - ≥ the thickness of the track and studs.
  - To be the same material as the track and studs.
- Shear values are not summed in the following detail:
  - Where multiple panels with different shear values are applied to the same side of the wall.
- Shear values are summed in the following detail:
  - Where panels of equal shear value are applied to both sides of the wall.
- Where panels with different shear values are applied to each side of a wall, the following applies:
  - The greater of the following determines the total design shear value of the detail:
    2 × the lesser design shear value.
    The larger of the 2 design shear values.

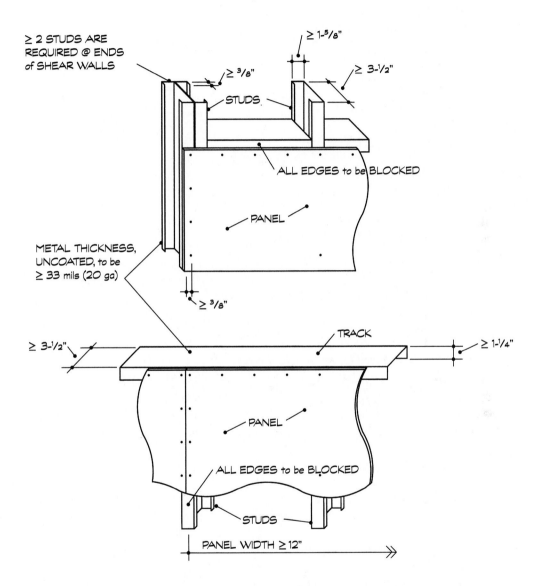

≥ 2 STUDS ARE
REQUIRED @ ENDS
of SHEAR WALLS

≥ ³/₈"

STUDS

≥ 1-⁵/₈"

≥ 3-¹/₂"

ALL EDGES to be BLOCKED

PANEL

METAL THICKNESS,
UNCOATED, to be
≥ 33 mils (20 ga)

≥ ³/₈"

TRACK

≥ 3-¹/₂"

≥ 1-¹/₄"

PANEL

ALL EDGES to be BLOCKED

STUDS

PANEL WIDTH ≥ 12"

Fig. 2211.2.2. Requirements for steel-framed shear walls.

2211 Cold-Formed Steel Light-Framed Shear Walls

2211.2.2.1 Sheet steel sheathing

- Sheet steel sheathing is governed as follows:
  - It is permitted on the following framing to resist forces as listed below:
    Framing:
      Cold-formed steel framing.
    Forces:
      Wind and seismic.
  - Thickness is to be as follows:
    ≥ 0.018" as follows:
      Where fasteners are spaced at sheet edges as follows:
        6" where the following forces are resisted:
          Wind or seismic.
    ≥ 0.027" as follows:
      Where fasteners are spaced at sheet edges as follows:
        4", 3", 2" seismic forces are resisted.
        4" where wind forces are resisted.

  Note: The following are cited as governing sheet steel sheathing:
    ASTM A 653 SS Grade 33, "Specification for Steel Sheet, Zinc-Coated Galvanized or Zinc-Iron Hot-Dip Process."
    ASTM A 792 SS Grade 33, "Specification for Steel Sheet, 55% Aluminum-Zinc Alloy-Coated by the Hot-Dip Process."
    ASTM A 875 SS Grade 33, "Specification for Steel Sheet Zinc-54% Aluminum Alloy-Coated by the Hot-Dip Process."
    The following are cited as listing nominal shear values for sheet steel sheating.
    IBC Table 2211.2(1), "Nominal Shear Values for Wind Forces in Pounds per Foot for Shear Walls Framed with Cold-Formed Steel Studs."
    IBC Table 2211.2(3), "Nominal Shear Values for Seismic Forces in Pounds per Foot for Shear Walls Framed with Cold-Formed Steel Studs."

  - Other requirements for sheet steel sheathing are shown in the following illustrations.

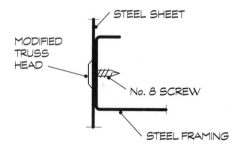

Fig. 2211.2.2.1A. Attachment screw requirements for sheet steel sheathing on cold-formed shear wall steel framing.

2211 Cold-Formed Steel Light-Framed Shear Walls

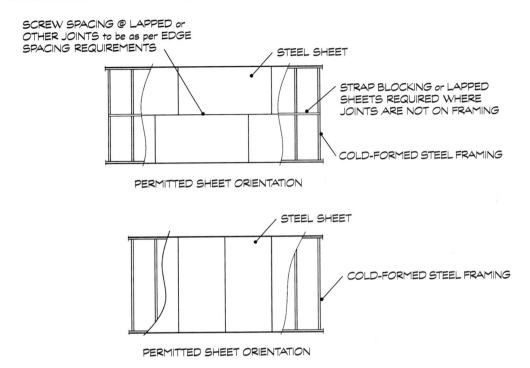

SCREW SPACING @ LAPPED or
OTHER JOINTS to be as per EDGE
SPACING REQUIREMENTS

STEEL SHEET

STRAP BLOCKING or LAPPED
SHEETS REQUIRED WHERE
JOINTS ARE NOT ON FRAMING

COLD-FORMED STEEL FRAMING

PERMITTED SHEET ORIENTATION

STEEL SHEET

COLD-FORMED STEEL FRAMING

PERMITTED SHEET ORIENTATION

Fig. 2211.2.2.1B. Permitted orientations of sheet steel panels on shear wall framing.

2211.2.2.2 Wood structural panel sheathing *(part 1 of 2)*

- Wood structural panel sheathing is governed as follows:
  - It is permitted on the following framing to resist forces as listed below:
    Framing:
      Cold-formed steel framing.
    Forces:
      Wind and seismic.

  - Shear values are provided in the previous section.

    Note: The following are cited as listing nominal shear values for sheet steel sheathing:
      IBC Table 2211.2(1), "Nominal Shear Values for Wind Forces in Pounds per Foot for Shear Walls Framed with Cold-Formed Steel Studs."
      IBC Table 2211.2(3), "Nominal Shear Values for Seismic Forces in Pounds per Foot for Shear Walls Framed with Cold-Formed Steel Studs."

  - Panels must be made with exterior glue.

    Note: The following are cited as alternatives with which the panels must comply:
      DOC PS1, "Construction and Industrial Plywood."
      DOC PS2, "Performance Standard for Wood-Based Structural-Use Panels."

2211 Cold-Formed Steel Light-Framed Shear Walls

2211.2.2.2 Wood structural panel sheathing *(part 2 of 2)*

- ○ Increases in shear values are not permitted based on the following:
  Duration of load.

  Note: Chapter 23, "Wood," is cited as governing increases based on duration of load.

- ○ Other requirements for wood panel sheathing are shown in the following illustrations.

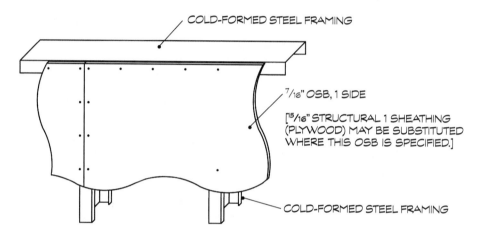

COLD-FORMED STEEL FRAMING

$^{7}/_{16}$" OSB, 1 SIDE

[$^{15}/_{16}$" STRUCTURAL 1 SHEATHING (PLYWOOD) MAY BE SUBSTITUTED WHERE THIS OSB IS SPECIFIED.]

COLD-FORMED STEEL FRAMING

WOOD STRUCTURAL PANEL SHEATHED SHEAR WALL

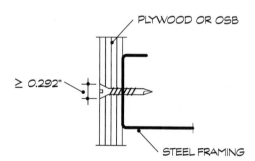

PLYWOOD OR OSB

≥ 0.292"

STEEL FRAMING

Fig. 2211.2.2.2A. Permitted panel substitution and attachment screw requirements for wood structural panel sheathing on cold-formed shear wall steel framing.

2211 Cold-Formed Steel Light-Framed Shear Walls

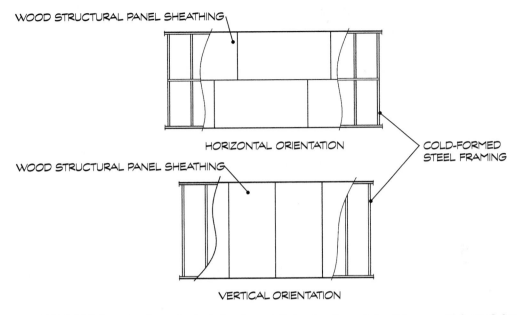

Fig. 2211.2.2.2B. Permitted panel orientation for wood structural panel sheathing on cold-formed shear wall steel framing.

2211.2.2.3 Gypsum board panel sheathing

- Gypsum board panel sheathing is governed as follows:
  - It is permitted on the following framing to resist forces as listed below:
    Framing:
      Cold-formed steel framing.
    Forces:
      Wind and seismic.

    Note: 1617.6, "Seismic-force-resisting systems," is cited as governing walls subject to seismic forces.

  - Gypsum board combined with other materials is governed as follows:
    Shear values of the various applied sheathing materials are not summed as follows:
      In cases other than those described in this chapter.

    Note: IBC Table 2211.2(2), "Nominal Shear Values for Wind Forces in Pounds per Foot for Shear Walls Framed with Cold-Formed Steel Studs Faced with Gypsum Board," is cited as providing shear values for these walls.

  - Other requirements for gypsum board sheathing are shown in the following illustrations.

    Note: ASTM C 954, "Specification for Steel Drill Screws for the Application of Gypsum Panel Products or Metal Plaster Bases to Steel Studs from 0.033 Inch to 0.112 Inch in Thickness."

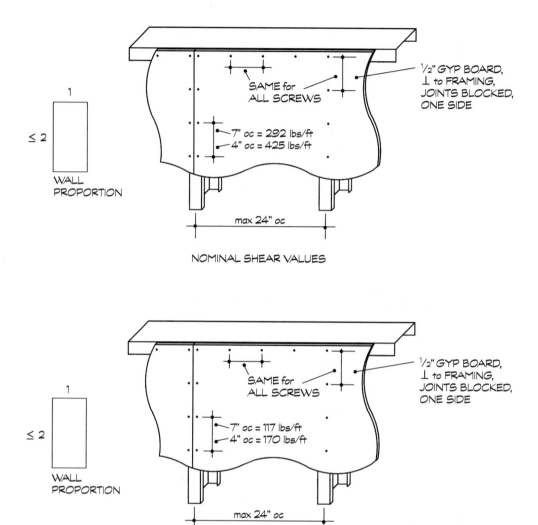

Fig. 2211.2.2.3A. Shear values for shear walls framed with cold-formed steel studs and gypsum board on one side, subject to wind. Values shown are shear values for a similar wall with gypsum board on two sides ÷ 2. *[Based on IBC Table 2211.2(2)]*

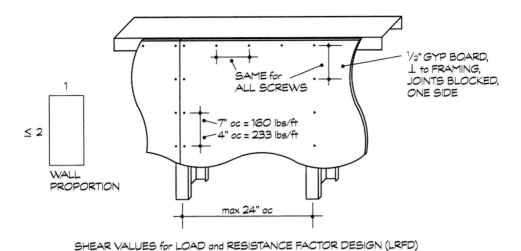

SHEAR VALUES for LOAD and RESISTANCE FACTOR DESIGN (LRFD)

Fig. 2211.2.2.3B. Shear values for shear walls framed with cold-formed steel studs and gypsum board on one side, subject to wind. Values shown are shear values for a similar wall with gypsum board on two sides ÷ 2. *[Based on IBC Table 2211.2(2)]*

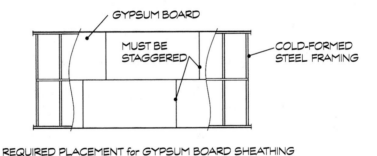

Fig. 2211.2.2.3C. Gypsum board orientation and fastening for cold-formed steel-framed shear walls.

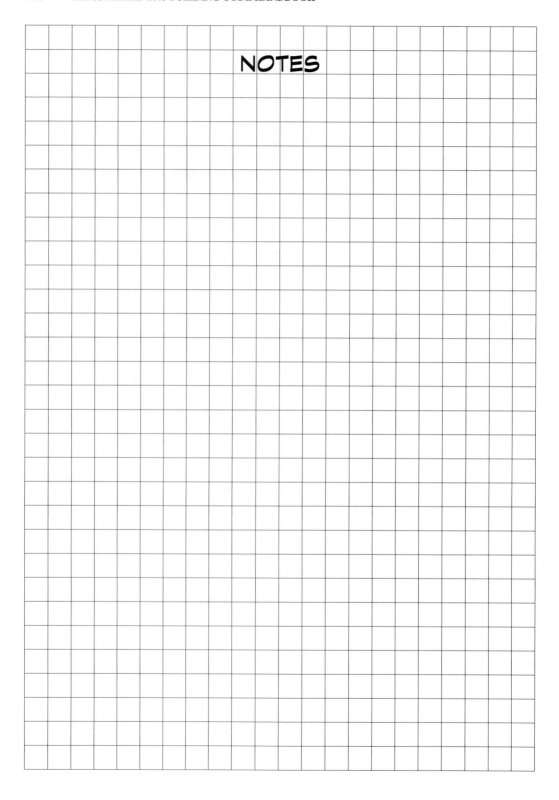

NOTES

23

Wood

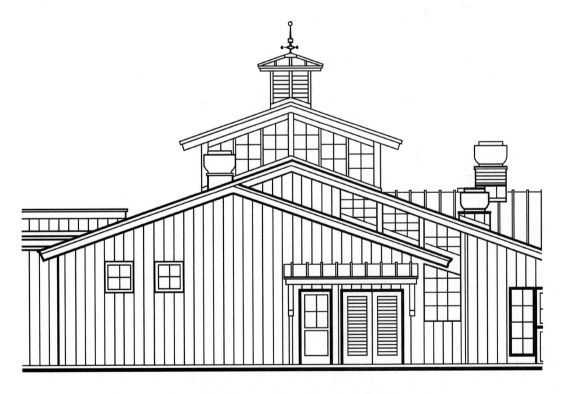

Central Kitchen. Lompoc Unified School District.
Lompoc, California. *(partial elevation)*
Phillips Metsch Sweeney Moore Architects. Santa Barbara, California.

2304 General Construction Requirements

2304.6 Wall sheathing

- This section addresses wall sheathing in wood-framed construction.
- Framing for buildings must be sheathed by one of the following materials:
  - The following materials specified elsewhere in the code:
    Weather boarding.
    Stucco.
  - Materials shown in details provided in this section.
  - Other material as follows:
    Approved.
    Of equal strength and durability.

  Note: The following are cited as sources of requirements for sheathing indicated above:
  Section 1405, "Installation of Wall Coverings."
  Section 2510, "Lathing and Furring for Cement Plaster (Stucco)."
  IBC Table 2304.6, "Minimum Thickness of Wall Sheathing," is the basis of the following details.
  The following are cited as governing wood structural panels which are not illustrated in this section:
  Table 2308.9.3(2), "Exposed Plywood Panel Siding."
  Table 2308.9.3(3), "Wood Structural Panel Wall Sheathing."
  The following are cited as governing M-S "Exterior Glue" and M-2 "Exterior Glue" particle board, which are not illustrated in this section:
  Table 2306.4.3, "Allowable Shear for Particle Board Shear Wall Sheathing."
  Table 2308.9.3(5), "Allowable Spans for Particle Board Wall Sheathing."

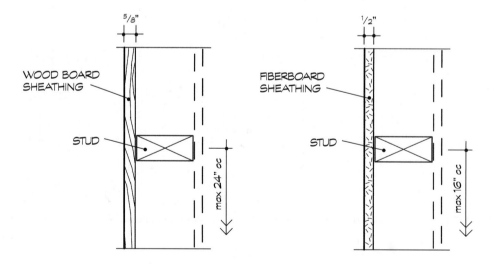

Fig. 2304.6A. Minimum thickness of wall sheathing. *[IBC Table 2304.6]*

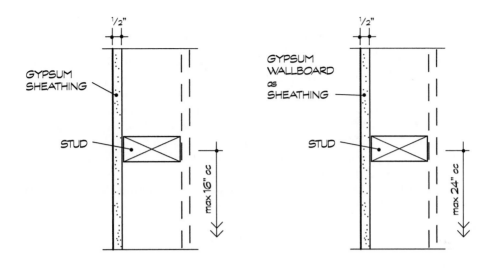

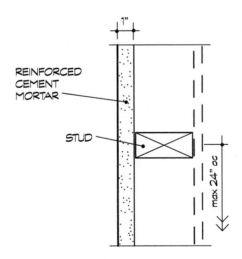

Fig. 2304.6B. Minimum thickness of wall sheathing. *[IBC Table 2304.6]*

2304 General Construction Requirements

2304.7.1 Structural floor sheathing

- Thicknesses required for structural floor sheathing are shown in the details provided.

    Note: IBC Table 2304.7(2), "Sheathing Lumber, Minimum Grade Requirements: Board Grade," is cited as governing floor sheathing. The table lists grading rules. The following are cited as the sources of requirements for the structural floor sheathing indicated above and are the basis of the details provided:

    IBC Table 2304.7(1), "Allowable Spans for Lumber Floor and Roof Sheathing."

    IBC Table 2304.7(3), "Allowable Spans and Loads for Wood Structural Panel Sheathing and Single-Floor Grades Continuous over Two or More Spans with Strength Axis Perpendicular to Supports."

    IBC Table 2304.7(4), "Allowable Span for Wood Structural Panel Combination Subfloor-Underlayment (Single Floor)."

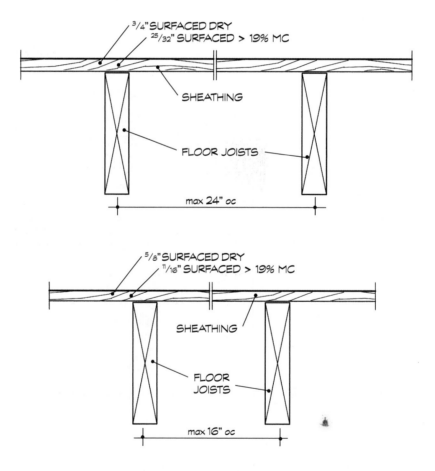

Fig. 2304.7.1A. Spans and minimum thicknesses for floor sheathing. *[IBC Table 2304.7(1)]*

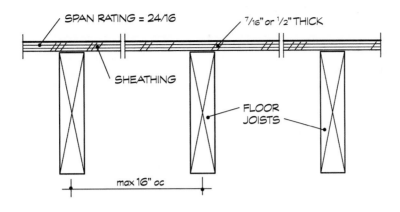

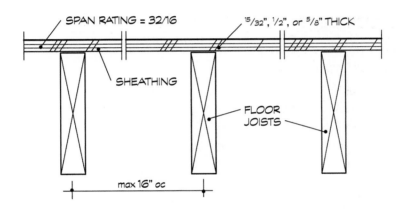

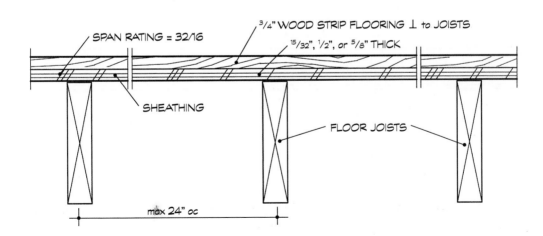

Fig. 2304.7.1B-1. Spans, loads, and minimum thicknesses for wood structural panel floor sheathing continuous over ≥ 2 spans, ⊥ to supports. *[IBC Table 2304.7(3)]*

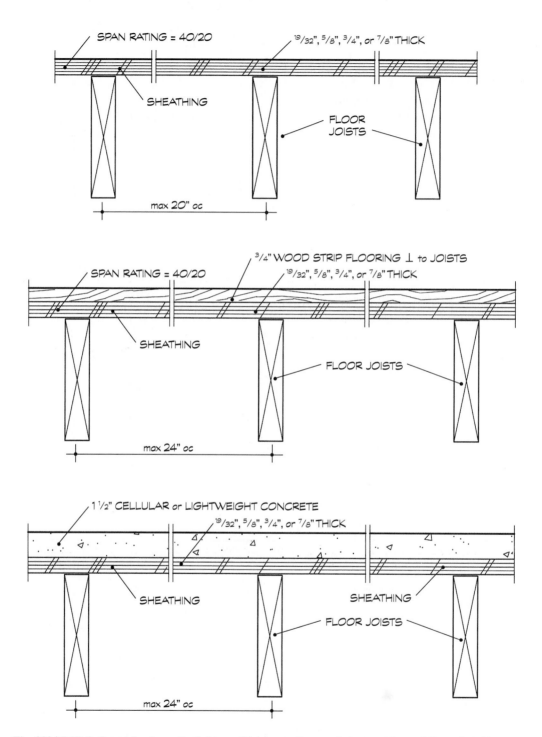

Fig. 2304.7.1B-2. Spans, loads, and minimum thicknesses for wood structural panel floor sheathing continuous over ≥ 2 spans, ⊥ to supports. *[IBC Table 2304.7(3)]*

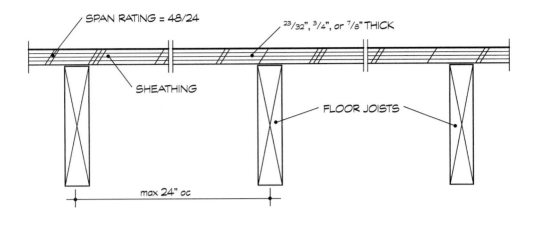

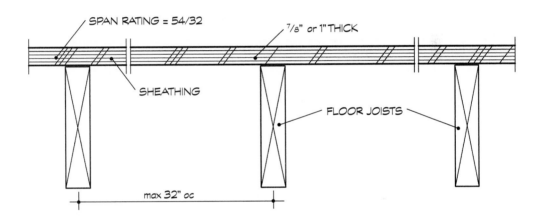

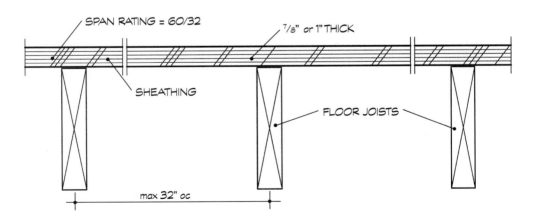

Fig. 2304.7.1B-3. Spans, loads, and minimum thicknesses for wood structural panel floor sheathing continuous over ≥ 2 spans, ⊥ to supports. *[IBC Table 2304.7(3)]*

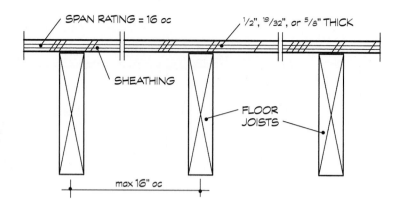

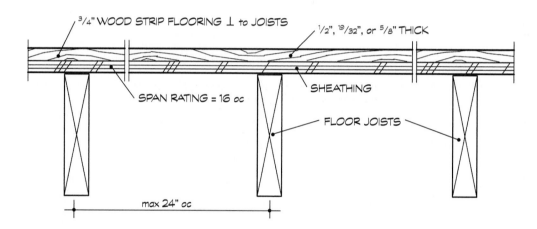

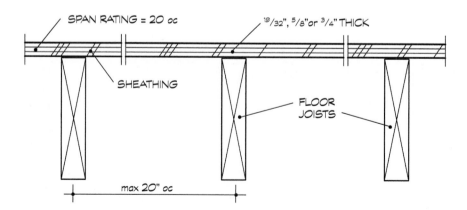

Fig. 2304.7.1B-4. Spans, loads, and minimum thicknesses for wood structural panel floor sheathing continuous over ≥ 2 spans, ⊥ to supports. *[IBC Table 2304.7(3)]*

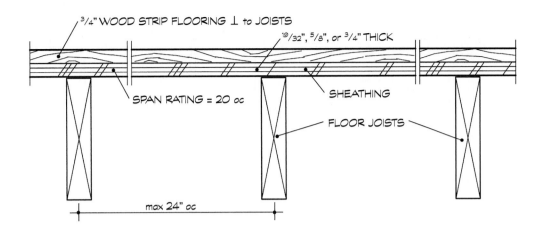

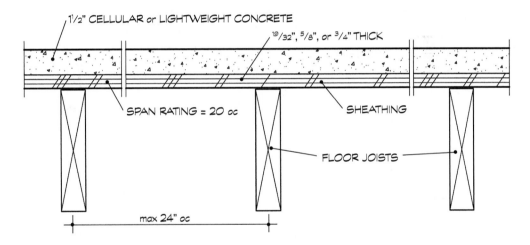

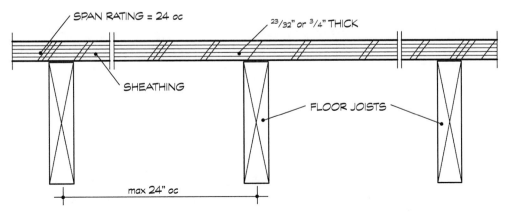

Fig. 2304.7.1B-5. Spans, loads, and minimum thicknesses for wood structural panel floor sheathing continuous over ≥ 2 spans, ⊥ to supports. *[IBC Table 2304.7(3)]*

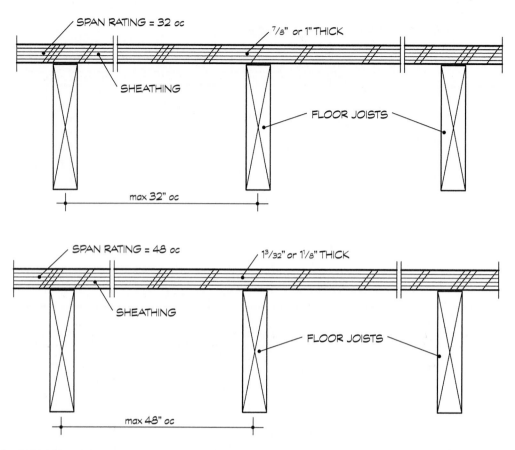

Fig. 2304.7.1B-6. Spans, loads, and minimum thicknesses for wood structural panel floor sheathing continuous over ≥ 2 spans, ⊥ to supports. *[IBC Table 2304.7(3)]*

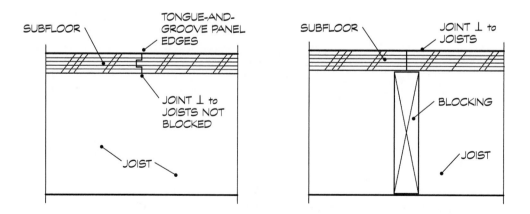

Fig. 2304.7.1C-1. Options for required edge support at subfloor panels. Subfloor panels in IBC Table 2304.7(4) require one of the edge support details shown in Figs. 2304.71C-1 and C-2.

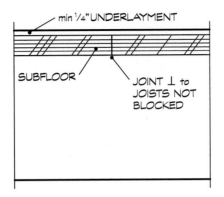

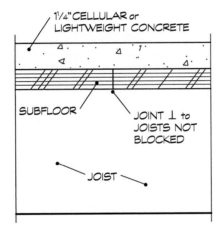

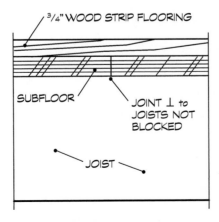

Fig. 2304.7.1C-2. Options for required edge support at subfloor panels. Subfloor panels in IBC Table 2304.7(4) require one of the edge support details shown in Figs. 2304.71C-1 and C-2.

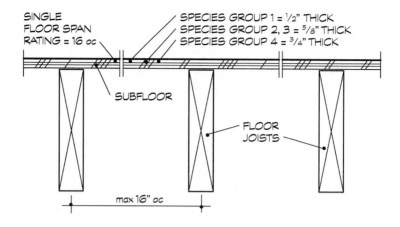

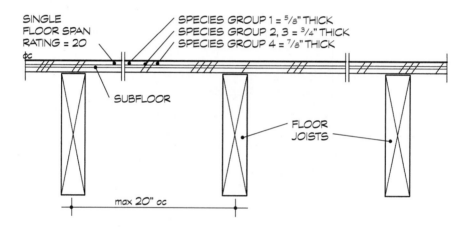

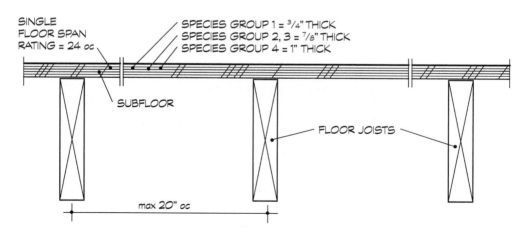

Fig. 2304.7.1D. Spans and minimum thicknesses of combination subfloor-underlayment (single floor) panels continuous over ≥ 2 spans, ⊥ to supports. *[IBC Table 2304.7(4)]*

2304 General Construction Requirements

2304.7.2 Structural roof sheathing

- Thicknesses required for structural roof sheathing are shown in the details provided.
- Wood structural panel roof sheathing must be bonded as follows:
  - With exterior grade glue.

    Note: IBC Table 2304.7(2), "Sheathing Lumber, Minimum Grade Requirements: Board Grade," is cited as governing roof sheathing. The table lists grading rules. The following are cited as the sources of requirements for the structural roof sheathing indicated above and are the basis of the details provided:
    IBC Table 2304.7(1), "Allowable Spans for Lumber Floor and Roof Sheathing."
    IBC Table 2304.7(3), "Allowable Spans and Loads for Wood Structural Panel Sheathing and Single-Floor Grades Continuous over Two or More Spans with Strength Axis Perpendicular to Supports."
    IBC Table 2304.7(5), "Allowable Load (psf) for Wood Structural Panel Roof Sheathing Continuous over Two or More Spans and Strength Axis Parallel to Supports."

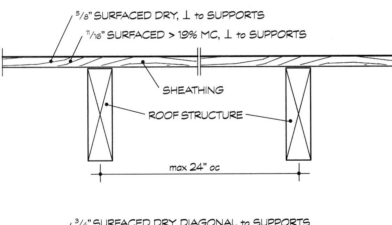

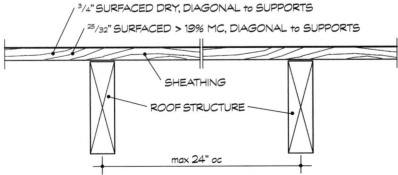

Fig. 2304.7.2A. Spans and minimum thicknesses for roof sheathing. *[IBC Table 2304.7(1)]*

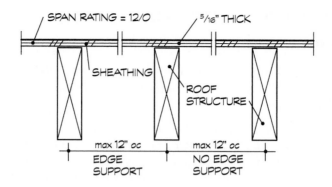

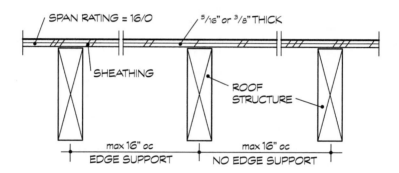

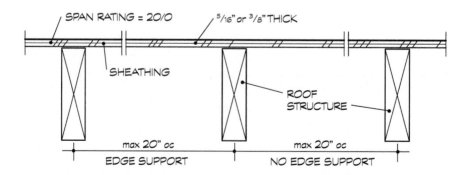

Fig. 2304.7.2B-1. Spans, loads, and minimum thicknesses for wood structural panel roof sheathing continuous over ≥ 2 spans, ⊥ to supports. *[IBC Table 2304.7(3)]*

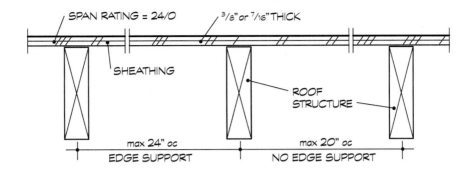

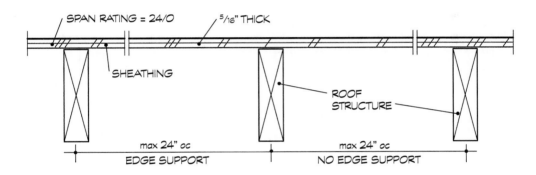

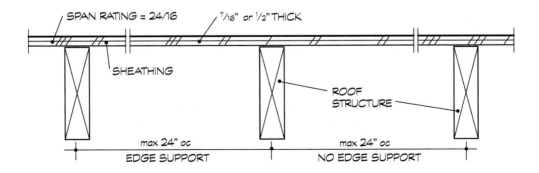

Fig. 2304.7.2B-2. Spans, loads, and minimum thicknesses for wood structural panel roof sheathing continuous over ≥ 2 spans, ⊥ to supports. *[IBC Table 2304.7(3)]*

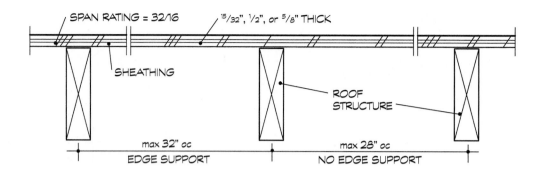

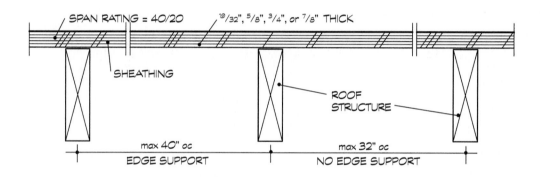

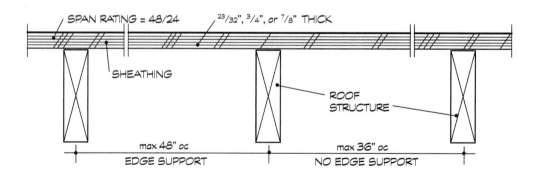

Fig. 2304.7.2B-3. Spans, loads, and minimum thicknesses for wood structural panel roof sheathing continuous over ≥ 2 spans, ⊥ to supports. *[IBC Table 2304.7(3)]*

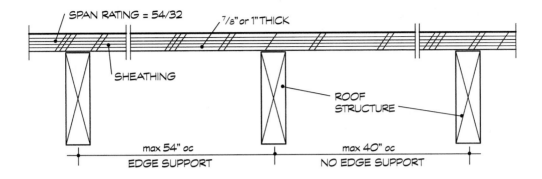

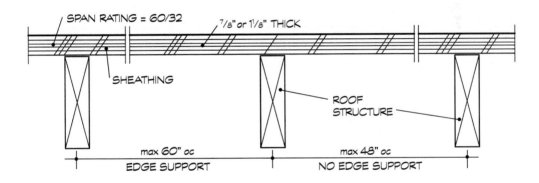

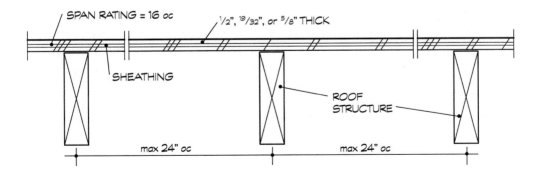

Fig. 2304.7.2B-4. Spans, loads, and minimum thicknesses for wood structural panel roof sheathing continuous over ≥ 2 spans, ⊥ to supports. *[IBC Table 2304.7(3)]*

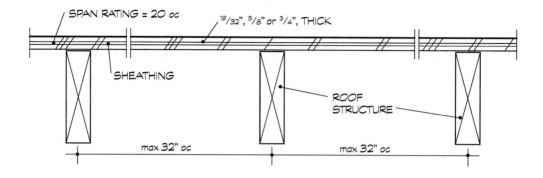

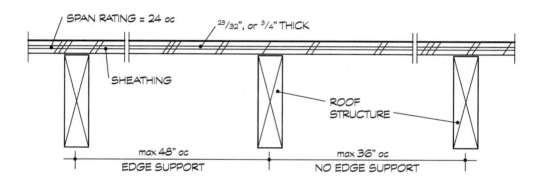

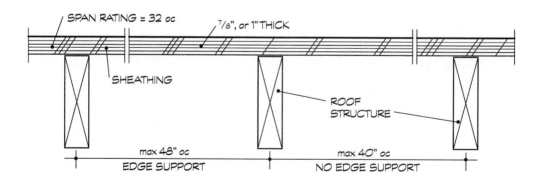

Fig. 2304.7.2B-5. Spans, loads, and minimum thicknesses for wood structural panel roof sheathing continuous over ≥ 2 spans, ⊥ to supports. *[IBC Table 2304.7(3)]*

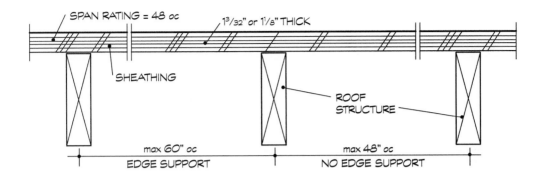

Fig. 2304.7.2B-6. Spans, loads, and minimum thicknesses for wood structural panel roof sheathing continuous over ≥ 2 spans, ⊥ to supports. *[IBC Table 2304.7(3)]*

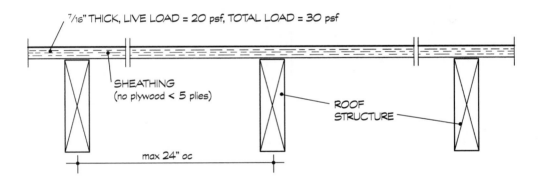

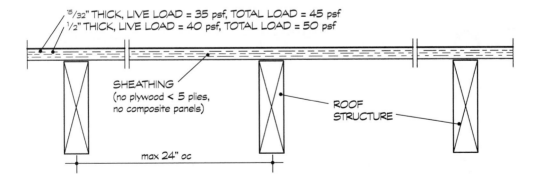

Fig. 2304.7.2C-1. Spans, loads, and minimum thicknesses for wood structural 1 roof sheathing panels continuous over ≥ 2 spans, ⊥ to supports. *[IBC Table 2304.7(5)]*

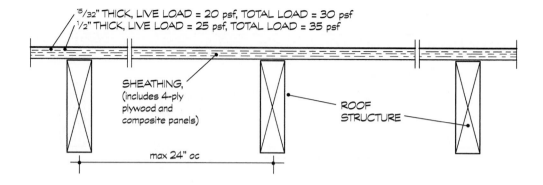

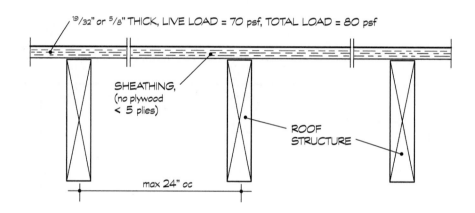

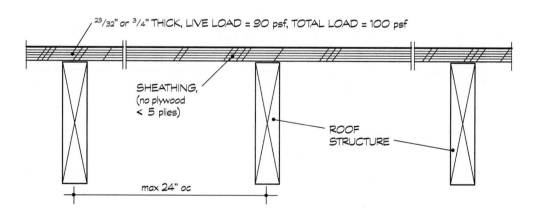

Fig. 2304.7.2C-2. Spans, loads, and minimum thicknesses for wood structural 1 roof sheathing panels continuous over ≥ 2 spans, ⊥ to supports. *[IBC Table 2304.7(5)]*

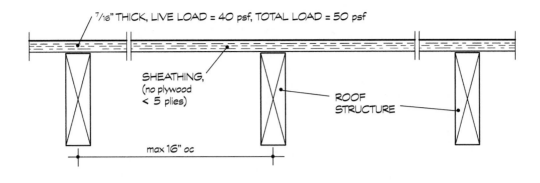

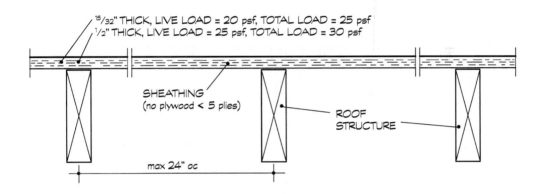

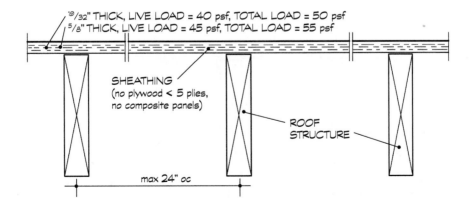

Fig. 2304.7.2C-3. Spans, loads, and minimum thicknesses for wood panel roof sheathing (other than structural 1 sheathing) continuous over ≥ 2 spans, ⊥ to supports. *[IBC Table 2304.7(5)]*

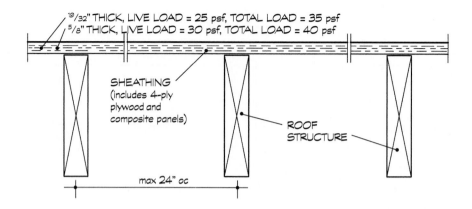

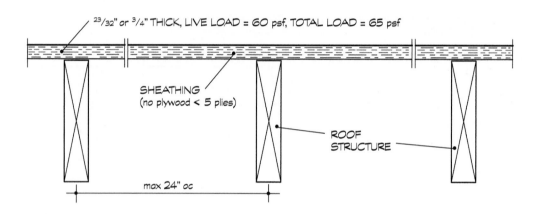

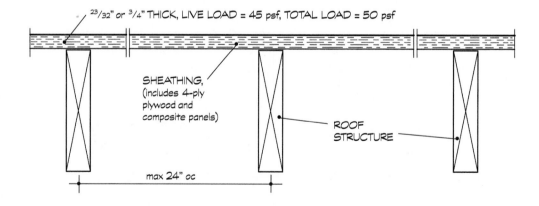

Fig. 2304.7.2C-4. Spans, loads, and minimum thicknesses for wood panel roof sheathing (other than structural 1 sheathing) continuous over ≥ 2 spans, ⊥ to supports. *[IBC Table 2304.7(5)]*

2308 Conventional Light-Frame Construction

2308.9.1 Size, height and spacing

- Utility-grade studs are governed as follows:
  - Spacing must be ≤ 16" on center.
  - They may not support more than the following:
    A ceiling and a roof.
  - Length is limited as follows:
    ≤ 8' for exterior walls.
    ≤ 8' for load-bearing walls.
    ≤ 10' for interior walls.
    ≤ 10' for nonload-bearing walls.
- Other studs are governed as shown in the details provided.

    Note: IBC Table 2308.9.1, "Size, Height and Spacing of Wood Studs," is cited as the source of requirements and is the basis for the following details.

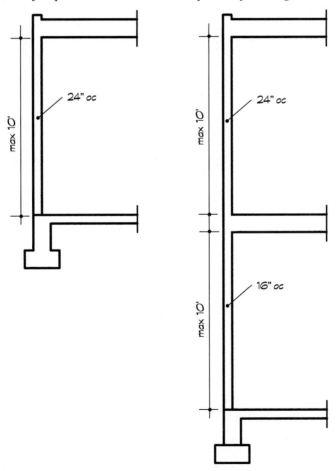

Fig. 2308.9.1A. Maximum height between lateral supports for 2"× 4" wood studs in load-bearing walls.

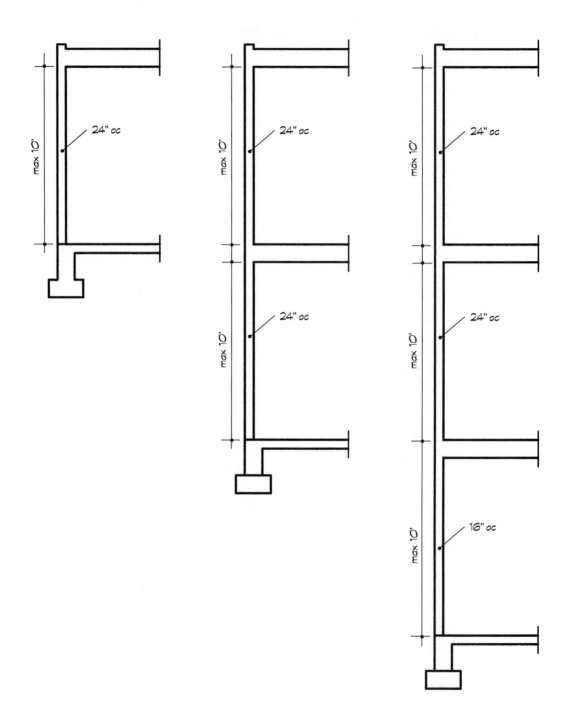

Fig. 2308.9.1B. Maximum height between lateral supports for 3"× 4" wood studs in load-bearing walls.

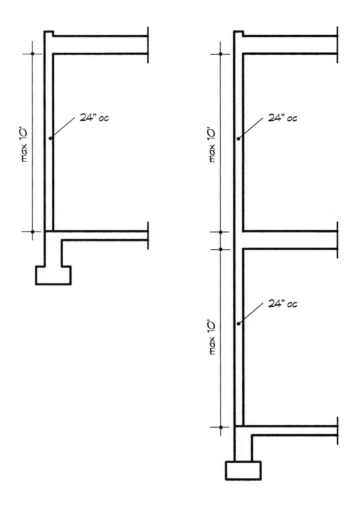

Fig. 2308.9.1C. Maximum height between lateral supports for 2″× 5″ wood studs in load-bearing walls.

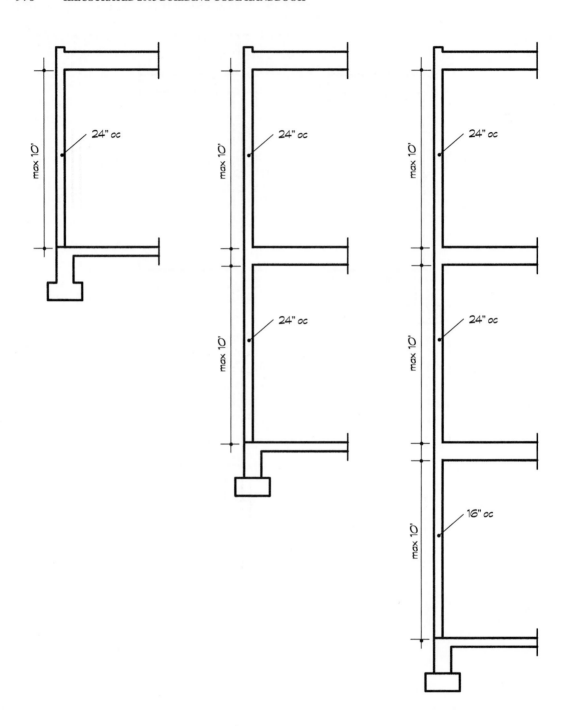

Fig. 2308.9.1D. Maximum height between lateral supports for 2"× 6" wood studs in load-bearing walls.

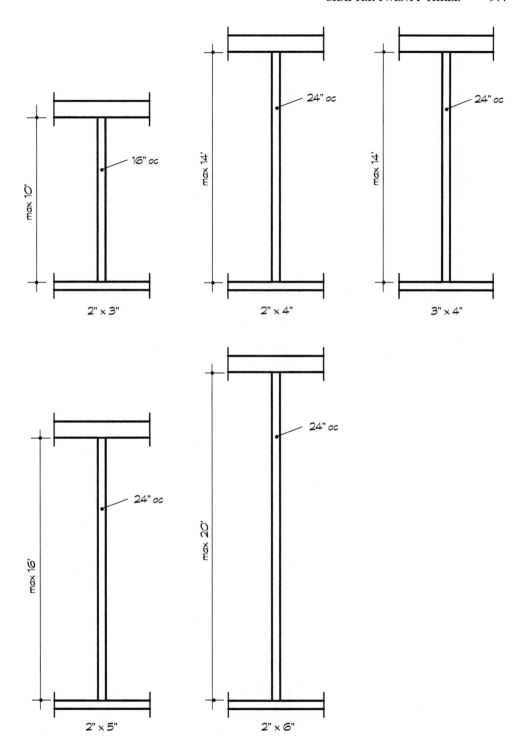

Fig. 2308.9.1E. Maximum height between lateral supports for wood studs in nonload-bearing walls.

2308 Conventional Light-Frame Construction

2308.9.3 Bracing *(part 1 of 3)*

- Braced wall lines must consist of the following:
    - Braced wall panels as follows:
        - Panels must meet the following requirements of this section:
            - Location within the wall.
            - Type of bracing.
            - Amount of bracing.

    Note: The following are cited as sources of requirements for braced wall panels:
    IBC Fig. 2308.9.3, "Basic components of the lateral bracing system."
    IBC Table 2308.9.3(1), "Braced Wall Panels."

- Braced wall panels must be located as follows:
    - In one of the following positions:
        - Aligned with each other.
        - Offset ≤ 4'.
    - ≤ 8' from each end of a braced wall line.
    - ≤ 12'- 6" from each end of a braced wall line as follows:
        - Where a designed collector is provided.
- Braced wall panels must be identified on construction drawings.
- Braced wall panels must be detailed as follows:
    - Vertical joints of panel sheathing must fall on studs.
    - Adjacent panels must be fastened to the same framing member as follows:
        - Where edges meet.
    - Horizontal joints must fall on blocking or other framing as follows:
        - Blocking or other framing must be one of the following:
            - The same size as the studs.
            - The size specified by installation requirements for the sheathing material.
    - Blocking is required under braced wall lines in the following case:
        - Where the joists below are ‖ to braced wall lines.
    - Sole plates must be nailed to floor framing.
    - Top plates must be nailed to the framing above.

    Note: 2308.3.2, "Braced wall panel connections," is cited as governing sole plate and top
    plate connections to adjacent framing.

- Cripple walls must meet the following bracing requirements:
    - Where stud height ≥ 1'-2":
        - Where located in Seismic Design Category A, B, or C:
            - Requirements are the same for full height walls.
        - Where located in Seismic Design Category D or E:
            - Requirements other than those for full height walls apply.

    Note: 2308.9.4.1, "Bracing," is cited as the source of requirements for cripple walls as
    indicated above.

2308 Conventional Light-Frame Construction

2308.9.3 Bracing *(part 2 of 3)*

- Braced wall panels must be constructed as one of the following systems:
  - Continuous diagonal lumber braces with the following characteristics:
    Nominal 1" × 4".
    Let into the following:
      Top plates.
      Bottom plates.
      Intervening studs.
    Installed at an angle as follows:
      $\geq 45°$ and $\leq 60°$ from the horizontal.

  Note: IBC Table 2304.9.1, "Fastening Schedule," is cited as governing the size, type, and location of fastener required for the bracing system indicated above.

  - Wood boards with the following characteristics:
    $\geq {}^{5}/_{8}$" net thickness.
    Installed diagonally on studs as follows:
      Studs spaced ≤ 24" on center.
    Length of panel (measured horizontally) must be $\geq 4'$.
    Where studs are spaced ≤ 16" on center:
      Panel must span ≥ 3 stud spaces.
    Where studs are spaced ≤ 24" on center:
      Panel must span ≥ 2 stud spaces.
  - Wood structural panel sheathing as shown on the details provided.

  Note: The following are cited as governing the structural panels indicated above and are the basis of the details provided:
      IBC Table 2308.9.3(2), "Exposed Plywood Panel Siding."
      IBC Table 2309.9.3(3), "Wood Structural Panel Wall Sheathing."

  - Fiberboard sheathing panels with the following characteristics:
    $\geq \frac{1}{2}$" thickness.
    Installed as follows on studs spaced ≤ 16" on center:
      Vertically.
      Horizontally.
    Length of panel (measured horizontally) must be $\geq 4'$.
    Panel must span ≥ 3 stud spaces.

  Note: The following are cited as governing the fastening of the fiberboard panels indicated above:
      2306.4.4, "Fiberboard shear walls."
      IBC Table 2308.9.3(4), "Allowable Shear Values (plf) for Wind or Seismic Loading on Vertical Diaphragms of Fiberboard Sheathing Board Construction for Type V Construction Only."

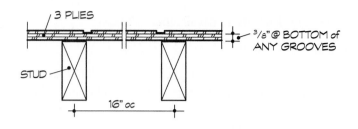

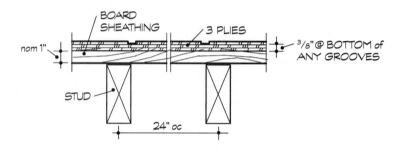

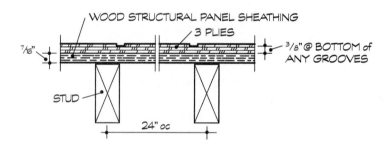

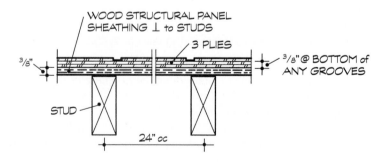

Fig. 2308.9.3A-1. Span, plies, and minimum thickness of exposed plywood siding applied directly to studs or over sheathing. *[IBC Table 2308.9(2)]*

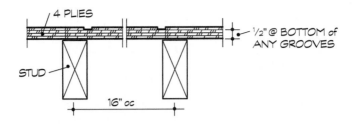

Fig. 2308.9.3A-2. Span, plies, and minimum thickness of exposed plywood siding applied directly to studs or over sheathing. *[IBC Table 2308.9(2)]*

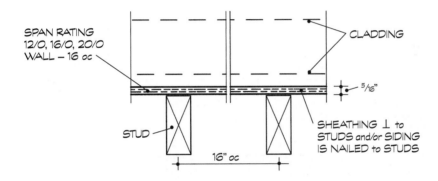

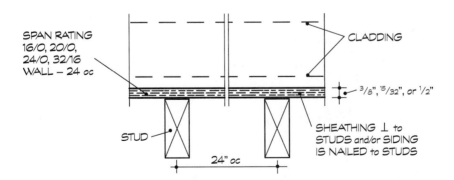

Fig. 2308.9.3B-1. Span and minimum thickness of wood structural wall sheathing not exposed to weather. *[IBC Table 2308.9(3)]*

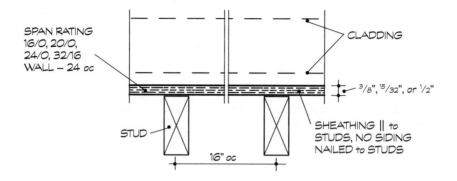

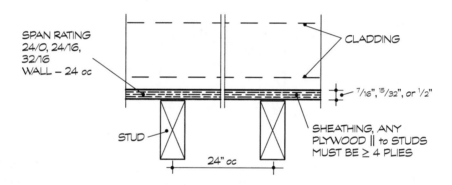

Fig. 2308.9.3B-2. Span and minimum thickness of wood structural wall sheathing not exposed to weather.
[IBC Table 2308.9(3)]

2308 Conventional Light-Frame Construction

2308.9.3 Bracing *(part 3 of 3)*

○ Gypsum board as follows:
　　Types:
　　　Sheathing.
　　　Wallboard.
　　　Veneer base.
　　Requirements:
　　　½" thick.
　　　4' wide.
　　　Nailed 7" on center to studs ≤ 24" on center.
　　　Where applied to one side of a bracing panel:
　　　　Length must be ≥ 8' (measured horizontally).
　　　Where applied to both sides of a bracing panel:
　　　　Length must be ≥ 4' (measured horizontally).

> *Note: IBC Table 2306.4.5, "Allowable Shear for Wind or Seismic Forces for Shear Walls of Lath and Plaster or Gypsum Board Wood Framed Wall Assemblies," is cited as governing the fastening of gypsum board as indicated above.*

○ Particleboard wall sheathing panels with the following characteristics as shown in the details provided in this section:
　　Length of panel (measured horizontally) must be ≥ 4':
　　　Where studs are spaced ≤ 16" on center:
　　　　Panel must span ≥ 3 stud spaces.
　　　Where studs are spaced ≤ 24" on center:
　　　　Panel must span ≥ 2 stud spaces.

> *Note: IBC Table 2308.9.3(5), "Allowable Spans for Particleboard Wall Sheathing," is cited as governing particleboard wall sheathing and is the basis of the details provided in this section.*

○ Portland cement plaster as follows:
　　On studs ≤ 16" on center.
　　Length of panel (measured horizontally) must be ≥ 4'.
　　Panel must span ≥ 3 stud spaces.

> *Note: Section 2510, "Lathing and Furring for Cement Plaster (Stucco)," is cited as governing the application of portland cement plaster as indicated above.*

○ Hardboard panel siding as follows:
　　Length of panel (measured horizontally) must be ≥ 4'.
　　Where studs are spaced ≤ 16" on center:
　　　Panel must span ≥ 3 stud spaces.
　　Where studs are spaced ≤ 24" on center:
　　　Panel must span ≥ 2 stud spaces.

> *Note: 2303.1.6, "Hardboard," is cited as a source of requirements.*
> *IBC Table 2308.9.3(6), "Hardboard Siding," is cited as a source of requirements.*

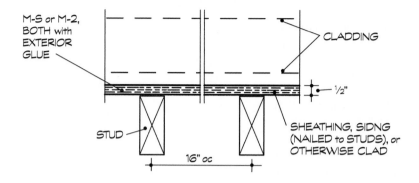

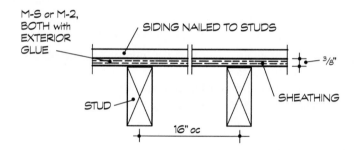

Fig. 2308.9.3C. Span and minimum thickness of particleboard wall sheathing not exposed to weather.
[IBC Table 2308.9(5)]

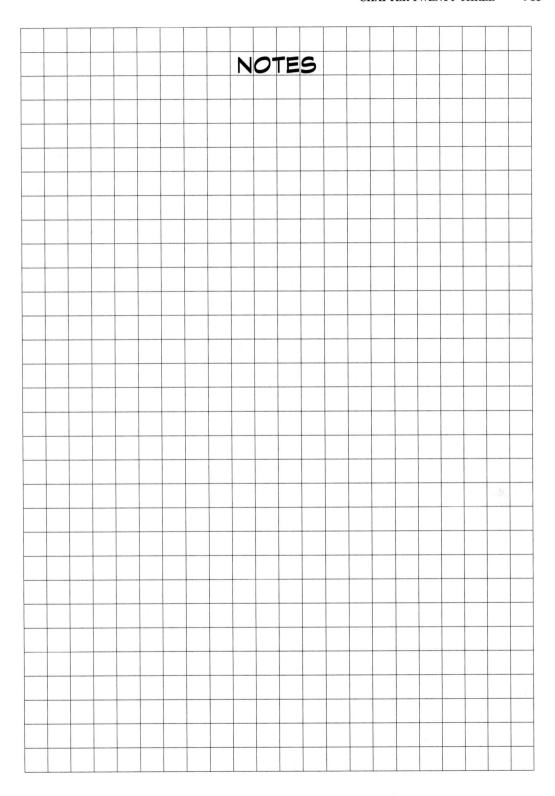

NOTES

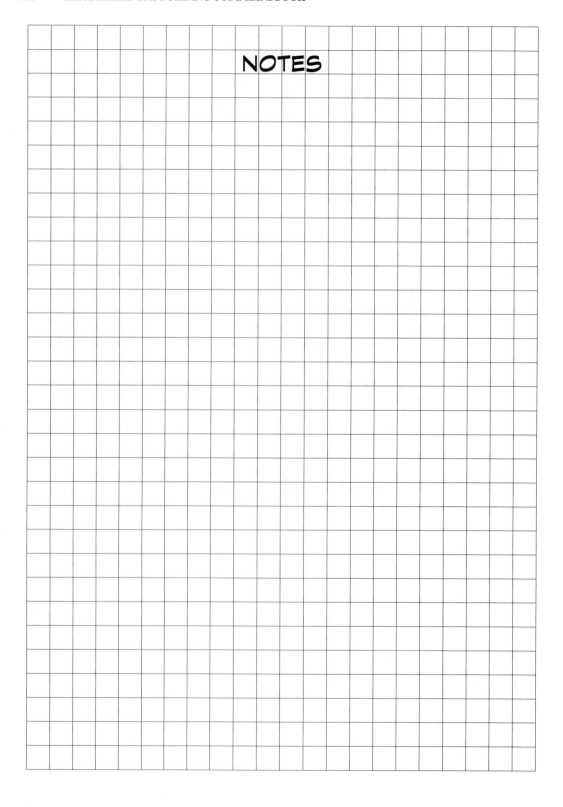

NOTES

24

Glass and Glazing

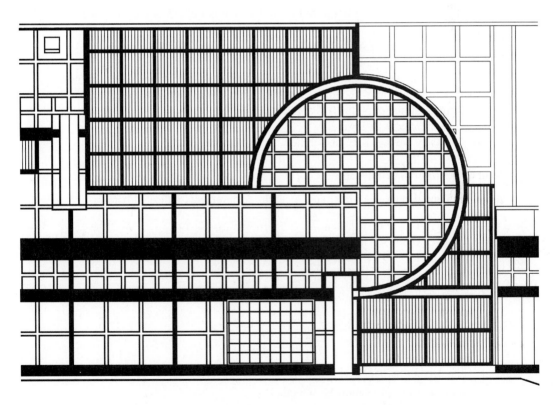

Lubrication Engineers, Inc. Wichita, Kansas. *(partial elevation)*
Gossen Livingston Associates, Inc. Architecture. Wichita, Kansas.

2403 General Requirements for Glass

2403.3 Framing

- A glass edge qualifies as having a firm support where deflection due to the loading indicated below is limited as follows:
  - Deflection:
    The edge deflection ⊥ to a pane of glass may not be > either of the following:
    $^1/_{175}$ the length of the glass edge.
    ¾".
  - Loading:
    Where the larger of the following loads is applied where loads are combined:
    The positive load.
    The negative load.

  Note: Section 1605, "Load Combinations."

2403.4 Interior glazed areas

- Deflection of interior glazing in the following location is limited as indicated below:
  - Location:
    Adjacent to a walking surface.
  - Deflection:
    The differential deflection of adjacent unsupported edges is governed as follows:
    Deflection must be ≤ the thickness of the glass in the following case:
    Where a force of 50 lbs/ft is applied as follows:
    Horizontally to 1 panel.
    At any point ≤ 3'-6" above the walking surface.

2403.5 Louvered windows or jalousies

- In the following conditions, glass must meet the requirements indicated below:
  - Conditions:
    Glass:
    Float.
    Wired.
    Patterned.
    Locations:
    Louvered windows.
    Jalousies.
  - Requirements:
    Glass must be ≥ $^3/_{16}$" thick.
    Glass must be ≤ 4' long.
    Exposed edges of glass must be smooth.
    Wire glass may not be used as follows:
    Where wire is exposed on longitudinal edges.
    Where other glass types are used, the following applies:
    Design must be provided to the building official for approval.

2405 Sloped Glazing and Skylights

2405.1 Scope

- This section applies to the following glazing where sloped as indicated below:
  - Glazing:
    Glass.
    Transparent materials.
    Translucent materials.
    Opaque glazing materials.
    Glazing materials in the following:
      Skylights.
      Roofs.
      Sloped walls.
  - Slope:
    Where sloped > 15 degrees from vertical plane.

2405.2 Allowable glazing materials and limitations

- The following materials are permitted in sloped glazing:
  - Laminated glass with one of the following:
    A polyvinyl butyral interlayer ≥ 30 mils thick.
    An equivalent interlayer.
  - Wired glass.
  - Light-transmitting plastics.

    Note: Section 2607, "Light-Transmitting Plastic Wall Panels," is cited as governing these plastics.

  - Heat-strengthened glass.
  - Fully tempered glass.
  - Annealed glass as follows:
    Where there is no walking surface below.
    Where any walking surface below is protected from falling glass.
    In commercial or detached noncombustible greenhouses as follows:
      Used only for growing plants.
      Closed to the public.
      Height of greenhouse at ridge is ≤ 30' above grade.

    Note: 2405.3, "Screening," exceptions 2 and 3, are cited as governing annealed glass and are summarized above.
    Section 2610, "Light-Transmitting Plastic Skylight Glazing," is cited as the source of additional requirements for plastic skylights.
    2101.2.5, "Glass masonry," is cited as governing glass block installations.

2405 Sloped Glazing and Skylights

2405.3 Screening *(part 1 of 2)*

- Screens are not required under fully tempered glass in the following case:
  - Where the glazing occurs between floors as follows:
    - Glazing is sloped ≤ 30 degrees from a vertical plane.
    - Highest point of glass is ≤ 10' above the walking surface.
- Screens are not required below the following glazing for the conditions indicated below:
  - Glazing:
    - Any glazing including annealed glass.
  - Conditions:
    - Where one of the following conditions applies:
      - Where there is no walking surface below.
      - Where any walking surface below is protected from falling glass.
- Screens are not required below the following glazing in the locations indicated below:
  - Glazing:
    - Any glazing including annealed glass.
  - Locations:
    - In commercial or detached noncombustible greenhouses as follows:
      - Used only for growing plants.
      - Closed to the public.
      - Height of greenhouse at ridge is ≤ 30' above grade.
- Screens are not required in the following locations for the conditions indicated below:
  - Locations:
    - In occupancies R-2, R-3, R-4.
  - Conditions:
    - Area of each pane of glass is ≤ 16 sf.
    - Highest point of glass is ≤ 12' above either of the following:
      - A walking surface.
      - Any other area which may be accessed.
    - Where glazing is fully tempered glass:
      - Glass thickness is ≤ $^3/_{16}$".
    - Where glazing is laminated glass:
      - One of the following interlayers must be provided:
        - Polyvinyl butyral ≥ 15 mils thick.
        - An equivalent interlayer.

2405 Sloped Glazing and Skylights

2405.3 Screening *(part 2 of 2)*

- Screens as indicated below are required under the following sloped glazing:
  - ○ Glazing:
      Includes the following glass in the formats listed below:
        Glass:
          Heat-strengthened glass.
          Fully tempered glass.
        Formats:
          Glazing with a single layer of glass.
          The bottom layer among multiple layers of glass.
  - ○ Screens:
      Must be able to support 2 × the weight of the glazing.
      Must be securely fastened to framing.
      Must be installed ≤ 4" of the glass.
      Must be noncombustible.
      Must be ≥ #12 B&S gage (0.0808") mesh ≤ 1" × 1".
      Where located in a corrosive atmosphere:
        Equivalent noncorrosive screening is required.

2405.4 Framing *(part 1 of 2)*

- The following must be noncombustible in Type I and II construction:
  - ○ Frames for sloped glazing.
  - ○ Frames for skylights.
- In environments with acid fumes that damage metals, the following applies:
  - ○ The following components may be constructed of the materials listed below:
      Components:
        Sash and frames of skylights.
        Sash and frames of sloped glazing.
      Materials:
        Approved pressure-treated wood.
        Other approved noncorrosive material.
- Curbs for skylights are governed as follows:
  - ○ Occupancy R-3 has the following requirements regarding curbs:
      On roofs sloping ≥ 3:12 curbs are not required.
      On roofs sloping < 3:12 curbs are required as follows:
        Skylights must be mounted ≥ 4" above the roof on a curb.
        Curb must be constructed according to one of the following:
          As required for the framing.
          As per manufacturer's instructions.

2405 Sloped Glazing and Skylights

2405.4 Framing *(part 2 of 2)*

      ○ In other locations, the following is required regarding curbs:

         Where the roof slope is < 45° the following applies:

            Curbs ≥ 4" high are required for skylights.

            Curbs must be constructed as required for the framing.

    • Framing supporting skylights and sloped glazing must be designed as follows:

      ○ To resist tributary roof loads assigned by the code.

       Note: Chapter 16, "Structural Design," is cited as the source of tributary roof loads.

> **Case study: Fig. 2405.4.** The roof of the occupancy B building slopes 4:12, thus requiring a 4" curb at skylights. Such a curb is provided as indicated in the illustration. Consequently the skylight is in compliance with code requirements.

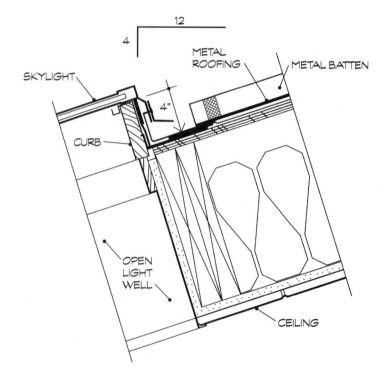

Fig. 2405.4. Detail at skylight. Central Kitchen. Lompoc Unified School District. Lompoc, California. Phillips Metsch Sweeney Moore Architects. Santa Barbara, California.

2406 Safety Glazing

2406.3 Hazardous locations *(part 1 of 3)*

- This section addresses the requirement for safety glazing where glazing is used.
- Safety glazing is not required in nonhazardous locations as noted in the next section.

  Note: 2406.3.1, "Exceptions," lists locations not hazardous for glazing.

- The following locations require safety glazing:
  - Sliding door units as follows:
      Sliding panels.
      Fixed panels.
  - Sliding and bifold closet doors.
  - Storm doors.
  - Unframed swinging doors.
  - In the following elements at the bathing-type locations listed below:
      Elements:
        Doors.
        Enclosures.
        Any building wall serving as an enclosure as follows:
          Where the lowest exposed glazing is < 5' above the standing surface.
      Locations:

      | Hot tubs | Whirlpools | Saunas |
      | Steam rooms | Bathtubs | Showers |

- The following glazing near doors is governed as indicated below:
  - Glazing:
      Fixed or operable.
      Adjacent to a door with both the following characteristics:
        Exposed glazing is ≤ 2' from the door as follows:
          Measured on the shortest line to the nearest edge of the closed door.
        Lowest exposed glazing is < 5' above the walking surface.
  - Requirements:
      The following conditions do not require safety glazing:
        Where the glazing is decorative glass.
        Where there is a wall or barrier as follows:
          Between the door and the glazing.
        Where the door opens to one of the following spaces ≤ 3' deep:
          Closet.
          Storage.

  Note: 2406.3, "Hazardous locations," item 7, is cited as governing this glazing.

  Where the glazing is ⊥ to the closed door where both the following apply:
    In 1- and 2-family dwellings.
    In occupancy R-2.
  Other conditions require safety glazing.

Case study: Fig. 2406.3. Safety glazing is required on either side of the entry doors since it is within 2' of the door. The glazing above the door is not required to be safety glazing as it is above a height of 5'. Safety glazing is required in the swinging doors. Tempered glass is provided in the doors and on each side of the doors, thus, the entry is in compliance with the code.

Fig. 2406.3. Partial elevation at east entry. Hot Springs Police Department New Headquarters. Hot Springs National Park, Arkansas. Cromwell Architects Engineers. Little Rock, Arkansas.

2406 Safety Glazing

2406.3 Hazardous locations *(part 2 of 3)*

- Safety glazing in swinging doors is governed as follows:
  - It is not required in swinging jalousie doors.
  - It is not required where the glazing is decorative glass.
  - It is required in other swinging doors.

    Note: 2406.3.1, "Exceptions," is cited as the source of requirements for jalousies without safety glazing.

- The following glazing is governed as indicated:
  - The following glazing is not required to be safety glazing:
    - That which is protected by a bar as follows:
      - Bar has a vertical dimension ≥ 1½".
      - Bar is able to resist a 50-lb/ft load applied horizontally as follows:
        - Without deflecting to contact the glazing.
      - Bar is located as follows:
        - On the side of glazing to which there is access.
        - ≥ 2'-10" and ≤ 3'-2" above the walking surface.
    - The exterior pane of multiple layers of glazing as follows:
      - Where the lowest exposed glazing is ≥ 25' above the following:
        - Above any of the following surfaces adjacent to the exterior of the glazing:
          - Grade.
          - Roof.
          - Walking surface.
          - Other horizontal or sloped surface.
  - The following glazing is governed elsewhere in this section:
    - That which is required by this section to have safety glazing as follows:
      - Where glazing is < 5' above a standing surface in the following locations:
        - Bathing-type locations.
        - Near doors.
  - Glazing in locations other than those indicated above is governed as follows:
    - Decorative glass is not required to be safety glazing.
    - Otherwise, safety glazing is required where all of the following conditions apply:
      - Exposed surface has all the following characteristics:
        - Area of any pane is > 9 sf.
        - Bottom edge is < 1'-6" above the floor.
        - Top edge is > 3' above the floor.
      - Plane of glazing is ≤ 3' from a walking surface as follows:
        - Measured horizontally.

2406 Safety Glazing

2406.3 Hazardous locations *(part 3 of 3)*

- Safety glazing is required for the following components in the locations listed below:
    - Components:
        The following components with any area or height are included:
        Structural baluster panels.
        Nonstructural in-fill panels.
    - Locations:
        Guards and railings.
- Safety glazing is required in the following locations where the conditions listed apply:
    - Locations:
        Walls and fences as follows:
        Enclosing the following both indoors and outdoors:
        Swimming pools.
        Hot tubs and spas.
    - Conditions:
        Where all of the following conditions apply:
        Bottom edge of glazing is < 5' above the walking surface as follows:
        On the side where water is contained.
        Glazing is ≤ 5' from the edge of the water as follows:
        Measured horizontally.
    - Glazing adjacent to the following elements is governed as indicated below:
        Elements:
        Stairways and ramps.
        Landings.
        Requirements:
        Safety glazing is not required where the following conditions apply:
        The side of the element has the following:
        Guard or handrail as follows:
        With one of the following components:
        Balusters or in-fill panels.
        Located ≥ 1'-6" from the glazing.

    Note: The following are cited as governing the guards and handrails:
    Section 1012, "Guards."
    1607.7, "Loads on handrails, guards, grab bars and vehicle barriers."

    Safety glazing is required where the glazing is located with both of the following:
    Glazing is ≤ 3' from a walking surface as follows:
    Measured horizontally.
    Bottom edge of glazing is < 5' above the adjacent walking surface.
    Safety glazing is required at stairways where it is located with both of the following:
    Glazing is ≤ 5' from the bottom stairway tread as follows:
    Measured horizontally in any direction.
    Bottom edge of glazing is < 5' above the tread nosing.

2406 Safety Glazing

2406.3.1 Exceptions

- The following are not hazardous locations requiring safety glazing:
  - Openings in doors as follows:
    Able to pass a 3" sphere.
  - Decorative glass.

    Note: 2406.3, "Hazardous locations," item 1, 6, or 7 is cited as specifying locations and conditions wherein decorative glass need not be safety glazing.

  - Curved glazing as follows:
    In revolving doors.
  - Glazed doors as follows:
    In commercial refrigeration.
  - Glass block.

    Note: 2101.2.5, "Glass masonry," is cited as governing glass block.

  - Louvered glazing as follows:
    Windows.
    Jalousies.

    Note: 2403.5, "Louvered windows or jalousies," is cited as governing this glazing.

  - The following glazing located as indicated below:
    Glazing:
      Mirrors.
      Other glass panels.
    Location:
      On a surface providing the following:
        Support across the entire back of the glazing.

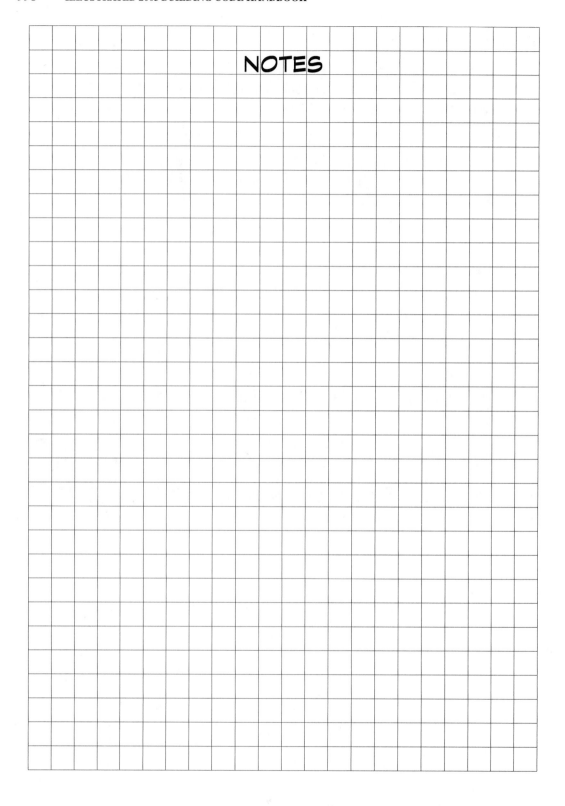

NOTES

25

Gypsum Board and Plaster

Hoyt Street Properties. Portland Oregon. *(partial elevlation)*
Ankrom Moisan Associated Architects. Portland, Oregon.

2502 Definitions

2502.1 Definitions *(part 1 of 2)*

- **Cement plaster**
  - One of the following mixtures:
    - Portland cement, aggregate, other approved materials.
    - Portland cement, hydrated lime, aggregate, other approved materials.
    - Blended cement, aggregate, or other approved materials.
    - Blended cement, hydrated lime, aggregate, other approved materials.
    - Masonry cement, aggregate, other approved materials.
    - Plastic cement, aggregate, other approved materials.
  - Other approved materials are as specified in the code.

- **Exterior surfaces**
  - Surfaces exposed to the weather.

- **Gypsum board**
  - Any of the following:
    - Gypsum wallboard.
    - Gypsum sheathing.
    - Gypsum veneer plaster base.
    - Exterior gypsum soffit board.
    - Predecorated gypsum board.
    - Water-resistant gypsum backing board.

  Note: The following are cited as listing standards governing gypsum board:
  > *IBC Table 2506.2, "Gypsum Board Materials and Accessories."*
  > *IBC Table 2507.2, "Lath, Plastering Materials and Accessories."*
  > *Chapter 35, "Referenced Standards."*

- **Gypsum plaster**
  - Any of the following:
    - Calcined gypsum.
    - A mixture of the following:
      - Calcined gypsum.
      - Lime.
      - Aggregate.
    - Other approved materials.

- **Gypsum veneer plaster**
  - Gypsum plaster as follows:
    - Applied to an approved base.
    - Applied in 1 or more layers.
    - Usually ≤ ¼" thick.

- **Interior surfaces**
  - Surfaces not exposed to the weather.

2502 Definitions

2502.1 Definitions *(part 2 of 2)*

- **Weather-exposed surfaces**
  - The following surfaces are not included:
    Ceilings and roof soffit surfaces as follows:
      Enclosed by the following components that extend ≥ 12" below such surfaces:
        Walls.
        Fascia.
        Bulkheads.
        Beams.
    Walls or parts of walls under a roof as follows:
      In an area that is not enclosed.
      Set back from the roof edge as follows:
        A distance ≥ 2 × the height of the open space under the roof edge.
    Parts of ceilings and roof soffits located as follows:
      A horizontal distance ≥ 10' from the outer edges of the following:
        The ceiling or roof soffit.
  - Otherwise, the following surfaces where exposed to the weather are included:
    Walls.
    Ceilings.
    Floors.
    Roofs.
    Soffits.
    Similar surfaces.

- **Wire backing**
  - Horizontal strands of wire as follows:
    Attached to surfaces of vertical supports.
    Wire is taut.
    Covered with building paper.
    Serves as a backing for cement plaster.

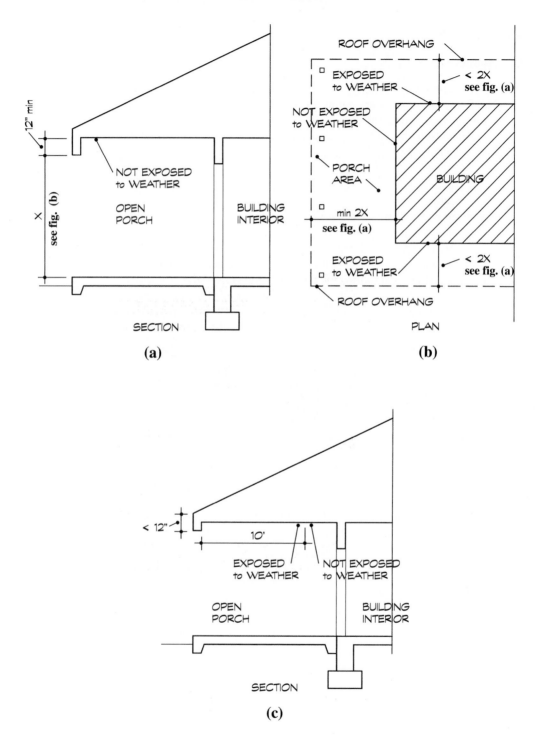

Fig. 2502.1. Conditions of exposure conditions for ceilings, soffits, and walls.

2504 Vertical and Horizontal Assemblies

2504.1.1 Wood framing

- The wood supports for the following be ≥ 2" in any dimension:
  - Lath.
  - Gypsum board.
- Wood stripping or furring is governed as follows:
  - Where applied to solid backing the following size is required:
    ≥ 1"× 2".
  - Otherwise, the following size is required:
    ≥ 2" in any dimension.

2504.1.2 Studless partitions

- The required thicknesses of the following vertical studless partitions are ≥ 2":
  - Solid plaster on the following:
    ³/₈" rib metal lath.
    ¾" rib metal lath.
    ½" long-length gypsum lath.
  - Gypsum board partitions.

2508 Gypsum Construction

2508.2 Limitations

- The following materials may not be exposed directly to the weather:
  - Gypsum wallboard.
  - Gypsum plaster.
- Gypsum wallboard may not be used in the following locations:
  - With direct exposure to water.
  - With exposure to continuous high humidity.
- Gypsum sheathing may be installed in the following location:
  - On exterior surfaces.

  Note: ASTM C 1280, "Specification for Application of Gypsum Sheathing," is cited as governing gypsum sheathing.

2508.2.1 Weather protection

- Weather protection must be provided prior to the installation of the following:
  - Gypsum wallboard.
  - Gypsum lath.
  - Gypsum plaster.

2508.3 Single-ply application

- The following parts of gypsum board must fall on framing members:
  - Edges ‖ to framing members.
  - Ends ‖ to framing members.
- The following parts of gypsum board are governed as indicated below:
  - Parts:
    Edges.
    Ends.
  - Requirements:
    They need not touch adjacent panels in the following case:
    In concealed spaces as follows:
    Where there is no requirement for the following:
    Fire-resistance-rated construction.
    Shear resistance.
    Diaphragm resistance.
    In other locations they must be in contact with adjacent panels.

2508 Gypsum Construction

2508.3.1 Floating angles

- Where the following conditions apply, the fastening of gypsum board is governed as indicated below:
  - Conditions:
    The assembly is not intended to resist shear.
    The assembly does not require a fire-resistance rating.
  - Requirements:
    Fasteners are not required at the following locations:
      Top plates of walls.
      Bottom plates of walls.
    Fasteners are not required at the perimeters of the following:
      Ceilings.
      Soffits.
- Fastener heads may not break the following:
  - The face paper on the gypsum board.

2508.4 Joint treatment

- This section addresses the following details in fire-resistance-rated assemblies:
  - Joints between gypsum board panels.
  - Fasteners in gypsum board panels.
- The details need not be finished so as to seal them in any of the following cases:
  - Where the details will have a decorative finish such as follows that would seal them:
    Wood paneling.
    Battens.
    Acoustical finishes.
    Similar applications.
  - In one-layer assemblies as follows:
    Where joints fall on wood framing.
  - Where any of the following gypsum board products are used:
    Square edge.
    Tongue-and-groove (V-edge).
    Backing board.
    Sheathing.
  - In multiple-layer assemblies as follows:
    Where joints of adjacent layers are offset.
  - In assemblies which were tested for fire resistance as follows:
    Without the details being sealed.
- In other cases the details must be finished so as to seal them.

2508 Gypsum Construction

2508.5 Horizontal gypsum board diaphragm ceilings

- A horizontal diaphragm ceiling may be created by the following:
  - Gypsum board applied wood joists.

    Note: IBC Table 2508.5, "Shear Capacity for Horizontal Wood Framed Gypsum Board Diaphragm Ceiling Assemblies," is cited as governing these diaphragms.

2508.5.1 Diaphragm proportions

- Horizontal diaphragm ceilings must have the following proportions:
  - ≤ 1½:1 as defined at its edges by shear walls.
- The following conditions are not allowed for the diaphragm:
  - Rotation or cantilevers.

2508.5.2. Installation

- Installation of horizontal diaphragm ceilings is governed as follows:
  - Gypsum board must be applied ⊥ to the joists.
  - Joints between the ends of gypsum board panels have the following requirement:
    Adjacent courses must have end joints on different joists.

2508.5.3 Blocking of perimeter edges

- Blocking of horizontal diaphragm ceilings are governed as follows:
  - The perimeter of the gypsum board ceiling must be blocked as follows:
    With wood ≥ 2"× 6" as follows:
    Installed with the wider dimension horizontal in the following location:
    Over the wall top plate as follows:
    To provide a nailing surface for the gypsum board ≥ 2" wide.

2508.5.4 Fasteners

- Fasteners in horizontal diaphragm ceilings have the following requirements:
  - Gypsum board must be secured in the following manner:
    Fasteners must be spaced ≤ 7" oc as follows:
    At all supports and perimeter blocking.
    Fasteners must be located ≤ ³⁄₈" from the following:
    Edge of the gypsum board as applicable.
    End of the gypsum board as applicable.

    Note: IBC Table 2508.5, "Shear Capacity for Horizontal Wood Framed Gypsum Board Diaphragm Ceiling Assemblies," is cited as governing the fasteners.

2508.5.5 Lateral force restrictions

- A gypsum board diaphragm may not be used to resist forces from the following:
  - Masonry or concrete construction.

2509 Gypsum Board in Showers and Water Closets

2509.2 Base for tile

- This section addresses the base required under tile and or panels.
- Water-resistant gypsum backing board is required as a substrate in the following case:
  - Where gypsum board is used as a base in the following locations:
    Bathtub areas.
    Shower compartment walls.
    Water closet compartment walls.
  - At other walls and ceilings, the following applies:
    Regular gypsum board may be used as a base.

    Note: The following are cited as governing regular gypsum board used as a base:
    GA-216, "Application and Finishing of Gypsum Board."
    ASTM C 840, "Specification for Application and Finishing of Gypsum Board."

2509.3 Limitations

- This section addresses water-resistant gypsum backing board.
- Such boards may not be used as follows:
  - Over a vapor retarder in the following areas:
    Bathtub compartments.
    Shower compartments.
  - In any of the following areas:
    Those directly exposed to water.
    Those exposed to continuous high humidity.
- Such boards ½" thick may not be used as follows:
  - On ceilings where supports are > 12" on center.
- Such boards ⅝" thick may not be used as follows:
  - On ceilings where supports are 16" on center.

2510 Lathing and Furring for Cement Plaster (Stucco)

2510.5.1 Support of lath

- Solid backing is required for lath and attachments as follows:
  - Where lath on a vertical surface extends between the following:
    Rafters or similar projections.

2510.5.2.1 Use of gypsum board as a backing board

- Use of the following materials as backing board is governed as indicated below:
  - Materials:
    Gypsum lath or wallboard.
  - Requirements:
    Such materials may be used as a backing for cement plaster as follows:
    Where the following materials are used in the locations indicated below:
    Materials:
    Weather-resistant barrier between lath and sheathing.
    One of the following types of lath:
    Self-furred metal lath.
    Self-furred wire fabric lath.
    Locations:
    On horizontal supports of ceilings or roof soffits.
    On interior walls.
    Such materials may not be used as backing for cement plaster in other cases.

2510.5.2.2 Use of gypsum sheathing backing

- Gypsum sheathing may be used as a backing for cement plaster where the following are used:
  - Weather-resistant barrier between lath and sheathing.
  - Metal or wire fabric lath.

    Note: 2510.6, "Weather-resistant barriers," is cited as governing such barriers.

2510.5.3 Backing not required

- Wire backing is not required behind the following:
  - Expanded metal lath.
  - Paperbacked wire fabric lath.

2510.6 Weather-resistant barriers

- Where such barriers are installed over wood-based sheathing, the following applies:
  - A weather-resistive vapor permeable barrier as follows must be included:
    Performance to be ≥ 2 layers of Grade D paper.
  - Weather-resistant barriers are to be installed as specified elsewhere in the code.

    Note: 1404.2, "Weather-resistive barrier," is cited as governing such barriers.

2511 Interior Plaster

2511.2 Limitations

- Plaster may not be applied directly to the following:
  - Fiber insulation board.
- Cement plaster applied to the following materials is governed as indicated below:
  - Materials:
    - Gypsum lath.
    - Gypsum plaster.
  - Requirements:
    - Such materials must be protected by a water-resistive barrier.
    - Direct application to such materials is not permitted.

  Note: The following are cited as sources of applicable requirements, a partial summary of which is provided above:
  2510.5.1, "Support of lath."
  2510.5.2, "Use of gypsum backing board."

2511.3 Grounds

- Where used, grounds must establish the required thickness for plaster.
- Plaster thickness is measured from the following:
  - Face of lath.
  - Face of other bases as applicable.

  Note: The following are cited as governing the required thickness of plaster:
  ASTM C 842, "Specification for Application of Interior Gypsum Plaster."
  ASTM C 926, "Specification for Application of Portland Cement Based Plaster."

2511.5 Wet areas

- Showers and public toilets require the following wall surfaces:
  - Smooth.
  - Nonabsorbent.

  Note: The following are cited as sources of applicable requirements, a partial summary of which is provided above:
  1210.2, "Walls."
  1210.3, "Showers."

- Wood framing must be protected with an approved moisture barrier as follows:
  - Where the interior of walls and partitions have all of the following characteristics:
    - Covered with one of the following materials:
      - Cement plaster.
      - Tile of similar material.
    - Subject to splashed water.

2512 Exterior Plaster

2512.1 General

- Cement plaster is required to be applied as follows:
  - In ≥ 3 coats as follows:
    - Where applied over any of the following:
      - Metal lath.
      - Wire fabric lath.
  - In ≥ 2 coats as follows:
    - Where applied over any of the following:
      - Masonry.
      - Concrete.
      - Gypsym board.
    - Where both the following conditions exist:
      - The plaster is of adequate thickness.
      - Where the plaster is covered by any of the following:
        - A veneer.
        - Other facing material.
        - A second wall.

    Note: 2510.5, "Backing," is cited as governing the backing for cement plaster.
    ASTM C 926, "Specification for Application of Portland Cement Based Plaster,"
    is cited as reporting the thickness of the plaster, which is adequate for the purpose
    noted above.

2512.1.1 On-grade floor slab

- On the following assemblies, exterior plaster is governed as indicated below:
  - Assemblies:
    - Wood framing on a concrete slab-on-grade.
    - Steel framing on a concrete slab-on-grade.
  - Requirements:
    - The plaster must cover the lath and paper.
    - The plaster may not extend below the lath and paper.
  - The installation of the following components must also comply with standards other than the code:
    - Lath.
    - Paper.
    - Flashing.
    - Drip screeds.

    Note: ASTM C 1063, "Specification for Installation of Lathing and Furring to Receive
    Interior and Exterior Portland Cement Based Plaster," is cited as governing the
    components listed above.

2512 Exterior Plaster

2512.1.2 Weep screeds

- Weep screeds are required for exterior cement plaster as follows:
  - Screeds must drain trapped water to the exterior.
  - Screed requirements are shown on the detail below.

  Note: ASTM C 926, "Specification for Application of Portland Cement Based Plaster," is cited as governing weep screeds.

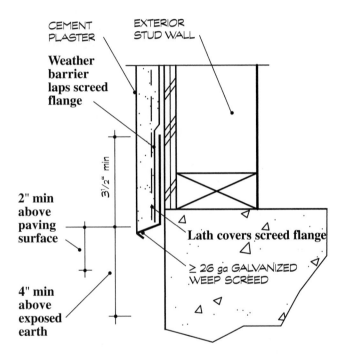

Fig. 2512.1.2. Cement plaster weep screed requirements.

2512 Exterior Plaster

2512.2 Plasticity agents

- The following substances may not be added to the stucco mixtures indicated below:
  - Substances:
    Lime.
    Plasticizers.
  - Mixtures:
    With plastic cement.
    With masonry cement.
- In other cases plasticity agents may be added to stucco mixtures as follows:
  - Where approved.
  - In quantities that are approved.
- The following plasticizers may be added to the stucco mixtures indicated below:
  - Plasticizers:
    Hydrated lime.
    Lime putty.
  - Mixtures:
    Cement plaster.
    Cement lime plaster.

  Note: ASTM C926, "Specification for Application of Portland Cement Based Plaster," is cited as governing the amounts of the plasticizers that may be added.

2512.3 Limitations

- Gypsum plaster is not permitted as follows:
  - In exterior applications.

2512.5 Second-coat application

- The second coat of exterior cement plaster is governed as follows:
  - It must be applied to the required thickness.
  - It must be rodded and floated to a roughness as follows:
    Adequate for bonding with the finish coat.
    Roughness is limited to $1/4$" variation under a 5' straight edge in any direction.

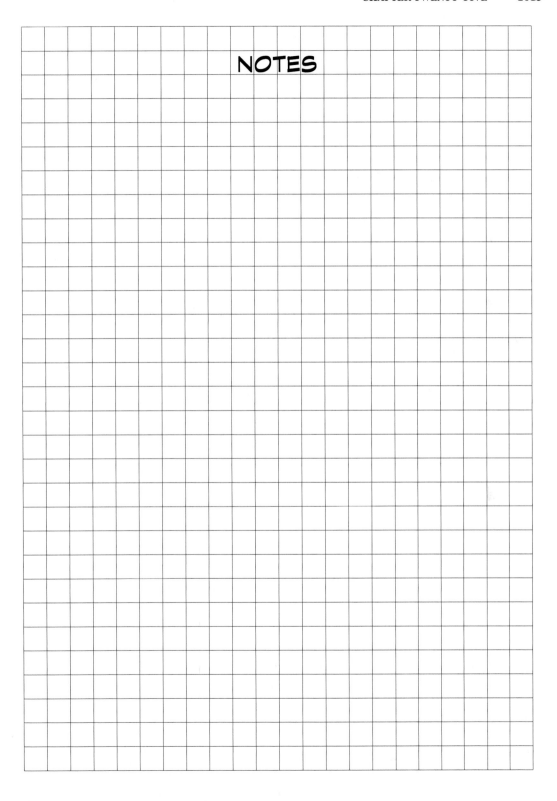

NOTES

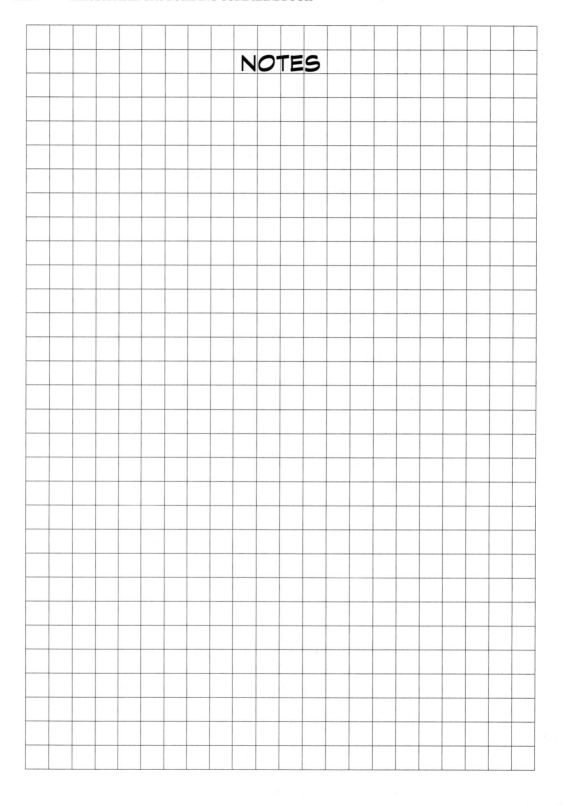

NOTES

26

Plastic

Alterations to 209 Main Street. Annapolis, Maryland.
Alt Breeding Schwarz, Architects, LLC. Annapolis, Maryland.

2603 Foam Plastic Insulation

2603.4 Thermal barrier

- Foam plastic insulation need not be separated from the interior of a building where specifically permitted by the code.

  Note: The following are cited as sources of conditions wherein such insulation need not be separated from the interior:
  2603.4.1, "Thermal barrier not required."
  2603.8, "Special approval."

- Otherwise, foam plastic insulation must be separated from the interior of a building as follows:
  - By the following thermal barrier:
    - Barrier must limit temperature rise as follows:
      - Average temperature rise on the unexposed surface is limited by the following:
        - $\leq 250°F$ after 15 minutes of fire exposure.
    - Barrier must remain in place for ≥ 15 minutes of fire exposure.
  - Other requirements are shown in the detail provided.

  Note: ASTM E 119, "Test Methods for Fire Tests of Building Construction and Materials," is cited as governing temperature rise as indicated above.
  Section 717, "Concealed Spaces," is cited as governing such spaces.
  The following are cited as governing a barrier's performance in a fire:
  FM 4880, "American National Standard for Evaluating Insulated Wall or Wall and Roof/Ceiling Assemblies, Plastic Interior Finish Materials, Plastic Exterior Building Panels, Wall/Ceiling Coating Systems, Interior and Exterior Finish Systems."
  UL 1040, "Fire Test of Insulated Wall Construction."
  UL 1715, "Fire Test of Interior Finish Material."
  NFPA 286, "Standard Method of Fire Test for Evaluating Contribution of Wall and Ceiling Interior Finish to Room Fire Growth."

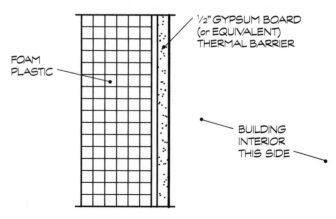

Fig. 2603.4. Thermal barrier.

2603 Foam Plastic Insulation

2603.4.1.1 Masonry or concrete construction

- This section addresses thermal barriers between foam plastic insulation and building interiors.
- Such a thermal barrier is not required in the following walls where conditions indicated below apply:
  - Walls:
    Concrete.
    Masonry.
  - Conditions:
    Where the insulation is covered on both sides by ≥ 1" of one of the the following materials:
    Concrete.
    Masonry.

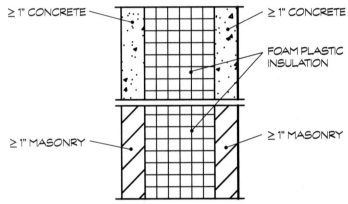

Fig. 2603.4.1.1. Alternative to thermal barrier.

2603.4.1.2 Cooler and freezer walls

- This section addresses thermal barriers between foam plastic insulation and building interiors.
- Such a thermal barrier is not required in walls of cooler and freezer walls where all of the following conditions apply:
  - The foam plastic insulation is tested in a thickness ≥ 4" to have the following properties:
    Flame spread index ≤ 25.
    Smoke-developed index ≤ 450.
  - The foam plastic insulation has the following temperature thresholds:
    Flash ignition temperature is ≥ 600°F.
    Self-ignition temperature is ≥ 800°F.
  - Cooler or freezer is sprinklered.
  - Where located in a building:
    The portion of the building containing the cooler or freezer is sprinklered.
  - Other requirements are shown on the following illustration.

2603 Foam Plastic Insulation

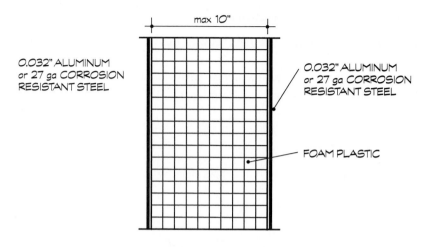

Fig. 2603.4.1.2. Alternative to thermal barriers in cooler and freezer walls.

2603.4.1.3 Walk-in coolers

- This section addresses thermal barriers between foam plastic insulation and building interiors.
- Where buildings are not sprinklered, the following applies to walk-in coolers and freezers:
  - A thermal barrier is not required where all of the following conditions are present:
    The sum of cooler and/or freezer floor areas is ≤ 400 sf.
    The foam plastic flame spread is ≤ 75.
    The foam plastic conforms to requirements shown in the detail provided.
  - Thicker foam plastic is permitted where meeting requirements shown in the following detail.

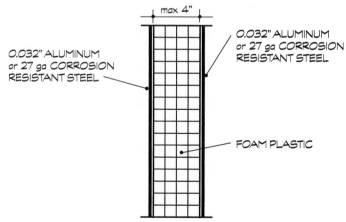

Fig. 2603.4.1.3. Alternative to thermal barrier in walk-in coolers.

2603 Foam Plastic Insulation

2603.4.1.4 Exterior walls — one-story buildings

- This section addresses thermal barriers between foam plastic insulation and building interiors.
- Such barriers are not required where all of the following conditions apply:
  - The foam plastic has the following properties:
    Flame spread index is ≤ 25.
    Smoke-developed index is ≤ 450.
  - Building is sprinklered as per NFPA 13.
  - Other requirements are met as shown in the following detail.

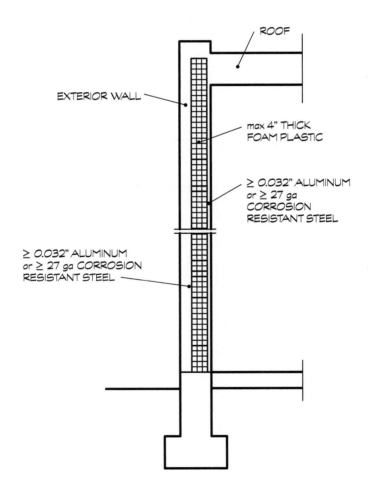

Fig. 2603.4.1.4. Alternative to a thermal barrier in exterior walls of 1-story buildings.

2603 Foam Plastic Insulation

2603.4.1.5 Roofing

- This subsection addresses thermal barriers between foam plastic insulation and building interiors.
- Such a barrier is not required where foam plastic insulation is used as follows:
  - Where the plastic is part of a roof assembly meeting all of the following conditions:
    Assembly is one of the following:
      Class A.
      Class B.
      Class C.
    The assembly with the plastic insulation passes required tests.

  Note: The following tests are cited as alternative standards of which the assembly indicated above must pass one:
      FM 4450, "Approved Standard for Class 1 Insulated Steel Deck Roofs."
      UL 1256, "Fire Test of Roof Deck Construction."

- The insulation does not require a thermal barrier for conditions shown in the following detail.

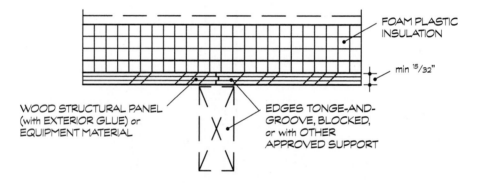

Fig. 2603.4.1.5. Roof sheathing not requiring a thermal barrier.

2603.4.1.6 Attics and crawl spaces

- This section addresses thermal barriers between foam plastic insulation and building interiors.
- Such a barrier is not required in the following spaces for conditions indicated below:
  - Spaces:
    The following locations where accessed only for utility service:
      Attics.
      Crawl spaces.
  - Conditions:
    Foam insulation is protected against ignition as shown in the details provided.

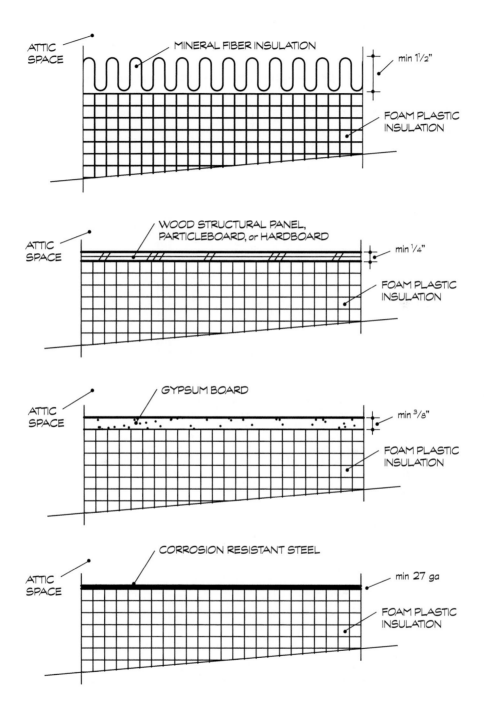

Fig. 2603.4.1.6. Alternatives to a thermal barrier at attics and crawl spaces. Orientation varies for crawl spaces and some attics.

2603 Foam Plastic Insulation

2603.4.1.7 Doors not required to have a fire protection rating

- This section addresses thermal barriers between foam plastic insulation and building interiors.
- Such a barrier is not required in doors with the following insulation and as shown in the detail below:
  - Foam plastic insulation must have the following properties:
    Flame spread index ≤ 75.
    Smoke-developed index ≤ 450.

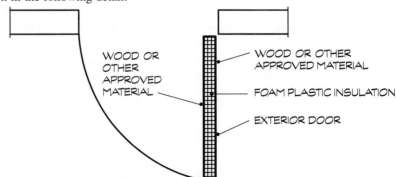

Fig. 2603.4.1.7. Door facing material where no fire protection rating is required.

2603.4.1.8 Exterior doors in buildings of Group R-2 or R-3

- This section addresses thermal barriers between foam plastic insulation and building interiors.
- Such barriers are not required in doors filled with foam insulation as follows:
  - Entrance doors as follows:
    In the following occupancies:
      R-2, R-3.
    To individual dwelling units.
    That do not require a fire-resistance rating.
    As shown in the following detail.

Fig. 2603.4.1.8. Exterior door facing at R-2 and R-3 where no fire-resistance rating is required.

2603 Foam Plastic Insulation

2603.4.1.9 Garage doors

- This section addresses thermal barriers between foam plastic insulation and building interiors.
- Such barriers are not required in garage doors filled with foam insulation where all of the following conditions are met:
  ○ Insulation has the following properties:
      Flame spread index is ≤ 75.
      Smoke developed index is ≤ 450.
  ○ Garage serves 1- or 2-family dwelling.
  ○ Garage may be either of the following:
      Attached.
      Detached.

  Note: 2603.3, "Surface-burning characteristics," is cited as governing foam insulation, a partial summary of which is provided above.

- A thermal barrier is not required for the following garage doors filled with foam insulation:
  ○ Garage doors that do not require a fire-resistance rating as follows:
      With facing materials shown in the detail provided.
      Other facing materials must meet required standards.

  Note: DASMA 107, "Room Fire Test Standard for Garage Doors Using Foam Plastic Insulation," is cited as the standard that other facings must meet.

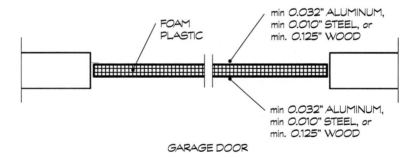

Fig. 2603.4.1.9. Garage door with foam insulation.

2603 Foam Plastic Insulation

2603.4.1.10 Siding backer board

- This section addresses thermal barriers between foam plastic insulation and building interiors.
- Such a barrier is not required for foam plastic insulation with all of the following characteristics:
  - Insulation of ≤ 2000 Btu/sf.
  - Used as a backing for siding.
  - Meeting conditions shown in the detail provided.

  Note: NFPA 259, "Test Method for Potential Heat of Building Materials," is cited as the test for determining Btu/sf.

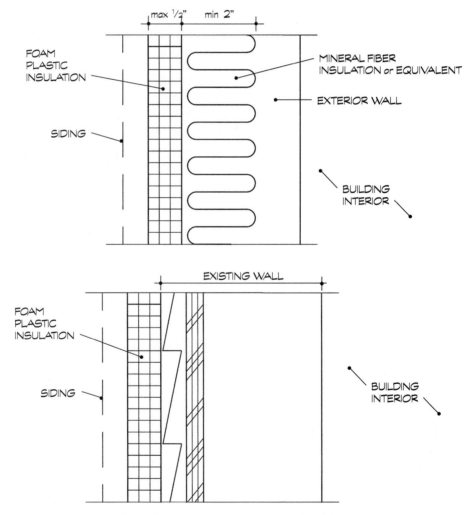

Fig. 2603.4.1.10. Permitted uses of foam plastic insulation as a backing for siding.

<u>2604 Interior Finish and Trim</u>

2604.2.2 Thickness

- Size limitations of interior trim of foam plastic are shown on the illustration provided.

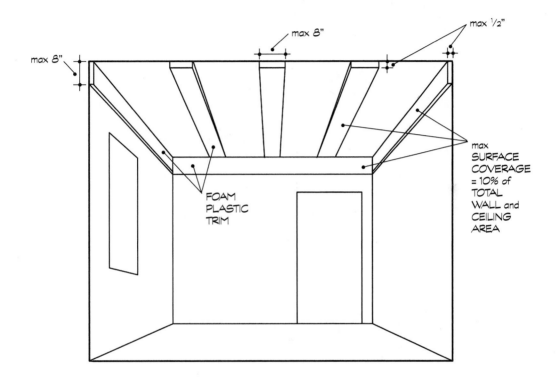

Fig. 2604.2.2. Foam plastic as interior trim.

2604.2.3 Area limitation

- Limitations of surface coverage for trim of foam plastic are shown in Fig. 2604.2.2.

2605 Plastic Veneer

2605.2 Exterior use

- Plastic veneer on building exteriors must meet the following requirements:
  - Physical aspects are governed as follows:
    - In Type VB construction:
      - The following are not limited where the walls do not have a fire-resistance rating:
        - Area of plastic panel.
        - Minimum separation distance between panels.
        - Smoke-density.
    - Otherwise, plastic must meet the requirements shown in the illustration below.

Note: 2606.4, "Specifications," is cited as governing exterior plastic veneer.

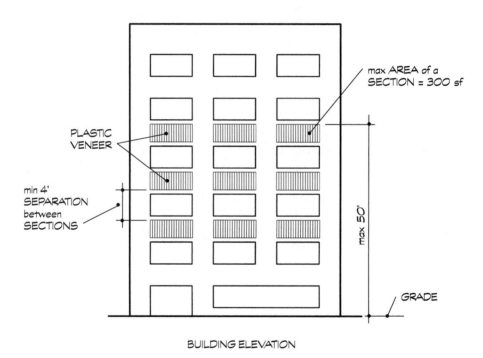

BUILDING ELEVATION

Fig. 2605.2. Building façade with plastic panels applied.

2606 Light-Transmitting Plastics

2606.7.1 Support

- Light-transmitting plastic diffusers must be supported from overhead construction as follows:
  - By hangers as shown in the following detail.

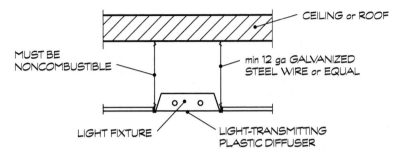

Fig. 2606.7.1. Supports for right-transmitting plastic diffusers.

2606.7.3 Size limitations

- Individual panels of light-transmitting plastics are limited in size as follows:
  - Length must be ≤ 10'.
  - Area must be ≤ 30 sf.
- A partial list of dimensions meeting size limitations is provided below:

Table 2606.7.3   Maximum Sizes of Light-Transmitting Plastic Panels

Width	Length	Width	Length	Width	Length
3'-0"	10'-0"	3'-10"	7'-9"	4'-8"	6'-5"
3'-1"	9'-8"	3'-11"	7'-7"	4'-9"	6'-3"
3'-2"	9'-5"	4'-0"	7'-6"	4'-10"	6'-2"
3'-3"	9'-2"	4'-1"	7'-4"	4'-11"	6'-1"
3'-4"	9'-0"	4'-2"	7'-2"	5'-0"	6'-0"
3'-5"	8'-9"	4'-3"	7'-0"	5'-1"	5'-10"
3'-6"	8'-6"	4'-4"	6'-11"	5'-2"	5'-9"
3'-7"	8'-4"	4'-5"	6'-9"	5'-3"	5'-8"
3'-8"	8'-2"	4'-6"	6'-8"	5'-4"	5'-7"
3'-9"	8'-0"	4'-7"	6'-6"	5'-5"	5'-6"

2606 Light-Transmitting Plastics

2606.7.5 Electrical lighting fixtures

- Light-transmitting plastic diffusers in light fixtures located in the following areas are governed as indicated below:
  - Areas:
    Required exits.
    Required corridors.
  - Requirements:
    Where the building is not sprinklered as per NFPA 13:
    Area of plastic must be ≤ 30% of the ceiling area as follows:
    A partial list of minimum on-center spacing of various fixtures is provided below. Details showing common layouts that meet minimums are provided on the following pages.

  Note: The following are cited, one of which must govern the plastic panels above:
  Chapter 8, "Interior Finishes."
  2606.7.2, "Installation," which governs service temperatures.

Table 2606.7.5   Minimum Center-to-Center Spacing of Plastic Diffusers in Ceilings of Exits and Corridors

	Width of ceiling					
Diffuser size	3'	4'	5'	6'	7'	8'
1' × 4'	4'-5"	3'-4"	2'-8"	2'-3"	1'-11"	1'-8"
1' × 8'	8'-11"	6'-8"	5'-4"	4'-5"	3'-10"	3'-4"
2' × 2'	4'-5"	3'-4"	2'-8"	2'-3"	1'-11"	1'-8"
2' × 4'	8'-11"	6'-8"	5'-4"	4'-5"	3'-10"	3'-4"
2' × 8'	17'-9"	13'-4"	10'-8"	8'-11"	7'-7"	6'-8"
4' × 4'	17'-9"	13'-4"	10'-8"	8'-11"	7'-7"	6'-8"

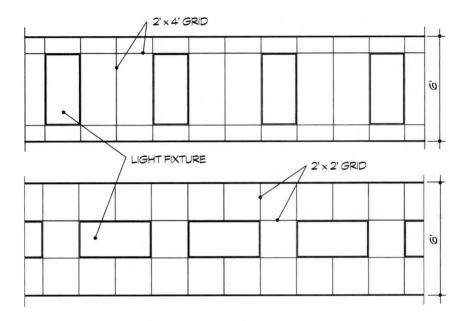

Fig. 2606.7.5A. Reflected ceiling plans with 22% fixture coverage.

Case study:

Fig. 2606.7.5A. Plastic diffusers at the ceiling light fixtures are limited to 30% of the ceiling area. The corridor shown in this school is 8' wide. This means that the difussers cannot be closer than 3'- 4" as indicated in the handbook Table 2606.7.5. Since the actual spacing of the fixtures is 12' oc, they comply with the code requirement. The actual ceiling coverage of the fixtures is < 9%.

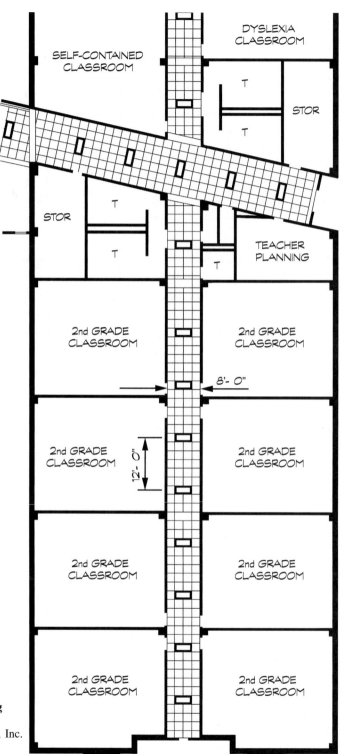

Fig. 2606.7.5B. Partial reflected ceiling plan. New Jasper Pre-K–2nd Grade School. Jasper, Texas. PBK Architects, Inc. Houston, Texas.

2606 Light-Transmitting Plastics

2606.12 Solar collectors

- This section addresses light-transmitting plastics as covers on solar collectors.
- Such plastic covers are limited in area as follows:
  - Where thickness is ≤ 0.010":
    The total area of any type plastic must be ≤ ¹/₃ the roof area.
  - Where thickness is > 0.010":
    The total area of type CC1 plastics as follows must be ≤ ¹/₃ the roof area:
      Such as polycarbonate.
    The total area of type CC2 plastics as follows must be ≤ ¼ the roof area:
      Such as acrylic.
- Other requirements are shown on the illustration provided.

  Note: 2606.4, "Specifications," lists the properties and standards for CC1 and CC2 plastics, which are based on burning characteristics.

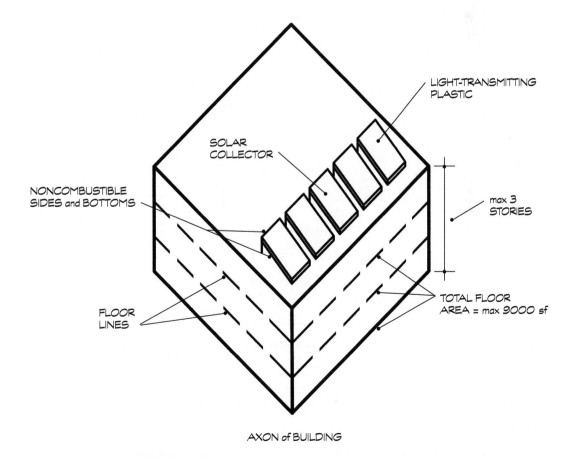

LIGHT-TRANSMITTING PLASTIC

SOLAR COLLECTOR

NONCOMBUSTIBLE SIDES and BOTTOMS

max 3 STORIES

FLOOR LINES

TOTAL FLOOR AREA = max 9000 sf

AXON of BUILDING

Fig. 2606.12. Building limits for roof-top solar collectors with light-transmitting plastic covers.

2607 Light-Transmitting Plastic Wall Panels

2607.3 Height limitation

- This section addresses light-transmitting plastic panels on exterior building walls.
- The height of such panels is not limited where all of the following apply:
  - Where building is sprinklered as per NFPA 13.
  - Where panel size is limited according to the following:
    Fire separation distance.
    Class of plastic.

  Note: 2607.5, "Automatic sprinkler system," is cited as the source of requirements necessary for panels to have unlimited height as indicated above.

- Height requirement of other exterior wall panels is shown on the illustration provided.

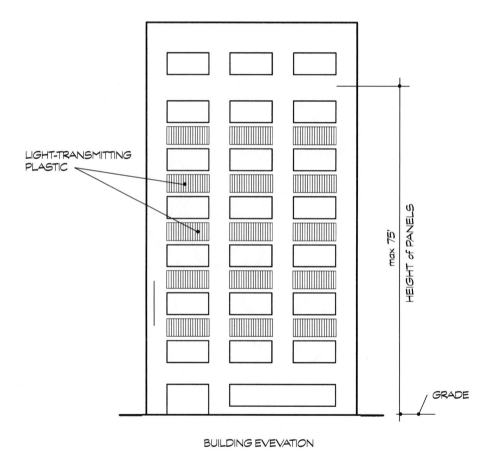

BUILDING EVEVATION

Fig. 2607.3. Maximum height for light-transmitting plastic on a building façade.

2607 Light-Transmitting Plastic Wall Panels

2607.4 Area limitation and separation

- This section addresses light-transmitting plastic panels on exterior building walls.
- This section does not apply to plastic veneers used as exterior siding in Type V construction.

  Note: Section 1406, "Combustible Materials on the Exterior Side of Exterior Walls," is cited as the source of requirements for the plastic siding as indicated above.

- This section does not apply to plastic wall panels in greenhouses.

  Note: 704.8, "Allowable area of openings," is cited as the source of requirements for unprotected openings, which governs greenhouses.

- The following are shown on the illustrations provided with this section:
  - Maximum area of an individual plastic panel on a building façade.
  - Minimum vertical and horizontal distances between panels as follows:
      Separation may be provided by either of the following:
      Distances shown in the illustrations provided with this section.
      A flame barrier as shown in the illustration provided with this section.
- The maximum % of wall area in any story that a plastic panel may cover is the smaller of the following:
  - The maximum % of unprotected openings permitted by the code.
  - The maximum % shown in the illustrations provided with this section.

  Note: 704.8, "Allowable area of openings," is cited as the source listing the maximum % of unprotected openings permitted in a building façade.

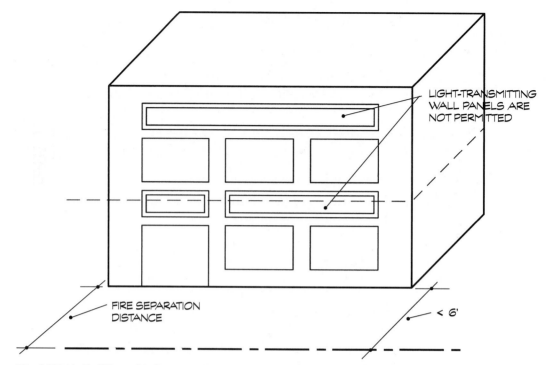

Fig. 2607.4A. Building with fire separation distance < 6'.

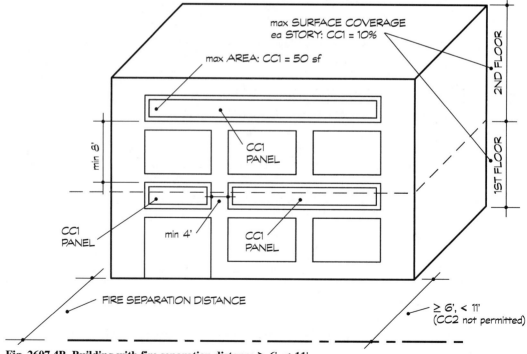

Fig. 2607.4B. Building with fire separation distance ≥ 6', < 11'.

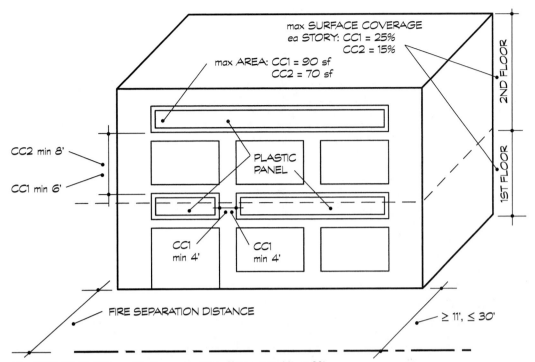

Fig. 2607.4C. Building with fire separation distance ≥ 11', ≤ 30'.

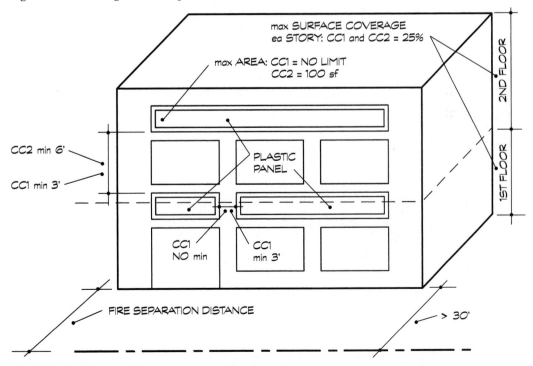

Fig. 2607.4D. Building with fire separation distance > 30'.

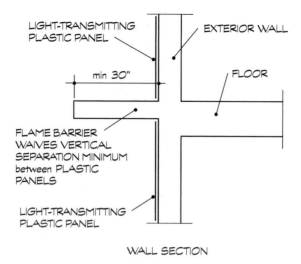

Fig. 2607.4E. Flame barrier at exterior wall.

Case study: Fig. 2607.4F. The CC1 light-transmitting plastic wall panels located above the lower roof are in a wall of high 1st-floor space. Neither the distance between panels nor the area of the panels is governed for this type plastic, as indicated by IBC Table 2607.4. The panel coverage is < 50% of the exterior wall area (which continues beyond the elevation shown), thus, meeting this code limitation.

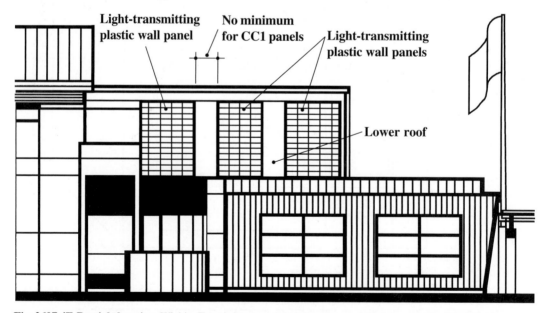

Fig. 2607.4F. Partial elevation. Wichita Transit Storage, Administration, and Maintenance Facility. Wichita, Kansas. Wilson Darnell Mann, P.A., Architects. Wichita, Kansas.

2607 Light-Transmitting Plastic Wall Panels

2607.5 Automatic sprinkler system

- This section addresses light-transmitting plastic panels on exterior building walls.
- The maximum % of wall area in any story that a plastic panel may cover is the smaller of the following:
  - The maximum % of unprotected openings permitted by the code.
  - The maximum % shown in the illustrations provided with this section.
  - 50%.

    Note: 704.8, "Allowable area of openings," is cited as the source listing the maximum % of unprotected openings permitted in a building façade.

  - There are no height limitations to the plastic panels meeting the above requirements.

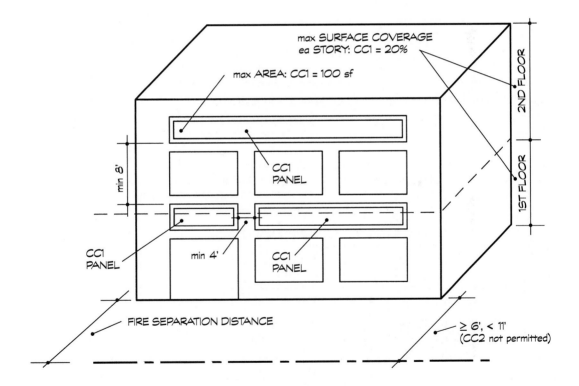

Fig. 2607.5A. Building with fire separation distance ≥ 6', < 11'; building sprinklered.

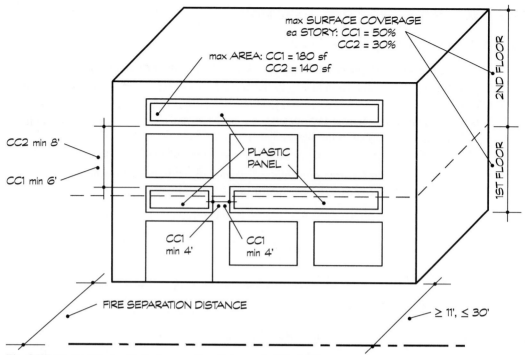

Fig. 2607.5B. Building with fire separation distance ≥ 11', ≤ 30'.

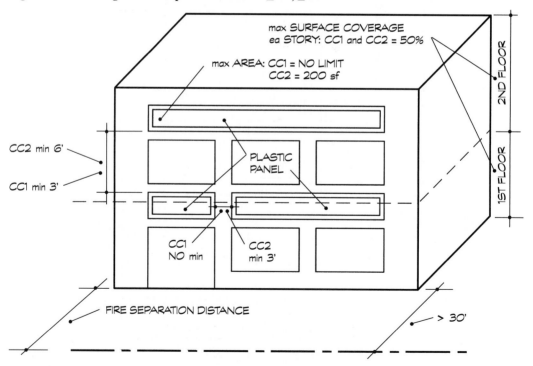

Fig. 2607.5C. Building with fire separation distance > 30'; building sprinklered.

2608 Light-Transmitting Plastic Glazing

2608.2 Buildings of other types of construction

- This section addresses light-transmitting plastic glazing in buildings other than Type VB construction.
- Where openings in exterior walls are not required to be protected, the following applies:
  - Requirements for light-transmitting plastic glazing are shown on the illustrations provided with this section as follows:
    Required vertical separation may be provided by either of the following:
    Distances shown in the illustrations provided with this section.
    A flame barrier as shown in the illustrations provided with this section.

> *Note: Section 704, "Exterior Walls," is cited as the source specifying conditions wherein exterior walls must be protected.*
> *Section 2606, "Light-Transmitting Plastics," is cited as governing the light-transmitting glazing noted above.*
> *903.3.1.1, "NFPA 13 sprinkler systems," is cited as governing the sprinklers required for reduced restrictions for plastic glazing.*

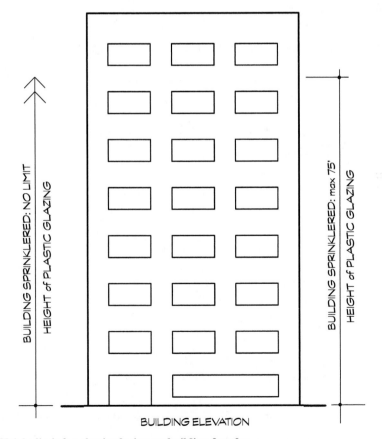

Fig. 2608.2A. Height limit for plastic glazing on building façades.

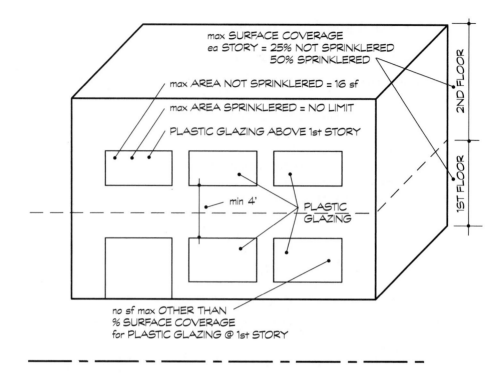

max SURFACE COVERAGE
ea STORY = 25% NOT SPRINKLERED
50% SPRINKLERED

max AREA NOT SPRINKLERED = 16 sf

max AREA SPRINKLERED = NO LIMIT

PLASTIC GLAZING ABOVE 1st STORY

min 4'

PLASTIC
GLAZING

2ND FLOOR

1ST FLOOR

no sf max OTHER THAN
% SURFACE COVERAGE
for PLASTIC GLAZING @ 1st STORY

Fig. 2608.2B. Plastic glazing limits.

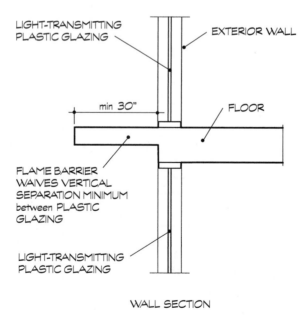

LIGHT-TRANSMITTING
PLASTIC GLAZING

EXTERIOR WALL

min 30"

FLOOR

FLAME BARRIER
WAIVES VERTICAL
SEPARATION MINIMUM
between PLASTIC
GLAZING

LIGHT-TRANSMITTING
PLASTIC GLAZING

WALL SECTION

Fig. 2608.2C. Plastic glazing limits.

2609 Light-Transmitting Plastic Roof Panels

2609.2 Separation

- This section addresses light-transmitting plastic roof panels.
- The separation of plastic roof panels is not required in the following cases:
  - In low-hazard buildings such as the following:

    The following swimming pool buildings:

      ≤ 5000 sf.

      With a fire separation distance ≥ 10'.

    The following greenhouses:

      Used to grow plants for one of the following purposes:

        On a production basis.

        For research.

      No public access.

      With a fire separation distance ≥ 4'.
- Otherwise, separation requirements for plastic roof panels are as shown in the illustrations provided with this section.

  Note: 2609.4, "Area limitations," exception 2 or 3, is cited as the source waiving the requirements for roof panel separation for the cases indicated above.
  903.3.1.1, "NFPA 13 sprinkler systems," is cited as governing the sprinklers required for waiving separation requirements for plastic roof panels.

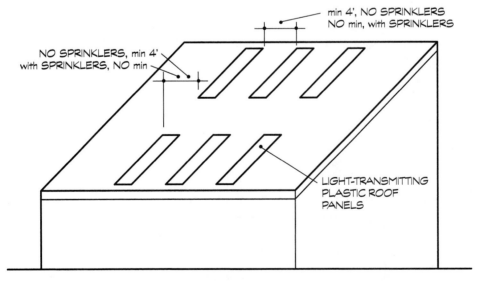

Fig. 2609.2A. Minimum separation of light-transmitting plaster roof panels measured in a horizontal plane.

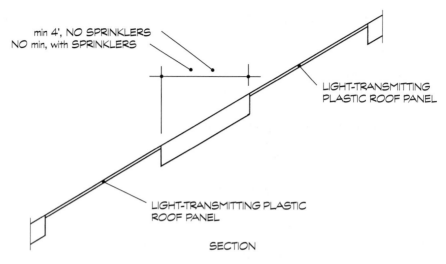

min 4', NO SPRINKLERS
NO min, with SPRINKLERS

LIGHT-TRANSMITTING
PLASTIC ROOF PANEL

LIGHT-TRANSMITTING PLASTIC
ROOF PANEL

SECTION

Fig. 2609.2B. Minimum separation of light-transmitting plastic roof panels measured in a horizontal plane.

2609.3 Location

- This section addresses light-transmitting plastic roof panels.

- The requirement for locating plastic roof panels is shown in the illustration provided for the following case:
  - Where exterior wall openings are required to be protected.

    Note: 704.8, "Allowable area of openings," is cited as the source defining conditions wherein exterior wall openings must be protected.

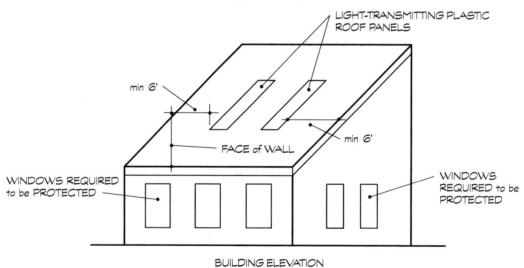

LIGHT-TRANSMITTING PLASTIC
ROOF PANELS

min 6'

min 6'

FACE of WALL

WINDOWS REQUIRED
to be PROTECTED

WINDOWS
REQUIRED to be
PROTECTED

BUILDING ELEVATION

Fig. 2609.3. Plastic roof panels near walls where windows need to be protected.

2609 Light-Transmitting Plastic Roof Panels

2609.4 Area limitations *(part 1 of 5)*

- This subsection addresses light-transmitting plastic roof panels.
- This section does not apply to the following structures:
  - Low-hazard structures such as the following:
    - The following swimming pool buildings:
      - ≤ 5000 sf.
      - With a fire separation distance ≥ 10'.
  - The following greenhouses:
    - Used to grow plants for one of the following purposes:
      - On a production basis.
      - For research.
    - No public access.
    - With a fire separation distance ≥ 4'.
  - Roof coverings over the following:
    - In occupancy R-3:
      - Terraces.
      - Patios.
- Otherwise, areas of plastic roof panels are limited as shown in the tables and illustration provided with this section.

  Note: IBC Table 2609.4, "Area Limitations for Light-Transmitting Plastic Roof Panels," is cited as the source of area limitations and is the basis for the tables provided with this section.

  903.3.1.1, "NFPA 13 sprinkler systems," is cited as governing the sprinklers necessary for increasing area limitations for plastic roof panels.

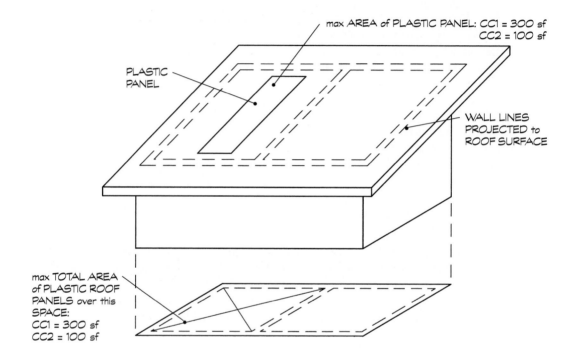

max AREA of PLASTIC PANEL: CC1 = 300 sf
CC2 = 100 sf

PLASTIC
PANEL

WALL LINES
PROJECTED to
ROOF SURFACE

max TOTAL AREA
of PLASTIC ROOF
PANELS over this
SPACE:
CC1 = 300 sf
CC2 = 100 sf

Fig. 2609.4. Maximum size of light-transmitting plastic roof panels.

2609 Light-Transmitting Plastic Roof Panels

2609.4 Area limitations *(part 2 of 5)*

- A partial list of maximum sizes for the following CC1-class plastic roof panels is shown below:
  - Panels must be ≤ 300 sf each for buildings with no sprinklers.

Table 2609.4a		Maximum Roof Panel Sizes for CC1 Plastics with No Sprinklers					
Given width	Max. length	Given width	Max. length	Given width	Max. length	Given width	Max. length
1'-0"	300'-0"	6'-0"	50'-0"	11'-0"	27'-3"	16'-0"	18'-9"
1'-4"	225'-6"	6'-4"	47'-4"	11'-4"	26'-5"	16'-4"	18'-4"
1'-8"	180'-0"	6'-8"	45'-0"	11'-8"	25'-8"	16'-8"	18'-0"
2'-0"	150'-0"	7'-0"	42'-10"	12'-0"	25'-0"	17'-0"	17'-7"
2'-4"	128'-6"	7'-4"	40'-11"	12'-4"	24'-3"	17'-4"	17'-3"
2'-8"	112'-6"	7'-8"	39'-1"	12'-8"	23'-8"	17'-8"	16'-11"
3'-0"	100'-0"	8'-0"	37'-6"	13'-0"	23'-0"	18'-0"	16'-8"
3'-4"	90'-0"	8'-4"	36'-0"	13'-4"	22'-6"	18'-4"	16'-4"
3'-8"	81'-9"	8'-8"	34'-7"	13'-8"	21'-11"	18'-8"	16'-0"
4'-0"	75'-0"	9'-0"	33'-4"	14'-0"	21'-5"	19'-0"	15'-9"
4'-4"	69'-3"	9'-4"	32'-1"	14'-4"	20'-11"	19'-4"	15'-6"
4'-8"	64'-3"	9'-8"	31'-0"	14'-8"	20'-5"	19'-8"	15'-3"
5'-0"	60'-0"	10'-0"	30'-0"	15'-0"	20'-0"	20'-0"	15'-0"
5'-4"	56'-3"	10'-4"	29'-0"	15'-4"	19'-6"	20'-4"	14'-9"
5'-8"	52'-11"	10'-8"	28'-1"	15'-8"	19'-1"	20'-8"	14'-6"

- A partial list of maximum sizes for the following CC1-class plastic roof panels is shown below:
  - Panels must be ≤ 600 sf each for sprinklered buildings.

Table 2609.4b		Maximum Roof Panel Sizes for CC1 Plastics on Sprinklered Buildings					
Given width	Max. length	Given width	Max. length	Given width	Max. length	Given width	Max. length
1'-0"	600'-0"	7'-0"	85'-8"	13'-0"	46'-1"	19'-0"	31'-7"
1'-6"	400'-0"	7'-6"	80'-0"	13'-6"	44'-5"	19'-6"	30'-9"
2'-0"	300'-0"	8'-0"	75'-0"	14'-0"	42'-10"	20'-0"	30'-0"
2'-6"	240'-0"	8'-6"	70'-7"	14'-6"	41'-4"	20'-6"	29'-3"
3'-0"	200'-0"	9'-0"	66'-8"	15'-0"	40'-0"	21'-0"	28'-6"
3'-6"	171'-5"	9'-6"	63'-1"	15'-6"	38'-8"	21'-6"	27'-10"
4'-0"	150'-0"	10'-0"	60'-0"	16'-0"	37'-6"	22'-0"	27'-3"
4'-6"	133'-4"	10'-6"	57'-1"	16'-6"	36'-4"	22'-6"	26'-8"
5'-0"	120'-0"	11'-0"	54'-6"	17'-0"	35'-3"	23'-0"	26'-1"
5'-6"	109'-1"	11'-6"	52'-2"	17'-6"	34'-3"	23'-6"	25'-6"
6'-0"	100'-0"	12'-0"	50'-0"	18'-0"	33'-4"	24'-0"	25'-0"
6'-6"	92'-3"	12'-6"	48'-0"	18'-6"	32'-5"	24'-6"	24'-5"

2609 Light-Transmitting Plastic Roof Panels

2609.4 Area limitations *(part 3 of 5)*

- A partial list of maximum areas for the following CC1-class plastic roof panels is shown below:
  - Sum of panel areas must be ≤ 30% of floor area served in buildings with no sprinklers.

Table 2609.4c   Maximum Total Area Permitted for Roof Panels of CC1 Plastics with No Sprinklers

Floor area (sf)	Maximum panel area (sf)	Floor area (sf)	Maximum panel area (sf)	Floor area (sf)	Maximum panel area (sf)	Floor area (sf)	Maximum panel area (sf)
100	30	1300	390	2500	750	3700	1110
200	60	1400	420	2600	780	3800	1140
300	90	1500	450	2700	810	3900	1170
400	120	1600	480	2800	840	4000	1200
500	150	1700	510	2900	870	4100	1230
600	180	1800	540	3000	900	4200	1260
700	210	1900	570	3100	930	4300	1290
800	240	2000	600	3200	960	4400	1320
900	270	2100	630	3300	990	4500	1350
1000	300	2200	660	3400	1020	4600	1380
1100	330	2300	690	3500	1050	4700	1410
1200	360	2400	720	3600	1080	4800	1440

- A partial list of maximum areas for the following CC1-class plastic roof panels is shown below:
  - Sum of panel areas must be ≤ 60% of floor area served in sprinklered buildings.

Table 2609.4d   Total Aggregate Area Permitted for Roof Panels of CC1 Plastics with Sprinklers

Floor area (sf)	Maximum panel area (sf)	Floor area (sf)	Maximum panel area (sf)	Floor area (sf)	Maximum panel area (sf)	Floor area (sf)	Maximum panel area (sf)
100	60	1300	780	2500	1500	3700	2220
200	120	1400	840	2600	1560	3800	2280
300	180	1500	900	2700	1620	3900	2340
400	240	1600	960	2800	1680	4000	2400
500	300	1700	1020	2900	1740	4100	2460
600	360	1800	1080	3000	1800	4200	2520
700	420	1900	1140	3100	1860	4300	2580
800	480	2000	1200	3200	1920	4400	2640
900	540	2100	1260	3300	1980	4500	2700
1000	600	2200	1320	3400	2040	4600	2760
1100	660	2300	1380	3500	2100	4700	2820
1200	720	2400	1440	3600	2160	4800	2880

2609 Light-Transmitting Plastic Roof Panels

2609.4 Area limitations *(part 4 of 5)*

- A partial list of maximum sizes of the following CC2-class plastic roof panels is shown below:
  - Panels must be ≥ 100 sf each for buildings with no sprinklers.

Table 2609.4e		Maximum Roof Panel Sizes for CC2 Plastics with No Sprinklers					
Given width	Max. length	Given width	Max. length	Given width	Max. length	Given width	Max. length
1'-0"	100'-0"	3'-6"	28'-6"	6'-0"	16'-8"	8'-6"	11'-9"
1'-2"	85'-8"	3'-8"	27'-3"	6'-2"	16'-2"	8'-8"	11'-6"
1'-4"	75'-0"	3'-10"	26'-1"	6'-4"	15'-9"	8'-10"	11'-3"
1'-6"	66'-8"	4'-0"	25'-0"	6'-6"	15'-4"	9'-0"	11'-1"
1'-8"	60'-0"	4'-2"	24'-0"	6'-8"	15'-0"	9'-2"	10'-10"
1'-10"	54'-6"	4'-4"	23'-1"	6'-10"	14'-7"	9'-4"	10'-8"
2'-0"	50'-0"	4'-6"	22'-2"	7'-0"	14'-3"	9'-6"	10'-6"
2'-2"	46'-1"	4'-8"	21'-5"	7'-2"	13'-11"	9'-8"	10'-4"
2'-4"	42'-10"	4'-10"	20'-8"	7'-4"	13'-7"	9'-10"	10'-2"
2'-6"	40'-0"	5'-0"	20'-0"	7'-6"	13'-4"	10'-0"	10'-0"
2'-8"	37'-6"	5'-2"	19'-4"	7'-8"	13'-0"	10'-2"	9'-10"
2'-10"	35'-3"	5'-4"	18'-9"	7'-10"	12'-9"	10'-4"	9'-8"
3'-0"	33'-4"	5'-6"	18'-2"	8'-0"	12'-6"	10'-6"	9'-6"
3'-2"	31'-7"	5'-8"	17'-7"	8'-2"	12'-2"	10'-8"	9'-4"
3'-4"	30'-0"	5'-10"	17'-1"	8'-4"	12'-0"	10'-10"	9'-2"

- A partial list of maximum sizes for the following CC2-class plastic roof panels is shown below:
  - Panels must be ≤ 200 sf each for sprinklered buildings.

Table 2609.4f		Maximum Roof Panel Sizes for CC2 Plastics on Sprinklered Buildings					
Given width	Max. length	Given width	Max. length	Given width	Max. length	Given width	Max. length
1'-0"	200'-0"	5'-0"	40'-0"	9'-0"	22'-2"	13'-0"	15'-4"
1'-4"	150'-0"	5'-4"	37'-6"	9'-4"	21'-5"	13'-4"	15'-0"
1'-8"	120'-0"	5'-8"	35'-3"	9'-8"	20'-8"	13'-8"	14'-7"
2'-0"	100'-0"	6'-0"	33'-4"	10'-0"	20'-0"	14'-0"	14'-3"
2'-4"	85'-8"	6'-4"	31'-7"	10'-4"	19'-4"	14'-4"	13'-11"
2'-8"	75'-0"	6'-8"	30'-0"	10'-8"	18'-9"	14'-8"	13'-7"
3'-0"	66'-8"	7'-0"	28'-6"	11'-0"	18'-2"	15'-0"	13'-4"
3'-4"	60'-0"	7'-4"	27'-3"	11'-4"	17'-7"	15'-4"	13'-0"
3'-8"	54'-6"	7'-8"	26'-1"	11'-8"	17'-1"	15'-8"	12'-9"
4'-0"	50'-0"	8'-0"	25'-0"	12'-0"	16'-8"	16'-0"	12'-6"
4'-4"	46'-1"	8'-4"	24'-0"	12'-4"	16'-2"	16'-4"	12'-2"
4'-8"	42'-10"	8'-8"	23'-1"	12'-8"	15'-9"	16'-8"	12'-0"

2609 Light-Transmitting Plastic Roof Panels

2609.4 Area limitations *(part 5 of 5)*

- A partial list of maximum areas for the following CC2-class plastic roof panels is shown below:
  - ○ Sum of panel areas must be ≤ 25% of floor area served in buildings with no sprinklers.

Table 2609.4g		Maximum Total Area Permitted for Roof Panels of CC2 Plastics with No Sprinklers					
Floor area (sf)	Maximum panel area (sf)	Floor area (sf)	Maximum panel area (sf)	Floor area (sf)	Maximum panel area (sf)	Floor area (sf)	Maximum panel area (sf)
100	25	1300	325	2500	625	3700	925
200	50	1400	350	2600	650	3800	950
300	75	1500	375	2700	675	3900	975
400	100	1600	400	2800	700	4000	1000
500	125	1700	425	2900	725	4100	1025
600	150	1800	450	3000	750	4200	1050
700	175	1900	475	3100	775	4300	1075
800	200	2000	500	3200	800	4400	1100
900	225	2100	525	3300	825	4500	1125
1000	250	2200	550	3400	850	4600	1150
1100	275	2300	575	3500	875	4700	1175
1200	300	2400	600	3600	900	4800	1200

- A partial list of maximum areas for the following CC2-class plastic roof panels is shown below:
  - ○ Sum of panel areas must be ≤ 50% of floor area served in sprinklered buildings.

Table 2609.4h		Total Aggregate Area Permitted for Roof Panels of CC2 Plastics with Sprinklers					
Floor area (sf)	Maximum panel area (sf)	Floor area (sf)	Maximum panel area (sf)	Floor area (sf)	Maximum panel area (sf)	Floor area (sf)	Maximum panel area (sf)
100	50	1300	650	2500	1250	3700	1850
200	100	1400	700	2600	1300	3800	1900
300	150	1500	750	2700	1350	3900	1950
400	200	1600	800	2800	1400	4000	2000
500	250	1700	850	2900	1450	4100	2050
600	300	1800	900	3000	1500	4200	2100
700	350	1900	950	3100	1550	4300	2150
800	400	2000	1000	3200	1600	4400	2200
900	450	2100	1050	3300	1650	4500	2250
1000	500	2200	1100	3400	1700	4600	2300
1100	550	2300	1150	3500	1750	4700	2350
1200	600	2400	1200	3600	1800	4800	2400

2610 Light-Transmitting Plastic Skylight Glazing

2610.2 Mounting

- This section addresses skylights with light-transmitting plastic glazing.
- Curbs are not required for skylights as follows:
  - Where the roof slopes ≥ 3:12 in either of the following locations:
    In occupancy R-3.
    Where unclassified roof coverings are allowed.
- Neither of the following materials is required at the edge of a skylight where the condition indicated below applies:
  - Materials:
    Metal.
    Noncombustible material.
  - Condition:
    Where unclassified roof coverings are allowed.
- Otherwise, skylights are governed as follows:
  - Curbs are required for skylights as shown in the detail below.
  - Where edges are not constructed as per the detail provided, the following applies:
    Edge must be shown to resist combustion upon exposure to a standard test flame.

  Note: The following are cited as governing exposure of the skylight edge to a test flame.
  One of the standards must be used. A Class B brand is specified for the test.
  ASTM E 108, "Test Methods for Fire Tests of Roof Coverings."
  UL 790, "Tests for Fire Resistance of Roof Covering Materials."

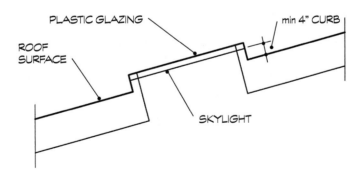

Fig. 2610.2. Required curb for light-transmitting plastic glazing in skylights.

2610 Light-Transmitting Plastic Skylight Glazing

2610.3 Slope

- This section addresses skylights with light-transmitting plastic glazing.
- This section does not apply to skylights that are shown to resist combustion upon exposure to a standard test flame.

> *Note: The following are cited as governing exposure of the skylight to a test flame. One of the standards must be used. A Class B brand is specified for the test.*
> *ASTM E 108, "Test Methods for Fire Tests of Roof Coverings."*
> *UL 790, "Tests for Fire Resistance of Roof Covering Materials."*

- Requirements for other skylights are shown on the details provided on the following pages.
- A partial list of mounting heights required for domed skylights is provided with this section.
- Dome-shaped skylights must have a rise ≥ 10% of its longest span as indicated in the following partial list of rise requirements.

Table 2610.3   **Required Rise of Domed Skylight vs. Span**

Span	Minimum rise	Span	Minimum rise	Span	Minimum rise	Span	Minimum rise
≤ 2'-6"	3"	3'-10"	$4^5/_8$"	5'-2"	$6^1/_4$"	6'-6"	$7^{13}/_{16}$"
2'-7"	$3^1/_8$"	3'-11"	$4^3/_4$"	5'-3"	$6^5/_{16}$"	6'-7"	$7^{15}/_{16}$"
2'-8"	$3^1/_4$"	4'-0"	$4^{13}/_{16}$"	5'-4"	$6^7/_{16}$"	6'-8"	8"
2'-9"	$3^5/_{16}$"	4'-1"	$4^{15}/_{16}$"	5'-5"	$6^1/_2$"	6'-9"	$8^1/_8$"
2'-10"	$3^7/_{16}$"	4'-2"	5"	5'-6"	$6^5/_8$"	6'-10"	$8^1/_4$"
2'-11"	$3^1/_2$"	4'-3"	$5^1/_8$"	5'-7"	$6^3/_4$"	6'-11"	$8^5/_{16}$"
3'-0"	$3^5/_8$"	4'-4"	$5^1/_4$"	5'-8"	$6^{13}/_{16}$"	7'-0"	$8^7/_{16}$"
3'-1"	$3^3/_4$"	4'-5"	$5^5/_{16}$"	5'-9"	$6^{15}/_{16}$"	7'-1"	$8^1/_2$"
3'-2"	$3^{13}/_{16}$"	4'-6"	$5^7/_{16}$"	5'-10"	7"	7'-2"	$8^5/_8$"
3'-3"	$3^{15}/_{16}$"	4'-7"	$5^1/_2$"	5'-11"	$7^1/_8$"	7'-3"	$8^3/_4$"
3'-4"	4"	4'-8"	$5^5/_8$"	6'-0"	$7^1/_4$"	7'-4"	$8^{13}/_{16}$"
3'-5"	$4^1/_8$"	4'-9"	$5^3/_4$"	6'-1"	$7^5/_{16}$"	7'-5"	$8^{15}/_{16}$"
3'-6"	$4^1/_4$"	4'-10"	$5^{13}/_{16}$"	6'-2"	$7^7/_{16}$"	7'-6"	9"
3'-7"	$4^5/_{16}$"	4'-11"	$5^{15}/_{16}$"	6'-3"	$7^1/_2$"	7'-7"	$9^1/_8$"
3'-8"	$4^7/_{16}$"	5'-0"	6"	6'-4"	$7^5/_8$"	7'-8"	$9^1/_4$"
3'-9"	$4^1/_2$"	5'-1"	$6^1/_8$"	6'-5"	$7^3/_4$"	7'-9"	$9^5/_{16}$"

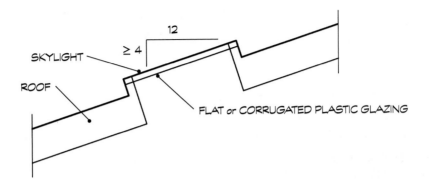

Fig. 2610.3A. Minimum slope of flat or corrugated light-transmitting plastic skylight glazing.

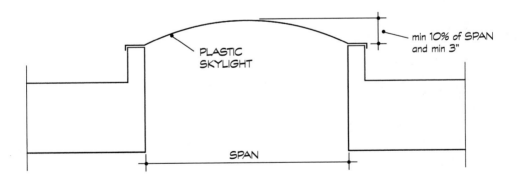

Fig. 2610.3B. Minimum rise of dome-shaped light-transmitting plastic skylight glazing.

2610 Light-Transmitting Plastic Skylight Glazing

2610.4 Maximum area of skylights

- This section addresses skylights with light-transmitting plastic glazing.
- Area limitations of this section do not apply to skylights in the following cases:
  - Where the building is sprinklered as per NFPA 13.
  - Where the building is equipped with the following:
    Smoke vents.
    Heat vents.

  Note: Section 910, "Smoke and Heat Vents," is cited as governing such devices as indicated above.

- Otherwise, the table below provides a partial list of maximum sizes permitted for skylights as follows:
  - Area inside the curb must ≤ 100 sf for an individual skylight.

Table 2610.4   Maximum Sizes Permitted for Skylights

Given width	Max. length	Given width	Max. length	Given width	Max. length	Given width	Max. length
1'-0"	100'-0"	3'-6"	28'-6"	6'-0"	16'-8"	8'-6"	11'-9"
1'-2"	85'-8"	3'-8"	27'-3"	6'-2"	16'-2"	8'-8"	11'-6"
1'-4"	75'-0"	3'-10"	26'-1"	6'-4"	15'-9"	8'-10"	11'-3"
1'-6"	66'-8"	4'-0"	25'-0"	6'-6"	15'-4"	9'-0"	11'-1"
1'-8"	60'-0"	4'-2"	24'-0"	6'-8"	15'-0"	9'-2"	10'-10"
1'-10"	54'-6"	4'-4"	23'-1"	6'-10"	14'-7"	9'-4"	10'-8"
2'-0"	50'-0"	4'-6"	22'-2"	7'-0"	14'-3"	9'-6"	10'-6"
2'-2"	46'-1"	4'-8"	21'-5"	7'-2"	13'-11"	9'-8"	10'-4"
2'-4"	42'-10"	4'-10"	20'-8"	7'-4"	13'-7"	9'-10"	10'-2"
2'-6"	40'-0"	5'-0"	20'-0"	7'-6"	13'-4"	10'-0"	10'-0"
2'-8"	37'-6"	5'-2"	19'-4"	7'-8"	13'-0"	10'-2"	9'-10"
2'-10"	35'-3"	5'-4"	18'-9"	7'-10"	12'-9"	10'-4"	9'-8"
3'-0"	33'-4"	5'-6"	18'-2"	8'-0"	12'-6"	10'-6'	9'-6"
3'-2"	31'-7"	5'-8"	17'-7"	8'-2"	12'-2"	10'-8"	9'-4"
3'-4"	30'-0"	5'-10"	17'-1"	8'-4"	12'-0"	10'-10"	9'-2"

2610 Light-Transmitting Plastic Skylight Glazing

2610.5 Aggregate area of skylights *(part 1 of 3)*

- This section addresses skylights with light-transmitting plastic glazing.
- The sum of the areas of skylights on a roof is limited based on the size of the floor area served, as shown in the illustration provided with this section.
- Higher limits are permitted where one of the following is present:
  - Sprinklers as per NFPA 13.
  - Smoke and heat vents.

    Note: Section 910, "Smoke and Heat Vents," is cited as governing such devices as indicated above.

- Tables are provided on the following pages with partial lists of skylight sizes complying with the limits of this section.

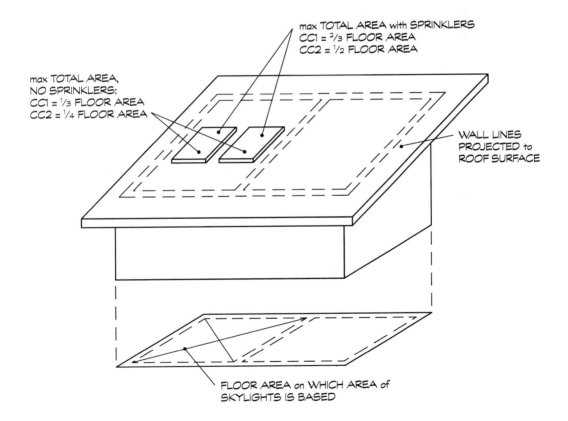

Fig. 2610.5A. Maximum area of skylights with light-transmitting plastic glazing.

2610 Light-Transmitting Plastic Skylight Glazing

2610.5 Aggregate area of skylights *(part 2 of 3)*

- The maximum permitted sum of skylight areas with CC1-class plastic is as follows:
  - Total area be $\leq \frac{1}{3}$ the floor area served where no sprinklers or vents are provided.

Table 2610.5a   **Maximum Total Skylight Area for CC1 Plastics with No Sprinklers or Vents**

Floor area (sf)	Maximum panel area (sf)	Floor area (sf)	Maximum panel area (sf)	Floor area (sf)	Maximum panel area (sf)	Floor area (sf)	Maximum panel area (sf)
100	33.33	1300	433.33	2500	833.33	3700	1233.33
200	66.67	1400	466.67	2600	866.67	3800	1266.67
300	100.00	1500	500.00	2700	900.00	3900	1300.00
400	133.33	1600	533.33	2800	933.33	4000	1333.33
500	166.67	1700	566.67	2900	966.67	4100	1366.67
600	200.00	1800	600.00	3000	1000.00	4200	1400.00
700	233.33	1900	633.33	3100	1033.33	4300	1433.33
800	266.67	2000	666.67	3200	1066.67	4400	1466.67
900	300.00	2100	700.00	3300	1100.00	4500	1500.00
1000	333.33	2200	733.33	3400	1133.33	4600	1533.33
1100	366.67	2300	766.67	3500	1166.67	4700	1566.67
1200	400.00	2400	800.00	3600	1200.00	4800	1600.00

- The maximum permitted sum of skylight areas with CC1-class plastic is as follows:
  - Total area be $\leq \frac{2}{3}$ the floor area served with sprinklers or vents provided.

Table 2610.5b   **Maximum Total Skylight Area for CC1 Plastics with Sprinklers or Vents**

Floor area (sf)	Maximum panel area (sf)	Floor area (sf)	Maximum panel area (sf)	Floor area (sf)	Maximum panel area (sf)	Floor area (sf)	Maximum panel area (sf)
100	66.67	1300	866.67	2500	1666.67	3700	2466.67
200	133.33	1400	933.33	2600	1733.33	3800	2533.33
300	200.00	1500	1000.00	2700	1800.00	3900	2600.00
400	266.67	1600	1066.67	2800	1866.67	4000	2666.67
500	333.33	1700	1133.33	2900	1933.33	4100	2733.33
600	400.00	1800	1200.00	3000	2000.00	4200	2800.00
700	466.67	1900	1266.67	3100	2066.67	4300	2866.67
800	533.33	2000	1333.33	3200	2133.33	4400	2933.33
900	600.00	2100	1400.00	3300	2200.00	4500	3000.00
1000	666.67	2200	1466.67	3400	2266.67	4600	3066.67
1100	733.33	2300	1533.33	3500	2333.33	4700	3133.33
1200	800.00	2400	1600.00	3600	2400.00	4800	3200.00

2610 Light-Transmitting Plastic Skylight Glazing

2610.5 Aggregate area of skylights *(part 3 of 3)*

- The maximum permitted sum of skylight areas with CC2-class plastic is as follows:
  - Total area be $\leq \frac{1}{4}$ the floor area served where no sprinklers or vents are provided.

Table 2610.5c   Maximum Total Skylight Area for CC2 Plastics with No Sprinklers or Vents

Floor area (sf)	Maximum panel area (sf)	Floor area (sf)	Maximum panel area (sf)	Floor area (sf)	Maximum panel area (sf)	Floor area (sf)	Maximum panel area (sf)
100	25	1300	325	2500	625	3700	925
200	50	1400	350	2600	650	3800	950
300	75	1500	375	2700	675	3900	975
400	100	1600	400	2800	700	4000	1000
500	125	1700	425	2900	725	4100	1025
600	150	1800	450	3000	750	4200	1050
700	175	1900	475	3100	775	4300	1075
800	200	2000	500	3200	800	4400	1100
900	225	2100	525	3300	825	4500	1125
1000	250	2200	550	3400	850	4600	1150
1100	275	2300	575	3500	875	4700	1175
1200	300	2400	600	3600	900	4800	1200

- The maximum permitted sum of skylight areas with CC2-class plastic is as follows:
  - Total area be $\leq \frac{1}{2}$ the floor area served with sprinklers or vents provided.

Table 2610.5d   Maximum Total Skylight Area for CC2 Plastics with Sprinklers or Vents

Floor area (sf)	Maximum panel area (sf)	Floor area (sf)	Maximum panel area (sf)	Floor area (sf)	Maximum panel area (sf)	Floor area (sf)	Maximum panel area (sf)
100	50	1300	650	2500	1250	3700	1850
200	100	1400	700	2600	1300	3800	1900
300	150	1500	750	2700	1350	3900	1950
400	200	1600	800	2800	1400	4000	2000
500	250	1700	850	2900	1450	4100	2050
600	300	1800	900	3000	1500	4200	2100
700	350	1900	950	3100	1550	4300	2150
800	400	2000	1000	3200	1600	4400	2200
900	450	2100	1050	3300	1650	4500	2250
1000	500	2200	1100	3400	1700	4600	2300
1100	550	2300	1150	3500	1750	4700	2350
1200	600	2400	1200	3600	1800	4800	2400

Case study: Fig. 2610.5B. There are 4 light-transmitting polycarbonate (CC1) plastic skylights serving the atrium shown. The area of each 10' ×10' skylight is not limited due to the fact that the building is sprinklered. The aggregate area of the skylights is limited to $^2/_3$ of the area they serve (twice the $^1/_3$ limit for nonsprinklered buildings). In this case, the 400 sf total area of the 4 skylights is < the 1410 sf limit. Separation of the skylights is not governed since the building is sprinklered. The skylights are in compliance with code requirements.

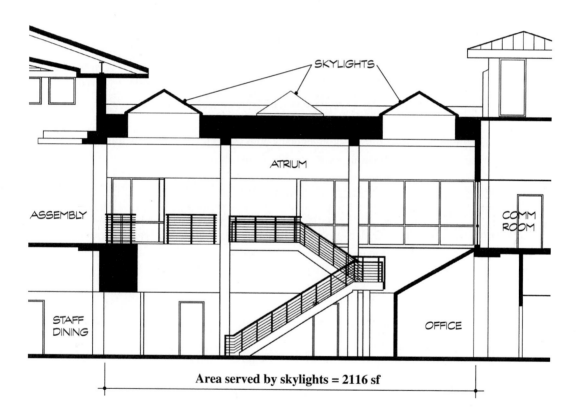

Area served by skylights = 2116 sf

Fig. 2610.5B. Section at atrium. Lee's Summit Police and Court Facility. Lee's Summit, Missouri. The Hollis and Miller Group, Inc. Lee's Summit, Missouri.

2610 Light-Transmitting Plastic Skylight Glazing

2610.6 Separation

- This section addresses skylights with light-transmitting plastic glazing.
- This section does not address the following:
  - Buildings sprinklered as per NFPA 13.
  - In occupancy R-3 with both the following characteristics:
    Multiple skylights above the same space.
    Sum of areas $\leq$ 100 sf.
- Otherwise, skylights must be separated as shown in the illustration below.

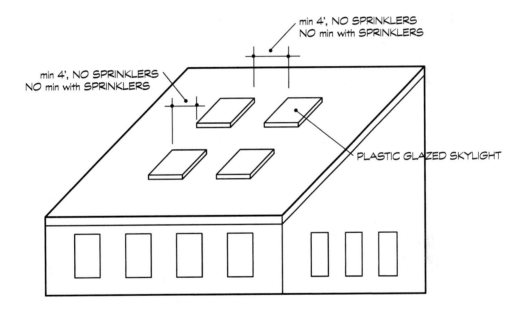

Fig. 2610.6. Minimum separation of skylights with light-transmitting plastic glazing measured in a horizontal plane.

2611 Light-Transmitting Plastic Interior Signs

2611.2 Aggregate area

- Wall signs of light-transmitting plastics in covered mall buildings may not be > 20% of the wall area as follows:
  - A partial list of signs within this limit is provided below:

Table 2611.2   Areas of Interior Signs Permitted Based on Wall Area

Wall area (sf)	Sign area (sf)	Wall area (sf)	Sign area (sf)	Wall area (sf)	Sign area (sf)	Wall area (sf)	Sign area (sf)
73	14.60	85	17.00	97	19.40	109	21.80
74	14.80	86	17.20	98	19.60	110	22.00
75	15.00	87	17.40	99	19.80	111	22.20
76	15.20	88	17.60	100	20.00	112	22.40
77	15.40	89	17.80	101	20.20	113	22.60
78	15.60	90	18.00	102	20.40	114	22.80
79	15.80	91	18.20	103	20.60	115	23.00
80	16.00	92	18.40	104	20.80	116	23.20
81	16.20	93	18.60	105	21.00	117	23.40
82	16.40	94	18.80	106	21.20	118	23.60
83	16.60	95	19.00	107	21.40	119	23.80
84	16.80	96	19.20	108	21.60	120	24.00

2611.3 Maximum area

- Wall signs of light-transmitting plastics in covered mall buildings may not be > 24 sf as follows:
  - A partial list of signs within this limit is provided below:

Table 2611.3   Dimensions of Interior Signs ≤ 24 sf in Area

Width	Length	Width	Length	Width	Length	Width	Length
1'-0"	24'-0"	2'-0"	12'-0"	3'-0"	8'-0"	4'-0"	6'-0"
1'-1"	22'-1"	2'-1"	11'-6"	3'-1"	7'-9"	4'-1"	5'-10"
1'-2"	20'-6"	2'-2"	11'-1"	3'-2"	7'-7"	4'-2"	5'-9"
1'-3"	19'-2"	2'-3"	10'-8"	3'-3"	7'-4"	4'-3"	5'-7"
1'-4"	18'-0"	2'-4"	10'-3"	3'-4"	7'-2"	4'-4"	5'-6"
1'-5"	16'-11"	2'-5"	9'-11"	3'-5"	7'-0"	4'-5"	5'-5"
1'-6"	16'-0"	2'-6"	9'-7"	3'-6"	6'-10"	4'-6"	5'-4"
1'-7"	15'-1"	2'-7"	9'-3"	3'-7"	6'-8"	4'-7"	5'-2"
1'-8"	14'-4"	2'-8"	9'-0"	3'-8"	6'-6"	4'-8"	5'-1"
1'-9"	13'-8"	2'-9"	8'-8"	3'-9"	6'-4"	4'-9"	5'-0"
1'-10"	13'-1"	2'-10"	8'-5"	3'-10"	6'-3"	4'-10"	4'-11"
1'-11"	12'-6"	2'-11"	8'-2"	3'-11"	6'-1"	4'-11"	4'-10"

2611 Light-Transmitting Plastic Interior Signs

2611.4 Encasement

- This section addresses interior signs of light-transmitting plastic wall signs in covered mall buildings.
- Edge requirements for such signs are shown in the illustration provided.

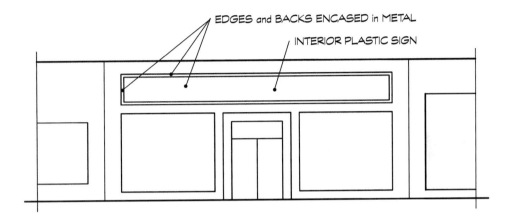

Fig. 2611.4. Light-transmitting plastic wall signs in covered mall buildings.

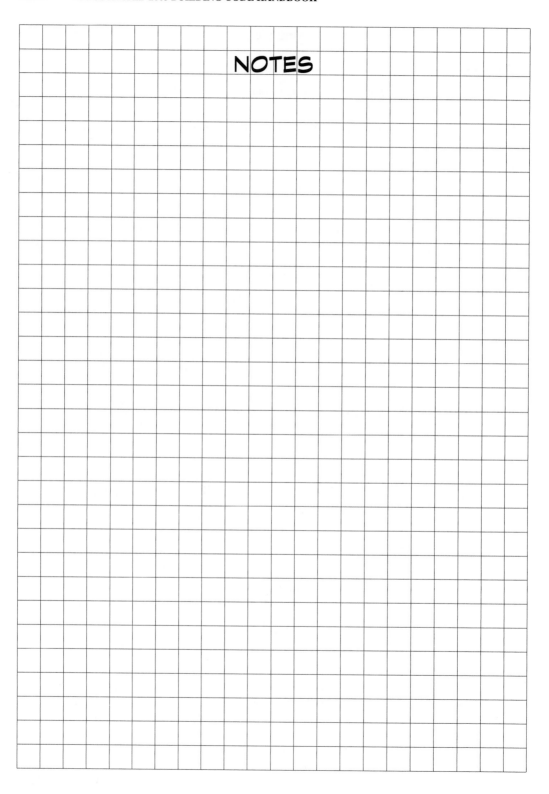

NOTES

27

Electrical

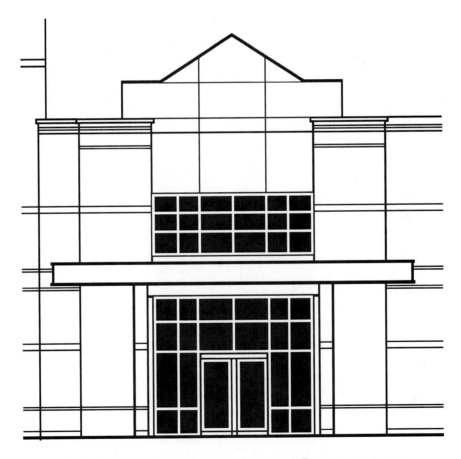

Methodist Community Health Center. Sugar Land, Texas. *(partial elevation)*
HKS, Inc., Architects, Engineers, Planners. Dallas, Texas.

2702 Emergency and Standby Power Systems

2702.2 Where required *(part 1 of 3)*

- This section indicates the need for the follwing systems by reporting the requirements of the individual sections cited in the code:
  - Emergency power systems.
  - Stand-by power systems.
- Emergency power systems are required for the following:
  - Voice communication systems in occupancy A.

    Note: 907.2.1.2, "Emergency power," is cited as governing these systems.

  - Exit signs.

    Note: 1011.5.3, "Power source," is cited as governing exit signs.

  - Means of egress illumination.

    Note: 1006.3, "Illumination emergency power," is cited as governing means of egress illumination.

  - Semiconductor fabrication facilities.

    Note: 415.9.10, "Emergency power systems," is cited as governing these facilities.

  - Exit signs in temporary tents and membrane structures.

    Note: International Fire Code is cited as governing these exit signs.

  - Occupancies with highly toxic and toxic materials.

    Note: International Fire Code is cited as governing these occupancies.

  - Occupancies with pyrophoric materials as follows:
    Where silane gas is located.

    Note: International Fire Code is cited as governing these occupancies.

  - High-rise buildings for the following:
    Exit signs.
    Means of egress lighting.
    Elevator car lighting.
    Emergency voice/alarm communication systems.
    Fire detection systems.
    Fire alarm systems.

    Note: 403.11, "Emergency power systems," is cited as identifying systems required in high-rise buildings and is partially summarized above.

2702 Emergency and Standby Power Systems

2702.2 Where required *(part 2 of 3)*

- Underground buildings for the following:
  Emergency voice/alarm communication systems.
  Fire alarm systems.
  Fire detection systems.
  Elevator car lighting.
  Means of egress lighting.
  Exit sign illumination.

  Note: 405.10, "Emergency power," is cited as governing these systems.

- Doors in occupancy I-3.

  Note: 408.4.2, "Power-operated doors and locks," is cited as governing these doors.

- Standby power systems are required for the following:
  - Smoke control systems.

  Note: 909.11, "Duct smoke detectors," is cited as governing these systems.

  - Elevators that are in an accessible means of egress.

  Note: 1007.4, "Elevators," is cited as governing these systems.

  - Horizontal sliding doors.

  Note: 1008.1.3.3, "Horizontal sliding doors," is cited as governing these doors.

  - Auxiliary inflation systems for membrane structures.

  Note: 3102.8.2, "Standby power," is cited as governing these auxiliary systems.

  - Occupancies with organic peroxides as follows:
    Where silane gas is located.

  Note: International Fire Code is cited as governing these occupancies.

  - Emergency voice/alarm communication systems as follows:
    In covered mall buildings > 50,000 sf.

  Note: 402.12, "Standby power," is cited as governing covered mall buildings and is summarized above.

  - High-rise buildings for the following:
    Fire command center.
    Fire pumps.
    Emergency voice/alarm communication systems.
    Lighting for mechanical equipment rooms.
    Elevators.

  Note: 403.10, "Standby power, "is cited as identifying systems required in high-rise buildings and is partially summarized above.

2702 Emergency and Standby Power Systems

2702.2 Where required *(part 3 of 3)*

- Underground buildings for the following:
  Smoke control.
  Ventilation equipment for smokeproof enclosures.
  Fire detection equipment for smokeproof enclosures.
  Fire pumps.
  Elevatrors.

  Note: 405.9, "Standby power," is cited as governing these systems.

- Airport traffic control towers for the following:
  Pressurization equipment.
  Mechanical equipment.
  Lighting.
  Elevator operation.
  Fire alarms.
  Fire detection systems.

  Note: 412.1.5, "Standby power," is cited as governing these systems.

- Elevators.

  Note: 3003.1, "Standby power," is cited as governing elevators.

- Smoke-proof enclosures.

  Note: 909.20, "Smokeproof enclosures," is cited as governing these enclosures.

- One of the following systems is required in the location indicated below:
  - Systems:
    Emergency power system.
    Standby power system.
  - Location:
    Occupancies with hazardous materials.

  Note: 415.5.4, "Standby or emergency power," is cited as governing these types of power for occupancies with hazardous materials.

NOTES

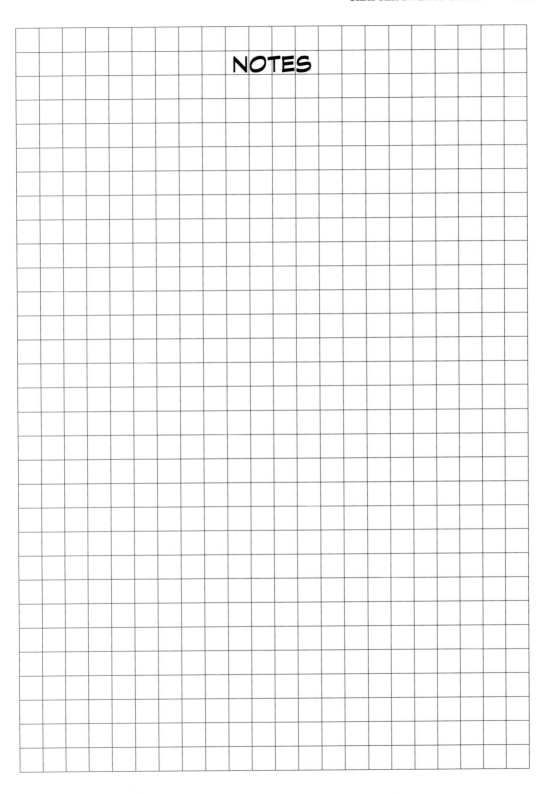

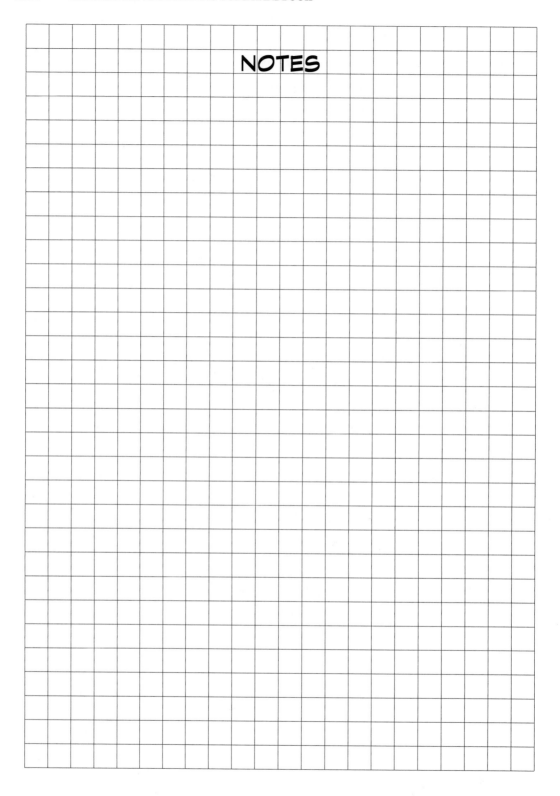

NOTES

28

Mechanical Systems

Glad Tidings Assembly of God Church. Naticoke, Pennsylvania.
Mullins and Weida, Architect and Associate. Bear Creek, Pennsylvania.

2801 General

2801.1 Scope

- The following components are governed by the codes indicated below:
  - Components:
    Mechanical appliances.
    Mechanical equipment.
    Mechanical systems.
  - Codes:
    International Mechanical Code.
    International Fuel Gas Code.
- The following components are governed by the codes indicated below:
  - Components:
    Masonry chimneys.
    Fireplaces.
    Barbecues.
  - Codes:
    Chapter 21, "Masonry."
    International Mechanical Code.

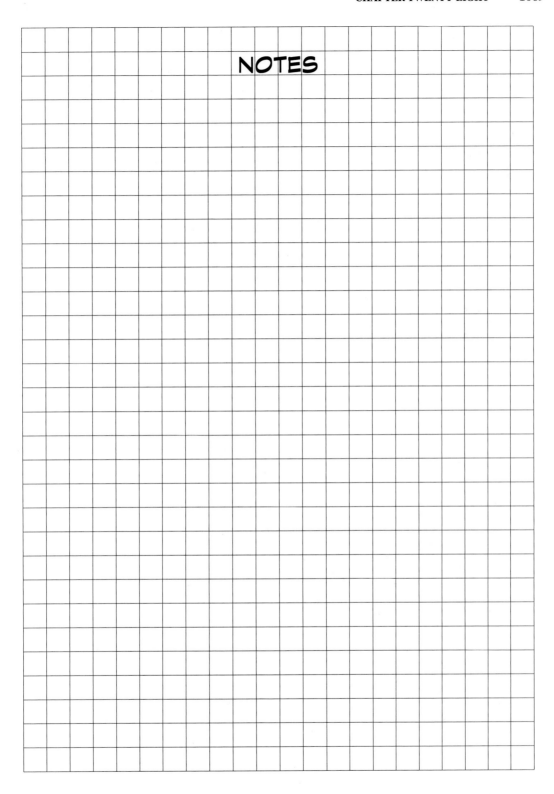

NOTES

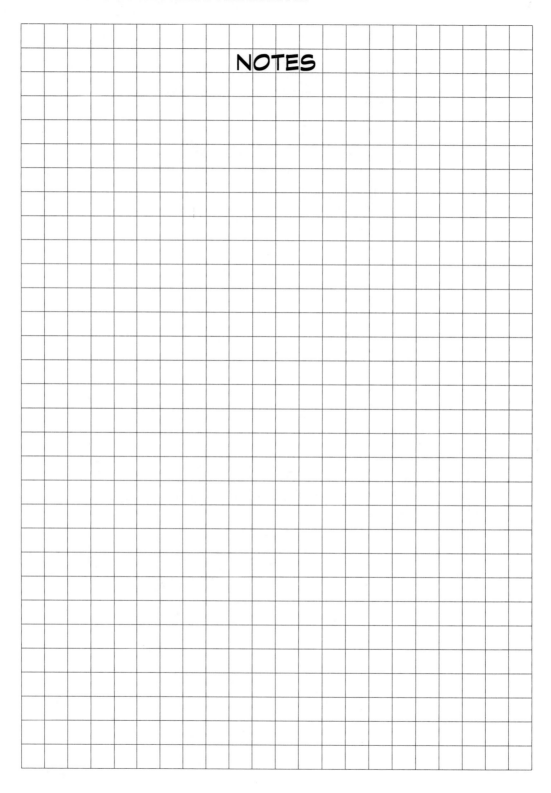

NOTES

29

Plumbing Systems

Creston Elementary Multipurpose Building. Creston, California.
Phillips Metsch Sweeney Moore Architects. Santa Barbara, California.

2902 Minimum Plumbing Facilities

2902.1 Minimum number of fixtures *(part 1 of 14)*

- Partial lists of plumbing fixtures required in each occupancy are provided in this section as follows:
  - The code includes data which can be used to determine the number of fixtures required for occupant counts > provided in these tables.
- Minimums for occupancies not listed will be determined by the building official.
- Where not indicated otherwise ≥ 1 service sink is required for all occupancies.
- In each toilet room urinals may be installed in lieu of ≤ ½ the required water closets.
- Drinking fountains are not required where restaurants serve water.
- Drinking fountains are not required where bottled-water coolers are provided.

> *Note: IBC Table 2902.1, "Minimum Number of Required Plumbing Facilities," is cited as governing the number of occupants served.*
> *Chapter 3, "Use and Occupancy Classification," is cited as applicable.*
> *The following sections of the International Plumbing Code are cited:*
> *419.2, "Substitution for water closets," permits the substitution of urinals for water closets as summarized above.*
> *410.1, "Approval," permits omitting drinking fountains as summarized above.*

Table 2902.1a   Occupancies A-1 and A-3: Minimum Plumbing Fixtures Required

Occupant count	WC men	WC women	Lavs	DF	Occupant count	WC men	WC women	Lavs	DF
1–65	1	1	1	1	751–780	7	12	4	2
66–125	1	2	1	1	781–800	7	13	4	2
126–130	2	2	1	1	801–845	7	13	5	2
131–195	2	3	1	1	846–875	7	14	5	2
196–200	2	4	1	1	876–910	8	14	5	2
201–250	2	4	2	1	911–975	8	15	5	2
251–260	3	4	2	1	976–1000	8	16	5	2
261–325	3	5	2	1	1001–1040	9	16	6	3
326–375	3	6	2	1	1041–1105	9	17	6	3
376–390	4	6	2	1	1106–1125	9	18	6	3
391–400	4	7	2	1	1126–1170	10	18	6	3
401–455	4	7	3	1	1171–1200	10	19	6	3
456–500	4	8	3	1	1201–1235	10	19	7	3
501–520	5	8	3	2	1236–1250	10	20	7	3
521–585	5	9	3	2	1251–1300	11	20	7	3
586–600	5	10	3	2	1301–1365	11	21	7	3
601–625	5	10	4	2	1366–1375	11	22	7	3
626–650	6	10	4	2	1376–1400	12	22	7	3
651–715	6	11	4	2	1401–1430	12	22	8	3
716–750	6	12	4	2	1431–1495	12	23	8	3

Source: IBC Table 2902.1.

2902 Minimum Plumbing Facilities

2902.1 Minimum number of fixtures *(part 2 of 14)*

Table 2902.1b   Occupancy A-2 Nightclubs, Bars, etc.: Minimum Plumbing Fixtures Required

Occupant count	WC men	WC women	Lavs	DF	Occupant count	WC men	WC women	Lavs	DF
1–40	1	1	1	1	226–240	6	6	4	1
41–75	2	2	1	1	241–280	7	7	4	1
76–80	2	2	2	1	281–300	8	8	4	1
81–120	3	3	2	1	301–320	8	8	5	1
121–150	4	4	2	1	321–360	9	9	5	1
151–160	4	4	3	1	361–375	10	10	5	1
161–200	5	5	3	1	376–400	10	10	6	1
201–225	6	6	3	1	401–440	11	11	6	1

Source: IBC Table 2902.1.

Table 2902.1c   Occupancy A-2 Restaurants: Minimum Plumbing Fixtures Required

Occupant count	WC men	WC women	Lavs	DF	Occupant count	WC men	WC women	Lavs	DF
1–75	1	1	1	1	376–400	6	6	2	1
76–150	2	2	1	1	401–450	6	6	3	1
151–200	3	3	1	1	451–500	7	7	3	1
201–225	3	3	2	1	501–525	7	7	3	2
226–300	4	4	2	1	526–600	8	8	3	2
301–375	5	5	2	1	601–675	9	9	4	2

Source: IBC Table 2902.1.

- The following plumbing fixtures must be made available when the church is occupied:
  - Located in adjacent buildings owned and controlled by the church.

Table 2902.1d   Occupancy A-3, Places of Worship: Minimum Plumbing Fixtures Required

Occupant count	WC men	WC women	Lavs	DF	Occupant count	WC men	WC women	Lavs	DF
1–75	1	1	1	1	451–525	4	7	3	1
76–150	1	2	1	1	526–600	4	8	3	1
151–200	2	3	1	1	601–675	5	9	4	1
201–225	2	3	2	1	676–750	5	10	4	1
226–300	2	4	2	1	751–800	6	11	4	1
301–375	3	5	2	1	801–825	6	11	5	1
376–400	3	6	2	1	826–900	6	12	5	1
401–450	3	6	3	1	901–975	7	13	5	1

Source: IBC Table 2902.1.

2902 Minimum Plumbing Facilities

2902.1 Minimum number of fixtures *(part 3 of 14)*

Table 2902.1e   Occupancy A-3 Passenger Terminals and Transportation Facilities: Minimum Fixtures Required

Occupant count	WC	Lavs	DF	Occupant count	WC	Lavs	DF
1–500	1	1	1	7,501–8,000	16	11	8
501–750	2	1	1	8,001–8,250	17	11	9
751–1,000	2	2	1	8,251–8,500	17	12	9
1,001–1,500	3	2	2	8,501–9,000	18	12	9
1,501–2,000	4	3	2	9,001–9,500	19	13	10
2,001–2,250	5	3	3	9,501–9,750	20	13	10
2,251–2,500	5	4	3	9,751–10,000	20	14	10
2,501–3,000	6	4	3	10,001–10,500	21	14	11
3,001–3,500	7	5	4	10,501–11,000	22	15	11
3,501–3,750	8	5	4	11,001–11,250	23	15	12
3,751–4,000	8	6	4	11,251–11,500	23	16	12
4,001–4,500	9	6	5	11,501–12,000	24	16	12
4,501–5,000	10	7	5	12,001–12,500	25	17	13
5,001–5,250	11	7	6	12,501–12,750	26	17	13
5,251–5,500	11	8	6	12,751–13,000	26	18	13
5,501–6,000	12	8	6	13,001–13,500	27	18	14
6,001–6,500	13	9	7	13,501–14,000	28	19	14
6,501–6,750	14	9	7	14,001–14,250	29	19	15
6,751–7,000	14	10	7	14,251–14,500	29	20	15
7,001–7,500	15	10	8	14,500–15,000	30	20	15

Source: IBC Table 2902.1.

2902 Minimum Plumbing Facilities

2902.1 Minimum number of fixtures *(part 4 of 14)*

Table 2902.1f **Occupancies A-4 and A-5 Coliseums, Arenas, Stadiums, Amusement Parks, etc.: 1–1500 Seats: Minimum Plumbing Fixtures Required**

Occupant count	WC men	WC women	Lavs men	Lavs women	DF	Occupant count	WC men	WC women	Lavs men	Lavs women	DF
1–40	1	1	1	1	1	751–760	11	19	4	6	1
41–75	1	2	1	1	1	761–800	11	20	4	6	1
76–80	2	2	1	1	1	801–825	11	21	5	6	1
81–120	2	3	1	1	1	826–840	12	21	5	6	1
221–150	2	4	1	1	1	841–880	12	22	5	6	1
151–160	3	4	1	2	1	881–900	12	23	5	6	1
161–200	3	5	1	2	1	901–920	13	23	5	7	1
201–225	3	6	2	2	1	921–960	13	24	5	7	1
226–240	4	6	2	2	1	961–975	13	25	5	7	1
241–280	4	7	2	2	1	976–1000	14	25	5	7	1
281–300	4	8	2	2	1	1001–1040	14	26	6	7	2
301–320	5	8	2	3	1	1041–1050	14	27	6	7	2
321–360	5	9	2	3	1	1051–1080	15	27	6	8	2
361–375	5	10	2	3	1	1081–1120	16	28	6	8	2
376–400	6	10	2	3	1	1121–1160	16	29	6	8	2
401–440	6	11	3	3	1	1161–1200	16	30	6	8	2
441–450	6	12	3	3	1	1201–1240	17	31	7	9	2
451–480	7	12	3	4	1	1241–1275	17	32	7	9	2
481–520	7	13	3	4	1	1276–1280	18	32	7	9	2
521–525	7	14	3	4	1	1281–1320	18	33	7	9	2
526–560	8	14	3	4	1	1321–1350	18	34	7	9	2
561–600	8	15	3	4	1	1351–1360	19	34	7	10	2
601–640	9	16	4	5	1	1361–1400	19	35	7	10	2
641–675	9	17	4	5	1	1401–1425	19	36	8	10	2
676–680	10	17	4	5	1	1426–1440	20	36	8	10	2
681–720	10	18	4	5	1	1441–1480	20	37	8	10	2
721–750	10	19	4	5	1	1481–1500	20	38	8	10	2

Source: IBC Table 2902.1.

2902 Minimum Plumbing Facilities

2902.1 Minimum number of fixtures *(part 5 of 14)*

Occupancies A-4 and A-5 Coliseums, Arenas, Stadiums, Amusement Parks, etc.:
Table 2902.1g   1501–4600 Seats: Minimum Plumbing Fixtures Required

Occupant count	WC men	WC women	Lavs men	Lavs women	DF	Occupant count	WC men	WC women	Lavs men	Lavs women	DF
1501–1560	21	39	8	11	2	3061–3120	34	65	16	21	4
1561–1600	21	40	8	11	2	3121–3150	34	66	16	21	4
1601–1620	21	40	9	11	2	3151–3180	34	66	16	22	4
1621–1650	22	41	9	11	2	3181–3200	35	67	16	22	4
1651–1680	22	41	9	12	2	3201–3240	35	67	17	22	4
1681–1740	22	42	9	12	2	3241–3300	35	68	17	22	4
1741–1800	23	43	9	12	2	3301–3360	36	69	17	23	4
1801–1860	23	44	10	13	2	3361–3400	36	70	17	23	4
1861–1920	24	45	10	13	2	3401–3420	36	70	18	23	4
1921–1950	24	46	10	13	2	3421–3450	37	71	18	23	4
1951–1980	24	46	10	14	2	3451–3480	37	71	18	24	4
1981–2000	25	47	10	14	2	3481–3540	37	72	18	24	4
2001–2040	25	47	11	14	3	3541–3600	38	73	18	24	4
2041–2100	25	48	11	14	3	3601–3660	38	74	19	25	4
2101–2160	26	49	11	15	3	3661–3720	39	75	19	25	4
2161–2200	26	50	11	15	3	3721–3750	39	76	19	25	4
2201–2250	26	50	12	15	3	3751–3780	39	76	19	26	4
2251–2220	26	50	12	16	3	3781–3800	40	77	19	26	4
2221–2280	27	51	12	16	3	3801–3840	40	77	20	26	4
2281–2340	27	52	12	16	3	3841–3900	40	78	20	26	4
2341–2400	28	53	12	16	3	3901–3960	41	79	20	27	4
2401–2460	28	54	13	17	3	3961–4000	41	80	20	27	4
2461–2540	29	55	13	17	3	4001–4020	41	80	21	27	5
2541–2550	29	56	13	17	3	4021–4050	42	81	21	27	5
2551–2580	29	56	13	18	3	4051–4080	42	81	21	28	5
2581–2600	30	57	13	18	3	4081–4140	42	82	21	28	5
2601–2640	30	57	14	18	3	4141–4200	43	83	21	28	5
2641–2700	30	58	14	18	3	4201–4260	43	84	22	29	5
2701–2760	31	59	14	19	3	4261–4320	44	85	22	29	5
2761–2800	31	60	14	19	3	4321–4350	44	86	22	29	5
2801–2820	31	60	15	19	3	4351–4380	44	86	22	30	5
2821–2850	32	61	15	19	3	4381–4400	45	87	22	30	5
2851–2880	32	61	15	20	3	4401–4440	45	87	23	30	5
2881–2940	32	62	15	20	3	4441–4500	45	88	23	30	5
2941–3000	33	63	15	20	3	4501–4560	46	89	23	31	5
3001–3060	33	64	16	21	4	4561–4600	46	90	23	31	5

Source: IBC Table 2902.1.

2902 Minimum Plumbing Facilities

2902.1 Minimum number of fixtures *(part 6 of 14)*

Table 2902.1h   Occupancy B Business: Minimum Plumbing Fixtures Required

Occupant count	WC	Lavs	DF	Occupant count	WC	Lavs	DF
1–25	1	1	1	371–400	9	7	4
26–40	2	1	1	401–450	10	7	5
41–50	2	2	1	451–500	11	8	5
51–100	3	3	1	501–530	12	8	6
101–130	4	3	2	531–550	12	9	6
131–150	4	4	2	550–600	13	9	6
151–200	5	4	2	601–610	14	9	7
201–250	6	4	3	611–650	14	10	7
251–280	7	5	3	651–690	15	10	7
281–300	7	6	3	691–700	15	11	7
301–350	8	6	4	701–750	16	11	8
351–370	9	6	4	751–770	17	11	8

Source: IBC Table 2902.1.

Table 2902.1i   Occupancy E Educational: Minimum Plumbing Fixtures Required

Occupant count	WC	Lavs	DF	Occupant count	WC	Lavs	DF
1–50	1	1	1	1001–1050	21	21	11
51–100	2	2	1	1051–1100	22	22	11
101–150	3	3	2	1101–1150	23	23	12
151–200	4	4	2	1151–1200	24	24	12
201–250	5	5	3	1201–1250	25	25	13
251–300	6	6	3	1251–1300	26	26	13
301–350	7	7	4	1301–1350	27	27	14
351–400	8	8	4	1351–1400	28	28	14
401–450	9	9	5	1401–1450	29	29	15
451–500	10	10	5	1451–1500	30	30	15
501–550	11	11	6	1501–1550	31	31	16
551–600	12	12	6	1551–1600	32	32	16
601–650	13	13	7	1601–1650	33	33	17
651–700	14	14	7	1651–1700	34	34	17
701–750	15	15	8	1701–1750	35	35	18
751–800	16	16	8	1751–1800	36	36	18
801–850	17	17	9	1801–1850	37	37	19
851–900	18	18	9	1851–1900	38	38	19
901–950	19	19	10	1901–1950	39	39	20
951–1000	20	20	10	1951–2000	40	40	20

Source: IBC Table 2902.1.

2902 Minimum Plumbing Facilities

2902.1 Minimum number of fixtures *(part 7 of 14)*

- Factory and industrial occupancies require the following facilities, where required by the manufacturer, and other fixtures as shown in the partial table below:
  - Emergency eyewash stations.
  - Emergency showers.

Table 2902.1j

Occupancies F-1 and F-2 Factory and Industrial: Minimum Plumbing Fixtures Required

Occupant count	WC	Lavs	DF	Occupant count	WC	Lavs	DF
1–100	1	1	1	801–900	9	9	3
101–200	2	2	1	901–1000	10	10	3
201–300	3	3	1	1001–1100	11	11	3
301–400	4	4	1	1101–1200	12	12	3
401–500	5	5	2	1201–1300	13	13	4
501–600	6	6	2	1301–1400	14	14	4
601–700	7	7	2	1401–1500	15	15	4
701–800	8	8	2	1501–1600	16	16	4

Source: IBC Table 2902.1.

Table 2902.1k   Occupancy I-1 Residential Care: Minimum Plumbing Fixtures Required

Occupant count	WC	Lavs	Bathtub/ shower	DF	Occupant count	WC	Lavs	Bathtub/ shower	DF
1–8	1	1	1	1	41–48	5	5	6	1
9–10	1	1	2	1	49–50	5	5	7	1
11–16	2	2	2	1	51–56	6	6	7	1
17–20	2	2	3	1	57–60	6	6	8	1
21–24	3	3	3	1	61–64	7	7	8	1
25–30	3	3	4	1	65–70	7	7	9	1
31–32	4	4	4	1	71–72	8	8	9	1
33–40	4	4	5	1	73–80	8	8	10	1

Source: IBC Table 2902.1.

- Fixtures for patients in occupancy I-2 hospitals and ambulatory nursing homes are governed as follows:
  - Employee toilets are separate from patient toilets as follows:
    They are not governed by the following requirements or table.
  - 1 toilet room may serve 2 adjacent rooms where all of the following conditions apply:
    Toilet has 1 lavatory and 1 water closet.
    Toilet is directly accessed from each room with provisions for privacy.
  - Otherwise, the following is required for each patient room:
    1 water closet and 1 lavatory.
  - 1 service sink is required for each floor.
  - Other fixtures are required as shown in the following table.

2902 Minimum Plumbing Facilities

2902.1 Minimum number of fixtures *(part 8 of 14)*

Table 2902.1l   Occupancy I-2 Hospitals, Ambulatory Nursing Homes:
Minimum Fixtures Required for Patients

Patient count	Bathtub/ shower	DF	Patient count	Bathtub/ shower	DF	Patient count	Bathtub/ shower	DF
1–15	1	1	166–180	12	2	331–345	23	4
16–30	2	1	181–195	13	2	346–360	24	4
31–45	3	1	196–200	14	2	361–375	25	4
46–60	4	1	201–210	14	3	376–390	26	4
61–75	5	1	211–225	15	3	391–400	27	4
76–90	6	1	226–240	16	3	401–405	27	5
91–100	7	1	241–255	17	3	406–420	28	5
101–105	7	2	256–270	18	3	421–435	29	5
106–120	8	2	271–285	19	3	436–450	30	5
121–135	9	2	286–300	20	3	451–465	31	5
136–150	10	2	301–315	21	4	466–480	32	5
151–165	11	2	316–330	22	4	481–495	33	5

Source: IBC Table 2902.1.

- Fixtures for institutional employees other than residential care are governed as follows:
  o Employee toilets are separate from patient toilets.
  o A service sink is not required to serve employees.
  o Bathing facilities are not required for employees.
  o Otherwise, fixture requirements are as shown in the partial table below:

Table 2902.1m   Occupancy I Institutional Employees Other Than Residential Care:
Minimum Fixtures Required for Employees

Employee count	WC	Lavs	DF	Employee count	WC	Lavs	DF
1–25	1	1	1	126–140	6	4	2
26–35	2	1	1	141–150	6	5	2
36–50	2	2	1	151–175	7	5	2
51–70	3	2	1	176–200	8	6	2
71–75	2	2	1	201–210	9	6	3
76–100	4	3	1	211–225	9	7	3
101–105	5	3	2	226–245	10	7	3
106–125	5	4	2	246–250	10	8	3

Source: IBC Table 2902.1.

2902 Minimum Plumbing Facilities

2902.1 Minimum number of fixtures (*part 9 of 14*)

- Fixtures for institutional visitors other than residential care are governed as follows:
  - A service sink is not required to serve visitors.
  - Bathing facilities are not required for visitors.
  - Otherwise, fixture requirements are as shown in the partial table below:

Table 2902.1n   Occupancy I Institutional Visitors Other Than Residential Care: Minimum Plumbing Fixtures Required for Vistors

Visitor count	WC	Lavs	DF	Visitor count	WC	Lavs	DF
1–75	1	1	1	201–225	3	3	1
76–100	2	1	1	226–300	4	3	1
101–150	2	2	1	301–375	5	4	1
151–200	3	2	1	376–400	6	4	1

Source: IBC Table 2902.1.

- Fixtures for inmates of prisons are governed as follows:
  - Employee toilets are separate from inmate toilets and are not governed by guidelines for inmates or the table below.
  - 1 water closet for each cell.
  - 1 lavatory for each cell.
  - Other fixtures are required as shown in the partial table below:

Table 2902.1o   Occupancy I-3 Prisons: Minimum Fixtures Required for Inmates

Inmate count	Bathtub/ shower	DF	Inmate count	Bathtub/ shower	DF	Inmate count	Bathtub/ shower	DF
1–15	1	1	211–225	15	3	436–450	30	5
16–30	2	1	226–240	16	3	451–465	31	5
31–45	3	1	241–255	17	3	466–480	32	5
46–60	4	1	256–270	18	3	481–495	33	5
61–75	5	1	271–285	19	3	496–500	34	5
76–90	6	1	286–300	20	3	501–510	34	6
91–100	7	1	301–315	21	4	511–525	35	6
101–105	7	2	316–330	22	4	526–540	36	6
106–120	8	2	331–345	23	4	541–555	37	6
121–135	9	2	346–360	24	4	556–570	38	6
136–150	10	2	361–375	25	4	571–585	39	6
151–165	11	2	376–390	26	4	586–600	40	6
166–180	12	2	391–400	27	4	601–615	41	7
181–195	13	2	401–405	27	5	616–630	42	7
196–200	14	2	406–420	28	5	631–645	43	7
201–210	14	3	421–435	29	5	646–660	44	7

Source: IBC Table 2902.1.

2902 Minimum Plumbing Facilities

2902.1 Minimum number of fixtures *(part 10 of 14)*

- Fixtures for inmates of the following I-3 occupancies the following are governed as indicated below and as listed in the following table:
  - Occupancies:
    Reformatories.
    Detention and correctional centers.
  - Employee toilets are separate from inmate toilets and are not governed here.
  - Otherwise, fixture requirements are as shown in the partial table below.

Table 2902.1p

Occupancy I-3 Reformatories, Detention Centers, Correctional Centers: Minimum Plumbing Fixtures Required for Inmates

Inmate count	WC	Lavs	Bathtub/ shower	DF	Inmate count	WC	Lavs	Bathtub/ shower	DF
1–15	1	1	1	1	106–120	8	8	8	2
16–30	2	2	2	1	121–135	9	9	9	2
31–45	3	3	3	1	136–150	10	10	10	2
46–60	4	4	4	1	151–165	11	11	11	2
61–75	5	5	5	1	166–180	12	12	12	2
76–90	6	6	6	1	181–195	13	13	13	2
91–100	7	7	7	1	196–200	14	14	14	2
101–105	7	7	7	2	201–210	14	14	14	3

Source: IBC Table 2902.1.

- Fixtures for I-4 occupancies including adult day care and child care are governed as follows:
  - Employee toilets are separate from patient toilets as follows:
    They are not governed by the following requirements or table below.
  - Day nurseries require only 1 bathtub.
  - Otherwise, fixture requirements are as shown in the partial table below:

Table 2902.1q

Occupancy I-4, Adult Day Care and Child Care: Minimum Plumbing Fixtures Required for Patients

Patient count	WC	Lavs	Bathtub/ shower	DF	Patient count	WC	Lavs	Bathtub/ shower	DF
1–15	1	1	1	1	106–120	8	8	8	2
16–30	2	2	2	1	121–135	9	9	9	2
31–45	3	3	3	1	136–150	10	10	10	2
46–60	4	4	4	1	151–165	11	11	11	2
61–75	5	5	5	1	166–180	12	12	12	2
76–90	6	6	6	1	181–195	13	13	13	2
91–100	7	7	7	1	196–200	14	14	14	2
101–105	7	7	7	2	201–210	14	14	14	3

Source: IBC Table 2902.1.

2902 Minimum Plumbing Facilities

2902.1 Minimum number of fixtures *(part 11 of 14)*

Table 2902.1r   Occupancy M Mercantile: Minimum Plumbing Fixtures Required

Occupant count	WC	Lavs	DF	Occupant count	WC	Lavs	DF
1–500	1	1	1	1501–2000	4	3	2
501–750	2	1	1	2001–2250	5	3	3
751–1000	2	2	1	2251–2500	5	4	3
1001–1500	3	2	2	2501–3000	6	4	3

Source: IBC Table 2902.1.

- The following R-1 occupancies are governed as indicated below:
  - Occupancies:
      Hotels.
      Motels.
      Transient borading houses.
  - Requirements:
      The following fixtures are required in each guest room:
        1 water closet.
        1 lavatory.
        1 bathtub/shower.
- The following S-1 and S-2 occupancies are governed as indicated below and by the following partial table:
  - Occupancies:
      Storage of goods.
      Warehouses.
      Storehouses.
      Freight depots.
      Moderate-hazard storage.
  - Requirements:
      The following must be provided where required by the function of the occupancy:
        Emergency eyewash stations.
        Emergency showers.

Table 2902.1s   Occupancy S-1 and S-2 Storage: Minimum Plumbing Fixtures Required

Occupant count	WC	Lavs	DF	Occupant count	WC	Lavs	DF
1–100	1	1	1	301–400	4	4	1
101–200	2	2	1	401–500	5	5	1
201–300	3	3	1	501–600	6	6	1

Source: IBC Table 2902.1.

2902 Minimum Plumbing Facilities

2902.1 Minimum number of fixtures *(part 12 of 14)*

Occupancy R-2 Dorms, Fraternities, Sororities, Nontransient Boarding Houses:
Occupancy R-4 Residential Care/Assisted Living Facilities:
Table 2902.1t   1–360 Occupants: Minimum Plumbing Fixtures Required

Occupant count	WC	Lavs	Bathtub/ shower	DF	Occupant count	WC	Lavs	Bathtub/ shower	DF
1–8	1	1	1	1	181–184	19	19	23	2
9–10	1	1	2	1	185–190	19	19	24	2
11–16	2	2	2	1	191–192	20	20	24	2
17–20	2	2	3	1	193–200	20	20	25	2
21–24	3	3	3	1	201–208	21	21	26	3
25–30	3	3	4	1	209–210	21	21	27	3
31–32	4	4	4	1	211–216	22	22	27	3
33–40	4	4	5	1	217–220	22	22	28	3
41–48	5	5	6	1	221–224	23	23	28	3
49–50	5	5	7	1	225–230	23	23	29	3
51–56	6	6	7	1	231–232	24	24	29	3
57–60	6	6	8	1	233–240	24	24	30	3
61–64	7	7	8	1	241–248	25	25	31	3
65–70	7	7	9	1	249–250	25	25	32	3
71–72	8	8	9	1	251–256	26	26	32	3
73–80	8	8	10	1	257–260	26	26	33	3
81–88	9	9	11	1	261–264	27	27	33	3
89–90	9	9	12	1	265–270	27	27	34	3
91–96	10	10	12	1	271–272	28	28	34	3
97–100	10	10	13	1	273–280	28	28	35	3
101–104	11	11	13	2	281–288	29	29	36	3
105–110	11	11	14	2	289–290	29	29	37	3
111–112	12	12	14	2	291–296	30	30	37	3
113–120	12	12	15	2	297–300	30	30	38	3
121–128	13	13	16	2	301–304	31	31	38	4
129–130	13	13	17	2	305–310	31	31	39	4
131–136	14	14	17	2	311–312	32	32	39	4
137–140	14	14	18	2	313–320	32	32	40	4
141–144	15	15	18	2	321–328	33	33	41	4
145–150	15	15	19	2	329–330	33	33	42	4
151–152	16	16	19	2	331–336	34	34	42	4
153–160	16	16	20	2	337–340	34	34	43	4
161–168	17	17	21	2	341–344	35	35	43	4
169–170	17	17	22	2	345–350	35	35	44	4
171–176	18	18	22	2	351–352	36	36	44	4
177–180	18	18	23	2	353–360	36	36	45	4

Source: IBC Table 2902.1.

2902 Minimum Plumbing Facilities

2902.1 Minimum number of fixtures *(part 13 of 14)*

Occupancy R-2 Dorms, Fraternities, Sororities, Nontransient Boarding Houses:
Occupancy R-4 Residential Care/Assisted Living Facilities:
Table 2902.1u   361–720 Occupants: Minimum Plumbing Fixtures Required

Occupant count	WC	Lavs	Bathtub/ shower	DF	Occupant count	WC	Lavs	Bathtub/ shower	DF
361–368	37	37	46	4	541–544	55	55	68	6
369–370	37	37	47	4	545–550	55	55	69	6
371–376	38	38	47	4	551–552	56	56	69	6
377–380	38	38	48	4	553–560	56	56	70	6
381–384	39	39	48	4	561–568	57	57	71	6
385–390	39	39	49	4	569–570	57	7	72	6
391–392	40	40	49	4	571–576	58	58	72	6
393–400	40	40	50	4	577–580	58	58	73	6
401–408	41	41	51	5	581–584	59	59	73	6
409–410	41	41	52	5	585–590	59	59	74	6
411–416	42	42	52	5	591–592	60	60	74	6
417–420	42	42	53	5	593–600	60	60	75	6
421–424	43	43	53	5	601–608	61	61	76	7
425–430	43	43	54	5	609–610	61	61	77	7
431–432	44	44	54	5	611–616	62	62	77	7
433–440	44	44	55	5	617–620	62	62	78	7
441–448	45	45	56	5	621–624	63	63	78	7
449–450	45	45	57	5	625–630	63	63	79	7
451–456	46	46	57	5	631–632	64	64	79	7
457–460	46	46	58	5	633–640	64	64	80	7
461–464	47	47	58	5	641–648	65	65	81	7
465–470	47	47	59	5	649–650	65	65	82	7
471–472	48	48	59	5	651–656	66	66	82	7
473–480	48	84	60	5	657–660	66	66	83	7
481–488	49	49	61	5	661–664	67	67	83	7
489–490	49	49	62	5	665–670	67	67	84	7
491–496	50	50	62	5	671–672	68	68	84	7
497–500	50	50	63	5	673–680	68	68	85	7
501–504	51	51	63	6	681–688	69	69	86	7
505–510	51	51	64	6	689–690	69	69	87	7
511–512	52	52	64	6	691–696	70	70	87	7
513–520	52	52	65	6	697–700	70	70	88	7
521–528	53	53	66	6	701–704	71	71	88	8
529–530	53	53	67	6	705–710	71	71	89	8
531–536	54	54	67	6	711–712	72	72	89	8
537–540	54	54	68	6	713–720	72	72	90	8

Source: IBC Table 2902.1.

2902 Minimum Plumbing Facilities

2902.1 Minimum number of fixtures *(part 14 of 14)*

- The following occupancies are governed as indicated below:
  - Occupancies:
    R-2 apartment houses.
    R-3 1- and 2-family dwellings.
  - Requirements:
    The following plumbing fixtures listed below are required for each dwelling unit:
    1 water closet.
    1 lavatory.
    1 bathtub/shower.
    1 kitchen sink.
    Drinking fountains are not required.
    A service sink is not required.
    Automatic clothes washer connections as indicated in the following table:

Table 2902.1v — **Occupancy R-2 Apartment Houses: / Occupancy R-3 1- and 2-Family Dwellings: / Minimum Automatic Clothes Washer Connections Required**

Dwelling unit count	Connections required	Dwelling unit count	Connections required	Dwelling unit count	Connections required
20	1	220	9	320	17
30	2	230	10	330	18
40	3	240	11	340	19
50	4	250	12	350	20
60	5	260	13	360	21
80	6	280	14	380	22
90	7	290	15	390	23
100	8	300	16	400	24

Source: IBC Table 2902.1.

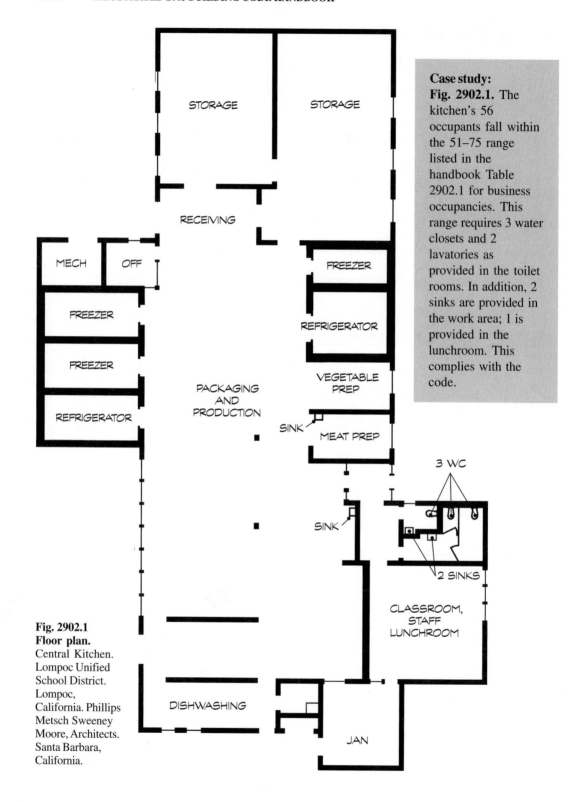

STORAGE

STORAGE

RECEIVING

MECH

OFF

FREEZER

REFRIGERATOR

FREEZER

FREEZER

VEGETABLE PREP

REFRIGERATOR

PACKAGING AND PRODUCTION

SINK

MEAT PREP

SINK

3 WC

2 SINKS

CLASSROOM, STAFF LUNCHROOM

DISHWASHING

JAN

Case study:
Fig. 2902.1. The kitchen's 56 occupants fall within the 51–75 range listed in the handbook Table 2902.1 for business occupancies. This range requires 3 water closets and 2 lavatories as provided in the toilet rooms. In addition, 2 sinks are provided in the work area; 1 is provided in the lunchroom. This complies with the code.

Fig. 2902.1
Floor plan.
Central Kitchen. Lompoc Unified School District. Lompoc, California. Phillips Metsch Sweeney Moore, Architects. Santa Barbara, California.

2902 Minimum Plumbing Facilities

2902.2 Separate facilities

- Separate sex toilet facilities are not required for the following cases:
  - Private facilities.
  - For occupancies with ≤ 15 employees.
  - In buildings or tenant spaces where occupant load is ≤ 15 including both of the following:
    Employees.
    Customers.
  - In mercantile occupancies as follows:
    With ≤ 50 occupants.
- Otherwise, where toilet fixtures are required, separate sex facilities must be provided.

2902.3 Number of occupants of each sex

- Where not specified otherwise, distribution of the following facilities must be as indicated below:
  - Facilities:
    Water closets.
    Lavatories.
    Showers or bathtubs.
  - Distribution:
    Facilities must be distributed between sexes in one of the following ways:
    Equally.
    According to anticipated distribution of the sexes in the occupant load as follows:
    Supporting statistical data is required.
    Must be approved by the building official.

2902 Minimum Plumbing Facilities

2902.4 Location of employee toilet facilities in occupancies other than assembly or mercantile

- The following toilet facilities are governed as indicated below:
    - Toilets:
        Where provided as indicated below for employees working in the following locations:
            Work locations:
                Storage structures.
                Kiosks.
            Toilet location:
                In an adjacent structure.
    - Requirements:
        Adjacent structure must have one of the following characteristics:
            Under same ownership or lease as is the work location.
            Under same control is as the work location.
        Travel distance from the work location to the toilet facilities must be as follows:
            ≤ 500'.
- In other cases, employee toilet facilities are governed as follows:
    - In occupancies other than A or M, the following applies:
        Access to toilet facilities must be from within the employees' work area.
        Employee toilet facilities must be one of the following:
            Separate from public customer facilities.
            Combined with public facilities.

2902.4.1 Travel distance

- Occupancies A and M are not governed by this section.
- In occupancy F, required toilet facilities need not be located as indicated below, where approved by the building official.
- In other occupancies, required toilet facilities must be located as follows:
    - ≤ 1 story above or below the employees' work area.
    - ≤ 500' travel distance from the employees' work area.

2902.5 Location of employee toilet facilities in mercantile and assembly occupancies
  (part 1 of 2)

- Employee toilet facilities are not required in the following location:
    - In tenant spaces where toilets are otherwise provided as follows:
        Where travel distance between the following points is ≤ 300':
            Main entrance to tenant space.
            Central toilet area.
        Central toilet area is located ≤ 1 story above or below the tenant space.

2902 Minimum Plumbing Facilities

2902.5 Location of employee toilet facilities in mercantile and assembly occupancies
(part 2 of 2)

- In other cases, employee toilets are required in buildings and tenant spaces as follows:
    - Restaurants.
    - Nightclubs.
    - Places of public assembly.
    - Mercantile occupancies.
- Employee toilet facilities may be separate or combined with public customer facilities.
- Required toilet facilities must be located as follows:
    - $\leq$ 1 story above or below the employees' work area.
    - $\leq$ 500' travel distance from the employees' work area in other than a covered mall.
    - $\leq$ 300' travel distance from the employees' work area in a covered mall.

2902.6 Public facilities

- Buildings and tenant spaces for public use must have toilet facilities for the public as follows:
    - Toilet facilities must be located as follows:
        $\leq$ 1 story above or below the space requiring toilet facilities.
        $\leq$ 500' travel distance to the toilet facilities.

2902.6.1 Covered malls

- Covered mall buildings require toilet facilities as follows:
    - Travel distance to toilets must be $\leq$ 300'.
    - Required toilet facilities must be provided in one of the following locations:
        In each individual store.
        In a central toilet area.
    - Travel distance to central toilet facilities is measured from the following:
        The main entrance of each store or tenant space.

2902.6.3 Pay facilities

- Required toilet facilites must be free of charge.
- Any pay toilet facilites must be in excess of the required number of facilities.

2902.6.4 Signage

- Each toilet room entrance requires the following signage:
    - Room's gender designation as follows:
        Must be legible.
        Must be visible.

    Note: ICC A117.1, "Accessible and Usable Buildings and Facilities," is cited as governing these signs.

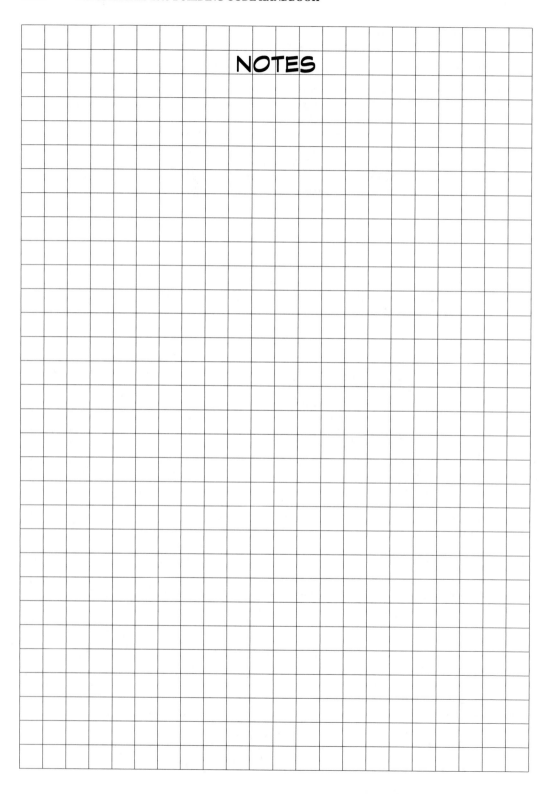

NOTES

30

Elevators and Conveying Systems

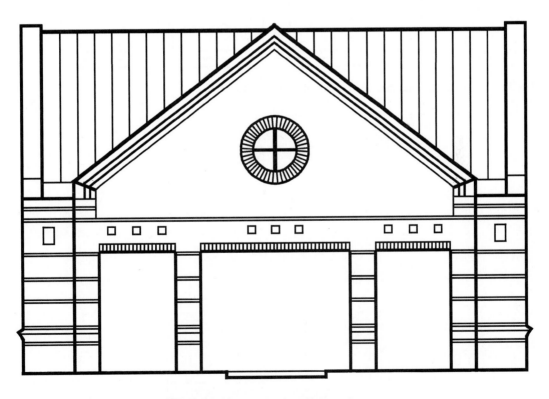

Christus St. Michael Health Care Center. Texarkana, Texas. *(partial elevation)*
Watkins Hamilton Ross Architects, Inc. Houston, Texas.

3002 Hoistway Enclosures

3002.2 Number of elevator cars in a hoistway

- The number of elevators permitted in a hoistway is shown in the illustrations below.

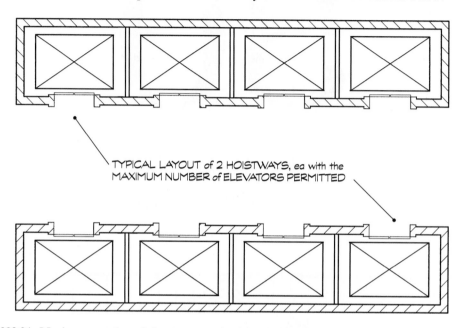

TYPICAL LAYOUT of 2 HOISTWAYS, ea with the
MAXIMUM NUMBER of ELEVATORS PERMITTED

Fig. 3002.2A. Maximum number of elevators permitted in a hoistway.

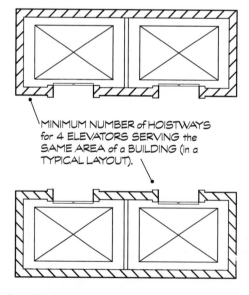

MINIMUM NUMBER of HOISTWAYS
for 4 ELEVATORS SERVING the
SAME AREA of a BUILDING (in a
TYPICAL LAYOUT).

Fig. 3002.2B. Minimum number of hoistways.

3002 Hoistway Enclosures

3002.3 Emergency signs

- Signs at elevators prohibiting use of elevators during a fire are not required as follows:
  - Where elevators are part of an accessible means of egress.

  Note: 1007.4, "Elevators," is cited as governing elevators as indicated above.

- Otherwise, a sign is required by each elevator call button as follows:
  - Sign must be approved.
  - Sign must be a standardized design.
  - Sign must state the message shown on the illustration below.

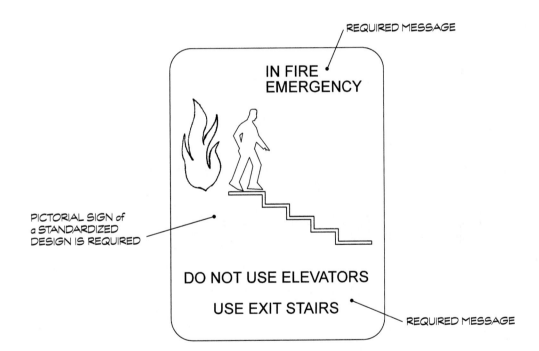

Fig. 3002.3. Acceptable pictorial design for a sign required to be posted at elevators prohibiting elevator use during fire.

3002 Hoistway Enclosures

3002.4 Elevator car to accommodate ambulance stretcher

- In buildings ≥ 4 stories, the following applies:
  - ≥ 1 elevator must be provided as follows:
    For fire department emergency access to all floors.
    Size to be as indicated in the detail below.
    Must be identified with signs as shown in the following detail.

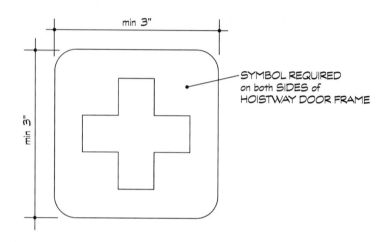

Fig. 3002.4A. Symbol required at elevator design for fire department use.

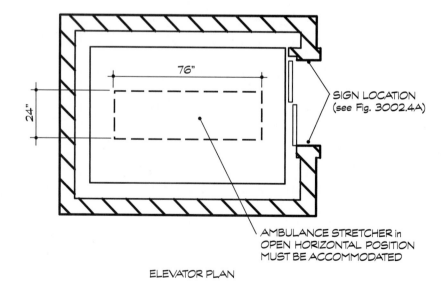

Fig. 3002.4B. Plan of elevator accommodating an ambulance stretcher.

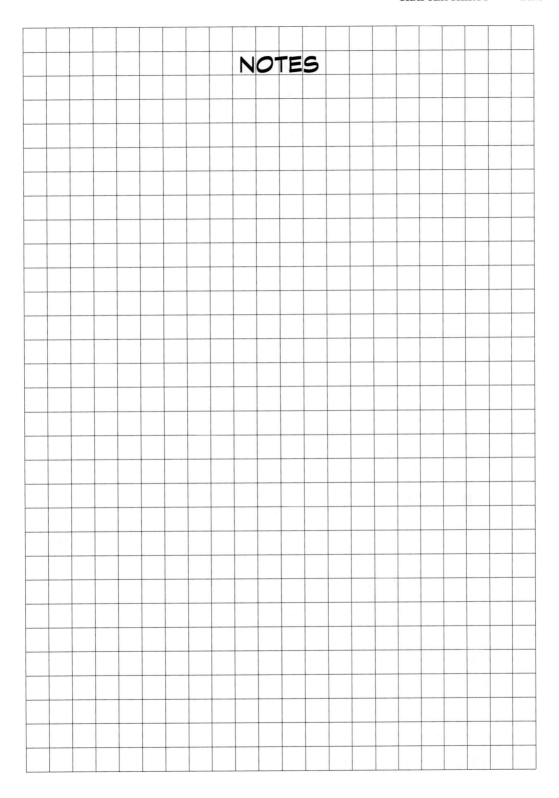

NOTES

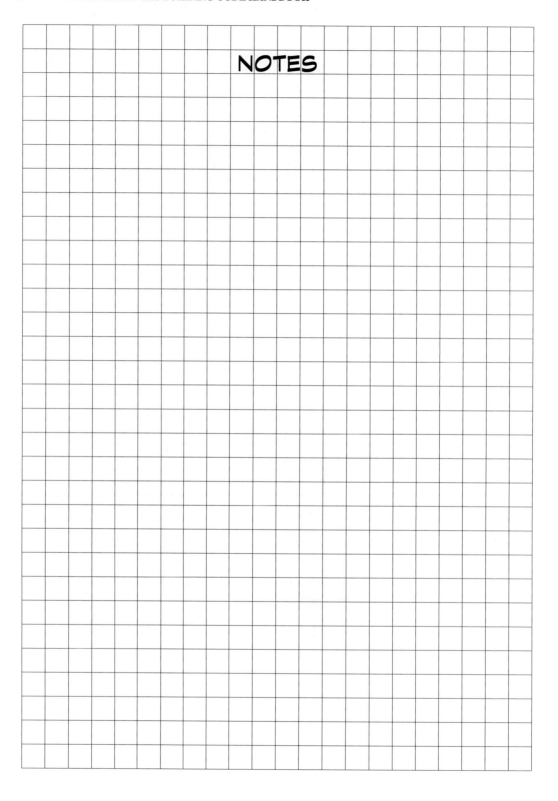

31

Special Construction

AmberGlen Business Center. Hillsboro, Oregon. *(partial elevation)*
Ankrom Moisan Associated Architects. Portland, Oregon.

3104 Pedestrian Walkways and Tunnels

3104.5 Fire barriers between pedestrian walkways and buildings *(part 1 of 2)*

- This section applies to pedestrian walkways connecting buildings as follows:
  - At grade.
  - Above grade.
  - Below grade.
- Where exterior walls of the connected buildings are required to have a fire-resistance rating > 2 hrs, the following applies:
  - The walkway must be sprinklered as per NFPA 13.

  Note: Section 704, "Exterior Walls," is cited as the source governing the fire-resistance ratings of exterior walls.

- This section does not require a fire-resistance rating for walls of the following heights where they have any of the additional conditions indicated below:
  - Heights:
    - Walls separating a pedestrian walkway from a building as follows:
      - Height complies with both of the following where not sprinklered:
        - ≤ 3 stories and ≤ 40'.
      - Height complies with both of the following where sprinklered:
        - ≤ 5 stories and 55'.
      - Height is ≥ 8'.
  - Conditions:
    - Where connected buildings are ≥ 10' apart and all of the following apply:
      - Walkway is sprinklered as per NFPA 13.
      - Any glass in the wall and doors separating the walkway from building is as follows:
        - One of the following types of glass is used:
          - Tempered.
          - Wired.
          - Laminated.
      - Glass is protected by NFPA 13 sprinklers as follows:
        - Sprinklers can wet the whole interior surface of the glass.
      - Glass is mounted as follows:
        - In a gasketed frame.
        - So that the frame can deflect without breaking the glass as follows:
          - Prior to activation of the sprinklers.
      - No obstructions exist between sprinklers and glass.
    - Where connected buildings are ≥ 10' apart and all of the following apply:
      - Both side walls of the walkway must be open as follows:
        - ≥ 50%.
      - Open area is uniformly distributed.
      - Open area prevents the accumulation of the following:
        - Smoke and toxic gases.
    - Where buildings are on the same lot.

  Note: 503.1.3, "Buildings on same lot," is cited as governing such buildings.

3104 Pedestrian Walkways and Tunnels

3104.5 Fire barriers between pedestrian walkways and buildings *(part 2 of 2)*

- In other cases, walkways must be separated from the connected buildings as shown in the illustration below.

    Note: Section 715, "Opening Protectives," is cited as governing the fire protection rating required for windows as noted in the illustration.

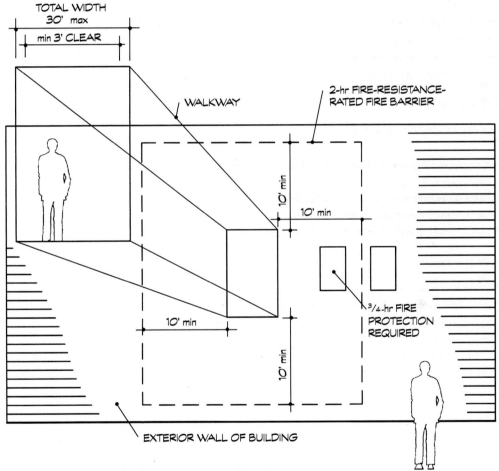

Fig. 3104.5. Pedestrian walkway, dimensions, and fire barrier at building.

3104 Pedestrian Walkways and Tunnels

3104.7 Egress

- Pedestrian walkways serving as a required exit are governed as follows:
  - They must be able to be accessed at all times.

3104.8 Width

- Width of pedestrian walkways must be as shown in the previous illustration.

3104.9 Exit access travel

- This section addresses pedestrian walkways and tunnels.

- Exit access travel distance within such elements is governed as follows:

Type of walkway	Sprinklered	Not sprinklered
Tunnel	≤ 200'	≤ 200'
Pedestrian walkway	≤ 250'	≤ 200'
Pedestrian walkway, both sides open ≥ 50%	≤ 400'	≤ 300'

- Sprinklers are to be as per NFPA 13.

3104.10 Tunneled walkway

- A separation is required between the following elements as indicated below:
  - Elements:
    Tunneled walkway.
    Building to which the tunneled walkway connects.
  - Separation:
    Must be ≥ 2 hr fire-resistance-rated construction.
    Openings require protection.

  Note: IBC Table 715.3, "Fire Door and Fire Shutter Fire Protection Ratings," is cited as governing the openings in the separation construction.

3104.11 Ventilation

- The following vents for the elements listed below have the requirement indicated:
  - Vents:
    Smoke.
    Heat.
  - Elements:
    Enclosed walkways.
    Tunneled walkways.
  - Requirement:
    They must meet requirements as for occupancy F-1.

  Note: Section 910, "Smoke and Heat Vents," is cited as governing the vents.

3106 Marquees

3106.2 Thickness

- The vertical dimension of a marquee is as shown in the illustrations below.

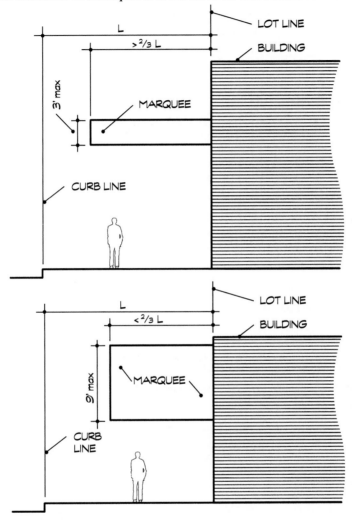

Fig. 3106.2. Maximum vertical dimension of marquees.

3106.5 Construction

- A marquee must be supported entirely from the building.
- A marquee must be constructed of noncombustible materials.
- A marquee's structure must be protected from deterioration.
- A marquee must meet structural requirements of the code.

Note: Chapter 16, "Structural Design," is cited as governing the structure of a marquee.

3109 Swimming Pool Enclosures and Safety Devices

3109.3 Public swimming pools

- Public swimming pools must be enclosed by a fence as shown in the following detail.

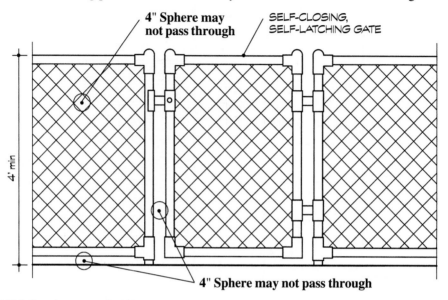

Fig. 3109.3. Barriers around public swimming pools.

3109.4.1 Barrier height and clearances

- This section addresses residential swimming pools.
- Such pools must be enclosed by a barrier as shown in the following details.

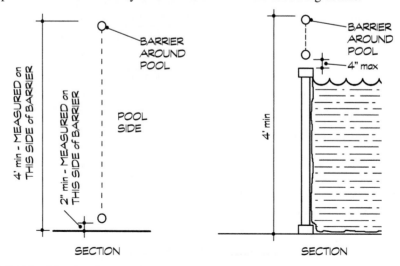

Fig. 3109.4.1. Residential swimming poor barrier height and clearances.

3109 Swimming Pool Enclosures

3109.4 1.1 Openings

- This section addresses barriers enclosing residential swimming pools.
- Openings in the required barrier must be as shown in the following detail.

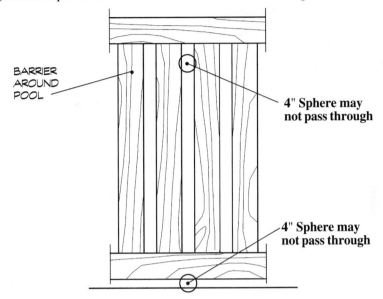

Fig. 3109.4 1.1. Openings in barriers around residential swimming pools.

3109.4.1.2 Solid barrier surfaces

- This section addresses barriers enclosing residential swimming pools.
- Where a required barrier is solid, the surface must be as shown in the following detail.

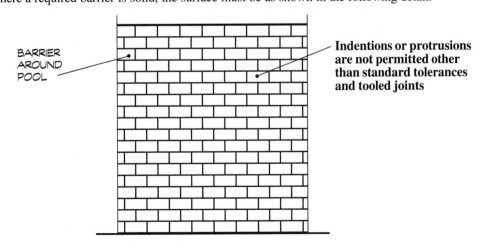

Fig. 3109.4.1.2. Solid barrier surfaces around residential swimming pools.

3109 Swimming Pool Enclosures

3109.4.1.3 Closely spaced horizontal members

- This section addresses barriers enclosing residential swimming pools.
- Requirements for barriers constructed of the following are shown in the detail below:
  - Horizontal members as follows:
    Vertical distance between tops of members is < 3'-9".
  - Vertical members.

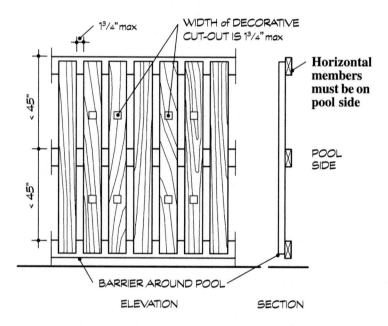

Fig. 3109.4.1.3. Closely spaced horizontal members in barriers around residential swimming pools.

3109.4.1.4 Widely spaced horizontal members

- This section addresses barriers enclosing residential swimming pools.
- Requirements for barriers constructed of the following are shown in the detail provided with this section:
  - Horizontal members as follows:
    Vertical distance between tops of members is ≥ 3'-9".
  - Vertical members.

3109 Swimming Pool Enclosures

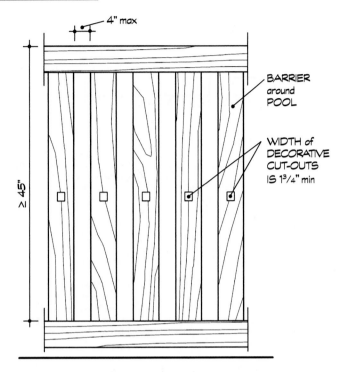

Fig. 3109.4.1.4. Widely spaced horizontal members in barriers around residential swimming pools.

3109.4.1.5 Chain link dimensions

- This section addresses barriers enclosing residential swimming pools.
- Requirements for chain link fencing are shown on the following details.

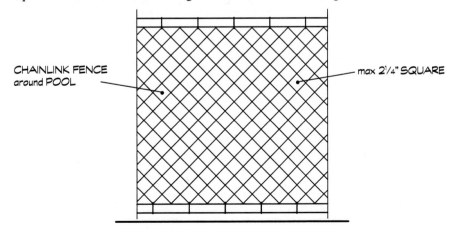

Fig. 3109.4.1.5A. Chain link dimensions in fences around residential swimming pools.

3109 Swimming Pool Enclosures

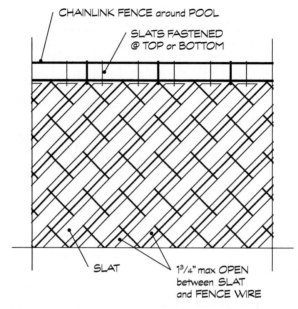

Fig. 3109.4.1.5B. Chain link dimensions at slats in fences around residential swimming pools.

3109.4.1.6 Diagonal members

- This section addresses barriers enclosing residential swimming pools.
- The limitation of openings for barriers with diagonal members is shown in the following detail.

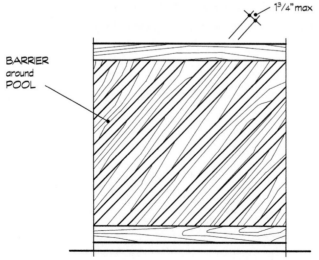

Fig. 3109.4.1.6. Diagonal members in barriers around residential swimming pools.

3109 Swimming Pool Enclosures

3109.4.1.7 Gates

- Requirements for access gates in barriers are shown in the following detail.

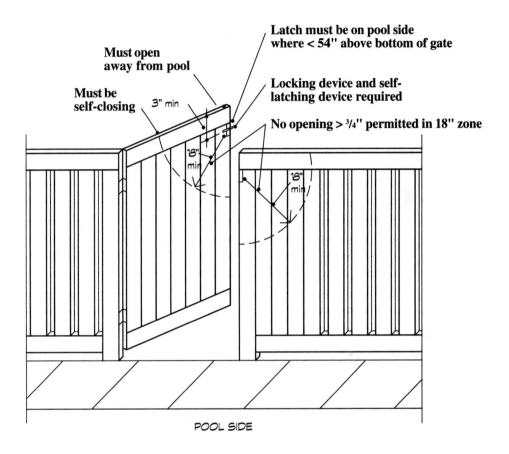

Fig. 3109.4.1.7. Gates in barriers around residential swimming pools.

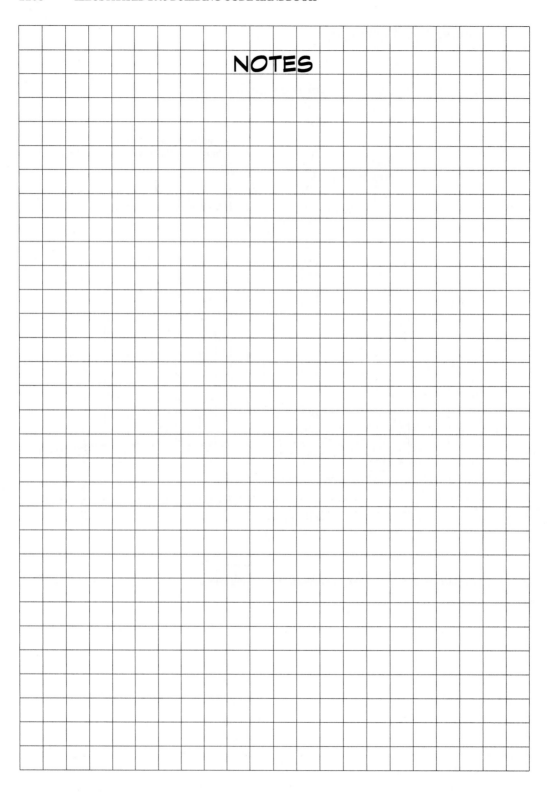

NOTES

32

Encroachments into the Public Right-of-Way

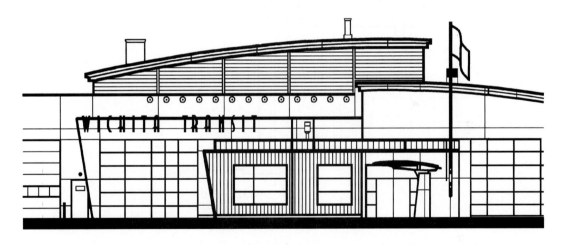

Wichita Transit Storage, Administration, and Maintenance Facility.
Wichita, Kansas. *(partial elevation)*
Wilson Darnell Mann, P.A., Architects. Wichita, Kansas.

3202 Encroachments

3202.1.1 Structural support

- The following detail shows where a foundation may project beyond the property line.
- Otherwise, foundations may not project beyond the property line.

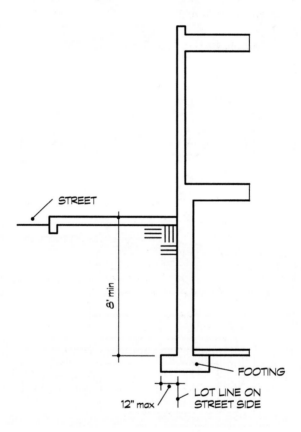

Fig. 3202.1.1. Projection of foundation over property line.

3202 Encroachments

3202.2 Encroachments above grade and below 8 feet in height

- Only the following elements may project into the public right-of-way within a height of 8':
  - Steps.
  - Architectural features.
  - Awnings.

    Note: The following are cited as governing the elements that may project into the public right-of-way within a height of 8':
    3202.2.1, "Steps."
    3202.2.2, "Architectural features."
    3202.2.3, "Awnings."

- Doors and window may not project into the public right of way within a height of 8'.

3202.2.1 Steps

- Requirements for steps that encroach on the public right-of-way are shown in the following illustration.

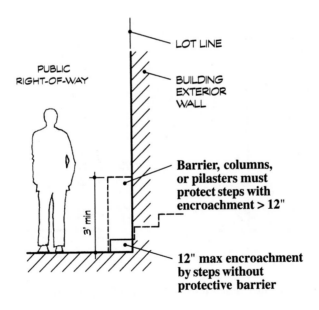

Fig. 3202.2.1. Projection of steps into the public right-of-way.

3202 Encroachments

3202.2.2 Architectural features

- Projection of the following features into the public right-of-way is limited as shown in the illustration below:
    - The following features are limited to a projection of ≤ 12":
        Columns.
        Pilasters.
    - The following details are limited to a projection of ≤ 4":
        Belt courses.
        Lintels.
        Sills.
        Architraves.
        Pediments.

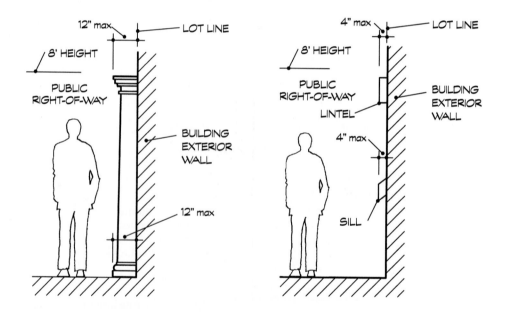

Fig. 3202.2.2. Projection of architectural features into the public right-of-way.

3202 Encroachments

3202.2.3 Awnings

- The required clearance for an awning projecting into the public right-of-way is shown in the following illustration.

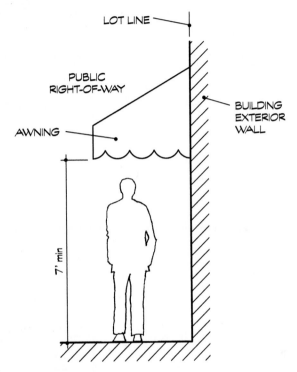

Fig. 3202.2.3. Projection of awnings into the public-right-of-way.

3202.3.1 Awnings, canopies, marquees and signs

- This section addresses encroachments into the public-right-of way above a height of 8'.
- The following elements are governed as indicated below:
  - Elements:
    Awnings.
    Canopies.
    Marquees.
    Signs.
  - Requirements:
    Elements must meet code structural requirements.
    Clearance requirements are shown in the following illustrations.

  Note: Chapter 16, "Structural Design," is cited as governing the structure of the elements indicated above.

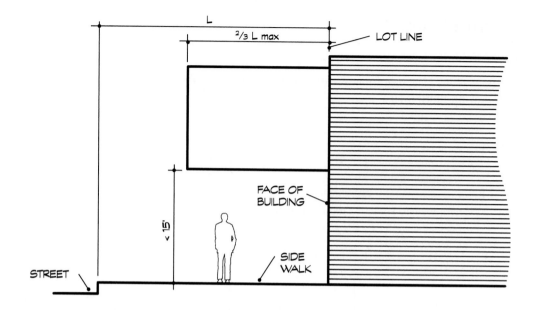

Fig. 3202.3.1A. Projection of awnings, canopies, marquees, and signs into the public right-of-way at a height ≥ 8' and < 15'.

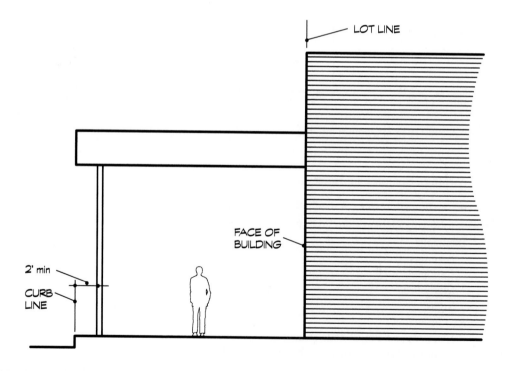

Fig. 3202.3.1B. Columns supporting awnings, canopies, marquees, and signs that project into the public right-of-way.

3202 Encroachments

3202.3.2 Windows, balconies, architectural features and mechanical equipment

- The following elements that project into the public right-of-way are governed as indicated below:
  - Elements:
    Windows.
    Balconies.
    Architectural features.
    Mechanical equipment.
  - Requirements:
    Where located above 8', the limit of encroachment is indicated as follows:
    In the illustration provided with this section.
    In the partial table below as based on the following:
    1" of encroachment is permitted for each 1" of height above 8'.
    ≤ 4' of encroachment is permitted.

Encroachment into Public Right-of-Way Permitted:
Table 3202.3.2   Windows, Balconies, Architectural Features, Mechanical Equipment

Vertical	Projection	Vertical	Projection	Vertical	Projection
8'-1"	0'-1"	9'-5"	1'-5"	10'-9"	2'-9"
8'-2"	0'-2"	9'-6"	1'-6"	10'-10"	2'-10"
8'-3"	0'-3"	9'-7"	1'-7"	10'-11"	2'-11"
8'-4"	0'-4"	9'-8"	1'-8"	11'-0"	3'-0"
8'-5"	0'-5"	9'-9"	1'-9"	11'-1"	3'-1"
8'-6"	0'-6"	9'-10"	1'-10"	11'-2"	3'-2"
8'-7"	0'-7"	9'-11"	1'-11"	11'-3"	3'-3"
8'-8"	0'-8"	10'-0"	2'-0"	11'-4"	3'-4"
8'-9"	0'-9"	10'-1"	2'-1"	11'-5"	3'-5"
8'-10"	0'-10"	10'-2"	2'-2"	11'-6"	3'-6"
8'-11"	0'-11"	10'-3"	2'-3"	11'-7"	3'-7"
9'-0"	1'-0"	10'-4"	2'-4"	11'-8"	3'-8"
9'-1"	1'-1"	10'-5"	2'-5"	11'-9"	3'-9"
9'-2"	1'-2"	10'-6"	2'-6"	11'-10"	3'-10"
9'-3"	1'-3"	10'-7"	2'-7"	11'-11"	3'-11"
9'-4"	1'-4"	10'-8"	2'-8"	12'-0"	4'-0"

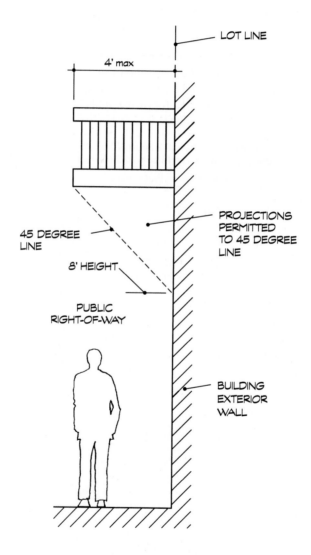

Fig. 3202.3.2. Projection of windows, balconies, architectural features, and mechanical equipment into the public right-of-way.

3202 Encroachments

3202.3.3 Encroachments 15 feet or more above grade

● Encroachments ≥ 15' above grade are governed as shown in the following illustration.

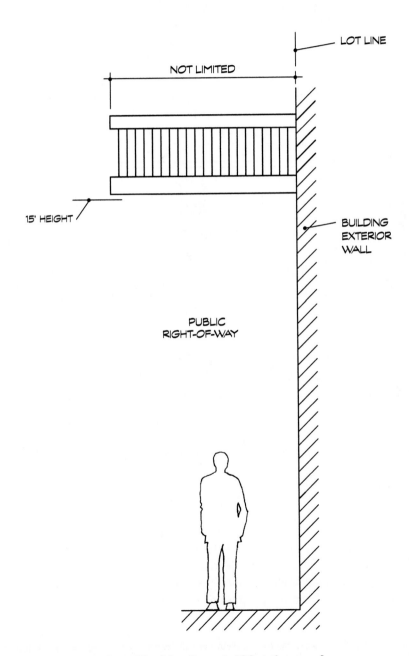

Fig. 3202.3.3. Projections into the public right-of-way ≥ 15 feet above grade.

3202 Encroachments

3202.3.4 Pedestrian walkways

- Pedestrian walkways over a public right-of-way are governed as follows:
  - Must be approved by the authority having jurisdiction.
  - Clearance required is shown in the following illustration.

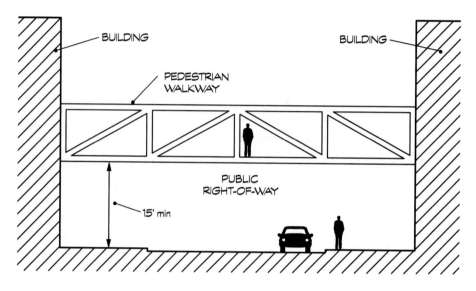

Fig. 3202.3.4 Pedestrian walkways over the public right-of-way.

3202.4 Temporary encroachments

- The following elements installed for ≤ 7 months in any calendar year are governed as indicated below:
  - Elements:
    Vestibules.
    Storm enclosures.
  - Requirements:
    Must be approved by the authority having jurisdiction.
    Encroachment permitted into a public right-of-way is shown as follows:
      In the illustration provided with this section.
- Temporary entrance awnings are governed as indicated in the illustration provided with this section.

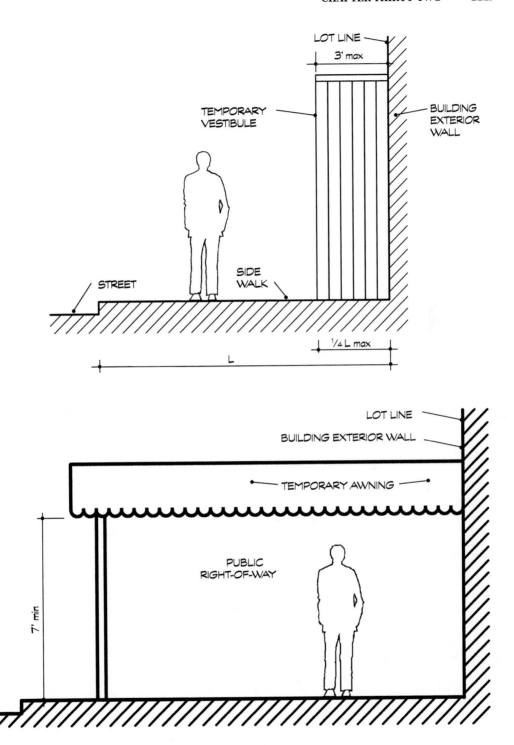

Fig. 3202.4. Temporary projections into the public right-of-way.

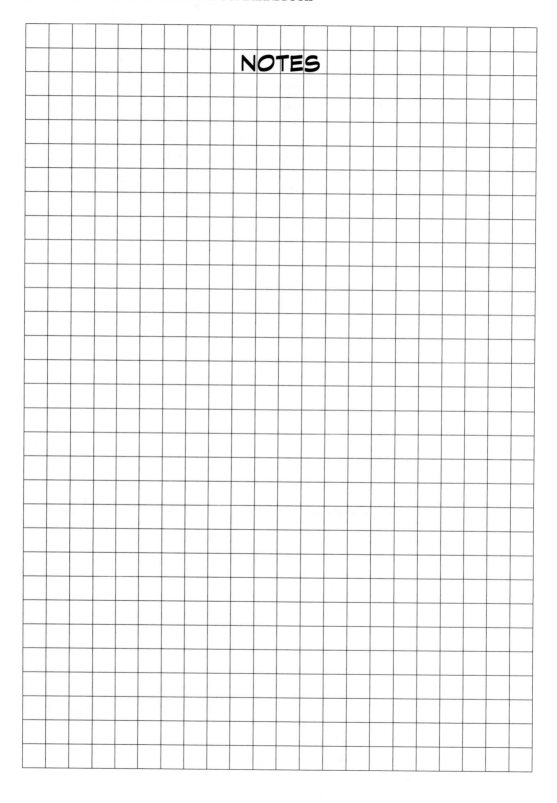

33

Safeguards during Construction

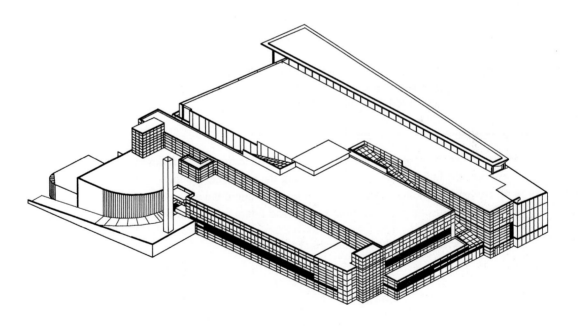

University of Connecticut New Downtown Campus at Stamford, Connecticut.
Perkins Eastman Architects, P.C. New York, New York.

3304 Site Work

3304.1 Excavation and fill

- Excavation and fill must be accommodated to protect the following:
  - Life safety.
  - Property.
- Stumps and roots must be removed as follows:
  - In the area to be occupied by the building:
    - To a depth of ≥ 12" below grade.
- The following wood forms used for concrete must be removed before the building is used for any purpose:
  - Forms in the ground.
  - Forms between foundations sills and grade.
- Prior to completion of construction, the following must be removed:
  - Loose or miscellaneous wood as follows:
    - Where in contact with grade under the building.

3304.1.1 Slope limits

- Permanent fill must slope as follows:
  - ≤ 1:2.
- Permanent slopes for excavated grade must comply with one of the following:
  - A gradient ≤ 1:2.
  - Other slopes are permitted where both of the following apply:
    - Slope is justified by documentation from a soil investigation.
    - Slope is approved by the building official.

3304.1.2 Surcharge

- Fill or other surcharge may be placed against a building only as follows:
  - Where the building is capable of resisting the additional loading.
- Where existing footings can be affected by excavation, the following applies:
  - Footings must be protected from present and future movement by one of the following:
    - Underpinning.
    - Otherwise protected against settlement.

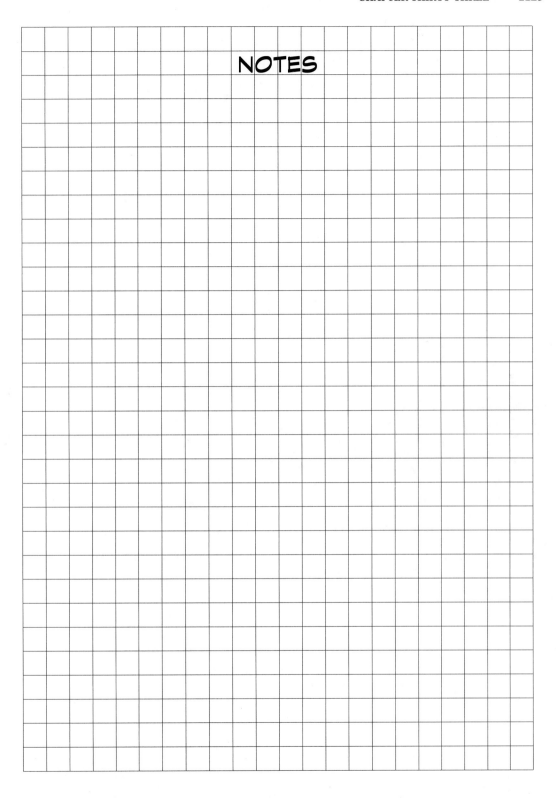

NOTES

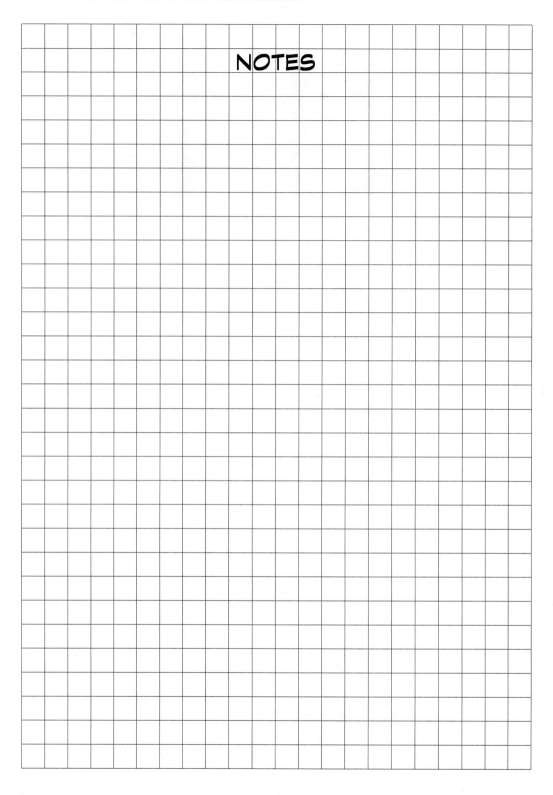

NOTES

34

Existing Structures

Lake Forest City Hall Renovation and Addition. Lake Forest, Illinois.
David Woodhouse Architects. Chicago, Illinois.

3403 Additions, Alterations or Repairs

3403.4 Stairways

- Stairway construction in an existing building is not required to meet requirements for stairways in new construction where all of the following conditions apply:
  - Where the stairway construction is one of the following types:
    An alteration.
    A replacement.
  - Where existing conditions do not permit a reduction in the following:
    Pitch.
    Slope.

Case study: Fig. 3403.4. The stairway is part of the existing portion of the renovation project. The winders, which would be prohibited in new construction by Section 1009, "Stairways and Handrails," are permitted to remain in this stairway alteration. This is possible since the stairway space is restricted by the existing construction, which does not permit the additional steps that would be necessary to eliminate the winders.

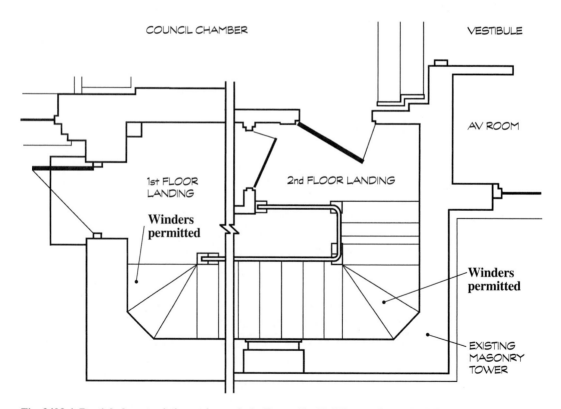

Fig. 3403.4. Partial plan at existing stairway. Lake Forest City Hall Renovation and Addition. Lake Forest, Illinois. David Woodhouse Architects. Chicago, Illinois.

3409 Accessibility for Existing Buildings

3409.7.4 Ramps

- This section addresses alterations to existing buildings.
- Where space does not permit compliance with standard ramp slopes, ramps are governed as shown in the details below.

> Note: 1010.2, "Slope," is cited as governing standard ramp slopes that may not be met due to space limitations.
>
> IBC Table 3409.7.4, "Ramps," is cited as the source of requirements for ramps that cannot meet the standard slope requirements.

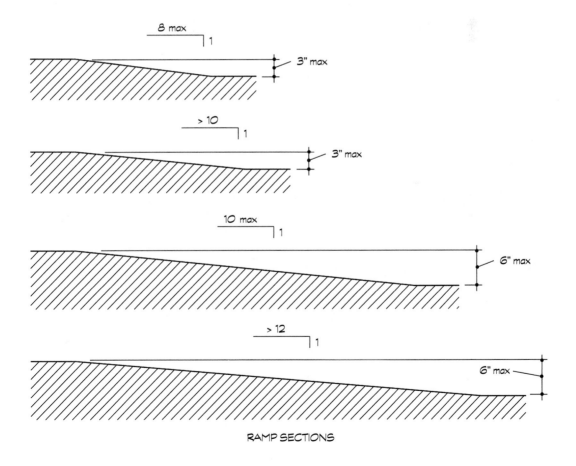

RAMP SECTIONS

Fig. 3409.7.4. Ramps for accessibility in existing buildings.

3409 Accessibility for Existing Buildings

3409.8 Historic buildings

- This section series applies to historic buildings as follows:
  - Where subject to either of the following:
    Alterations.
    Change of occupancy.
  - Where compliance with standard requirements for the following facilities would adversely affect historic value as indicated below:
    Facilities:
      Accessible routes.
      Accessible ramps.
      Accessible entrances.
      Accesible toilet facilities.
    Historic value:
      Where approved by the authority having jurisdiction.
  - Where alternative access requirements are technically feasible.

    Note: The following are cited as providing alternative requirements:
    3409.8.1, "Site arrival points."
    3409.8.2, "Multilevel buildings and facilities."
    3409.8.3, "Entrances."
    3408.9.4, "Toilet and bathing facilities."
    3408.9.5, "Ramps."

3409.8.1 Site arrival points

- The following is an alternative access requirement for historic buildings:
  - ≥ 1 accessible route between the following locations is required:
    An accessible site arrival point.
    An accessible building entrance.

3409.8.2 Multilevel buildings and facilities

- The following is an alternative access requirement for historic buildings:
  - ≥ 1 accessible route between the following locations is required:
    An accessible building entrance.
    An accessible entrance to public spaces as follows:
      On the same level as the accessible building entrance.

3409 Accessibility for Existing Buildings

3409.8.3 Entrances

- The following is an alternative access requirement for historic buildings:
  - ○ ≥ 1 main entrance must be accessible as follows:
    Where an accessible main entrance is not possible, one of the following applies:
      A nonpublic entrance must be accessible as follows:
        Entrance may not be locked while the building is occupied.
      Another entrance must be accessible as follows:
        Where the entrance is locked one of the following is required:
          A notification system.
          A remote monitoring system.
  - ○ Signs are required at the following entrances addressing accessibility.

    Note: Section 1110, " Signage," is cited as governing the signs.

3409.8.4 Toilet and bathing facilities

- The following is an alternative access requirement for historic buildings:
  - ○ Where toilets are provided, the following is required:
    ≥ 1 must be accessible.

    Note: 1109.2.1, "Unisex toilet and bathing rooms." is cited as governing this toilet.

3409.8.5 Ramps

- The following is an alternative access requirement for historic buildings:
  - ○ Slope requirement for ramp runs ≤ 2' is shown in the following detail.

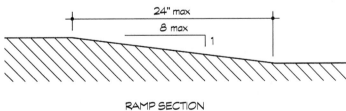

RAMP SECTION

Fig. 3409.8.5. Ramps in historic buildings.

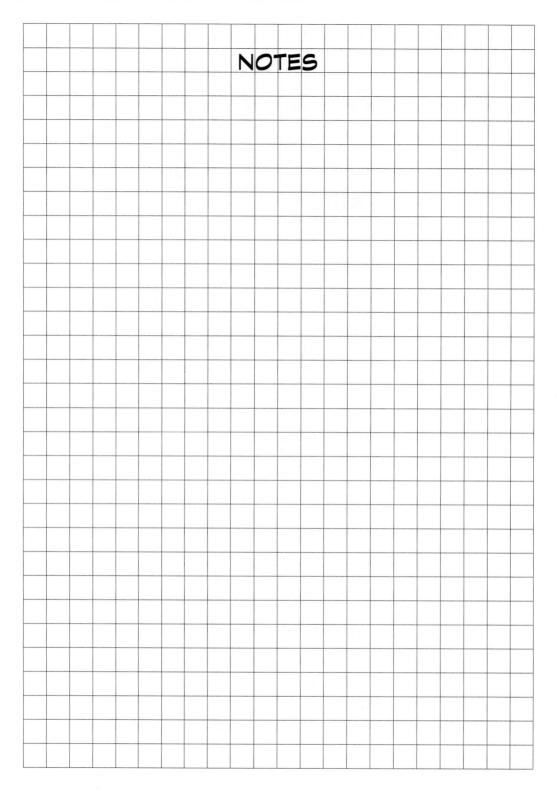

NOTES

35

Referenced Standards

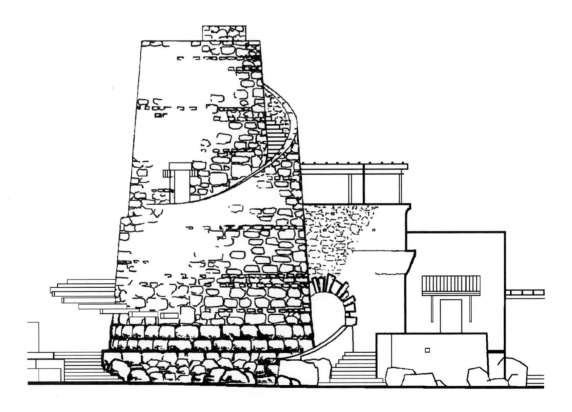

Lady Bird Johnson Wildflower Center. Austin, Texas. *(partial elevation)*
Overland Partners, Inc. San Antonio, Texas.

Referenced Standards

Below are agencies providing standards cited in the code including title abbreviations and contact information.

- **AA**

  Aluminum Association
  900 19th Street, NW, Suite 300
  Washington, DC 20006

  Web site: www.aluminum.org
  Fax: 202-862-5164
  Tel: 202-862-5100

- **AAMA**

  American Architectural
  Manufacturers Association
  1827 Walden Office Square, Suite 550
  Schaumberg, IL 60173

  Web site: www.aamanet.org
  Fax: 847-303-5774
  Tel: 847-303-5664

- **ACI**

  American Concrete Institute
  38800 Country Club Drive
  Farmington Hills, MI 48333

  Web site: www.aci-int.org
  Fax: 248-848-3701
  Tel: 248-848-3700

- **AF&PA**

  American Forest & Paper Association
  1111 19th St., NW, Suite 800
  Washington, DC 20036

  Web site: www.afandpa.org
  e-mail: info@afandpa.org
  Fax: 202-463-2700
  Tel: 202-463-2471
  Tel: 800-878-8878

- **AHA**

  American Hardwood Association
  1210 West NW Highway
  Palatine, IL 60067

  Tel: 847-934-8800

- **AISC**

  American Institute of Steel Construction
  One East Wacker Drive, Suite 3100
  Chicago, IL 60601-2001

  Web site: www.aisc.org
  Fax: 312-670-5403
  Tel: 312-670-2400

- **AISI**

  American Iron and Steel Institute
  1140 Connecticut Avenue, Suite 705
  Washington, DC 20036-4700

  Web site: www.steel.org
  Tel: 202-452-7100

Referenced Standards

- **AITC**

  American Institute of Timber Construction
  7012 S. Revere Parkway, Suite 140
  Englewood, CO 80112

  Web site: www.aitc-glulam.org
  e-mail: info@aitc-glulam.org
  Fax: 303-792-0669
  Tel: 303-792-9559

- **ALI**

  Automotive Lift Institute
  P.O. Box 33116
  Indialantic, FL 32903-3116

  Web site: www.autolift.org
  e-mail: info@autolift.org
  Fax: 321-722-9931
  Tel: 321-722-9993

- **ANSI**

  American National Standards Institute
  25 West 43rd Street, Fourth Floor
  New York, NY 10036

  Web site: www.ansi.org
  e-mail: info@ansi.org
  Fax: 212-398-0023
  Tel: 212-642-4900

- **APA**

  Engineered Wood Association
  P.O. Box 11700
  Tacoma, WA 98411-0700

  Web site: www.apawood.org
  e-mail: help@apawood.org
  Fax: 253-565-7265
  Tel: 253-565-6600

- **ASAE**

  American Society of Agricultural Engineers
  2950 Niles Road
  St. Joseph, MI 49085-9659

  Web site: www.asae.org
  e-mail: hq@asae.org
  Fax: 269-429-3852
  Tel: 269-429-0300

- **ASCE/SEI**

  American Society of Civil Engineers
  1801 Alexander Bell Drive
  Reston, VA 20191-4400

  Web site: www.asce.org
  Fax: 703-295-6222
  Tel: 800-548-2723

  Structural Engineering Institute
  1801 Alexander Bell Drive
  Reston, VA 20191-4400

  Web site: www.seinstitute.org
  e-mail: sei@asce.org
  Fax: 703-295-6361
  Tel: 703-295-6195

- **ASME**

  American Society of Mechanical Engineers
  Three Park Avenue
  New York, NY 10016-5990

  Web site: www.asme.org
  e-mail: infocentral@asme.org
  Fax: 212-591-7674
  Tel: 212-591-7000
  Tel: 800-843-2763

Referenced Standards

- **ASTM**

  American Society for Testing and Materials   Web site: www.astm.org
  100 Barr Harbor Drive   e-mail: infoctr@astm.org
  West Conshohocken, PA 19428-2959   Fax: 610-832-9555
                                                Tel: 610-832-9500

- **AWPA**

  American Wood-Preservers' Association   Web site: www.awpa.com
  P.O. Box 5690   e-mail: awpa@itexas.net
  Grandbury, TX 76049-0690   Fax: 817-326-6306
                                                Tel: 817-326-6300

- **AWS**

  American Welding Society   Web site: www.aws.org
  550 NW LeJeune Road   e-mail: info@aws.org
  Miami, FL 33126   Fax: 305-443-7559
                                                Tel: 305-443-9353
                                                Tel: 800-443-9353

- **BHMA**

  Builders Hardware Manufacturers'   Web site: www.buildershardware.com
  Association   e-mail: info@buildershardware.com
  355 Lexington Avenue, 17th Floor   Fax: 212-370-9047
  New York, NY 10017-6603   Tel: 212-297-2100

- **CGSB**

  Canadian General Standards Board   Web site: www.pwgsc.gc.ca/cgsb
  Place du Portage III-6B1   Fax: 819-956-5644
  11 Laurer Street   Tel: 819-956-0425
  Hull, Quebec, Canada K1A 1G6

- **CPSC**

  U.S. Consumer Product Safety Commission   Web site: www.cpsc.gov
  4330 East-West Highway   e-mail: info@cpsc.gov
  Bethesda, MD 20814-4408   Fax: 301-504-0124
                                                Tel: 301-504-6816
                                                Tel: 800-638-2772

- **CSSB**

  Cedar Shake and Shingle Bureau   Web site: www.cedarbureau.org
  P.O. Box 1178   e-mail: info@cedarbureau.com
  Sumas, WA 98295-1178   Fax: 604-820-0266
                                                Tel: 604-820-7700

Referenced Standards

- **DASMA**

  Door and Access Systems Manufacturer's
  Association International
  1300 Summer Avenue
  Cleveland, OH 44115-2851

  Web site: www.dasma.com
  e-mail: dasma@dasma.com
  Fax: 216-241-0105
  Tel: 216-241-7333

- **DOC**

  U.S. Department of Commerce
  National Institute of Standards
  and Technology
  1401 Constitution Avenue, NW
  Washington, DC 20230

  Web site: www.commerce.gov
  e-mail: devans@doc.gov
  Tel: 301-975-6478

- **DOL**

  U.S. Department of Labor
  c/o Superintendent of Documents
  U.S. Government Printing Office
  Washington, DC 20402-9325

  Web site: www.gpo.gov
  e-mail: gpoaccess@gpo.gov
  Fax: 202-512-1262
  Tel: 202-512-1530
  Tel: 888-293-6498

- **DOTn**

  U.S. Department of Transportation
  400 7th Street, SW
  Washington, DC 20590

  Web site: www.dot.gov
  e-mail: dot.comments@ost.dot.gov
  Tel: 202-366-4000

- **FEMA**

  Federal Emergency Management Agency
  Federal Center Plaza
  500 C Street, SW, Room 824
  Washington, DC 20472-0001

  Web site: www.fema.gov
  e-mail: eipa@fema.gov
  Tel: 202-566-1600

- **FM**

  Factory Mutual
  Standards Laboratories Department
  1151 Boston-Providence Turnpike
  P.O. Box 9102
  Norwood, MA 02062

  Web site: www.fmglobal.com
  e-mail: information@fmglobal.com
  Fax: 781-255-4218
  Tel: 781-255-4200

- **GA**

  Gypsum Association
  810 First Street NE, #510
  Washington, DC 20002-4268

  Web site: www.gypsum.org
  e-mail: info@gysum.org
  Fax: 202-289-3707
  Tel: 202-289-5440

Referenced Standards

- **HPVA**

  Hardwood Plywood Veneer Association
  1825 Michael Faraday Drive
  P.O. Box 2789
  Reston, VA 20195-0789

  Web site: www.hpva.org
  e-mail: hpva@hpva.org
  Fax: 703-435-2537
  Tel: 703-435-2900

- **ICC**

  International Code Council
  5203 Leesburg Pike, Suite 708
  Falls Church, VA 22041

  Web site: www.iccsafe.org
  e-mail: staff@iccsafe.org
  Fax: 703-379-1546
  Tel: 703-931-4533

- **NAAMM**

  National Association of Architectural
  Metal Manufacturers
  8 South Michigan Avenue, Suite 1000
  Chicago, IL 60603

  Web site: www.naamm.org
  e-mail: naamm@gss.net
  Fax: 312-332-0706
  Tel: 213-332-0405

- **NCMA**

  National Concrete Masonry Association
  13750 Sunrise Valley Drive
  Herndon, VA 22171-4662

  Web site: www.ncma.org
  e-mail: recepti@ncma.org
  Fax: 703-713-1910
  Tel: 703-713-1900

- **NFPA**

  National Fire Protection Association
  1 Batterymarch Park
  P.O. Box 9101
  Quincy, MA 02269-9101

  Web site: www.nfpa.org
  Fax: 617-770-0700
  Tel: 617-770-3000

- **NIST**

  National Institute of Standards and
  Technology
  100 Bureau Drive, Stop 3460
  Gaithersburg, MD 20899-3460

  Web site: www.nist.gov
  e-mail: inquiries@nist.gov
  Tel: 301-975-6478

- **PCI**

  Precast/Prestressed Concrete Institute
  175 W. Jackson Boulevard, Suite 1859
  Chicago, IL 60604-9773

  Web site: www.pci.org
  e-mail: info@pci.org
  Fax: 312-786-0353
  Tel: 312-786-0300

Referenced Standards

- **PTI**

  Post-Tensioning Institute
  8601 N. Black Canyon Hwy., Suite 103
  Phoenix, AZ 85021

  Web site: www.post-tensioning.org
  e-mail: info@post-tensioning.org
  Fax: 602-870-7541
  Tel: 602-870-7540

- **RMA**

  Rubber Manufacturers Association
  1400 K Street, NW, #900
  Washington, DC 20005

  Web site: www.rma.org
  Fax: 202-682-4854
  Tel: 202-682-4800
  Tel: 800-220-7622

- **RMI**

  Rack Manufacturers Institute
  8720 Red Oak Boulevard, Suite 201
  Charlotte, NC 28217

  Web site: www.mhia.org/rmi/pr3.htm
  e-mail: infosinger@mhia.org
  Fax: 704-676-1199
  Tel: 704-676-1190

- **SJI**

  Steel Joist Institute
  3127 10th Avenue, North Ext.
  Myrtle Beach, SC 29577-6760

  Web site: www.steeljoist.org
  e-mail: sji@steeljoist.org
  Fax: 843-626-5565
  Tel: 843-626-1995

- **SPRI**

  Single-Ply Roofing Institute
  77 Rumford Avenue, Suite 3-B
  Waltham, MA 02543

  Web site: www.spri.org
  e-mail: info@spri.org
  Fax: 781-647-7222
  Tel: 781-647-7026

- **TIA**

  Telecommunications Industry Association
  2500 Wilson Boulevard, Suite 300
  Arlington, VA 22201-3834

  Web site: www.tiaonline.org
  e-mail: tia@tia.eia.org
  Fax: 703-907-7727
  Tel: 703-907-7700

- **TMS**

  The Masonry Society
  3970 Broadway, Unit 201-D
  Boulder, CO 80304-1135

  Web site: www.masonrysociety.org
  e-mail: info@masonrysociety.org
  Fax: 303-541-9215
  Tel: 303-939-9700

- **TPI**

  Truss Plate Institute
  583 D'Onofrio Drive, Suite 200
  Madison, WI 53719

  Web site: www.tpinst.org
  Tel: 608-833-5900

Referenced Standards

- **UL**

  Underwriters Laboratories
  333 Pfingsten Road
  Northbrook, IL 60062-2096

  Web site: www.ul.com
  e-mail: northbrook@us.ul.com
  Fax: 847-272-8129
  Tel: 847-272-8800

- **ULC**

  Underwriters Laboratories of Canada
  7 Underwriters Road
  Toronto, Ontario, Canada M1R 3B4

  Web site: www.ulc.ca
  e-mail: ulcinfo@ulc.ca
  Fax: 416-757-9540
  Tel: 416-757-3611
  Tel: 800-4636-852

- **WDMA**

  Window and Door Manufacturers
  Association
  1400 East Touhy Avenue, Suite 470
  Des Plaines, IL 60018

  Web site: www.wdma.com
  e-mail: admin@wdma.com
  Fax: 847-299-1286
  Tel: 847-299-5200
  Tel: 800-223-2301

- **WRI**

  Wire Reinforcement Institute, Inc.
  942 Main Street, Suite 300
  Hartford, CT 06103

  Web site:
  www.wirereinforcementinstitute.org
  Fax: 860-808-3009
  Tel: 800-552-4974

NOTES

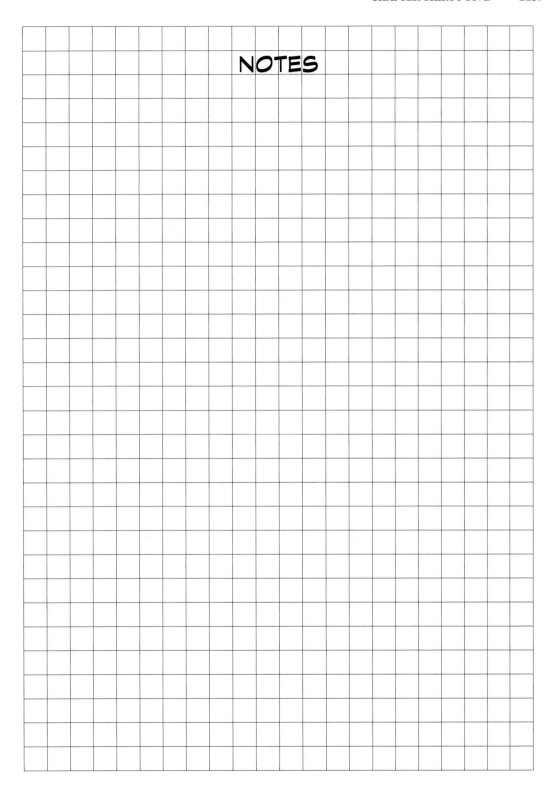

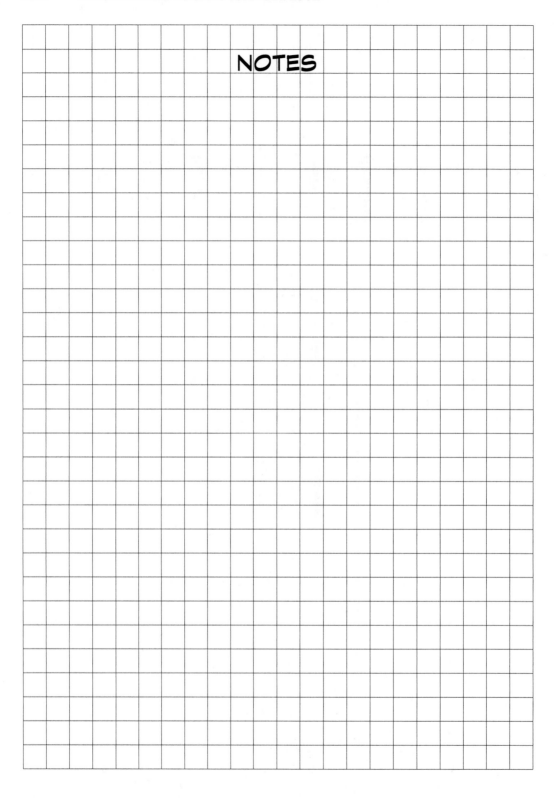

NOTES

Appendix

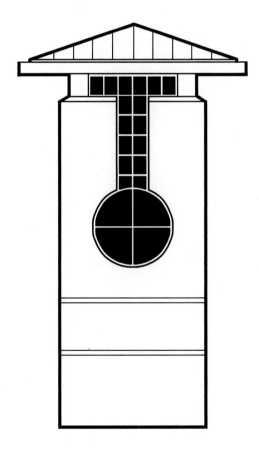

Lee's Summit Police and Court Facility. Lee's Summit, Missouri. *(partial elevation)*
The Hollis and Miller Group, Inc. Lee's Summit, Missouri.

Appendix A:
Abbreviations

These abbreviated terms may appear in both upper- and
lowercase forms in the text, tables, and drawings.

act	actual	*dr*	door
admin	administration	*ea*	each
all	allowable	*elec*	electrical
bd	board	*elev*	elevation
bldg	building	*eq*	equal
bm	beam	*equip*	equipment
Btu	British thermal unit	*exist*	existing
cmu	concrete masonry unit	*ext*	exterior
col	column	*fdn*	foundation
conc	concrete	*fe*	fire extinguisher
conf	conference	*fec*	fire extinguisher cabinet
const	construction	*fin*	finish
cu ft	cubic foot or feet	*flr*	floor
cu in	cubic inch or inches	*ft*	foot or feet
df	drinking fountain	*ga*	gage
dia	diameter	*galv*	galvanized
dim	dimension	*gyp*	gypsum

horiz	horizontal		*r*	radius
ht	height		*rec*	reception
IBC	*International Building Code*		*recpt*	reception
insul	insulation		*ref*	refrigerator
int	interior		*reinf*	reinforcing
j	janitor		*req'd*	required
jan	janitor		*rm*	room
lav	lavatory		*sched*	schedule
lb	pound		*sec*	secretary
lbs/ft	pounds per foot		*sf*	square foot or feet
lbs/ft	pounds per feet		*sht*	sheet
m	men		*sq cm*	square centimeters
max	maximum		*sq in*	square inch or inches
mech	mechanical		*stl*	steel
mezz	mezzanine		*sto*	storage
mgr	manager		*stor*	storage
min	minimum		*struct*	structural
na	not applicable		*t*	toilet
no.	number		*typ*	typical
nom	nominal		*ul*	unlimited
np	not permitted		*vert*	vertical
oc	on center		*vest*	vestibule
occ	occupancy		*w*	women
occ	occupants		*wc*	water closet
off	office		*wd*	wood
opng	opening		*wt*	weight
psf	pounds per square foot		*wwf*	welded wire fabric
psi	pounds per square inch		*wwm*	welded wire mesh

Appendix B:
Symbols

@	at
<	less than
>	greater than
≥	greater than or equal to
≤	less than or equal to
⊥	perpendicular to
‖	parallel to
°	degrees, temperature
°	degrees, radial
÷	divide by
×	multiply by
=	equal to
%	percent
'	foot or feet
"	inch or inches

Index

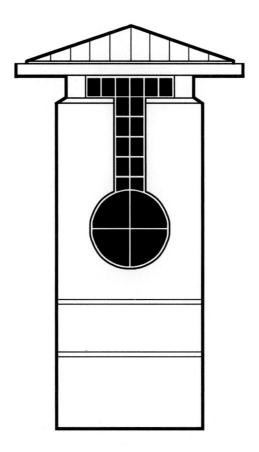

Lee's Summit Police and Court Facility. Lee's Summit, Missouri. *(partial elevation)*
The Hollis and Miller Group, Inc. Lee's Summit, Missouri.

Index

A

Access to unoccupied spaces:
attics, 685; crawl spaces, 685; mechanical appliances, 685

Accessibility, 448:
areas of refuge, 454; communication, 456; construction sites, 604; continuity, 450; day care, 606; detached dwellings, 604; detention facilities, 606; elevators, 452; employee work areas, 603; equipment spaces, 605; existing buildings, 603; exit stairways, 451–452; four or more stories, 451; fuel-dispensing systems, 606; Group R-1, 606; identification, 458; instructions, 458; limited access spaces, 605; locations, 603; platform lifts, 454; raised areas, 604; separation, 456; signage, 458; single occupant structures, 605; size, 456; utility buildings, 604

Accessible entrances, 612:
dwelling units, 613; entrances for inmates, 613; from elevated walkways, 612; from tunnels, 612; location, 612; parking garages, 612; restricted entrances, 612; service entrances, 613; sleeping units, 613; tenant spaces, dwelling units, and sleeping units, 613

Accessible facilities, 646:
assembly area, 655; check-out aisles, 657; clear floor space, 649; coat hooks, 655; controls, 658–659; detectable warnings, 655; dispersion, 656; dressing rooms, 657; drinking fountains, 652; elevators, 652; fitting rooms, 657; folding shelves, 655; food service, 658; kitchens and kitchenettes, 652; lifts, 652–654; location, 649; locker rooms, 657; lockers, 654; operable windows, 659; privacy, 649; recreation facilities, 660; sales counters, 658; seating at counters, 656; seating at tables, 656; seating at work surfaces, 656; service counters, 658; shelving and display units, 654; sinks, 650; stairways, 660; storage, 654; toilets and bathing, 646–647; unisex bathing, 649; unisex toilets, 648; unisex toilets and bathing, 648; waiting lines, 658; water closet, 650

Accessible route, 607:
connected spaces, 608; employee work areas, 610; location, 611; multilevel facilities, press boxes, 610; security barriers, 611; site, 608; site arrival points, 607

Adult care facility, 51

Aluminum, 848

Area modifications:
area determination, 152; area modifications, 143; basements, 143; frontage increase, 143–146; open space limits, 149; sprinkler increase, 149–151; width limits, 149

Assembly:
aisle accessways, 585–589; aisle handrails, 591–592; aisle obstructions, 585; aisle risers, 590; aisle surface, 590; aisle termination, 584; aisle treads, 590; aisle

B

C

F

L

M

N

O

P

R

S

T

U

Y

V

W

ABOUT THE AUTHOR

Terry L. Patterson is a licensed architect and a tenured professor of architecture at the University of Oklahoma. He has more than 30 years of professional experience and more than 25 years of teaching experience. A resident of Norman, Oklahoma, Terry is also a widely published author.